A broadly inclusive, evangelical commentary on Daniel that at the same time engages respectfully and thoroughly the critical issues without partisanship, argument, or accusation. This is one of a kind!
—RONALD W. PIERCE, professor of Old Testament, Talbot School of Theology

Widder provides well-reasoned evangelical positions on critical matters and her comments are thorough, clear, and accessible. Her translations are carefully crafted to convey the nuances of the Hebrew and Aramaic, and it is clear she has a deep familiarity with the book. Her facility in discourse-linguistic analysis is evident throughout, making it a wonderful contribution to the series.
—JOHN COOK, professor of Old Testament and Semitic languages and
director of Hebrew language Instruction, Asbury Theological Seminary

A new day for Daniel studies. If persons were trapped until they preached through Daniel—which describes the way many approach such a series—and only one commentary was allowed, it's an easy choice. Wendy Widder's commentary combines her expertise in Hebrew and Aramaic and builds on her series of important studies on Daniel over the past decade. She never minimizes interpretive difficulties. But Wendy leads us past the long- line of interpretive cul-de-sacs created by earlier commentators on Daniel. Anyone who wants to understand and teach Daniel and trust the Most High God needs to start here.
—GARY EDWARD SCHNITTJER, distinguished professor of Old Testament, Cairn University

A masterful introduction followed by close analysis at the microlevel, clear discourse analysis at the microlevel, and stimulating biblical theological treatment at the intertextual level. And Widder's ability to link all of this to the big idea at each point makes for stimulating reading—I literally read it straight through. Henceforth, it's my go-to commentary on Daniel.
—DALE BRUEGGEMANN, retired missionary and educator

I have come to appreciate the clarity and precision of Dr. Widder's writing over the years, so it is with great pleasure that I commend her latest work on Daniel. Readers of this volume will find a solid command of the challenging issues surrounding Daniel blended with up-to-date insights from discourse analysis and linguistic approaches to the Hebrew and Aramaic text.
—STEVEN RUNGE, scholar in residence, Clear Bible

Widder provides a close reading of the text of Daniel, highlighting the essential features of the book's clauses in its original languages. By auditing how the book creates its discourse, she builds a solid platform for moving from grammar and syntax towards meaning and theological interpretation. Students will appreciate the attention to detail, as well as the wider connections Widder makes between different parts of the book of Daniel. Widder does not shy away from the difficult critical issues, of which there are many. She presents multiple perspectives, which she evaluates with generosity, while also being up front with the conservative Christian framework within which she is working. Christian exegetes and preachers will find both food for thought and good guidance for their analysis and preaching endeavors.
—GEORGE ATHAS, director of research, Moore Theological College

DANIEL

Zondervan Exegetical Commentary on the Old Testament

Editorial Board

General Editor
Daniel I. Block
Gunther H. Knoedler Professor Emeritus of Old Testament, Wheaton College

Associate Editors
Hélène Dallaire
Professor of Old Testament and Director of Messianic Judaism Programs, Denver Seminary

Stephen Dempster
Associate Professor of Religious Studies, Crandall University

Jason S. DeRouchie
Research Professor of Old Testament and Biblical Theology, Midwestern Baptist Theological Seminary

Miles V. Van Pelt
Alan Belcher Professor of Old Testament and Biblical Languages, Reformed Theological Seminary

Zondervan Editors
Katya Covrett
Lee Fields

DANIEL
God's Kingdom Will Endure

ZONDERVAN
Exegetical Commentary
ON THE
Old Testament
A DISCOURSE ANALYSIS OF THE HEBREW BIBLE

WENDY WIDDER

Daniel I. Block, General Editor

ZONDERVAN ACADEMIC

Daniel
Copyright © 2023 by Wendy L. Widder

Requests for information should be addressed to:
Zondervan, 3900 Sparks Dr. SE, Grand Rapids, Michigan 49546

Zondervan titles may be purchased in bulk for educational, business, fundraising, or sales promotional use. For information, please email SpecialMarkets@Zondervan.com.

Library of Congress Cataloging-in-Publication Data

Names: Widder, Wendy, 1968- author.
Title: Daniel : a discourse analysis of the Hebrew Bible / Wendy L. Widder.
Other titles: Zondervan exegetical commentary on the Old Testament
Description: Grand Rapids : Zondervan, 2023. | Series: Zondervan exegetical commentary on the Old Testament | Includes bibliographical references and index.
Identifiers: LCCN 2023001555 | ISBN 9780310942368 (hardcover)
Subjects: LCSH: Bible. Daniel--Commentaries. | Rhetoric in the Bible. | Hebrew language--Discourse analysis. | BISAC: RELIGION / Biblical Commentary / Old Testament / Prophets | RELIGION / Biblical Commentary / General
Classification: LCC BS1555.53 .W532 2023 | DDC 224/.507--dc23/eng/20230519
LC record available at https://lccn.loc.gov/2023001555

> The Hebrew text is from Deut 31:11–13, which highlights the importance of "hearing" the voice of Scripture:
>
> When all Israel comes to appear before יהוה your God at the place he will choose, you shall read this *Torah* before them in their hearing. Assemble the people—men, women and children, and the foreigners residing in your towns—so they can *listen* and learn to fear יהוה your God and follow carefully all the words of this *Torah*. Their children, who do not know this *Torah*, must *hear* it and learn to fear יהוה your God as long as you live in the land you are crossing the Jordan to possess. (NIV, modified)

All Scripture quotations, unless otherwise indicated, are the author's own translations. Scripture quotations noted as NIV are taken from The Holy Bible, New International Version®, NIV®. Copyright © 1973, 1978, 1984, 2011 by Biblica, Inc.® Used by permission of Zondervan. All rights reserved worldwide. www.Zondervan.com. The "NIV" and "New International Version" are trademarks registered in the United States Patent and Trademark Office by Biblica, Inc.® • Scripture quotations marked ESV are taken from the ESV® Bible, *The Holy Bible, English Standard Version*®. Copyright © 2001, 2016 by Crossway, a publishing ministry of Good News Publishers. Used by permission. All rights reserved. • Scripture quotations marked NASB are taken from the *New American Standard Bible*®. Copyright © 1960, 1962, 1963, 1968, 1971, 1972, 1973, 1975, 1977, 1995 by The Lockman Foundation. Used by permission. (www.Lockman.org). • Scripture quotations designated NET are taken from the *NET Bible*®. Copyright ©1996–2017 by Biblical Studies Press, L.L.C. http://netbible.com. All rights reserved. • Scripture quotations marked NJPS are taken from *Tanakh: The Holy Scriptures: The New JPS Translation according to the Traditional Hebrew Text*. Copyright © 1985, 1999 by the Jewish Publication Society. • Scripture quotations marked NRSV are taken from the *New Revised Standard Version Bible*. Copyright ©1989 Division of Christian Education of the National Council of the Churches of Christ in the United States of America. Used by permission. All rights reserved.

Any internet addresses (websites, blogs, etc.) and telephone numbers in this book are offered as a resource. They are not intended in any way to be or imply an endorsement by Zondervan, nor does Zondervan vouch for the content of these sites and numbers for the life of this book.

All rights reserved. No part of this publication may be reproduced, stored in a retrieval system, or transmitted in any form or by any means—electronic, mechanical, photocopy, recording, or any other—except for brief quotations in printed reviews, without the prior permission of the publisher.

Cover design: Tammy Johnson
Interior design: Beth Shagene

Printed in the United States of America

To Rick,
who brought the radiance of summer into my fall

Contents

Illustrations xi
Series Introduction xiii
Author's Preface and Acknowledgments xvii
Abbreviations xix
Select Bibliography xxv

Translation of Daniel 1
Introduction to Daniel 23
Commentary on Daniel 43

MACRO UNIT 1
God's Kingdom in Exile: The Conflict Begins (1:1–21) 43
    1. Daniel 1:1–21 45

MACRO UNIT 2
The Superiority of God and His Kingdom (2:1–7:28) 79
    2. Daniel 2:1–49 81
    3. Daniel 3:1–30 140
    4. Daniel 3:31–4:34[4:1–37] 195
    5. Daniel 5:1–6:1[5:31] 246
    6. Daniel 6:2–29[1–28] 296
    7. Daniel 7:1–28 348

MACRO UNIT 3
Encouragement until God's Eternal Kingdom Comes
(8:1–12:13) 403
    8. Daniel 8:1–27 405
    9. Daniel 9:1–27 451
  10. Daniel 10:1–12:13............................. 496

    Ancient Sources Index 543
    Subject Index.. 567
    Author Index.. 573

Illustrations

Figures

1. Date Formulae in Daniel 39
2. Parallel Accounts in Daniel 3:31–4:34[4:1–37] 220

Tables

2.1. The Identities of the Kingdoms in Daniel 2 115
7.1. Vision Block 1 (Dan 7:1–6) 355
7.2. Vision Block 2 (Dan 7:7–12) 364
7.3. Vision Block 3 (Dan 7:13–28) 375
7.4. The Identities of the Kingdoms in Daniel 2 and 7 386
8.1. Vision Block 1 (Dan 8:1–4) 410
8.2. Vision Block 2 (Dan 8:5–14) 417
8.3. Vision Block 3 (Dan 8:15–27) 426
8.4. The Greek View of the Kingdoms in Daniel 2, 7, and 8 432
8.5. The Roman View of the Kingdoms in Daniel 2, 7, and 8 433

Series Introduction

Prospectus

Modern audiences are often taken in by the oratorical skill and creativity of preachers and teachers. However, they tend to forget that the authority of proclamation is directly related to the correspondence of the key points of the sermon to the message the biblical authors were trying to communicate. Since we confess that "all Scripture [including the entirety of the Old Testament] is God-breathed and is useful for teaching, rebuking, correcting and training in righteousness, so that [all God's people] may be thoroughly equipped for every good work" (2 Tim 3:16–17), it seems essential that those who proclaim its message should pay close attention to the rhetorical agendas of biblical authors. Too often modern readers, including preachers, are either baffled by Old Testament texts, or they simply get out of them that for which they are looking. Many commentaries available to pastors and teachers try to resolve the dilemma either through word-by-word and verse-by-verse analysis or synthetic theological reflections on the text without careful attention to the flow and argument of that text.

The commentators in this series recognize that too little attention has been paid to biblical authors as rhetoricians, to their larger rhetorical and theological agendas, and especially to the means by which they tried to achieve their goals. Like effective communicators in every age, biblical authors were driven by a passion to communicate a message. So we must inquire not only what that message was but also what strategies they used to impress their message on their hearers' ears. This reference to "hearers" rather than to readers is intentional, since the biblical texts were written to be heard. Not only were the Hebrew and Christian Scriptures composed to be heard in the public gathering of God's people, but they were also written before the invention of moveable type, and few would have had access to their own copies of the Scriptures. While the contributors to this series acknowledge with Paul that every Scripture—that is, every passage in the Hebrew Bible—is God-breathed, we also recognize that the inspired authors possessed a vast repertoire of rhetorical and literary strategies. These included not only the special use of words and figures of speech but also the deliberate selection, arrangement, and shaping of ideas.

The primary goal of this commentary series is to help serious students of

Scripture, as well as those charged with preaching and teaching the Word of God, to hear the messages of Scripture as biblical authors intended them to be heard. While we recognize the timelessness of the biblical message, the validity of our interpretation and the authority with which we teach the Scriptures are related directly to the extent to which we have grasped the message intended by the author in the first place. Accordingly, when dealing with specific texts, the authors of the commentaries in this series are concerned with three principal questions: (1) What are the principal theological points the biblical writers are making? (2) How do biblical writers make those points? (3) What significance does the message of the present text have for understanding the message of the biblical book within which it is embedded and the message of the Scriptures as a whole? The achievement of these goals requires careful attention to the way ideas are expressed in the Old Testament, including the selection and arrangement of materials and the syntactical shaping of the text.

To most readers syntax operates primarily at the sentence level. But recent developments in biblical study, particularly advances in rhetorical and discourse analysis, have alerted us to the fact that syntax operates also at the levels of the paragraph, the literary unit being analyzed, and the composition as a whole. Discourse analysis, also called macro syntax, studies the text beyond the level of the sentence (sentence syntax), where the paragraph serves as the basic unit of thought. Those contributing to this series recognize that this type of study may be pursued in a variety of ways. Some will prefer a more bottom-up approach, where clause connectors and transitional features play a dominant role in analysis. Others will pursue a more top-down approach, where genre or literary form begins the discussion. However, we all understand that both approaches are required to understand fully the method and the message of the text. For this reason, the ultimate value of discourse analysis is that it allows the text to set the agenda in biblical interpretation.

One of the distinctive goals for this series is to engage the biblical text using some form of discourse analysis to understand not only what the text says but also how it says it. While attention to words or phrases is still essential, contributors to this commentary series will concentrate on the flow of thought in the biblical writings, both at the macroscopic level of entire compositions and at the microscopic level of individual text units. In so doing we hope to help other readers of Scripture grasp both the message and the rhetorical force of Old Testament texts. When we hear the message of Scripture, we gain access to the mind of God.

Format of the Commentary

The format of this series is designed to achieve the goals summarized above. Accordingly, each volume in the series will begin with an introduction to the book being explored. In addition to answering the usual questions of date, authorship, and provenance of the composition, commentators will highlight what they consider to be the main theological themes of the book and then discuss broadly how the style and structure of the book develop those themes. This discussion will include a coherent outline of the contents of the book, demonstrating the contribution each part makes to the development of the principal themes.

The commentaries on individual text units that follow will repeat this process in greater detail. Although complex literary units will be broken down further, the commentators will address the following issues.

1. **Main Idea of the Passage:** A one- or two-sentence summary of the key ideas the biblical author seeks to communicate.
2. **Literary Context:** A brief discussion of the relationship of the specific text to the book as a whole and to its place within the broader arguments.
3. **Translation and Exegetical Outline:** Commentators will provide their own translations of each text, formatted to highlight the discourse structure of the text and accompanied by a coherent outline that reflects the flow and argument of the text.
4. **Structure and Literary Form:** An introductory survey of the literary structure and rhetorical style adopted by the biblical author, highlighting how these features contribute to the communication of the main idea of the passage.
5. **Explanation of the Text:** A detailed commentary on the passage, paying particular attention to how the biblical authors select and arrange their materials and how they work with words, phrases, and syntax to communicate their messages. This will take up the bulk of most commentaries.
6. **Canonical and Theological Significance:** The commentary on each unit will conclude by building bridges between the world of the biblical author and other biblical authors and with reflections on the contribution made by this unit to the development of broader issues in biblical theology—particularly on how later Old Testament and New Testament authors have adapted and reused the motifs in question. The discussion will also include brief reflections on the significance of the message of the passage for readers today.

The way this series treats biblical books will be uneven. Commentators on smaller books will have sufficient scope to answer fully each of the issues listed above on each unit of text. However, limitations of space preclude full treatment of every text for the larger books. Instead, commentators will guide readers through ##1–4 and 6 for every literary unit, but Explanation of the Text (#5) will be selective, generally limited to twelve to fifteen literary units deemed most critical for hearing the message of the book.

In addition to these general introductory comments, we should alert readers of this series to several conventions that we follow. First, the divine name in the Old Testament is presented as YHWH. The form of the name—represented by the Tetragrammaton, יהוה—is a particular problem for scholars. The practice of rendering the divine name in Greek as κύριος (=Heb. אֲדֹנָי, "Adonay") is carried over into English translations as "Lord," which represents Hebrew יהוה and distinguishes it from "Lord," which represents Hebrew אֲדֹנָי. But this creates interpretive problems, for the connotations and implications of referring to someone by name or by title are quite different. When rendered as a name, English translations have traditionally vocalized יהוה as "Jehovah," which combines the consonants of יהוה with the vowels of אֲדֹנָי. However, today non-Jewish scholars often render the name as "Yahweh," recognizing that "Jehovah" is an artificial construct.

Second, frequently the verse numbers in the Hebrew Bible differ from those in our English translations. Since the commentaries in this series are based on the Hebrew text, the Hebrew numbers will be the default numbers. Where the English numbers differ, they will be provided in square brackets (e.g., Joel 4:12[3:12]).

Third, when discussing specific biblical words or phrases, these will be represented in Hebrew font and in translation, except where the transliterated form is used in place of an English term, either because no single English expression captures the Hebrew word's wide range meaning (e.g., *ḥesed* for חֶסֶד, rather than "lovingkindness"), or when it functions as a title or technical expression not readily captured in English (e.g., *gōʾēl* for גֹּאֵל, rather than "kinsman redeemer").

Daniel I. Block, general editor

Author's Preface and Acknowledgments

When I was asked to contribute this volume to the ZECOT series, my first response was "But I'm already writing on Daniel for the Story of God series." Assured that was not a problem, I accepted the challenge of following up one Daniel commentary with another, twice as long, without plagiarizing myself. On this second focused journey through the book, I marveled afresh at the depth and breadth of the book's relevance, and I am profoundly grateful to have been entrusted with the privilege of writing on the book of Daniel again.

The focus of this commentary series is discourse analysis and, as noted in the series introduction, approaches to discourse analysis vary from scholar to scholar. In my study of the discourse of Daniel, I used as my framework the work that Steve Runge has done, along with Josh Westbury, on the discourse of both Testaments. I had the privilege of working down the hall from Steve and Josh when we were all employed by Faithlife Corporation (then Logos Bible Software). Steve was always willing to chat, and I greatly appreciated his helpful perspective as I was beginning this project. Josh was especially helpful with specific questions I had with respect to Daniel, as he did much of the work on Daniel in the *Lexham Discourse Hebrew Bible*. I am grateful to both of them for sharing their expertise as I cut my "discourse analysis teeth" on the early chapters of Daniel.

One of the peculiarities of the book of Daniel is its dual languages—Biblical Hebrew and Biblical Aramaic. Scholars have done substantial work on the discourse features of Biblical Hebrew, but since Biblical Aramaic has such a small corpus, significantly fewer resources exist specific to Aramaic discourse. While the two languages are related, the syntax of Aramaic presents its own unique challenges. Thus I was delighted to discover in the fall of 2018 that John Cook was about to publish a full-length book on the Aramaic text of Ezra and Daniel. John completed his PhD studies at the University of Wisconsin–Madison shortly after I began mine, and I am thankful that God's providence allowed us to cross paths for even that brief time. John generously shared the PDF of his *Aramaic Ezra and Daniel: A Handbook on the Aramaic Text* many months before its publication, and his expertise helped me navigate some of the difficulties of Aramaic syntax.

All translations of Daniel texts throughout the commentary are mine, unless otherwise noted. Quotations from the rest of the Bible are from the NIV with one modification to align better with the preference of this commentary series and my personal preference: the NIV uses "Lord" for the divine name "YHWH," so I have substituted "YHWH" in every such occurrence. I have chosen other English translations for a handful of biblical quotations and have noted them as appropriate.

Special thanks to my editors, Daniel Block and Miles Van Pelt, whose patience and prayer saw me through to the end of this project, which coincided with a prolonged season of upheaval in my life—as well as with a fair bit of chaos and delay brought on by a global pandemic. Miles was always quick to respond to my queries, and Dan is a deep well in the field of Old Testament studies. Their thoughtful interaction with my manuscript enriched the final product, and I am honored to have had the privilege of working with both of them. I deeply appreciate the team at Zondervan, whose interest in my work made this project possible. My college friend Mark Vroegop was also kind enough to share a PDF of his book *Dark Clouds, Deep Mercy: Discovering the Grace of Lament* before its publication, another generous act that provided an empathetic pastoral guide through biblical lament. I am also indebted to the Department of Hebrew at the University of the Free State (Bloemfontein, South Africa), whose funds for my research associateship helped with expenses.

I started this project in a season of emptiness, with no idea how I would find the time, energy, and extra expertise needed to complete it. Into that emptiness, God poured abundance beyond anything I had expected or even thought possible. My friends Dave and Emmylou Grosser loved me from afar and then up close as I braved a new life in their town. Emmylou's steady friendship, clear thinking, and expertise in Old Testament studies buoyed me on difficult days. Dan and Ruthanne Crapo opened their hearts and their eyes to see how they might help in their own unique way. My new family at Grace CRC in Inver Grove Heights offered hearty encouragement and warm love week after week after week. And Rick, the biggest and best surprise God ever pulled on me, turned *my* life into *our* life. His companionship, unconditional love, and enthusiastic support enable and enrich me every day.

My cup runneth over. Thanks be to God, and may his glorious kingdom fill the earth . . . soon.

Wendy Widder
December, 2020

Abbreviations

Exhaustive lists of abbreviations for books of the Bible, pseudepigrapha, rabbinic works, papyri, classical works, and the like are readily available in sources such as *The SBL Handbook of Style* and not all are included here.

General

AD	*anno Domini* (in the year of our Lord)
BA	Biblical Aramaic
BCE	Before the Common Era
BH	Biblical Hebrew
ca.	*circa*, approximately
cf.	*confer*, compare
ch(s).	chapter(s)
ed(s).	editor(s), edited by
e.g.	*exempli gratia*, for example
esp.	especially
fig.	figure
i.e.	*id est*, that is
pf.	perfect, perfective
p(p).	page(s)
ptc.	participle
trans.	translator(s), translation, translated by
v(v).	verse(s)

Bibliographic

AB	Anchor Bible
ACCS:OT	Ancient Christian Commentary on Scripture: Old Testament
AJSL	*American Journal of Semitic Languages and Literatures*

ANET	*Ancient Near Eastern Texts Relating to the Old Testament.* Edited by James B. Pritchard. 3rd ed. Princeton: Princeton University Press, 1969
Ant.	*Jewish Antiquities*
ApOTC	Apollos Old Testament Commentary
BASOR	*Bulletin of the American Schools of Oriental Research*
BBR	*Bulletin for Biblical Research*
BCBC	Believers Church Bible Commentary
BECNT	Baker Exegetical Commentary on the New Testament
BETL	Bibliotheca Ephemeridum Theologicarum Lovaniensium
BHHB	Baylor Handbook on the Hebrew Bible
BTCB	Brazos Theological Commentary on the Bible
BZAW	Beihefte zur Zeitschrift für die alttestamentliche Wissenschaft
CBQ	*Catholic Biblical Quarterly*
CHANE	Culture and History of the Ancient Near East
ConcC	Concordia Commentary
COS	*The Context of Scripture.* Edited by William W. Hallo. 3 vols. Leiden: Brill, 1997–2002
CTJ	*Calvin Theological Journal*
DLNT	*Dictionary of the Later New Testament and Its Developments.* Edited by Ralph P. Martin and Peter H. Davids. Downers Grove: IL: InterVarsity Press, 1997
DOTPr	*Dictionary of the Old Testament: Prophets.* Edited by J. Gordon McConville and Mark Boda. Downers Grove, IL: Intervarsity Press, 2012
DOTWPW	*Dictionary of the Old Testament: Wisdom, Poetry, & Writings.* Edited by T. Longman III and P. Enns. Downers Grove, IL: Inter-Varsity Press, 2008
DTIB	*Dictionary for Theological Interpretation of the Bible.* Edited by Kevin J. Vanhoozer. Grand Rapids: Baker Academic, 2005.
EBC	Expositor's Bible Commentary
EDBT	*Evangelical Dictionary of Biblical Theology.* Edited by Walter A. Elwell. Grand Rapids: Baker Books, 1996
EvQ	*Evangelical Quarterly*
FRLANT	Forschungen zur Religion und Literatur des Alten und Neuen Testaments
GKC	*Gesenius' Hebrew Grammar.* Edited by Emil Kautzsch. Translated by Arther E. Cowley. 2nd ed. Oxford: Clarendon, 1910
HDR	Harvard Dissertations in Religion
HS	*Hebrew Studies*
HSM	Harvard Semitic Monographs
IBC	Interpretation: A Bible Commentary for Teaching and Preaching

IBHS	*An Introduction to Biblical Hebrew Syntax*, Bruce K. Waltke and Michael O'Connor. Winona Lake, IN: Eisenbrauns, 1990
ICC	International Critical Commentary
IEJ	*Israel Exploration Journal*
JA	*Journal Asiatique*
JAOS	*Journal of the American Oriental Society*
JBL	*Journal of Biblical Literature*
JETS	*Journal of the Evangelical Society*
JHebS	*Journal of Hebrew Scriptures*
Joüon	Joüon, Paul. *A Grammar of Biblical Hebrew.* Translated and revised by T. Muraoka. 2 vols. Rome: Pontifical Biblical Institute, 1991
JSOT	*Journal for the Study of the Old Testament*
JSP	*Journal for the Study of the Pseudepigrapha*
JSS	*Journal of Semitic Studies*
JTS	*Journal of Theological Studies*
LDHB	*The Lexham Discourse Hebrew Bible: Introduction*
LHBOTS	The Library of Hebrew Bible/Old Testament Studies
NAC	New American Commentary
NICNT	New International Commentary on the New Testament
NICOT	New International Commentary on the Old Testament
NIDOTTE	*New International Dictionary of Old Testament Theology and Exegesis.* Edited by Willem A. VanGemeren. 5 vols. Grand Rapids: Zondervan, 1997
NIGTC	New International Greek Testament Commentary
NIVAC	New International Version Application Commentary
NovT	*Novum Testamentum*
NSBT	New Studies in Biblical Theology
NSKAT	Neuer Stuttgarter Kommentar, Altes Testament
OTB	Overtures to Biblical Theology
OTE	*Old Testament Essays*
OTL	Old Testament Library
RCS:OT	Reformation Commentary on Scripture, Old Testament
SAIS	Studies in Aramaic Interpretation of Scripture
SBLEJL	Society of Biblical Literature Early Judaism and Its Literature
SHBC	Smyth & Helwys Bible Commentary
SOGBC	Story of God Bible Commentary
TAPA	*Transactions of the American Philological Association*
TDOT	*Theological Dictionary of the Old Testament.* Edited by G. Johannes Botterweck and Helmer Ringgren. Translated by John T. Willis et al. 17 vols. Grand Rapids: Eerdmans, 1974–2021

TOTC	Tyndale Old Testament Commentaries
TynBul	*Tyndale Bulletin*
USQR	*Union Seminary Quarterly Review*
VT	*Vetus Testamentum*
VTSup	Supplements to Vetus Testamentum
WBC	Word Biblical Commentary
WTJ	*Westminster Theological Journal*
ZAW	*Zeitschrift für die alttestamentliche Wissenschaft*
ZIBBC:OT	Zondervan Illustrated Bible Backgrounds Commentary: Old Testament

Bible Texts and Versions

BHS	*Biblia Hebraica Stuttgartensia.* Edited by Karl Elliger and Wilhelm Rudolph. Stuttgart: Deutsche Bibelgesellschaft, 1983
ESV	English Standard Version
KJV	King James Version
JPS	Jewish Publication Society OT 1917
LXX	Septuagint
MSG	*The Message*
MT	Masoretic Text
NAB	New American Bible
NAC	New American Commentary
NASB	New American Standard Bible
NET	New English Translation
NIV	New International Version
NJPS	*Tanakh: The Holy Scriptures: The New JPS Translation according to the Traditional Hebrew Text*
NRSV	New Revised Standard Version
NT	New Testament

Books of the Bible

Gen	Genesis
Exod	Exodus
Lev	Leviticus
Num	Numbers
Deut	Deuteronomy
Josh	Joshua

Judg	Judges
1–2 Sam	1–2 Samuel
1–2 Kgs	1–2 Kings
1–2 Chr	1–2 Chronicles
Neh	Nehemiah
Ps(s)	Psalm(s)
Prov	Proverbs
Eccl	Ecclesiastes
Song	Song of Solomon/Songs
Isa	Isaiah
Jer	Jeremiah
Lam	Lamentations
Ezek	Ezekiel
Dan	Daniel
Hos	Hosea
Mic	Micah
Nah	Nahum
Hab	Habakkuk
Zeph	Zephaniah
Hag	Haggai
Zech	Zechariah
Mal	Malachi
Matt	Matthew
Rom	Romans
1–2 Cor	1–2 Corinthians
Gal	Galatians
Eph	Ephesians
Phil	Philippians
Col	Colossians
1–2 Thess	1–2 Thessalonians
1–2 Tim	1–2 Timothy
Heb	Hebrews
Jas	James
1–2 Pet	1–2 Peter
Rev	Revelation

Extrabiblical Literature

1 En.	1 Enoch

1QH	Hodayot/Thanksgiving Hymns
1–2 Macc	1–2 Maccabees
2 Bar.	2 Baruch
2 Esd	2 Esdras
Sanh.	Sanhedrin

Select Bibliography

Baldwin, Joyce G. *Daniel.* TOTC 21. Downers Grove, IL: InterVarsity Press, 1978.

Bar-Efrat, Shimon. *Narrative Art in the Bible.* New York: T&T Clark, 2004.

Berlin, Adele. *Poetics and Interpretation of Biblical Narrative.* Winona Lake, IN: Eisenbrauns, 1994.

Calvin, John. *Daniel.* A Geneva Series Commentary. Translated from Latin (1561). Repr., Calvin Translation Society, 1852–53. Repr., Carlisle, PA: Banner of Truth Trust, 1995.

Chapell, Bryan. *The Gospel According to Daniel: A Christ-Centered Approach.* Grand Rapids, Baker Books: 2014.

Collins, John J., ed. *Apocalypse: The Morphology of a Genre. Semeia* 14. Missoula, MT: Scholars Press, 1979.

Collins, John J. *Daniel.* Hermeneia. Minneapolis: Fortress, 1993.

Collins, John J., and Peter W. Flint. *The Book of Daniel: Composition and Reception.* 2 vols. Leiden: Brill, 2001.

Cook, John A. *Aramaic Ezra and Daniel: A Handbook on the Hebrew Text.* BHHB. Waco, TX: Baylor University Press, 2019.

———. "Grammar and Theology in Daniel 3:16–18." *BBR* 28.3 (2018): 367–380.

Evans, Craig A. "Daniel in the New Testament: Visions of God's Kingdom." Pages 490–527 in *The Book of Daniel: Composition and Reception.* Vol. 2. Edited by John J. Collins and Peter W. Flint. Leiden: Brill, 2001.

Fewell, Danna Nolan. *Circle of Sovereignty: Plotting Politics in the Book of Daniel.* Nashville: Abingdon, 1991.

Goldingay, John E. *Daniel.* WBC 30. Dallas: Word, 1989.

Goldingay, John E. *Daniel.* Rev. ed. WBC 30. Grand Rapids: Zondervan Academic, 2019.

Gooding, David W. "The Literary Structure of the Book of Daniel and Its Implications," *TynBul* 32 (1981): 60–61.

Goswell, Greg. "The Temple Theme in the Book of Daniel." *JETS* 55.3 (2012): 509–20.

Greidanus, Sidney. *Preaching Christ from Daniel: Foundations for Expository Sermons.* Grand Rapids: Eerdmans, 2012.

Hartman, Louis F., and Alexander A. DiLella, *The Book of Daniel.* AB 23. Garden City, NY: Doubleday, 1978.

Hill, Andrew E. *Daniel.* EBC 8. Grand Rapids: Zondervan, 2008.

Korner, Ralph J. "'And I Saw . . .' An Apocalyptic Literary Convention for Structural Identification in the Apocalypse." *NovT* 42.2 (April, 2000): 160–83.

Lacocque, André. *The Book of Daniel.* Translated by David Pellauer. London: SPCK, 1979.

Lederach, Paul M. *Daniel.* BCBC. Scottdale, PA: Herald, 1994.

Lenglet, Adrien. "La structure litteraire de Daniel 2–7." *Biblica* 53.2 (1972): 169–90.

Li, Tarsee. *The Verbal System of the Aramaic of Daniel: An Explanation in the Context of Grammaticalization*. SAIS 8. Leiden: Brill, 2009.

Long, V. Philips. *The Art of Biblical History*. Grand Rapids: Zondervan, 1994.

Longman, Tremper III. *Daniel*. NIVAC. Grand Rapids: Zondervan, 1999.

Lucas, Ernest C. *Daniel*. ApOTC 20. Downers Grove, IL: InterVarsity Press, 2002.

Lucas, Ernest C. "Daniel." Pages 518–71 in *ZIBBC:OT* 4. Edited by John H. Walton. Grand Rapids: Zondervan, 2009.

Millard, A. R. "Daniel 1–6 and History." *EvQ* 49 (1977): 67–73.

Miller, Cynthia L. *The Representation of Speech in Biblical Hebrew Narrative: A Linguistic Analysis*. HSM 55. Winona Lake, IN: Eisenbrauns, 2003.

Miller, Stephen R. *Daniel*. NAC 18. Nashville: Broadman & Holman, 1994.

Montgomery, James A. *A Critical and Exegetical Commentary on the Book of Daniel*. ICC. New York: Scribner's Sons, 1927.

Muraoka, Takamitsu. *A Biblical Aramaic Reader with an Outline Grammar*. Leuven: Peeters, 2015.

Newsom, Carol A., with Brennan W. Breed. *Daniel: A Commentary*. OTL. Louisville: Westminster John Knox, 2014.

Oppenheim, A. Leo. "The Interpretation of Dreams in the Ancient Near East." *TAPA* 46, *n.s.*; Philadelphia: The American Philosophical Society, 1956.

Pace, Sharon. *Daniel*. SHBC 17. Macon, GA: Smyth & Helwys, 2008.

Porteous, Norman W. *Daniel: A Commentary*. OTL. Philadelphia: Westminster, 1976.

Runge, Steven E. *Discourse Grammar of the Greek New Testament: A Practical Introduction for Teaching and Exegesis*. Peabody, MA: Hendrickson.

Runge, Steven E., and Joshua R. Westbury, eds. *LDHB*. Bellingham, WA: Lexham, 2012.

Seow, C. L. *Daniel*, Westminster Bible Companion. Louisville: Westminster John Knox, 2003.

Steinmann, Andrew E. *Daniel*. ConcC St. Louis: Concordia, 2008.

Sternberg, Meir. *The Poetics of Biblical Narrative: Ideological Literature and the Drama of Reading*. Bloomington: Indiana University Press, 1985.

Tomasino, Anthony J. *Judaism Before Jesus: The Events and Ideas That Shaped the New Testament World*. Downers Grove, IL: InterVarsity Press, 2003.

Towner, W. Sibley. *Daniel*. IBC. Atlanta: John Knox, 1984.

Walton, John H. "The Four Kingdoms of Daniel." *JETS* 29.1 (1986): 25–36.

Walvoord, John. *Daniel: The Key to Prophetic Revelation*. Chicago: Moody, 1971.

Wells, Samuel, and George Sumner, *Esther and Daniel*. BTCB. Grand Rapids: Brazos, 2013.

Westbury, Josh. "Quotative Frames and the Power of Redundancy." https://academic.logos.com/quotative-frames-and-the-power-of-redundancy/

Widder, Wendy L. *Daniel*. SOGBC. Grand Rapids: Zondervan, 2016.

Wills, Lawrence M. *The Jew in the Court of a Foreign King: Ancient Jewish Court Legends*. HDR 26. Minneapolis: Fortress, 1990.

Wiseman, D. J. *Nebuchadrezzar and Babylon*. Oxford: Oxford University Press, 1985.

Wiseman, D. J., et al. *Notes on Some Problems in the Book of Daniel*. London: Tyndale Press, 1965.

Young, Edward J. *The Prophecy of Daniel: A Commentary*. Grand Rapids: Eerdmans, 1949.

Translation of Daniel

Daniel 1

1:1 In the third year of the reign of Jehoiakim, king of Judah, Nebuchadnezzar, king of Babylon, came to Jerusalem, and he laid siege to it. ²And the Lord gave into his hand Jehoiakim, king of Judah, and some of the vessels of the house of God, and he brought them into the land of Shinar (to) the house of his god(s)—the vessels he brought into the house of the treasury of his god(s).

³Then the king said to Ashpenaz, chief of his officials, to bring some of the sons of Israel—some of the royal seed and some of the nobles—⁴youths in whom there was no blemish, good looking, skilled in all wisdom, knowers of knowledge, discerners of knowledge, and who had the ability to stand in the palace of the king—and to teach them the literature and language of the Chaldeans. ⁵The king appointed for them a daily ration from the king's food and from the wine he drank, and they would be trained three years. Then some of them would stand in the presence of the king.

⁶Among them—from the sons of Judah—were Daniel, Hananiah, Mishael, and Azariah. ⁷And the commander of the officials assigned to them names. And he assigned for Daniel "Belteshazzar," and for Hananiah "Shadrach," and for Mishael "Meshach," and for Azariah "Abednego." ⁸But Daniel made up his mind that he would not defile himself with the king's food and with the wine he drank, so he sought from the commander of the officials that he might not defile himself. ⁹And God gave Daniel favor and compassion before the commander of the officials, ¹⁰but the commander of the officials said to Daniel, "I am afraid of my lord, the king who appointed your food and your drink, for why should he see your faces thinner than the (other) young men who are your age? Then you would endanger my head with the king."

¹¹So Daniel said to the guard, whom the commander of the officials had appointed over Daniel, Hananiah, Mishael, and Azariah, ¹²"Please test your servants for ten days: let us be given some vegetables that we may eat and [let us be given] water that we may drink. ¹³Then let our appearance and the appearance of the young men eating the king's food be observed by you, and according to what you see, deal with your servants."

[14]So he listened to them in this matter, and he tested them ten days. [15]At the end of the ten days, their appearance was seen to be better and fatter in flesh than all the young men eating the king's food. [16]So the guard took away their food and the wine they drank, and he gave them vegetables. [17]And as for these four young men, God gave them knowledge and skill in all literature and wisdom. And Daniel understood all visions and dreams.

[18]And at the end of the days when the king said to bring them in, the commander of the officials brought them in before Nebuchadnezzar. [19]And the king spoke with them, and there was not found among all of them any like Daniel, Hananiah, Mishael, and Azariah. And they stood before the king. [20](In) every matter of wisdom and understanding which the king sought from them, he found them ten times better than all the magicians and the conjurers who were in all his kingdom. [21]And so Daniel was (there) until the first year of Cyrus the king.

Daniel 2

[2:1]In the second year of the reign of Nebuchadnezzar, Nebuchadnezzar dreamed dreams. His spirit was troubled, and his sleep left him. [2]And the king said to call the magicians and enchanters and sorcerers and Chaldeans to tell the king his dreams. They came and they stood before the king.

[3]The king said to them, "A dream I have dreamed, and troubled is my spirit to know the dream.

[4]The Chaldeans spoke to the king *(Aramaic)*, "O King, live forever! Tell the dream to your servants, and the interpretation we will declare."

[5]Responding, the king said to the Chaldeans, "The word from me is firm: If you do not make known to me the dream and its interpretation, you will be dismembered, and your houses will be made a rubbish heap. [6]But if the dream and its interpretation you declare, gifts and reward and great honor you will receive from me. Therefore, the dream and its interpretation declare to me."

[7]They answered a second time, saying, "Let the king tell the dream to his servants, and the interpretation we will declare."

[8]Responding, the king said, "For certain I know that you are buying time. Because you have perceived that the word from me is firm—[9]that if the dream you do not make known to me, there is one decree for you—a lying and corrupt word you have agreed to speak before me until the time changes. Therefore, the dream say to me, and I will know that its interpretation you will declare."

[10]The Chaldeans answered the king, saying, "There is not a man on earth who is able to declare the matter of the king, hence no king—great and powerful—has asked a matter like this of any magician or sorcerer or Chaldean. [11]The matter that the king

asks is difficult, and there is no other who can declare it to the king except the gods, whose dwelling place is not with flesh."

[12] Because of this, the king, in great agitation and anger, said to destroy all the wise men of Babylon. [13] The decree went out, and the wise men were being executed, and they sought Daniel and his friends to be killed.

[14] Then Daniel replied with counsel and discretion to Arioch, chief of the guards of the king who went out to kill the wise men of Babylon. [15] Responding, he said to Arioch, the officer of the king, "Why is the decree from the king so harsh?"

[16] Then Arioch made known the matter to Daniel. And Daniel went and petitioned the king that he might give him time to declare the interpretation to the king.

[17] Then Daniel went to his house and to Hananiah, Mishael, and Azariah—his companions—the matter he made known [18] in order to seek compassion from the God of Heaven concerning this mystery, so that they might not destroy Daniel and his companions with the rest of the wise men of Babylon.

[19] Then to Daniel—in the vision of the night—the mystery was revealed. Then Daniel blessed the God of Heaven. [20] Responding, Daniel said, "May the name of God be blessed from forever to forever because of the wisdom and might that are his. [21] He changes the times and seasons, deposes kings and raises up kings, gives wisdom to wise men and knowledge to those with understanding. [22] He reveals the deep things and the hidden things, he knows what is in the darkness, and the light with him is encamped. [23] You, the God of my fathers, I praise and laud, who have given me the wisdom and the might. Now you have made known to me what we asked of you—that is, the matter of the king you made known to us."

[24] Therefore, Daniel went to Arioch, whom the king appointed to destroy the wise men of Babylon. He came, and thus he said to him, "The wise men of Babylon do not destroy. Take me before the king, and the interpretation to the king I will declare."

[25] Then Arioch in haste brought Daniel before the king, and thus he said to him, "I have found a man from the sons of the exile of Judah, who the interpretation to the king will make known."

[26] Responding, the king said to Daniel (whose name was Belteshazzar), "Are you able to make known to me the dream that I dreamed and its interpretation?"

[27] Responding, Daniel said before the king, "No wise men, sorcerers, magicians, diviners are able to declare to the king the mystery that the king asks. [28] However, there is a God in heaven who reveals mysteries. And he has made known to King Nebuchadnezzar what will be in the latter days. Your dream and the visions of your head upon your bed are this. [29] As for you, O king, your thoughts upon your bed came up—what will be after this; the revealer of mysteries made known to you what will be. [30] And as for me, not on account of wisdom that I have more than all the living this mystery was revealed to me, but in order that the interpretation to the king may be made known, and the thoughts of your heart you may know.

³¹"You, O king, were looking, and oh! One great statue—that image was great and its splendor was surpassing—was standing before you, and its appearance was frightening. ³²That statue—its head was of fine gold, its chest and its arms were of silver, its belly and its thighs were of bronze, ³³its legs were of iron; as for its feet, they were partly of iron and partly of clay. ³⁴You were looking until a stone was cut out, not by hands. It struck the statue on its feet of iron and clay, and it shattered them. ³⁵Then the iron, the clay, the bronze, the silver, and the gold fell to pieces as one, and they were like chaff from threshing floors of summer. The wind lifted them and no trace of them could be found. But the stone which shattered the statue became a great mountain, and it filled all the land.

³⁶"This is the dream, and its interpretation we will tell the king. ³⁷You, O king, are the king of kings, to whom the God of Heaven has given the kingdom, the power, and the strength, and the honor. ³⁸And wherever they may dwell, the sons of man, the beast of the field, and the birds of heaven he has given into your hand, and he made you to rule over all of them. You are the head of gold. ³⁹After you will arise another kingdom, inferior to you, and another, third kingdom—of bronze—[will arise], which will rule over all the earth. ⁴⁰The fourth kingdom will be strong like iron. Just as iron shatters and grinds everything, so, as iron that smashes, it will shatter and smash all these. ⁴¹And that which you saw—the feet and toes—partly of potter's clay and partly of iron, will be a divided kingdom. And some of the firmness of the iron will be in it, just as you saw the iron mixed with the soft clay. ⁴²As for the toes of the feet, some of them are iron and some of them are clay; part of the kingdom will be strong, and part of it will be brittle. ⁴³Those that you saw—the iron mixed with the soft clay—will be mixed in the seed of man, but they will not stick to one another, just as iron does not mix with clay. ⁴⁴In the days of those kings, the God of Heaven will raise up a kingdom that will never be destroyed, and the kingdom will not be left to another people. It will shatter and put an end to all these kingdoms. But as for it, it will stand forever, ⁴⁵just as you saw that from the mountain a stone was cut, which was not [cut] by hands, and it shattered the iron, the bronze, the clay, the silver, and the gold.

"A great God has made known to the king what will happen after this. The dream is certain, and its interpretation is sure."

⁴⁶Then King Nebuchadnezzar fell on his face and to Daniel paid homage. He commanded an offering and incense to be offered to him. ⁴⁷Responding, the king said to Daniel, "Surely, as for your god, he is god of gods and lord of kings and the revealer of mysteries, since you were able to reveal this mystery."

⁴⁸Then the king made Daniel great, and many gifts he gave him. He made him ruler over all the province of Babylon and chief prefect over all the wise men of Babylon. ⁴⁹And Daniel sought of the king, and he appointed Shadrach, Meshach, and Abednego over the affairs of the province of Babylon, but Daniel was in the court of the king.

Daniel 3

³:¹Nebuchadnezzar the king made an image of gold; its height was sixty cubits; its breadth was six cubits. He set it up in the plain of Dura in the province of Babylon. ²Then Nebuchadnezzar the king sent to assemble the satraps, the prefects and the governors, the counselors, the treasurers, the judges, the magistrates, and all the high officials of the province to come to the dedication of the image, which Nebuchadnezzar the king had set up. ³Then the satraps, the prefects and the governors, the counselors, the treasurers, the judges, the magistrates, and all the high officials of the province were assembling for the dedication of the image, which Nebuchadnezzar the king had set up, and they were standing before the image, which Nebuchadnezzar had set up.

⁴And the herald was calling loudly: "To you it is said, peoples, nations, and languages! ⁵At the time that you hear the sound of the horn, the flute, lyre, the trigon, harp, pipe, and all kinds of music, you are to fall down and pay homage to the image of gold, which Nebuchadnezzar the king has set up. ⁶But whoever does not fall down and pay homage at that moment will be thrown into the midst of the furnace of blazing fire."

⁷Therefore, at that time, when all the peoples began hearing the sound of the horn, the flute, lyre, the trigon, harp, and all kinds of music, all the peoples, nations, and languages were falling down (and) paying homage to the image of gold, which Nebuchadnezzar the king had set up.

⁸Therefore, at that time, certain Chaldeans came forward and accused the Jews. ⁹They answered, saying to Nebuchadnezzar the king, "O king, live forever. ¹⁰You, O king, made a decree that every man who hears the sound of the horn, the flute, lyre, the trigon, harp, and pipe, and all kinds of music should fall down and pay homage to the image of gold. ¹¹But whoever does not fall down and pay homage will be thrown into the midst of the furnace of blazing fire. ¹²There are certain Jews whom you appointed over the administration of the province of Babylon—Shadrach, Meshach, and Abednego. These men have not paid attention to you, O king. Your gods they do not serve, and the image of gold which you have set up they are not paying homage to."

¹³Then Nebuchadnezzar in rage and fury said to bring Shadrach, Meshach, and Abednego. So these men were brought before the king. ¹⁴Responding, Nebuchadnezzar said to them, "Is it true, Shadrach, Meshach, and Abednego, my gods you do not serve, and to the image of gold which I set up you are not paying homage? ¹⁵Now, if you are ready, at the time you hear the sound of the horn, the flute, lyre, the trigon, harp, and bagpipe, and all kinds of music, you will fall down and pay homage to the image that I have made. But if you do not pay homage, at that moment you will be thrown to the midst of the furnace of blazing fire, and who is a god who will deliver you from my hand?"

¹⁶Shadrach, Meshach, and Abednego answered, saying to the king, "Nebuchadnezzar, we do not need concerning this word to respond to you ¹⁷whether our God whom we serve is able to deliver us. From the furnace of blazing fire and from your hand, O king, he may deliver, ¹⁸but if not, let it be known to you, O king, that your gods we do not serve and to the image of gold which you have set up we will not pay homage."

¹⁹Then Nebuchadnezzar was filled with fury and the image of his face was changed against Shadrach, Meshach, and Abednego. Responding, he said to heat the furnace seven times more than was proper to heat it. ²⁰And to certain mighty men who were in his army he said to bind Shadrach, Meshach, and Abednego to cast into the furnace of blazing fire.

²¹Then those men were bound in their coats, trousers, hats, and clothing, and they were cast into the midst of the furnace of blazing fire. ²²Because of this—because the command of the king was so harsh, and the furnace was heated excessively—those men who carried up Shadrach, Meshach, and Abednego, the flame of the fire killed them. ²³But those three men—Shadrach, Meshach, and Abednego—fell into the midst of the furnace of blazing fire bound.

²⁴Then Nebuchadnezzar the king was alarmed, and he rose in haste. Responding, he said to his high officials, "Did we not cast three men into the midst of the furnace bound?"

Responding, they said to the king, "Certainly, O king!"

²⁵Responding, he said, "Look! I am seeing four men, loosened, walking in the midst of the fire, and there is no injury on them. And the appearance of the fourth is like a son of the gods."

²⁶Then Nebuchadnezzar approached the door of the furnace of blazing fire. Responding, he said, "Shadrach, Meshach, and Abednego, servants of the Most High God, come out and come here!"

Then Shadrach, Meshach, and Abednego were coming out from the midst of the fire. ²⁷Assembling, the satraps, prefects, governors, and high officials of the king were seeing those men, that the fire did not have power over their bodies, the hair of their heads was not singed, their coats were not affected, and the smell of fire was not on them.

²⁸Responding, Nebuchadnezzar said, "Blessed be the God of Shadrach, Meshach, and Abednego, who sent his angel and delivered his servants who trusted in him, and the command of the king violated, and gave their bodies, because they would not serve and would not worship any god except their God. ²⁹By me a decree is made that any people, nation, or language who speaks negligence against the God of Shadrach, Meshach, and Abednego will be dismembered, and his house will be made into a dung heap, because there is no other God who is able to deliver like this."

³⁰Then the king prospered Shadrach, Meshach, and Abednego in the province of Babylon.

Daniel 3:31–4:34[4:1–37]

³:³¹"Nebuchadnezzar the king to all peoples, nations, and languages, which live in all the earth: May your peace increase! ³²It seemed good to me to declare the signs and the wonders which the Most High God did with me. ³³How great are his signs! And how mighty are his wonders! His kingdom is an everlasting kingdom, and his dominion is from generation to generation.

⁴:¹"I, Nebuchadnezzar, was at ease in my house, and [I was] flourishing in my palace. ²A dream I saw, and it was frightening me. And [I saw] fantasies upon my bed, and the visions of my head terrified me. ³I made a decree to bring before me all the wise men of Babylon, who could make known to me the interpretation of the dream. ⁴Then the magicians, enchanters, Chaldeans, and diviners were coming, and the dream I was saying before them, but its interpretation they were not making known to me.

⁵"At last Daniel came before me (whose name is Belteshazzar, like the name of my god, and in whom is a spirit of the holy gods), and the dream I told him. ⁶'Belteshazzar, chief of the magicians, who I know that a spirit of the holy gods is in you, and no mystery baffles you, consider my dream that I saw, and say its interpretation. ⁷These were the visions of my head upon my bed:

'I was looking, and oh! A tree was in the middle of the earth, and its height was great. ⁸The tree grew great, and it became strong. Its height was reaching to the heavens, and its visibility was [reaching] to the end of the whole earth. ⁹Its foliage was beautiful, and its fruit was abundant, and food for all was on it. Under it the beasts of the field were seeking shade, and in its branches the birds of the heavens dwelled, and from it all flesh was being sustained.

¹⁰'I was looking in the visions of my head upon my bed, and oh! A watcher—that is, a holy one—was descending from the heavens. ¹¹He was calling out loudly, and thus he was saying, "Chop down the tree, and cut off its branches! Strip its foliage, and scatter its fruit! Let the beasts flee from under it, and the birds from its branches. ¹²But the stump of its roots leave in the ground, and with a band of iron and bronze in grass of the field. And with the dew of the heavens let it become wet, and with the beasts let its portion be with the grass of the ground. ¹³Let its heart be changed from a man, and let a beast's heart be given to him, and let seven periods of time pass over him. ¹⁴By a decree of watchers is the message, and a command of holy ones is the decision, in order that the living may know that the Most High is ruler over the kingdom of mankind, and to whomever he wishes, he gives it, and the lowliest of men he sets over it."

¹⁵'This dream I, King Nebuchadnezzar, saw. Now you, Belteshazzar, say the interpretation. As none of the wise men of my kingdom are able to make known the interpretation to me, but you are able, for a spirit of the holy gods is in you.'"

¹⁶Then Daniel, whose name was Belteshazzar, was appalled for a short time, and his thoughts were alarming him. Responding, the king said, "Belteshazzar, do not let the dream or its interpretation alarm you."

Responding, Belteshazzar said, "My lord, may the dream be for those who hate you, and its interpretation for your adversaries. ¹⁷The tree that you saw, which grew great and became strong, and whose height reached to the heavens, and whose visibility [reached] to all the earth;

¹⁸and whose foliage was beautiful, and whose fruit was abundant, and on which was food for all;

under which dwelled the beasts of the field, and in whose branches lived the birds of the heavens

¹⁹—you are it, O king, who have grown great and become strong; and whose greatness has become great and has reached to the heavens, and whose dominion is to the end of the earth.

²⁰That which the king saw—a watcher, a holy one, descending from the heavens, and saying, *'Chop down the tree, and destroy it! But the stump of its roots leave in the ground—and with a band of iron and bronze in the grass of the field—and with the dew of the heavens let it become wet, and with the beasts of the field let its portion be until seven times pass over him.'*

²¹—this is the interpretation, O king, and it is the decree of the Most High that has come upon my lord, the king:

²²"You will be driven from mankind, and your dwelling place will be with the beasts of the field. You will be fed grass like cattle, and some of the dew of the heavens will be making you wet. Seven times will pass over you until you know that the Most High is ruler over the kingdom of mankind, and to whomever he wishes, he gives it. ²³And as it was said to leave the stump of the tree's roots, your kingdom remains for you from when you acknowledge that heaven is sovereign. ²⁴Therefore, O king, may my counsel be pleasing to you—break off your sins with righteousness, and your iniquities (break off) with showing mercy to the poor—perhaps there may be a lengthening of your prosperity."

²⁵All this came upon Nebuchadnezzar the king. ²⁶At the end of twelve months, he was walking on [the roof of] the palace of the kingdom of Babylon. ²⁷Responding, the king said, "Is this not Babylon the great, which I myself have built for a royal house, by the strength of my power and for the glory of my majesty?"

²⁸While the word was in the mouth of the king, a voice came down from the heavens, "To you it is said, Nebuchadnezzar the king: *The kingdom has departed from you, ²⁹and from mankind you are driven, and with the beasts of the field is your dwelling. You will be fed grass like cattle, and seven times will pass over you until you acknowledge that the Most High is ruler over the kingdom of mankind, and to whomever he wishes, he gives it."*

³⁰At that moment, the word about Nebuchadnezzar was fulfilled, and from mankind he was driven, and he was eating the grass like cattle, and some of the dew of the heavens was making his body wet, until his hair grew long like eagles' and his nails [grew] like birds.'

³¹"At the end of the days, I, Nebuchadnezzar, lifted my eyes to the heavens. And as my reason to me was returning, the Most High I blessed, and the one who lives forever I praised and honored, whose dominion is an everlasting dominion, and whose kingdom is from generation to generation. ³²All the inhabitants of the earth are considered nothing, and according to his will he does with the host of the heavens and the inhabitants of the earth. There is no one who can strike his hand and say to him, 'What have you done?' ³³At the time that my reason was returning to me, and for the glory of my kingdom, my majesty and my splendor were returning to me, and my counselors and my magistrates were seeking me; over my kingdom I was established, and surpassing greatness was added to me. ³⁴Now I, Nebuchadnezzar, praise and exalt and glorify the king of the heavens, whose every work is true, and whose ways are just, and who the ones walking in pride is able to humble."

Daniel 5:1–6:1[5:31]

⁵:¹Belshazzar the king made a great feast for a thousand of his noblemen, and in front of the thousand, he was drinking wine. ²Belshazzar said, with the taste of the wine, to bring the vessels of gold and silver that Nebuchadnezzar his father had taken from the temple that was in Jerusalem, so the king and his noblemen, his wives and his concubines, could drink with them. ³Then they brought the vessels of gold that had been taken from the temple which was the house of God which was in Jerusalem, and the king and his noblemen, his wives and his concubines, drank with them. ⁴They drank the wine, and they praised the gods of gold and silver, bronze, iron, wood, and stone.

⁵At that moment, fingers of a human hand appeared, and they were writing opposite the lampstand on the plaster of the wall of the palace of the king. The king was watching the back of the hand which was writing. ⁶Then the king—his countenance changed, and his thoughts were alarming him, and the joints of his loins were loosening, and his knees were knocking together. ⁷The king was calling loudly to bring the conjurers, the Chaldeans, and the diviners. Responding, the king said to the wise men of Babylon, "Any man who reads this writing and makes known its interpretation to me will be clothed with purple, and a necklace of gold will be around his neck, and he will have power as third in the kingdom."

⁸Then all the wise men of the king were coming in, but they were not able to read the writing or make its interpretation known to the king.

⁹Then King Belshazzar was greatly alarmed, and his countenance was changing, and his noblemen were becoming perplexed. ¹⁰The queen, because of the words of the king and his noblemen, came to the banquet house. Responding, the queen said, "O king, live forever. Do not let your thoughts alarm you, and do not let your countenance be changed. ¹¹There is a man in your kingdom who has a spirit of the holy gods in him. In the days of your father, illumination, insight, and wisdom like the wisdom of the gods were found in him. ¹²King Nebuchadnezzar, your father, appointed him chief of the magicians, conjurers, Chaldeans, and diviners—your father, the king. Because an extraordinary spirit and knowledge, and insight for interpreting dreams, declaring riddles, and 'untying knots' were found in this Daniel, for whom the king appointed the name 'Belteshazzar,' now let Daniel be called, that the interpretation he might declare."

¹³Then Daniel was brought in before the king. Responding, the king said to Daniel, "Are you that Daniel, who is one of the sons of the exile of Judah, which my father the king brought from Judah? ¹⁴I have heard about you that a spirit of the gods is in you, and illumination, insight, and great wisdom are found in you. ¹⁵Just now the wise men and conjurers were brought before me that they might read this writing and make known to me its interpretation. But they are not able to make known the interpretation of the words. ¹⁶But I myself have heard about you, that you are able to interpret interpretations and to loosen knots. So, if you are able to read the writing and make its interpretation known to me, you will be clothed with purple, and a necklace of gold will be around your neck, and you will have power as third in the kingdom."

¹⁷Then responding, Daniel said before the king, "Let your gifts be for yourself, and give your rewards to another. Nevertheless, I will read the writing to the king, and I will make known the interpretation to him. ¹⁸As for you, O king—the Most High God gave the kingdom and the greatness and the honor and the majesty to Nebuchadnezzar your father. ¹⁹Because of the greatness which he gave him, all peoples, nations, and languages were trembling and in fear before him; whom he wished he killed; and whom he wished he let live; and whom he wished he exalted; and whom he wished he humiliated. ²⁰And when his heart was lifted up, and his spirit hardened so that he acted proudly, he was deposed from the throne of his kingdom, and the glory was taken from him. ²¹From the sons of man he was driven, and his heart was like the beasts, and his dwelling was with wild donkeys, and grass was fed to him like cattle. And from the dew of heaven his body was wet until he acknowledged that the Most High God is ruler over the kingdom of man and whomever he wishes, he establishes over it.

²²"But you, his son, Belshazzar, did not humble your heart, even though you knew all this. ²³But over the Lord of heaven you exalted yourself, and the vessels of his house they have brought before you. And you and your noblemen, your wives and

concubines, are drinking wine with them. And the gods of silver and gold, bronze, iron, wood and stone which do not see, and do not hear, and do not know, you praised. But the God in whose hand is your life and all your ways, him you have not honored. ²⁴Then from him the back of the hand was sent, and this writing was written. ²⁵This is the writing that was written: *Mene, mene, tekel, upharsin.* ²⁶This is the interpretation of the message: *Mene:* God has numbered your kingdom and brought an end to it. ²⁷*Tekel:* You have been weighed on the balances and you have been found lacking. ²⁸*Peres:* Your kingdom has been divided and given to the Medes and Persians."

²⁹Then Belshazzar said [gave orders], and Daniel was clothed with purple, and a necklace of gold was around his neck, and a proclamation was made about him that he was the third ruler in the kingdom. ³⁰On that very night Belshazzar the Chaldean king was killed, ⁶:¹and Darius the Mede received the kingdom at about the age of sixty-two.

Daniel 6:2–29[1–28]

⁶:²It seemed good to Darius to establish over the kingdom 120 satraps who would be in all the kingdom. ³And over them were three overseers (which Daniel was one of them) to whom these satraps were to give account, and the king would not suffer harm.

⁴Then this Daniel was distinguishing himself among the overseers and satraps. Because an extraordinary spirit was in him, the king was intending to set him over all the kingdom. ⁵Then the overseers and satraps began seeking a cause to find against Daniel concerning the kingdom, but no cause or corruption were they able to find. Because he was trustworthy, no negligence or corruption did they find concerning him.

⁶Then those men were saying, "We will not find against this Daniel any cause unless we find (it) against him with respect to the law of his God." ⁷Then these overseers and satraps came by collusion to the king, and were saying thus to him, "O Darius the king, live forever. ⁸All the overseers of the kingdom, the prefects and the satraps, the counselors and the governors have consulted together to establish a statute of the king and to enforce a prohibition that anyone who seeks a petition from any god or man except you for thirty days, O king, will be thrown to the den of lions. ⁹Now, O king, you should establish the prohibition and sign the document, which cannot be changed, according to the law of the Medes and Persians which cannot be annulled." ¹⁰Therefore, King Darius signed the document, that is, the prohibition.

¹¹But Daniel, when he knew that the document had been signed, went to his house. His windows were opened in his upper chamber facing Jerusalem, and three

times a day he would kneel on his knees, praying and praising before his God, as he had been doing before this. ¹²Then those men came by collusion, and they found Daniel seeking and imploring before his God. ¹³Then they approached [the king], and they were saying before the king concerning the prohibition of the king, "Did you not write a prohibition that any man who seeks from any god or man except you for thirty days, O king, will be thrown into the den of lions?"

Responding, the king said, "The matter is certain, according to the law of the Medes and Persians, which cannot be annulled."

¹⁴Then they answered, saying before the king, "Daniel, who is one of the exiles of Judah, does not pay heed to you, O king, or to the prohibition which you signed. But three times in a day he makes his petition."

¹⁵Then the king, when he heard the word, was very distressed, and set [his] mind upon Daniel to deliver him. Until the sun went down, he was struggling to rescue him.

¹⁶Then those men came by collusion to the king, and they were saying to the king, "Know, O king, that a law of the Medes and Persians is that any prohibition or statute which the king establishes cannot be changed."

¹⁷Then the king gave the order, and they brought Daniel, and they threw (him) to the den of lions. Responding, the king said to Daniel, "Your God, whom you serve continually—may he deliver you."

¹⁸A stone was brought, and it was set over the mouth of the den. And the king sealed it with his signet ring and with the signet ring of his noblemen, so that nothing concerning Daniel would be changed. ¹⁹Then the king went to his palace. He passed the night without food, and he did not summon entertainment for himself. His sleep fled from him.

²⁰Then arising at daybreak, at dawn, the king went with haste to the lions' den. ²¹As he drew near to the den, he cried out to Daniel with a troubled voice. Responding, the king said to Daniel, "Daniel, servant of the living God, has your God whom you serve continually been able to deliver you from the lions?"

²²Then Daniel with the king spoke, "O king, live forever! ²³My God sent his angel, and he shut the mouth of the lions, and they did not harm me. Inasmuch as before him I was found to be innocent, so also before you, O king, I have not done harm."

²⁴Then the king was exceedingly glad concerning him, and he gave the order concerning Daniel to bring up from the den. So Daniel was brought up from the den, and no harm was found on him, who had trusted in his God. ²⁵The king gave the order and they brought those men who accused Daniel, and they threw them, their sons, and their wives to the lions' den. They did not reach the bottom of the den before the lions overpowered them and crushed all their bones.

²⁶Then Darius the king wrote to all peoples, nations, and languages, which were living in all the land: "May your peace abound! ²⁷By me a decree is made that in the whole dominion of my kingdom they must tremble and fear before the God of

Daniel—who is the living and enduring God forever, and whose kingdom will not be destroyed, and whose dominion is until the end. ²⁸He delivers, and he rescues, and he does signs and wonders in the heavens and on the earth—who has delivered Daniel from the power of the lions."

²⁹Then this Daniel prospered in the reign of Darius, that is, in the reign of Cyrus the Persian.

Daniel 7

¹In the first year of Belshazzar, king of Babylon, Daniel saw a dream and visions of his head upon his bed. Then the dream he wrote down; the beginning of the account he said. ²Responding, Daniel said, "I was looking in my vision in the night, and oh! The four winds of heaven were stirring up the great sea. ³Four great beasts were coming up from the sea, each different from the other. ⁴The first one was like a lion, but it had wings of an eagle. I was looking until its wings were plucked, and it was lifted from the ground, and it was set upon its feet like a man. And a human heart was given to it.

⁵"And oh!—another beast, a second one, resembling a bear, but to one side it was raised up. And three ribs were in its mouth, between its teeth. And thus they said to it, 'Arise! Eat much meat!'

⁶"After this, I was looking, and oh!—another, like a leopard! But it had four wings of a bird on its back, and the beast had four heads, and dominion was given to it.

⁷"After this I was looking in the visions of the night, and oh!—a fourth beast, dreadful and terrifying and exceedingly strong! It had great teeth of iron. It was eating, and it was crushing, and it was trampling the rest with its feet. And it was different from all the beasts that were before it. It had ten horns. ⁸I was considering the horns, and oh! Another horn, a little one, came up among them. And three of the former horns were uprooted before it. And oh! Eyes like the eyes of a man were on this horn, and a mouth speaking great things.

⁹"I was looking, until thrones were set up, and an Ancient of Days sat. His garment was white like snow, and the hair on his head was white like wool. His throne had flames of fire; its wheels were burning fire. ¹⁰A river of fire was gushing and coming out from before him. A thousand of thousands were attending him, and a myriad of myriads was standing before him. The court sat, and books were opened.

¹¹"I was looking then from (the time of) the sound of the great words that the horn was speaking, I was looking until the beast was killed, and its body was destroyed, and it was given to the burning of the fire. ¹²As for the rest of the beasts, their dominion was taken away, but a prolonging in life was given to them until a season and a time.

¹³"I was looking in the visions of the night, and oh! With the clouds of heaven one

like a son of man was coming. He came up to the Ancient of Days, and they presented him before him. ¹⁴And to him was given dominion and glory and a kingdom, and all peoples, nations, and languages will serve him. His dominion is an eternal dominion that will not pass away, and his kingdom (is one) that will not be destroyed.

¹⁵"My spirit was distressed—I, Daniel—within me, and the visions of my head were alarming me. ¹⁶I approached one of those standing by, and I sought from him the truth concerning all this. He spoke to me, so that he might make known to me the interpretation of the matter. ¹⁷'These great beasts, which they are four, are four kings. They will arise from the earth, ¹⁸but the holy ones of the Most High will receive the kingdom, and they will possess the kingdom forever and forever and ever.'

¹⁹"Then I desired to make certain concerning the fourth beast, which was different from all of them—(it was) exceedingly dreadful; its teeth were of iron, and its claws were of bronze. It was eating, and crushing, and trampling the rest under its feet—²⁰and concerning the ten horns, which were on its head. And [concerning] the other which came up and three fell before it. And as for that horn—it had eyes and a mouth speaking great things. And its appearance was larger than its associate(s).

²¹"I was looking, and that horn was making war with the holy ones, and it was overcoming them ²²until the Ancient of Days came, and judgment was given for the holy ones of the Most High. And the time came, and the holy ones took possession of the kingdom.

²³"Thus he said, 'The fourth beast will be a fourth kingdom on the earth that will be different from all kingdoms, and will devour all the earth, and will trample it down, and will crush it. ²⁴As for the ten horns—from this kingdom ten kings will arise, and another will arise after them. He will be different from the previous ones. He will subdue three kings, ²⁵and he will speak words against the Most High, and he will wear out the holy ones of the Most High. And he will intend to change times set by law. They will be given into his hand until a time, times, and half a time. ²⁶The court will sit, and his dominion they will take away, in order to destroy and abolish until the end. ²⁷And the kingdom, the dominion, and the greatness of the kingdoms under all the heavens will be given to the people of the holy ones of the Most High. Their kingdom is an everlasting kingdom, and all dominions will serve and obey them.'

²⁸"At this point was the end of the account. As for me, Daniel, my thoughts were greatly alarming me, and my countenance was changing upon me. But I kept the matter in my heart."

Daniel 8

¹"In the third year of the reign of Belshazzar the king, a vision appeared to me—I, Daniel—after the one that appeared to me previously. ²And I looked in the vision,

and while I was looking, I was in Susa the citadel, which is in Elam the province. I looked in the vision, and I myself was along the canal of Ulai.

³"I lifted my eyes, and I looked—and oh! A single ram was standing in front of the canal. It had two horns. The horns were long, but one was longer than the other, and the longer one was coming up later. ⁴I saw the ram charging westward and northward and southward, and no animal could stand before it; and there was none who could deliver from its hand. It did as it pleased, and it magnified itself.

⁵"I was considering, and oh! A billy goat of the goats was coming from the west across the face of all the earth, and nothing was touching the ground. The billy goat had a prominent horn between his eyes. ⁶He came up to the ram that had two horns, which I saw standing before the canal, and he ran toward it in his raging strength. ⁷I saw him reach the side of the ram, and he was enraged at it. He struck the ram, and he broke its two horns. There was no power in the ram to stand against him. He threw it to the ground and trampled it. And no one delivered the ram from his hand.

⁸"The billy goat of the goats magnified himself exceedingly, but when he was strong, the great horn was broken, and four prominent ones came up in its place to the four winds of heaven. ⁹From one of them went out a smaller horn, and it grew exceedingly great to the south and to the east and to the Beautiful. ¹⁰It grew as far as the host of heaven, and it caused some of the host and some of the stars to fall to the earth, and it trampled them. ¹¹Even to the commander of the host it magnified itself, and from him was taken away 'the continual,' and the place of his sanctuary was thrown down. ¹²And the host was being given over, alongside 'the continual,' on account of transgression, and it was casting truth to the ground. It did, and it was successful.

¹³"I heard a holy one speaking, and another holy one said to that one, the one speaking, 'How long is the vision—"the continual" and the transgression that desolates, the giving over of both a sacred place and a host for trampling?'

¹⁴"And he said to me, 'Until 2,300 evenings and mornings, then a sacred place will be put right.'

¹⁵"And so it was that when I, Daniel, saw the vision, I sought understanding. And oh! Standing in front of me was one with the appearance of a man. ¹⁶I heard the voice of a man between the Ulai. He called, and he said, 'Gabriel, explain the vision to this man.'

¹⁷"And he came near where I was standing. And when he came, I was terrified, and I fell on my face. He said to me, 'Understand, son of man, that the vision is for an end time.'

¹⁸"As he spoke with me, I fell into a deep sleep, my face to the ground. He touched me, and he set me upright where I was standing. ¹⁹He said, 'Look, I am letting you know what will be at the end of the indignation, because at an appointed time will be an end. ²⁰The ram, which you saw with the two horns, represents the kings of Media

and Persia. ²¹And the shaggy goat is the king of Greece. As for the great horn which was between his eyes—it is the first king. ²²As for the broken one and the four that rose in its place—four kingdoms will arise from a nation, but not with its power. ²³In the latter part of their rule when the transgressors have reached full measure, a king will arise—fierce of face and who understands riddles. ²⁴His power will be mighty, but not with his own power. He will destroy extraordinarily. He will be successful, and he will do. He will destroy mighty men and a holy people. ²⁵By his shrewdness, he will cause deceit to succeed by his hand. In his own mind, he will make himself great. He will destroy many at ease, and against the prince of princes he will stand. But without human hand, he will be shattered.

²⁶"'The vision of the evenings and the mornings, which has been said—it is true. But as for you, seal up the vision, for it belongs to many days.'

²⁷"But I, Daniel, was undone, and I was sick for days. Then I arose, and I did the work of the king. I was appalled about the vision, but there was no one to explain."

Daniel 9

¹"In the first year of Darius, son of Ahasuerus, from Median descent, who was made king over the kingdom of the Chaldeans, ²in the first year of his reign, I, Daniel, understood in the scrolls the number of years, which was the word of YHWH to Jeremiah the prophet, for the fullness of the desolation of Jerusalem—seventy years.

³"And I set my face to the Lord God to seek by prayer and supplication, with fasting and sackcloth and ashes. ⁴I prayed to YHWH my God, and I confessed, and I said, 'Ah, Lord, the great and awesome God, keeping covenant and lovingkindness to those who love him and keep his commandments, ⁵we have sinned, and we have done wrong. We have done wickedly, and we have rebelled, turning from your commandments and your judgments. ⁶We did not listen to your servants, the prophets, who spoke in your name to our kings, our princes, and our fathers, and to all the people of the land.

⁷"To you, O Lord, belongs righteousness, but to us belongs open shame, as this day—to the men of Judah and to those dwelling in Jerusalem and to all Israel, those who are near and those who are far away in all the lands, where you scattered them there because of the treachery which they committed against you. ⁸YHWH, to us belongs open shame—to our kings, to our princes, and to our fathers, because we sinned against you. ⁹To the Lord our God belongs compassion and forgiveness, although we have rebelled against him.

¹⁰'We did not listen to the voice of YHWH our God to walk in his torah, which he gave to us by the hand of his servants the prophets. ¹¹All Israel transgressed your torah, turning aside, not listening to your voice, and the curse and the oath has

gushed over us, which is written in the Torah of Moses, the servant of God, because we have sinned against him. ¹²And he fulfilled his words which he spoke against us and against our rulers, which ruled us, to bring on us great calamity, which has not been done under all the heaven like what has been done in Jerusalem. ¹³As it is written in the Torah of Moses, all this calamity came upon us. Yet we have not tried to appease YHWH our God by turning from our iniquity and giving attention to your truth. ¹⁴YHWH kept watch over the calamity, and he brought it upon us, for righteous is YHWH our God over all his deeds which he has done, and we did not listen to his voice.

¹⁵'And now, O Lord our God, who brought your people out from the land of Egypt with a strong hand and made a name for yourself, as at this day, we have sinned. We have been wicked. ¹⁶O Lord, according to all your righteous acts, let your anger and your wrath turn from your city, Jerusalem, the mountain of your holiness, for, on account of our sins and the iniquities of our fathers, Jerusalem and your people have become a reproach to all those around us.

¹⁷'But now, listen, our God, to the prayer of your servant and to his supplications, and shine your face upon your desolate sanctuary, for the sake of the Lord. ¹⁸Incline, my God, your ear and listen! Open your eyes and see our desolations and the city which your name is called over it! For not on account of our righteousness are we pleading our supplications before you, but on account of your great mercy [we are pleading]. ¹⁹O Lord, please listen! O Lord, please forgive! O Lord, give attention and act—Do not delay for your sake, my God, because your name is called over your city and over your people.'

²⁰"And while I was speaking and praying and confessing my sin and the sin of my people, Israel, and presenting my supplication before YHWH my God on behalf of the holy mountain of my God—²¹while I was speaking in prayer, the man Gabriel, whom I had seen in the vision at the beginning, wearied with weariness, approached me at the time of the evening offering.

²²"He instructed and he spoke with me, and he said, 'Daniel, now I have come forth to instruct you in understanding. ²³At the beginning of your supplication, a word went out, and I, even I, came to declare [it], for you are treasured. Consider the word and understand the vision. ²⁴Seventy weeks are determined for your people and for your holy city to finish the transgression, and to make an end of sin, and to atone for iniquity, and to bring in everlasting righteousness, and to seal up vision and prophet, and to anoint a holy of holies. ²⁵Know and understand: From the going out of a word to restore and to build Jerusalem until an anointed one, a ruler, will be seven weeks. And for sixty-two weeks it will be rebuilt with a plaza and a moat, but in distressed times. ²⁶And after the sixty-two weeks, an anointed one will be cut off and have nothing. And the city and the holy place, the people of the ruler who is coming will destroy, and its end will come with a flood. And until (the) end will be

war; desolations are determined. ²⁷He will confirm a covenant for the many for one week. But in the middle of the week he will stop sacrifice and offering, and upon the wing of abominations will be a desolator, until complete destruction—one that is decreed—pours out on the desolator.'"

Daniel 10–11

¹In the third year of Cyrus, king of Persia, a word was revealed to Daniel, whose name was called Belteshazzar. True was the word—and a great conflict. But he understood the word, and he had an understanding about the vision.

²"In those days, I, Daniel, was mourning for three weeks of days. ³Pleasant bread I did not eat, and meat and wine did not enter my mouth. I did not anoint myself at all until the fullness of three weeks of days.

⁴"On the twenty-fourth day of the first month, I was along the bank of the great river—that is the Tigris—⁵and I lifted my eyes, and I looked, and oh! A man clothed in linen! His waist was girded with gold of Uphaz. ⁶His body was like topaz. His face was like the appearance of lightning, and his eyes were like torches of fire. His arms and legs were like the gleam of burnished bronze, and the sound of his words was like the sound of a tumult.

⁷"And I, Daniel, alone saw the vision. The men who were with me did not see the vision. However, a great fear fell upon them, and they fled to hide themselves, ⁸and I alone remained. I saw this great vision, and no strength remained in me. My vigor was changed for ruin, and I did not retain strength. ⁹I heard the sound of his words, and as I heard the sound of his words, I fell on my face into a deep sleep, and my face was on the ground.

¹⁰"And oh! A hand touched me, and it set me trembling on my knees and palms of my hands. ¹¹He said to me, 'Daniel, highly favored man, understand the words which I am about to speak to you. Stand in your place, for now I have been sent to you.' And when he spoke this word with me, I stood trembling.

¹²"And he said to me, 'Do not be afraid, Daniel, for from the first day when you set your heart to understand and to humble yourself before your God, your words were heard, and I have come on account of your words. ¹³But the prince of the kingdom of Persia was standing against me for twenty-one days, and, to my surprise, Michael, one of the chief princes, came to help me, since I alone was left there beside the kings of Persia. ¹⁴But I came to help you understand what will happen to your people in the latter days, for the vision is for days yet to come.'

¹⁵"When he spoke with me according to these words, I bowed my face to the ground, and I was unable to speak. ¹⁶Then oh! One with the likeness of the sons of men was touching my lips, and I opened my mouth, and I spoke. I said to the one

standing before me, 'My lord, on account of the vision, my pangs have come upon me, and I have not retained any strength. ¹⁷How is the servant of this my lord able to speak with this my lord? As for me, from now no strength remains in me, and breath is not left in me.'

¹⁸"The one with the appearance of a man touched me again, and he strengthened me. ¹⁹He said, 'Do not be afraid, dearly loved man. Peace be yours. Be strong, yes, be strong.'

"And when he had spoken with me, I was strengthened. And I said, 'May my lord speak for you have strengthened me.'

²⁰"And he said, 'Do you know why I came to you? But now I will return to fight with the prince of Persia, I must go forth—Oh! The prince of Greece is coming. ²¹However, I will tell you what is inscribed in a book of truth. There is no one supporting me against these—except Michael, your prince. [**Daniel 11**] ¹I, in the first year of Darius the Mede, arose to strengthen and be protection for him. ²But now truth I will tell you:

'Listen, another three kings are arising for Persia, and the fourth will gain much more wealth than all of them. And when he has become strong in his wealth, he will stir up everything—that is, the kingdom of Greece. ³A king of strength will arise. He will rule with great authority, and he will do as he pleases. ⁴But when he has arisen, his kingdom will be broken, and it will be divided to the four winds of the heavens—but not to his descendants and not according to his authority which he ruled, for his kingdom will be uprooted and (given) to others besides these.

⁵'And the king of the south and one of his princes will grow strong, and he will grow strong over him. And he will rule. His dominion will be a great dominion. ⁶At the end of years they will ally, and the daughter of the king of the south will come to the king of the north to make an agreement. But she will not retain the strength of arm, and he will not stand, or his arm. And she will be given over, and the ones who brought her, and he who fathered her, and he who supported her in that time. ⁷One of the shoots from her root will arise in his place, and he will come to the army, and he will enter the fortress of the king of the north, and he will deal with them, and he will prevail. ⁸And also their gods with their molten images, with their precious vessels of silver and gold into captivity he will take to Egypt. And he for years will withdraw from the king of the north.

⁹"Then he [the king of the north] will come into the realm of the king of the south, but he will return to his own land. ¹⁰But his sons will mobilize and gather a multitude of great power. It will keep coming and overflow and pass through and return and wage war as far as (his) fortress. ¹¹But the king of the south will be enraged, and he will go out, and he will fight with him, with the king of the north. He will raise up a great multitude, but the multitude will be given into his hand. ¹²When the multitude is carried away, his heart will be lifted up, and he will throw down tens of thousands,

but he will not remain strong. ¹³Again, the king of the north will raise up a multitude greater than the first, and at the time of the end, some years, he will again come with a great army and abundant supplies. ¹⁴And in those times, many will stand against the king of the south, and the sons of the violent ones of your people will be lifted up to establish a vision, but they will stumble.

¹⁵"Then the king of the north will come, and heap up an assault ramp, and he will capture a fortified city. And the strength of the south will not stand, not even his choice troops. There will be no strength to stand. ¹⁶The one coming against him will do as he pleases. No one will stand before him. He will stand in the Beautiful Land, and destruction will be in his hand. ¹⁷He will set his face to come with the power of his entire kingdom, and a proposal with him, and he will make it. And the daughter of women he will give him to ruin it [the kingdom], but it will not stand, and it will not be for him. ¹⁸Then he will set his face to coastlands, and he will capture many. But a commander will stop his scorn against him—moreover, he will return his scorn to him. ¹⁹So he will set his face to the fortresses of his land, but he will stumble, and he will fall, and he will not be found.

²⁰"Then one will stand in his place, who sends out a tax collector for the splendor of the kingdom. But within few days he will be shattered, but not in anger and not in battle. ²¹Then in his place will stand a despicable person, but the honor of kingdom will not be given to him. He will come with ease, and he will seize the kingdom by intrigues. ²²The overflowing forces will be overwhelmed before him, and they will be broken—and also a ruler of a covenant. ²³And after he makes an alliance with him, he will act deceitfully. He will go up, and he will become powerful with a few people. ²⁴With ease and into the richest province he will come, and he will do what his fathers and his fathers' fathers had not done. Booty and plunder and property to them he will distribute, and against fortified cities he will devise his plans—but only for a time. ²⁵He will stir up his power and his heart against the king of the south with his great army, and the king of the south will prepare for battle with his very great and large army, but he will not stand, because plans will be devised against him. ²⁶The ones eating his choice food will break him, and his army will overflow, and many will fall slain. ²⁷As for these two kings—their hearts will be for evil, and at the same table lies they will speak, but it will not succeed, for still there will be an end at an appointed time.

²⁸"Then he will return to his land with great wealth, but his heart will be against the holy covenant. He will take action, and he will return to his land. ²⁹At an appointed time he will return, and enter the south, but the latter will not be like the former—³⁰The ships of Kittim will come against him, and he will be humbled. He will return, and he will be angry against the holy covenant. He will take action, and then he will return. He will show regard for those who abandon the holy covenant. ³¹Forces from him will arise, and they will desecrate the sanctuary fortress. They will

remove the daily sacrifice, and they will set up the abomination that desolates. ³²The wicked ones of the covenant he will pollute with smooth words, but the people who know their God will be strong, and they will act. ³³And the wise of the people will instruct the many, but they will stumble by the sword, by fire, by captivity, or by plunder for days. ³⁴And when they stumble, they will be given a little help, and many will join them insincerely. ³⁵But some of the wise will stumble, to refine them, and to purify, and to make them pure until an end time, for it is still for the appointed time.

³⁶'The king will do as he pleases, and he will exalt himself. He will make himself greater than any god, and against the God of gods he will speak great things. He will prosper until wrath is finished, for that which is decreed has been done. ³⁷The gods of his fathers he will not regard—nor the one beloved of women. He will not regard any god, for he will magnify himself against them all. ³⁸But a god of fortresses instead he will honor, and a god which his fathers did not know he will honor with gold and with silver and with costly stones, and with treasures. ³⁹He will act against a fortress of fortresses with a foreign god. The one he regards he will show great honor, and he will make them ruler over the many, and the land he will divide up for a price. ⁴⁰But at an end time, the king of the south will make war with him. The king of the north will storm against him with chariot and horsemen and with many ships. He will enter the lands, and he will overflow, and he will cross over, ⁴¹and he will enter the Beautiful Land. And many will stumble, but these will be rescued from his hand— Edom, Moab, and the chief sons of Ammon. ⁴²He will stretch out his hand against the lands, and the land of Egypt will not escape. ⁴³He will rule over the hidden treasures of gold and silver and all the treasures of Egypt. The Libyans and Cushites will be in his steps. ⁴⁴Then reports will alarm him from the east and the north, and he will go out in great fury to destroy and to devote many to destruction. ⁴⁵He will pitch his royal tents between the seas and the beautiful holy mountain, but he will come to his end, and there will be no one to help him.

Daniel 12

¹'At that time Michael will arise, the great prince standing over the sons of your people. It will be a time of distress which has not been from the beginning of a nation until that time. And at that time your people will be delivered—all the ones found written in the book. ²And many of those sleeping in the dusty earth will arise—these to life everlasting, and these to shame and to everlasting abhorrence. ³The wise will shine like the shining of the expanse of the heavens, and the ones who make many righteous like the stars forever and ever.

⁴'But now, Daniel, keep these words secret, and seal the scroll until a time of the end. Many will roam about, and knowledge will increase.'

⁵"I looked—I, Daniel—and oh! Two others were standing, one on this bank of the river, and one on that bank of the river. ⁶And he said to the man clothed in linen, who was above the waters of the river, 'How long until the end of the wonders?' ⁷Then I heard the man clothed in linen, who was above the waters of the river, and he raised his right hand and his left hand to the heavens, and he swore by the life of the Eternal One, that for an appointed time, appointed times, and half, and at the completion of the breaking of the power of the holy people all these things will be completed.

⁸"As for me, I heard but I did not understand, so I said, 'My lord, what will be after these things?'

⁹"And he said, 'Go, Daniel, for hidden and sealed are the words until an end time. ¹⁰Many will be purged, purified, and refined. But the wicked will do wickedness, and none of the wicked will understand, but the wise will understand. ¹¹From the time the daily sacrifice is taken away and the desolating abomination is set up there will be 1,290 days. ¹²Happy is the one who waits and reaches 1,335 days. ¹³And now, go to the end and rest, and you will stand for your inheritance at the end of days.'"

Introduction to Daniel

God's Kingdom Will Endure

The book of Daniel features some of the best-known stories in the Bible, as well as some of its most enduring eschatological images. Together the stories of four Judean captives (chs. 1–6) and the visions of future events (chs. 7–12) weave a masterful portrayal of God's sovereignty over all the earth. The book showcases the supremacy of God's eternal kingdom as he shows himself to be superior to all other gods in his knowledge, power, law, and kingship.

A pervasive message of the book is that God's sovereign rule may not always be obvious, but nonetheless he alone rules a kingdom that will endure. His kingdom will ultimately destroy all human kingdoms, and his superior king will reign with his people over an indestructible kingdom forever. Until that day, his people live and often suffer in exile among the kingdoms of the world, but they can endure with courage and confidence as they await the coming fullness of God's eternal kingdom.

Daniel in the Canon

In most English Bibles, the book of Daniel follows the prophetic book of Ezekiel and precedes the Book of the Twelve (Hosea–Malachi).[1] It is considered one of the four so-called Major Prophets: Isaiah, Jeremiah, Ezekiel, Daniel. However, in the Hebrew canon, the book of Daniel is not included with the Prophets[2] but is in the collection of Writings—a collection of books we typically consider to be poetry

---

1. The placement of Daniel after Ezekiel in most English Bibles aligns with the most common arrangement of the Septuagint (LXX), the Greek translation of the Hebrew Bible. Though the LXX was translated by 100 BCE, the evidence for canonical order does not occur until the middle of the second-century CE in Christian canonical lists and in manuscripts of the fourth century and later.

2. The "Prophets" (נְבִיאִים) in the Hebrew canon consists of the Former Prophets (Joshua, Judges, 1–2 Samuel, 1–2 Kings) and the Latter Prophets (Isaiah, Jeremiah, Ezekiel, and the Twelve).

(Job, Psalms, Proverbs, Ecclesiastes, Song of Songs, Lamentations) or historical narrative (Ruth, Chronicles, Ezra, Nehemiah, Esther).

While the history behind these respective canons is not relevant here, it is worth considering why the book of Daniel appears in different places. Generally speaking, the English/Greek canon and the Hebrew canon are organized according to the genre of each book. Thus, in English Bibles, Daniel is categorized as a prophetic book, while in the Hebrew canon, it falls between Esther and Ezra and so is categorized more or less as a book of historical narrative. The reason for these different categorizations likely stems from the dual genres evident in the book of Daniel. Chapters 1–6 are historical in nature, recounting by way of narrative several experiences of Daniel and his friends in Babylonian exile. Chapters 7–12 are visionary literature—specifically, apocalyptic visions with prophetic significance. In light of these drastically different genres, it seems that the Hebrew canon classified the entire book according to the genre of its first half, placing the book alongside narrative books that recount the history of the Jews after the exile: Ezra, Nehemiah, Esther.[3] By contrast, the canon reflected in most English Bibles classified it according to the genre of the second half of the book, placing Daniel among the Prophets.[4]

Genre

The order of books in the English/Greek and the Hebrew canons appears to reflect a focus on one of the book's two distinct genres—broadly described as narrative and prophetic. The first six chapters are stories, narratives about Daniel and his three friends in exile in Babylon. The last six chapters are visions that Daniel received during his time as an exile.

While the English/Greek canon draws attention to Daniel's prophetic role, he was not a typical prophet. In Old Testament Israel, prophets were YHWH's commissioned mouthpieces, clearly seen in the refrain that appears throughout the prophetic books: "Thus says YHWH."[5] The prophets' primary task was calling the people to covenant

---

3. The two books of Chronicles record a second version of the Samuel–Kings history, but they appear in the Writings because the Chronicler wrote during the postexilic period, reframing Israel's history for a new, postexilic generation. The placement of the book of Daniel in the Writings does not mean that the canon compilers did not consider the man Daniel a prophet. That Second Temple Jews did in fact consider him a prophet is evident in Jesus's first-century-AD reference to "Daniel the prophet" (Matt 24:15), the declaration of Josephus that Daniel was "one of the greatest of the prophets" (*Ant.* 10.11.7 [Whiston]), the mention of "Daniel the Prophet" in 4Q174, and early rabbinic sources (John J. Collins, *Daniel*, Hermeneia [Minneapolis: Fortress, 1993], 52). By the time of the Babylonian Talmud (ca. AD 500), however, Daniel—though highly esteemed—was not considered a prophet (b. Sanh. 93b–94).

4. An additional reason posited for the placement of Daniel in the Writings is that the book was written after the collection of Prophets was closed. Proponents of the late-date authorship of the book (see Author and Date below) offer this in support of a second-century-BCE date. However, attempts to specify the process and timing of canonization are inconclusive.

5. כֹּה אָמַר אֲדֹנָי יהוה (also [יהוה] כֹּה־אָמַר יהוה; see, e.g., Isa 7:7; 31:4; Jer 2:5; Ezek 2:4; Amos 1:3; Mic 2:3).

faithfulness, confronting and condemning their sin, and urging them to repent. The book of Daniel gives no evidence that Daniel even interacted with his people outside the palace, where he served as a royal courtier for idolatrous foreign kings.

Daniel better fits the model of a biblical wise man than a prophet of YHWH. It is in the narrative chapters of the book (chs. 1–6) that the narrator portrays Daniel navigating the challenges of exilic life as he remained faithful to the law of his God. This collection of narratives reflects an ancient Near Eastern storytelling genre in which wise and pious captives serve and succeed in foreign royal courts. Called "court stories," these accounts describe either a conflict or a contest in the royal court. In the former, the foreign captive faces danger because of his/her character or faith, and in the latter the captive faces and solves a challenging problem that the king's experts are unable to solve. In both conflicts and contests, the foreign courtier rises to the occasion and demonstrates superiority over the abilities of the king's regular staff. Because of the courtier's success, the king bestows great rewards.[6]

The stories in Dan 1–6 fit loosely in the genre of ancient Near Eastern court stories, where foreign captives are proven innocent after being unjustly accused. In the book of Daniel, Daniel and his friends face accusations of faithfulness to their God instead of to the king, and they are indeed guilty (chs. 3 and 6). Nonetheless, they are also delivered from death and then handsomely rewarded by the king. One scholar notes of these conflicts that "there is a basic conflict, which no happy ending may really resolve. The danger of a new crisis of life and death remains a permanent fixture."[7] While Daniel succeeds under one king (Nebuchadnezzar), another potentially hostile foreign king waits in the wings—first Belshazzar and then Darius. Such deviations from the typical plotline of ancient Near Eastern court stories take the focus off Daniel the wise man and put it on Daniel's God. Neither Daniel nor his friends are the central characters of the book of Daniel. That position belongs to God, and the intent of every court story is to show his superiority over the gods of exile.

The visions in the second half of the book are prophetic in that they reveal future events, though, as noted above, Daniel was not a typical Old Testament prophet nor were his visions typical prophetic visions. The visions he received served a different primary function than calling God's people to repentance. A more exact genre classification of Dan 7–12 requires first considering the broader category of which prophecy is a part: visionary literature, a genre in which "the things . . . pictured by the writer at the time of writing exist in the imagination, not in empirical reality."[8]

---

6. The best-known court story of the ancient Near East is Ahiqar, an Aramaic story of a foreign sage in the Assyrian royal court. In the Bible, the stories of Joseph in Pharaoh's court (Gen 41–42), Esther in the court of Persian Ahasuerus, and Nehemiah in Artaxerxes's court (Neh 1–2) are often classified as court stories.

7. Andreas Bedenbender, "Seers as Mantic Sages in Jewish Apocalyptic (Daniel and Enoch)" in *Scribes, Sages, and Seers: The Sage in the Eastern Mediterranean World*, ed. Leo G. Perdue, FRLANT 219 (Göttingen: Vandenhoeck & Ruprecht, 2008), 264.

8. Leland Ryken, *How to Read the Bible as Literature . . . and Get More Out of It* (Grand Rapids: Zondervan, 1984), 165.

The subgenre of prophetic literature is the best description of what comprises most of the Old Testament prophetic books. However, the visionary literature in the book of Daniel better fits another subgenre: apocalyptic literature. Apocalyptic literature is familiar to New Testament readers since the book of Revelation is an apocalypse.[9]

Apocalyptic literature was prevalent during the Second Temple period and into the Christian era (ca. 250 BCE–AD 250) and exhibits recognizable characteristic features and themes. These include the extensive use of symbolism, the periodization of history, pessimism about the present and optimism about the future, the persecution of the righteous, cosmic destruction, resurrection, and re-creation.[10] Many apocalypses included *ex eventu* prophecy and so were also pseudonymous.[11] In the late 1970s, biblical scholars especially interested in apocalyptic literature formulated a definition of the genre to guide future study. In their words, apocalyptic literature is "a genre of revelatory literature with a narrative framework, in which a revelation is mediated by an otherworldly being to a human recipient, disclosing a transcendent reality which is both temporal, insofar as it envisages eschatological salvation, and spatial insofar as it involves another, supernatural world."[12] David Hellholm adds a helpful nuance to this definition, noting that apocalyptic literature is "intended for a group in crisis with the purpose of exhortation and/or consolation by means of divine authority."[13] Said another way, apocalyptic literature reveals information from the divine realm to a human by way of a heavenly mediator (often an angel). This revelation involves the supernatural, heaven, and the future, and is often embedded in a story. The purpose of such literature was to encourage or comfort oppressed people with the sovereignty of God.

Apocalyptic literature was born of its time—widespread oppression of the Jews who lived according to their religious convictions. It assured them of a future salvation that included the destruction of their oppressors and the establishment of a righteous new order. Its vision of future reward and judgment encouraged God's people to remain true to him no matter what it cost. Apocalyptic literature was an encoded genre—an extensive matrix of symbolism that would have been clear to the original audience but opaque to outsiders (including later interpreters).[14]

The apocalyptic literature in Daniel is an early exemplar, its character falling some-

---

9. The book of Revelation has the distinction of being the first book in antiquity to self-designate as an apocalypse (Greek ἀποκάλυψις, meaning "revelation, disclosure").

10. For a more detailed description of features shared by apocalyptic texts, see Daniel I. Block, "Preaching Old Testament Apocalyptic to a New Testament Church," *CTJ* 41 (2006), 17–52.

11. See further below on Author and Date.

12. John J. Collins, ed., *Apocalypse: The Morphology of a Genre, Semeia* 14 (Missoula, MT: Scholars Press, 1979), 9.

13. David Hellholm, "The Problem of Apocalyptic Genre and the Apocalypse of John," *Semeia* 36 (1986), 27.

14. Lucas describes this symbolism, saying, "The symbols carry a colour, a feel and an emotional charge that arise from their cultural role. This makes them a powerful form of communication within their original context, but a puzzling one outside it" (Ernest C. Lucas, *Daniel*, ApOTC 20 [Downers Grove, IL: InterVarsity Press, 2002], 196).

where between the prophetic literature of the Old Testament and the apocalypses of Second Temple literature. Daniel received visions from God like other Old Testament prophets, and much of the book's imagery reflects that of other prophetic writings, especially that of Ezekiel. But the book also has what one scholar has called "an ad hoc, experimental character. The combination of tales and visions does not conform to any clear precedent and, indeed, does not become a recurrent feature of the genre."[15] The best description of the visions in chs. 7–12 may be "apocalyptic prophecy"—that is, it reflects both subgenres of visionary literature but is not wholly one or the other.

Author and Date

The book of Daniel, like most Old Testament books, has no ascription of authorship. While the vision reports in the second half of the book are written in the first-person voice of Daniel, some of them are embedded in third-person narratives written by an anonymous author (e.g., 7:1; 10:1). All the stories in the first half of the book are written in the voice of an anonymous third-person narrator.

Nonetheless, the traditional view of authorship is that Daniel himself wrote the entire book while he was an exile in Babylon during the sixth century BCE.[16] His audience consisted of Jews living in the diaspora, and his purpose for writing was to encourage them to live as faithful followers of YHWH no matter what it might cost them, because their God was king of all the earth—not just king of the land and people of Israel.

The first recorded challenge to this view appears in the writings of Porphyry, a third-century philosopher and religious skeptic, who argued that Daniel's visions contained "narrated past events" which the author of the book had himself lived through.[17] Porphyry's conclusions—namely, that the book of Daniel is pseudepigraphic and

---

15. Collins, *Daniel*, 58. This nonconformity for many conservative scholars includes the absence of pseudonymity and *ex eventu* prophecy, two traits often found in other apocalypses. See further on Author and Date.

16. The name "Daniel" appears in the Bible outside the book of Daniel seven times. Three of these are unrelated to the historical figure of the exile (1 Chr 3:1; Ezra 8:2; Neh 10:7[6]), and one is Jesus's reference in the Olivet Discourse to "the prophet Daniel" (Matt 24:15). The remaining three occurrences are in the exilic book of Ezekiel, where the prophet mentions "Daniel" among the righteous Noah and Job (14:14, 20) and again in an oracle against the king of Tyre (28:3). The identity of Ezekiel's "Daniel" is debated, but it may well be that he is referring to the historical figure of the book of Daniel. For the discussion, see Daniel I. Block, *The Book of Ezekiel: Chapters 1–24*, NICOT (Grand Rapids: Eerdmans, 1997), 446–50; and Block, *The Book of Ezekiel: Chapters 25–48*, NICOT (Grand Rapids: Eerdmans, 1998), 96–97.

17. P. M. Casey, "Porphyry and the Origin of the Book of Daniel," *JTS* 27.1 (1976): 15–33. Porphyry's particular opposition to Christianity was its claim that the Bible is God's inspired word. Thus, he highlighted what he perceived to be contradictions between the Old and New Testaments and even among the apostles themselves. In so doing, he hoped to discredit the divine nature of the Bible. Porphyry's writings against Christianity were lost to the book-banning-and-burning by the Holy Roman Empire, so what we know of his argument on the authorship of Daniel comes by way of Jerome's commentary on Daniel. This means that sorting out both sides of the debate requires sifting through the polemics of both men.

dates to the Maccabean era (second century BCE)—all but disappeared from history until the rise of critical biblical scholarship in the eighteenth century, and today most critical scholars agree with Porphyry's conclusions. They consider the book a product of an anonymous Jew (or group of Jews[18]) living in Palestine during the second century BCE and suffering through the hellish events of the Antiochene persecution that ultimately led to the Maccabean revolt in 167 BCE.

The most significant factors that caused critical scholars to question the traditional view of Danielic authorship were historical difficulties, primarily in the accounts of Dan 1–6, and the nature of the prophecy in Daniel's visions. These are discussed in detail as appropriate in the commentary that follows, but for our purposes here, the historical difficulties are taken as evidence that the author of the stories lived far removed in time and even place from their context in the sixth century BCE, and so he understandably got some historical details wrong.[19] By contrast, the laser-sharp precision of prophecies in the visions of chs. 7–12 (and especially in Dan 11) about events in second-century-BCE Syria-Palestine seems to put the author in the thick of those tumultuous events.

Critical scholars credit the precision of these prophecies to the literary device of *vaticinium ex eventu* prophecy—that is, "speaking after the event." Use of this device goes hand in hand with pseudonymity: an author/prophet adopts the name of a venerable and well-known historical person who "predicts" what is really history to the author. When the "prophecy" reaches the author's own time, it shifts from narrating history to predicting the future—and so may be subject to error. With respect to the authorship of Daniel, this shift happens in Dan 11:40, where the author predicts details of Antiochus IV's downfall that do not correlate with the historical record (11:40–45). An author's purpose for using this device would have varied, but in the visions of Daniel, the purpose would have been to encourage those suffering under Antiochus IV that their God—the one who controlled history from the time of Persia (Dan 11:2) until the present—was also in control of their future.

By way of analogy, if I were to use this literary device to write a "prophecy" of the United States from its inception to the present, I would adopt the persona of a well-known and well-respected person who lived in late-eighteenth-century America—such as George Washington—and through that person's voice, I would recount my *historical* perspective as his *prophetic* perspective. Thus, Washington's "prophecy" would be accurate and could be quite detailed until it reached the time of my writing it. Any prophecy from that point on would be genuinely predictive—and so subject to error. My purpose in using this literary device might be to encourage

---

18. The identity of this group is typically understood to be "the wise" (הַמַּשְׂכִּילִים) of Dan 11:33–35 and 12:3, though there is no consensus on who comprised "the wise." See further the discussion in Collins, *Daniel*, 66–69.

19. Many of the historical difficulties dissolve when considered in light of narrative features and authorial purposes. See in the commentary.

Christians disheartened by the trajectory of secularism and the flourishing of evil in our own country that the God who has controlled history to this point is also active in the present and will take care of the future.

While we may think this a strange (or even deceptive) way to prophesy about the future or to recount history, it is a known genre in the literature of the ancient Near East.[20] The question for evangelical scholars committed to a high view of Scripture is whether God would have used such a literary device in his inspired word and to what extent he would have used it. Some scholars argue that the genre is deceptive, and God certainly would not have used it.[21]

But we should not be so hasty in dismissing the possibility since we cannot be sure the genre was, in fact, deceptive. Our knowledge of ancient genres is limited, and it may be that the original audience of Daniel understood how *ex eventu* prophecy worked and expected less of it than we do in terms of predictive precision. Furthermore, they may have been familiar with pseudonymity as an author's way to ground his perspective in a particular theological tradition. If this were true, then an anonymous second-century-BCE author writing under sixth-century-BCE Daniel's name would not have been trying to hoodwink his audience into accepting an undeserving (or fraudulent) text; rather, he would have been situating himself within an accepted theological tradition.

Additionally, it is not our task to say which genres God may or may not find acceptable for his inspired word. Our task as readers is to understand genres and read accordingly, not judge their appropriateness. Esteemed textual critic Bruce Metzger offers the following caution about genre and biblical interpretation:

> Instead of beginning with declarations of what is licit and what is illicit, one is likely to make more progress by considering the theological problem from a historical and literary point of view. It must be acknowledged that the inspiration of the Scriptures is consistent with any kind of form of literary composition that was in keeping with the character and habits of the speaker or writer. Whatever idiom or mode of expression he would use in ordinary speech must surely be allowed him when moved by the Holy Spirit. Rhetoric, poetry, drama, allegory, saga, legend, or any other form of serious discourse that would be rightly understood in a merely human production, cannot be excluded on *a priori* grounds from one divinely inspired. Even the most rigorously formulated doctrine of inspiration would admit that the dramatic composition of the Book of Job and the Song of Songs ascribes to historical personages discourses not literally uttered by them.[22]

---

20. See further on chs. 10–12, especially n50xxx.

21. See, e.g., James M. Hamilton Jr., *With the Clouds of Heaven: The Book of Daniel in Biblical Theology*, NSBT, ed. D. A. Carson (Downers Grove, IL: InterVarsity, 2014), 37; Stephen R. Miller, *Daniel*, NAC 18 (*n.p.*: Broadman & Holman, 1994), 24–33.

22. Bruce M. Metzger, "Literary Forgeries and Canonical Pseudepigrapha," *JBL* (1972): 21–22. More recently, John Walton says, "Remember that genres cannot be true or false, errant or inerrant; they are what they are. If such a genre was recognized in the ancient world and readers would have understood

Aside from the question of genre appropriateness, some evangelicals equate this view of Danielic authorship with a denial of genuine predictive prophecy—that is, they assume all scholars holding a late-date view deny that an exilic Daniel could have accurately predicted future events and with such astonishing detail. This certainly describes the view of many critical scholars, but it is unfair and uncharitable to assume all scholars sympathetic to a second-century-BCE authorship share this perspective. There are evangelical scholars with high views of Scripture's inspiration and authority on both sides of the issue; the date of Daniel should not be a litmus test for orthodoxy.

Evangelical scholars with a late-date view of authorship often question the purpose of the detailed prophecy in ch. 11 given to a sixth-century-BCE Daniel. It is unlike other biblical prophecy, reading more like a history book without names and places filled in. Scholars wonder if this atypical prophecy would be better understood in a different way from other biblical prophecy. These scholars do not question God's ability to reveal a detailed future to Daniel, but rather they question his reason for doing so. They wonder what significance such a prophecy would have had for Daniel or his original audience.

It is wise to exercise caution whether we are evaluating an ancient genre or trying to determine God's purposes. In my view, the answer to the question of Danielic authorship is probably somewhere between the early date and the late date and may well reflect several hands. That is, it is not necessary to say one person wrote the book at a specific point in time (the book itself makes no such claim). Some biblical books give evidence of multiple authorial/editorial hands over a long period of time, and we simply cannot recreate the compositional history of books we find in our Bible today. All we can do is examine the text we have, consider the historical/cultural contexts it appears to reflect, and do our best to determine its author and original audience.

Daniel's exact role in the book that bears his name is unknown. Does belief in the inspiration, authority, and infallibility of Scripture require that Daniel wrote every word, or can we accept that Daniel's experiences in exile were recorded by someone else? Can we accept that other faithful Jews could have adopted and adapted his exilic experiences to speak God's Word into their specific contexts? While we may have varying levels of comfort with different theories of inspiration, authorship, and compositional history, the historical church has affirmed the canonicity of the book[23]—regardless of how exactly it came to be shaped the way it is in its respective canons.[24]

---

the nature of that genre, it would be perfectly legitimate for a communicator to use that genre. It would not be considered deceptive if there were a common understanding of how the genre worked" (John H. Walton and D. Brent Sandy, *The Lost World of Scripture: Ancient Literary Culture and Biblical Authority* [Downers Grove, IL: InterVarsity, 2013], 232).

23. Note that the Greek text (and so the Roman Catholic and Orthodox canons, which derive from the Greek) of Daniel includes three passages that are not in the MT: (1) the Prayer of Azariah and the Song of the Three Men (in Dan 3); (2) the story of Susanna (a separate chapter); (3) the stories of Bel and the dragon (a separate chapter).

24. For a thought-provoking discussion of the evangelical doctrine of Scripture and issues in the production of the Bible, see Walton and Sandy, *The Lost World of Scripture*.

The position of this commentary is that the book of Daniel reflects real events that happened to a real Daniel in Babylonian exile, and that the prophecies recorded in the visions are accurate. However, I am not willing to say who recorded these events, who compiled the book into its present form, and what editorial adaptations may have happened during the book's compositional history. Nor do I consider these issues critical to understanding the meaning and significance of the book.[25]

Language and Structure

In the Masoretic Text, the book of Daniel begins in Hebrew, but in ch. 2 the language changes to Aramaic, which continues through the end of ch. 7.[26] Hebrew resumes in ch. 8 and continues through the rest of the book. While Daniel is not the only Old Testament book with a significant portion of Aramaic alongside its Hebrew, the presence of it in Daniel is not easily explained.[27]

Several theories have been proposed for this linguistic phenomenon, but none has gained consensus. Collins categorizes the various proposals into four groups.[28] In the first group are those who posit that one author wrote the book using two languages for reasons essentially lost to history (e.g., perhaps the court stories were written in

---

25. Similarly, see Walton: "We affirm that there was a real Daniel who lived in the sixth century and served in the courts of kings from the time of Nebuchadnezzar to the time of Cyrus. We accept that the narratives about his life reflect real events in a real past, though, as always, reported through the accepted conventions for narrative in that time. These narratives would likely have existed in individual documents for some time before being compiled into the literary work that we know.... In Daniel 7, the vision is reported by someone else (Dan 7:2), but is then reported in the first person. In chapters 8–10 the oracular experiences are presented in the first person with no recognized outside reporter, though Daniel 10:1 does refer to Daniel in the third person. Chapter 11 makes no explicit claims, but chapter 12 picks up again with Daniel from verse 4 on.... we are not trying to sort out which parts should be attributed to whom. We are quite willing to proceed on faith rather than skepticism with regard to God's willingness and ability to give the specific details of the Hellenistic period to Daniel in the sixth century. The question concerns how clearly that claim is made. Is it possible that a follower of Daniel some centuries later expanded Daniel's oracle in chapter 10 to include the details in chapter 11? We could not rule it out. Whether the oracle was given two centuries before the events or two months before the events would make little difference" (Walton and Sandy, *The Lost World of Scripture*, 231–32).

26. Aramaic is documented as early as the tenth century BCE, and its use spans the balance of Old Testament history. Scholars have tried to determine where the Aramaic of Daniel falls in the history of the language—and so resolve the debate over the date of the book—but the Aramaic that appears in Daniel (Imperial Aramaic) dates as early as 700 BCE and continued in use until about 200 BCE. Since the Aramaic chapters of the book (chs. 2–7) are often thought to be older than the Hebrew chapters (chs. 1, 8–12), and since many late-date advocates think the second-century-BCE author compiled chs. 1–6 from a collection of stories that had been in circulation, either the early date or the late date of authorship is plausible. Another language factor that arises in dating the book of Daniel is the presence of several Persian and Greek loanwords. However, scholars generally agree that these are compatible with either date.

27. The Old Testament book of Ezra also includes several chapters of Aramaic (4:8–6:18; 7:12–26), but in those contexts, it appears in diplomatic correspondence between Persian administrators in Mesopotamia and Jews in Palestine. Since Aramaic was the lingua franca of the Persian period, it is not surprising to find it used in the administrative correspondence in Ezra. (Additional Aramaic in the Old Testament is a single phrase [Gen 31:47] and a single verse [Jer 10:11].)

28. See Collins, *Daniel*, 12–13, for a more detailed discussion of these theories.

Aramaic because they involved gentile kings, while the visions were composed in Hebrew because they concerned Jews, or perhaps the author switched languages in Dan 2:4b to make the speech of the Chaldeans more authentic and then did not switch back until Dan 8). The second group of proposals entails the idea that the book was originally written in Hebrew but quickly translated into Aramaic for non-Hebrew readers. Then when some Hebrew chapters were lost, they were just replaced with chapters from the Aramaic edition. In a third group are theories that propose the book was first written in Aramaic, but at some later time several chapters were translated into Hebrew so that the book of Daniel would be included in the canon. A final category includes theories suggesting that the Aramaic material is older and was simply incorporated into a Hebrew composition without the labor of translation.

While some of these proposals might be plausible if the presence of two languages appeared to be ad hoc, none of them provides a good explanation for the fact that the two languages are integral to the structure of the book. The six Aramaic chapters (chs. 2–7) form a widely recognized chiastic structure. A chiasm (or chiasmus), derived from the Greek letter *chi* (χ), is an "X-like" literary structure in which parallel portions (chapters, in this case) are arranged in an inverted order. The structure in the book of Daniel appears as follows:

Chapter 1—Prologue (Hebrew)
Chapters 2–7—Stories about Jews in Gentile nations (Aramaic)
A Nebuchadnezzar dreams about a statue (four earthly kingdoms and a fifth eternal kingdom) (ch. 2)
  B Faithful Jews (Shadrach, Meshach, and Abednego) face death for refusing to bow to the king's statue (ch. 3)
    C A proud gentile king (Nebuchadnezzar) is humbled and restored (ch. 4)
    C' A proud gentile king (Belshazzar) is humbled and destroyed (ch. 5)
  B' A faithful Jew (Daniel) faces death for refusing to pray to anyone but God (ch. 6)
A' Daniel dreams about four earthly kingdoms and a fifth eternal kingdom (ch. 7)
Chapters 8–12—Prophecies about Jews back in the land (Hebrew)

This use of two languages creates a clear compositional structure and indicates that their presence in a single book is not an accident of translational history.[29]

---

29. While some scholars propose additional chiastic structures in the book (see, e.g., Andrew E. Steinmann, *Daniel*, ConcC [St. Louis: Concordia, 2008], 21–25; David W. Gooding, "The Literary Structure of the Book of Daniel and Its Implications," *TynBul* 32 [1981]: 43–80; Hamilton, *With the Clouds of Heaven*, 77–83), the chiasm in chs. 2–7 has near universal consensus among scholars. The credit for "discovery" of this chiasm goes to Adrien Lenglet, "La structure litteraire de Daniel 2–7," *Biblica* 53.2 (1972): 169–90.

The relationship of these two languages to the book's two genres also suggests intention. The book has six chapters of Aramaic and six chapters of Hebrew. It has six chapters of narrative and six chapters of apocalyptic. But these genres and languages do not correspond. Chapter 1 is narrative in Hebrew. Chapters 2–6 are narrative in Aramaic. Chapter 7 is apocalyptic in Aramaic. Chapters 8–12 are apocalyptic in Hebrew. Chapter 7 is the misfit in the structure, sharing the apocalyptic genre with chapters 8–12 but the language and chiastic structure of the narrative chapters. We will return to a discussion of chapter 7 below.

The use of two languages in the book of Daniel serves a literary purpose. The chapters of the Aramaic chiasm primarily recount events that took place in the royal courts of Babylon and its successors during the exilic tenure of Daniel and his three friends. Aramaic was the lingua franca of the day, used both in the royal court and in the daily life of Judean exiles outside the royal court. Its use in the chapters pertaining to life in exile reflects the people's experience as foreigners. The shift back to Hebrew in chs. 8–12 corresponds to the contents of Daniel's visions in those final chapters: he was seeing the future of his people back in the land of Israel. Accordingly, we would expect ch. 1 to be in Aramaic rather than Hebrew. However, most commentators consider Dan 1 to function as a prologue to the entire book, introducing the main characters, the setting, and the primary themes. This may explain the use of Hebrew there.

But the use of Aramaic does more than represent the life of God's people in exile. The chiastic structure of the Aramaic chapters sets forth themes that carry throughout the book and perhaps even shape how we should read and understand the book's message. The focus of a chiastic structure is found at its center, and the message at the center is the heart of the author's larger message. In the Aramaic chiasm of Daniel, the center chapters are Dan 4 and Dan 5. Both of these chapters recount God's humbling of a proud human king—Nebuchadnezzer in Dan 4 and Belshazzar in Dan 5. Two kings who overreached their God-given authority were brought low by the one who alone is sovereign. He had raised them up and given them their power, but when they refused to acknowledge his higher kingship, he took them down. A central message of the book of Daniel is God's sovereignty over all other kings, on whom he bestows great power. However, with this power comes responsibility and accountability: all kings will answer to God for their use (or abuse) of power.

On either side of these central stories are two accounts that further explore the relationship between the divine king and human kings and two accounts that illustrate how citizens of God's kingdom can live faithfully under human kings. The chapters that frame the chiasm (chs. 2 and 7) provide a cosmic look at human kingdoms, and they are shown to be both magnificent (ch. 2) and arrogantly evil (ch. 7). Goldingay says the dream of Dan 2 "offered world rulers a vision of their position as a God-given calling," but Dan 7's vision reminds rulers that they are accountable to God.[30] Chapters 3 and 6 feature examples of what it might look like to remain faithful to the divine king while serving human kings. Nebuchadnezzar was hostile toward Shadrach, Meshach, and Abednego as they sought to serve their God (ch. 3). Darius was amenable to Daniel, but he was captive to forces greater than his good intentions (ch. 6). In both chapters, God's followers were faithful, no matter the cost.[31]

From this chiastic collection of stories illustrating divine and human kingship, as well as the cost of faithfulness, the book of Daniel shifts to its apocalyptic visions. The primary focus of the visions is the suffering God's people would endure at the hands of gentile kings *after* the exile. During the years of exile as portrayed in Dan 1–6, Daniel and his three friends had been able to influence the gentile overlords they served for good. But in the visions of Dan 7–12, God's people must endure their persecution and remain faithful, awaiting their coming reward and the sure punishment of their oppressors. In Daniel's visions, he saw attacks on God and his people that went far beyond anything Daniel's people had experienced at the hands of their exilic captors. While these two sections of the book have different emphases, they nonetheless share themes introduced and illustrated in the Aramaic chiasm. They both highlight the hubris of human rulers who fail to acknowledge God's sovereignty, and they both show such rulers ultimately brought low by him. They both find hope in the sovereignty of God and his eternal kingdom, and they both illustrate God's people standing firm in their faith no matter the cost. Together the sections represent "two ends of the spectrum of the experience of the godly person living in a pagan society."[32] Sometimes we can be active in society and culture and remain faithful to our Christian convictions. But sometimes it is not possible to do both, and faithfulness to God may mean that we suffer, even unto death.[33]

The hinge that holds these two sections of the book together is Dan 7. Daniel's vision of the four beasts and then the throne room of God lies at the heart of the book and defies any attempt at a tidy division of the book into genre or language. It holds the book together by the interlocking of its genre and its language, and it furnishes the book's grandest display of God's eternal kingdom and his people's reward. Willis calls the chapter "a theological center of gravity that seems to pull the entire book together around the triumph of divine sovereignty"[34]—a triumph that revolves

---

30. John Goldingay, *Daniel*, rev. ed., WBC 30 (Grand Rapids: Zondervan Academic, 2019), 354. Unless otherwise noted, all Goldingay references are taken from this edition.

31. Of the themes in the chiasm, Goldingay says, "Daniel 3–6 portrays [human kings] as inclined to make themselves into God; they are thus also inclined to put mortal pressure on those who are committed to God (chs. 3; 6), but they are themselves on the way to catastrophe (chs. 4; 5)" (*Daniel*, 354).

32. Lucas notes that this reality "parallels the difference in ethos between Paul's positive view of the Roman government in Rom. 13 and John's negative view of it in Rev. 13. Both situations present challenges and temptations to test the faithfulness of those seeking to remain true to their vision of God" (*Daniel*, 195).

33. Lucas, *Daniel*, 195.

34. Amy C. Merrill Willis, *Dissonance and the Drama of Divine Sovereignty*, LHBOTS 520 (New York: T&T Clark, 2010), 62.

around "one like a son of man" and the saints receiving the everlasting kingdom. This vision offers the book's first hope for what lay beyond any current or future suffering, and this hope is designed to encourage faithful endurance for the people of God.[35]

Significance of the Book

In the biblical story of Israel, the book of Daniel falls "between the times"—that is, its setting is in the years of exile, after God's chosen people had lost their land and before he restored them to it. Exile was the worst possible scenario for the people of Israel. It signaled a broken covenant and the loss of everything that made them the unique people of God: land, Davidic king, and the temple—YHWH's presence with them. Exile was punishment for a long history of unfaithfulness to the Mosaic covenant.

From this place of loss and punishment comes the book of Daniel, with its stories of four Judean youths succeeding and thriving in the court of a gentile king. We are never told what Daniel and his friends were like before exile—that is, were they among the idolatrous masses that ignored the prophets' calls to repentance, or were they among the precious few who kept the covenant with YHWH? The book of Daniel is not particularly concerned with the history that brought Daniel and his friends to exile.[36] It is concerned with their present and future. Their present—that is, life in exile—is depicted in the colorful stories of Dan 1–6. They are brave, wise, and faithful, and they prosper, rising to high positions in a foreign land. Their future—that is, life after exile—comes into view with Daniel's wild visions in chs. 7–8. The revelations of chs. 9–12 add greater clarity to that future—and what Daniel saw disturbed him deeply.

The cause of Daniel's angst is never explained, but his prayer in ch. 9 reveals quite a bit about what he was thinking. As he reflected on Jeremiah's prophecy about the seventy-year exile, he prayed for restoration (e.g., Jer 25:1–15; 29:1–14). He prayed that YHWH would restore his people, his city, and his temple—for his own name's sake. Daniel does not detail what "restoration" looked like to him, but we can probably assume he had in mind the prophets' words of glorious restoration. Daniel awaited the end of exile and a magnificent resettlement in the land of Israel.

God answered Daniel's prayer in Dan 9 with further revelation. He sent Gabriel with the startling message that the seventy years of Babylonian exile were just part of a much greater exile: seventy times seven—an exponentially greater fullness of time. The end of exile that Daniel awaited was not the end he had anticipated.

---

35. See further below on Dan 7.
36. Daniel's prayer in Dan 9 is the only place where the book addresses the people's culpability.

But this greater exile would be of a different nature than the seventy-year exile. The years of Babylonian exile were literal and punitive—that is, the people lived away from their land because they were being punished for national sin. The greater exile would be nonliteral and also nonpunitive: the visions Daniel saw took place when God's people lived back in their land, and the suffering was inflicted on those who were faithful to the covenant, while those who were unfaithful escaped the suffering (Dan 11:30–35). In the Old Testament, exile was where God's people landed when they broke the covenant, but Daniel's visions reveal an exile where God's people find themselves in "exile" for *keeping* covenant.

In light of this redefinition of exile, the book of Daniel also affirms foundational truths for God's people living in exile. It shows them who their God is and who they are as citizens of his eternal kingdom. It helps them understand what to expect in exile and how they should live in it.

The book of Daniel reveals the God of Israel as the sovereign king of a world-encompassing eternal kingdom. He is king of all kings. Throughout the book he is called by names "that make explicit that he is not merely a peculiarly Jewish god but the God in/of heaven, King/Lord of heaven, God of gods, Lord of Lords, great God, living God, God On High, august, awesome, and fiery." Yet this majestic and glorious God is not far from his people: "he is also our God, my God, your God, the God of the covenant, the fathers' God, one who is compassionate and forgiving."[37]

He is revealed as the Most High God who rules over all kings. His knowledge is shown to be superior to theirs. His power far surpasses theirs. His law is life-giving and good, while their own laws hold them captive. His king rules all peoples, nations, and languages forever, while their reigns are territorial and fleeting. The greatest rulers of the world are subject to him, dependent on his good pleasure for their lives and lordship. Yet this great God, this King of all kings, often chooses to veil himself and even to stay his hand. He acts behind the scenes, and sometimes he appears not to act at all. But the book of Daniel repeatedly affirms that this God does everything at exactly the right time (8:19; 11:27, 29, 35; cf. 7:12). The course of world events is never out of his control.

The book of Daniel also illustrates what it means to be people of this eternal kingdom. While God's covenant people await the fullness of his rule on earth, they live in exile and expectation. In their lands of exile, God's people serve human kings who demonstrate varying responses to their God-delegated authority and so also to his people. Sometimes God's people can thrive, while other times they will suffer. Sometimes they will be able to influence their culture for good, but other times they will be silenced and even destroyed. Whatever their circumstances, God's people can

---

37. Goldingay, *Daniel*, 581.

be assured that more is going on behind the scenes than they can see; behind their earthly battles are heavenly battles—all part of a cosmic conflict that will continue until God's eternal kingdom fills the earth. The book of Daniel assures God's people that when that consummation comes, it will bring vindication and reward—judgment of the oppressors, resurrection, and inheritance of the kingdom.

These visions of the future were for Daniel's people—the Old Testament people of God, Israel—but the book of Daniel also hints that the coming eternal kingdom will encompass others. The entire book is set in exile, where gentile kings offer praise to God, and Daniel's vision in ch. 7 reveals "all peoples, nations, and languages" worshiping "one like a son of man" around the fiery throne (7:13, 14). The book does not address how this comes to be, but the prevalence of the idea prompted one commentator to argue that the entire book of Daniel is "an extended theological reflection on the status, purpose and destiny of the Gentiles."[38]

And that is where we live. On the other side of the cross, as followers of Jesus Christ, we live in exile in Babylon—wherever in the twenty-first-century world we find ourselves. We live under foreign overlords, human kings whose values rarely reflect those of God's eternal king and kingdom. We face the challenge of faithfulness when our respective cultures and societies make demands on us that violate the life-giving law of God. Some of us suffer greatly for following the King of kings.

While we await the fullness of God's kingdom on earth—the New Jerusalem filled with Jew and gentile alike because of the finished work of Christ—we live in both exile and expectation. We live with the confidence that the God of all gods and the King of all kings is in control. We believe that at just the right time, the rule of YHWH will become the reality of the world, and at just the right time, the Son of Man will open the scroll (Rev 5:6–9). The twenty-four elders, the myriads of angels, and "every creature in heaven and on earth and under the earth and on the sea, and all that is in them" will sing "praise and honor and glory and power" to the Lamb forever (Rev 5:13). And we will live and reign with him forever!

Matters of Methodology

A central feature of this commentary series is discourse analysis, but since approaches to discourse analysis vary from scholar to scholar, an overview of the methodology followed here is necessary. First, in terms of translation, I have leaned toward a formally equivalent translation throughout. This means that my translation

---

38. Samuel Wells and George Sumner, *Esther and Daniel*, BTCB (Grand Rapids: Brazos Press, 2013), 117. Sumner wrote the Daniel portion of the commentary.

is wooden in places, but my purpose is to preserve (as much as possible) some features of the text that would otherwise be lost in translation.

Second, my analysis of the text is based on the clausal unit, which by definition has one and typically only one verbal form. Clausal units include the Hebrew (and Aramaic) verbless clause, a "to be" predication that lacks a form of the "to be" verb: for example, יְהוָה מֶלֶךְ has no verb, but it is properly translated "YHWH *is* king." In terms of my clausal analysis, I have made exceptions for date formulae, which are not formally considered clauses since they neither contain verbs nor are they verbless clauses. Each date formula is charted in my translation as a separate clause and is dependent on an independent clause that follows it.

Third, the relationship between the clauses is depicted by indentation on the translation charts. Independent clauses (also called main clauses) *in the voice of the third-person narrator* begin at the far right margin (Hebrew text; far left for English text), and dependent clauses (also called subordinate clauses) are indented in relationship to their governing clause. Independent clauses *in embedded speech* are indented once to indicate their dependence, as it were, on the narrator's speech frame (see, e.g., 1:10). As a rule, I have defined the nature of a clause by its syntax. However, in some instances, I have allowed semantics to overrule syntax, and the translation charts will reflect this in their (non)indentation of clauses (e.g., see on Dan 6:2[1]).

Organization and Outline of the Book of Daniel

The primary organization of the book of Daniel and the approach followed in this commentary is that of its chiastic structure in correlation with its two languages (see outlines below). However, a secondary way of organizing the book that can be especially helpful in an overview such as this is according to the date formulae that occur throughout the book. There are nine date formulae, each based on the regnal year of a king (1:1, 21; 2:1; 7:1; 8:1; 9:1–2; 10:1, 11:1), one additional chronological reference (10:4), and an undated reference to a king's reign (6:29[28]). Considering the book according to its chronology makes clear the overlap between the narrative stories set in the royal court (chs. 1–6) and Daniel's visions (chs. 7–12). See figure 1.

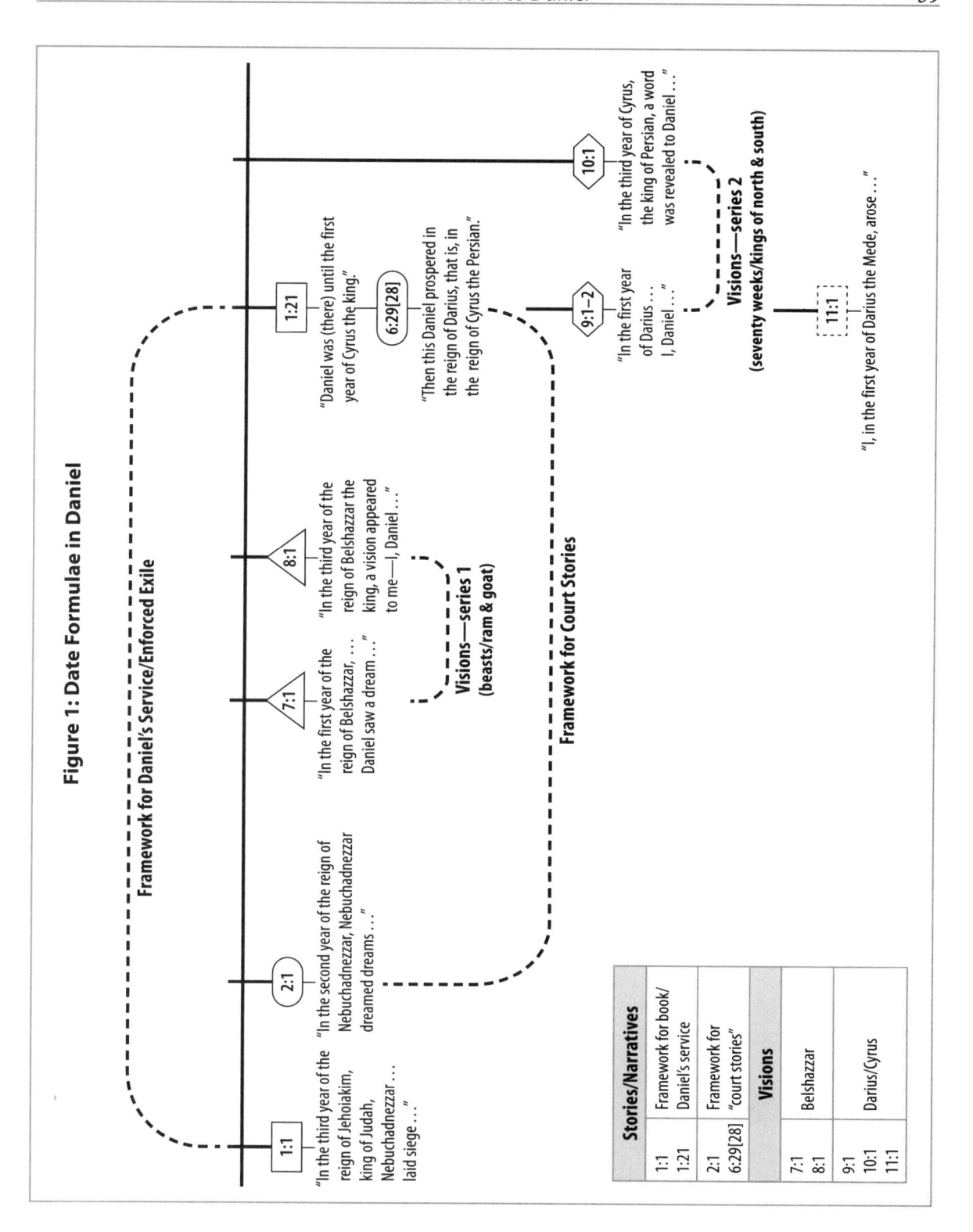

Figure 1: Date Formulae in Daniel

1:1 — "In the third year of the reign of Jehoiakim, king of Judah, Nebuchadnezzar ... laid siege ..."

2:1 — "In the second year of the reign of Nebuchadnezzar, Nebuchadnezzar dreamed dreams ..."

1:21 — "Daniel was (there) until the first year of Cyrus the king."

6:29[28] — "Then this Daniel prospered in the reign of Darius, that is, in the reign of Cyrus the Persian."

Framework for Daniel's Service/Enforced Exile

Framework for Court Stories

7:1 — "In the first year of the reign of Belshazzar, ... Daniel saw a dream ..."

8:1 — "In the third year of the reign of Belshazzar the king, a vision appeared to me—I, Daniel ..."

Visions—series 1 (beasts/ram & goat)

9:1–2 — "In the first year of Darius ... I, Daniel ..."

10:1 — "In the third year of Cyrus, the king of Persian, a word was revealed to Daniel ..."

Visions—series 2 (seventy weeks/kings of north & south)

11:1 — "I, in the first year of Darius the Mede, arose ..."

Stories/Narratives	
1:1	Framework for book/ Daniel's service
1:21	
2:1	Framework for "court stories"
6:29[28]	
Visions	
7:1	Belshazzar
8:1	
9:1	Darius/Cyrus
10:1	
11:1	

Brief Outline

God's Kingdom Will Endure

    I. Macro Unit 1: God's Kingdom in Exile: The Conflict Begins (1:1a–21)
        A. God Establishes His Kingdom in Exile (1:1a–21)
    II. Macro Unit 2: The Superiority of God and His Kingdom (2:1a–7:28d)
        A. God's Superior Knowledge and His Eternal Kingdom (2:1a–49c)
        B. God's Superior Power and His Servants' Faithfulness (3:1a–30)
        C. A Humbled King and His Restored Power (3:31a–4:34e[4:1a–37e])
        D. A Humbled King and His Rescinded Power (5:1a–6:1[5:31])
        E. God's Superior Law and His Servant's Faithfulness (6:2a–29[1a–28])
        F. God's Superior King and Eternal Kingdom (7:1a–28d)
    III. Macro Unit 3: Encouragement until God's Eternal Kingdom Comes (8:1a–12:13c)
        A. God's Leash on Evil (8:1a–27f)
        B. Repentance and God's Promise of Restoration (9:1a–27d)
        C. The Ultimate Conflict and God's Final Victory (10:1a–12:13c)

Complete Outline

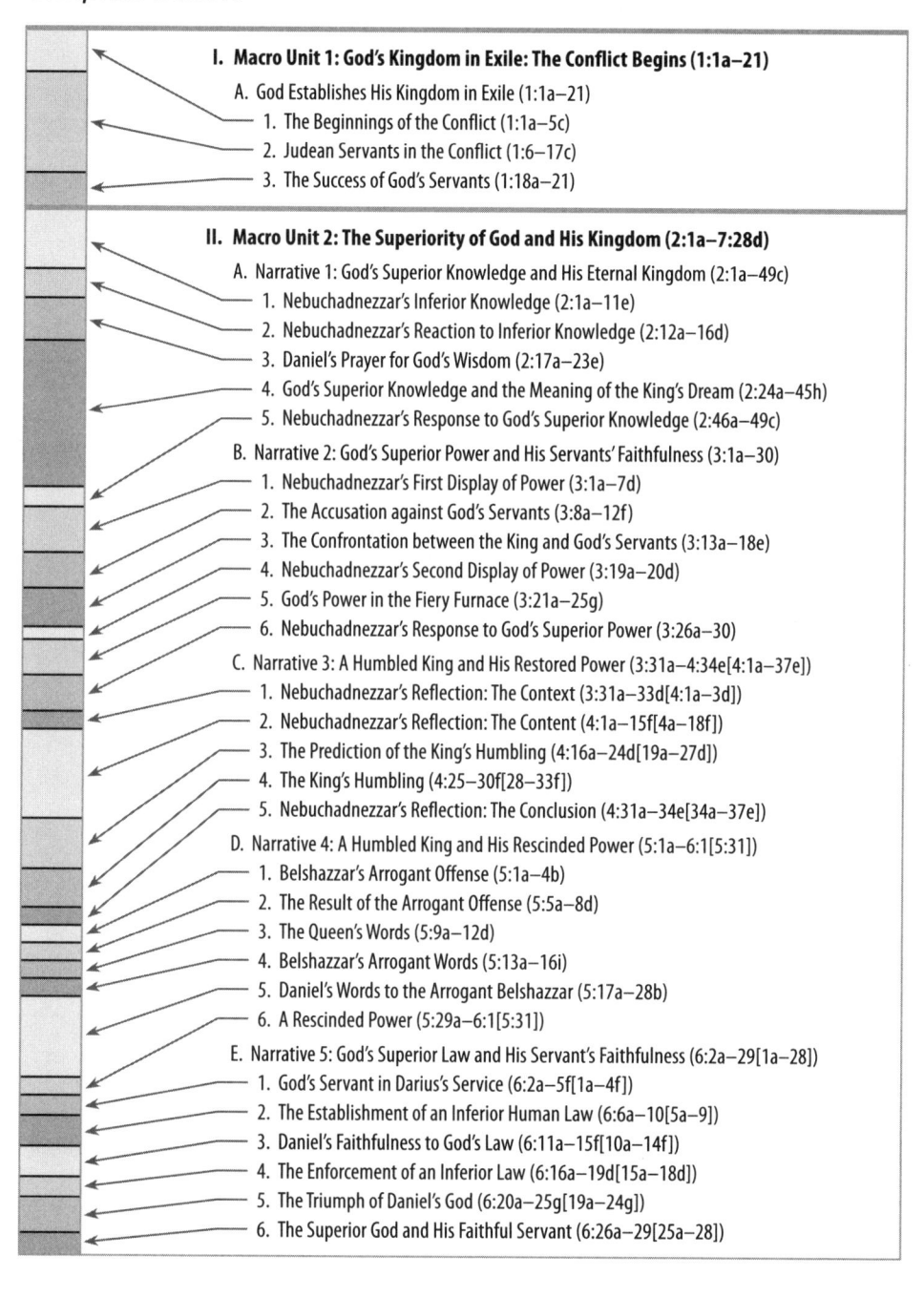

I. Macro Unit 1: God's Kingdom in Exile: The Conflict Begins (1:1a–21)
    A. God Establishes His Kingdom in Exile (1:1a–21)
        1. The Beginnings of the Conflict (1:1a–5c)
        2. Judean Servants in the Conflict (1:6–17c)
        3. The Success of God's Servants (1:18a–21)

II. Macro Unit 2: The Superiority of God and His Kingdom (2:1a–7:28d)
    A. Narrative 1: God's Superior Knowledge and His Eternal Kingdom (2:1a–49c)
        1. Nebuchadnezzar's Inferior Knowledge (2:1a–11e)
        2. Nebuchadnezzar's Reaction to Inferior Knowledge (2:12a–16d)
        3. Daniel's Prayer for God's Wisdom (2:17a–23e)
        4. God's Superior Knowledge and the Meaning of the King's Dream (2:24a–45h)
        5. Nebuchadnezzar's Response to God's Superior Knowledge (2:46a–49c)
    B. Narrative 2: God's Superior Power and His Servants' Faithfulness (3:1a–30)
        1. Nebuchadnezzar's First Display of Power (3:1a–7d)
        2. The Accusation against God's Servants (3:8a–12f)
        3. The Confrontation between the King and God's Servants (3:13a–18e)
        4. Nebuchadnezzar's Second Display of Power (3:19a–20d)
        5. God's Power in the Fiery Furnace (3:21a–25g)
        6. Nebuchadnezzar's Response to God's Superior Power (3:26a–30)
    C. Narrative 3: A Humbled King and His Restored Power (3:31a–4:34e[4:1a–37e])
        1. Nebuchadnezzar's Reflection: The Context (3:31a–33d[4:1a–3d])
        2. Nebuchadnezzar's Reflection: The Content (4:1a–15f[4a–18f])
        3. The Prediction of the King's Humbling (4:16a–24d[19a–27d])
        4. The King's Humbling (4:25–30f[28–33f])
        5. Nebuchadnezzar's Reflection: The Conclusion (4:31a–34e[34a–37e])
    D. Narrative 4: A Humbled King and His Rescinded Power (5:1a–6:1[5:31])
        1. Belshazzar's Arrogant Offense (5:1a–4b)
        2. The Result of the Arrogant Offense (5:5a–8d)
        3. The Queen's Words (5:9a–12d)
        4. Belshazzar's Arrogant Words (5:13a–16i)
        5. Daniel's Words to the Arrogant Belshazzar (5:17a–28b)
        6. A Rescinded Power (5:29a–6:1[5:31])
    E. Narrative 5: God's Superior Law and His Servant's Faithfulness (6:2a–29[1a–28])
        1. God's Servant in Darius's Service (6:2a–5f[1a–4f])
        2. The Establishment of an Inferior Human Law (6:6a–10[5a–9])
        3. Daniel's Faithfulness to God's Law (6:11a–15f[10a–14f])
        4. The Enforcement of an Inferior Law (6:16a–19d[15a–18d])
        5. The Triumph of Daniel's God (6:20a–25g[19a–24g])
        6. The Superior God and His Faithful Servant (6:26a–29[25a–28])

F. Narrative 6: God's Superior King and Eternal Kingdom (7:1a–28d)
   1. Vision Block 1: The Three Beasts (7:1a–6e)
   2. Vision Block 2: The Fourth Beast (7:7a–12b)
   3. Vision Block 3: One Like a Son of Man (7:13a–28d)

III. Macro Unit 3: Encouragement until God's Eternal Kingdom Comes (8:1a–12:13c)

A. Narrative 1: God's Leash on Evil (8:1a–27f)
   1. Vision Block 1: The Two-Horned Ram (8:1a–4e)
   2. Vision Block 2: The Billy Goat of the Goats (8:5a–14b)
   3. Vision Block 3: The Interpretation of the Vision of the Evenings and the Mornings (8:15a–27f)

B. Narrative 2: Repentance and God's Promise of Restoration (9:1a–27d)
   1. The Context of Repentance (9:1a–3b)
   2. Daniel's Prayer of Repentance (9:4a–19f)
   3. The Revelation of Restoration (9:20a–27d)

C. Narrative 3: The Ultimate Conflict and God's Final Victory (10:1a–12:13c)
   1. Vision Block 1: The Vision of a Heavenly Messenger (10:1a–11:2a)
   2. Vision Block 2: The Revelation from the Book of Truth (11:2b–12:4d)
   3. Vision Block 3: The Vision of Two Others (12:5a–13c)

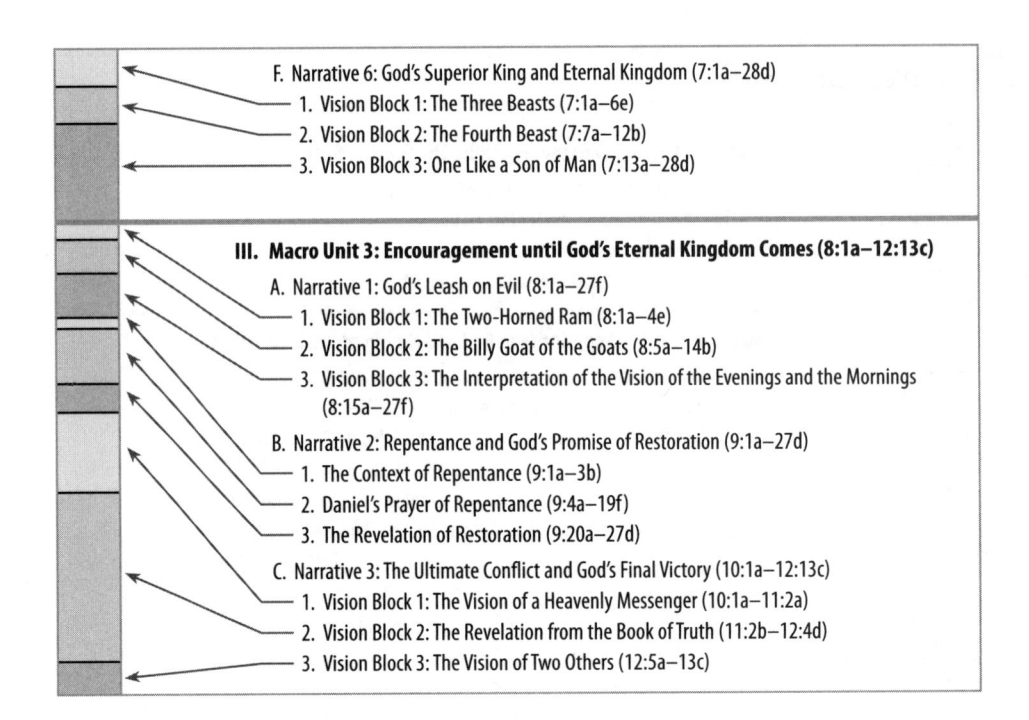

MACRO UNIT 1

Daniel 1:1a–21

God's Kingdom in Exile:
The Conflict Begins

Main Idea of the Macro Unit

The opening macro unit of the book of Daniel introduces the clash of kings and cultures that dominates the book. It reveals that such conflicts reflect a greater conflict—that of the one true God versus the many gods worshiped by people everywhere. This macro unit also reveals that this greater conflict is no conflict at all. The God of Israel is actively working his plan behind the scenes. In Dan 1, he infiltrates the idolatrous kingdom of Babylon by allowing his temple vessels and his human vessels to be carried away into exile, into the heart of the foreign god's territory. But through these vessels, he places his presence in the palace of the foreign king and in the temple of the Babylonian god. The faithfulness of his servants despite the onslaught of Babylonian enculturation positions them to represent him well in their foreign context.

Literary Context of the Macro Unit

Daniel 1 functions as a prologue for the book by setting its historical and cultural context, introducing its main characters, and establishing its key themes. In the unusual two-language structure of the book, ch. 1 stands by itself in Hebrew before the six chapters of Aramaic (see pp. 31–35). The six Aramaic chapters, arranged in a chiastic structure, comprise the heart of the book and develop themes of divine and human kingship and how God's people should live in the tension that is often present between the two. Daniel 1 introduces these themes in its portrayal of King Nebuchadnezzar of Babylon, King Jehoiakim of Judah, the Lord, and four captive Judeans: Daniel, Hananiah, Mishael, and Azariah.

> **I. Macro Unit 1: God's Kingdom in Exile: The Conflict Begins (1:1a–21)**
>   A. God Establishes His Kingdom in Exile(1:1a–21)
> II. Macro Unit 2: The Superiority of God and His Kingdom (2:1a–7:28d)
> III. Macro Unit 3: Encouragement until God's Eternal Kingdom Comes (8:1a–12:13c)

Daniel 1:1a–21

A. God Establishes His Kingdom in Exile

Main Idea and Literary Context

Please see the Main Idea and the Literary Context for Macro Unit 1.

1. The Beginnings of the Conflict (1:1a–5c)

Main Idea of the Passage

Daniel 1:1a–5c traces the events that initiated the Babylonian exile: the transfer of God's sacred vessels—temple and human—from Jerusalem to a foreign land. In these world-shattering events, the passage also affirms God's sovereignty and presence in exile.

Literary Context

Daniel 1:1a–5c functions in at least two ways in its broader literary context. First, it establishes the historical and geographical backdrop for macro unit 1 (Dan 1) and the entire book. The date formula of 1:1 provides the beginning point for the book's events, and the events of the passage explain how it is that God's people happen to be in a foreign place for the duration of the book. The opening passage also interprets these historical events, laying out a theme that dominates the book: while it may look like Israel's God had been defeated by the Babylonian king and his god, things were not what they seemed. The people of God were in exile because their God handed them over to Nebuchadnezzar. Not only had Israel's God not lost control of the circumstances "on the ground," he had orchestrated them.

The second function of Dan 1:1a–5c is introducing the main characters of the macro unit and book. Babylonian Nebuchadnezzar is the representative gentile king in a book where gentile monarchs will play an important role. The "sons of Israel" (1:3b) are representative of the people of God in exile. Encounters between these representative characters drive the book. This passage also reveals the king's strategy with respect to the exiles—namely, to own them, mind and body (1:4c–5c). The remainder of the macro unit will demonstrate the strategy of the representative exiles: to remain faithful to their God.

> A. God Establishes His Kingdom in Exile (1:1a–21)
> → **1. The Beginnings of the Conflict (1:1a–5c)**
>   2. Judean Servants in the Conflict (1:6–17c)
>   3. The Success of God's Servants (1:18a–21)

Translation and Exegetical Outline

(See page 47.)

Structure and Literary Form

In the opening narrative of the book of Daniel, seven main clauses trace the actions of Nebuchadnezzar and the Lord (אֲדֹנָי) in the fateful events associated with the Babylonian siege of Jerusalem. Nebuchadnezzar is both the grammatical subject and the agent of six of the verbs (1:1b–c, 2b–c, 3a, 5a), while the Lord is the grammatical subject and agent[1] of only one (1:2a). An eighth main clause (1:5c) furnishes the target of the king's actions in 1:3a–5b—namely, a group of captives groomed for royal service.

The text opens with a date formula (1:1a) that establishes the historical starting point of the book and, more immediately, the context for the chapter. This clause is subordinate to the independent clause that immediately follows (1:1b):

---

1. A grammatical subject is not always the agent—that is, the one responsible for the action of the verb. For example, subjects of passive verbs are the recipients of the action, not the agents of it (see, e.g., vv. 12b, 13a).

Daniel 1:1a–5c

1a		In the third year of the reign of Jehoiakim, king of Judah,	**I. God's Kingdom in Exile: The Conflict Begins (1:1a–21)** A. God Establishes His Kingdom in Exile (1:1a–21) 1. The Beginnings of the Conflict (1:1a–5c) a. The Historical Setting (1:1a–2c) (1) The Timing (1:1a)
1b		Nebuchadnezzar, king of Babylon, came to Jerusalem,	(2) Nebuchadnezzar's Conquest (1:1b–c)
1c		and he laid siege to it.	
2a		And the Lord gave into his hand Jehoiakim, king of Judah, and some of the vessels of the house of God,	(3) The Lord's Gift (1:2a)
2b		and he brought them into the land of Shinar (to) the house of his god(s)	(4) The King's Plunder (1:2b–c)
2c		—the vessels he brought into the house of the treasury of his god(s).	
3a		Then the king said to Ashpenaz, chief of his officials,	b. The King's Strategy (1:3a–5c) (1) The King's Orders (1:3a–4c) (a) The Human Plunder (1:3a–4b)
3b		to bring some of the sons of Israel—some of the royal seed and some of the nobles—	
4a		youths in whom there was no blemish, good looking, skilled in all wisdom, knowers of knowledge, discerners of knowledge,	
4b		and who had the ability to stand in the palace of the king—	
4c		and to teach them the literature and language of the Chaldeans.	(b) The Educational Plan (1:4c)
5a		The king appointed for them a daily ration from the king's food and from the wine he drank,	(2) The King's Menu (1:5a)
5b		and they would be trained three years.	(3) The Timeline (1:5b)
5c		Then some of them would stand in the presence of the king.	(4) The Goal (1:5c)

"Nebuchadnezzar . . . came [בָּא] to Jerusalem." The purpose for his coming was to besiege it (וַיָּצַר, 1:1c).

The outcome of Nebuchadnezzar's efforts was that the Lord gave (וַיִּתֵּן, 1:2a) him a partial victory. This is the first of three occurrences of נתן, "to give," with the Lord/God as the grammatical subject in the chapter (1:2a, 9, 17b). The three נתן clauses establish a subtle but important theme in the book: God is behind events that, on the surface, appear to be caused by someone else—such as a more powerful king (and god), in the case of Jehoiakim's and Jerusalem's apparent defeat.

The text resumes with Nebuchadnezzar's action with respect to his "plunder" (i.e., God's gift): he brought them (וַיְבִיאֵם, 1:2b) to his country and deposited the vessels (הֵבִיא, 1:2c) in the treasury of his god. The first clause leaves ambiguous exactly what part of his plunder went to Shinar, while the second clause makes explicit that it was the temple vessels (אֶת־הַכֵּלִים), the fronted object of the clause.

The next paragraph begins with a *wayyiqtol* verb form (וַיֹּאמֶר), advancing the action of Nebuchadnezzar by describing his orders with respect to the human plunder from his conquest of Jerusalem (1:3a). His chief official was to do two things, expressed with infinitives: bring (לְהָבִיא, 1:3b) the captives and teach them (וּלְלַמְּדָם, 1:4c). A second *wayyiqtol* verb form (וַיְמַן, 1:5a) continues the king's action with respect to his captives: he appoints a special diet for them. This independent clause is followed by another infinitive (וּלְגַדְּלָם, 1:5b), which functions as a finite verb and also summarizes the king's strategy for the captives.[2] The purpose of the training was that the captives would serve in the king's court.

Explanation of the Text

a. The Historical Setting (1:1a–2c)

The first main event of the book of Daniel is reported in the first independent clause (1:1b): "Nebuchadnezzar, king of Babylon, came to Jerusalem." A date formula precedes it (1:1a) and gives the timing of the main event—namely, the siege of Jerusalem by Nebuchadnezzar, king of Babylon.[3] This date formula is the first of eight such formulae that provide structure for the book.[4] This first formula links the events that follow to the reign of the Judean king Jehoiakim, while the rest of the

---

2. The verb in v. 5b is an infinitive (וּלְגַדְּלָם), but here it functions as the equivalent of a finite verb and represents action successive to the *wayyiqtol* in v. 5a (וַיְמַן). Compare Job 34:8, and see Bruce K. Waltke and M. O'Connor, *An Introduction to Biblical Hebrew Syntax* (Winona Lake, IN: Eisenbrauns, 1990), 611. See further below on 1:5.

3. Depending on the timing of the siege (see the commentary below), Nebuchadnezzar may only have been heir apparent to his father's throne at the time; Nebuchadnezzar ascended to the throne in late 605 BCE after his father, Nabopolassar, died. If this was the case, the author of Daniel refers to him as "king" in "an anticipatory sense" (Tremper Longman III, *Daniel*, NIVAC [Grand Rapids: Zondervan, 1999], 43). For the purposes of the book, Nebuchadnezzar was king.

4. See Date Formulae in Daniel (fig. 1) in the introduction. There are nine formulae, but two of them refer to the same regnal year and corresponding events in the span of two verses (9:1–2; the first year of Darius).

formulae are tied to the regnal years of gentile kings (Nebuchadnezzar [2:1], Belshazzar [7:1; 8:1], Darius [9:1; 11:1], and Cyrus [1:21; 10:1]). The events of the first two verses initiate the demise of Judah and the beginning of exile. The date formulae after 1:1 are tied to gentile kings because the rest of the book is set in Babylon.

Jehoiakim came to the throne in the aftermath of his father's death. Josiah had been killed at Megiddo in 609 BCE when he confronted the army of Pharaoh Neco, who was en route to help the Assyrians fight the Babylonians. Josiah's immediate successor was his son Jehoahaz, but three months into Jehoahaz's reign, Neco deposed him and made Josiah's second son, Jehoiakim, king instead (2 Kgs 23:29-35; 609-598 BCE). Jehoiakim remained an Egyptian vassal until the Babylonians under Nebuchadnezzar routed the Egyptians at Carchemish in 605 BCE. For the next three years Jehoiakim was vassal to Nebuchadnezzar. Then in 601 BCE he rebelled against his Babylonian overlord, a decision that ultimately brought an unhappy Nebuchadnezzar to besiege Jerusalem during 598/597 (2 Kgs 24:1-7).[5]

Jehoiakim was the reason for the 598 BCE siege, but he appears to have died before the effort quashed his rebellion, and his son Jehoiachin was the one to surrender to Nebuchadnezzar a mere three months and ten days after assuming his father's throne (2 Kgs 24:8-12). When all was said and done, Jehoiakim "slept with his fathers" (2 Kgs 24:6);[6] Jehoiachin was in Babylonian exile (2 Kgs 24:12-16); and a third son of Josiah—Zedekiah—became Nebuchadnezzar's choice for Judean king (2 Kgs 24:17). Zedekiah holds the distinction of being the last king of Judah; the capital city of Jerusalem fell in 587 BCE.

The timing of Jehoiakim's "third year" in Dan 1:1 is a vexing problem. It is typically understood to refer to 605 BCE, when Nebuchadnezzar's army was on military campaign in Syria-Palestine. However, this date presents several challenges. The first challenge is what appears to be a textual inconsistency. Jeremiah 25:1 equates Jehoiakim's *fourth* year with Nebuchadnezzar's *first* year—meaning the events of Dan 1:1 would predate Nebuchadnezzar's rise to the throne. A possible solution to this conundrum is a difference between systems of dating regnal years. In the Babylonian system, reflected in Dan 1:1, the king's accession year was separate from the first year of his reign: accession year, year 1, year 2, year 3. In the Judean system, reflected in Jer 25:1, the king's accession year *was* the first year of his reign: accession/year 1, year 2, year 3, year 4.[7] In this case, the third year of Jehoiakim in 605 BCE coincided with the accession year of Nebuchadnezzar.[8]

---

5. In addition to being a headache for Nebuchadnezzar, Jehoiakim was largely unpopular among his own people because he squandered national funds to rebuild his palace, and he used forced labor to do it (Jer 22:13-17). The prophet Jeremiah accused him of idolatry, social injustice, greed, murder, oppression, and covenant violation (Jer 22:1-17; 25-26; 36).

6. Second Chronicles 36:6 records that Nebuchadnezzar bound Jehoiakim with shackles to take him to Babylon, but it does not specify that he ever left Judah, much less arrived in Babylon. It is more likely that he died and was buried in the land of Israel.

7. D. J. Wiseman et al., *Notes on Some Problems in the Book of Daniel* (London: Tyndale, 1965), 16-18.

8. If 605 BCE is the correct date historically for the siege and subsequent deportation of Daniel and his friends, then one could speculate—as Block does—that in God's providence, Daniel's advance arrival in Babylon and his establishment in the royal court before the mass deportation could help account for the Judeans' settlement in good circumstances by the river Kebar (Ezek 1:1; 3:15): "Why should the Judaeans have been settled within the vicinity of Babylon (rather than far away), be given a large tract of fertile land, and granted the level of independence necessary to maintain their own ethnic identity and social cohesion? Daniel may have been the answer to this question"—much like Joseph was the advance party so Jacob's clan could settle in desirable Goshen ("Preaching Old Testament Apocalyptic to a New Testament Church," 25-26). What is clear from extrabiblical textual evidence is that the Judean

A second challenge is that the extrabiblical evidence for a 605 BCE siege of Jerusalem is slim, and the chronology is difficult. Nebuchadnezzar's army was on the move in Syria-Palestine in early 605, but the primary source for this data (the Babylonian Chronicle) refers only generally to Babylonian successes in the region, without mentioning Jerusalem or Jehoiakim. During the same year, Nebuchadnezzar's father, Nabopolassar, died in Babylon, and the warring heir returned home for his own coronation. The timing of the campaign in Syria-Palestine and Nebuchadnezzar's coronation in Babylon leaves a very small window in which he could have defeated Jehoiakim back in Palestine.

However, these difficulties are not insurmountable, since Nebuchadnezzar's presence would not have been required for the events described in 1:1. The actions of his army would be credited to him, whether he was physically present or not.[9] Furthermore, the activity described in 1:1 need not refer to a formal military siege; it could simply mean they "showed hostility."[10] If this is the sense of the word in 1:1, Nebuchadnezzar could have sent enough of his army to persuade Jehoiakim to give up before he made matters worse. If Jerusalem was among the cities attacked by Nebuchadnezzar's army during the 605 BCE campaign, then 1:1 recounts Jehoiakim's shift from Egyptian to Babylonian vassalage.[11]

Another possible solution to the chronological challenge of the date in Dan 1:1 is that Jehoiakim's third year refers not to the third year of his appointment by Pharaoh Neco or even to the third year of his Babylonian vassalage, but rather to the third year after he rebelled against Nebuchadnezzar in 601 BCE and seems to have asserted Judean independence (cf. 2 Kgs 23:36–24:6).[12] In this case, Jehoiakim's "third year" would have been 598 BCE, and the siege of Dan 1:1 is the same siege of 2 Kgs 24:10.[13] This is attractive from a historical perspective, given the lack of extrabiblical evidence for a 605 BCE siege, but it also fits within a discourse pattern of the book: linking key events to the first and third years of kings' reigns (cf. Dan 7:1; 8:1; 9:1; 10:1; 11:1; the only exception is 2:1). This pattern may actually provide a hint that the dates in Daniel are not intended to be precise. Goldingay suggests that "first" and "third" may be more concrete ways of saying "at the beginning" or "not long after the beginning" of a king's reign.[14] The similarity of dates at key transitions throughout the book may be the narrator's literary way of affirming God's sovereignty in history[15]—God was in charge when a king began his reign, and he remained active and in control even after the king had established himself.

If the siege of Dan 1:1 is the 598/597 BCE siege, one might protest that Jehoiakim was not the king that Nebuchadnezzar defeated (1:2). However, connecting the events to his reign rather than to his successor's is appropriate since Jehoiakim was the reason for the Babylonian assault; Jehoiachin

---

community thrived during their time in Babylon, though the historical reasons for this thriving remain speculative. For a recent study of the Judeans in Babylonian exile based on archival cuneiform sources, see Tero Alstola, *Judeans in Babylonia: A Study of Deportees in the Sixth and Fifth Centuries BCE*, CHANE 109 (Leiden: Brill, 2020).

9. Lucas, *Daniel*, 51.

10. D. J. Wiseman, *Nebuchadrezzar and Babylon* (Oxford: Oxford University Press, 1985), 23, and Longman, *Daniel*, 44–45.

11. See further Lucas, *Daniel*, 50–52.

12. Iain Provan, V. Philips Long, and Tremper Longman III, *A Biblical History of Israel* (Louisville: Westminster John Knox, 2003), 381n112.

13. This siege is also recorded in the *Babylonian Chronicles* (Chronicle 5, line 12; A. K. Grayson, *Assyrian and Babylonian Chronicles* [Winona Lake, IN: Eisenbrauns, 2000], 102).

14. Goldingay, *Daniel*, 152–53. In his discussion, Goldingay cites J. B. Segal, "Numerals in the Old Testament," *JSS* 10 (1965): 2–20, though Segal only says that the number three "represents the basic notion of plurality in human action and thought" (19). He does not specifically address the use of "first year" or "third year."

15. Goldingay, *Daniel*, 152–53.

barely had time to size his crown before his reign was over.¹⁶

Regardless of whether Dan 1:1 refers to 605 or 598 BCE, Jehoiakim's third year sets the *terminus a quo* for the book's events, and specifically, for the period of time in which the narratives of chs. 1–6 occur. The end of ch. 1 provides the *terminus ad quem*: the first year of Cyrus (1:21). These two dates span the length of the enforced exile: it began with the siege and first captives to Babylon, and it officially ended with the decree of Cyrus that allowed Jewish exiles to return to their homeland (539–538 BCE).

In the worldview of the ancient Near East, the outcome of a conflict like the one described in Dan 1:1 showcased the superiority of the victorious king and his god. Kings waged war on behalf of their gods to increase their deities' territories,¹⁷ and when one king was victorious over another king, it demonstrated his god's victory over the god(s) of the conquered king. Nebuchadnezzar's transfer of vessels from the Jerusalem temple to the treasury of his god in Babylon (1:2b–c) illustrates this. From all appearances, Nebuchadnezzar's god had defeated Jehoiakim's.

But the text refutes this idea with the main clause of 1:2a (. . . וַיִּתֵּן) and its introduction of a new character into the events: אֲדֹנָי. The title itself means "lord" or "master," and the form אָדוֹן is commonly used in the Old Testament for earthly masters (e.g., of Joseph in Gen 45:8; Moses in Num 11:28; David in 1 Kgs 1:17). The same form also appears in reference to God (e.g., Josh 3:11; Ps 114:7), but the more commonly used form is אֲדֹנָי, which is used only for God (e.g., Gen 18:3; Isa 38:16; Ps 35:17). The occurrence of אֲדֹנָי in Daniel is limited to Dan 1:2 and to Daniel's prayer in ch. 9 (9:3–4, 7, 15–17, 19).¹⁸ By using this title to introduce God, the narrator hints that this new character is really the one in charge—not either of the human kings he has already introduced. This is the one who is truly and absolutely Lord and Master—not just in Israel, but over all the earth. Goldingay summarizes, "The titles 'the Lord' and 'God' with their absolute implications belong only to Yahweh; the exile happened by the act of this sovereign God who is also Israel's God, not Nebuchadnezzar's."¹⁹

The action of the Lord in 1:2a makes explicit what this title implies and also provides the key to understanding the events reported in the opening verses. The Lord "gave" (נתן) Jehoiakim and some of the temple vessels into Nebuchadnezzar's hand.²⁰ What appears on the surface to be the defeat of a lesser king (Jehoiakim) by a greater king (Nebuchadnezzar) was actually the gift of an even greater king—*the* Lord, *the* Master (cf. Jer 27:6).

The statement that the Lord gave Jehoiakim, "king of Judah," into Nebuchadnezzar's hand says more than necessary to convey the simple facts. The reader already knows who Jehoiakim is (1:1a), so the overspecification that he is "king of Judah" serves a purpose other than identification.²¹ By restating

---

16. Another viewpoint that considers the date in terms of its larger narrative purpose is that of George Athas, who argues that "the narrative couches this siege in 606/5 BCE" even though there was not actually a siege at that time. The narrator's purpose for setting the beginning of the exile in 605 BCE relates to the timing of the seventy "weeks" in Dan 9. See further George Athas, "In Search of the Seventy 'Weeks' of Daniel 9," *JHebS* 9.2 (2009): 2–20.

17. Jeffrey J. Niehaus, *Ancient Near Eastern Themes in Biblical Theology* (Grand Rapids: Kregel, 2008), 30–31.

18. The most common epithet for Israel's God in Daniel is "God," Hebrew אֱלֹהִים, *ĕlōhîm*. The divine name, YHWH, occurs only in ch. 9.

19. Goldingay, *Daniel*, 152.

20. This is the first of three occurrences of the phrase "the Lord/God gave (נתן)" in ch. 1 (vv. 2, 9, 17).

21. Steven E. Runge and Joshua R. Westbury, eds., *LDHB* (Bellingham, WA: Lexham Press, 2012), 2.1 Overspecification.

who Jehoiakim is—namely, the Davidic king—the narrator invites the reader to pause and consider the significance of who Jehoiakim is and what the Lord is doing. Jehoiakim, Judah, and Jerusalem belong to the Lord, yet he is the one who hands them over. The following paraphrase highlights the significance of the overspecification: "The Lord gave Jehoiakim—yes, you read that right, *his very own Davidic king*—and his sacred temple vessels into the hand of an idol-worshiping foreign king." This is counterintuitive and even seems to be a violation of the Davidic covenant. God should not be doing this, from a human perspective. If he has the power to give Jehoiakim into Nebuchadnezzar's hand, would he also not have the power to keep him out of it?

The action of the Lord in 1:2a sets what appears to be a defeat in its proper context. Nebuchadnezzar is the dominant agent throughout this section: he comes, he besieges, he takes plunder back to Babylon, and he issues orders about the captives. But this single action of the Lord casts the entire exile as God's decision and under God's control. The king of Judah has been handed over, but the *real* king of Judah—nay, the king of all the world—remains on the throne. Later in the book, we will get the backstory for these events; we will understand the secondary causation for the exile (i.e., the people's sin; 9:4–19), but here in this opening scene, we see only the primary causation: God did it.

The mention of the vessels of the house of God as part of the Lord's "gift" to Nebuchadnezzar serves at least three purposes. First, in conjunction with the rest of 1:2, it confirms that—to all appearances—Nebuchadnezzar was the victorious king. Fighting on behalf of the apparent victorious god, he did what any ancient Near Eastern king would have done: transfer sacred plunder to his god's temple. Second, as Newsom says, the vessels were "the portable symbol of divine presence" and power for the Jews, who did not have physical representations of their God[22]—and mentioning them here hints to the reader that God did not just hand over his king, vessels, and people for Nebuchadnezzar to do with as he pleased. He went *with* them to Babylon, a reality that plays out in the rest of the book. Finally, mention of the vessels sets up the account in ch. 5 of Belshazzar, whose blasphemous use of the same vessels precipitates his demise (5:2–5).

The next main clause explains what Nebuchadnezzar did with what the Lord had given him: "and he brought them into the land of Shinar" (1:2b). At first read, this statement sounds like Nebuchadnezzar took everything the Lord had given him—the temple vessels and Jehoiakim—to the land of Shinar. However, the clause that follows clarifies the situation by fronting the object, "the vessels" (וְאֶת־הַכֵּלִים, 1:2c). Fronting a thematic element draws extra attention to it,[23] and in this case, by placing "the vessels" at the beginning of what appears to be a simple restatement (i.e., what Nebuchadnezzar did with the plunder), the narrator provides the referent for "them" in 1:2b. The vessels he took to Shinar. The defeated Jehoiakim was most likely left and buried in Judah (see p. 49n6 above).

"Shinar" in 1:2b is rendered "Babylon" in some English translations because Shinar, an infrequently used name for Babylon,[24] is unfamiliar to many readers, and it occurs nowhere else in the book of Daniel. However, by referring to Nebuchadnezzar's home as Shinar, the narrator calls to mind its most

---

22. Carol A. Newsom, *Daniel: A Commentary*, OTL (Louisville: Westminster John Knox, 2014), 40–41. See 2 Kgs 24:13; 25:13–17; Jer 27:16–22; 28:1–9; 2 Chr 36:7, 10, 18.

23. Runge and Westbury, *LDHB*, 5.1 Topical Frames.
24. Genesis 10:10; 11:2; 14:1, 9; Josh 7:21; Isa 11:11; and Zech 5:11.

notable occurrence in the Bible—Gen 11:1–9, which tells the story of the tower of Babel and the birth of Babylon. The book of Daniel will recount the death of Babylon, and by invoking the name "Shinar," the narrator invites the reader to consider what follows in light of the earlier story.

On the plains of Shinar in Gen 11, a group of settlers embarked on building a city with a tall tower. The tower was likely a ziggurat, part of a larger temple complex, and it would have functioned as a staircase for the gods to come down and receive gifts (i.e., food and drink) from their worshipers.[25] As part of the temple complex, the ziggurat was sacred space—that is, a place where people had access to the presence of the divine.[26]

Ancient Near Eastern people constructed temples in part to glorify the name of the gods they housed. This perspective is evident in the Bible's description of Solomon's temple (e.g., 1 Kgs 3:2; 5:3–5; 8:16–29).[27] The builders at Shinar, however, were more concerned about their own name than the name of their god (Gen 11:4). Rather than constructing sacred space for the glory and reputation of their god, they built it for their own benefit and betterment—a failure to recognize their place as people dependent on the divine. They blurred the lines between humanity and deity, and God judged them for it, confusing their language and so prompting them to scatter.[28]

In the book of Daniel, Babylonian kings also blur the lines between humanity and deity. Nebuchadnezzar may have honored his victorious god in ch. 1 by placing the Jerusalem temple vessels in his treasury, but in ch. 3 he will act more like a god himself (see, e.g., Dan 3:15). In ch. 4, he will be severely judged for his pride—namely, his profound failure to acknowledge his place before the Most High God. In ch. 5, the "son" and inferior successor of the great Nebuchadnezzar will outdo him in at least one respect—his profound failure to acknowledge his utter dependence on the Most High God for his every breath (5:22–23).

At Shinar in Gen 11, humans blurred the lines between deity and humanity; in the book of Daniel, Babylonian kings will act like gods. On the plains of Shinar, God judged the pride of the tower builders; in the book of Daniel, he judges the pride of kings who ruled the empire that grew out of the ill-fated efforts at Shinar. Ultimately, in the theology of the book of Daniel, Babylon falls because of royal pride, an appropriate end to the city that began at Shinar.[29]

---

25. John H. Walton, "The Mesopotamian Background of the Tower of Babel Account and Its Implications," *BBR* 5 (1995): 162.

26. Longman and Walton argue that much of what lies behind Gen 11 and the rest of the theological history in Gen 1–11 is a concern for divine presence and the order it brings: "After ordering the cosmos to be sacred space (Gen 1; 'sacred space' is the result of God's presence) and then setting up Eden as the place of his residence (and therefore as sacred space), access to that sacred space is lost when Adam and Eve decide they want to be the center of order. From this point on, people consistently follow their inclinations toward making themselves the center of order, which instead leads to increasing disorder. God responds with correctives that are order bringing. Though sin and its resultant disorder have been introduced, that negative impact is overshadowed by the larger reality that people have lost access to God's presence" (Tremper Longman III and John H. Walton, *The Lost World of the Flood: Mythology, Theology, and the Deluge Debate* [Downers Grove, IL: IVP Academic, 2018], 115).

27. "The idea that construction of sacred space ought to make a name for deity is reflected both in the ANE literature, such as in the names of ziggurats or temples, and in the biblical ideology" (Longman and Walton, *The Lost World of the Flood*, 133).

28. The name "Babel" (בָּבֶל) is an ironic mispronunciation of a Hebrew word meaning "to confuse" (בלל).

29. Christopher J. H. Wright comments on the use of "Shinar" in Dan 1:2, "It was an unusual name for that region of the world, first used to describe the land where the Tower of Babel had been built (Gen 11:1–9). It was like some ghastly time-warp, as if God had put history in reverse and taken Israel right back before Abraham was even heard of, back to the land which God had called Abraham to *leave*. Something

Three of Nebuchadnezzar's four actions in these opening verses are described with the same verb: בוא. First, he came (בָּא; *qal* pf.) to Jerusalem to besiege it (1:1b). In the aftermath of the assault, he brought (וַיְבִיאֵם; *hiphil wayyiqtol*; 1:2b) his plunder to Shinar, depositing (הֵבִיא; *hiphil* pf.; 1:2c) it in the temple treasury of his god. He came and went, having accomplished what he set out to do. But what happens between his coming and going in the narrative minimizes his success: the Lord gave it to him. Nebuchadnezzar may appear to be the primary agent, but in fact, the Lord is.[30]

These opening verses focus on the encounter between two earthly kings. While the first king, Jehoiakim of Judah, is of no consequence in the book, the narrator's inclusion of him helps foreground the book's theological concern with kings and kingdoms.[31] The verses also introduce the most important character in the book—the one whose unseen involvement bespeaks his sovereignty over the circumstances.

b. The King's Strategy (1:3a–5c)

The narrative continues with the main clause of 1:3a, in which Nebuchadnezzar directs the chief of his officials concerning heretofore unmentioned human plunder from Judah (1:3b–5b).[32] The purpose of these directions is that the Judeans would be qualified to serve the king (1:5c).

To this point in the narrative, the narrator has referred to Nebuchadnezzar by name (1:1b) and as the implicit subject of the verb (i.e., "he," 1:1c, 2b–c). While 1:1b introduced him into the narrative by name and identified him as "king of Babylon," here in 1:3a he is simply "the king" (הַמֶּלֶךְ). This change of reference—from a proper name to a generic reference—shifts the center of attention away from Nebuchadnezzar.[33] In the verses that follow, the center of attention will be the "sons of Israel" (1:3b), young men from the royalty and nobility of Judah.

Rather than calling the young men "sons of Judah," the narrator identifies them as Israelites—that is, members of YHWH's covenant people. Although the divine name "YHWH" does not occur until ch. 9, the presence of Israel's covenant partner is just below the surface of the narrative in ch. 1. The temple vessels remained his in a foreign land (see Dan 5:1–5, 22–23), and so did the human vessels that were in covenant with him. The Lord/YHWH may have handed them over into captivity, but he did not stay behind when Nebuchadnezzar relocated *his* belongings to Babylon.

Ashpenaz, the king's official, receives two directives from Nebuchadnezzar—to bring (לְהָבִיא, 1:3b) and to teach (וּלְלַמְּדָם, 1:4c) the youths. The first of these gives us the "who and why" of the order. The young captives were the cream of the Judean crop, described with a litany of terms that befit ancient Near Eastern sages: they were attractive and with-

---

was surely very, very wrong. Everything had gone backwards. History seemed out of control. Had God himself lost control?" (*Hearing the Message of Daniel: Sustaining Faith in Today's World* [Grand Rapids: Zondervan, 2017], 24; Wright's words assume a location in southeast Mesopotamia for Abraham's Ur, while many scholars consider the location to be in northwest Mesopotamia—though there is no consensus on the exact location.)

30. Newsom notes: "Throughout the rest of the story, Nebuchadnezzar and his officials are associated with the verb *bô'* (vv. 3, 18 [twice]), whereas God is consistently associated with the verb *nātan* (vv. 9, 17). Thus the reader knows what Nebuchadnezzar does not know: the God of Israel is the effective agent in history, not Nebuchadnezzar" (*Daniel*, 41).

31. Newsom, *Daniel*, 40. Newsom notes that "king" occurs some 187 times in the book, and "reign" occurs 69 times.

32. The verb is אמר, "to say," but we could easily translate "command," since when a king "says" something to one of his officials, he is probably not just making conversation.

33. Cf. how 1 Sam 2:19 refers to Hannah as "his [Samuel's] mother." Runge and Westbury, *LDHB*, 2.6 Changed Reference.

out physical defect; they were mentally superior and had exceptional aptitude.³⁴ The king wanted the best of the best as royal advisers in his court (לַעֲמֹד בְּהֵיכַל הַמֶּלֶךְ, 1:4b; cf. 1:5c).

The second directive provides the "how" of the order, the process by which the foreign youths would become qualified to serve as royal courtiers. Ashpenaz was to teach the captives "the language and literature of the Chaldeans" (1:4c), an education that entailed more than learning a foreign language and mastering Babylonian lore. Although the spoken language of Babylon was Aramaic (and thus similar to the Hebrew spoken by the Judean captives), the king's advisers also needed to know Akkadian, the language of Babylon's literary tradition and the courtiers' professional literature. Akkadian is not an easy language. It requires the "learning of hundreds of symbols and the rules for their use. This was achieved by first copying simple exercises set by the teacher, and then copying important literary texts, many of which were religious in nature."³⁵ This educational process could rightfully be called enculturation: "The school was an ideological molder of minds, the place where future members of the bureaucracy were socialized, where they received a common stock of ideas and attitudes which bound them together as a class and in many ways separated them from their original backgrounds."³⁶ Nebuchadnezzar intended to make the select sons of Israel some of Babylon's finest civil servants.

The rationale provided by the text for the king's directive (1:4b) may have been but part of a larger strategy. The Babylonian king may also have intended to use the captive youths as political hostages. At this point in the Babylonian-Judean conflict, Nebuchadnezzar wanted "to control Judah without actually taking it over."³⁷ After the captives' three years of rigorous education and enculturation, the king could have sent some of them back to their homeland as propaganda tools. This practice was known in ancient Rome, where the state "[took] the children of other close relatives of client states and [held] them 'hostage.' This practice was not punishment as much as security against rebellion. As these hostages lived in Rome, a high-ranking Roman family became their patron and they became acclimated to Roman ways, with the idea that they would be friends of Rome when they returned to their native lands."³⁸ If this was part of Nebuchadnezzar's plan, the narrator's silence about it is probably because only the stated rationale is relevant to the purposes of the book.

The narrative action resumes with the main clause of 1:5a (וַיְמַן): the king ordered a rich, royal diet for the captives. By setting this directive as a main clause and not as part of the orders just given to Ashpenaz, the narrator brings to the reader's attention the issue that will be the impetus for the captives' actions later in the chapter (1:8–17). The dependent clause that follows sets three years as the

---

34. An earlier Egyptian text uses similar language to describe an ideal scribe: he was to be "choice of heart, persevering in counsel. . . . a youth distinguished of appearance and pleasing of charm, who can explain the difficulties of the annals like him who composed them." See "A Satirical Letter," trans. John A. Wilson (*ANET*, 475).

35. Lucas, *Daniel*, 53.

36. Piotr Michalowski, "Charisma and Control: On Continuity and Change in Early Mesopotamian Bureaucratic Systems," in *The Organization of Power: Aspects of Bureaucracy in the Ancient Near East*, ed. McGuire Gibson and Robert D. Biggs (Chicago: Oriental Institute of the University of Chicago, 1987), 63. Michalowski's comments are about scribal training specifically, but they are also applicable to the training of royal advisors. For more information about the nature of education in the ancient Near East, see David M. Carr, *Writing on the Tablet of the Heart: Origins of Scripture and Literature* (Oxford: Oxford University Press, 2005).

37. Longman, *Daniel*, 47.

38. Longman, *Daniel*, 48–49n21.

time frame for the training (1:5b). Most translations and commentators read the infinitive in 1:5b as the third in a series of infinitives describing the king's orders to Ashpenaz—he was to (1) bring the captives (לְהָבִיא, 1:3b); (2) teach them the language and literature of Babylon (וּלְלַמְּדָם, 1:4c); and (3) train them for three years (וּלְגַדְּלָם, 1:5b). While semantically it seems to fit as part of these instructions, syntactically it is set apart and dependent on the main clause of 1:5a (not the main clause of 1:3a). The author could have included it in the series of clauses dependent on 1:3a, but he chose instead to subordinate it to the independent clause about the king's appointment of the captives' food. This choice reflects the significance of the king's food and the role it was meant to play in the enculturation of the captives. Indeed, the narrative that follows supports the idea that the king's food—not any other aspect of their enforced regimen—was *the* issue for the captives.

The final independent clause of the opening unit (1:1–5) summarizes the purpose of the training: "some of"[39] the youths would stand before the king (יַעַמְדוּ לִפְנֵי הַמֶּלֶךְ, 1:5c). This statement reaches back to 1:4b, where the youths were selected because of their aptitude for service in the king's palace (לַעֲמֹד בְּהֵיכַל הַמֶּלֶךְ), and it looks ahead to 1:19c, where the youths will stand before the king to be assessed and then to serve, if they measure up (וַיַּעַמְדוּ לִפְנֵי הַמֶּלֶךְ).

2. Judean Servants in the Conflict (1:6–17c)

Main Idea of the Passage

Daniel 1:6–17 introduces four Judean exiles who remain faithful to God despite being captives-in-training for royal service to a foreign king. The passage demonstrates God's sovereignty over their circumstances and his blessing in the midst of them.

Literary Context

Daniel 1:6–17 is the heart of the narrative in ch. 1, and it accomplishes at least two goals in its broader literary context. First, it introduces four specific "sons of Israel" (1:3b), the Judeans who will be representative of God's exilic people in the events of the book, and it demonstrates their commitment to remain

---

39. מִקְצָת is also in v. 2, where it refers to "some of" the temple vessels. Here, it refers to "some of" the human vessels (note the masculine-plural suffix).

faithful to God in the midst of the defiling circumstances of exile. This section reveals their character and what the reader might expect from them in the chapters to follow.

Second, these verses continue a theme established in the preceding section—namely, that things are not what they appear to be. When the curtain rises on Daniel, Hananiah, Mishael, and Azariah, the stage has already been set for the Judean exiles to be entirely owned by the Babylonian king (1:3–5). However, in telling their story, the narrator subtly reinforces that God—not the king—is directing the events. The king is none the wiser, but the reader knows God is at work and that his sovereignty, which dictated national events in 1:1–2, also encompasses the day-to-day routine of his individual servants.

A. God Establishes His Kingdom in Exile (1:1a–21)
   1. The Beginnings of the Conflict (1:1a–5c)
→ **2. Judean Servants in the Conflict (1:6–17c)**
   3. The Success of God's Servants (1:18a–21)

Translation and Exegetical Outline

(See pages 58–59.)

Structure and Literary Form

This passage opens by introducing by name the four Judeans at the heart of the narrative (1:6). Three elements structure the rest of the passage: occurrences of the verb שׂים, "to set, place" (1:7a–b, 8a), statements that "God gave" (נתן) something to someone (1:9, 17b), and sections of reported speech (1:10b–f, 12–13).

The verb שׂים occurs in three consecutive independent clauses (1:7a–b, 8a). The first two explain that the commander of the officials changed the names of the Judeans (1:7a–b), an act that helps set up the problem of the narrative addressed in the third שׂים clause (1:8a): Daniel makes a decision with respect to the enculturation of the captives (see also 1:3–5). The next independent clause describes the action Daniel took because of this decision (1:8c). These two independent clauses with Daniel as the agent are each followed by a relative clause detailing the reason for his action: not defiling himself (1:8b–d).

Daniel 1:6–17c

			2. Judean Servants in the Conflict (1:6–17c)
			a. The Four Sons of Judah (1:6–7b)
			(1) Hebrew Identities (1:6)
6	וַיְהִ֣י בָהֶ֗ם מִבְּנֵ֣י יְהוּדָ֔ה דָּנִיֵּ֥אל חֲנַנְיָ֖ה מִֽישָׁאֵ֥ל וַעֲזַרְיָֽה׃	Among them—from the sons of Judah—were Daniel, Hananiah, Mishael, and Azariah.	
			(2) Babylonian Identities (1:7a–b)
7a	וַיָּ֧שֶׂם לָהֶ֛ם שַׂ֥ר הַסָּרִיסִ֖ים שֵׁמ֑וֹת	And the commander of the officials assigned to them names.	
7b	וַיָּ֨שֶׂם לְדָנִיֵּ֜אל בֵּ֣לְטְשַׁאצַּ֗ר וְלַחֲנַנְיָה֙ שַׁדְרַ֔ךְ וּלְמִֽישָׁאֵ֖ל מֵישַׁ֑ךְ וְלַעֲזַרְיָ֖ה עֲבֵ֥ד נְגֽוֹ׃	And he assigned for Daniel "Belteshazzar," and for Hananiah "Shadrach," and for Mishael "Meshach," and for Azariah "Abednego."	
			b. The Decision of the Exiles (1:8a–17c)
			(1) The King's Defiling Table (1:8a–b)
8a	וַיָּ֤שֶׂם דָּנִיֵּאל֙ עַל־לִבּ֔וֹ	But Daniel made up his mind	
8b	אֲשֶׁ֧ר לֹֽא־יִתְגָּאַ֛ל בְּפַתְבַּ֥ג הַמֶּ֖לֶךְ וּבְיֵ֣ין מִשְׁתָּ֑יו	↑ that he would not defile himself with the king's food and with the wine he drank,	
			(2) Daniel's First Attempt (1:8c–10f)
			(a) The Request (1:8c–d)
8c	וַיְבַקֵּשׁ֙ מִשַּׂ֣ר הַסָּרִיסִ֔ים	so he sought from the commander of the officials	
8d	אֲשֶׁ֖ר לֹ֥א יִתְגָּאָֽל׃	↑ that he might not defile himself.	
			(b) God's Gift (1:9)
9	וַיִּתֵּ֤ן הָֽאֱלֹהִים֙ אֶת־דָּ֣נִיֵּ֔אל לְחֶ֖סֶד וּֽלְרַחֲמִ֑ים לִפְנֵ֖י שַׂ֥ר הַסָּרִיסִֽים׃	And God gave Daniel favor and compassion before the commander of the officials,	
			(c) The Commander's Response (1:10a–f)
10a	וַיֹּ֜אמֶר שַׂ֤ר הַסָּרִיסִים֙ לְדָנִיֵּ֔אל	but the commander of the officials said to Daniel,	
10b	יָרֵ֤א אֲנִי֙ אֶת־אֲדֹנִ֣י הַמֶּ֔לֶךְ	"I am afraid of my lord, the king	
10c	אֲשֶׁ֣ר מִנָּ֔ה אֶת־מַאֲכַלְכֶ֖ם וְאֶת־מִשְׁתֵּיכֶ֑ם	who appointed your food and your drink,	
10d	אֲשֶׁ֡ר לָמָּה֩ יִרְאֶ֨ה אֶת־פְּנֵיכֶ֜ם זֹעֲפִ֗ים מִן־הַיְלָדִים֙	for why should he see your faces thinner than the (other) young men	
10e	אֲשֶׁ֣ר כְּגִֽילְכֶ֔ם	← who are your age?	
10f	וְחִיַּבְתֶּ֥ם אֶת־רֹאשִׁ֖י לַמֶּֽלֶךְ׃	Then you would endanger my head with the king."	

Daniel 1:1a–21

11a	So Daniel said to the guard,	(3) Daniel's Second Attempt (1:11a–14b)
11b	whom the commander of the officials had appointed over Daniel, Hananiah, Mishael, and Azariah,	(a) The Target (1:11a–b)
12a	"Please test your servants for ten days:	(b) The Test (1:12a–13c)
12b	let us be given some vegetables	
12c	that we may eat	
12d	and [let us be given] water	
12e	that we may drink.	
13a	"Then let our appearance and the appearance of the young men eating the king's food be observed by you,	
13b	and according to what you see,	
13c	deal with your servants."	
14a	So he listened to them in this matter,	(c) The Guard's Response (1:14a–b)
14b	and he tested them ten days.	
15	At the end of the ten days, their appearance was seen to be better and fatter in flesh than all the young men eating the king's food.	(4) The Result (1:15–17c) (a) Superior Appearance (1:15)
16a	So the guard took away their food and the wine they drank,	(b) A New Regimen (1:16a–b)
16b	and he gave them vegetables.	
17a	And as for these four young men,	(c) God's Gifts (1:17a–c)
17b	God gave them knowledge and skill in all literature and wisdom.	
17c	And Daniel understood all visions and dreams.	

The statement that God "gave" (נתן) something to someone first appears in 1:2a, where the Lord gave Jehoiakim and some of the temple vessels into Nebuchadnezzar's hand.[40] In this section, it occurs two more times (1:9, 17b), reminding readers that God drives the events of the chapter (and by implication, the rest of the book). In the first of these two occurrences (1:9), God gave Daniel favor with the commander of the officials, the one who had changed his name and the one of whom Daniel had made his request (1:8c–d). The second occurrence falls at the end of the section (1:17b), where God gave the four Judeans the knowledge and skills necessary to succeed in their foreign environment.

The central section of the passage includes two instances of reported speech, the first by the commander of the officials to Daniel (1:10b–f) and the second by Daniel to the guard in charge of the four Judeans (1:12–13). These speeches develop the plot, but they also provide windows into the thoughts, interests, and motivations of their speakers.[41]

The passage concludes with a summary of what became of the four men introduced at the beginning of the section (1:17b–c; cf. 1:6). Using a left-dislocation structure ("And as for these four young men," 1:17a)—that is, information syntactically outside the main clause (1:17b) but referred to in the main clause—the narrator "introduce[s] something that is too complex to include in the main clause, where it might otherwise cause confusion."[42] God gave these four young men success in their Babylonian education (1:17b; cf. 1:4c), and Daniel was also able to understand visions and dreams (1:17c).

Explanation of the Text

a. The Four Sons of Judah (1:6–7b)

The opening passage of the book (1:1–5) introduced Israelite exiles into the narrative in general terms. In this section, four young men from that group move to the fore, identified by name and then renamed before they become part of the plotline that occupies the rest of the chapter. These characters, and especially Daniel, will be part of the book's larger narrative, and what is revealed about them here creates the context for their roles in future chapters.

While the larger group was called the "sons of Israel," these men specifically are from the tribe of Judah (מִבְּנֵי יְהוּדָה, 1:6a). Even their names help to identify them as God's people: Daniel, "God is my judge"; Hananiah, "YHWH has acted graciously"; Azariah, "YHWH has helped"; Mishael, probably "Who is like God" or "who is what God is?"[43]

---

40. See above on Dan 1:2 for discussion about the use of אֲדֹנָי, "the Lord."

41. "All speech reflects and exposes the speaker, while it sometimes also brings to light qualities of the person being addressed (or reveals the speaker's opinion of that person). What people say witnesses not only to their thoughts, feelings, etc., but is often slanted to accord with the character, mood, interests and status of their interlocutor" (Shimon Bar-Efrat, *Narrative Art in the Bible* [New York: T&T Clark, 2004], 64–65).

42. Runge and Westbury, *LDHB*, 5.7 Left Dislocation.

43. Lucas, *Daniel*, 53.

As captives in Babylon, their names are changed to praise gods such as Bel and Nabu: Belteshazzar, Shadrach, Meshach, and Abednego.[44] The renaming of the Judean exiles signaled their new identity as subjects of the Babylonian king and also implied their allegiance to him and his gods.

It may be troubling to us that the young men apparently did not object to this reidentification. It may also trouble us that the narrator does not indicate that they put up a fight against other objectionable aspects of their education, such as learning the art of divination. The Mosaic Law strictly forbade the practice of reading signs and omens to decipher the will of the gods (e.g., Lev 19:26; 1 Sam 15:23; Jer 14:14), yet the Judeans must have learned it and, we learn at the end of the chapter, learned it so well that they even excelled at it.

To this point in the narrative, the Judeans have apparently submitted to every aspect of their education, such that their assimilation to the idolatrous Babylonian culture appears to be complete. But the narrator is about to challenge this conclusion. For the second time in the chapter, a set of circumstances requires reinterpretation (cf. 1:1–2 and see comments there). Earlier in the chapter, Nebuchadnezzar's possession of God's temple vessels suggested that the Babylonian king's god had defeated the God of Israel. This time, it is four human vessels that appear to be under the control of the Babylonian king. Appearances even suggest that they have compromised their faith in YHWH, the God of Israel, along the exilic way. But the narrator will soon show us once again that things are not as they seem.

b. The Decision of the Exiles (1:8a–17c)

The narrator describes the name-changing action by the commander of the officials, likely the same person responsible for the education of the exiles from Israel (1:3a), in a pair of independent שׂים clauses ("to set, place," 1:7a–b) and a third independent שׂים clause describing Daniel's response—not to the new names but to another aspect of the enculturation: eating from the king's table (1:8a).

Newsom translates all three שׂים clauses with "decided" and highlights the narrator's subtle wordplay, in which the same word (שׂים) describes the name-changing action by the head of staff (1:7–8) and Daniel's determination not to defile himself with the royal food and drink. She calls the double names of the exiles "an index of the double identities experienced by all exiles, immigrants, and colonized peoples, who must continually negotiate the sometimes-conflicting claims of the two cultures to which they belong," noting that the שׂים clauses illustrate both the Judean captives and the Babylonian official navigating the tensions created by their cultural divide: "the head of staff is diminishing the 'foreignness' of the Judean exiles in their new Babylonian context, and Daniel is asserting a nonnegotiable mark of Judean identity."[45]

To this point in the narrative, Daniel and his fellow exiles have been pawns in the hand of a conquering king. They have been brought in (1:3b) to be educated (1:4c), trained (1:5b), and fed from the king's table (1:5a); and they have had their names changed

---

44. It is not entirely clear what these new names meant. If, as suggested here, they were names extolling Babylonian gods, "Belteshazzar" may mean "Bel, protect his life" or "Lady, protect the king," and "Abednego" may be a corruption or wordplay of a name meaning "servant of Nabu" or "servant of the shining one" (see, e.g., Goldingay, *Daniel*, 156–57; Collins, *Daniel*, 141; A. R. Millard, "Daniel 1–6 and History," *EvQ* 49 [1977], 72). There is no consensus on the meanings of "Shadrach" and "Me-shach," though Millard offers "I am very fearful (of God)" and "I am of little account," respectively, for the two names ("Daniel 1–6 and History," 72). Some scholars think the Hebrew narrator of Daniel creatively twisted the foreign names so they were actually "corrupted forms of names extolling pagan gods" (Lucas, *Daniel*, 53). A third, satirical view is that the names are Babylonian gibberish to parody Babylonian culture.

45. Newsom, *Daniel*, 47.

(1:7). Now for the first time in the text, the narrator moves Daniel from a passive to an active role. He decides what he must do—or what he must *not* do—and then he goes about implementing his decision.

The reason for Daniel's decision not to eat or drink from the king's table is made clear in two relative clauses: he did not want to defile, or ritually contaminate, himself (אֲשֶׁר לֹא־יִתְגָּאָל; 1:8b–d). What is not clear is why the king's fare would have been defiling. While the food would have been offered to idols and its preparation would have violated Jewish food laws, this would have been true of all the king's food—even the vegetables, which Daniel felt free to eat. And neither of these objections would have applied to the king's wine.[46]

It is possible that Daniel chose a battle he could win. He could not have refused to participate in the educational training, and he needed this training to serve well where God had put him. He also may not have been successful had he protested the change of his name, and it may well be that the name changes were a non-issue for the exiles, since we know that by the end of exile, prominent and respected Jews like Sheshbazzar and Zerubbabel have Babylonian names.[47] Perhaps in the daily routine of his diet Daniel saw a stand he could feasibly take. Longman suggests that the reason for refusing the food had more to do with *who* was feeding the four Judeans than *what* they were feeding them:

> Their minds as well as their bodies are being fed by the Babylonian court. If they prosper, then to whom should they attribute their development and success? The Babylonians. However, by refusing to eat the food of the king, they know it is not the king who is responsible for the fact that "they looked healthier and better nourished than any of the young men who ate the royal food" (1:15). Their robust appearance, usually attained by a rich fare of meats and wine, is miraculously achieved through a diet of vegetables. Only God could have done it.[48]

If this was the case, then Daniel's resolution was less about taking a public stand than making a private decision to remember his life source during the three years of total immersion training. Every time they ate, Daniel and his friends would be reminded that although they could not choose to avoid the idolatrous Babylonian culture, they could choose to be nourished by the King of kings rather than the king of Babylon.

While all four named exiles participate in the vegetables and water regimen, it is Daniel who assumes leadership of the group. The narrator summarizes his action by saying he sought out the commander of the officials "that he might not defile himself" (אֲשֶׁר לֹא יִתְגָּאָל; 1:8d). He does not detail how Daniel went about this, nor does he report what Daniel specifically asked, but the narrator's summary suggests that Daniel may have explained why he considered the king's food objectionable—namely, that it was defiling.

The next independent clause advances the

---

46. See Lucas, *Daniel*, 54, and Longman, *Daniel*, 52, for further discussion of the food issue. The food resolution of ch. 1 may have been a temporary decision lasting only for the three years of training, since during the reign of Cyrus (10:3), a mourning Daniel abstains from food he apparently ate regularly: choice food (i.e., meat and wine). This assumes that the beginning and ending dates of Daniel's service presented in ch. 1 (1:1, Jehoiakim's third year; 1:21, Cyrus's first year) only delimit the years of enforced exile and say nothing about Daniel's potential service beyond that point. If the chronologies of 1:21 and 10:1 are read literally, however, then one could argue that Daniel's royal service was finished by the time of his fasting in 10:3, so he may have had control over his own food preparation then. See Collins: "Daniel 10:3 clearly presupposes that Daniel normally partook of meat and wine when these were no longer furnished from the table of the king" (*Daniel*, 143).

47. Collins, *Daniel*, 140–41.

48. Longman, *Daniel*, 53.

narrative, giving us cause to think Daniel will receive what he has asked: God gave (וַיִּתֵּן הָאֱלֹהִים) Daniel favor and compassion with the Babylonian commander (1:9). This second of three "God gave" statements in the chapter reminds us that God is behind the circumstances of the chapter (cf. 1:2a; 1:17b); surely such God-given favor will compel the commander to accede to Daniel's request.

The narrator provides the commander's response in reported speech (1:10b–f). Reported speech in the biblical text should not be read as a transcription of what was really said; no one was there with stylus and tablet taking notes. Rather, like everything else in biblical narrative, the narrator shapes reported speech to emphasize certain elements and influence the reader's interpretation of the speaker and the events. Bar-Efrat describes reported speech this way:

> Conversations in biblical narrative are never precise and naturalistic imitations of real-life conversations. They are highly concentrated and stylized, are devoid of idle chatter, and all the details they contain are carefully calculated to fulfil a clear function. Moreover, the conversations are sometimes so compressed that the details we want or expect to find in them are missing.[49]

The commander's response begins with a verbless clause with predicate-subject word order: יָרֵא אֲנִי (1:10b). The expected word order is subject-predicate, so by placing the predicate first, the narrator focuses the entire clause on this element: that is, the commander's fear.[50] Everything the commander says is framed by this fear. He fears "my lord, the king." It would have been sufficient to say he fears the king, since every reader knows who the king is and why he might induce fear. But the overspecification of the king as "my lord" provides a narrative contrast to the other "lord" in the chapter—the Lord of 1:2a, the one who has mastery over all the chapter's events. That same Lord, Lord of all the earth, had even caused the commander of the officials to be favorably inclined toward the Judean exile, but his fear of "my lord, the king," אֲדֹנִי הַמֶּלֶךְ, drove his response to Daniel's request. He feared for his life if the king had cause to think he had not followed orders. Without the narrator's preemptive statement that God had given Daniel favor with the commander of officials, we might interpret his response to Daniel as the absence of God's favor on his followers, who were trying to do the right thing before their God. But instead the narrator subtly reminds us that God is behind the events of the chapter—even when they do not unfold as one might expect they should if God is behind them.

The commander may not have done what Daniel asked, but Newsom suggests that God's favor nonetheless led him to give Daniel the space to try another tactic, while also protecting himself from what he feared—namely, the king:

> Not only does the head of staff show Daniel sympathy and kindness by not using his knowledge of Daniel's proposed resistance against him, but he also protects himself by replying to Daniel with the words of an impeccably loyal servant of the king who respects the king's commands. At the same time, by focusing only on the criterion of Daniel's appearance rather than explicitly denying Daniel's request, he gives the courtier's equivalent of a wink.

---

49. Bar-Efrat, *Narrative Art in the Bible*, 148.

50. Grammarians also describe this word order as a "clause of classification," in contrast to a "clause of identification"—that is, it answers the question, "What is the subject like?" (*IBHS*, 130–32).

Daniel has been given space to pursue his request, so long as the criterion of good appearance can be met—and so long as the head of staff does not have to know about the arrangements.⁵¹

In the narrative-advancing main clause of 1:11a, Daniel approached the guard who had charge of the day-to-day routine of the four Judeans. In this second request, the narrator reports Daniel's speech and so provides a window into his character and motivation (1:12–13). In Daniel's initial request, we do not know how the request was presented, though it appears Daniel told the commander the food would be defiling (1:8c–d). In this second attempt, Daniel proposed a test and said nothing about the reason for it.

With appropriate respect, indicated by the נָא particle on the verb and the self-referential expression "your servants" (נַס־נָא אֶת־עֲבָדֶיךָ, 1:12a),⁵² Daniel asked for ten days of vegetables and water. Ten days was long enough to make a difference, but not long enough to result in what the commander had feared—that is, haggard-looking exiles. Then the guard could assess their appearance in comparison to the other captives and decide whether to keep feeding them vegetables.

Early in the chapter, the narrator described the exiles as exceptional (1:3b–4b), heaping up terms common to wisdom traditions of the ancient Near East, and here in Daniel's actions and words we see his skills at work. Daniel found the right way to do the right thing—wisdom in action. He is "the incarnation of a wise man—a man who knows how to navigate life. He knows the right action for the right situation; he knows the right word to effect a godly result."⁵³

The narrator does not report, as he had with the commander, that God gave Daniel favor with the guard. Yet the guard agrees to Daniel's proposal. We are not told why, but we can speculate that somehow he benefitted from it. Perhaps the extra four servings from the king's table went home with him at day's end. Regardless, the test was successful, and ten days later the Judean exiles were healthier in appearance than the others: "better and fatter in flesh than all the young men eating the king's food" (1:15). The guard saw no good reason to require they eat the king's food, so he took it away—and quite possibly kept it for himself—and gave them vegetables instead (1:16).

The book of Daniel casts Daniel as another, greater Joseph, especially in chs. 2 and 4, but hints of it are also in ch. 1.⁵⁴ Thematically, both are Hebrew exiles serving in foreign courts; both are good looking (Gen 39:6; Dan 1:4); both exhibit great wisdom (Gen 41:39; Dan 1:4, 20); both enjoy God's blessing in their respective environments (Gen 39:2–6; Dan 1:17–20).⁵⁵ Another hint of the Joseph story in Dan 1 is the description of the Judean exiles after the ten-day dietary test (Dan 1:15), when they are said to be בְּרִיאֵי בָשָׂר, "fat of flesh," an expression used elsewhere only in Gen 41 to describe the fat cows of Pharaoh's dream. The narrator may have employed this description to suggest that just as

---

51. Newsom, *Daniel*, 49.

52. The function of the נָא particle in Hebrew is a matter of debate. The interpretation here assumes a precative function—that is, it expresses the wish or desire of the speaker (*IBHS*, 34.7a; cf. also GKC §105b [308]; Joüon §105c [322–23]). Another understanding of the form is that it expresses a logical consequence: that is, it "denote[s] that the command in question is a logical consequence, either of an immediately preceding statement or of the general situation in which is it uttered" (Thomas O. Lambdin, *Introduction to Biblical Hebrew* [New York: Scribner's Sons, 1971], 170).

53. Longman, *Daniel*, 54.

54. See IN DEPTH: A Theological Paradigm for God's Work among the Nations: The Court Stories of Daniel (Dan 2) and Joseph (Gen 41) in Canonical Context on pp. 123–37.

55. Robert Gnuse, "The Jewish Dream Interpreter in a Foreign Court: The Recurring Use of a Theme in Jewish Literature," *JSP* 17 (1990): 40.

the fat cows in Pharaoh's dreams represented years of plenty for Egypt, so the presence of the Judean exiles precipitated "years of plenty" for the Babylonian royal court—the gentile kings would benefit from their presence.

The section ends with a summary of the four Judeans' status. The narrator uses a left dislocation structure in 1:17a to introduce the topic of the four young men: "And as for these four young men." This structure sets information outside the syntax of the main clause (1:17b) and allows the narrator to "introduce something that is too complex to include in the main clause, where it might otherwise cause confusion."[56] The main clause can then simply refer to the four men with a suffixed pronoun (לָהֶם).

For the third time in the chapter, the narrator reports that "God gave" someone something (1:17b). In this final instance, God gave the Judeans ability to excel in the king's service. The young men had been selected for royal training because they were exceptional, but the narrator indicates that God enabled them to succeed above and beyond their normal capacities. By placing this statement immediately after the report of the exiles' stand against the king's defiling food, the narrator implies that God especially blessed them for their faithfulness.[57] Daniel is uniquely gifted with the ability to understand all kinds of visions and dreams, a skill that is integral to the next chapter and throughout the book.

In this section, the author of Daniel has once again demonstrated who is really in control despite appearances. The Babylonian king does not ultimately rule over Daniel and his friends; they are subject to a more powerful king whose subtle "gifts" (נתן; 1:9, 17b) demonstrate his faithfulness to his people and his power over a formidable king.

3. The Success of God's Servants (1:18a–21)

Main Idea of the Passage

Daniel 1:18–21 demonstrates the outcome of the king's educational efforts to prepare the Judean captives for royal service. The four youths emerged at the head of the class, showing that it was possible for God's people to do more than merely survive exile: they could also thrive there because God was ultimately in control of their circumstances.

---

56. Again we cite Runge and Westbury, *LDHB*, 5.7 Left Dislocation.

57. Goldingay disputes that the Judeans' exceptional abilities are related to their faithfulness. In the first edition of his *Daniel* (Dallas: Word, 1989), he explicitly says, "v 17 does not follow from v 16 as a reward of faithfulness or a fruit of asceticism" and the abilities described "denote supernaturally revealed knowledge," in contrast to the rational wisdom of 1:4 (p. 20). The text of Dan 1 mentions them in preparation for the following chapters. In the revised edition of Goldingay's *Daniel* (Grand Rapids: Zondervan Academic, 2019), these comments are gone, but in their place is a much lengthier discussion in the same vein: "By allowing the young men to be open to alien learning, but then portraying their learning as superior, Daniel makes the same points as Isa 47, perhaps more strongly. It asserts that there is insight about life, history, and politics . . . that only God endows" (171).

Literary Context

Daniel 1:18–21 is the closing unit of the book's first macro unit (Dan 1), and it accomplishes at least two things in this broader context. First, it provides the results of the king's efforts in the chapter to train captives for royal service—and specifically, to train the four Judean youth Daniel, Hananiah, Mishael, and Azariah. The section puts the exclamation point on the chapter's storyline by showing that those who declined the king's rich food not only survived his efforts to own them—they surpassed the abilities of their colleagues.

Second, the passage works in tandem with the chapter's opening section to set the parameters for the book's chronology. Daniel is among the captives taken from Jerusalem in Jehoiakim's third year (1:1–5), and he is in the royal court through Persian Cyrus's first year (1:21). The backdrop of the book is Babylonian exile, an exile imposed by Nebuchadnezzar and his successors that officially concluded with the decree of Cyrus that captive people could return to their homelands (539 BCE).

> A. God Establishes His Kingdom in Exile (1:1a–21)
>   1. The Beginnings of the Conflict (1:1a–5c)
>   2. Judean Servants in the Conflict (1:6–17c)
> → **3. The Success of God's Servants (1:18a–21)**

Translation and Exegetical Outline

(See page 67.)

Structure and Literary Form

The narrative of the third and final section in macro unit 1 (Dan 1:1–21) unfolds in a series of independent clauses (1:18c, 19a–c, 20b, 21). In this section, the narrator describes the setting of Nebuchadnezzar's examination (1:18a–19a), its results (1:19b–c), and the success of the Judean exiles in the royal court (1:20a–c). A final independent clause provides the length of Daniel's service (1:21).

The section opens with subordinate temporal clauses (1:18a–b), establishing the background for the first main clause (1:18c) and positioning what follows in the context of the chapter's events (cf. 1:5b–c). The second independent clause describes

Daniel 1:18a–21

18a	וּלְמִקְצָת הַיָּמִים אֲשֶׁר־אָמַר הַמֶּלֶךְ	And at the end of the days when the king said	3. The Success of God's Servants (1:18a–21)
18b	לַהֲבִיאָם ←	↑ to bring them in,	a. Nebuchadnezzar's Test (1:18a–19a)
			(1) The Timing (1:18a–b)
18c	וַיְבִיאֵם שַׂר הַסָּרִיסִים לִפְנֵי נְבֻכַדְנֶצַּר׃	the commander of the officials brought them in before Nebuchadnezzar.	(2) The Presentation (1:18c)
19a	וַיְדַבֵּר אִתָּם הַמֶּלֶךְ	And the king spoke with them,	(3) The Examination (1:19a)
19b	וְלֹא נִמְצָא מִכֻּלָּם כְּדָנִיֵּאל חֲנַנְיָה מִישָׁאֵל וַעֲזַרְיָה	and there was not found among all of them any like Daniel, Hananiah, Mishael, and Azariah.	b. Nebuchadnezzar's Discovery (1:19b–20c)
			(1) The Four Exiles Excel (1:19b)
19c	וַיַּעַמְדוּ לִפְנֵי הַמֶּלֶךְ׃	And they stood before the king.	(2) The Four Exiles Serve the King (1:19c)
20a	וְכֹל דְּבַר חָכְמַת בִּינָה אֲשֶׁר־בִּקֵּשׁ מֵהֶם הַמֶּלֶךְ ←	↓ (In) every matter of wisdom and understanding which the king sought from them,	(3) The Superiority of the Exiles (1:20a–c)
20b	וַיִּמְצָאֵם יָדוֹת עֶשֶׂר עַל כָּל־הַחַרְטֻמִּים הָאַשָּׁפִים	he found them ten times better than all the magicians and the conjurers	
20c	אֲשֶׁר בְּכָל־מַלְכוּתוֹ׃ ←	↑ who were in all his kingdom.	
21	וַיְהִי דָּנִיֵּאל עַד־שְׁנַת אַחַת לְכוֹרֶשׁ הַמֶּלֶךְ׃	And so Daniel was (there) until the first year of Cyrus the king.	c. Daniel's Continuing Service (1:21)

the main event of the section—that is, the king's examination of the captives (1:19a). The subsequent clause summarizes what the examination revealed: the four Judeans stood head and shoulders above the other candidates for royal service (1:19b). The main clause in 1:19c discloses that the king's educational regimen had accomplished its goal (cf. 1:5c): the exiles had been trained so that they could stand before the king, and the narrator announces that the Judeans do. Furthermore, the Judeans continued to excel, outshining all the king's courtiers (1:20b–c). This declaration is introduced with a left-dislocation structure in 1:20a (information syntactically outside the main clause but referred to in the main clause) so the narrator can "introduce something that is too complex to include in the main clause, where it might otherwise cause confusion."[58] In this case, he introduces the areas in which the king found the Judeans superior. The section concludes with a final independent clause, in which the narrator sets the span of Daniel's time in royal service (1:21) and provides an endpoint for the enforced exile that began in 1:1 (i.e., the third year of Jehoiakim).

Explanation of the Text

a. Nebuchadnezzar's Test (1:18a–19a)

The chapter moves toward its climax in this section by pointing to two earlier clauses in the chapter. First, the section's opening temporal clause reports that the days which the king had ordered have ended (1:18a–b), a reference to the three years of training the king commanded for the captured Jerusalem nobility. At the end of this training, the exiles were to stand in the presence of the king (1:5b–c), and so the narrator reports that the end has come (1:18a–b). Second, the king had initially ordered the commander of the officials to "bring" (לְהָבִיא; 1:3b) some of the Judean nobility for the purpose of indoctrination. Here the commander again "brings" the exiles (וַיְבִיאֵם; 1:18c), but this time he brings them into Nebuchadnezzar's presence. The commander of the officials brought the exiles from Jerusalem to Babylon and now he brings them to the king himself. It is the day of reckoning, and the success of Daniel earlier in the chapter (1:8–17) has prepared the reader well to expect a similar outcome here.

For the first time since 1:1, the narrator names the king in 1:18c—the commander presents the exiles to "Nebuchadnezzar." This change of referent brings Nebuchadnezzar to center stage for the examination of the exiles. His presence has surely been felt throughout the chapter since he was the one who issued the orders (1:3–5), but he has not been actively involved in the education of the exiles. He ordered it and assumed it was happening, but at this point, he becomes involved. By including the detail that the king himself conducted the examination interviews (1:19a), the narrator characterizes Nebuchadnezzar "as someone who likes to be in control of the process from beginning to end."[59] To this point in the narrative, the king has had no rea-

---

58. Again from Runge and Westbury, *LDHB*, 5.7 Left Dislocation.

59. Newsom, *Daniel*, 51.

son to think he has not maintained complete control of the circumstances surrounding the human plunder from Jerusalem. However, Newsom notes "the delicious irony of the story"—that while Nebuchadnezzar naturally assumes he has control of his underlings, the details of the narrative reveal that he does not. His officials have, without his knowledge, acted contrary to what he commanded. So, "the king who would be always in control does not, in fact, control his servants in all respects." More important to the narrative, however, is that "there is another monarch, far more powerful and far more in control of events than Nebuchadnezzar, who has prepared these exceptional young men for his service."[60]

b. Nebuchadnezzar's Discovery (1:19b–20c)

The purpose of the examination was to test the exiles' worthiness to "stand in the presence of the king" (1:5c; cf. 1:4b).[61] They had been chosen for their abilities to do so (1:4b), but the examination would determine if they had also achieved the necessary qualifications to do so (1:5c). The narrator reports that they did: the Judeans were at the top of the class; there was none like the four men (1:19b).

The outcome of this examination was that the four young men "stood before the king" (1:19c), a statement that creates an *inclusio* with 1:5c. The events that transpire between these two statements (1:6–17) disclose to the reader how the Judeans became qualified to stand before the king. One might have expected to read of their travails learning Akkadian or their wrestling with Babylonian lore or their interacting with other would-be courtiers. But these young men were not, as the king thought, simply in training to be his advisers; they were being prepared by a greater king to be his vessels in a foreign court. So the narrator relates a foundational story of their faithfulness to the God of Israel when outside forces conspired against such loyalty. The events of the chapters to follow will test their mettle: they will find themselves in the wrong place at the wrong time (ch. 2); they will encounter hostile enterprising colleagues (ch. 3); and they will face conspiracy (ch. 6). The opening chapter of the book grounds their responses in all the circumstances to follow in the decision they made not to eat the king's rich food, their resolution to be sustained by their God.

The statement in 1:20b ("he found them ten times better than all the magicians and the conjurers") indicates that not only had the Judeans surpassed the abilities of their fellow captives, but in the course of their service to the king, they surpassed even the cream of the Babylonian crop. Every time the king sought advice from his courtiers, he found the Judeans' counsel superior to everyone else's. In this superlative statement, the narrator foreshadows the superiority of Israel's God that the rest of the book will substantiate.[62]

Nebuchadnezzar may have sought "to extinguish the very remembrance of God," but that same God is the triumphant one in this opening chapter.[63] Furthermore, that same God will bless the foreign king through the presence of his faithful servants in the Babylonian court. God's people may

---

60. Newsom, *Daniel*, 51.
61. "Stand in the presence of" (עֲמֹד לִפְנֵי) is a common expression for servitude to a king (e.g., Gen 41:46; 1 Sam 16:21; Jer 52:12).
62. Chapters 2 and 4 will especially demonstrate the superiority of Daniel (and his God) to the king's other wise men.
63. John Calvin, *Daniel*, A Geneva Series Commentary, trans. from Latin (1561; repr., Calvin Translation Society, 1852–53; repr., Carlisle, PA: Banner of Truth Trust, 1995), 114.

be trapped in an idolatrous, foreign land, but he was right there with them. And through his divine presence, God blessed his people, and through them, he blessed their captors. The "defeated" God of Israel was alive and well during the captivity of his people, working as he so often does—behind the scenes, through the weak and powerless.

c. Daniel's Continuing Service (1:21)

The chapter ends with a chronological note about the duration of Daniel's service. He served until the first year of Cyrus, the Persian king who defeated the Babylonians in 539 BCE.[64] This statement does not mean that Daniel's service in the foreign court ended in the first year of Cyrus: the account of the lions' den in ch. 6 happens during the reign of Darius, and ch. 10 allows that he may have still been serving during the third year of Cyrus (10:1). Rather, the statement in 1:21 functions as a rhetorical device that places Daniel in the foreign court for the duration of the "enforced exile,"[65] a period of time that ended when Cyrus issued a decree allowing exiles of foreign countries to return to their homelands.[66] To postexilic generations of Jews, the very name "Cyrus" meant the end of exile, a counterpoint to "Nebuchadnezzar," whose name "spell[ed] invasion, siege, defeat, plundering, exile. . . . 'Nebuchadnezzar' brings the day of Yahweh's abandoning his people to darkness and wrath, a historical experience and at the same time a pointer to ultimate darkness and wrath. 'Cyrus suggests deliverance and freedom, restoration and rebuilding, the joy of going home."[67] The end of exile brought about through Cyrus was the working out of God's intentions (Isa 45:1–8; Ezra 1:1–4; 2 Chr 36:22–23).[68]

Daniel 1:21 says that Daniel was there at work in exile, from start to finish, and the subtle message of the entire chapter is that so was God. His hand steered events from Jehoiakim's defeat to Daniel's treatment in exile and the success of the Judean youth in the Babylonian court.

The historical circumstances said otherwise, but Israel's God had not been defeated. Instead, he was the one in control. At three key points in the chapter, the narrator explicitly states that "God gave" something to someone, statements that relativize "military power, political power, and the power of human insight."[69]

Canonical and Theological Significance

The Strength of the Weak God

Throughout the Old Testament, God stuns onlookers with displays of his power. His "strong hand and outstretched arm" (Ps 136:12; Jer 32:21) routs Pharaoh's army

---

64. Babylon's demise is recorded in Dan 5:30–6:1[5:31], where "Darius the Mede" receives the kingdom. Darius is mentioned several times in the book (6:1[5:31]; ch. 6; 9:1; 11:1), but his identity is a difficulty in Daniel. See the discussion in ch. 5, n95.

65. Lucas, *Daniel*, 56. Jeremiah refers to God's judgment against Babylon and subsequent restoration of Israel after seventy years of servitude (Jer 25:12–14; 29:10). For the period of seventy years, see on 9:2.

66. See further on 10:1.
67. Goldingay, *Daniel*, 172.
68. Newsom, *Daniel*, 52.
69. Goldingay, *Daniel*, 171, paraphrasing W. H. Joubert on Dan 1 in *Power and Responsibility in the Book of Daniel* (PhD diss., University of South Africa, 1980).

at the exodus (Exod 7–15); sends clouds of Jericho dust billowing over the land of Canaan (Josh 6:1–27); makes the Canaanites melt in fear (Exod 15:15; Josh 2:9, 24); and incinerates a pile of soaked stones atop Mount Carmel (1 Kgs 18:20–40). In the New Testament, Jesus serves up a feast for thousands from a single sack (Matt 14:13–21; Mark 8:1–10; Luke 9:10–17; John 6:1–15); brings the dead to life (e.g., Mark 5:35–43; Luke 7:11–17; John 11:1–44); heals the lame, blind, crippled, and mute (Matt 15:29–31); and strolls across a dark stormy sea (Matt 14:22–33; Mark 6:45–52). In Acts his apostles will continue this headline-grabbing activity during the earliest days of the church (e.g., Acts 3:1–10; 5:12–16; 9:36–43), and the book of Revelation puts the exclamation point on these accounts with its predicted displays of divine power.

But a strong undercurrent in the biblical story is that God's activity in history is usually far less sensational. He moves like a soft breeze; he speaks in a barely audible voice. He works through the small, the weak, the socially inconsequential, and the marginalized: the widow at Zarephath (1 Kgs 17:8–16); the cowering Gideon (Judg 6:11–7:25); the boy David (1 Sam 17); the Samaritan woman (John 4:39–42); the Galilean fishermen (Acts 2:14–41; 3:1–10; 4:13–22).

Even more astounding in the biblical narrative is that he sometimes works through what appears to be his own weakness. This is the case in Dan 1:1–5, where the ancient Near Eastern headlines surely would have proclaimed that the God of Israel had been defeated by the superior god of Nebuchadnezzar. Centuries earlier, the shell-shocked Israelites watched the despised Philistines carry the ark of YHWH's covenant away to the temple of their god (1 Sam 4:1–5:2). The Philistine god Dagon had bested the God of the Israelites, and his possession of the ark proved it. Or so the Philistines thought until the next morning when they found their god "bowed" down before the ark. The morning after that he had lost his head and hands from "bowing" down again (1 Sam 5:3–4). Lest the humbled Dagon forfeit any more body parts, his worshipers quickly sent the ark of Israel's God back where it belonged.

The events of Dan 1 include no such humor, humbling, or change of fortune. The narrative does, however, deliver a subtle interpretation of the world-shattering events that aligns them with the earlier "defeat." Things were not what they seemed. The defeat of Jehoiakim and the loss of the temple vessels did not represent the defeat of Israel's God. Rather—just as he had been in Philistine territory—God was in control of the circumstances in Jerusalem and in Babylon, directing them according to his own plan and purpose, however inscrutable those may have been to people in the midst of them.

As devastating as the loss of the ark was in premonarchic Israel and the loss of the Davidic king and temple vessels (and eventually the entire land) was in the days of Babylonian exile, they only foreshadowed the story at the climax of the canon. If ever the God of Israel appeared to have lost to the enemy, it was on Good Friday when the Son of God could not, apparently, save himself or convince his Father to do so (Matt 27:40–43, 46).

Yet the Gospels affirm repeatedly that the death of Jesus was no surprise to him or to God (Matt 16:21; 17:22–23; 20:17–19; 26:2; Mark 8:31; Luke 9:22, 44–45; 18:31–3). While Jesus may have pleaded for another way, he knew it would not be. However, he had also predicted his resurrection. His disciples managed to miss this, just as they had missed the thrice-spoken prophecy of his death. But when Friday's shock and Saturday's sorrow gave way to Sunday, they realized their God had not lost after all. What had appeared to be defeat was instead the ultimate victory (Acts 4:27–28).

Luther considered the cross the most complete revelation of God, simultaneously revealing him to be all loving and all mysterious. Historian Mark Noll summarizes Luther's view: "At the cross the creation itself took hold of the Creator; the creation entombed the Creator. At the cross the loftiest heights came down to the deepest depths; at the cross the hands of men pierced the hands that made humankind. There could be no greater mystery."[70] This revelation, Luther contended, should be our undoing: "to realize that the cross was where God had most completely revealed himself was then to realize that any hope for the self would involve a secondary crucifixion of the sinful self."[71] In other words, when we see this "weak" God, we realize his sovereignty and our own insufficiency. It is when we come to the end of ourselves that "God's strength begins, provided faith is present and waits on him."[72]

God's people who lived through the events of Dan 1:1–5 must have wondered why their God had allowed himself to be defeated. Sometimes we may be tempted to wonder the same thing as we skim the endless stream of atrocities in our news feeds. But the cross defies such despair. The cross redefines power and weakness. The cross changes everything, guaranteeing that victory belongs to our God and assuring us that one day we will see him return with power and great glory—never to be considered "weak" again.

Lord of All the Earth

The introduction of God into the Daniel narrative as "the Lord" (אֲדֹנָי; see on 1:2) establishes one of the themes of the book: he is Lord of all the earth, not just the God of conquered King Jehoiakim and the territory of Judah. In a world that considered gods to be rulers of designated territories, Israel's God claimed to be Lord of all lords and King of all kings. The heavens are his throne and the earth is his footstool (Isa 66:1).

---

70. Mark A. Noll, *Turning Points: Decisive Moments in the History of Christianity* (Grand Rapids: Baker Books, 1997), 169.

71. Noll, *Turning Points*, 169.

72. Luther, "The Magnificat," *Luther's Works* 21:340. Cited in Noll, *Turning Points*, 170n12.

In the book of Daniel, Israel's God is frequently called the Most High/Most High God (3:26; 3:32[4:2]; 4:14[17]; 5:18, 21; 7:25), and in ch. 2, he is repeatedly called "the God of heaven" (2:18–19, 37, 44). His wisdom and power supersede those of his "competitors" in Babylon (2:27–29, 47; 3:28–29; 4:15[18]; 5:7–8, 14–17). His dominion and glory alone last forever (3:33[4:3]; 4:31–32[34–35]; 6:27[26]; 7:14, 27). He shares wisdom, power, dominion, and even glory with humans, but he also holds them accountable for what they do with it (2:20–23, 37–38; 4:25–34[28–37]). His unchanging law renders powerless a rigid man-made law and brings life rather than death (6:5–24[4–23]). In the second half of the book, his wisdom, power, dominion, and glory lie beneath the surface of the narrative, much as they do in the book's opening verses. His people will endure unspeakable anguish (7:21–25; 8:24–25; 9:26–27; 11:30–43; 12:1); his city will be overrun (7:25; 8:9–14; 9:24–27; 11:31–35); and he himself will suffer profound loss (8:10–14). But in all this calamity, he remains the Lord, Lord of all the earth. His sovereignty may be subtle in the narrative,[73] but it is nonetheless assured (7:9–14, 26; 12:1–3).

The theme of Israel's God being Lord of all the earth reverberates throughout the biblical canon, from its first verses to its final pages. In Gen 1, God is transcendent over his creation. He has no competitors as he speaks order into cosmic chaos. He faces no struggle against astral deities or writhing monsters of the sea. At his word, the world falls into its place in an ordered universe, and he effortlessly and lavishly stocks it with everything needed for the flourishing of his image-bearers. Sixty-six books and untold millennia later, the theme of his lordship culminates with a great multitude representing every tribe, nation, and language singing "Hallelujah!"; the cosmic enemy being cast into the lake of fire; and the dwelling place of God encompassing the earth (Rev 19:1–10; 20:7–15; 21:1–4).

Between the bookends of these resounding proclamations unfolds the story of God's people on earth—a story in which he calls a childless man and his barren wife to a land he promises to give him and his descendants. He covenants to be the God of Abraham, Isaac, and Jacob, but it is clear in the biblical story that he is not confined to the territory of the promised land. Several generations after he made his covenant with Abraham, he neutralized the power of Egypt's gods, making sure that Pharaoh and all Egypt knew that he was YHWH (Exod 7:5, 17; 8:18[22]; 14:4, 18). During the years of kingship in Israel, he corrected Syrian king Ben-Hadad's assumption that he could defeat YHWH on the plains since Israel's God was a god of the hills (1 Kgs 20:28); Ben-Hadad ended up pleading for his life after his army was decimated on the plains. In the southern kingdom a century and a half later, YHWH

---

73. In the visions of Dan 7–8, passive verbs hint that God is at work: the lion's wings are plucked and the creature is lifted to its feet; the bear is ordered to devour; the leopard is given dominion; three horns are uprooted; the fourth beast will be slain, destroyed, and burned; the host and the daily sacrifice were given over to the little horn. Throughout the visions, "appointed times" are all in God's hands (8:19; 11:27, 29, 35; cf. 7:12).

answered Hezekiah's entreaty that he, God of all the kingdoms of the earth, deliver Jerusalem from Sennacherib and the Assyrians (2 Kgs 19:14–19). In the pages of the New Testament, Paul proclaims that God has seated Jesus at his right hand, "far above all rule and authority, power and dominion, and every name that is invoked, not only in the present age but also in the one to come" (Eph 1:21). That is cosmic lordship.

We live in a world often ruled by tyrants, and we wonder at the power granted them. We long for the day when YHWH fully and finally makes his enemies a footstool for his feet (Ps 110:1; cf. Luke 20:43; Acts 2:35; 7:49; Heb 10:13). Until then, we recognize that this cosmic God works his plan on earth through his chosen vessels—be they followers of his or not (e.g., Nebuchadnezzar [Jer 27:6] and Cyrus [Isa 44:28–45:1]). He did indeed give his vessels and his people into the hand of Nebuchadnezzar, but not without purpose. It was through those vessels—in the temple and in the palace—that the God of Israel would make himself known to the reigning powers of the day. His people were not alone in exile; he was there and he was active. And so too for us—God is present and active, and he makes himself known through us as we daily demonstrate his lordship in a world awash with other gods.

Lord of Individual Circumstances

Daniel 1 makes clear that the Lord, Lord of all the earth, orchestrated the international circumstances that led to the demise of his holy city, Davidic king, and temple (1:1–2). In claiming this, the book resonates with the rest of the canon: no power can thwart the Lord, and no opponent takes him by surprise. He is on the cosmic throne, and the earth is his footstool (Isa 66:1; Matt 5:35). But the book of Daniel likewise asserts that the Lord of all the earth is also Lord of individual people and their particular circumstances. Daniel, Hananiah, Mishael, and Azariah were four victims of events so far beyond their control they could not even delude themselves into thinking otherwise (as humans are prone to do). Kings rose and fell around the Judeans, leaving them powerless in their wake and subject to the surging waves of captivity. With no recourse, no option but submission, they embarked on the journey of diaspora—living in a culture born of values foreign to the ways of their God.

But that same God was Lord of their circumstances in diaspora. His sovereignty is a bedrock truth the narrator brings home three times in Dan 1 through repetition of the simple expression "God gave." The first time, God's "gift" functioned at the level of headline news—he "gave" his king into the hand of King Nebuchadnezzar. In the next two occurrences, God's "gifts" operated at the mundane level of good will and, we might say, good grades: he gave Daniel favor in the eyes of his overlord, and he gave the four Judeans knowledge and skills to excel in their training for Babylonian royal service.

It can be easy to overlook the "little" ways God is at work in our lives or to dismiss his fingerprints as coincidences or natural consequences. Most of us probably acknowledge that he is present and active, but we also tend to give ourselves a lot of credit for the way life goes. When it goes according to our plan, we thank God for his blessing (if we think of it), and when it does not go as we hoped, we ask him to fix it. This is not in itself bad, as long as we recognize that he is weaving *all* of it together according to his good plan. What we consider good, what we consider bad—he is behind all of it. God does not superimpose his blessing on our self-made lives; he builds them from the bottom up. This means that rather than praying, "Bless me, Lord, in all I do today," we would reflect reality better if we prayed, "Lord, help me see your work in my life today and live faithfully in the midst of it."

Because God is Lord over our individual circumstances, we can trust that he knows what he is doing, and we can live with childlike trust in our caring Father. As Paul told the Athenians on Mars Hill, we live and move and have our being in the God who made the world (Acts 17:24–28). He makes our hearts pump and our lungs expand. He sets a table before us. Whether we acknowledge it or not, we depend on him for every breath and every morsel.

Daniel acknowledged such dependence in his resolution not to eat the king's fare, but this kind of dependence has never come easily to humans. Adam and Eve's refusal to trust that what God had provided was good set the rest of us on a course of self-sufficient destruction. We expend anxious energy pursuing what we will eat, what we will drink, and what we will put on, when God has said life is more than food and we cannot live on bread alone (cf. Matt 6:25; Deut 8:2–3; 29:5[6]).

Daniel's test is our test. Can we, *will* we trust that what God provides—whether meager or much—is what we need? We can live with both plenty and in poverty when we understand the source of our life (Phil 4:12). Calvin says it well: "We ought to consider our life sustained neither by bread nor any other food but by the secret blessing of God. . . . This, at least, is certain: whatever food we feed on, we are nourished and sustained by God's gratuitous power."[74] Because the Lord of all the earth is also Lord over our individual circumstances, we can trust that he knows what he is doing, and we can live in the quiet confidence of his good care.

Living in Diaspora and Longing for the Shalom of Home

Set in the earliest days of the Jewish diaspora, the book of Daniel has long been treasured among those living in both literal and nonliteral diaspora—that is, those who are driven from their homes and homelands and those who remain in their homelands but find themselves in cultures with worldviews and values foreign to

---

74. John Calvin, *Commentaries on Daniel*, in RCS:OT 12 (Downers Grove, IL: InterVarsity Press, 2012), 247.

their own. Learning to survive and even thrive in places far from "home" is a challenge we all face to some degree.

As many as seventy-nine million people worldwide have been forcibly displaced, and millions more are considered stateless—that is, they do not have benefits of national citizenship anywhere.[75] The fates of such people vary: some never return home; some return to a home they hardly recognize; some spend the rest of their lives in refugee camps; some gain citizenship in a new country.

Most Jews of the sixth-century-BCE diaspora never returned to the land of Israel. Instead they and their descendants lived scattered among the nations (cf. Ps 44:12[11]; Jer 30:11; Ezek 36:19; Zech 10:9). The longings that characterize this age of diaspora find voice in many of the psalms, and especially in the Psalms of Ascents (Pss 120–34).[76] Cries for peace in a land of liars and warmongers (Ps 120), for justice and the freedom to flourish (Ps 122), for God's mercy in the face of endless contempt (Ps 123), and for relief from great suffering (Ps 129) permeate the collection. Dozens of other psalms reflect a similar desperation. Endangered people cry out to God for refuge, security, protection, and even rescue. When the world shakes and quakes beneath them, people need sure footing. They need a place to hide. Such a place is only found in God (e.g., Pss 11, 28, 31, 34, 61, 141–44), and so in God they trust and for God they wait. The New Testament completes this picture by anchoring this hope in Christ. Displaced, endangered people who are "in Christ" have a sure foundation and a sure hope, no matter how far from home they are.

Many of us will never know this kind of displacement, the literal loss of home and country. We may spend our entire lives in the same country, city, and even house. And yet we too find ourselves in foreign lands, in cultures with values antithetical to those we hold as believers. The degrees of antithesis differ, but the question of how to navigate one's culture and be true to one's faith is relevant to every believer in every culture. What is the relationship between faith and culture?[77] How do God's people live in a relatively friendly culture without assimilating to the point of being indistinguishable? How do God's people live in a place that is hostile to the gospel? How do we salt and light our respective cultures?

For some, Daniel offers the prime example of how to navigate a foreign culture.

---

75. These figures are from the end of 2019. "Figures at a Glance," UNHCR: The UN Refugee Agency (https://www.unhcr.org/en-us/figures-at-a-glance.html).

76. The origin of this collection is uncertain, but the songs may have been used by diaspora Jews longing for God's restoration of Jerusalem.

77. The classic book on this topic is H. Richard Niebuhr's *Christ and Culture* (New York: Harper & Row, 1951). Niebuhr identifies five responses Christians can take with respect to Christ's place in culture: Christ of culture; Christ against culture; Christ the transformer of culture; Christ above culture; and Christ and culture in paradox. Daniel best fits the "Christ the transformer of culture" response. Lucas says this response "recognizes the social dimension of God's redemptive purpose and seeks to work with it by an involvement that does not assimilate to culture, but confronts it with the aim of transforming it. Learning about a culture (e.g. studying the literature and language of the Chaldeans) is not the same thing as assimilating to it, but is the essential basis for a critical involvement in it" (*Daniel*, 58).

But Daniel's approach is only one of several, and it may not be the best way for everyone. Situations differ and each requires wisdom and discernment. In the early postexilic communities of Ezra and Nehemiah, isolationism was the best way the covenant community could survive; it needed to learn and conform itself to God's long-forgotten standards. By contrast, the best answer for Daniel and Esther was to engage their idolatrous cultures so God could transform them. Each approach was appropriate in its context, places where God's people had lost their control—a situation not unlike the church faces in many places today.

Living faithfully in an alien culture requires discernment and wisdom. It requires that we ask repeatedly what it means to be *in* our particular part of the world but not *of* it. It demands that we wrestle with how to love God and neighbor. It calls for us to consider what lines to draw and what lines might need to be redrawn.

Regardless of the answer we reach about how to engage and disengage with our culture, we share the calling to be a blessing wherever we are. The idea that God's people should be a blessing is rooted in the Abrahamic covenant. God promised to bless Abraham, but he also said Abraham would be a blessing to all the families of the earth. Paul makes clear that the salvation of the gentiles was the definitive fulfillment of this promise (Gal 3:7–9), but there have been lesser fulfillments throughout the history of God's people, Jew and gentile: Joseph blessed the Egyptians (Gen 40–42); the Israelite slave girl blessed her Aramean master (2 Kgs 5); Daniel blessed the Babylonian and Medo-Persian rulers; and postbiblical history is filled with names like Francis of Assisi, George Mueller, Amy Carmichael, Mother Teresa, and the ten Boom family—followers of Jesus whose very presence blessed those around them. Paul describes this blessing as a fragrance—the fragrance of Christ, spread wherever we go (2 Cor 2:14). Such a metaphor challenges us to consider what the world "smells" when we are around.

Whether we are forcibly displaced or just entirely out of place in our respective cultures, we all long for ultimate shalom, the day when heaven comes to earth and we live here forever with God in a world where we will all flourish. Shalom Home. Until then, our callings are the same. Live faithfully. Hope in God. Be a blessing wherever in the world we find ourselves. Bear the fragrance of Christ.

MACRO UNIT 2

Daniel 2:1a–7:28d

The Superiority of God and His Kingdom

Main Idea of the Macro Unit

The second macro unit of the book of Daniel consists of the Aramaic portion of the book—chs. 2–7. Arranged in a chiastic structure,[1] these chapters primarily involve events that transpired in the royal courts of Babylon and later Persia and involved the four Judean exiles. Written in the lingua franca of the Jews' exilic world, the Aramaic chapters represent the life of God's people in a foreign land.[2] Taken as a whole, these chapters develop themes that drive the entire book: they illustrate how the sovereign ruler of an everlasting kingdom brings arrogant human rulers low, and they demonstrate how God's people can remain faithful no matter the hostility or suffering they face under idolatrous regimes.

Literary Context of the Macro Unit

There are three macro units in the book of Daniel: ch. 1, chs. 2–7, and chs. 8–12. The first functions as a prologue for the book, and the second develops themes that prepare the way for the third. The second macro unit is a chiasm of six chapters that focus on the dynamic between divine and human kingship and also illustrate how God's followers can live faithfully under foreign rulers. These themes carry into the

---

1. Parallel chapters are 2 and 7, 3 and 6, and 4 and 5.
2. On the significance of the Aramaic chiastic structure in Daniel, see the introduction (pp. 31–35).

apocalyptic visions of chs. 8–12, which are primarily concerned with the intense suffering that God's people face under gentile kings, and especially under Seleucid king Antiochus IV Epiphanes in the second-century BCE. These sufferings surpass their suffering in exile, and their ability to influence their rulers for good—as Daniel and his friends do in the first half of the book—diminishes: the faithful can only endure and look forward to their everlasting reward.

The stories in chs. 2–6 are often classified as court stories, a storytelling genre of the ancient Near East. Such tales/stories recount episodes in which wise and pious captives serve in foreign courts, and they typically follow one of two plotlines: recounting a conflict in the royal court, where the foreign captive faces danger and even death because of his/her character or faith, or telling of a contest in which the captive courtier solves a perplexing problem that royal experts are unable to solve. The foreign captive is then rewarded by the king for exhibiting superior wisdom. The stories in Dan 2–6 fit loosely in the genre of court story, deviating in ways that draw attention away from the captive hero and focus instead on the hero's God, the central character of the book of Daniel. Each court story in Daniel shows Israel's God working through the wit and wisdom of the four captive Judeans to showcase his own superiority over all other gods.[3]

> I. Macro Unit 1: God's Kingdom in Exile: The Conflict Begins (1:1a–21)
> **II. Macro Unit 2: The Superiority of God and His Kingdom (2:1a–7:28d)**
>   A. Narrative 1: God's Superior Knowledge and His Eternal Kingdom (2:1a–49c)
>   B. Narrative 2: God's Superior Power and His Servants' Faithfulness (3:1a–30)
>   C. Narrative 3: A Humbled King and His Restored Power (3:31a–4:34e[4:1a–37e])
>   D. Narrative 4: A Humbled King and His Rescinded Power (5:1a–6:1[5:31])
>   E. Narrative 5: God's Superior Law and His Servant's Faithfulness (6:2a–29[1a–28])
>   F. Narrative 6: God's Superior King and Eternal Kingdom (7:1a–28d)
> III. Macro Unit 3: Encouragement until God's Eternal Kingdom Comes (8:1a–12:13c)

---

3. For more on the use of court stories in the book of Daniel, see the introduction (p. 25).

Daniel 2:1a–49c

A. Narrative 1: *God's Superior Knowledge and His Eternal Kingdom*

Main Idea of Narrative 1 (2:1a–49c)

Nebuchadnezzar, the reigning king of Babylon in Dan 2, learns significant information about the future from a troubling dream, but more importantly, he discovers that true wisdom and power reside not with his experts but with the God of Heaven. This God grants both wisdom and power to humans for times and seasons but retains the right to take both away. His kingdom alone will endure forever.

Literary Context of Narrative 1 (2:1a–49c)

Daniel 2 is the first of six Aramaic chapters in the book. It follows the Hebrew prologue of ch. 1 and begins a series of five consecutive narratives about encounters between the Judean exiles and gentile kings (chs. 2–6). As such, it is typically classified as a court tale and specifically, a court contest.[1] Chapter 1 introduced the four captive men and set the context for their exemplary civil service. Chapter 2 is set in the royal court, and through Daniel's initiative and intervention, it showcases the superiority of Israel's God.

As part of the Aramaic chiasm of chs. 2–7, it stands parallel with the account of Daniel's vision in ch. 7 (four beasts out of the sea), and together they illustrate God's global reign and sole claim to everlasting dominion, power, and glory.

---

1. See further the Literary Context of the Macro Unit (pp. 79–80) and the introduction (p. 25).

> II. Macro Unit 2: The Superiority of God and His Kingdom (2:1a–7:28d)
> → **A. Narrative 1: God's Superior Knowledge and His Eternal Kingdom (2:1a–49c)**
> B. Narrative 2: God's Superior Power and His Servants' Faithfulness (3:1a–30)
> C. Narrative 3: A Humbled King and His Restored Power (3:31a–4:34e[4:1a–37e])
> D. Narrative 4: A Humbled King and His Rescinded Power (5:1a–6:1[5:31])
> E. Narrative 5: God's Superior Law and His Servant's Faithfulness (6:2a–29[1a–28])
> F. Narrative 6: God's Superior King and Eternal Kingdom (7:1a–28d)

1. Nebuchadnezzar's Inferior Knowledge (2:1a–11e)

Main Idea of the Passage

Daniel 2:1–11 demonstrates the inadequacy of Babylonian wisdom and prepares the way for Israel's God to showcase his sole claim to true wisdom and power—both of which he bestows on human rulers.

Literary Context

Daniel 2:1–11 is the opening section of the narrative that comprises ch. 2. As such, it functions in at least two ways in its broader literary context. First, it introduces a twofold conflict of the narrative: King Nebuchadnezzar has had a troubling dream, and his experts are unable to recount or interpret it. Second, by highlighting this inadequacy of the Babylonian experts and their gods, the section prepares the way for Daniel and his God to resolve the king's conflict throughout the rest of the chapter.

> A. Narrative 1: God's Superior Knowledge and His Eternal Kingdom (2:1a–49c)
> → **1. Nebuchadnezzar's Inferior Knowledge (2:1a–11e)**
> 2. Nebuchadnezzar's Reaction to Inferior Knowledge (2:12a–16d)
> 3. Daniel's Prayer for God's Wisdom (2:17a–23e)
> 4. God's Superior Knowledge and the Meaning of the King's Dream (2:24a–45h)
> 5. Nebuchadnezzar's Response to God's Superior Knowledge (2:46a–49c)

Translation and Exegetical Outline

(See pages 84–86.)

Structure and Literary Form

The first narrative of the book's Aramaic chiasm (chs. 2–7) opens with a scene-setting exchange between King Nebuchadnezzar and his advisers, the Chaldeans (2:1–11). Six subsections carry the story forward in this opening exchange: 2:1–3, 4, 5–6, 7, 8–9, and 10–11. In the first of these (2:1–3), the narrator introduces the problem and the king's proposed solution. The opening subsection concludes with a reported speech of the king (2:3), and the remaining five subsections continue the narrator's use of reported speech to relate the encounter between the king and his advisers. These speeches develop the plot, but they also provide windows into the thoughts, interests, and motivations of their speakers.[2]

The text of the book of Daniel shifts from Hebrew to Aramaic in 2:4b and continues in this language for the remainder of the chiastic structure that dominates the book (chs. 2–7). The switch in languages is signaled at the end of 2:4a in the quotative frame for the Chaldeans' first speech, and it begins in 2:4b with their first words.[3]

Explanation of the Text

a. The Background (2:1a–3d)

An opening date formula (2:1a; cf. 1:1a) establishes the historical setting for the account in Dan 2: it happened in the second year of Nebuchadnezzar's reign. This temporal clause is subordinate to the independent clause that immediately follows (2:1b; "Nebuchadnezzar dreamed [חָלַם] dreams"). Two subsequent independent clauses detail the result of the king's dreaming: the *wayyiqtol* of 2:1c (וַתִּתְפָּעֶם) says he was troubled,[4] and the noun phrase that begins the next clause (וּשְׁנָתוֹ, "and his sleep," in the clause וּשְׁנָתוֹ נִהְיְתָה עָלָיו, "and his sleep left him," 2:1d) focuses on the ultimate result of his troubling dreams—he could not sleep.

The narrator uses the plural "dreams" (חֲלֹמוֹת; 2:1b, 2c), but when the king speaks in 2:3, he will use the singular "dream" (חֲלוֹם), as will everyone else after him in the narrative. Perhaps he had a series of dreams, as Pharaoh did in Gen 41, but

---

2. See ch. 1, n41.
3. For the significance of this chiastic structure, see further the introduction (pp. 31–35).
4. The Pharaoh of Joseph's day was also "troubled" (פעם) by dreams (Gen 41:8; cf. Ps 77:5). For the relationship between Gen 41 and Dan 2, see further IN DEPTH: A Theological Paradigm for God's Work among the Nations: The Court Stories of Daniel (Dan 2) and Joseph (Gen 41) in Canonical Context" on pp. 123–37.

Daniel 2:1a–11e

II. The Superiority of God and His Kingdom (2:1a–7:28d)
　A. Narrative 1: God's Superior Knowledge and His Eternal Kingdom (Dan 2:1a–49c)
　　1. Nebuchadnezzar's Inferior Knowledge (2:1a–11c)
　　　a. The Background (2:1a–3d)
　　　　(1) The Timing (2:1a)
　　　　(2) The Problem (2:1b–d)

1a	וּבִשְׁנַת שְׁתַּיִם לְמַלְכוּת נְבֻכַדְנֶצַּר	In the second year of the reign of Nebuchadnezzar,
1b	חָלַם נְבֻכַדְנֶצַּר חֲלֹמוֹת	Nebuchadnezzar dreamed dreams.
1c	וַתִּתְפָּעֶם רוּחוֹ	His spirit was troubled,
1d	וּשְׁנָתוֹ נִהְיְתָה עָלָיו׃	and his sleep left him.
2a	וַיֹּאמֶר הַמֶּלֶךְ	And the king said
2b	לִקְרֹא לַחַרְטֻמִּים וְלָאַשָּׁפִים וְלַמְכַשְּׁפִים וְלַכַּשְׂדִּים	to call the magicians and enchanters and sorcerers and Chaldeans

　　　　(3) The Proposed Solution (2:2e–3d)

2c	לְהַגִּיד לַמֶּלֶךְ חֲלֹמֹתָיו	to tell the king his dreams.
2d	וַיָּבֹאוּ	They came
2e	וַיַּעַמְדוּ לִפְנֵי הַמֶּלֶךְ׃	and they stood before the king.
3a	וַיֹּאמֶר לָהֶם הַמֶּלֶךְ	The king said to them,
3b	חֲלוֹם חָלָמְתִּי	"A dream I have dreamed,
3c	וַתִּפָּעֶם רוּחִי	and troubled is my spirit
3d	לָדַעַת אֶת־הַחֲלוֹם׃	to know the dream."

　　　b. The Chaldeans' First Response (2: 4a–d)

4a	וַיְדַבְּרוּ הַכַּשְׂדִּים לַמֶּלֶךְ אֲרָמִית	The Chaldeans spoke to the king (*Aramaic*),
4b	מַלְכָּא לְעָלְמִין חֱיִי	"O King, live forever!
4c	אֱמַר [חֶלְמָא] (חֶלְמָה) לְעַבְדָיךְ	Tell the dream to your servants,
4d	וּפִשְׁרָא נְחַוֵּא׃	and the interpretation we will declare."

Daniel 2:1a–49c 85

c. The King's First Threat (2:5a–6c)
  (1) The First Condition (2:5a–f)

5a	עָנֵה ↓	↓ Responding,
5b	מַלְכָּא וְאָמַר [לְכַשְׂדָּיֵא] (לְכַשְׂדָּאֵי)	the king said to the Chaldeans,[2]
5c	מִלְּתָה מִנִּי אַזְדָּא	"The word from me is firm:
5d	הֵן לָא תְהוֹדְעוּנַּנִי ↓	If you do not make known to me the dream and its interpretation,
5e	חֶלְמָא וּפִשְׁרֵהּ	
5f	הַדָּמִין תִּתְעַבְדוּן וּבָתֵּיכוֹן נְוָלִי יִתְּשָׂמוּן׃	you will be dismembered, and your houses will be made a rubbish heap.
6a	וְהֵן חֶלְמָא וּפִשְׁרֵהּ תְּהַחֲוֹן	But if the dream and its interpretation you declare,
6b	מַתְּנָן וּנְבִזְבָּה וִיקָר שַׂגִּיא תְּקַבְּלוּן מִן־קֳדָמָי	gifts and reward and great honor you will receive from me.
6c	לָהֵן חֶלְמָא וּפִשְׁרֵהּ הַחֲוֹנִי׃	Therefore, the dream and its interpretation declare to me."

d. The Chaldeans' Second Response (2:7a–c)

7a	עֲנוֹ תִנְיָנוּת וְאָמְרִין	They answered a second time, saying,
7b	מַלְכָּא חֶלְמָא יֵאמַר לְעַבְדוֹהִי	"Let the king tell the dream to his servants,
7c	וּפִשְׁרָה נְהַחֲוֵה׃	and the interpretation we will declare."

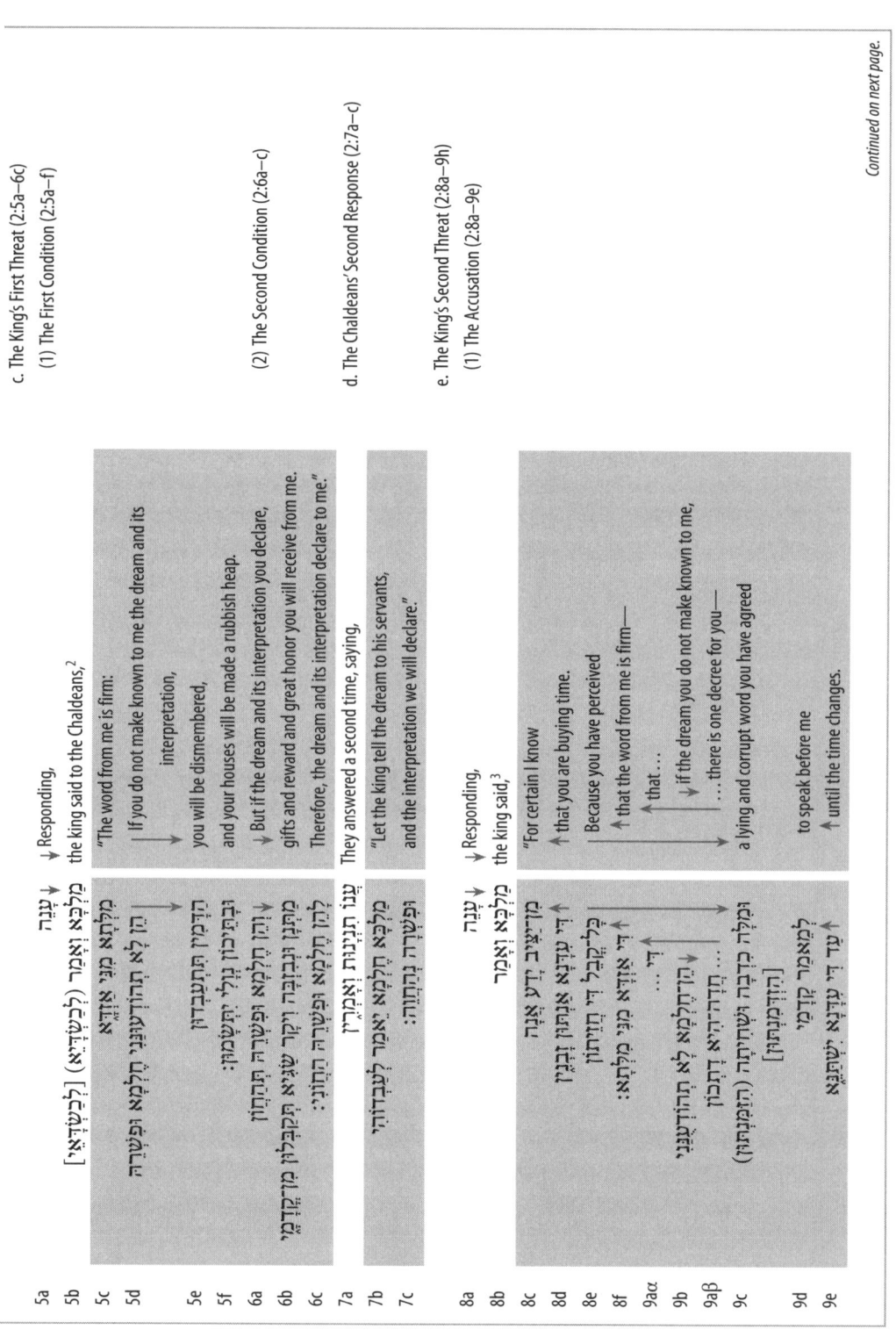

e. The King's Second Threat (2:8a–9h)
  (1) The Accusation (2:8a–9e)

8a	עָנֵה ↓	↓ Responding,
8b	מַלְכָּא וְאָמַר	the king said,[3]
8c	מִן־יַצִּיב יָדַע אֲנָה	"For certain I know
8d	דִּי עִדָּנָא אַנְתּוּן זָבְנִין	that you are buying time.
8e	כָּל־קֳבֵל דִּי חֲזֵיתוֹן	Because you have perceived
8f	דִּי אַזְדָּא מִנִּי מִלְּתָא׃	← that the word from me is firm—
9aα	דִּי ...	that....
9b	הֵן חֶלְמָא לָא תְהוֹדְעֻנַּנִי	↓ if the dream you do not make known to me,
9aβ	... חֲדָה־הִיא דָתְכוֹן	← ...there is one decree for you—
9c	וּמִלָּה כִדְבָה וּשְׁחִיתָה [הִזְמִנְתּוּן] (הִזְדְּמִנְתּוּן)	a lying and corrupt word you have agreed
9d	לְמֵאמַר קֳדָמַי	to speak before me
9e	עַד דִּי עִדָּנָא יִשְׁתַּנֵּא	← until the time changes.

Continued on next page.

---

1. אֲרָמִית, "Aramaic," in the MT is likely a scribal note that signals the shift from Hebrew (1:1–2:4a) to Aramaic. The Aramaic continues through 7:28, and Hebrew resumes in 8:1.
2. For explanation of the translation of v. 5a–b, see on 2:5 in commentary.
3. See on 2:5 in commentary.

Continued from previous page.

9f	לִ֗י תֵאמְר֣וּן חֶלְמָ֔א	Therefore, the dream say to me,
9g	וְאִנְדַּ֕ע	and I will know
9h	↑ דִּ֥י פִשְׁרֵ֖הּ תְּהַחֲוֻנַּֽנִי׃	↑ that its interpretation you will declare."

(2) The Demand (2:9f–h)

f. The Chaldeans' Third Response (2:10a–11e)

(1) The First Protest (2:10a–e)

10a	עֲנ֨וֹ כַשְׂדָּאֵ֤י קֳדָם־מַלְכָּא֙ [אָמְרִ֔ין] וְאָמְרִ֔ין	The Chaldeans answered the king, saying,
10b	לָֽא־אִיתַ֤י אֲנָשׁ֙ עַל־יַבֶּשְׁתָּ֔א	"There is not a man on earth
10c	↑ דִּ֚י מִלַּ֣ת מַלְכָּ֔א יוּכַ֖ל לְהַחֲוָיָ֑ה	↑ who ... is able ↑ to declare the matter of the king,
10d	כָּל־קֳבֵ֗ל דִּ֚י כָּל־מֶ֙לֶךְ֙ רַ֣ב וְשַׁלִּ֔יט	hence no king—great and powerful—has asked a matter
10e	מִלָּ֤ה כִדְנָה֙ לָ֣א שְׁאֵ֔ל לְכָל־חַרְטֹּ֖ם וְאָשַׁ֥ף וְכַשְׂדָּֽי׃	like this of any magician or sorcerer or Chaldean.

(2) The Second Protest (2:11a–e)

11aα	וּמִלְּתָ֛א ...	The matter ...
11b	דִֽי־מַלְכָּ֥ה שָׁאֵ֖ל	↑ that the king asks,
11aβ	יַקִּירָ֑ה	... is difficult,
11c	וְאָחֳרָן֙ לָ֣א אִיתַ֔י	and there is no other
11d	↑ דִּ֥י יְחַוִּנַּ֖הּ קֳדָ֣ם מַלְכָּ֑א לָהֵ֣ן אֱלָהִ֔ין	↑ who can declare it to the king except the gods,
11e	↑ דִּ֚י מְדָ֣רְה֔וֹן עִם־בִּשְׂרָ֖א לָ֥א אִיתֽוֹהִי׃	↑ whose dwelling place is not with flesh."

only one remained in his mind enough to trouble him. Or perhaps he was in something of a trance.[5] Pace suggests two effects of the narrator's use of the plural: first, it may indicate the significance of the dream and its "debilitating effects" on the king; second, it may link the chapter's events to other dream texts—namely, Nebuchadnezzar's tree dream in Dan 4 and Pharaoh's dream about corn and cows in Gen 41.[6]

The setting of the troubling dream early in Nebuchadnezzar's reign invites the idea that the dream troubled the young king because it somehow threatened the security of his reign.[7] It also raises a chronological difficulty between chs. 1 and 2, a difficulty commentators have discussed since ancient times.[8] In ch. 1, Nebuchadnezzar brings Judeans to Babylon for three years of training, and in ch. 2, one of those captives (Daniel) is among the royal advisers in the king's *second* year—before Daniel could have completed his years of training (cf. 2:12–13). If Daniel interpreted the dream of ch. 2 and was promoted to a supervisorial position (2:48), he would surely have been finished with his training since the king would hardly have made a trainee a supervisor. Scholars dating back to at least the Reformation have offered solutions to this problem:[9]

Year of Daniel's Training	Year of Nebuchadnezzar's Reign
First year	Accession year (taking captives)
Second year	First year
Third year	Second year (the dream)

---

5. James A. Montgomery, *A Critical and Exegetical Commentary on the Book of Daniel*, ICC (New York: Scribner's Sons, 1927), 142.

6. Sharon Pace, *Daniel*, SHBC 17 (Macon, GA: Smyth & Helwys, 2008), 50. Seow agrees that the use of plural "dreams," in spite of the fact that the king clearly had only one dream, intends to echo the two dreams that Pharaoh had in Gen 41 (C. L. Seow, "From Mountain to Mountain: The Reign of God in Daniel 2," in *A God So Near: Essays on Old Testament Theology in Honor of Patrick D. Miller*, ed. Brent A. Strawn and Nancy Bowen [Winona Lake, IN: Eisenbrauns, 2003], 358). There are, as most scholars note, many similarities between Dan 2 and Gen 41, suggesting that the author of Daniel did intend to compare and contrast the two captive Hebrew men. See further IN DEPTH: A Theological Paradigm for God's Work among the Nations: The Court Stories of Daniel (Dan 2) and Joseph (Gen 41) in Canonical Context, pp. 123–37.

7. Newsom, *Daniel*, 66–67.

8. See Newsom (*Daniel*, 66) and Collins (*Daniel*, 154–55) for a summary of explanations commentators have offered since antiquity.

9. Calvin, for example (*Daniel*, 115). Many commentators include variations of the chart here, but the one here is based on Edward J. Young, *The Prophecy of Daniel: A Commentary* (Grand Rapids: Eerdmans, 1949), 56; his work was based on S. R. Driver, *The Book of Daniel* (Cambridge: Cambridge University Press, 1900), 17. Critical scholars tend to reject this attempt to harmonize (e.g., Collins, *Daniel*, 154–55). For discussion of accession years and systems of dating, see on Dan 1:1.

Seow considers the chronological marker another link to the Gen 41 account of Joseph and Pharaoh: "Poignantly, too, the setting of the story in the second year of Nebuchadnezzar's reign (v. 1), that is, the second year of Daniel's exile, echoes the fact that Joseph was called upon to interpret the Pharaoh's dreams after only two years of captivity in a foreign country (Gen 41:1)" ("From Mountain to Mountain," 358). Thus he considers explanations that address the discrepancy of dating between Dan 1 and 2 (e.g., different calendars, origin of the stories, etc.) unconvincing and unnecessary. The larger point is that Daniel succeeded not on account of his Chaldean education, which was incomplete when he bested the Babylonian sages. Rather his success "calls attention to the triumph of divine wisdom and foreknowledge conveyed through a lowly exile, a faithful servant of God" (359). Like Joseph before him, during the second year of his exile, he "would enlighten his mighty captor and save others from death" ("From Mountain to Mountain," 358–59).

Fewell offers another suggestion about the dating of ch. 2 relative to ch. 1. First, she says the narrator intends it to be read as a flashback; that is, this dream occurs in the middle of Daniel's three-year training. She says this explains why the king does not appear to know him (2:25–26). It also increases the monstrosity of the king's order to destroy the Babylonian royal advisers: "Not only is he willing to kill all the fully fledged sages for the failure of a few to accomplish the impossible, but his order extends even to those who are merely preparing to become his future advisers" (Danna Nolan Fewell, *Circle of Sovereignty: Plotting Politics in the Book of Daniel* [Nashville: Abingdon,

Assuming the conclusion of the chart above (i.e., the captives' third year of training was Nebuchadnezzar's second year) and the literary contexts of chs. 1 and 2, it is possible that the Judeans had concluded their three years of training and passed their examination before the king with flying colors (1:18–20), but still were not among the wise men summoned in ch. 2 for any number of historical reasons the text does not tell us (e.g., Did they have to acquire a certain amount of on-the-job experience to be among this elite group?). We know the king found them superior to "all the magicians and the conjurers who were in all his kingdom" (1:20), but hyperbole is certainly at work in that assessment. Part of the point of the ch. 1 narrative is that the exilic foursome thrived and excelled in the foreign court because God's hand was behind their circumstances. At the end of their training, they are in the king's service (1:19), but they apparently are not among the go-to group summoned by Nebuchadnezzar in ch. 2.[10] After his troubling dream a short time after the captives entered his service, the king summoned his regular advisers, who could not meet his demands. Daniel then stepped forward, succeeded, and was promoted over his Babylonian colleagues. He also requested that the king give his three friends high governmental positions.

That Nebuchadnezzar was troubled by his dream reflects the theology of ancient Mesopotamia (and many parts of the world today) that dreams could be messages from the gods. The gods used dreams and other natural phenomena to "write" their plans for the world.[11] Understanding these divine plans required correctly reading the signs or, in this case, interpreting the dream. However, most signs were written in a language known only to experts, who used divination to decipher what the gods had said.[12]

1991], 26–27). Fewell then argues that Daniel's promotion at the conclusion of the chapter creates narrative tension, since we might have expected Daniel to return and finish his training, but instead he and his friends are immediately made part of the court and given high positions. Chapters 1 and 2 thus "stand in tension with one another and raise the question of the narrator's reliability. Does Daniel become successful because his special wisdom and ability are of constant, but general assistance to Nebuchadnezzar, as the narrator tells us in chapter 1? Or does Daniel become successful because, on this particular occasion, he so impresses the king with his ability and diplomacy that the king mistakes him for divine and his partial truth [Fewell describes Daniel's interpretation as "the version of diplomacy," p. 35] for the whole truth?" (*Circle of Sovereignty*, 37).

10. We know the king suspects that this group of wise men may lie to him (2:9), but whether they had done so in the past we cannot be sure. His suspicion (and perhaps their guilt) may mean his unprecedented demand of them in ch. 2 was an excuse to do away with them. Since they had no recourse to pass his test, the king could carry out his threat, be rid of them, and summon a new group of advisers to deal with the pressing issue of his dream. If indeed this was his plan, he made it impossible to carry out when he ordered the execution of *all* Babylon's wise men (2:12).

11. Many Westerners shy away from such belief, but in African belief systems of today, many believe "serious dreams are a means of communication between this world and the spirit world of the ancestors, divinities, and the High God" ("Dreams," in *Africa Bible Commentary: A One-Volume Commentary Written by 70 African Scholars*, ed. Tokunboh Adeyemo [Grand Rapids: Zondervan, 2006], 993). This perspective extends to African Christian theology, in which dreams may be regarded as authentic communication from God.

12. The ancients believed that divine messages, the methods for interpreting them, and the interpretations themselves all came from the gods. Two ancient Near Eastern texts make this clear. First, in *History of Babylonia*, third-century-BCE priest Berossus recounts the history of mankind based on Sumerian and Akkadian myths. He tells how merman-like monster Oannes (also known as Adapa or "Wise One") came ashore in prehistoric Babylonia, followed by six similar creatures—the *apkallu*. The god of intelligence, Ea (also known as Enki), had created these seven demigods as his envoys of knowledge to primitive humans. Oannes gave mortals the gift of knowledge in writing, science, architecture, law, mathematics, and agriculture—knowledge that had belonged exclusively to the gods. But Ea kept some knowledge back from humans, including knowledge of the future and the revelation of certain secrets. Such knowledge was only accessible through divination techniques. In an Akkadian text about antediluvian king Enmeduranki, the gods Shamash and Adad taught the king the crafts of oil and liver divination and how to hold a cedar

In Dan 2:2, the troubled Babylonian king did what every ancient king would have done: he called his royal advisers (the *wayyiqtol* of 2:2a [וַיֹּאמֶר] and its infinitive complement in 2:2b [לִקְרֹא]), whose task is stated by the infinitive of 2:2c—telling the king his dreams (לְהַגִּיד). The text identifies these experts as magicians, enchanters, sorcerers, and "Chaldeans."[13] The combined skill sets of this group included dream interpretation, occultic arts, and reading animal livers and entrails. Each title technically represents a different expertise,[14] but the point of the list is not to detail the array of skills and assess the potential of each expert to interpret the king's dream. Rather, the narrative effect of the list is that the king had Babylon's best at his disposal. Whatever the king's problem, someone should have had the solution. And yet, as the story unfolds, none of the advisers will be able to help, a situation that sets up the entrance of Daniel and the God of Israel. Babylon's best and brightest had failed, their gods unable to help them.

The next two clauses report that the advisers came (וַיָּבֹאוּ, 2:2d) and stood (וַיַּעַמְדוּ, 2:2e) in the king's presence (cf. 1:5, 19). The remainder of this first section of the narrative unfolds through dialogue between the king and his advisers. Like everything else in biblical narrative, dialogue (reported speech) is shaped by the narrator to emphasize certain elements and influence the reader's interpretation of both the speaker and the events. In this case, the account is "characterized by mutual misinterpretation" that produces potential disaster.[15]

The narrator moves the dream to center stage by positioning the word חֲלוֹם at the beginning of the initial clause of the king's report to his advisers (2:3b): "A dream I have dreamed." In this first exchange, the king does not explicitly tell his advisers what he wants—that is, he wants them to tell him the dream and its interpretation (2:5–6). Instead, he merely says he is troubled to know the dream. On one hand, the king's "request" appears straightforward, and his advisers think they understand exactly what he wants. On the other hand, his words are ambiguous enough to set up the miscommunication that follows.

b. The Chaldeans' First Response (2:4a–d)

The advisers, collectively called "Chaldeans" throughout the dialogue (cf. 2:5b, 10a), respond to the king as expected—both in terms of how they address him and what they ask. First, they follow the protocol for how subordinates address the king:

---

rod for divination purposes. Then Enmeduranki passed this knowledge to wise men of key Mesopotamian cities. Dreams, techniques for divination, and the interpretations they rendered were all believed to be divinely sourced. (Berossus's *History of Babylonia* is only available in fragmentary references from other Greek writers. Excerpts are available in I. P. Cory, *The Ancient Fragments* [London: Pickering, 1828; HTML ed. by Christopher M. Weimer, December 2002] and accessible online [e.g., www. https://www.sacred-texts.com/cla/af/af02.htm]. See also Jean Bottéro, *Mesopotamia: Writing, Reasoning, and the Gods*, trans. Zainab Bahrani and Marc Van De Mieroop [Chicago: University of Chicago Press, 1992], 246–49.)

13. "Chaldeans" is a technical term here, not a reference to the people from Chaldea (an area just south of Babylon), a special class of priest-scholars, who were experts in astrology.

14. Magicians' expertise was the occultic arts, including astrology, sorcery, and exorcism. They were also skilled in hydromancy (mixing liquids in a divining cup and interpreting the message therein), haruspicy (reading animal entrails), hepatoscopy (reading animal livers), augury (tracking the behavior of sacred animals and interpreting its meaning), and oneiromancy (dream interpretation). Enchanters appear to have been priests who communicated with the spirit world (including the dead) via magic spells and incantations. Sorcerers' specialty was witchcraft: using charms, incantations, and spells to manipulate supernatural powers for good or evil. For further description, see C. Van Dam, "Divination, Magic," *DOTPr*: 159–62.

15. Newsom, *Daniel*, 68.

"O King, live forever" (2:4b; cf. 3:9; 5:10; 6:6[5]; 21[20]).[16] Then they ask the king to tell them the dream so they can declare its meaning (2:4c–d). They use the imperative אֲמַר, but since the context does not suggest any impropriety on their part, we assume their imperative is a request and not a command.

In other biblical accounts of troubling dreams, the dreamers specify that they want to know the interpretation (cf. Dan 4; Gen 40–41), and although Nebuchadnezzar did not make this explicit initially (2:3), his advisers knew what was expected of them—or until this day, they thought they did. The king would report his dream to them, and they would use their expertise to divine its significance. This recounting of the dream was as much for the benefit of the king as for his interpreters, since the act of speaking a dream dispelled any evil effects it may have had on the dreamer.[17]

The Chaldeans' response marks the beginning of the Aramaic portion of Daniel, and the transition is signaled by the clause-final word אֲרָמִית, commonly translated "in Aramaic" (2:4a; e.g., ESV, NASB, NRSV, NJPS). While the advisers probably did respond to the king in Aramaic, the lingua franca of their day, the notation is most likely an editorial marker that scribes used to indicate the shift in language that will continue until Hebrew resumes in 8:1.[18]

This first response by the Chaldeans introduces an important theme in the chapter: "declaring" (חוה) the dream/interpretation (2:4d, 6a–c, 7c, 9h, 10d, 11d, 16d, 24h, 27cβ; cf. 2:5d, 7b, 9a–f, 25d, 26e). The frequent placement of the verb חוה in clause-final position (2:6a, 6c, 7c, 9h, 10d), especially in the dialogue between the king and the royal advisers, highlights its significance. The driving question of the chapter is "Where is true knowledge found?" Who can provide the king with knowledge of the dream? Who can declare to him what he wants to know? The first part of the answer clearly demonstrated in 2:1–11 is "Not the Babylonian experts."

c. The King's First Threat (2:5a–6c)

The king's response to his advisers' request is introduced by a multiverb frame (also called a "redundant quotative frame")—that is, it uses more than one speaking verb to set up the direct speech: עֲנֵה מַלְכָּא וְאָמַר (2:5a–b). English translations deal with this frame in different ways. Many choose to use only one English verb to represent the two Hebrew forms (e.g., "replied to" in NASB and NIV; "answered" in NRSV), while others retain two separate verbs in translation (e.g., "answered and said" in ESV and KJV).

In many languages, the discourse effect of such a frame is that it creates a pause in the narrative just before something important or surprising.[19] This is the case in Biblical Hebrew, where the multiverb frame employing both ענה and אמר (ענה + אמר) "seems to signal the most salient or important

---

16. Seow notes that "the emptiness of their courtesy will become all too obvious" in the unfolding narrative: "Nebuchadnezzar's kingship can hardly be an eternal one! He has no control over time, much less eternity" ("From Mountain to Mountain," 361).

17. A. Leo Oppenheim, "The Interpretation of Dreams in the Ancient Near East," *TAPA* 46, n.s. (Philadelphia: American Philosophical Society, 1956), 219. See also Collins, *Daniel*, 156.

18. For a discussion on why the book of Daniel has Aramaic at all, see the introduction, pp. 31–35.

19. Runge and Westbury, *LDHB*, 1.5 Redundant Quotative Frames. See also Steven E. Runge, *Discourse Grammar of the Greek New Testament: A Practical Introduction for Teaching and Exegesis* (Peabody, MA: Hendrickson), 145–52; and see Josh Westbury, "Quotative Frames and the Power of Redundancy" (https://academic.logos.com/quotative-frames-and-the-power-of-redundancy/) for numerous Old Testament examples of the effect of redundancy on discourse.

response in the conversation."²⁰ Additionally, if the frame occurs twice in a single conversation, it introduces the speaker's refusal to a request.²¹

However, the situation seems to be different in Biblical Aramaic. Whereas in Hebrew the single-verb frame is most common and the multiverb frame signals something particularly significant in the discourse, in the Aramaic portion of Daniel the speech frames are predominately multiverb frames. The most frequent combination is the one that is here in 2:5, ענה + אמר, and it occurs in nearly every instance of direct speech. This makes it implausible that its presence alone signals "the most salient or important response in the conversation."²²

However, the Aramaic ענה + אמר frames are not all the same. Rather, they occur in three formats in Daniel: with two participles (as in 2:5); with two perfect verbs; and with a perfect ענה and a participle אמר.²³ So, although the mere presence of a multiverb frame does not appear to be noteworthy (as in BH), the choice of one format over another may be. In his analysis of Aramaic speech frames in Daniel, Cook concludes that the most common format (i.e., two participles) has been conventionalized in Daniel,²⁴ while shifts away from this dominant frame appear to be significant in the discourse. He specifically addresses the five instances of the perfect ענה with the participle אמר (Dan 2:7, 10; 3:9, 16; 6:14[13]):

[I]n each of the five cases, the use of this framing correlates with a salient and dispreferred response. In 2:7 and 10, the king's counselors push back on the king's demands. . . . Daniel 3:9 and 6:14 introduce the charges against the three friends and Daniel, respectively, being both a dispreferred response in the king's eyes and salient inasmuch as the charges drive the whole storyline in each case. Finally, in 3:16 the perfect-participle frame introduces the friends' climactic speech of resistance to the king's demand, again being both dispreferred and highly salient.²⁵

---

20. Cynthia L. Miller, *The Representation of Speech in Biblical Hebrew Narrative: A Linguistic Analysis*, HSM 55 (Winona Lake, IN: Eisenbrauns, 2003), 321. See her full discussion on pp. 320–22. Miller's example is contained in the exchange between Abraham's servant and Laban and Bethuel when the servant wants to take their sister/daughter Rebecca to be Isaac's wife. The redundant quotative frame ענה + אמר is in Gen 24:50: ויען לבן ובתואל ויאמרו מיהוה יצא הדבר.

21. Miller, *The Representation of Speech in Biblical Hebrew Narrative*, 322. Miller's example is in Gen 27:34–40, where Isaac twice responds to Esau's distraught requests for a blessing in the wake of Jacob's deception. Both of Isaac's responses (Gen 27:37, 39) are introduced by ענה + אמר, and both are answers Esau does not want to receive.

22. To this point in the narrative of Daniel, the *wayyiqtol* has controlled the flow of the narrative and our understanding of the book's discourse. However, Aramaic does not employ the *wayyiqtol* or any similar form in its narrative, a fact that increases the significance of other discourse features of the text.

23. The occurrences of the ענה + אמר frame in the Aramaic of Daniel are as follows: two participles (2:5, 8, 15, 20, 26–27, 47; 3:14, 19, 24–26, 28; 4:16[19], 27[30]; 5:7, 13, 17; 6:13[12], 17[16], 21[20]; 7:2); two perfect verbs (5:10); a perfect ענה and a participle אמר (2:7, 10; 3:9, 16; 6:14[13]).

24. He further argues that the two-participle format of the frame (as here in 2:5) represents two distinct clauses, where the first participle (ענה) is a "scene-setting" word in initial position. The noun/subject between the verbs (מַלְכָּא) is the syntactic subject of the second verb (ואמר), and the *waw* is a phrase-boundary marker (as in Dan 2:12 and Gen 22:4). Thus, I have translated 2:5 and all other instances of the two-participle format as two clauses, with the first as a "scene-setting" adjunct to the main clause: "Responding, the king said . . ." See further John A. Cook, *Aramaic Ezra and Daniel: A Handbook on the Hebrew Text*, BHHB (Waco, TX: Baylor University Press, 2019), 10–12.

25. Cook, *Aramaic Ezra and Daniel*, 11. See full discussion on pp. 10–12. Cook makes no suggestion about the significance of the frame with two perfect verbs in Dan 5:10 (the only place this frame occurs); given the paucity of data, it is hard to know what to say of it. See further the commentary on these five occurrences. (See also Westbury, "Quotative Frames and the Power of Redundancy.")

In 2:5, the king refuses to do what his advisers have just requested, and he does so with an iron fist. First, he alerts them to the certainty of what he is about to say (2:5c), and then he offers two conditional statements. In the "if" clause of each condition, the king lays out the expected action (תְּהוֹדְעוּנַּנִי, "make known to me," 2:5d; תְּהַחֲוֹן, "declare," 2:6a) with its objects (חֶלְמָא וּפִשְׁרֵהּ, "the dream and its interpretation," 2:5d, 6a). If they do not do what he asks, one thing will result (2:5e–f); if they do, another thing will result (2:6b). The results are extremes—the negative involves dismemberment and destruction (2:5e–f; cf. Ezra 6:11), and the positive offers heaps of rewards (2:6b). Such a combination of threat and promise is widely known in the ancient Near East (even in the blessings and curses of Israel's own covenant).[26]

While the pattern of threat and promise is well attested, this speech from Nebuchadnezzar is a heavy-handed overreaction. When he told his advisers that he had had a troubling dream, they responded as would have been expected: Tell us the dream and we will interpret it. This was part of their training, and this was, in part, why the king employed them. But nothing could have prepared them for the king's reaction. Interpreting dreams was what they did; reporting dreams was not. The advisers will later rightly protest that this demand was simply not in their realm of expertise or experience.[27]

In the absence of backstory, we cannot be sure why the king is demanding this.[28] In 2:9, he offers an explanation (see below), but it is insufficient to account for his impossible demand. For the moment, the narrator leaves us with the feeling that Nebuchadnezzar is out of his head, a feeling that the rest of 2:1–12 and ch. 3 will validate. This is a king of extremes, a maniacal monarch who severely overreacts to situations that seem like business-as-usual in the Babylonian government.

d. The Chaldeans' Second Response (2:7a–c)

The Chaldeans' second response to the king is also introduced by a multiverb frame consisting of אמר + ענה, but unlike the previous example (see 2:5 above), this frame is one of five exceptions to the typical format in Daniel and so is likely to have discourse significance—specifically, it signals the dispreferred response: the king would like them to tell him the dream, and they would like to make the king happy and so avoid dismemberment. They can do neither. The speech frame also includes the word תִּנְיָנוּת, "a second time." The significance of this word is not that they are responding for the second time, but that their second response is the same as the first (cf. 2:4c–d).

Their near verbatim response does have one subtle difference. The Chaldeans switch from using the second-person ("Tell the dream to your servants," 2:4c) to employing the third person ("Let the king tell the dream to his servants," 2:7b), signaling another level of politeness. The king's volatility put his advisers on pins and needles. They hope to diffuse the situation before matters get worse.

---

26. A similar pattern of promise and threat is found in Darius I's Behistun inscription, "which invokes the friendship of Ahura Mazda and plentiful family for those who honor the inscription and the reverse for those who do not" (Collins, *Daniel*, 157). This inscription on a cliff in western Iran, commissioned by Darius the Great between 522 and 486 BCE, is a lengthy trilingual inscription with a large relief of a conquering King Darius.

27. Had the king been more accommodating, the diviners could have requested time to seek an oracle from the gods, in which the relevant deity would hopefully reveal the dream.

28. The text is unclear about Nebuchadnezzar's motives and whether he remembered the contents of the dream. See further Goldingay, *Daniel*, 197–98; and Longman, *Daniel*, 77–78.

e. The King's Second Threat (2:8a–9h)

But their caution seems to have the opposite effect. In the king's third speech (cf. 2:3 and 5–6), he again refuses to do what his advisers request, but this time we learn the reason for his demand: he suspects his wise men have lied to him in the past, and he wants to be sure he gets the truth for this troubling dream. He will know they are telling the true interpretation if they can also tell him his dream.

The king's desire for confirmation of the dream's interpretation is not unusual in itself. Dreams were considered the least scientific means of divination because they were internal to the dreamer—that is, they could not be observed by an objective witness as, for example, animal livers and entrails could.[29] Even the ancients knew that sometimes people have wacky dreams that mean little except, perhaps, you should have skipped the spicy midnight snack. Because of such subjectivity, dreams were considered less reliable sources of divine knowledge, and dreamers often sought confirmation of an interpretation from a more trusted method of divination.[30] Nebuchadnezzar was troubled enough by his dream to summon his government officials, so he likely believed it carried state significance[31]—all the more reason to make sure he could trust the interpretation. But the method of confirmation he demanded was unprecedented.

f. The Chaldeans' Third Response (2:10a–11e)

The narrator frames the Chaldeans' desperate third response with the same speech frame as their second response—the atypical speech frame in Daniel that likely signals another dispreferred response.[32] This time the group protests that no one except the gods could do what the king asked. Daniel will later affirm that they are correct (2:27). However, then they tell the king that the gods' "dwelling place is not with flesh" (2:11e). This is a strange aside by the wise men, because ancient people built temples *so that* their gods would dwell with them. We need go no further than the Bible to see this illustrated. When YHWH covenanted with Israel to be their God and they his people, he also said he would dwell among them (e.g., Exod 29:45–46; Deut 16:11; 1 Kgs 6:13). They constructed the tabernacle and later the temple for exactly this purpose. Perhaps Nebuchadnezzar's panicked advisers meant their gods were not present to help with the king's request, or perhaps they were not thinking or speaking clearly.[33] Whatever the case, their protest prepares the way for Daniel, who came to be known as one in whom the "spirit of the holy gods" dwelled (Dan 4:5[8], 6[9], 15[18]; 5:11, cf. 5:14).[34]

In this opening exchange between the king and the Chaldeans, the narrator sets up the conflict that

---

29. Most revelatory dreams that kings received had clear information about a future event. Such a dream (commonly called a "message dream") occurs in the Bible in 1 Kgs 3:5–15, where Solomon has a dream/vision in which God asks him what he wants. Solomon requests wisdom, and God grants him riches, honor, and potentially a long life. Symbolic dreams, however, were more likely to need an interpreter (although the meanings of symbolic dreams could also be obvious; e.g., Joseph's dreams of bowing sheaves and stars in Gen 37).

30. For more on dreams in the ancient Near East, see Oppenheim, "The Interpretation of Dreams in the Ancient Near East." See also Jean Bottéro, *Religion in Ancient Mesopotamia*, trans. Teresa Lavender Fagan (Chicago: University of Chicago Press, 2001): 176–86.

31. Goldingay, *Daniel*, 196.

32. The atypical speech frame is ענה (perfect) + אמר (participle) and occurs five times in Daniel. See on 2:5 above.

33. Critical scholar Collins suggests that their failure "to turn to the gods for help, either by prayer or by ritual" is "contrived to sharpen the contrast with Daniel" (*Daniel*, 157).

34. Pharaoh also said this of Joseph (Gen 41:38).

drives the storyline of the chapter. First, an internal conflict rages in the Babylonian king because of a troubling dream. This leads to a conflict between him and his experts when they prove unequal to the task he lays before them: declare his dream and its interpretation. Their inability underlies the driving question of the chapter: where are true knowledge and wisdom found?

2. Nebuchadnezzar's Reaction to Inferior Knowledge (2:12a–16d)

Main Idea of the Passage

Daniel and his friends find themselves in mortal danger on account of the king's decree to destroy all the wise men of Babylon after his royal advisers were unable to recount his troubling dream.

Literary Context

The first section of ch. 2 laid out the primary problem in the narrative: the king wanted someone to tell him the contents and meaning of his troubling dream, but his own experts were unable to meet his demands (2:1–11). The inability of Babylonian wisdom prepares the way for Daniel later in the chapter to succeed where the wise men failed (2:24–45). This second section of the narrative falls between the identification of the chapter's driving problem and the description of its eventual solution, and it functions in at least three ways in its broader literary context. First, it brings Daniel and his friends into the story by introducing a more pressing problem that befalls the Judean exiles (i.e., they will be killed with the rest of Babylon's wise men). Second, it again demonstrates Daniel's shrewd discernment (cf. 1:11–13). Third, it sets the context for Daniel's prayer and praise in the third section (2:17–23), a section that expounds the theme of the chapter and even the book.

> A. Narrative 1: God's Superior Knowledge and His Eternal Kingdom (2:1a–49c)
>   1. Nebuchadnezzar's Inferior Knowledge (2:1a–11e)
>   2. **Nebuchadnezzar's Reaction to Inferior Knowledge (2:12a–16d)**
>   3. Daniel's Prayer for God's Wisdom (2:17a–23e)
>   4. God's Superior Knowledge and the Meaning of the King's Dream (2:24a–45h)
>   5. Nebuchadnezzar's Response to God's Superior Knowledge (2:46a–49c)

Translation and Exegetical Outline

(See page 96.)

Structure and Literary Form

The second section of the narrative that comprises ch. 2 continues with the fallout of the earlier exchange between King Nebuchadnezzar and his advisers, the Chaldeans (2:1–11). In this section (2:12a–16d), the king responds to the inability of his advisers to do what he demands—namely, tell him the contents of his dream as well as its meaning. Three subsections develop the story line in this section: 2:12a–13d, 14a–15c, and 15d–16d. In the first, the king reacts with rage and issues a decree to destroy all of Babylon's wise men, including Daniel and his friends; the narrator sets this command in indirect speech (2:12). The second subsection relates the exchange between Daniel and Arioch, as the Judean exile demonstrates his shrewd discretion; the narrator sets Daniel's inquiry in direct speech (2:15a–c). In the final subsection, the narrator reports that Daniel petitions the king for time to declare the interpretation (2:16).

Daniel 2:12a–16d

12a	כׇּל־קֳבֵל דְּנָה מַלְכָּא בְּנַס וּקְצַף שַׂגִּיא וַאֲמַר	Because of this, the king, in great agitation and anger, said[1]	2. Nebuchadnezzar's Reaction to Inferior Knowledge (2:12a–16d)
12b	לְהוֹבָדָה לְכֹל חַכִּימֵי בָבֶל׃	↑ to destroy all the wise men of Babylon.	a. The King's Order (2:12a–13d)
13a	וְדָתָא נֶפְקַת	The decree went out,	(1) The King's Rage and Command (2:12a–b)
13b	וְחַכִּימַיָּא מִתְקַטְּלִין	and the wise men were being executed,	(2) The Sentence of the Wise Men (2:13a–b)
13c	וּבְעוֹ דָּנִיֵּאל וְחַבְרוֹהִי	and they sought Daniel and his friends	(3) The Sentence of Daniel and His Friends (2:13c–d)
13d	לְהִתְקְטָלָה׃	↑ to be killed.	
14a	בֵּאדַיִן דָּנִיֵּאל הֲתִיב עֵטָא וּטְעֵם לְאַרְיוֹךְ רַב־טַבָּחַיָּא דִּי מַלְכָּא	Then Daniel replied with counsel and discretion to Arioch, chief of the guards of the king	b. Daniel's Inquiry (2:14a–15c)
14b	דִּי נְפַק	who went out	(1) Daniel's Shrewdness (2:14a–c)
14c	לְקַטָּלָה לְחַכִּימֵי בָּבֶל׃	↑ to kill the wise men of Babylon.	
15a	עָנֵה	Responding,	(2) Daniel's Question (2:15a–c)
15b	וְאָמַר לְאַרְיוֹךְ שַׁלִּיטָא דִי־מַלְכָּא	he said to Arioch, the officer of the king,[2]	
15c	עַל־מָה דָתָא מְהַחְצְפָה מִן־קֳדָם מַלְכָּא	"Why is the decree from the king so harsh?"	
15d	אֱדַיִן מִלְּתָא הוֹדַע אַרְיוֹךְ לְדָנִיֵּאל׃	Then Arioch made known the matter to Daniel.	c. Daniel's Petition (2:15d–16d)
16a	וְדָנִיֵּאל עַל	And Daniel went	(1) Arioch's Response (2:15d)
16b	וּבְעָה מִן־מַלְכָּא	and petitioned the king	(2) Daniel's Request (2:16a–d)
16c	דִּי זְמָן יִנְתֵּן־לֵהּ	↑ that he might give him time	
16d	וּפִשְׁרָא לְהַחֲוָיָה לְמַלְכָּא׃	↑ to declare the interpretation to the king.	

1. See commentary on 2:12 and see further Cook, *Aramaic Ezra and Daniel*, 115, 128.
2. See on 2:5 in commentary.

Explanation of the Text

a. The King's Order (2:12a–13d)

The second section of the ch. 2 narrative opens with a reason/result frame, "because of this," כָּל־קֳבֵל דְּנָה (2:12a), where "this" refers to the wise men's response to the king—their overall refusal and inability to do what he asked and their declaration that the king's demand was impossible (2:10–11). This response prompted the king's decree that they be destroyed, a decree that was issued בְּנַס וּקְצַף שַׂגִּיא, "in great agitation and anger" (2:12a–b).[35]

To this point in the narrative, we have only seen the king's rage in his rash and harsh words. Now the narrator explicitly attributes outrageous anger to him (בְּנַס וּקְצַף שַׂגִּיא; 2:12a), and in that anger, he issued a decree to destroy all of Babylon's wise men. There is no logic to what the king does. If he kills all his wise men, he will not have anyone to help him understand his dream. But the narrator is not concerned to portray a rational, thoughtful Nebuchadnezzar; this is a monarch who acts and overreacts without thinking.[36]

The king's orders are passed down, and as the executions are being carried out (participle מִתְקַטְּלִין, 2:13b), we learn for the first time that the orders target Daniel and his friends for destruction along with the rest of the Babylonian wise men. Clause 2:13c begins with an impersonal active verb, "they sought" (וּבְעוֹ), a form that can be translated as a passive verb with the object as the subject: "Daniel and his friends were sought" (e.g., NAB, NJPS). The king's henchmen could have been used as the subject of the active verb, but since the focus of the narrative event is Daniel and his friends, the narrator left the subject unspecified.[37]

b. Daniel's Inquiry (2:14a–15b)

Daniel actively enters the scene in 2:14a, after the transitional conjunction בֵּאדַיִן, "then." Daniel is said to have "replied" (הֲתִיב) to Arioch, an interesting verb choice when no one has spoken to Daniel in the narrative. It may function in the same way as ענה, "to answer," sometimes does—that is, prefacing a response to a situation or information (see, e.g., on 2:20 below). We can speculate what the king's chief guard might have said as he made his rounds and reached Daniel since we know what

---

35. My translation understands בְּנַס וּקְצַף שַׂגִּיא as a prepositional phrase, with the preposition בְּ on a noun נַס. The verse has one main verb (וַאֲמַר). Most English translations render v. 12 as two independent clauses: "because of this, the king was exceedingly angry" and "he gave orders to destroy all the wise men" (see, e.g., ESV, NASB, NIV), a reading based on understanding בְּנַס, an otherwise unattested root, as a synonym for קְצַף, "to get angry." The two words are read as a verbal hendiadys—a two-for-one expression—with the adverb שַׂגִּיא, "exceedingly." By contrast, in my translation, נַס is not a verb but a noun related to the adjective נסיס (attested in the Aramaic of Gen 40:6 [Tg. Onq.]), and the waw on וַאֲמַר is a phrase-boundary marker (not a coordinating conjunction; see p. 91n24 above). See further Cook, *Aramaic Ezra and Daniel*, 128.

36. Miller suggests motives for Nebuchadnezzar's desire to dispose of his advisers (*Daniel*, 82), but regardless of the historical reasons, the narrator paints the king as maniacal, a portrait he will further develop in ch. 3.

37. Many readers of Daniel have wondered why the Judeans were not summoned with the original group of wise men (2:2). In the book's chronology, they were still in their three years of training (cf. 2:1), but in terms of the narrative, the reason for their absence is not important. In literary terms, however, their absence is crucial because it sets up the conflict at the center of the story (Lucas, *Daniel*, 71–72). This central conflict is the question of where true wisdom is found and who has access to it. For twelve verses, the best of Babylon has paraded its incompetence to access knowledge from heaven. The rest of the chapter will focus on Daniel and his God, the one who reveals wisdom and distributes power.

the royal order was, but the narrator provides no help for the first of several times in this section.

The actual words to which Daniel may have been replying are not important, but Daniel's words and the manner in which he spoke them are. The narrator signals this importance in at least three ways: first, he states that Daniel replied and how (2:14a); second, he puts Daniel's response in the form of direct speech (2:15c); third, he includes an otherwise superfluous quotative frame for Daniel's speech (2:15a–b; 2:14a could have introduced his speech).

Daniel replied with "counsel and discretion" (עֵטָא וּטְעֵם, 2:14a), a description that matches what we already know of Daniel from ch. 1 (1:8–14). He is calm, cool, and collected when the executioner arrives—a sharp contrast with the "bluster and disbelief [and] bewildered helplessness"[38] of the royal advisers throughout the previous section. Daniel "models insight and piety" and is "shrewd and astute before Aryok."[39] The fact that Daniel is carrying on a conversation at all with the executioner may be surprising; that he can do so with such aplomb is impressive. He neither pleads for his life nor protests his innocence—as most of us probably would have done. Rather, without a whiff of fear, he asks the executioner for the backstory of the king's decree.

The narrator further highlights the significance of Daniel's speech by his overspecification of Daniel's conversation partner. The narrator first named and identified the man to whom Daniel issued his request in 2:14a–c: Arioch, the king's chief guard and the one responsible to carry out the king's order. But in the quotative frame of 2:15a–b, the narrator renames and reidentifies "Arioch, the officer of the king." This information is not necessary in itself; rather, it highlights the role of Arioch in the narrative as the instrument of the king—an idea that will reemerge in 2:24–25.

c. Daniel's Petition (2:15d–16d)

Daniel's earlier astute dealings with royal staff (1:8–14) prepare us for Arioch's response and the narrator's matter-of-fact recounting that the chief guard told Daniel what he wanted to know (2:15d). With the necessary information, Daniel then petitions the king for time and receives it (2:16). The narrator does not explain the process by which Daniel made this petition, leaving commentators to speculate that the Judean marched into the throne room and asked—a clear violation of court protocol and a possible death sentence (cf. Esth 4:8–11). The narrator's silence may leave room for such a bold move, but it does not require it. Lucas notes that an ancient reader may just have assumed Daniel followed protocol,[40] and Goldingay observes that the language of 2:16 does not require that he even saw the king in person; he could have received permission through a senior court official.[41] In any case, the process is not important to the narrator; the outcome is: Daniel received time, an ironic twist in a story where his beleaguered colleagues were accused of trying to "buy time" (2:8).[42]

---

38. Goldingay, *Daniel*, 209.
39. Goldingay, *Daniel*, 209.
40. Lucas, *Daniel*, 72.
41. "But does v. 16 require that he actually saw the king, which would normally involve using the term קדם מלכא 'before the king,' as in vv. 24, 25?" (Goldingay, *Daniel*, 179n16.a.).
42. Goldingay (*Daniel*, 178n8.a.) and Newsom (*Daniel*, 69–70) discuss the nature of Nebuchadnezzar's accusation that his advisers were trying to buy time, noting that the English idiom "to buy time" carries meaning that the Aramaic does not. First, the Aramaic word עִדָּן does not refer to time in the abstract but rather to a specific time. Second, the king accuses them of buying "the time" (עִדָּנָא), a definite period. Newsom says the king's words in 2:8–9 indicate "that he sees the sages as motivated by the certainty of the king's ultimatum and decree. Thus to 'buy the time,' that is, to possess or own it, seems to be

Daniel 2:12–16 is a terse section of narrative with many gaps, lingering questions, and unreported speech. Why did the king demand the death of *all* the wise men, even those who may have still been in training or were perhaps working as apprentices? Why did Arioch entertain Daniel's question and bother to answer the condemned man? What explanation did he give to Daniel? How did Daniel gain access to the king, and how did he get the furious king to give him time? Why is so much speech *not* reported: the king's order (2:12); the decree itself (2:13a); the executioners' hunt (2:13b–d); Arioch's response to Daniel (2:15d); and Daniel's petition to the king (2:16). Of all the possible spoken words, the narrator gives voice to only one: Daniel's query to Arioch (2:14a–15c). The king spoke three times in the previous section (2:3, 5–6, 8–9), but in this section the narrator sends him to the background. He is not named, and his deadly decree—a vital piece of the plot—appears only via indirect speech.

Daniel is the key character in this scene. He is the only character to whom the narrator assigns direct speech, and the narrator introduces the speech with extensive description. In these few verses, the narrator contrasts Daniel with the rest of the king's wise men:

> The so-called experts have shown themselves fools lacking the diplomatic adroitness to handle the king, but Daniel has it; he gets his way where they could not. They were refused time to devise a solution to the conundrum for themselves; he is granted time to seek a revelation from God. They were dismissed for their self-confessed helplessness; he is accepted for his expectation that he can do something.[43]

As the narrative continues, the narrator will further develop this portrait of Daniel as a wise statesman and extraordinary sage.

3. Daniel's Prayer for God's Wisdom (Dan 2:17a–23e)

Main Idea of the Passage

Daniel 2:17a–23e shows what Daniel does with the time afforded him by the king to interpret the dream (2:16): he recruits his companions to seek God's mercy, and when God reveals the dream to him, Daniel praises God for his wisdom and power and for his sovereign choice to bestow both on whomever he will.

---

an idiom designating a strategy to gain control of the situation" (69). Later in the chapter, Daniel's doxology puts "changing times and seasons" parallel to "removing and installing kings" (2:21), suggesting to Newsom that "'until the time changes' may be a euphemistic way of referring to the king's demise and replacement by another monarch" (69). Thus, the king was afraid that his advisers were conspiring against him and would "give him a falsely benign interpretation of an ominous dream. Relying on their advice, he would then fail to take the necessary measures that could deflect the evil portent, thus leading to his overthrow and death" (70).

43. Goldingay, *Daniel*, 209–10.

Literary Context

The first two sections of ch. 2 laid out the primary problem in the narrative (the king's troubling dream; 2:1–11) and a secondary problem that involved Daniel and his friends (the death sentence for Babylon's wise men; 2:12–16). This third section of the narrative shows Daniel's response to the crisis and functions in at least three ways in its broader literary context. First, in the narrative it foreshadows the content and meaning of the king's dream (2:24–45), and it also summarizes the message of the whole chapter. Finally, in the context of the book of Daniel, this section expounds the primary theme of the entire book.

> A. Narrative 1: God's Superior Knowledge and His Eternal Kingdom (2:1a–49c)
>   1. Nebuchadnezzar's Inferior Knowledge (2:1a–11e)
>   2. Nebuchadnezzar's Reaction to Inferior Knowledge (2:12a–16d)
> ➡ **3. Daniel's Prayer for God's Wisdom (2:17a–23e)**
>   4. God's Superior Knowledge and the Meaning of the King's Dream (2:24a–45h)
>   5. Nebuchadnezzar's Response to God's Superior Knowledge (2:46a–49c)

Translation and Exegetical Outline

(See page 101.)

Structure and Literary Form

The third section of the narrative in ch. 2 follows Daniel's actions after his confrontation with Arioch (2:14–15) and his request for time to interpret the dream (2:16). Two main sections comprise the passage: Daniel's response when he is granted time (2:17–18) and his prayer of praise when the mystery of the king's dream is revealed to him (2:19–23). The second section includes a lengthy embedded poem that is also direct speech (2:20c–23e).

The conjunction אֱדַיִן, "then," and two clauses with perfect verbs (הוֹדַע, אֲזַל) begin the passage (2:17a–b), describing Daniel's actions. Two successively subordinate clauses detail the purpose of Daniel's action (2:18a–b). Then two clauses beginning with אֱדַיִן open the second section, indicating God's answer to the Judeans' prayer

Daniel 2:17a–23e

	Aramaic	English	Outline
			3. Daniel's Prayer for God's Wisdom (2:17a–23e)
			a. Daniel's Response to the Crisis (2:17a–18b)
17a	אֱדַיִן דָּנִיֵּאל לְבַיְתֵהּ אֲזַל	Then Daniel went to his house	
17b	וְלַחֲנַנְיָה מִישָׁאֵל וַעֲזַרְיָה חַבְרוֹהִי מִלְּתָא הוֹדַע׃	and to Hananiah, Mishael, and Azariah—his companions—the matter he made known	
18a	וְרַחֲמִין לְמִבְעֵא מִן־קֳדָם אֱלָהּ שְׁמַיָּא עַל־רָזָה דְּנָה	in order to seek compassion from the God of Heaven concerning this mystery,	
18b	דִּי לָא יְהֹבְדוּן דָּנִיֵּאל וְחַבְרוֹהִי עִם־שְׁאָר חַכִּימֵי בָבֶל׃	so that they might not destroy Daniel and his companions with the rest of the wise men of Babylon.	
			b. Daniel's Doxology (2:19a–23e)
			(1) The Mystery Revealed (2:19a)
19a	אֱדַיִן לְדָנִיֵּאל בְּחֶזְוָא דִי־לֵילְיָא רָזָה גֲלִי	Then to Daniel—in the vision of the night—the mystery was revealed.	
			(2) The Frame (2:19b–20b)
19b	אֱדַיִן דָּנִיֵּאל בָּרִךְ לֶאֱלָהּ שְׁמַיָּא׃	Then Daniel blessed the God of Heaven.	
20a	עָנֵה דָנִיֵּאל	Responding,[1]	
20b	וְאָמַר	Daniel said,	
			(3) Daniel's Blessing (2:20c–d)
20c	לֶהֱוֵא שְׁמֵהּ דִּי־אֱלָהָא מְבָרַךְ מִן־עָלְמָא וְעַד־עָלְמָא	"May the name of God be blessed from forever to forever	
20d	דִּי חָכְמְתָא וּגְבוּרְתָא דִּי לֵהּ־הִיא׃	because of the wisdom and might that are his.[2]	
			(4) God's Superior Power (2:21a–d)
21a	וְהוּא מְהַשְׁנֵא עִדָּנַיָּא וְזִמְנַיָּא	He changes the times and seasons,	
21b	מְהַעְדֵּה מַלְכִין	deposes kings	
21c	וּמְהָקֵים מַלְכִין	and raises up kings,	
21d	יָהֵב חָכְמְתָא לְחַכִּימִין וּמַנְדְּעָא לְיָדְעֵי בִינָה׃	gives wisdom to wise men and knowledge to those with understanding.	
			(5) God's Superior Wisdom (2:22a–c)
22a	הוּא גָּלֵא עַמִּיקָתָא וּמְסַתְּרָתָא	He reveals the deep things and the hidden things,	
22b	יָדַע מָה בַחֲשׁוֹכָא	he knows what is in the darkness,	
22c	וּנְהוֹרָא [וּנְהִירָא] עִמֵּהּ שְׁרֵא׃	and the light with him is encamped.[3]	
			(6) Daniel's Praise (2:23a–b)
23a	לָךְ אֱלָהּ אֲבָהָתִי מְהוֹדֵא וּמְשַׁבַּח אֲנָה	You, the God of my fathers, I praise and laud,	
23b	דִּי חָכְמְתָא וּגְבוּרְתָא יְהַבְתְּ לִי	who have given me the wisdom and the might.	
			(7) God's Answer (2:23c–e)
23c	וּכְעַן הוֹדַעְתַּנִי דִּי־בְעֵינָא מִנָּךְ	Now you have made known to me	
23d		what we asked of you—	
23e	דִּי־מִלַּת מַלְכָּא הוֹדַעְתֶּנָא׃	that is, the matter of the king you made known to us."	

1. See on 2:5 above.
2. "Although rare, the context demands a causal interpretation of the first דִּי phrases here, which is modified by the relative null-copula possessive clause signaled by the second דִּי" (Cook, *Aramaic Ezra and Daniel*, 135).
3. "[I]s encamped" is the translation of Tarsee Li, *The Verbal System of the Aramaic of Daniel: An Explanation in the Context of Grammaticalization* SAIS 8 (Leiden: Brill, 2009), 69.

(2:19a) and Daniel's response of praise (2:19b). A multiverb speech frame (2:20a–b) sets up the direct speech of Daniel's doxology.

Daniel's doxology, the embedded poem of this section, has five subsections: 20c–d, 21, 22, 23a–b, 23c–e. The final subsection functions as a conclusion in which Daniel explicitly states that God answered the prayer regarding the matter of the king. The first four subsections form the body of the poem and stand in a parallel structure: 2:20c–d and 2:23a–b are parallel; 2:21 and 2:22 are parallel. The first and fourth summarize why God is worthy of praise, and the second and third illustrate his power and wisdom.

Explanation of the Text

a. Daniel's Response to the Crisis (2:17a–18b)

While Daniel's doxology is the key component of this section of ch. 2—indicated by its genre,[44] length, and presentation as direct speech—Daniel himself is also central to the text. The narrator indicates Daniel's significance by referring to him four times with more specificity than required by the narrative (2:17a, 18b, 19b, 20b).[45]

Daniel goes to his house and friends, whose Hebrew names are placed in clause-initial position in 2:17b. Although these friends appeared in the ch. 2 narrative tangentially in 2:13c (i.e., as Daniel's friends, חַבְרוֹהִי, who were also on the chopping block), the narrator has not identified them by name since 1:19, when they completed their training and stood in service to the king. By placing them (in a prepositional phrase) first in the clause and using their Hebrew names, the narrator reintroduces them to the reader, calls to mind their experiences and exemplary standing in ch. 1, and perhaps creates a contrast between these Judean wise men and the rest of Babylon's wise men: this Hebrew quartet will seek compassion from the "God of Heaven,"[46] who will show himself to have no competitors among the gods of their colleagues. The king's wise men had claimed that gods did not dwell among people (2:11), by which they seem to have meant their gods were inaccessible. By contrast, the God of Heaven will show himself to be accessible.

He will also show himself to be merciful, which was the foundation of Daniel's request. Daniel tells his friends "the matter" (מִלְּתָא, 2:17b) so that they will all seek God's compassion, רַחֲמִין—the first word of 2:18a. This placement of the object רַחֲמִין in clause-initial position emphasizes the great need for God's

---

44. Prinsloo calls it poetry "in a sea of prose" (G. T. M. Prinsloo, "Two Poems in a Sea of Prose: The Content and Context of Daniel 2.20–23 and 6.27–28," *JSOT* 59 [1993]: 93–108).

45. The appearance of his name in v. 17a could also be considered an instance of overspecification since the narrator names Daniel in v. 16a and he would remain the expected antecedent of the pronoun in v. 17a.

46. "God of Heaven" is a frequent title for God in Dan 2 (vv. 18, 19, 37, 44) and other postexilic books (Ezra and Nehemiah). See also Gen 24:3, 7; Jonah 1:9; Rev 11:13; 16:11. Goldingay (*Daniel*, 198) calls it a parallel expression to the title "God On High" in Dan 3–7 (3:34[4:2]; 5:18, 21).

mercy and compassion; without it, the Judeans will die with the rest of the wise men (2:18b).[47]

For the first time in the book, the narrator uses the word "mystery" (רָזָה) to refer to the king's dream and interpretation (2:18a). Prior to this in the narrative, it has simply been "the matter" (מִלָּה, מִלְּתָא, 2:10, 11, 15, 17). The word רָזָה/רָז, a Persian loanword in both Hebrew and Aramaic, can refer to something kept hidden (e.g., Sir 8:18), reflecting what Daniel would have thought of the king's dream at this point in the narrative. However, the word is also used of cosmic and eschatological mysteries (e.g., in the Dead Sea Scrolls[48]), and since that is how it occurs later in Dan 2 (2:27, 28, 30, 47), the narrator likely used the word here to foreshadow the content of the king's dream.[49]

While the narrator will spend four verses on Daniel's praise for answered prayer, he has little interest in the actual prayer that precipitated that answer. The prayer is "twice removed" from the text: the words are not recorded, nor does the narrator explicitly say the men prayed.[50] He simply reports that Daniel told his companions about the king's decree so they would seek God's compassion in the matter (2:17–18), and the next clause states that the mystery was revealed to Daniel (2:19). The narrator's treatment of the situation suggests the actual petition is peripheral to the emphasis and focus of the text. The focus will be on Daniel's response to the "God of Heaven" for revealing the mystery (2:20–23).

b. Daniel's Doxology (2:19a–23e)

The central component of the chapter is Daniel's doxology of 2:20–23, a fact the narrator indicates by the change in genre, the length devoted to the praise, its presentation as direct speech, and the way he introduces it—namely, with a summary of what follows (2:19b). He also maintains the focus on Daniel by, first, placing the prepositional phrase לְדָנִיֵּאל, "to Daniel," immediately after the conjunction in 2:19a, and second, by overspecifying him (2:19b, 20b); he has already been named in 2:19a, so the repetition of his name in 2:19b and 2:20b is not essential information. Note that the speech frame in 2:20a–b includes the word עָנֵה when Daniel is not responding to or answering God in a conversation; rather he is "responding" to the revelation (see also 2:47).[51]

Daniel learns the mystery in a "vision of the night" (בְּחֶזְוָא דִי־לֵילְיָא), and while every reader knows God did it, the narrator puts him behind the scenes again (cf. 1:2, 9, 17): the mystery "was revealed" (רָזָה גֲלִי), a passive verb without an explicit agent. Fewell notes, "God does nothing that we can see. God says nothing that we can hear."[52] This narrative note also contrasts "his reception of the 'mystery' via a night vision with the mantic methods of divination the Chaldeans would have employed."[53]

Daniel's doxology is the first of four poems or doxologies in the Aramaic of chs. 2–6.[54] Prinsloo

---

47. "The word sequence of the sentence underscores the urgency of the plea . . . emphasizing the importance of God's role" (Pace, *Daniel*, 59). Fewell observes that "Daniel's primary motivation is self-preservation and the preservation of his friends. Only secondarily is he concerned with his professional colleagues who are, in the scheme of things, Daniel's potential rivals" (*Circle of Sovereignty*, 28).
48. See, e.g., 1QH 1:11–12, 1QM 14:14, 1QS 11:3–4, 1 QpHab 7:8 (Collins, *Daniel*, 159).

49. Newsom, *Daniel*, 71.
50. Daniel later explicitly states that God made known what the men had asked of him (2:23c–e).
51. Cook, *Aramaic Ezra and Daniel*, 134.
52. Fewell, *Circle of Sovereignty*, 28.
53. Cook, *Aramaic Ezra and Daniel*, 134.
54. See also 3:31–33[4:1–3], 4:31–32[34–35], and 6:26–28[25–27].

identifies four functions of this particular poem in the narrative: (1) the change in genre catches attention and so prepares the reader for something out of the ordinary; (2) the poem heightens tension by delaying the revelation of the dream to the reader; (3) it slows the pace of the narrative, again catching and focusing the reader's attention; (4) it makes an important theological statement: "Only God is wise and powerful. Only he can convey the meaning of mysteries. Only he really knows what is going to happen. Only he can convey such knowledge to people."[55]

Daniel's praise is a psalm of individual thanksgiving[56] in which he both declares and describes God's praise.[57] Thanksgiving psalms reflect a poet's gratitude for God's response to a specific request for help.[58] Typically these psalms report the specific distress encountered by the psalmist, but Daniel's doxology does not, perhaps because the threat is clear from the narrative context. The praise unfolds in five subsections (2:20c–d, 21, 22, 23a–b, 23c–e) that exhibit parallel structure (see Structure and Literary Form above). In the first set of parallel subsections (2:20c–d//2:23a–b), Daniel declares God's praise. With a jussive verb (לֶהֱוֵא, 2:20c), he praises God's name because wisdom and might are his (2:20d).[59] Then in the corresponding cola (2:23a–b), he praises God in first person (אֲנָה) for giving him wisdom and might. The second set of parallel subsections (2:21//2:22) then illustrates how God displays his power (2:21) and wisdom (2:22). His power is evident in his changing of times and seasons, his taking down and setting up of kings, and his bestowal of wisdom on people.[60] His wisdom is apparent in the deep hidden things he knows.

Daniel's doxology anticipates what follows in the next section of the narrative (2:24–45). His knowledge of the dream where Babylon's best fell short will testify that the God of Heaven is the true source of wisdom, and his interpretation will proclaim that the same God is also the true source of power—the one who has power and wisdom and bestows it on whomever he will. His declaration that God gave *him* wisdom and power (2:23b) also anticipates what follows. Daniel's wisdom is evident in his knowledge of the "mystery," and his power becomes apparent at the end of the chapter when the king bestows significant political power on the lowly exile (2:48).

The prayer of praise by the Judean exile also invokes the covenant between the God of Israel and Daniel. He begins by praising the "God of Heaven" (2:19b), a reference to the God who is sovereign over other gods, but he concludes by praising the אֱלָהּ אֲבָהָתִי, "the God of my fathers" (2:23a). This title highlights Daniel's belief that the transcendent God is the same God who chose to connect himself to a particular people—Daniel's people, Israel. Seow notes that the significance of Daniel's use of this designation for God lies in its earliest occurrences in the Bible. It first appears in the Bible in connection with God's self-revelation to Moses, where he revealed himself as YHWH, the God of Israel's ancestors (Exod 3:13–16; 4:5). The designation then appears throughout "the Deuteronomic tradition as a constant reminder of the ancient

---

55. Prinsloo, "Two Poems in a Sea of Prose," 101.

56. W. Sibley Towner, *Daniel*, IBC (Louisville: John Knox, 1984), 33.

57. Claus Westermann, *The Praise of God in the Psalms* (Richmond, VA: John Knox, 1965), 102.

58. Examples from the Psalter include Pss 9, 18, 30, 32, 34, 41, 66, 73, 92, 103, 116, 118, 138. See further Richard P. Belcher, Jr., "Thanksgiving, Psalms of," in *DOTWPW*, 805–8.

59. To praise "the name of God" is to praise God; his name presents his person (cf. Deut 12:5; 14:24; 2 Sam 7:13; 1 Kgs 8:16–20; Job 1:21; Neh 9:5; Pss 68:5[4]; 135:3).

60. "Wisdom" in this context is not the empirical, rational wisdom of Proverbs; it is supernatural insight received by direct revelation.

bond that Israel had with God." Given this broader biblical context, Daniel's doxology in Dan 2 draws on the fact "that 'the God of the fathers,' whose self-revelation to Moses enabled Moses to confront Pharaoh's awesome power, is now revealing again, this time through his servant in exile, who is to confront another powerful and oppressive ruler in history." The God of Israel's ancestors is the transcendent God, the one who "relates to a particular people and intervenes in history to deliver them."[61]

The narrator signals in multiple ways that Daniel's doxology is of heightened importance in the narrative. Its significance is that it contains the primary message of the narrative: wisdom and power are God's, and both are his to give and take. The significance of this doxology, however, extends beyond ch. 2, capturing the most important message of the entire book. God raises up kings and takes them down, beginning in 1:1–3. He confounds the "wise" in ch. 2, while giving wisdom to his servant Daniel. Throughout the book, he shares his wisdom, power, dominion, and even glory with people, but he also calls them to account for it. In the mire of human power struggles for control, his kingdom alone is eternal, and to him belong power, dominion, and glory.

4. God's Superior Knowledge and the Meaning of the King's Dream (2:24a–45h)

Main Idea of the Passage

In Daniel 2:24–45, Daniel tells Nebuchadnezzar the contents of his troubling dream, and he declares its interpretation, revealing that his God is the wise and powerful one who grants wisdom and power to human rulers—including the great king of Babylon.

Literary Context

This fourth section of ch. 2 is the climax of the chapter. It resolves the problem of the king's troubling dream, presented in section 1 (2:1–11), when Daniel reports the contents of the dream to the king and also tells him the meaning of the dream. The section also fully resolves the secondary problem presented in the second section (2:12–16)—that is, the death sentence for Babylon's wise men, including Daniel and his friends—in Daniel's encounter with the king.

In the macro unit of chs. 2–7, the king's dream stands parallel with Daniel's vision of four beasts from the sea in ch. 7. These outer chapters of the Aramaic

---

61. Seow, "From Mountain to Mountain," 363–64.

chiasm provide a wide-angle view on God's hand in human history; he is the one who is sovereign over all earthly kings and kingdoms, and his kingdom alone will endure forever.

> A. Narrative 1: God's Superior Knowledge and His Eternal Kingdom (2:1a–49c)
> 1. Nebuchadnezzar's Inferior Knowledge (2:1a–11e)
> 2. Nebuchadnezzar's Reaction to Inferior Knowledge (2:12a–16d)
> 3. Daniel's Prayer for God's Wisdom (2:17a–23e)
> ➡ **4. God's Superior Knowledge and the Meaning of the King's Dream (2:24a–45h)**
> 5. Nebuchadnezzar's Response to God's Superior Knowledge (2:46a–49c)

Translation and Exegetical Outline

(See pages 107–10.)

Structure and Literary Form

The fourth section of the narrative that comprises ch. 2 (2:24–45) consists of two subsections: the single verse of 2:24 and then the rest of the section, 2:25–45. In the first, Daniel addresses Arioch, intervening on behalf of himself, his friends, and all the wise men of Babylon, who were under a death sentence for their inability to meet the king's unprecedented demands. Daniel's words to the executioner are set as direct speech. The second subsection comprises most of the fourth section, and it consists of three units of direct speech: the first by Arioch to the king (2:25); the second by the king to Daniel (2:26); and the third by Daniel to the king (2:27–45).

The length of Daniel's speech to the king indicates its significance in the chapter. It begins with a prologue (2:27a–30d) in which Daniel vindicates the king's advisers (2:27c–e), extols the superiority of his God (2:28a–d), summarizes the significance of the king's dream (2:28e–29d), and dismisses any claim of his own superior ability (2:30). The speech continues with the report of Nebuchadnezzar's dream (2:31–36), a section that opens with the vocative "You, O king" (2:31a) and concludes with the dream's interpretation (2:37a–45h), a section that also opens with the vocative "You, O king" (2:37a).

Daniel 2:24a–45h

24a	כׇּל־קֳבֵל דְּנָה דָּנִיֵּאל עַל עַל־אַרְיוֹךְ	Therefore, Daniel went to Arioch,	4. God's Superior Knowledge and the Meaning of the King's Dream (2:24a–45h)
24b	דִּי מַנִּי מַלְכָּא	whom the king appointed	a. Daniel's Intervention (2:24a–h)
24c	לְהוֹבָדָה לְחַכִּימֵי בָבֶל	to destroy the wise men of Babylon.	
24d	אֲזַל	He came,	
24e	וְכֵן אֲמַר־לֵהּ	and thus he said to him,	
24f	לְחַכִּימֵי בָבֶל אַל־תְּהוֹבֵד	"The wise men of Babylon do not destroy.	
24g	הַעֵלְנִי קֳדָם מַלְכָּא	Take me before the king,	
24h	וּפִשְׁרָא לְמַלְכָּא אֲחַוֵּא:	and the interpretation to the king I will declare."	
25a	אֱדַיִן אַרְיוֹךְ בְּהִתְבְּהָלָה הַנְעֵל לְדָנִיֵּאל קֳדָם מַלְכָּא	Then Arioch in haste brought Daniel before the king,	b. The Dream and Its Interpretation (2:25a–45h)
25b	וְכֵן אֲמַר־לֵהּ	and thus he said to him,	(1) Arioch's Intervention (2:25a–d)
25c	דִּי־הַשְׁכַּחַת גְּבַר מִן־בְּנֵי גָלוּתָא דִּי יְהוּד	"I have found a man from the sons of the exile of Judah,	
25d	דִּי פִשְׁרָא לְמַלְכָּא יְהוֹדַע:	who the interpretation to the king will make known."	
26a	עָנֵה	Responding,	(2) The King's Question (2:26a–f)
26b	מַלְכָּא וְאָמַר לְדָנִיֵּאל[1]	the king said to Daniel[1]	
26c	דִּי שְׁמֵהּ בֵּלְטְשַׁאצַּר	(whose name was Belteshazzar),	
26d	הַאִיתָךְ כָּהֵל	"Are you able	
26e	לְהוֹדָעֻתַנִי חֶלְמָא [חֶזְוָה] . . . וּפִשְׁרֵהּ:	to make known to me the dream . . . and its interpretation?	
26f	דִּי חֲזֵית	that I dreamed"	
27a	עָנֵה	Responding,	(3) Daniel's Response (2:27a–45h)
27b	דָנִיֵּאל קֳדָם מַלְכָּא וְאָמַר[2]	Daniel said before the king,[2]	(a) The Prologue (2:27a–30d)

Continued on next page.

---

1. See commentary on 2:5.
2. See on commentary on 2:5.

108 — Macro Unit 2: The Superiority of God and His Kingdom

(a) The Prologue (2:27a–30d), cont.

(b) The Dream (2:31a–36b)

27cα	"the mystery …
27d	↳ that the king asks
27e	No wise men, sorcerers, magicians, diviners are able
27cβ	↰ … to declare to the king.
28a	However, there is a God in heaven
28b	↑ who reveals mysteries.
28c	And he has made known to King Nebuchadnezzar
28d	↳ what will be in the latter days.
28e	Your dream and the visions of your head upon your bed came up
29a	As for you, O king, your thoughts upon your bed came up
29b	⎯ what will be after this;
29c	the revealer of mysteries made known to you
29d	↑ what will be.
30aα	And as for me, not on account of wisdom …
30b	↑ that I have more than all the living
30aβ	… this mystery was revealed to me,
30c	but in order that the interpretation to the king may be made known,
30d	and the thoughts of your heart you may know.
31a	You, O king, were looking,
31bα	and oh! One great statue …
31c	⎯ that image was great
31d	and its splendor was surpassing⎯
31bβ	… was standing before you,
31e	and its appearance was frightening.
32a	That statue⎯
32b	its head was of fine gold,
32c	its chest and its arms were of silver,
32d	its belly and its thighs were of bronze,
33a	its legs were of iron;
33b	as for its feet, they were partly of iron and partly of clay.

Continued from previous page.

Daniel 2:1a–49c

34a		You were looking
34b		↱ until a stone was cut out, not by hands.
34c		It struck the statue on its feet of iron and clay,
34d		and it shattered them.
35a		Then the iron, the clay, the bronze, the silver, and the gold fell to pieces as one,
35b		and they were like chaff from threshing floors of summer.
35c		The wind lifted them
35d		and no trace of them could be found.
35eα		But the stone…
35f		↱ which shattered the statue
35eβ		…became a great mountain,
35g		and it filled all the land.
36a		This is the dream,
36b		and its interpretation we will tell the king.
37a		You, O king, are the king of kings,
37b		↱ to whom the God of Heaven has given the kingdom, the power, and the strength, and the honor.
38a		↳ And wherever they may dwell,
38b		the sons of man, the beast of the field, and the birds of heaven he has given into your hand,
38c		and he made you to rule over all of them.
38d		You are the head of gold.
39a		After you will arise another kingdom, inferior to you,
39b		and another, third kingdom—of bronze—[will arise],
39c		↱ which will rule over all the earth.
40a		The fourth kingdom will be strong like iron.
40b		↳ Just as iron shatters and grinds everything,
40c		so, as iron that smashes, it will shatter and smash all these.

(c) The Interpretation (2:37a–45h)

Continued on next page.

---

3. For further explanation of translation choices in these syntactically difficult verses (2:40–45), see Cook, *Aramaic Ezra and Daniel*, 150–61.

(c) The Interpretation (2:37a–45h), *cont.*

41a	And that which you saw—the feet and toes—partly of potter's clay and partly of iron,
41b	will be a divided kingdom.
41c	And some of the firmness of the iron will be in it,
41d	just as you saw the iron mixed with the soft clay.
42a	As for the toes of the feet, some of them are iron and some of them are clay;
42b	part of the kingdom will be strong,
42c	and part of it will be brittle.
43a	Those that you saw—the iron mixed with the soft clay—will be mixed in the seed of man,
43b	but they will not stick to one another,
43c	just as iron does not mix with clay.
44a	In the days of those kings, the God of Heaven will raise up a kingdom
44b	that will never be destroyed,
44c	and the kingdom will not be left to another people.
44d	It will shatter and put an end to all these kingdoms.
44e	But as for it, it will stand forever,
45a	just as you saw
45b	that from the mountain a stone was cut,
45c	which was not [cut] by hands,
45d	and it shattered the iron, the bronze, the clay, the silver, and the gold.
45e	A great God has made known to the king
45f	what will happen after this.
45g	The dream is certain,
45h	and its interpretation is sure."

Continued from previous page.

Explanation of the Text

a. Daniel's Intervention (2:24a–h)

After receiving an understanding of "the mystery" (2:19a), Daniel approached Arioch. At this point, the narrator could have simply reported that Daniel told Arioch he knew the meaning of the dream, so the official should take him to the king. Instead, he again overspecifies the identity of Arioch ("whom the king appointed to destroy the wise men of Babylon," 2:24b–c; Arioch is already known from 2:14–15, where the narrator also overspecified his identity), uses two clauses to report Daniel's action (2:24a and 2:24d), and sets Daniel's words in direct speech (2:24f–h) with a quotative frame that contains extraneous information (וְכֵן . . . לֵהּ, "and thus he said to him," 2:24e)—i.e., we know that he is speaking to Arioch.

The reason for all these narrative "extras" may be that Daniel, whom Arioch will identify to Nebuchadnezzar as one of the Judean exiles (2:25c), is about to issue what amounts to two orders to the king's high-ranking official. The first order is the more significant in context ("The wise men of Babylon do not destroy," לְחַכִּימֵי בָבֶל אַל־תְּהוֹבֵד, 2:24f), since the narrator has just reminded us that the king himself appointed Arioch to destroy the wise men. Now the lowly captive tells the king's official to disobey the king's order. While we might well assume the executions had already been stayed in light of the time Daniel apparently received from the king to make the interpretation known (2:16), the narrator uses this scene to subtly undermine the power and authority of the mighty Babylonian king: the king's official obeys the command of a mere captive. Without any of the expected politeness we might expect from a captive to a high-ranking royal official, Daniel tells Arioch to stop the slaughter and take him to the king (2:24f–g). Also of interest in Daniel's words is what comes first in his "order" to Arioch: the object of the verb, לְחַכִּימֵי בָבֶל, "the wise men of Babylon." By placing this first, the narrator suggests that the central concern of Daniel's coming to Arioch was the preservation of the wise men (including himself and his friends).[62]

b. The Dream and Its Interpretation (2:25a–45h)

Arioch does exactly what Daniel ordered, and he does it "in haste" (בְּהִתְבְּהָלָה, 2:25a)—a narrative detail that reminds us of the urgency of the situation. The narrator puts Arioch's response in language that echoes Daniel's command (cf. "take me before the king," הַעֲלַנִי קֳדָם מַלְכָּא [2:24g] and "(he) brought Daniel before the king," הַנְעֵל לְדָנִיֵּאל קֳדָם מַלְכָּא [2:25a]). Then the narrator frames Arioch's direct speech to the king with the same speech frame he used for Daniel's speech to Arioch, "thus he said to him" (וְכֵן אֲמַר־לֵהּ, 2:24e, 25b), both containing the same extraneous information (see above on 2:24). In this second instance, the narrator may be setting Arioch's speech alongside Daniel's to highlight its inaccuracy: Arioch implies to the king that he went looking for someone to interpret the dream and succeeded when he found Daniel, but the reader knows the initiative was all Daniel's. Arioch was just obeying the king's execution orders—and, in the narrator's view, not very well (see above on 2:24).

The king responds by querying Daniel, words

---

62. Cook, *Aramaic Ezra and Daniel*, 139.

the narrator sets in direct speech. Given that the focus of the entire chapter has been the problem of someone knowing the king's dream and being able to interpret it, the king's question brings the problem back to center stage before its resolution. In the introduction to the king's speech, the narrator also includes a clause overspecifying Daniel: "whose name was Belteshazzar" (דִּי שְׁמֵהּ בֵּלְטְשַׁאצַּר, 2:26c). This reminder of Daniel's Babylonian name represents a shift to the king's point of view—a point of view in which he owned the captive mind and body (see on 1:6–7). The irony in this context is that Daniel/Belteshazzar is about to speak on behalf of the one he really serves, the one who is the source of Nebuchadnezzar's power as well as the dream that troubled him.

Daniel responds to the king with the longest direct speech in a chapter packed with instances of direct speech (2:27–45).[63] The king had asked if he was able to tell him the dream and its interpretation (2:26d–f),[64] and Daniel repeats what the Chaldeans had told the king earlier—no human is able (2:10–11; 2:27c–e). The Chaldeans had also rightly said that the answer could only come from the divine realm. The real problem for the Babylonian professionals was that the dream came from the God of Israel, a god they could not manipulate or cajole. The Most High God bestows wisdom and power on whomever he chooses (2:20–23), and in this case, he gave it to his servant Daniel to make known the mystery he had revealed in a dream to Nebuchadnezzar.

Given the urgency of the king's demand, the reader might have expected Daniel to get to the point quickly. However, this narrator is in no hurry, and he again delays the resolution while Daniel refuses credit for what he is about to do (2:30),[65] clears the wise men of the king's charges (2:27c–e), and offers a preliminary explanation of what the king had dreamed and why (2:28c–d, 29). The effect of this ongoing delay is twofold: first, it heightens the suspense of the dream and its interpretation, and second, it keeps the chapter's main point in view: the true source of knowledge and power is the God in heaven. He is the one who reveals mysteries (2:28a–b, 29c).

Daniel's report divides into two major sections: the dream itself (2:31–36) and the interpretation (2:37–45). Each begins with a vocative ("You, O king," אַנְתָּה מַלְכָּא; 2:31a, 37a) that is not necessary to identify who is being addressed. These repeated vocatives help identify the sections of Daniel's speech, and they may also indicate Daniel's attempts to get the king's attention.[66]

The content of the dream divides into two major sections as well, each introduced with "you were looking" (חָזֵה הֲוַיְתָ, 2:31a, 34a). These comments cast the dream report from the king's point of view as it unfolded, a narrative move that Newsom says demonstrates the reliability of Daniel's information.[67] The first section of the dream report focuses on the appearance of the statue and the second section focuses on the stone and the encounter between the two. The description of

---

63. 2:3; 2:4; 2:5–6; 2:7; 2:9; 2:10–11; 2:15; 2:20–23; 2:24; 2:26; 2:27–45.

64. Arioch had merely said he had found someone to *interpret* the dream, but the king's query clarifies that Daniel had better be able to recount the dream as well (Fewell, *Circle of Sovereignty*, 30).

65. Cf. Joseph, who also refuted Pharaoh's belief that he could interpret dreams: "I cannot do it, but God will give Pharaoh the answer he desires" (Gen 41:16). See further IN DEPTH: A Theological Paradigm for God's Work among the Nations: The Court Stories of Daniel (Dan 2) and Joseph (Gen 41) in Canonical Context, pp. 123–37.

66. Runge and Westbury offer the colloquial English example, "Dude, listen to this!" *LDHB*, 2.3 Thematic Address.

67. Newsom, *Daniel*, 75. She also observes that not only does the king experience the dream, he himself is a figure in the dream.

the statue begins with אֲלוּ ("oh!"), an expression of surprise that increases anticipation for what follows. The syntax of the description also highlights the awesome nature of the statue, identifying the topic (צְלֵם חַד שַׂגִּיא, "one great statue") and then breaking into a description of its splendid greatness before completing the thought (קָאֵם לְקָבְלָךְ, "was standing before you"). In English, we would use em dashes for this syntax of interrupting one thought with another: "Oh! One great statue—that image was great and its splendor was surpassing—was standing before you" (2:31b–d).

The statue consisted of body parts in several different materials: gold head, silver torso, bronze midsection, iron legs with iron and clay feet. Large statues appeared across the ancient Near East, though they typically represented gods, whereas Nebuchadnezzar's seems to represent kings or kingdoms and even human history.[68] Fewell considers the statue in Nebuchadnezzar's dream to be an idol but not of a divine being. Rather, its human shape as well as the elements that comprise it indicates that the statue is an idol of humanity: "[the materials of the statue are] usually worked by human hands and valued by human society—gold and silver that adorn and give economic power, bronze and iron that make tools and weapons, and even pottery so necessary for literary and domestic purposes. . . . The top-heavy image is a symbol of a humanity that has over-reached itself."[69]

Juxtaposed to this awesome and terrifying image is the stone, a natural object devoid of any human influence. It is, as Fewell says, "a force that is completely 'other.'"[70] Yet, this natural object does unnatural—or supernatural—things: "It divorces itself from its surroundings, it propels itself against the image, it grows as if an organic entity, into a mountain that fills the entire earth," a mountain that also contrasts with the statue as a "raw and undomesticated" power that cannot be tamed.[71] This destruction of the statue by a stone has profound significance in the context of the Old Testament: "besides [a stone's] various physical meanings, as natural stone, ore, precious stone, weapon, or weight, 'eben is used symbolically as well to refer either to idols, who may be made of stone, or to the very God of Israel."[72] The stone of Nebuchadnezzar's dream calls to mind passages such as Isa 2:2–3, where the mountain of YHWH's temple is raised above the hills; Isa 11:9, which refers to YHWH's holy mountain and the earth being filled with the knowledge of YHWH; and Isa 6:3, where the whole earth is filled with YHWH's glory. In the Psalms, "the rock" or "my/their rock" is a commonly used name for God (Pss 18:2, 31 [צוּר], 46; 19:14; 28:1; 31:3–4[2–3] [צוּר]; סֶלַע]; 42:9; 62:3, 7–8[2, 6–7]; 71:3 [סֶלַע; צוּר]; 78:35; 89:27[26]; 92:15; 94:22; 95:1; 144:1). Although the Babylonian king would not have recognized the significance of the stone in his dream, Daniel and the Jewish audience of the book would have associated it with YHWH's rule.

This supernatural rock struck the statue at its most vulnerable place, the iron-clay feet, and pulverized it into bits of dust that blew away with the wind.[73] The statement that all the metals "fell to pieces as one" (דָּקוּ כַחֲדָה, 2:35a) indicates that,

---

68. Pace, *Daniel*, 67–68. A combination of metals representing different time periods is also known in ancient Near Eastern literature, though the iron-clay combination in Nebuchadnezzar's dream is unknown.

69. Fewell, *Circle of Sovereignty*, 34.

70. Fewell, *Circle of Sovereignty*, 34.

71. Fewell, *Circle of Sovereignty*, 34.

72. Pace, *Daniel*, 69.

73. The imagery of the smashed statue blowing away like chaff evokes Isaiah's likening of Israel "to a threshing sledge that turns mountains and hills into chaff" (Isa 41:14–15; Newsom, *Daniel*, 77; cf. C. L. Seow, *Daniel*, Westminster Bible Companion [Louisville: Westminster John Knox, 2003], 47).

although made up of many different parts and metals, the statue represented one thing. The dream report highlights the annihilation of the statue in 2:35d, where the subject (כָּל־אֲתַר) appears before the negated verb (לָא־הִשְׁתְּכַח), "underscoring that every last trace of the statue is gone: lit., 'any trace was not found.'"[74]

Daniel begins the dream's interpretation the same way he did the dream report (2:31a): "You, O king" (2:37a). This vocative, unnecessary in terms of meaning, delineates the next section and may also represent Daniel's attempt to get the king's attention.[75] Calling the king "the king of kings," Daniel praises Nebuchadnezzar for his expansive power. Yet this power is only derived from the God of Heaven who has given him kingship, power, strength, and honor (2:37b). The order of elements in Daniel's statement (2:37b) suggests the correct order of things—that is, the God of Heaven is the one who has power to bestow on whomever: אֱלָהּ שְׁמַיָּא ("the God of Heaven"), מַלְכוּתָא חִסְנָא וְתָקְפָּא וִיקָרָא ("the kingdom, the power, and the strength, and the honor"), יְהַב־לָךְ ("has given to you"). Daniel's description of Nebuchadnezzar's realm in 2:38 is difficult syntactically, but the emphasis is "on the fact that all the groups in the created order God has placed under Nebuchadnezzar's sovereignty," not on the dwelling places of each group.[76]

God is the subject of the verbs in this introductory praise, and he is the clear source of Nebuchadnezzar's power, a contrast to the behind-the-scenes way the narrator portrayed God's power in ch. 1 (e.g., 1:2).[77] In these words about Nebuchadnezzar's power, Daniel echoes themes from his doxology of God's sovereignty and bestowal of power on human kings (2:37a–38c; cf. 2:20–23).[78]

Daniel's opening praise of Nebuchadnezzar leads to the identification of the king as the head of gold (2:38d). This is almost as specific as the interpretation gets. The second kingdom is simply said to be inferior to Nebuchadnezzar, while the third kingdom will rule over all the earth, suggesting a kingdom even more expansive than Nebuchadnezzar's. The description of the fourth kingdom is the most extensive (2:40–43), indicating its relative importance in the dream.

Daniel's interpretation compares the fourth kingdom to iron, and just as iron smashes everything, so too will this kingdom. Then a final everlasting kingdom—the stone—shatters and puts an end to all the other kingdoms. Daniel concludes his interpretation by reminding Nebuchadnezzar of the dream's source (2:45e), significance (2:45f), and certainty (2:45g–h).

Although scholars have given much attention to identifying the four kingdoms of Nebuchadnezzar's dream, their exact identification is not crucial to the message of the dream or the chapter. The dream's main message is clear and transcends the historical referents for the kingdoms: all human kingdoms will ultimately be destroyed and overtaken by the everlasting kingdom of God. The dream illustrates the themes of Daniel's doxology earlier in the chapter.

---

74. Cook, *Aramaic Ezra and Daniel*, 149.

75. See p. 112n66 above.

76. The translation used here reads against the Masoretic accents; see further Cook, *Aramaic Ezra and Daniel*, 152–53. With respect to the groups of the created order, Cook notes the absence of "the fish of the sea" and comments: "The king's dominion over the wild animals . . . was demonstrated by the royal hunts, as would his dominion over the birds be illustrated by the refuge provided for them in the royal gardens and game parks. By contrast, the king can hardly be said to hold sovereignty over the fish of the sea, thus toning down the mythic-like portrayal of the king" (p. 153). See also Newsom, *Daniel*, 78.

77. Newsom, *Daniel*, 78.

78. Daniel's words also reflect texts that attribute Nebuchadnezzar's success to God (i.e., Jer 25:9; 27:5–6; 43:10; cf. Jer 28:14; Ezek 26:7), and they foreshadow Nebuchadnezzar's day of reckoning in ch. 4.

IN DEPTH: The Identities of the Kingdoms

Daniel's interpretation of the king's dream is straightforward, but relatively sparse. Its greatest interest is in the first and fourth kingdoms, with little said about the second and third. These gaps have left generations of Bible students to try sorting out the details. There are two main interpretations: the Greek and Roman views, named for their identification of the fourth kingdom. A third interesting but less widely held interpretation understands the dream to be about four kings, not kingdoms. For the most part historically, traditionalists have held the Roman view and non-traditionalists the Greek view, but all the views have their difficulties. The chart below shows the three interpretations alongside the details of the king's dream and Daniel's interpretation:

Table 2.1. The Identities of the Kingdoms in Daniel 2				
Nebuchadnezzar's Dream	**Daniel's Interpretation**	**The Roman View**	**The Greek View**	**The Four Kings View**
Gold head	Nebuchadnezzar	Babylon	Babylon/Nebuchadnezzar	Nebuchadnezzar
Silver chest	A second, inferior kingdom; arises after Nebuchadnezzar	Medo-Persia	Media	Belshazzar
Bronze belly/thighs	A third kingdom; rules over the whole earth	Greece	Persia	Darius
Iron legs Clay/iron feet	A fourth kingdom; crushes and breaks all the others; a divided kingdom (feet/toes), partly strong like iron and partly brittle, like iron mixed with soft clay	Rome; the iron-clay toes are usually said to be a revived Roman empire or an extension of the old Roman empire	Greece; begins with Alexander the Great; ends in history of intermarriages between dynasties succeeding Alexander	Cyrus
Rock	God's kingdom; endures forever and destroys all human kingdoms	God's kingdom; established at the first and second advents (birth and return of Christ)	God's kingdom; established at some point after the fall of Greece	God's kingdom and his people, specifically those in exile

The identification of the kingdoms is part of a larger interpretive puzzle in the book of Daniel. Chapters 2 and 7, the outer chapters of the Aramaic chiasm, both contain dreams/visions in which four entities (metals/statue in ch. 2 and beasts in ch. 7) are superseded by a fifth eternal entity. The vision of ch. 8 then includes two beasts related to the beasts of ch. 7. Because of the interconnectedness of these dreams/visions, I offer only a few comments here and delay further discussion until my comments on Dan 7–8.

Daniel identifies Nebuchadnezzar as the head of gold in Dan 2, and since ch. 7 includes a fairly clear identification of him as the first beast, nearly everyone agrees that Babylon (or Nebuchadnezzar specifically) is the first kingdom.[79] Then since the little horns of ch. 7 and ch. 8 (on the fourth beast and the goat, respectively) closely correspond to each other, and since the angelic interpreter of Daniel's vision in ch. 8 identifies the goat as the Greek empire (of Alexander the Great), it is reasonable to think that the fourth beast in Dan 7 is also Alexander's Greek empire (see Dan 8:21). Finally, the sordid history of intermarriage between the Ptolemies and Seleucids,[80] two dynastic inheritors of Alexander's empire, corresponds well to Daniel's interpretation of the statue's toes in Dan 2:43—that is, the mixture of iron and clay symbolized a mixing in marriages.[81]

This interconnectedness suggests a sequence of empires matching the Greek view (see table 2.1): Nebuchadnezzar/Babylon, Media, Persia, Macedonian Greece. This is the view I hold. However, the interpretation of Rome being the fourth kingdom has a long history, dating as early as Josephus.[82]

The third line of interpretation (the Four Kings View above) is that the four entities represented by the dream of ch. 2 and the vision of ch. 7 are not the same. However, they are related in that ch. 7 extends the pattern of ch. 2 to apply to a broader period of history. The four metals of ch. 2 represent the four kings in the book of Daniel: Nebuchadnezzar, Belshazzar, Darius, Cyrus. The attractiveness of this view lies in its attempt to read the dream in terms of its immediate context: in ch. 3, Nebuchadnezzar, the "head of gold," makes a grand show of his "golden greatness" by erecting a statue and commanding allegiance to it; in ch. 4, he exhibits his genuine greatness—at least, in theological terms—when he responds appropriately to the discipline of God and acknowledges the sovereignty of the Most High (4:31–32[34–35]); ch. 5 demonstrates the inferiority of the great king's successor Belshazzar ("after you will arise another kingdom, inferior to you," 2:39a); in the transition between chs. 5 and 6 and into ch. 6, Darius the Mede rules the whole earth (6:1, 26[5:31; 6:25]); then the narrative portion of the book closes with the mention of the fourth king, Cyrus

---

79. See Lucas (*Daniel*, 76) for a discussion of the fluid use of "kings" and "kingdoms" in these chapters.

80. The most readable resource I have found on this convoluted history is Anthony J. Tomasino, *Judaism Before Jesus: The Events and Ideas That Shaped the New Testament World* (Downers Grove, IL: InterVarsity Press, 2003). For much of the same history in a fictionalized account, see David A. deSilva, *Day of Atonement: A Novel of the Maccabean Revolt* (Grand Rapids: Kregel, 2015).

81. A stilted translation of Dan 2:43 makes this assertion more clear: "What you saw—the iron mixed with the potsherd of clay—they will be mixed by the seed of man, but they will not stick together, just as iron does not mix with clay."

82. Josephus, *Ant.* 10.10.4, Thackery. Lucas notes, however, that it was a new interpretation then that replaced an earlier interpretation (*Daniel*, 77). He also refers to 2 Esdras (4 Ezra) 12:11–12 as evidence that the interpretation was new.

the Persian (6:29[28]). The stone, cut from "the mountain" (2:45b), represents the lowly exiles, the elect people of God, who are effecting the reign of God that will one day fill the earth.[83]

In the end, every view has its shortcomings and inability to answer all the questions left by the textual gaps. In light of this and the emphasis of the narrative itself, Longman's comments are especially apt:

> We must entertain seriously the idea that the vision of Daniel 2 does not intend to be precise as it writes the history before it occurs. In other words, though it starts in the concrete present, it is a wrong strategy to proceed through history and associate the different stages of the statue with particular empires. The vision intends to communicate something more general, but also more grand: God is sovereign; he is in control despite present conditions.[84]

5. Nebuchadnezzar's Response to God's Superior Knowledge (2:46a–49c)

Main Idea of the Passage

Nebuchadnezzar responds to Daniel's dream interpretation by worshiping and rewarding him and by honoring his request to promote his three friends. The great Babylonian king declares that Daniel's ability to tell him the dream and its meaning show his God to be God of gods, lord of kings, and the one who can reveal mysteries.

Literary Context

This final section of the ch. 2 narrative is the denouement of the story. Daniel's interpretation (2:37–45) has satisfactorily resolved the problem of the king's dream,

---

83. Seow details this view in his article "From Mountain to Mountain." See also Goldingay (*Daniel*, 203–4, 214) and Seow (*Daniel*, 45–46). I find it tantalizing, especially given the narrative's emphasis in ch. 5 on Belshazzar's inferiority to Nebuchadnezzar. But ultimately, I think it falls short because the dream's great interest in the fourth kingdom is not reflected in the later narratives—that is, Cyrus only appears as a historical marker in the text, not a full-blown interest of the narrator (1:21; 6:29[28]; 10:1). There is another "four kings" view where the kings are Nebuchadnezzar, Amel-marduk, Neriglissar, and Nabonidus. See Collins (*Daniel*, 169) for the view and a critique.

84. Longman, *Daniel*, 82.

and in response Nebuchadnezzar rewards Daniel and his friends with promotions. These promotions form the backdrop for events that happen to the Judean exiles in subsequent chapters; their high positions and, in the case of Daniel, favor with the monarch, make them targets for jealous and conspiratorial colleagues to plot against them (chs. 3 and 6). The elevated position Daniel gained before Nebuchadnezzar in ch. 2 also sets up two future encounters between him and Babylonian kings: in ch. 4, Nebuchadnezzar will again seek his help to understand a troubling dream, and in ch. 5, Belshazzar will treat his predecessor's chief wise man with disregard and even disdain.

> A. Narrative 1: God's Superior Knowledge and His Eternal Kingdom (2:1a–49c)
>   1. Nebuchadnezzar's Inferior Knowledge (2:1a–11e)
>   2. Nebuchadnezzar's Reaction to Inferior Knowledge (2:12a–16d)
>   3. Daniel's Prayer for God's Wisdom (2:17a–23e)
>   4. God's Superior Knowledge and the Meaning of the King's Dream (2:24a–45h)
> ➡ **5. Nebuchadnezzar's Response to God's Superior Knowledge (2:46a–49c)**

Translation and Exegetical Outline

(See page 119.)

Structure and Literary Form

The fifth and final section of the ch. 2 narrative (2:46–49) has two subsections: the king's reaction to Daniel's recounting of the dream (2:46–47) and the promotion of the four Judean exiles (2:48–49). Each section begins with the temporal adverb אֱדַיִן(בְּ), "then" (2:46a, 48a). The first section recounts the king's reaction: Nebuchadnezzar worships Daniel (2:46) and acknowledges the superiority of his God with words the narrator sets in direct speech (2:47). In the second section, the king rewards Daniel (2:48) and then honors his request to promote Shadrach, Meshach, and Abednego (2:49).

Daniel 2:46a–49c

46a	בֵּאדַיִן מַלְכָּא נְבוּכַדְנֶצַּר נְפַל עַל־אַנְפּוֹהִי	Then King Nebuchadnezzar fell on his face	5. Nebuchadnezzar's Response to God's Superior Knowledge (2:46a–49c)
46b	וּלְדָנִיֵּאל סְגִד	and to Daniel paid homage.	a. The King's Reaction (2:46a–47e)
46c	וּמִנְחָה וְנִיחֹחִין אֲמַר	He commanded an offering and incense	(1) Worship (2:46a–d)
46d	לְנַסָּכָה לֵהּ׃	→ to be offered to him.	
47a	עָנֵה	→ Responding,	
47b	מַלְכָּא לְדָנִיֵּאל וְאָמַר	the king said to Daniel,[1]	(2) Acknowledgment of Daniel's God (2:47a–e)
47c	מִן־קְשֹׁט דִּי אֱלָהֲכוֹן הוּא אֱלָהּ אֱלָהִין וּמָרֵא מַלְכִין וְגָלֵה רָזִין	"Surely, as for your god, he is god of gods and lord of kings and the revealer of mysteries,	
47d	דִּי יְכֵלְתָּ	since you were able	
47e	לְמִגְלֵא רָזָה דְנָה׃	→ to reveal this mystery."	
48a	אֱדַיִן מַלְכָּא לְדָנִיֵּאל רַבִּי	Then the king made Daniel great,	b. The Exiles' Promotions (2:48a–49c)
48b	וּמַתְּנָן רַבְרְבָן שַׂגִּיאָן יְהַב־לֵהּ	and many gifts gave him.	(1) Daniel's Reward (2:48a–c)
48c	וְהַשְׁלְטֵהּ עַל כָּל־מְדִינַת בָּבֶל וְרַב־סִגְנִין עַל כָּל־חַכִּימֵי בָבֶל׃	He made him ruler over all the province of Babylon and chief prefect over all the wise men of Babylon.	
49a	וְדָנִיֵּאל בְּעָא מִן־מַלְכָּא	And Daniel sought of the king,	(2) Daniel's Request (2:49a–c)
49b	וּמַנִּי עַל עֲבִידְתָּא דִּי מְדִינַת בָּבֶל לְשַׁדְרַךְ מֵישַׁךְ וַעֲבֵד נְגוֹ	and he appointed Shadrach, Meshach, and Abednego over the affairs of the province of Babylon,	
49c	וְדָנִיֵּאל בִּתְרַע מַלְכָּא׃	but Daniel was in the court of the king.	

1. See on 2:5 above.

Explanation of the Text

a. The King's Reaction (2:46a–47e)

The final section of ch. 2 opens with the king reacting to Daniel's feat of recounting and interpreting his dream. Since the reader already knows who the king is, calling him "King Nebuchadnezzar" in 2:46a is an overspecification by the narrator, signaling a shift in key characters. Daniel was the central character in both the second and third sections (2:12–16; 2:17–23; see above), but now Nebuchadnezzar assumes that role in the narrative. The king falls on his face in a posture of worship and then offers gifts and incense to Daniel. Whether Nebuchadnezzar is worshiping Daniel or the deity he represents has been discussed since at least the time of Josephus (*Ant.* 10.211–212). He may simply be expressing his relief and satisfaction at the resolution Daniel has provided.[85] Given the king's words in 2:47, he is at the very least acknowledging Daniel's God. He does not praise Daniel for his ability but rather his God, whose superiority was made apparent in Daniel's ability to disclose the king's dream and its meaning. Seow observes that the king's gestures of worship illustrate the narrator's point that the reign of God is present in Daniel.[86]

The narrator sets the king's words of praise as direct speech (2:47a–b) and then opens the statement with מִן־קְשֹׁט דִּי אֱלָהֲכוֹן, "surely, as for your god" (2:47c)—a left dislocation structure that introduces the topic of his speech. This structure sets information outside the syntax of the main clause (. . . הוּא אֱלָהּ אֱלָהִין; 2:47c) and allows the narrator to emphasize the topic without increasing the complexity of the main clause. The main clause begins with the third masculine singular pronoun הוּא, a placement that also emphasizes the identity of Daniel's God as the topic of the king's praise.

Newsom observes that the king's words about Daniel's god involve three different acknowledgments. First, by calling him "god of gods," Nebuchadnezzar recognizes his power over other deities (cf. Deut 10:17; Ps 136:2). He also refers to him as "lord of kings," a title (also known from a Persian-era inscription[87]) that indicates Nebuchadnezzar's understanding of the "control of the history of earthly sovereignties" that Daniel's God had. The Babylonian king's final acknowledgment, evident in his words that Daniel's God is the "revealer of mysteries," is that his dream and Daniel's interpretation are divine revelations (2:28, 45; cf. 1QH 26.14–15).[88] The king's praise also returns to the theme of the chapter that the God of Israel is the true source of knowledge.

The king makes no comment about his dream or its meaning, so we cannot know with certainty

---

85. For a discussion of the material evidence for incense in the ancient Near East, see Alan Millard, "Incense—the Ancient Room Freshener: The Exegesis of Daniel 2:46," in *On Stone and Scroll: Essays in Honour of Graham Ivor Davies*, ed. James K. Aitken et al. (Berlin: de Gruyter, 2011), 111–22. Millard suggests that "the extravagant honour Nebuchadnezzar paid Daniel should be treated as the natural reaction of a relieved and satisfied despot" (121). The king's high honors reflected Daniel's promotion to a "quasi-royal position, in the style that would be recognized and which was not so very different from the position Belshazzar offered and gave to him [in ch. 5]" (121–22).

86. Seow, "From Mountain to Mountain," 371.

87. This is the Byblos marble inscription. See Frank M. Cross, "A Recently Published Phoenician Inscription of the Persian Period from Byblos," *IEJ* 29 (1979): 40–44.

88. Newsom, *Daniel*, 84.

his reaction to the dream that had so troubled him. However, given the timing of the chapter's events (his second year; 2:1), we can reasonably speculate what he may have been thinking. Nebuchadnezzar was a young king with a glorious reign ahead (he was the head of gold!). Whatever catastrophe of the future he may have seen in his troubling dream, it was not going to affect him. If this were indeed his response, Nebuchadnezzar would be much like good King Hezekiah, who was unfazed by Isaiah's prophecy of Jerusalem's destruction on somebody else's watch (2 Kgs 19).

b. The Exiles' Promotions (2:48a–49c)

Like the first subsection of this final section, the second begins with the temporal adverb אֱדַיִן (2:48a; cf. 2:46a). The king rewarded Daniel with political and religious authority. First, he set him over the entire province of Babylon, a prominent post in his government. Second, he appointed him chief prefect over all the wise men of Babylon; that is, he made him head over his assembly of religious experts. Nebuchadnezzar elevated the Judean exile above the men whose lives Daniel had saved by meeting the king's demand. Later in the book, a lofty promotion bestowed on him by King Darius will cause Daniel problems with his colleagues (6:4–5[3–4]). We are not told the reaction of the rest of wise men in the aftermath of the ch. 2 promotion, but since Daniel was responsible for saving their lives, one might think he was looked upon favorably.

Then for the second time in the chapter, Daniel makes a request of the king (cf. 2:16), and for the second time, the king gives him what he wants. Daniel requests that his three friends be made part of his administrative staff, and so the king assigns them posts in the province of Babylon.[89] Earlier in the chapter, the narrator called these three men by their Hebrew names: Hananiah, Mishael, and Azariah (2:17). In that context, Daniel was speaking to his three friends, so the use of Hebrew names was fitting. Here the context requires use of their Babylonian names: Nebuchadnezzar is appointing his civil servants Shadrach, Meshach, and Abednego to new positions in the Babylonian government.[90] The narrator may also have used their Babylonian names here in anticipation of ch. 3, since the promotion of the three men sets the stage for the events there. The narrator says Daniel was "in the court of the king," a place for men of high rank and honor.

In this second narrative of the book and the first narrative of the Aramaic chiasm (chs. 2–7), King Nebuchadnezzar of Babylon—great king of the ancient Near East—encounters the God of lowly Israel, the God who outranked his gods in his claim to wisdom and power. Through the king's dream and the inadequacy of Babylon's wise men, we see that Daniel's God is the source of true wisdom and power. Amazingly, he grants both to mere people for times and seasons that he alone determines. He stands alone as the eternal king, whose dominion will last forever.

---

89. See on Dan 2:1–3 for discussion of chronological difficulty of these promotions.

90. Interestingly, Daniel's Babylonian name, "Belteshazzar," is not used to reflect the king's point of view in ch. 2 (see, e.g., vv. 46–49). It only appears as a narrative aside (2:26). In ch. 4, the king uses the names "Daniel" and "Belteshazzar," but explains the two names (4:5–6[8–9], 15–16[18–19]), and in ch. 5 the queen mother also explains the two names (5:12).

Canonical and Theological Significance

Where Real Faith Lies

Nebuchadnezzar's dream of Dan 2 has challenged interpreters for centuries, and while the troubling dream creates the storyline of the chapter, it is not the narrator's focus. The dream and the events surrounding it are the vehicle for the primary message of the chapter: true wisdom and power belong to the God of Israel, who bestows both on human rulers. This message is expounded in Daniel's doxology (2:20–23), where God is extolled as the one who raises up and takes down rulers; who confounds the "wise" but gives wisdom to his faithful servants; who shares wisdom, power, dominion, and glory with people but calls them to account for what they do with it. He alone has an eternal kingdom, and to him alone belong all power, dominion, and glory.

Recognizing this about God only happens when we come to the end of human wisdom, when we recognize the insufficiency and finiteness of our own ability. It only happens when we recognize that we are not God, and we acknowledge that all the other gods we depend on (e.g., creativity, technology, hard work) are ultimately insufficient.

Daniel 2 brings us to the limits of human wisdom in its portrayal of Babylon's finest, who had no recourse to do what the king demanded. They could not access the knowledge needed, and their gods of silver and gold could not help them. The story of the wise men's miserable failure in conjunction with the contents of the king's dream calls to mind Isaiah's parody of the gods of the nations, gods that needed to be carried about or nailed to the floor to keep them from toppling over (Isa 40:19–20; 41:7; 44:12–13; 47:1–7). Such gods can neither explain the past nor reveal the future (Isa 44:7). Israel's God alone is wise, knowing and revealing hidden secrets (Isa 42:16; 45:3; 48:6). He is the God of gods, and no other god is able to bestow power and wisdom. All other gods stand (nailed to the floor) helpless before him.

There is comfort and refuge in God's incomparability. No matter how dire the circumstances, one day the rulers of the world and the inferior gods they represent will wither at God's breath and blow away like chaff (Isa 40:24). All nations and kings will bow before the servants of YHWH (Isa 49:7, 23; 60:10–14). Daniel 2, in its portrayal of human and divine weakness alongside the strength of Israel's God, illustrates Isaiah's message of hope.

It is easy to believe in God when he displays his power and his infinite wisdom is obvious. But the reality is that he often hides both.[91] While we probably always

---

91. See The Strength of the Weak God, pp. 70–72 above.

give lip service to his wisdom and power, the fact is that we are prone to embrace other gods and question both the wisdom and power of our God. He so often does things in ways we do not understand, and he so often fails to step in where we think he should—both on the grand stage of world events and in the little corners of the world we call our own. It is not hard to question his power when our daily newsfeed is awash with disaster and despotism. It is easy to question his wisdom when our life plans go badly awry. His power seems weak and his wisdom seems foolish.

And that seems to be exactly the way he likes it. When our God seems weak, it takes faith to believe he is strong. When he seems foolish, it requires faith to believe that he is wise. Walking with a God who does not always look like much is where real faith is found, and gratefully both the Bible and history provide plenty of examples of those who walked by faith with that God. Surrounded by such a great cloud of witnesses, so can we.

IN DEPTH: A Theological Paradigm for God's Work among the Nations: The Court Stories of Daniel (Dan 2) and Joseph (Gen 41) in Canonical Context[92]

Introduction

Readers have long recognized that the accounts of Daniel before Nebuchadnezzar in Dan 2 and Joseph before Pharaoh in Gen 41 have many similarities in plot, motif, and even language. Both feature kings with disturbing dreams from God that revealed the future (Gen 41:25; Dan 2:28–29, 45). Both young exiles demonstrate the superiority of their God by outshining the royal experts. Both captives deny superior ability and credit God with their knowledge (Gen 41:16; Dan 2:30). In both accounts, the onlookers believe the men's ability resulted from the "spirit of the holy gods" in them (Gen 41:38;[93] cf. Dan 2:11; 4:5[8], 15[18]). Finally, both Joseph and Daniel achieve great political power because of their royal service (Gen 41:39–46; Dan 2:48).

Twentieth-century scholars classified these biblical stories, along with the book of Esther, the stories of Bel and the Dragon, and 1 Esdras 3–4,[94] as "court

---

92. This excursus is adapted from an article: Wendy L. Widder, "The Court Stories of Joseph (Gen 41) and Daniel (Dan 2) in Canonical Context: A Theological Paradigm for God's Work among the Nations," *OTE* 27/3 (2014): 1112–28.

93. רוח אלהים in Gen 41:38.

94. The narrative of Bel and the Dragon consists of two stories that comprise one of the additional chapters/sections in the Greek text of Daniel (see n23 in the introduction). The stories both involve Daniel and Babylonian gods. In the first, Daniel exposes the absurdity of Bel/Marduk worship, and in the second,

narratives," noting that they share a basic plot and several motifs with other ancient Near Eastern stories.[95] Such narratives recount the intrigues and adventures of royal courtiers. In a narrower corpus of stories within this genre are tales of foreign courtiers who supplant the wisdom of the king's regular staff, succeed where it failed, and then receive handsome rewards for their efforts. The stories of Joseph and Daniel fall in this smaller category, the tales of royal courtiers.[96]

The purpose of court stories was likely manifold. First, like any well-told story, their intent was to entertain. Those most entertained by the success of a foreign captive would have been those who shared the hero's nationality. Such a success story was likely to foster the ethnic pride of a conquered people group by allowing them to share "vicarious pride in the figure of an exile who rose to the highest position in the kingdom."[97] Second, for the biblical accounts particularly, the stories showcase the superiority of the Israelite God as he worked through the wit and wisdom of Israelite youth. A third purpose behind the court tales may have been to encourage people in adversity to follow the virtuous model of characters such as Joseph and Daniel.[98] W. Lee Humphreys proposed that the stories illustrated a "lifestyle for diaspora," offering examples of Jews succeeding among the nations of the world.[99] While not every Jew would have expected to succeed to the extent of Joseph, Daniel, or Esther, the lives of these three "spoke a message of hope, which declared that Jews could serve foreign kings and bring help or salvation to their own people, as well as helping foreigners."[100]

---

he is thrown into the lions' den after he kills a dragon revered by the Babylonians. The book of 1 Esdras, also from the Greek text of the Old Testament, contains material from the book of Ezra. Chapters 3–4 tell the story of a contest among three young men serving as bodyguards to Persian King Darius I.

95. Collins credits Gunkel and Baumgartner as the first to make this classification for the biblical stories, grouping them in a genre that includes sections of Herodotus, Ktesias, Xenophon, and the *Thousand and One Nights* (*Daniel*, 39). Lists of the shared motifs among court stories are widely available (see, e.g., Goldingay, *Daniel*, 182–83; Collins, *Daniel*, 42–47). See also Susan Niditch and Robert Doran, "The Success Story of the Wise Courtier: A Formal Approach," *JBL* 96 [1977]: 180).

96. Collins, *Daniel*, 43. Elsewhere Richard D. Patterson describes the genre by saying "such stories deal with the exploits of a godly exile in a foreign court whose piety and wisdom enable him to emerge triumphantly from various tests and rise to personal prominence" ("Holding on to Daniel's Court Tales," *JETS* 36 [1993], 447). He further describes the narratives as usually involving "a specific test involving faith, morality, or compromise of covenantal standards" (447), but Patterson's description goes beyond that of critical scholarship, which does not include the criterion that the exile be godly or pious. Further, one might contest whether his criterion even applies to all the so-called court tales of the Old Testament (e.g., Joseph's appearance before Pharaoh does not seem to be a test of the Hebrew's faith, morality, or covenantal standards; nor does everyone agree that Esther qualified as a pious and godly exile in her captivity).

97. Collins, *Daniel*, 44. Lucas notes that the basis of such encouragement in Daniel's court tales "is not belief in some kind of inherent ethnic superiority, but trust in the Most High God, who rules supreme even over human rulers and their affairs" (*Daniel*, 27).

98. Pace says the stories "provide a sense of pride to the powerless and encouragement for the beleaguered to follow commandments and customs" (*Daniel*, 2).

99. W. Lee Humphreys, "Life-Style for Diaspora: A Study of the Tales of Esther and Daniel," *JBL* 92 (1973): 211–23.

100. Robert Gnuse, "From Prison to Prestige: The Hero Who Helps a King in Jewish and Greek Literature," *CBQ* 72 (2010), 31.

A fourth purpose for the biblical accounts in the Second Temple period could have been to affirm that foreign kings were still under God's rule: "The Jews would be led to confess that their God was still in charge of the world, even though tyrants held sway."[101]

The Joseph and Daniel accounts may well have been part of a "court narrative" genre, and they may also have served any or all of the purposes detailed above. However, their inclusion in the Bible requires that we understand them in their biblical contexts, not simply as isolated accounts in a literary vacuum. What do they each contribute to their textual surroundings? Why are two such similar stories included in the Hebrew Bible—would one have been sufficient? Furthermore, why is the second account, that of Daniel before Nebuchadnezzar, patterned so obviously after the first?[102] How do these two accounts contribute to Israel's portrayal of its God? To answer these questions, this excursus first considers the narratives of Gen 41 and Dan 2 in their respective contexts. Then it evaluates their relationship to each other and the role they play in the larger context of the Hebrew Bible in order to demonstrate, first, that the account of Daniel intends to portray God as even greater than the account of Joseph does, and, second, that the accounts together create a paradigm for God's work among the nations, where his people spend the majority of their history.

The Accounts in Context

Joseph before Pharaoh
The Story

In Gen 41 Pharaoh has a pair of dreams, which the narrator initially recounts for the reader (41:2–7). In the first, the Egyptian king was standing along the Nile River when seven fine and fat cows (יְפוֹת מַרְאֶה וּבְרִיאֹת בָּשָׂר) emerged from it and grazed among the reeds (41:2). Seven more cows came out of the river behind them, but they were ugly and scrawny (רָעוֹת מַרְאֶה וְדַקּוֹת בָּשָׂר) and hungry enough to eat a horse. Or seven fat cows (41:4–5). In the second dream, seven heads of grain came up good and fat (בְּרִיאוֹת וְטֹבוֹת) on one stalk (41:5). They were followed by seven heads of grain that were thin and "blasted by the

---

101. Gnuse, "From Prison to Prestige," 41.

102. The similarities between the stories are so extensive that it stretches the imagination to think the author of Daniel did not know and knowingly imitate the story of Joseph before Pharaoh. For discussions of what the accounts have in common, see, e.g., G. G. Labonté, "Genèse 41 et Daniel 2: question d'origine," in *The Book of Daniel in the Light of New Finding*, BETL 106, ed. A. S. van der Woude (Leuven: Leuven University Press, 1993), 271–84; Gnuse, "The Jewish Dream Interpreter in a Foreign Court," 40–41; and Matthew S. Rindge, "Jewish Identity under Foreign Rule: Daniel 2 as a Reconfiguration of Genesis 41," *JBL* 129 (2010): 88–89.

east wind" (41:6; cf. KJV, JPS; דַּקּוֹת וּשְׁדוּפֹת קָדִים). The seven thin heads swallowed the seven fat and full heads (הַבְּרִיאוֹת וְהַמְּלֵאוֹת; 41:7) before Pharaoh awoke. In the morning when his "spirit was troubled" (תִּפָּעֶם רוּחוֹ), Pharaoh summoned his experts—the magicians and wise men of Egypt—but they proved unable to help him (41:8). It was then that the chief cupbearer remembered what he had managed to forget for two full years—namely, how a lowly Hebrew servant had helped him by interpreting his own troubling dream (Gen 40). Joseph was hurriedly (וַיְרִיצֻהוּ; 41:14) brought to the king, who told the clean-shaven prisoner he had heard about his ability to interpret dreams. Denying such ability, Joseph nonetheless assured Pharaoh that God would respond to the king's anxiety (41:16).

Pharaoh then recounted his dream,[103] with slight variation from the narrator's version.[104] At the conclusion of the king's dream report, Joseph confirmed that the cows and the corn were the same dream and told the king that God had made known to him what he was going to do (41:25). Then Joseph repeated the dream, interpreting each element in turn. At the conclusion of his interpretation, Joseph provided the king with some unsolicited advice about appointing a wise and discerning man to oversee management of the crops during the coming feast and famine, effectively writing his own job description. Pharaoh extolled Joseph's wisdom and discernment, crediting his ability to the "spirit of God" in him. The Egyptian king promoted the prisoner to the palace, put him in charge of his house and the land of Egypt, turned over his signet ring, clothed him in fine clothes, slung a gold chain around his neck, and made him ride in the "second chariot" while Egyptians bowed before him. Then he changed his name to better befit an Egyptian overlord and gave him a priest's daughter for a wife (41:45). The narrator then reports the fulfillment of Pharaoh's dream, first describing the years of plenty—both in the land and in Joseph's house, where two sons were born—and then describing the years of famine.

The Context of Genesis 41

The account of Joseph before Pharaoh accomplishes at least two things in its immediate context. First and most obviously, it demonstrates to the reader the sovereignty of Joseph's God, who disrupts the world of a powerful ancient Near Eastern monarch and upends his kingdom with forces far beyond the control of

---

103. Pharaoh refers to the two dreams as if they were one (Gen 41:15, 17).

104. Meir Sternberg details the differences between the dream reports and suggests their significance. See his analysis of Gen 41 in *The Poetics of Biblical Narrative: Ideological Literature and the Drama of Reading* (Bloomington: Indiana University Press, 1985), 394–402.

Egypt's finest. Both the baffling dream and its spot-on fulfillment demonstrate God's sovereignty. The Egyptian experts do not understand the message of this God, much less have any power to thwart him. However, there is no indication that either Pharaoh or his experts acknowledged the sovereign superiority of Joseph's God. Rather, the praise goes to Joseph, in spite of his refusal to take credit for interpretive abilities (41:15–16).

A second purpose of the chapter is to establish Joseph as God's man in Pharaoh's court. Sternberg details how the narrative subtly communicates this through its series of dream reports. The reader first learns the dreams from the narrator, who presents the authoritative versions. Then the narrator says that Pharaoh reported the "dream"—singular—to his experts, who were unable to interpret "them"—plural (41:8). Sternberg suggests that behind this "grammatical clash . . . may lurk a perspectival clash," namely that Pharaoh thought the pair of dreams made one whole dream, while his advisors considered them separate dreams.[105] Pharaoh then reports the dream in detail to Joseph, and the differences between his rendering and the narrator's confirm that he has blurred the two dreams into a single dream. When Joseph repeats the dream, he sorts out Pharaoh's misreporting and "restores in interpretation what the dreamer himself disturbed in narration."[106] Sternberg argues that the narrator incorporates these multiple viewpoints, with their various discrepancies, in order to "establish Joseph's stature as God's elect rather than Pharaoh's":

> This chain of repetition develops a multiple and shifting play of perspectives: among the omniscient narrator's, the reader's, Pharaoh's, the magicians', Joseph's, and, most covert but also most dominant, God's. As far as the bare plot exigencies are concerned—the need to devise a causal sequence that will reverse Joseph's fortune from imprisonment to Grand Viziership—some of the members could be omitted or at least thoroughly reduced. . . . But what a naturalistic plot might allow, if not require, would mar the ideological plot that underlies the visible march of events and shapes the tale's theme and rhetoric.[107]

The Context of the Joseph Story

Beyond the immediate context of Gen 41, Joseph's impressive appearance before Pharaoh serves an important role in the larger Joseph narrative. Most notably, it puts Joseph in position for the fulfillment of his own dreams. In the

---

105. Sternberg, *The Poetics of Biblical Narrative*, 398.
106. Sternberg, *The Poetics of Biblical Narrative*, 400.
107. Sternberg, *The Poetics of Biblical Narrative*, 401.

first scene of the Joseph story, the favored son of Jacob has a pair of off-putting dreams that he recounts to his brothers and his father: their sheaves bowed to his in the first, and in the second, the sun, moon, and eleven stars bowed to him (Gen 37:5–10). From this point on in the narrative, Joseph knew little but trouble. First, after nearly killing him, his brothers settled for selling him into slavery. Then once in Egypt, Joseph had two false starts on his rise to fame. After a promising promotion that made him second in command in Potiphar's house, a falsely accused and implicated Joseph landed in prison. While there, he enjoyed the favor of the chief jailer, who made him second in command over the prisoners. Joseph's interpretation of dreams for the king's cupbearer and head chef gave him hope for release, but the cupbearer's bad memory left him forgotten in prison for an additional two years.

After this pair of ascents and descents for the Hebrew slave in Egypt, Gen 41 presents the third scene in what Wenham calls the "great triptych."[108] Joseph finally rises out of the pit and prison for the last time with his interpretation of Pharaoh's dreams, which sets in motion the fulfillment of his own dreams from years earlier. As second in command over Egypt, Joseph is in position for his bowing brothers. He is also set to steer Egypt through the ensuing years of plenty and scarcity. More importantly, God has put a man in place to preserve his own people, the people of Israel.[109]

The Context of Genesis and the Pentateuch

The Joseph narrative is both the culmination and conclusion of the book of Genesis, and it is also the transition to the book of Exodus and the rest of the Pentateuch. A masterfully told tale that fills nearly a third of the book, the Joseph narrative further develops all three elements of God's promise to Abraham: land, seed, and a relationship of blessing. Specifically, the account of Joseph before Pharaoh relates directly to one element of the Abrahamic promise and has clear repercussions for the other two. First, God had promised Abraham that he would be a blessing and in him all the families of the earth would be blessed (Gen 12:2–3). God's revelation to Joseph of the meaning of Pharaoh's dream and Joseph's subsequent advice made him a blessing. Abraham's great grandson,

---

108. Gordon J. Wenham, *Genesis 16–50*, WBC 2 (Waco, TX: Word, 1994), 389.

109. Joseph is not the only character in the larger narrative (Gen 37–50) that God uses to preserve his people. He sets up the long-term salvific preservation of Israel through the brother who shares the spotlight with Joseph—Judah, the one from whom Messiah would come. The dual redemptive roles of Joseph and Judah are important in their own right, but this essay focuses on Joseph exclusively since the textual connections between Daniel and Genesis specifically concern the interactions of God's people with gentile kings—a role Judah does not have.

the wise and discerning man appointed to manage Egypt's survival during the famine, blessed the people of Egypt and beyond. Second, with respect to the Abrahamic promise of descendants and land, Joseph's ascent to power in Gen 41 set the stage for him to save the descendants of Abraham—but to do so, they had to leave the land God had promised. Through Joseph, God prepared a haven for the Israelites to weather the famine, but Gen 47:27 reports that they did more than simply survive. While Egypt and the surrounding lands languished (47:13–26), the sons of Israel acquired land and were "fruitful and increased greatly in number" (47:27). The seed of Abraham, in jeopardy through most of the patriarchal narrative, appears to be in good stead for the first time by the end of Genesis, but they are living outside the land of promise.

Summary of Genesis 41 in Context

The account of Joseph before Pharaoh establishes him as God's man for that time in Israel's history. The narrative subtly demonstrates the superiority of Joseph's God over the powers of Egypt, and it also exhibits the superior wisdom of Joseph over his Egyptian "competition." No reason is given in the immediate context of Gen 41 for God's revelation to the king, except for Joseph's general pronouncement that God had made known to Pharaoh what he was going to do (41:25). It is only the broader context of the Joseph story, Genesis, and Exodus that shows Pharaoh's dreams to be part of a complex series of events that both preserved God's people and set them up for bondage in a foreign land.

Daniel before Nebuchadnezzar (Dan 2)
The Story

In Daniel 2 Nebuchadnezzar was troubled by dreams, so he summoned his experts (2:1–2). He demanded that they tell him his dreams as well as the interpretation (2:3–5) and threatened to dismember them if they failed (2:6). When he accused his wise men of conspiracy, they protested that only the gods could tell the king a dream and gods do not dwell among people. The king dismissed their protest and ordered the execution of all Babylon's wise men. This edict included Daniel and his Judean companions. Daniel requested time from the king, and when he and his friends sought God's mercy, God revealed the dream and its interpretation to Daniel (2:16–19). Daniel praised God for his sovereign wisdom and might (2:20–23), and then was taken in haste to Nebuchadnezzar. The king asked Daniel if he could tell him the dream and its interpretation, and Daniel confirmed what the wise men had said earlier: No person could, but God reveals secrets (2:27). Then he informed the king—twice—that God had made known to the king what would happen in the future (2:28–29). Daniel emphasized again that he only knew the dream and its meaning because God had told him—not because he had special wisdom (2:30). Then Daniel finally reported the dream of the magnificent statue. When he finished the interpretation, the king worshiped him and declared Daniel's God great for revealing the secret to Daniel: "Surely, as for your God, he is god of gods and lord of kings and the revealer of mysteries" (2:47). Nebuchadnezzar lavished gifts on Daniel and promoted him "over all the province of Babylon" and made him "chief prefect over all the wise men of Babylon" (2:48).

The Context of Daniel 2

The account of Daniel before Nebuchadnezzar in Dan 2 accomplishes several things in its immediate context. First, it establishes the superiority of Daniel (and his God) over his Babylonian colleagues. When they could not meet the king's demand, he could. They protested that no one could do what the king asked (a claim that Daniel affirms; 2:27); only the gods could, but they did not dwell among people.[110] Their protest prepares the way for Daniel to upstage the Babylonian experts by demonstrating access to a God who could reveal the dream and its interpretation.

Another purpose of Dan 2 is to establish God as the true source of wisdom and the sovereign over all human history. The first thirty verses focus on the source of wisdom. First the ineptitude of the Babylonian wise men takes center stage; they cannot access the knowledge the king demands (2:1–12). Then the narrator details Daniel's predicament and God's response, namely, sharing wisdom with Daniel (2:13–23). Then when Daniel finally arrived before the king to interpret the dream, he left no room for misunderstanding the source of the dream and its interpretation (2:24–30). Such mysteries belong solely to the God in heaven (2:28). The statue dream and its interpretation disclose that God is sovereign over human empires and the only eternal king whose dominion will endure forever.

The Context of Daniel

Daniel's success in ch. 2 confirms what the narrator reported in Dan 1:19–20, namely, that he was "ten times better" than the rest of the king's experts in every matter of wisdom and understanding. Although the most obvious demonstra-

---

110. See p. 93 above on the wise men's failure to turn to their gods for help.

tion of this would appear to be Daniel's revelation and interpretation of the dream, Daniel himself refutes this (2:26–28, 30). The wisdom and understanding were not his but had been given to him by God in response to his prayer (2:17–23, 30). Rather, Daniel's superiority is in view in 2:14, where the narrator reports that Daniel spoke to the executioner with "prudence and discretion" (ESV, NRSV; עֵטָא וּטְעֵם) about the king's decree, such that Arioch stopped, talked with him, and then allowed Daniel—under a death sentence—to go petition the king for time, the very thing the other wise men were denied (2:7–9). And Daniel received it (2:15–16). Behind this series of events is a careful negotiator, a man with superior skill. Daniel and his friends were spared, and ultimately the king got what he wanted because of Daniel's prudence and discretion.

Daniel 2 is also part of a larger context, the six-chapter block of Aramaic text in the book of Daniel (chs. 2–7):

A Chapter 2: Statue dream/four empires
  B Chapter 3: Jews face religious conflict/fiery furnace
    C Chapter 4: Tree dream/royal hubris
    C' Chapter 5: Handwriting on wall/royal hubris
  B' Chapter 6: Jew faces religious conflict/lions' den
A' Chapter 7: Beasts vision/four empires

For the purposes here, Nebuchadnezzar's statue dream in ch. 2 is related to Daniel's vision of the four beasts in ch. 7. Furthermore, the entire Aramaic chiasm is integral to the book's structure and even meaning.[111] Were it not for the chiasm, one could easily and convincingly divide the book between the narrative of chs. 1–6 and the apocalyptic/prophecy of chs. 7–12. However, ch. 7 confounds such a tidy division. It is bound in language and structure to what precedes, yet it is tied in theme, content, and genre to what follows.

The extremities of the chiasm—chs. 2 and 7—offer a wide-angle view of world history and God's control over it, a theme the book returns to repeatedly in its narrative accounts of vulnerable human kings and its visions of apocalyptic mayhem. God is revealed to be the source of true wisdom and power, and his kingdom will conquer all human kingdoms, fill the whole earth instead of just part of it, and alone endure forever. In ch. 2, God reveals himself to a gentile king as sovereign over all world powers, and in ch. 7, he does the same to

---

111. See the introduction for more on the significance of the Aramaic chiasm (pp. 31-35).

devout Daniel. Interestingly, neither recipient of this revelation understands it without divine assistance: Nebuchadnezzar, through the intermediary of Daniel, who received the dream and interpretation from God; and Daniel, through the intermediary of an angelic being.

Summary of Daniel 2 in Context

In Daniel's appearance before Nebuchadnezzar, God establishes his servant Daniel as superior over the Babylonian entourage of experts and reveals himself to be the true source of wisdom and the only one sovereign over human history. God alone has wisdom and power, and both are his to give and take. Daniel's magnificent doxology in Dan 2:20–23 captures the message that encompasses the entire book:

> Responding, Daniel said, "May the name of God be blessed from forever to forever because of the wisdom and power that are his. He changes the times and the seasons; deposes kings and raises up kings; gives wisdom to wise men and knowledge to those with understanding. He reveals the deep things and the hidden things, he knows what is in the darkness, and the light with him is encamped. You, the God of my fathers, I praise and laud, who have given me the wisdom and the might. Now you have made known to me what we asked of you—that is, the matter of the king you made known to us."

This message began in Dan 1:2, when God delivered Jehoiakim into the hand of Nebuchadnezzar, allowing his holy city to be destroyed, his temple to be torched, and his people carried into captivity. Throughout the book, God raises up kings and takes them down. He confounds the "wise" and gives wisdom and discernment to his faithful servants. He shares his wisdom, power, dominion, and even glory with humans, but he alone rules a kingdom that will destroy all human kingdoms, fill the earth, and endure forever.

Canonical Context of the Accounts

As detailed above, the accounts of Joseph before Pharaoh in Gen 41 and Daniel before Nebuchadnezzar in Dan 2 have significance in their immediate context, as well as in their larger contexts (i.e., the Joseph narrative and the book of Genesis; the Aramaic chiasm and the book of Daniel). But the similarities between the accounts and the clear patterning of one after the other require we also ask about the relationship they have to each other and the role they play in the Old Testament canon as it reflects the history of God's people. Building on the work of Matthew Rindge, who proposes that the account of Daniel before Nebuchadnezzar intends to portray Daniel as a greater Joseph, I suggest that it also means to portray a greater God. Further, the two accounts together create a paradigm for understanding God's work among the nations.

A Greater Joseph

Rindge identifies eighteen specific similarities between the plot structures of Gen 41 and Dan 2,[112] noting that "the numerous specific similarities (lexical and thematic) between these two narratives suggest that Daniel 2 is a conscious reworking of Genesis 41."[113] Rindge restricts his analysis to Dan 2 and Gen 41, but arguably, the author of Daniel evokes the Joseph account already in Dan 1, perhaps to foreshadow what's ahead in Dan 2. Thematically, both characters are Hebrew exiles serving in a foreign court, both are handsome (Gen 39:6; Dan 1:4); both demonstrate impressive wisdom (Gen 41:39; Dan 1:4, 20); both are blessed in their tasks (Gen 39:2–6; Dan 1:17–20).[114] If these broader themes do not trigger the reader's recognition of a possible connection, then one might think the description of Daniel and his friends after their dietary test would (Dan 1:15): after ten days of vegetables and water, the four Hebrews are said to be בְּרִיאֵי בָּשָׂר, "fat of flesh," an expression used elsewhere only in Gen 41 to describe the fat cows of Pharaoh's dream.

There are also differences between the portrayal of the characters in the accounts, and Rindge argues that this is where the greater significance lies. He argues that the differences "are consistent in nature, reflecting the existence of three distinct patterns," namely, dream interpretation, piety, and the nature of Joseph and Daniel's relationship to their respective foreign kings. In each area, Rindge shows that Daniel is presented as superior to Joseph,[115] suggesting that the account of Daniel before Nebuchadnezzar in Dan 2 reconfigures the account of Joseph before Pharaoh in Gen 41 in order to show Daniel to be a "new and improved" Joseph.[116] Rindge contends that this greater Joseph provides an ideal model for how Jews should relate to and function within a foreign empire—i.e., what Rindge calls "moderate resistance."[117]

---

112. Rindge, "Jewish Identity under Foreign Rule," 88–89.
113. Rindge, "Jewish Identity under Foreign Rule," 90.
114. Gnuse, "Jewish Dream Interpreter in a Foreign Court," 40.
115. Rindge, "Jewish Identity under Foreign Rule," 90–98.
116. Rindge, "Jewish Identity under Foreign Rule," 98. See also Goldingay (*Daniel*, 191), who compares the characters and events of Gen 41 and Dan 2 by saying, "[Dan 2] is like Gen 41, only more so" and then suggests "that Joseph could be seen as a type of Daniel."

117. "I say 'resistance' because he chooses to maintain his own dietary traditions. I say 'moderate' because, despite his rejection of the royal diet, Daniel nonetheless remains involved

A Greater God

The accounts of the two captives before foreign kings do more than present a message about one or both of the young Hebrews. As part of the portrayal of Israel's God, they also instruct the reader in the person, character, and activity of this God. The accounts are similar in their broad theological theme—namely, the sovereignty of God. However, a comparison of what God revealed to the pair of gentile kings and why he revealed it suggests that the account of Daniel before Nebuchadnezzar not only shows a greater Joseph, it shows a greater God.[118]

What God revealed to Pharaoh in Gen 41 was, essentially, a fourteen-year regional weather forecast and his control over it. For seven years, the rains would be plentiful along the Nile and the fields would overflow with crops. Then for seven years, the Nile river of life would not deliver. Famine would seize and all but strangle the land. By contrast, what God revealed to Nebuchadnezzar in Dan 2 was, essentially, the whole of human history and his sovereignty over it. The splendid and not-so-splendid human kingdoms would crumble before the one eternal kingdom that filled the whole earth, not just territories of it. In the former dream, God made known his sovereignty over regional weather patterns and the corresponding fertility of the land. In the latter, he revealed his sovereignty over all kingdoms and powers forever.

Why God revealed the dreams to the gentile kings is less clear in the texts. In Gen 41, Joseph simply tells Pharaoh that God has declared to Pharaoh what he is doing (41:25), and in Dan 2, Daniel tells Nebuchadnezzar that God has made known to the king what will happen (2:29). These answers tell us the general content of the dreams (i.e., future events), but neither tells us why God sent the dreams. We have to rely on the larger context for this. In the case of Pharaoh, the baffling dream brings Joseph to the mind of the cupbearer, who reports his ability to the king. Joseph's interpretation of the dream leads to his appointment over Egypt, which ultimately resulted in the sons of Israel moving there to survive the famine. In terms of Israel's history, we could say God sent the dream to Pharaoh so that the Israelites would survive. In the process, he also blessed Egypt too, preserving it through the wisdom of Joseph. In the case of Nebuchadnezzar, the purpose of the dream for the king specifically does not

---

in the Babylonian court. He still submits himself to the training of the 'Chaldeans' in language, literature, and education. Thus, Daniel offers a *via media* between the extremes witnessed in 1 Maccabees and Gen 41. He embraces neither the assimilation modeled by Joseph nor the rejection practiced by the Maccabees" (Rindge, "Jewish Identity under Foreign Rule," 103).

118. This is not to say that Joseph's God was somehow lesser than Daniel's God. Rather, by calling to mind the Joseph narrative, the Daniel narrative intends to portray God in a grander way with respect to his sovereignty and redemptive purposes.

come into focus until Dan 4, when he has his second dream, which I argue is a remedial lesson for a king who did not learn the first time that his kingdom was temporary and his power was relative and bestowed by a greater king. But the purpose of the dream goes beyond the circumstances of the Babylonian king. It reveals the coming kingdom of God, which breaks into history, destroys all human kingdoms, and fills the earth forever. In Pharaoh's dream, God made a way for the salvation of the starving Israelites and for the nations surrounding Egypt. In the latter, he reveals his coming, eternal kingdom, an event the New Testament says is inaugurated by Jesus, presented as the Savior of the world.

Both accounts reveal a sovereign God, but comparing the what and why of God's revelation to the gentile kings suggests that the Daniel account intends to show a greater God—that is, it magnifies the scope of both his sovereignty and salvation.[119]

A Paradigm for God's Work among the Nations

The accounts of Joseph before Pharaoh and Daniel before Nebuchadnezzar bookend the Old Testament story of Israel's life in the land of promise. Joseph's interpretation of Pharaoh's dream is the trigger event for moving the Israelites to Egypt, where they will enjoy royal favor and eventually suffer under royal oppression. Daniel's interpretation of Nebuchadnezzar's dream occurs early in the exilic period, when the people of God have lost the land of promise to the foreign invader. On either side of Israel's sustained presence in the land, the canon offers accounts with similar themes in which God sends a message to gentile kings and his servants encounter those kings specifically because of these revelations. In its canonical context, this pair of accounts provides a paradigm for God's interaction with "the nations," where most of the Bible's readers since the fall of Jerusalem in 587 BCE have lived.

In the previous section, we considered the significance of the specific messages God sent to Pharaoh and Nebuchadnezzar. Here, we consider the significance of the fact that God spoke to them at all at these points in history when Israel did not have possession of the promised land. I suggest three points of significance.

First, by speaking to the gentile kings whose influence most affected the Israelites (i.e., Pharaoh during the patriarchal period and Nebuchadnezzar during

---

119. I am not suggesting that Nebuchadnezzar's dream itself includes a message of salvation, either implicit or explicit. It is only when considered through the lens of the New Testament and the work of Christ recorded there that one might say, first, how the rock of Dan 2 comes to fill the earth and rule forever, and, second, how the Son of Man achieved salvation for the human race.

the Neo-Babylonian period), God sent a clear message to all involved that he was the God of the nations, not just Israel. Neither Pharaoh nor Nebuchadnezzar had met a God like this one. His messages eluded them and their experts, and the dreams' fulfillment exceeded any power they or their gods might have claimed. The God of Israel was also the God over Egypt and Babylon, whether or not they acknowledged his sovereignty.

Second, although the messages themselves were inscrutable to the gentile kings, God spoke in a language they understood—namely, dreams. Most revelatory dreams that kings received gave clear information about future events. A biblical example of such a "message dream" is in 1 Sam 3, where God calls three times to the sleeping Samuel so that he could tell the boy that he was about to judge Eli's family. Symbolic dreams were more likely to need an interpreter, although the meanings of symbolic dreams could also be obvious (e.g., Joseph's dreams of bowing sheaves and stars in Gen 37). In his Daniel commentary, Longman suggests that God spoke to Nebuchadnezzar in dreams because it was in dreams "that the Babylonian religion and Daniel's faith [came] closest," rather than speaking to him through something like the birth of a multiheaded ox.[120] The same could be said for God's revelation to Pharaoh.

A third point of significance about God's revelation to gentile kings is that he did not send the enigmatic messages until he had also put one of his servants in place to interpret the message. And even then, both texts are clear that the ability to explain the dreams came from God. Joseph and Daniel were only able to interpret the dreams because, in the language of the gentile kings, "the spirit of the holy gods" was in them (Gen 41:38 [רוּחַ אֱלֹהִים]; cf. Dan 2:11; 4:5[8], 15[18]). Their access to God's wisdom came from God himself, and God's wisdom was made available to the gentile kings through them.

The accounts of Joseph before Pharaoh in Gen 41 and Daniel before Nebuchadnezzar in Dan 2 reveal a God who bothers to communicate to gentile kings. In their respective contexts, the accounts each show the sovereignty of

---

120. Longman, *Daniel*, 77. Such an affinity between the gentile religions and Israel's religion likely also made the accounts more palatable to a Jewish audience, well-versed in God's view of the divination arts.

Karel van der Toorn considers it unusual for a royal courtier to be proficient in dream interpretation, and here the accounts of Daniel "seem to depart from the customs at the Assyrian and Babylonian courts. Although a Neo-Assyrian prayer to the sun-god speaks of the oneiromancer (*šāʾilu*) explaining a dream to the king, there is no mention of oneiromancers among the court sages, nor does any of their letters deal with the interpretation of royal dreams. It is not beyond the realm of possibility that the interpretation of dreams belonged to the expertise of the *bārû* or the . . . *ḫarṭibu*, but even if this were the case, difficult dreams play a minor to non-existent role in their correspondence" ("Scholars at the Oriental Court: The Figure of Daniel against Its Mesopotamian Background," in *The Book of Daniel: Composition and Reception*, vol. 1, ed. John J. Collins and Peter W. Flint [Leiden; Boston: Brill, 2001], 41–42).

God and his establishment of his man in the foreign court. Through his servants in captivity, God put the mighty foreign kings on alert that they depended on him for their lives and their kingdoms. The God of Israel did not appear to have an earthly kingdom at the times of Joseph and Daniel, but he nonetheless demonstrated his superiority over the gentile kings (who found the dreams inscrutable), all other gods (whose diviners were stymied), and the future. This YHWH may not have *looked* like much during the heyday of Egypt or Babylon, but in fact, he was Lord of all the earth.

Considered together in the context of Israel's historical and geographical situation, the pair of accounts creates a paradigm for God's work among the nations. God reached out to foreign kings through the murky means of revelatory dreams in order to make himself known. Knowing that the collective knowledge of the empires' finest interpreters would prove inadequate, he had already positioned his faithful servants—with access to the "spirit of the holy gods"—to interpret and explain the dreams.

Lord of the King of Kings

The city of Babylon enters the biblical narrative in Gen 11,[121] rises to imperial prominence during the time of the prophets, fades from the scene after the sixth-century-BCE ascendency of Persian Cyrus, and reemerges near the end of the New Testament—first as a code word for "Rome" and then as a symbol for the whole wicked world that opposes God and oppresses Christ's church (1 Pet 5:13; Rev 14:8; 16:19; 17:5; 18:2, 10, 21). In the theology of biblical authors, Babylon was the quintessentially sinful city: proud, idolatrous, defiant against God, and brutal in its treatment of his people.

Nebuchadnezzar stands as the representative of this city and the agent of its wickedness. He is the king who plundered the Jerusalem temple, took God's people captive, and torched the holy city. He is the one who threatened to kill Daniel and his three friends. Yet, in a brow-furrowing biblical twist, he is also the one twice given the title—by God himself, no less—"king of kings." In the first instance, the prophet Ezekiel speaks the words of God about the king who would conquer the Phoenician city of Tyre (Ezek 26:7), and in the second, Daniel declares the divine interpretation of the king's dream, telling him he is the "king of kings" (Dan 2:37a).[122] For many

---

121. See on Dan 1:2 above.

122. Besides Jesus and Nebuchadnezzar, the only other bearer of the title "king of kings" in the Bible is Artaxerxes, who uses the title for himself in a letter to Ezra (Ezra 7:12; cf. 1 Tim 6:15; Rev 17:14; 19:16).

New Testament believers, this lofty title cues a mental soundtrack of Handel's "Hallelujah": "And he shall reign for ever and ever . . . king of kings, forever! and ever!" We thrill with the superlative praise, and we might also scratch our heads over the title used of Nebuchadnezzar. After all, there can be only *one* "king of kings," and that one is Jesus. Why would God call Nebuchadnezzar, of all people, "king of kings"?

Perhaps because God uses the character Nebuchadnezzar to teach an important truth about his eternal kingdom. In the book of Daniel, the statement that Nebuchadnezzar is the "king of kings" begins the interpretation of a dream in which the king was meant to learn that even his splendid kingdom was derived and temporary. He may have been great (and he was), but he was only great because a greater king—the Lord of kings—made him so. By the end of the interpretation, the king sounds like he has heard the message—"Surely, as for your god, he is god of gods and lord of kings and the revealer of mysteries" (2:47c)—but the fiery furnace of ch. 3 will quickly demonstrate that the message went in one ear and right out the other. The king's tree dream in Dan 4 will resume with greater force the message of ch. 2 until he recognizes his dependence on the Lord of kings for his life, sanity, and power.

This title, "king of kings," taken together with another title given to Nebuchadnezzar in the Old Testament gives us a fuller picture of human dominion. Three times the prophet Jeremiah, speaking the words of YHWH, refers to Nebuchadnezzar as "my servant," putting the Babylonian despot in the same biblical company as Abraham, Jacob, Moses, David, and the prophets of Israel (Jer 25:9; 27:6; 43:10).[123] One scholar summarizes: "In the Hebrew Bible, there is no better company conceivable than these; at the same time, there is no candidate less likely for this title of honour than the Babylonian king Nebuchadnezzar."[124] The prophet Habakkuk famously questioned God's choice of Nebuchadnezzar as the cure for the sin that ailed Judah (Hab 1:12–2:1). Nonetheless the clear testimony of the Old Testament is that Nebuchadnezzar was chosen by YHWH to carry out a task in his universal plan—namely, to punish God's people and other nations of the world (Jer 46:25–26; cf. Ezra 5:12; Jer 21:7; Dan 1:2; 9:4–14). As the servant of YHWH, Nebuchadnezzar was "actually no more than a slave to the God of Israel, the nation that had been utterly defeated by him." [125] There was no reason to fear him; the one to fear was Nebuchadnezzar's master, YHWH.

---

123. Jeremiah 7:25 (the prophets); 30:10 (Jacob/Israel); 33:21 (David). Throughout the Old Testament, the appellation "my servant," referring to YHWH's servant, is used for Abraham (Gen 26:24), Moses (Num 12:7), Caleb (Num 14:24), Job (Job 1:8), Isaiah (Isa 20:3), Eliakim (Isa 22:20), Israel (Isa 41:8), Zerubbabel (Hag 2:23), and the coming Branch (Zech 3:8). "His servant" is used for Ahijah (1 Kgs 14:18), Elijah (2 Kgs 9:36), and Jonah (2 Kgs 14:25).

124. Klaas A. D. Smelik, "My Servant Nebuchadnezzar: The Use of the Epithet 'My Servant' for the Babylonian King Nebuchadnezzar in the Book of Jeremiah," *VT* 64 (2014), 112.

125. Smelik, "My Servant Nebuchadnezzar," 133.

When YHWH calls Nebuchadnezzar "king of kings," he reminds us that all power—even that of his greatest enemies—is derived power. When he calls him "my servant," he reminds us that every king and authority answers to someone greater than themselves. The eternal throne, power, and dominion belong to Jesus—a kingdom that began two thousand years ago with the birth of a baby in a lowly Bethlehem manger. But because that kingdom lacked the luster first-century Jews were looking for in their expected messiah, most people did not recognize God in their midst. They expected destruction of their enemies, restoration of his people, and a righteous rule over the whole earth forever. They expected power and great glory. Instead, they got an itinerant teacher from Nazareth ("Can anything good come from there?" John 1:46) who told stories comparing God's kingdom to small mustard seeds and slow-growing yeast, neither of which sounded very impressive (Matt 13:31–33).

The eternal kingdom had come with Jesus—the powers of the reigning prince shattered by his death and resurrection—but it began as the smallest of seeds in the womb of the virgin, and its growth through the body of Christ, the church, in the two millennia since has been slow, sometimes even stunted. We still await the full realization of Christ's glorious kingdom when, as the Lord and King of the king of kings, he will bring in the fullness of his reign by destroying every enemy: "Fallen! Fallen is Babylon the Great . . . never to be found again" (Rev 18:2, 21). Until that day, though, that kingship and lordship are far from evident: "Human rulers often flout God's laws and seem to have things entirely their own way." But for those who have eyes to see, there are signs of the kingdom at work in and through God's people.[126]

---

126. Lucas, *Daniel*, 80.

Daniel 3:1a–30

B. Narrative 2: *God's Superior Power and His Servants' Faithfulness*

Main Idea of Narrative 2 (3:1a–30)

Nebuchadnezzar makes a grand show of his power in Dan 3, demanding the allegiance of his subjects and challenging any god to deliver those who would defy him. The God of Shadrach, Meshach, and Abednego responds to the overweening king by delivering his faithful servants from the fiery furnace in spectacular fashion after they refuse to bow to the king's image and worship his gods. The Most High's superior power and the devotion of three Judean exiles to him in the face of certain death impress the king.

Literary Context of Narrative 2 (3:1a–30)

Daniel 3 is the second of six Aramaic chapters in the book. It is second in a series of five consecutive narratives about encounters between the Judean exiles and gentile kings (chs. 2–6). Like ch. 2, ch. 3 has its context among royal courtiers and the Babylonian king Nebuchadnezzar. Unlike the other four encounters with gentile kings in the Aramaic chiasm (chs. 2–7), ch. 3 features Shadrach, Meshach, and Abednego—the three Judean youth taken captive with Daniel in ch. 1. They also appeared in ch. 2 when Daniel asked his friends to pray for God's mercy (2:17–18), but Daniel is not part of their story in ch. 3.

As part of the chiasm of chs. 2–7, Dan 3 stands parallel with the account of Daniel's clash with Darius and his officials in ch. 6, and together these two sections illustrate how God's people should live under gentile rulers, whether those rulers are hostile to religious and cultural differences (as in Dan 3) or sympathetic (as in Dan 6).

Daniel 3 is usually classified as a court story, and specifically a court conflict.[1] The three men—Shadrach, Meshach, and Abednego—had been promoted (2:49) in the kingdom, and in this chapter, their rivals seize an opportunity to accuse them of treason. They are found guilty, but ultimately they are vindicated and receive an even greater promotion (3:30). Because the story involves a religious offense and not simply a political one, Goldingay notes that it may also qualify as a "confessor legend," in which heroes of faith defy a royal edict and face execution, because obeying the edict "would mean contravening a fundamental aspect of their religious commitment." In this particular story, the king himself investigates them and offers another opportunity to obey, "but he thereby only provides them with a chance to make their confession before the king himself, despite the reiterated threat of death. The penalty is duly exacted."[2]

> II. Macro Unit 2: The Superiority of God and His Kingdom (2:1a–7:28d)
>   A. Narrative 1: God's Superior Knowledge and His Eternal Kingdom (2:1a–49c)
> → **B. Narrative 2: God's Superior Power and His Servants' Faithfulness (3:1a–30)**
>   C. Narrative 3: A Humbled King and His Restored Power (3:31a–4:34e[4:1a–37e])
>   D. Narrative 4: A Humbled King and His Rescinded Power (5:1a–6:1[5:31])
>   E. Narrative 5: God's Superior Law and His Servant's Faithfulness (6:2a–29[1a–28])
>   F. Narrative 6: God's Superior King and Eternal Kingdom (7:1a–28d)

1. Nebuchadnezzar's First Display of Power (3:1a–7d)

Main Idea of the Passage

Daniel 3:1–7 puts a pompous Nebuchadnezzar on display, showcasing his disproportionate perception of his own power and setting him up to encounter the God who has even greater power.

---

1. See further the Literary Context of the Macro Unit (pp. 79–80) and the introduction (p. 25).

2. Goldingay, *Daniel*, 227.

Literary Context

Daniel 3:1–7 is the opening section of the narrative that comprises ch. 3. As such, it functions in at least three ways in its broader literary context. First, it draws from ch. 2's statue dream and the position of Nebuchadnezzar as the head of gold to create a context for the narrator's portrayal of Nebuchadnezzar in ch. 3—both in his construction of a golden image and in his own inflated self-perception. Second, it sets up the conflict of ch. 3, which will not be explicit until the second and third sections (3:8–12 and 13–18). The order to bow down to an image anticipates the possibility that someone will violate the king's order and face the threatened consequence. A third function of the opening section is introducing several words and phrases that will be repeated throughout this chapter and contribute to its key themes.

> B. Narrative 2: God's Superior Power and His Servants' Faithfulness (3:1a–30)
> → **1. Nebuchadnezzar's First Display of Power (3:1a–7d)**
> 2. The Accusation against God's Servants (3:8a–12f)
> 3. The Confrontation between the King and God's Servants (3:13a–18e)
> 4. Nebuchadnezzar's Second Display of Power (3:19a–20d)
> 5. God's Power in the Fiery Furnace (3:21a–25g)
> 6. Nebuchadnezzar's Response to God's Superior Power (3:26a–30)

Translation and Exegetical Outline

(See pages 143–44.)

Structure and Literary Form

The second narrative of the book's Aramaic chiasm (chs. 2–7[3]) opens with King Nebuchadnezzar's construction and dedication of a golden image (3:1–7).

---

3. For the significance of this chiastic structure, see further the introduction (pp. 31–35).

Daniel 3:1a–7d

B. Narrative 2: God's Superior Power and His Servant's Faithfulness (Dan 3:1a–30)

1. Nebuchadnezzar's First Display of Power (3:1a–7d)

   a. The Image of Gold (3:1a–d)

1a	Nebuchadnezzar the king made an image of gold;
1b	its height was sixty cubits;
1c	its breadth was six cubits.
1d	He set it up in the plain of Dura in the province of Babylon.

   b. The Dedication (3:2a–d)

2a	Then Nebuchadnezzar the king sent
2b	to assemble the satraps, the prefects and the governors, the counselors, the treasurers, the judges, the magistrates, and all the high officials of the province
2c	to come to the dedication of the image,
2d	which Nebuchadnezzar the king had set up.

   c. The Assembly (3:3a–d)

3a	Then the satraps, the prefects and the governors, the counselors, the treasurers, the judges, the magistrates, and all the high officials of the province were assembling for the dedication of the image,
3b	which Nebuchadnezzar the king had set up,
3c	and they were standing before the image,
3d	which Nebuchadnezzar had set up.

Continued on next page.

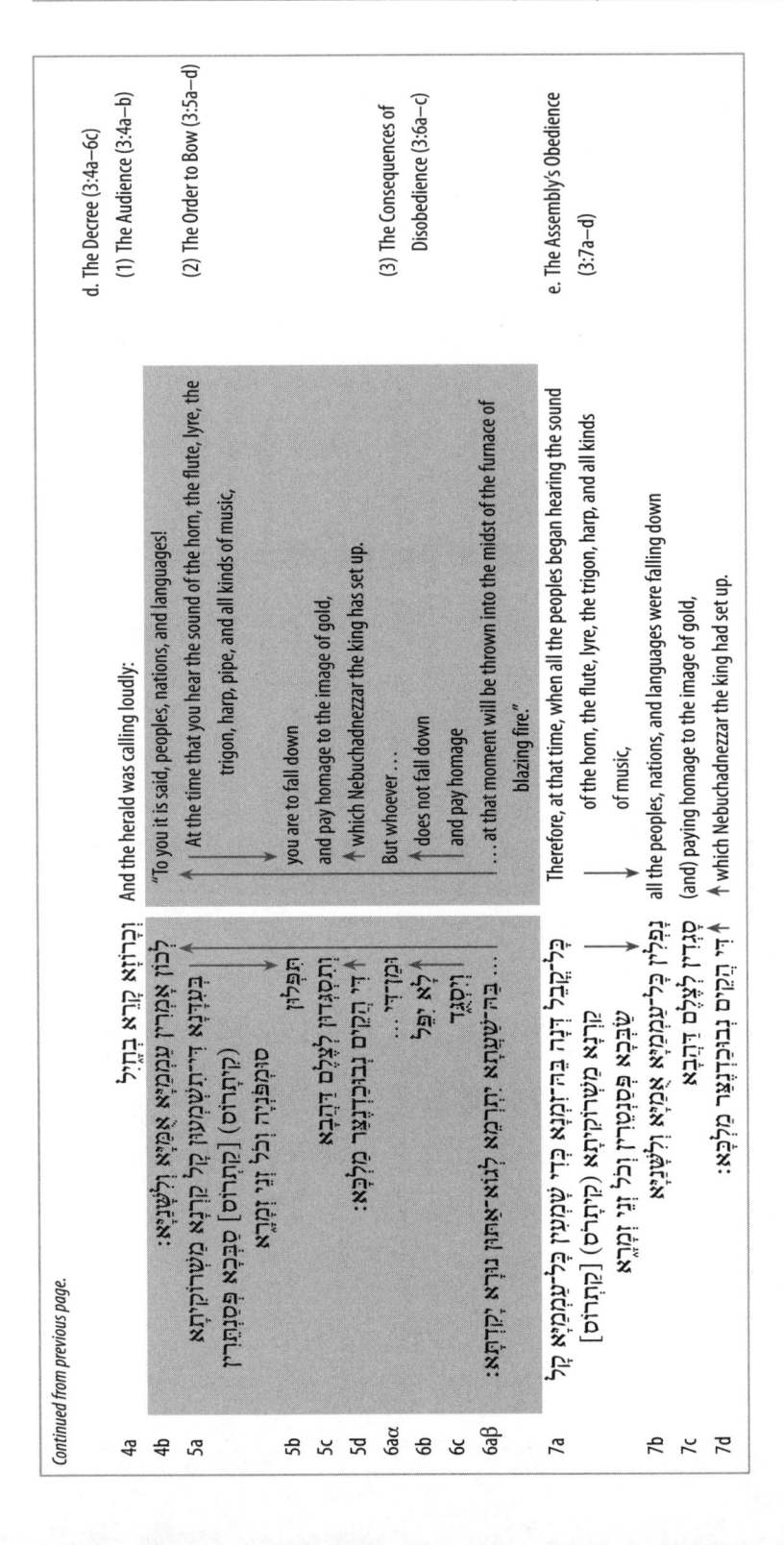

Macro Unit 2: The Superiority of God and His Kingdom

Continued from previous page.

d. The Decree (3:4a–6c)

(1) The Audience (3:4a–b)

4a And the herald was calling loudly:

4b "To you it is said, peoples, nations, and languages!

(2) The Order to Bow (3:5a–d)

5a At the time that you hear the sound of the horn, the flute, lyre, the trigon, harp, pipe, and all kinds of music,

5b you are to fall down

5c and pay homage to the image of gold,

5d which Nebuchadnezzar the king has set up.

6aα But whoever . . .

6b does not fall down

6c and pay homage

(3) The Consequences of Disobedience (3:6a–c)

6aβ . . . at that moment will be thrown into the midst of the furnace of blazing fire."

e. The Assembly's Obedience (3:7a–d)

7a Therefore, at that time, when all the peoples began hearing the sound of the horn, the flute, lyre, the trigon, harp, and all kinds of music,

7b all the peoples, nations, and languages were falling down

7c (and) paying homage to the image of gold,

7d which Nebuchadnezzar the king had set up.

Through the use of repetition, the narrator makes this image (צְלֵם) and the king's act of erecting it (דִּי הֲקֵים נְבוּכַדְנֶצַּר מַלְכָּא, "which Nebuchadnezzar the king set up," 3:2d, 3b, 5d, 7d; cf. 3:3d, 12e–f, 14e–f, 18d–e) tower over the first three sections of the narrative (3:1–7, 8–12, 13–18) before bringing to the fore the blazing furnace, the defiant faithfulness of Shadrach, Meshach, and Abednego, and the power of Israel's God in the final three sections (3:19–20, 21–25, and 26–30).

This first section, 3:1–7, begins with four independent clauses describing the king's image (צְלֵם, 3:1), including its material (gold, 3:1a), its height (sixty cubits, 3:1b), its breadth (six cubits, 3:1c), and its place of installation (on the plain of Dura, 3:1d). This description is followed by two subsections that echo each other (3:2 and 3:3). In the first (3:2), the narrator reports that the king issued an invitation to the dedication of the statue and then lists eight different groups of recipients. In the second (3:3), the narrator repeats the list in his report that all the invitees assembled for the dedication.

In the section's only instance of reported speech (3:4–6), the narrator gives voice to the herald who directed the assembled masses. The herald's statement includes the king's order to the crowd (3:5) and the announcement of the punishment that would result in the event of disobedience (3:6). The section concludes with the report that the assembled masses obeyed the order (3:7).

Two noteworthy narrative features that characterize ch. 3 are the repetition of several key phrases and lengthy lists. Both features are evident in this first section. The narrator introduces and repeats two lengthy lists: the first is the list of officials summoned to the dedication of the image ("the satraps, the prefects and the governors, the counselors, the treasurers, the judges, the magistrates, and all the high officials of the province," 3:2b and 3a; cf. 3:27b); the second is the list of musical instruments played at the dedication ("the horn, the flute, lyre, the trigon, harp, pipe, and all kinds of music," 3:5a and 3:7a, with a slight variation; cf. also 3:10c, 15b). A smaller list that occurs twice in this first section and then once in the final section is "peoples, nations, and languages" (3:4b, 7b, 29bα[4]). Words and phrases that this first section introduces and that are then repeated through much of the chapter include צְלֵם, "image" (3:1a, 2c, 3a, 3c, 5c, 7c, 10d, 12eα, 14eα, 15d, 18dα; cf. 19b); דִּי הֲקֵים נְבוּכַדְנֶצַּר מַלְכָּא, "which Nebuchadnezzar the king set up" (3:2d, 3b, 5d, 7d; cf. 3:3d, 12e–f, 14e–f, 18d–e); and אַתּוּן נוּרָא יָקִדְתָּא, "the furnace of blazing fire" (3:6aβ, 11aβ, 15g, 17d, 20d, 21b, 23a, 26a).

The repetition of key words or phrases, as well as the use and repetition of lengthy lists, is intentional and even integral to the narrator's purposes. At the surface level, this repetition lends a "resonant and rhythmic quality"[5] to the story and so invites audience participation and engagement. The predictability that results from such

---

4. The list in 3:29bα has singular nouns, whereas in v. 4b and v. 7b the nouns are plural.

5. Peter W. Coxon, "The 'List' Genre and Narrative Style in the Court Tales of Daniel," *JSOT* 35 (1986): 108, 110.

repetition makes the story fun to hear and easy to remember.[6] Further, the words and phrases targeted for repetition drive a key theme of the narrative: the foolishness of idolatry and those who engage in it.

At a deeper level, the repetition of the lengthy lists of administrators and instruments may be part of a satirical portrayal of pagan culture and behavior. In the events of Dan 3, the lists appear in the narrator's report of the king's command and in the subsequent obedience of his subjects, creating the impression that the king spoke and everyone mindlessly obeyed.[7] In his article about the function of the lists in Dan 3, Hector Avalos contends that the repetition of these lists is comedic and satirical "because it serves to expose the mechanistic and thoughtless behavior of the pagan worshippers, of the pagan government bureaucracy in particular, and because it elicits laughter in the process."[8] The bureaucracy of Nebuchadnezzar's Babylon appears to be a machine with unthinking subjects.

Taken together, the thematic repetition of key words, phrases, and lists associated with the king's administration may create a comedic portrayal of idolatry and those who participate in it—beginning with the king. Nebuchadnezzar may take himself very seriously, but we are laughing at him.[9]

---

6. Consider the repetition in children's stories like the "Three Little Pigs" and "Goldilocks and the Three Bears." In oral stories, such repetition contributes to memorability; in written stories, the predictability of the text assists early readers. In both, the repetition increases engagement and entertainment.

7. This mechanical obedience highlights the nonconformist actions of Shadrach, Meshach, and Abednego. Avalos notes, "The main source of the satire [in Dan 3] stems from the contrast between the mechanistic and automatic behavior of the pagans and the assertive and pious behavior of Shadrach, Meshach, and Abednego" (Hector I. Avalos, "The Comedic Function of the Enumerations of Officials and Instruments in Daniel 3," *CBQ* 53 (1991): 584.

8. Avalos bases his analysis of lists in Dan 3 on a view of comedy set forth by Henri Bergson. Avalos summarizes Bergson: "Bergson argued that simple mechanical iteration is a great source of comedy. When humans act as automatons or in an absentminded manner, they become subjects of comedy." Noting Bergson's emphasis on the social significance of comedy, namely "provoking laughter in social critique," Avalos says the word "satire" is a good way "to convey Bergson's ideas about the role of laughter in social critique" ("The Comedic Function of the Enumerations of Officials and Instruments in Daniel 3," 582).

9. Commentators see varying degrees of significance in the narrator's use of repetition. For example, in Goldingay's first edition of his Daniel commentary, he noted, "Several of the repetitions convey a humorous, mocking impression for the modern Western reader, and thus heighten a sense of satire about the story, but it is doubtful if they had this significance for the author and his readers (cf. the repetitions as a stylistic feature in Gen 1)" (*Daniel* [1989], 68). In his revised edition, he appears to concede that humor may underlie the repetition after all: "Repetition need not suggest mockery or humor . . . , but in this story several of the repetitions do convey a humorous, mocking impression, and thus heighten a sense of satire about the story. It is a 'parody of this ruthless king'" (*Daniel*, 229; citing David M. Gunn and Danna Nolan Fewell, "Nebuchadnezzar and the Three Jews," in *Narrative in the Hebrew Bible*, Oxford Bible Series [Oxford: Oxford University Press, 1993], 175). I think the significance of the repetition is evident in at least two ways: (1) what the repetition highlights—namely, the image and Nebuchadnezzar's act of setting it up; and (2) the chapter's relationship to Isaiah's portrayal of idolatry in Isa 44:9–20 and his assurance in 42:18–43:13 that YHWH is a God who delivers. See further below The Folly of Idolatry, pp. 189–91.

Explanation of the Text

a. The Image of Gold (3:1a–d)

Chapter 3 begins without a date formula (cf. 1:1; 2:1; 7:1; 8:1; 9:1; 10:1)[10] and without any transitional marker such as בֵּאדַיִן or אֱדַיִן, "then" (cf., Dan 2:14, 35, 46; 3:3, 13, 19, 21, 26, 30). Without a discernible break[11] it follows the narrative in ch. 2 of Nebuchadnezzar's dream about a magnificent multilayered metallic statue (2:31–33), a statue in which the king was represented as the head of gold (2:38). In this literary context, Nebuchadnezzar makes an image of gold. Whether the king's dream actually caused his image-making of ch. 3 is impossible to know, but regardless of the historical circumstances, the textual proximity of the two stories represents a narrative choice: by placing one seamlessly after the other, the narrator invites us to relate the two accounts.[12] When we read in 3:1a that "Nebuchadnezzar the king made an image of gold," we should have in our minds all the associations of the king's image in ch. 2:

> You, O king, were looking, and oh! One great statue—that image was great and its splendor was surpassing—was standing before you, and its appearance was frightening. That statue—its head was of fine gold, its chest and its arms were of silver, its belly and its thighs were of bronze, its legs were of iron; as for its feet, they were partly of iron and partly of clay. . . . You, O king, are the king of kings, to whom the God of Heaven has given the kingdom, the power, and the strength, and the honor. And wherever they may dwell, the sons of man, the beast of the field, and the birds of heaven he has given into your hand, and he made you to rule over all of them. You are the head of gold (2:31–33, 37–38).

We are justified in thinking as we begin the account in ch. 3 that the king who dreamed about a magnificent statue and his glorious position as the golden head is making an even more magnificent image (that is, a statue that is all gold instead of just topped with gold[13]) to display his greatness.[14]

The building and installation of statues were common in the ancient Mesopotamian world. Assyrian kings erected their likenesses to symbolize the extent of their dominion, and some later

---

10. The Greek versions begin Dan 3:1 with "in the eighteenth year." This date (586 BCE) matches the time frame of Jer 52:29, which reports the main deportation of Judean prisoners to Babylon. The date is likely inauthentic in Daniel; the Greek translators perhaps wanted to draw on another "repressive action by the king" to set up the events of Dan 3 (Collins, *Daniel*, 180).

11. Chapter divisions in the Bible were not developed until the Middle Ages, though our earliest manuscripts do indicate verse and paragraph breaks. There is a paragraph break between Dan 2 and Dan 3, but there are similar paragraph breaks within both chapters (e.g., after 2:45 and 3:23). Daniel 3 and the next three chapters all begin without temporal markers or date formulae.

12. Commentators since at least the time of Hippolytus (ca. AD 230) have suggested that Nebuchadnezzar's inspiration for his image was his dream in ch. 2. This is possible, but it is impossible to know historically, and the narrator does not explicitly connect the two events.

13. It is possible that the king's statue was solid gold, but more likely, it was gold-plated (cf. gold-plated items of the tabernacle, Exod 25–27; 30; cf. also 1 Kgs 6:20–35).

14. Pace suggests the juxtaposition of Dan 2 and Dan 3 invites an "appropriate comparison"—that the king built a statue covered entirely with gold when the statue in his dream had only a gold head "suggest[s] Nebuchadnezzar's defiance" and "portrays a king who learns nothing" from God's revelation in ch. 2 (*Daniel*, 89–90). Chapter 4 will follow this idea to its conclusion.

Hellenistic kings who deified themselves set up statues of themselves.[15] In Babylon, kings were not deified, but Nebuchadnezzar could well have made a statue representing his god. However, the narrator of Dan 3 chooses not to tell us *what* the king's image was. Whether it was of the king himself or of his god is ultimately irrelevant since we learn later that bowing before it indicated worship of Nebuchadnezzar's god(s) (3:12, 14).[16]

We can speculate what the king's image represented but focusing on this question misses the narrator's emphases. In two independent (verbless) clauses that follow the initial main clause in 3:1a, the narrator offers the measurements of the image (3:1b–c). Given the sparseness of description generally in biblical narrative, this information is noteworthy. If the narrator simply wanted us to know the image was immense and impressive, he could have echoed the description in ch. 2 and said the image was "great and its splendor was surpassing . . . and its appearance was frightening" (2:31). Instead, we first learn the height of the image: sixty cubits (90 feet), roughly the height of a ten-story building. The largest known statue in the ancient world, one of the Seven Wonders of the Ancient World, was the 105-foot-high bronze Colossus of Rhodes erected in 280 BCE. In terms of modern statues, the statue of Thomas Jefferson in the Jefferson Memorial in Washington, D.C. stands a mere nineteen feet tall, and Abraham Lincoln, were he to rise from his chair in the Lincoln Memorial, would only be twenty-eight feet tall. Copper Lady Liberty rises to 151 feet without her pedestal. Nebuchadnezzar's ninety-foot golden edifice is plenty tall to be considered great and of surpassing splendor.

In the third clause (3:1c), however, the narrator gives the width of the king's towering golden image: six cubits, or nine feet. At this point, the narrator's description might produce a grimace instead of inspiring awe: a man or god represented by a ninety-by-nine-foot statue would be incredibly tall and thin, even "abnormal and grotesque"[17]—a ninety-foot statue symbolizing an average sized man should be at least twenty feet wide.[18] It is possible the narrator exaggerated the statue's proportions to create a "satirical portrayal of paganism in this chapter,"[19] but in the literary context of the magnificent image of ch. 2, it is also possible the narrator means to poke fun at the king's perception of his own greatness.[20]

This self-aggrandizing act of the king is prefaced in 3:1a by overspecification of the main character: נְבוּכַדְנֶצַּר מַלְכָּא, "Nebuchadnezzar the king." Given that there is no definitive break between the dream

---

15. Collins discusses reports of numerous huge statues in the ancient world, including "those of Herodotus (1.183) concerning 'a sitting figure of Zeus, all of gold,' in the temple of Bel in Babylon and 'a figure of a man, twelve cubits high, entirely of solid gold,' in the same temple in the time of Cyrus. Diodorus (2.9) tells of three gold statues on top of the temple of Bel, one of which, representing Zeus, was forty feet high and weighed one thousand Babylonian talents. In the Seleucid period there was a huge statue of Apollo at Daphnae that was a copy of Phidias's statue of Zeus at Olympia" (*Daniel*, 180).

16. Goldingay notes that even if the image was that of Nebuchadnezzar, falling before it would imply acknowledgment of the king's god, just as Nebuchadnezzar's falling before Daniel after his interpretation of the dream (2:46) implied acknowledgment of Daniel's God (*Daniel*, 232). He also notes that the text's silence on what the statue represented "reflects its concern with the challenge it issued to the three Judahites and reflects the interwovenness and support of god, king, and nation" (*Daniel*, 232).

17. Lucas, *Daniel*, 89.

18. It is possible that the image constructed by the king consisted of an obelisk-like pedestal with a much smaller figure atop it; in this case, it would not be as disproportionate as the text implies (see, e.g., Ernest C. Lucas, "Daniel," in *ZIBBC:OT* 4, ed. John H. Walton [Grand Rapids: Zondervan, 2009], 536).

19. Lucas, *Daniel*, 89.

20. This seems even more likely given the story that follows in ch. 4—that is, the humbling of Nebuchadnezzar, who failed to learn the lesson of his dependence on the sovereign God of Israel. There is a thematic emphasis in the book of Daniel on the pride of human kings and God's responses to them.

account of Dan 2 and the image-making account of Dan 3 (see p. 147n14 above), no specification is required to identify the intended referent. Nebuchadnezzar was last mentioned by name in 2:46 and subsequently referred to as "the king" three times in 2:47–49. The overspecification here and throughout the chapter (i.e., 3:2a, 2d, 3b, 5d, 7d, 9a, 24a) casts Nebuchadnezzar in a negative light[21]—that is, he appears to think a bit too much of his royal power (see especially 3:15h–i and cf. 3:28c–e, 29e–g). In this first clause of the chapter, the narrator highlights a key theme of the chapter.

Thus the introductory verse of the chapter establishes what is most important to understanding the narrative that follows. What matters is that Nebuchadnezzar the king made this image and set it up. The statue, first mentioned here, is mentioned in nine more verses and always in some variation of "the image which Nebuchadnezzar the king set up" (צַלְמָא דִּי הֲקֵים נְבוּכַדְנֶצַּר מַלְכָּא; 3:2, 3, 5, 7, 10, 12, 14, 15, 18). The narrator offers no explicit motivation for the king's actions, nor does he provide the timing of the events that follow.[22] In the literary context, the concern of the narrator is that the reader bring impressions from ch. 2 into the reading of ch. 3.[23] In ch. 2, the king dreamed about a magnificent statue; in ch. 3, that king erects a statue that might, at first blush, appear more magnificent. However, upon closer examination, it portrays the disproportionate self-perception of the great king.[24] In both chapters, the God of Israel reveals himself to the gentile king: in ch. 2, Nebuchadnezzar sees a God who reveals mysteries, a God with wisdom that surpasses that of his gods; in ch. 3, he will discover a God with more power than any of his gods (3:15h–i, 28c–e, 29e–g).

b. The Dedication (3:2a–d)

After the image was made and installed, "Nebuchadnezzar the king" gave orders (3:2a–b) that his administrators attend a dedication ceremony. This second instance of overspecification of the king's name and title in as many verses (3:2a; cf. 3:1a) reinforces the impression from 3:1 that Nebuchadnezzar appears to think a bit too much of his royal power—a key theme of the chapter (3:1a, 2a, 2d, 3b, 5d, 7d, 9a, 24a; cf. 3:15h–i, 28c–e, 29e–g).

The narrator identifies seven types of summoned officials and probably lists them in order by rank.[25] The list, repeated verbatim in 3:3a and later in an adapted form (3:27), serves at least two purposes in the narrative. First, the litany of officials gives the impression that everyone who was anyone in

---

21. Runge and Westbury, *LDHB: Introduction*, 2.1. Overspecification.

22. See p. 147n10 above for the time frame and possible motivation of the Greek versions. Another common suggestion is that the erection and dedication of the image occurred early in the reign of Nebuchadnezzar and served to determine loyalty to the new administration. In this case, Walvoord summarizes the situation well: "The worship of the image was intended to be an expression of political solidarity and loyalty to Nebuchadnezzar rather than an intended act of persecution" (John Walvoord, *Daniel: The Key to Prophetic Revelation* [Chicago: Moody Press, 1971], 82). Goldingay proposes that the king was motivated by a desire to "consolidate the empire that the dream [of ch. 2] threatened" (*Daniel*, 231). Whatever the historical circumstances behind the statue, enough time has passed for Shadrach, Meshach, and Abednego—Judean "youth" (יְלָדִים) of

1:4, 17—to be described as "men" (גֻּבְרִין) in ch. 3 (vv. 12, 13, 21, 23, 24, 25, 27).

23. An additional relevant link between chs. 2 and 3 is the language used to describe Nebuchadnezzar's decree that attendees fall down and pay homage (תִּפְּלוּן וְתִסְגְּדוּן, 3:5b–c) to the image and the language in ch. 2's description of Nebuchadnezzar's response to Daniel (נְפַל עַל־אַנְפּוֹהִי וּלְדָנִיֵּאל סְגִד, 2:46a–b), who was representative of his God.

24. Nebuchadnezzar's greatness is not in question in the text; he is the head of gold on whom God bestowed great authority and power (see Dan 2:37–39; 4:17–20[20–23]; 5:18–19). The king's problem is his failure to acknowledge that his power and greatness are derived and the gift of the God of Heaven (see Dan 4:29[32]; 5:20–21).

25. Takamitsu Muraoka, *A Biblical Aramaic Reader with an Outline Grammar* (Leuven: Peeters, 2015), 46.

the king's administration was summoned. Second, combined with the overspecification of "Nebuchadnezzar the king," the list hints at the power of the king: he has all these administrators at his beck and call.[26]

The purpose of the assembly was to dedicate "the image which Nebuchadnezzar the king had set up" (3:2c–d). The word חֲנֻכָּא, "dedication," and its root, חנך, refer to the inauguration or first use of something, which may imply that after this inaugural event, Nebuchadnezzar's image may have served an ongoing function in the king's administration.[27]

c. The Assembly (3:3a–d)

The response to the king's summons was that everyone showed up. The narrator lists the elite line-up again (cf. 3:2b) and says they were assembling for the dedication (מִתְכַּנְּשִׁין). It is grammatically possible to translate מִתְכַּנְּשִׁין in the reflexive ("the [officials] were assembling" [cf. NIV] or "were gathering" [cf. ESV]) or the passive ("the [officials] were being assembled" [cf. NASB]). One could argue that the passive "were being assembled" better fits the context of officials responding to a royal command,[28] but given the narrator's description of the officials' obedience with almost exactly the same words as Nebuchadnezzar's command, he may mean to imply blind obedience: when the king spoke, his subjects fell in line (see Structure and Literary Form above and cf. 3:7 below). Of the repetition here, Fewell notes, "The precise people whom he summons are the precise people who assemble. Thus, through repetition, the narrator pictures a setting in which conformity is normative, disobedience is unthinkable."[29]

The progressive action of the translation "were assembling" expresses the Aramaic participle. While participles in Aramaic (and in Hebrew) eventually fulfill functions of perfects and imperfects alike,[30] Cook observes that in the Aramaic of Daniel, and particularly in Dan 3, participles are also used to express "pluractional events"—that is, they are "used to convey the 'in progress' status of multiple telic events distributed across multiple participants."[31] In ch. 3 the narrator expresses such concurrent activity by using participles here in 3:3 and in 3:4: the officials are assembling

---

26. The list may also function as a link to ch. 6: "the formal list presentation corresponds admirably with the concentric structure of the Aramaic chapters of Daniel as pointed out originally by A. Lenglet and confirmed by J. J. Collins. According to this view ch. 3 corresponds to ch. 6; both chapters contain lists of officials" (Coxon, "The 'List' Genre and Narrative Style in the Court Tales of Daniel," 98–99).

27. The Aramaic word חֲנֻכָּה, "dedication," is the same as the Hebrew word, which is used for the dedication of the altar (Num 7:10–11, 84, 88; 2 Chr 7:9), the temple (Ps 30:1; cf. 1 Kgs 8:63), and the rebuilt wall in Jerusalem (Neh 12:27). The intertestamental period saw the birth of Hanukkah, from the same word, an annual feast commemorating the rededication of temple after its cleansing by Judas Maccabees (see John 10:22).

28. See, e.g., Li, *The Verbal System of the Aramaic Daniel*, 72.

29. Fewell, *Circle of Sovereignty*, 39. Similarly, Newsom observes that "although . . . an enormous number of individual preparations, journeys, acts of coordination, and so forth would have been entailed for the event to take place, all of this activity is hidden from view. Similarly, the actual time required is collapsed. All that remains is command and obedience" (*Daniel*, 106).

30. "Functionally, the participle in BA is further along than in BH in its 'take over' of functions abandoned by the perfect and imperfect verb. Notably, the participle is the preferred encoding of stative verbs to express present states and for performative expressions instead of the perfect. . . . The participle is more frequently employed than the imperfect to express progressive/imperfective aspect in the past, present, or future and is preferred to the imperfect for expressing generic or habitual events. These functional expansions vis-à-vis the perfect and imperfect can all be found incipient in the Hebrew of Qohelet" (Cook, *Aramaic Ezra and Daniel*, 10).

31. Cook, *Aramaic Ezra and Daniel*, 10.

(מִתְכַּנְּשִׁין, 3:3a) and standing (קָיְמִין, 3:3c) before the image, while the herald is calling out (קָרֵא, 3:4a) instructions.[32]

d. The Decree (3:4a–6c)

With the assembly present and standing before "the image, which Nebuchadnezzar had set up" (3:3c–d), the dedication ceremony is ready to begin. The narrator uses direct speech for the king's decree, delivered by the herald, who bellows to the assembled dignitaries. The adverbial בְּחַיִל, "with strength" or "loudly" (3:4a), contributes to the portrayal of Nebuchadnezzar's greatness and the pomp of these events: the herald must shout to the masses gathered on the plain of Dura.

The herald's speech begins with "to you [they] are saying" (לְכוֹן אָמְרִין), a prepositional phrase followed by an active participle that functions as an impersonal plural (i.e., there is no explicit subject) and so is best translated as a passive: "to you it is said" (3:4b). The circumlocution here reflects that the herald represents the king in what he is about to say.

Three vocatives follow the herald's opening statement: "peoples, nations, and languages" (3:4b). Vocatives can be used to identify or clarify who is being addressed, but often they are used to draw attention to the addressees and characterize how the speaker perceives them.[33] In the context of Dan 3:4, it is not necessary to identify the audience since we already know who is assembled and that the herald is addressing them. Instead, the use of the vocatives here indicates the speaker's perception of his audience. In this case, it is the king's perception since the herald speaks on behalf of the king. The king perceives his audience as "peoples, nations, and languages," a grandiose way to think about one's payroll, but this perception aligns with the narrator's portrait of a king with an inflated sense of himself. The king considers his power great and expansive.

The directions given by the herald consist of two parts, each beginning with its own frame of reference that is followed by the section's main clause(s). In these two sections, the herald gives the expected behavior (3:5) and then addresses what happens in the unlikely event someone did not conform (3:6). In the first section, a temporal frame (3:5a) sets the context for obedience: "at the time that you hear . . . all kinds of music."[34] Two main clauses then instruct the audience to fall down and pay homage to the image (3:5b–c). The second section begins with a topical frame (3:6aα–c) that creates a contrast ("but," 3:6aα) and draws attention to those who do not fall down and pay homage to the image (3:6b–c). Then the main clause of this second section informs the audience of the consequences of disobedience: being thrown into "the furnace of blazing fire" (3:6aβ)—another phrase that will be oft-repeated in the narrative to follow (3:11aβ, 15g, 17c, 20d, 21b, 23a, 26a). The information about the penalty for disobedience gives a dramatic flourish to all that has happened in the chapter thus far. It also spells out more clearly the conflict in the chapter. From the opening verse, we had an inkling that the king was up to no good with this image, and when the herald announced the expectation that all subjects bow before the image, his words confirmed our suspicions. But it is the announcement

---

32. See further on 3:7, 26–27 below.
33. Runge and Westbury, *LDHB: Introduction*, 2.3 Thematic Address.
34. The use of musical instruments was more than fanfare for ceremonial occasions; it was an integral component of worship in the ancient Near East. See further Coxon, "The 'List' Genre and Narrative Style in the Court Tales of Daniel," 95–121.

of the consequences for disobedience that brings the conflict into sharper focus: now we strongly suspect that *someone* is going to be thrown into the blazing furnace.[35]

In the narrator's telling of the herald's proclamation, he again overspecifies the image and the king (3:5d; cf. 3:2d, 3b, 3c). No one at the assembly needed to be told that the image was gold (3:5c) or that "Nebuchadnezzar the king" had set it up (3:5d). They could see it with their own eyes, and they were at the dedication by order of the king. There are two effects of the overspecification in the proclamation representing the voice of the king. First, by drawing attention to the golden appearance of the statue, the king boasts about the magnificent nature of what he has made.[36] Second, by referring to himself as "Nebuchadnezzar the king" to a group of royal administrators, he asserts his power over them. By comparison, imagine a company meeting at which the CEO says, "Every employee needs to complete this survey, which I, the CEO, have distributed." The meaning is clear: "You will do this because I have power over you." In the context of Dan 3, the effect is obvious: Bow or else.

e. The Assembly's Obedience (3:7a–d)

The final subsection of Dan 3:1a–7d reports the response of the assembly to the proclamation of the herald, beginning with a reason/result phrase: כָּל־קֳבֵל דְּנָה, "therefore" (3:7a). In language that echoes the command, the narrator relates that כָּל־עַמְמַיָּא אֻמַּיָּא וְלִשָּׁנַיָּא, "all the peoples, nations, and languages" (3:7b; cf. 3:4b), were falling down and paying homage to the king's golden image when the music started.[37] The near verbatim report suggests that the assembled group followed the king's orders exactly. The repetition in 3:7 as well as throughout the first section (3:1–7) has a comedic function according to Avalos: "as soon as the instruments sound, the pagans genuflect en masse before a lifeless image without a second thought. In effect, the iteration of enumerations helps to portray those pagans as a version of Pavlov's dog."[38]

The opening section of the ch. 3 narrative (3:1–7) puts in place the elements that will shape the chapter: the king's pride, the towering but garish golden image, the automatic obedience of the royal officials, and the hint that not all will obey so willingly.

---

35. While the fiery furnace may strike us as an extreme form of punishment, burning is a known method of execution in Babylon (cf. Jer 29:22). A thousand years earlier in his famous law code, Babylonian Hammurabi mandated the same fate for those who committed a variety of crimes.

36. Given the ghastly proportions of the statue (see on 3:1), one can imagine there were more suppressed snickers in the audience than murmurs of awe.

37. Note the use of another "plurational event" expressed by participles: שָׁמְעִין, "began hearing" (v. 7a); נָפְלִין, "were falling down" (v. 7b); סָגְדִין, "were paying homage" (v. 7c). Cf. on 3:3 above.

38. Avalos, "The Comedic Function of the Enumerations of Officials and Instruments in Daniel 3," 585. See further above, "Structure and Literary Form."

2. The Accusation against God's Servants (3:8a–12f)

Main Idea of the Passage

Daniel 3:8–12 reveals both the identity of those who did not bow before the king's statue and the character of those who accuse them.

Literary Context

Daniel 3:8–12 is the second section of the narrative that comprises ch. 3. It follows the king's order to bow before the golden image or face the consequences and the subsequent report that "all the peoples, nations, and languages" obeyed (3:7b). This second section functions in at least two ways in its broader literary context. First, it furthers the plot by identifying "certain Jews" (3:12a) who have not conformed to the king's orders and thus may face the fiery furnace. Second, it introduces a new group of Chaldeans (cf. Dan 2:2, 4), enemies of the Jews in ch. 3, and it offers insight into their motivation and character.

> B. Narrative 2: God's Superior Power and His Servants' Faithfulness (3:1a–30)
>   1. Nebuchadnezzar's First Display of Power (3:1a–7d)
> → **2. The Accusation against God's Servants (3:8a–12f)**
>   3. The Confrontation between the King and God's Servants (3:13a–18e)
>   4. Nebuchadnezzar's Second Display of Power (3:19a–20d)
>   5. God's Power in the Fiery Furnace (3:21a–25g)
>   6. Nebuchadnezzar's Response to God's Superior Power (3:26a–30)

Translation and Exegetical Outline

(See pages 154.)

Daniel 3:8a–12f

		2. The Accusation against God's Servants (3:8a–12f)
8a	Therefore, at that time, certain Chaldeans came forward	a. The Summary (3:8a–b)
8b	and accused the Jews.	
9a	They answered, saying to Nebuchadnezzar the king,	b. The Setup (3:9a–11c)
9b	"O king, live forever.	(1) Addressing the King (3:9a–b)
10a	You, O king, made a decree	(2) Repeating the Decree (3:10a–11c)
10bα	that every man …	
10c	← who hears the sound of the horn, the flute, lyre, the trigon, harp, and pipe, and all kinds of music	
10bβ	… should fall down	
10d	and pay homage to the image of gold.	
11aα	But whoever …	
11b	← does not fall down	
11c	and pay homage	
11aβ	… will be thrown into the midst of the furnace of blazing fire.	
12a	There are certain Jews	c. The Accusation (3:12a–f)
12b	← whom you appointed over the administration of the province of Babylon—Shadrach, Meshach, and Abednego.	
12c	These men have not paid attention to you, O king.	
12d	Your gods they do not serve,	
12eα	and the image of gold …	
12f	← which you have set up	
12eβ	… they are not paying homage to."	

Structure and Literary Form

The second section of the narrative in ch. 3 (3:8a–12f) comprises two primary components: an introduction of the Chaldeans who will oppose the three Judean exiles, Shadrach, Meshach, and Abednego (3:8), and their accusation against them to the king, set in reported speech (3:9–12). The reported speech includes two subsections: first, the Chaldeans' repetition of the king's decree and the consequences of disobedience (3:10–11; cf. 3:5–6), followed by identification of the Jews as violators of the king's order (3:12). The reported speech also features repetition of several key elements introduced in the first section: the list of instruments played at the dedication (3:10c; cf. 3:5a, 7a); the צְלֵם דַּהֲבָא, "image of gold," דִּי הֲקֵימְתָּ, "which you set up" (3:10d, 12e–f; cf. 3:1a, 1d, 2c–d, 3a–d, 5c–d, 7c–d); and אַתּוּן נוּרָא יָקִדְתָּא, "the furnace of blazing fire" (3:11aβ; cf. 3:6aβ). This speech develops the plot, but as reported speech, it also provides a window into the thoughts, interests, and motivations of the accusatory Chaldeans.[39]

Explanation of the Text

a. The Summary (3:8a–b)

Daniel 3:8, the first verse in the second section (3:8–12), begins in the same way that Dan 3:7 did: כָּל־קֳבֵל דְּנָה בֵּהּ־זִמְנָא, "Therefore, at that time." Some ancient versions of the text do not have כָּל־קֳבֵל דְּנָה, "therefore" (or "accordingly") at the beginning of 3:8,[40] and so, many commentators have questioned its appropriateness in the context and consider it a scribal error in the Aramaic.[41] But others consider it original to the Aramaic, a "carefully coordinated" linking of the two scenes' actions. Newsom observes that the coordinated temporal phrases (of 3:7 and 8) suggest that the opponents of the Jews "did not just happen to notice [their] actions . . . but had been intentionally watching them, presumably knowing that the Jews might not comply with the king's command (cf. Dan 6:11–12)."[42]

The title "Chaldeans" may indicate the Babylonian ethnicity of the accusers and so reflect their ethnic hostility toward the Jews, or it may be a professional title (as in ch. 2; see p. 89n13 there) and so indicate professional jealousy (as in ch. 6; see further there). The narrator's statement that the Chaldeans "accused" the Jews reflects a colorful Aramaic idiom: they "ate the pieces" of the Jews.

---

39. See ch. 1, n41.
40. E.g., Theodotion and the Syriac.
41. Specifically, it is considered dittography: the scribe inadvertently copied the phrase from the beginning of 3:7 when his eye skipped from the בֵּאּ־זִמְנָא in 3:7 to the same in 3:8. See, e.g., Lucas, *Daniel*, 84, and Collins, *Daniel*, 176–77. Goldingay accepted this hypothesis in his first edition ([1989], 66), but in his revised edition, he concludes that the omission of the phrase in the ancient versions is more likely due to "unclarity about the logic of the 'so'" in v. 8 (*Daniel*, 225).
42. Newsom, *Daniel*, 106.

In context, it is a forward-pointing device that both summarizes and characterizes the words that follow. The Chaldeans did not just report to the king what they had observed; they accused the Jews, and they did so with venom.

The narrator does not provide the location of this event, but the king's response that the three men try again when the music played (3:15) suggests that the exchanges took place at "the king's ceremonial station, from which he has observed the spectacle."[43]

b. The Setup (3:9a–11c)

The narrator frames the accusation itself with a multiverb frame—that is, it uses more than one speaking verb to set up the quotation (עֲנוֹ וְאָמְרִין, 3:9a). As discussed at 2:5 above, the discourse effect of a such a frame in many languages is that it creates a pause in the narrative just before something particularly important or surprising. While this appears to be true in BH, the situation in BA seems to be different. In the Aramaic of Daniel, the speech frames are predominately multiverb frames and most frequently ענה + אמר, making it unlikely that its use signals the most important element of the conversation.

However, the speech frame in 3:9 is one of five exceptions to the format of the typical speech frame in Daniel, in which both ענה and אמר are participles. Here, ענה is a perfect, while אמר is a participle. As noted by Cook, the use of this divergent speech frame seems to correlate with "a salient and dispreferred response." Here in Dan 3:9, the frame sets up the charges against the three friends, which is "both a dispreferred response in the king's eyes and salient inasmuch as the charges drive the whole storyline."[44] Specifically, it identifies who has not obeyed the king's command.[45] As direct speech, it also reveals the character and motivations of the accusers.

The Chaldeans' speech begins with the near verbatim repetition of the herald's proclamation (3:10–11; cf. 3:4b–6aβ), repetition that reinforces the narrator's portrayal of mindless obedience to the king and is also part of the chapter's portrayal of Nebuchadnezzar's pomp and pride. By this point in the narrative, such repetition is sounding like mockery.

c. The Accusation (3:12a–f)

The information conveyed by the Chaldeans and the order in which they offer it indicate their malicious intent. First, the Chaldeans introduce Shadrach, Meshach, and Abednego into the narrative by reminding the king that he appointed "certain Jews" (גֻּבְרִין יְהוּדָאִין) to high-ranking positions (3:12a–b). Then they report the offense (3:12c–eβ): the Jews disregarded the king (3:12c), failed to serve his gods (3:12d), and did not pay homage to the image (3:12eα–β). The actual offense, according to the edict, was the Jews' failure to bow down to the image set up by the king, but the Chaldeans frame this fact with two additional accusations: the Jews disregarded the king (3:12c) and do not serve the king's gods (3:12d).

---

43. Newsom, *Daniel*, 107.

44. Cook, *Aramaic Ezra and Daniel*, 11. See further the commentary on 2:7 and 10 above and 3:16 and 6:14[13] below.

45. Readers often wonder where Daniel is in ch. 3. Some have suggested he was traveling or attending to palace duties, but given his rank as a chief provincial official (2:48), we would expect his presence at this ceremony where "everyone" was included (i.e., "all the high officials of the province," 3:2–3). Speculation about where he was is not useful since the narrator has no interest in the subject and provides nothing to help us; this account is about Shadrach, Meshach, and Abednego's trial.

This second accusation—that the Jews did not serve the king's gods—is evidence for the idea that the image represented Nebuchadnezzar's god. The clause itself begins with the topical frame לֵאלָהָךְ, "your gods." Fronting a thematic element either introduces a new concept or draws extra attention to a topic.[46] In this case, it is new information that worship of the image represented worship of Nebuchadnezzar's god. Also important is the use of the second-person possessive pronoun "your": Fewell notes that the Chaldeans "craftily voice the affront as a personal one" by calling the gods "your gods" rather than "our gods" or "Babylonians' gods."[47]

Newsom expands on Fewell's idea, observing that the last element of the speech is "the actual misdeed the Jews are alleged to have done." She comments on the significance of the two comments preceding—namely, that they interpret the Jews' act for the king: first, their refusal to bow to the statue represented their disdain for the king's authority—"a challenge to the king's majesty"; second, their action more comprehensively represents their refusal to revere or worship Nebuchadnezzar's god. Newsom concludes, "While the facts that the Chaldeans report are presumably true, they have framed them in such a way that they sound sinister to the king."[48]

The accusation of the Chaldeans may have been malicious, but insofar as Shadrach, Meshach, and Abednego did not bow down and worship the image set up by the king, they deserved death. Andrew Hill notes that the men were guilty of treason because they would not serve the king's god, and they were guilty of insubordination because they would not obey the king.[49] The story of the three Judeans in Dan 3 underscores the dilemma that diaspora Jews faced if they wanted to be faithful to their God but also be active in the social and political life of a foreign city—whether by choice or by force.[50]

3. The Confrontation between the King and God's Servants (3:13a–18e)

Main Idea of the Passage

Daniel 3:13–18 demonstrates the faithfulness of Shadrach, Meshach, and Abednego to their God in the face of death.

---

46. Runge and Westbury, *LDHB: Introduction*, 5.1 Topical Frames.
47. Fewell, *Circle of Sovereignty*, 43–44.
48. Newsom, *Daniel*, 108.
49. Andrew E. Hill, *Daniel*, EBC 8 (Grand Rapids: Zondervan, 2008), 79.
50. Lucas, *Daniel*, 90.

Literary Context

The first two sections of the narrative (3:1–7 and 8–12) set up the primary conflict of the chapter by showcasing Nebuchadnezzar's arrogance and by demonstrating the reflexive obedience of his officials. In the context created by these two sections, the third section (3:13–18) forms the heart of the narrative. As such, it functions in at least two ways in its broader literary context. First, it brings into clear focus the primary conflict of the chapter. When Nebuchadnezzar asks the rhetorical question of 3:15h–i, "Who is a god who will deliver you from my hand?" he gives voice to the inflated self-perception he has already demonstrated by his actions, and he sets up a showdown between himself and the God of the three Jews. Second, the third section illustrates what genuine faithfulness to God looks like. The response of Shadrach, Meshach, and Abednego to remain faithful to their God and to keep the first two commandments no matter what exemplifies how followers of God should face adversity.

> B. Narrative 2: God's Superior Power and His Servants' Faithfulness (3:1a–30)
>   1. Nebuchadnezzar's First Display of Power (3:1a–7d)
>   2. The Accusation against God's Servants (3:8a–12f)
> → **3. The Confrontation between the King and God's Servants (3:13a–18e)**
>   4. Nebuchadnezzar's Second Display of Power (3:19a–20d)
>   5. God's Power in the Fiery Furnace (3:21a–25g)
>   6. Nebuchadnezzar's Response to God's Superior Power (3:26a–30)

Translation and Exegetical Outline

(See pages 159–60.)

Structure and Literary Form

The third section of the narrative in ch. 3 (3:13a–18e) details the king's response to the accusation against the Jews by the Chaldeans and the subsequent confrontation between Nebuchadnezzar and Shadrach, Meshach, and Abednego. The heart of the narrative, this section consists of three subsections: 3:13, 14–15, and 16–18. The first of these subsections is the king's immediate reaction to the report that the Jews

Daniel 3:1a–30

Daniel 3:13a–18e

13a	בֵּאדַ֤יִן נְבוּכַדְנֶצַּר֙ בִּרְגַ֣ז וַחֲמָ֔ה אֲמַר֙	Then Nebuchadnezzar in rage and fury said
13b	לְהַיְתָיָה֙ לְשַׁדְרַ֣ךְ מֵישַׁ֔ךְ וַעֲבֵ֖ד נְג֑וֹ	to bring Shadrach, Meshach, and Abednego.
13c	בֵּאדַ֙יִן֙ גֻּבְרַיָּ֣א אִלֵּ֔ךְ הֵיתָ֖יוּ קֳדָ֥ם מַלְכָּֽא׃	So these men were brought before the king.
14a	עָנֵ֤ה	↓ Responding,
14b	נְבֻכַדְנֶצַּר֙ וְאָמַ֣ר לְה֔וֹן	Nebuchadnezzar said to them,[1]
14c	הַצְדָּ֕א שַׁדְרַ֥ךְ מֵישַׁ֖ךְ וַעֲבֵ֣ד נְג֑וֹ	"Is it true, Shadrach, Meshach, and Abednego,
14d	לֵֽאלָהַ֗י לָ֤א אִֽיתֵיכוֹן֙ פָּֽלְחִ֔ין	my gods you do not serve,
14eα	וּלְצֶ֧לֶם דַּהֲבָ֛א ...	and to the image of gold . . .
14f	דִּ֥י הֲקֵ֖ימֶת	← which I set up
14eβ	לָ֥א סָֽגְדִֽין׃	. . . you are not paying homage?
15a	כְּעַ֞ן הֵ֧ן אִֽיתֵיכ֣וֹן עֲתִידִ֗ין	Now, if you are ready,
15b	דִּ֣י בְעִדָּנָ֡א דִּֽי־תִשְׁמְע֡וּן קָ֣ל קַרְנָ֣א מַ֠שְׁרוֹקִיתָא (קיתרס) [קַתְר֨וֹס] שַׂבְּכָ֤א פְסַנְתֵּרִין֙ וְסוּמְפֹּ֣נְיָ֔ה וְכֹ֖ל זְנֵ֣י זְמָרָ֑א	at the time you hear the sound of the horn, the flute, lyre, the trigon, harp, and bagpipe, and all kinds of music,
15c	תִּפְּל֣וּן	you will fall down
15d	וְתִסְגְּדוּן֮ לְצַלְמָ֣א	and pay homage to the image
15e	דִֽי־עַבְדֵּת֒	← that I have made.
15f	וְהֵן֙ לָ֣א תִסְגְּד֔וּן	But if you do not pay homage,
15g	בַּהּ־שַׁעֲתָ֣ה תִתְרְמ֔וֹן לְגֽוֹא־אַתּ֥וּן נוּרָ֖א יָקִֽדְתָּ֑א	at that moment you will be thrown to the midst of the furnace of blazing fire,
15h	וּמַן־ה֣וּא אֱלָ֔הּ[2]	and who is a god
15i	דִּ֥י יְשֵֽׁיזְבִנְכ֖וֹן מִן־יְדָֽי׃	← who will deliver you from my hand?"

3. The Confrontation between the King and God's Servants (3:13a–18e)

   a. The King's Reaction (3:13a–c)

   b. The King's Speech (3:14a–15i)

      (1) The King's Question to the Jews (3:14a–f)

      (2) A Second Chance (3:15a–e)

      (3) The Consequence of Disobedience (3:15f–g)

      (4) The King's Challenge of the Jews' God (3:15h–i)

Continued on next page.

---

1. See commentary on 2:5.
2. Emended from *BHS* אֱלָ֔הּ.

Continued from previous page.

c. The Jews' Speech (3:16a–18c)

(1) The Non-defense (3:16a–17c)

16a	עֲנוֹ שַׁדְרַךְ מֵישַׁךְ וַעֲבֵד נְגוֹ	Shadrach, Meshach, and Abednego answered, saying to the king,
16b	וְאָמְרִין לְמַלְכָּא	
16c	נְבוּכַדְנֶצַּר לָא־חַשְׁחִין אֲנַחְנָה עַל־דְּנָה פִּתְגָם לַהֲתָבוּתָךְ׃	"Nebuchadnezzar, we do not need concerning this word
17aα		→ to respond to you
17b	הֵן אִיתַי אֱלָהַנָא …	← whether our God . . .
	דִּי־אֲנַחְנָא פָלְחִין	← whom we serve
17aβ	יָכִל	← . . . is able
17c	לְשֵׁיזָבוּתַנָא	← to deliver us.
17d	מִן־אַתּוּן נוּרָא יָקִדְתָּא וּמִן־יְדָךְ מַלְכָּא יְשֵׁיזִב׃	From the furnace of blazing fire and from your hand, O king, he may deliver,

(2) The Response (3:17d–18e)

18a	וְהֵן לָא	→ but if not,
18b	יְדִיעַ לֶהֱוֵא־לָךְ מַלְכָּא	let it be known to you, O king,
18c	דִּי לֵאלָהָךְ [אֱלָהָיִךְ] לָא־אִיתַנָא פָלְחִין	that your gods we do not serve
18dα	וּלְצֶלֶם דַּהֲבָא	and to the image of gold . . .
18e	דִּי הֲקֵימְתָּ	← which you have set up
18dβ	לָא נִסְגֻּד׃	. . . we will not pay homage."

had disobeyed his order—namely, rage (רְגַז וַחֲמָה, 3:13a). This rage fueled his order to summon the three Jews (לְהַיְתָיָה לְשַׁדְרַךְ מֵישַׁךְ וַעֲבֵד נְגוֹ, 3:13b). The second and third subsections are both recorded speech: first, the king's speech to Shadrach, Meshach, and Abednego (3:14–15), and second, the Jews' speech in response to the king (3:16–18).

The king's speech (3:14–15), the second subsection of the section, begins with Nebuchadnezzar's question to the three exiles: "Is it true . . . my gods you do not serve, and to the image of gold which I set up you are not paying homage?" (3:14c–eβ). This question is followed by his offer of a second chance (3:15a–e) and reiteration of the consequences of disobedience (3:15f–g). The king's speech concludes with a challenge to the God of the Jews: "And who is a god who will deliver you from my hand?" (3:15h–i).

The responding speech of Shadrach, Meshach, and Abednego in the third subsection (3:16a–18e) consists of two elements. First is their defense (more appropriately described as a non-defense) before the king: "Nebuchadnezzar, we do not need concerning this word to respond to you" (3:16a–17c). The second element is their declaration of continued defiance against the king's order: "your gods we do not serve and to the image of gold which you have set up we will not pay homage" (3:18c–dβ), regardless of what their God may or may not do (3:17d). This speech represents the Jews' only recorded speech in the entire narrative, as well as the only instance where they are active characters. The narrative focuses instead on the king's words and actions, as well as the words and actions of his other servants.

Explanation of the Text

a. The King's Reaction (3:13a–c)

Nebuchadnezzar's response to the Chaldeans' report was rage (בִּרְגַז וַחֲמָה, 3:13a), prompting him to summon the three defiant Jews. The description of the king as furiously angry is the first of two similar descriptions; the second begins the next section (הִתְמְלִי חֱמָא, "was filled with fury," 3:19a). Both are part of similar temporal clauses (בֵּאדַיִן נְבוּכַדְנֶצַּר . . .) and both describe the king's reaction to something he is told: in the first, he is responding to the Chaldeans' accusation that Shadrach, Meshach, and Abednego had not bowed to the image he set up (3:12), and in the second, he is responding to the declaration by the three Jews that they will not bow down (3:18). The king's rage rivals the heat of the furnace, which he will ultimately order heated "seven times more than was proper to heat it" (3:19e–f).

The description of Nebuchadnezzar's emotions here and elsewhere in ch. 3 (3:19a–b, 24a–b) is unique to him among the cast of characters in Dan 3. He is the only nonstatic character in the narrative—that is, he is the only one who shows emotions and undergoes change. The rest of the characters are collective, acting as groups (i.e., the Chaldeans, the officials, the three Jews, the soldiers), whereas Nebuchadnezzar is an individual character.⁵¹ His reported speech dominates the chapter, and at a pivotal place in the plot, the narrator even tells the story from his point of view (3:24–25). Newsom observes that this focus on Nebuchadnezzar is part of a larger role of the king in the book of Daniel—namely, he is the protagonist who undergoes a "gradual and at times painful education."⁵²

b. The King's Speech (3:14a–15i)

The king's speech consists of three main parts. First, he asks Shadrach, Meshach, and Abednego to confirm that the accusation is true: . . . הַצְדָּא (3:14c–eβ). Second, in a pair of conditional statements, he echoes the original decree, offering the Jews a second chance to conform or face the consequences of disobedience (. . . הֵן כְּעַן, 3:15a–e; . . . לָא וְהֵן, 3:15f–g). Third, he challenges any god to deliver the Jews from his punishment: וּמַן־הוּא אֱלָהּ . . . (3:15h–i).

The narrator frames the speech with the familiar speech frame: "Responding, Nebuchadnezzar said to them" (עָנֵה נְבוּכַדְנֶצַּר וְאָמַר לְהוֹן; 3:14a–b; cf. 3:9a).⁵³ What follows in the king's speech is his challenge to the Jews' God (3:15h–i), the main conflict in the narrative. As direct speech, the king's words will reveal more of his character and motivation.

Nebuchadnezzar begins his speech by addressing the three Jews by their court-appointed Babylonian names. This use of the vocative is not required since the reader already knows who the king is addressing (i.e., לְהוֹן, "to them," in the quotative frame; 3:14b), so the use here may serve two purposes. First, it indicates how the king perceives the three Jews—namely, as his court-appointed servants. Nebuchadnezzar had spent three years training these men and then had promoted them as a favor to Daniel (2:49), so perhaps he was a little peeved at their ingratitude. But more likely in the context of ch. 3, the raging king could not believe any of his servants would defy him. By reminding them of their place, Nebuchadnezzar expects their obedience.⁵⁴

The king repeats two of the offenses identified by the Chaldeans—first, that the three Jews did not serve his gods (3:14d), and second, that they did not pay homage to the image he had set up (3:14e–f). Without waiting for their response, Nebuchadnezzar offered the Jews a mulligan in the chapter's third repetition of the all-important edict.⁵⁵ A pair of conditional statements contains the king's offer. First, the king says, "Now, if you are ready . . ." (כְּעַן הֵן אִיתֵיכוֹן עֲתִידִין), a thought he never completes. However, the apodosis can be easily supplied based on the context—namely, "nothing will happen to you."⁵⁶ If, according to the second conditional statement, the three men did not (fall down and) pay homage (. . . וְהֵן לָא תִסְגְּדוּן, 3:15f), they would be cast into the furnace (3:15g).

The king's concluding question (3:15h–i) brings the primary conflict of the chapter into clear focus. Which god (and king) is most powerful? Which god can deliver? Who has the power over these three men who refuse to bow down? The word אֱלָהּ, "god," is indefinite ("a god," not "the god"), referring to any deity. Nebuchadnezzar is "challenging the power of deities to save from his own power."⁵⁷

---

51. The herald is an individual, but he acts on behalf of the king, not himself.
52. Newsom, *Daniel*, 100–101.
53. See on 2:5 above.
54. It is possible that the sing-song repetition of their names throughout the chapter is the narrator's ridicule of the Babylonian gods their names reflected. See p. 61n44 on Dan 1.
55. Cf. the herald's proclamation (vv. 4–6) and the Chaldeans' report (vv. 10–12). The narrator repeats much of the edict as well in his report that the people obeyed (v. 7).
56. Cf. similar structures in Exod 32:32 and Luke 13:9.
57. Cook, *Aramaic Ezra and Daniel*, 177.

The king's question in Dan 3 shows Nebuchadnezzar to be an arrogant king whose encounter with Israel's God will expose his pretensions of power. By claiming such power, Nebuchadnezzar elevates himself above any other god—even his own.

c. The Jews' Speech (3:16a–18e)

The response of Shadrach, Meshach, and Abednego in 3:16–18 to the king's challenge is their only recorded speech in the narrative, in contrast to Nebuchadnezzar, whose speech and actions dominate the chapter. The three Jews in the narrative are flat characters in literary terms, what Berlin calls type characters because they "are built around a single quality or trait. They do not stand out as individuals."[58] The three act as a group, and their single quality or trait is defiant faithfulness to their God.

The famous response of Shadrach, Meshach, and Abednego forms the heart of the narrative, and the narrator sets it up with the multiverb frame ענה + אמר, where ענה is a perfect and אמר is a participle. This is one of the exceptions to the typical format of the ענה + אמר frame, where both verbs are participles,[59] and as such, it likely signals "a salient and dispreferred response."[60] In this case, it introduces the speech in which Shadrach, Meshach, and Abednego resist the king's demand (his dispreferred response) and profess their unwavering commitment to their God (a highly salient element of the narrative).

The use of the vocative "Nebuchadnezzar" (3:16b) in Shadrach, Meshach, and Abednego's speech is not without debate. There are two ways to translate the end of 3:16a and the beginning of 3:16b, לְמַלְכָּא נְבוּכַדְנֶצַּר, and one's decision hinges on where the break between the clauses occurs. The first option (used here) breaks between לְמַלְכָּא, "to the king," and נְבוּכַדְנֶצַּר, "Nebuchadnezzar" (see also ESV, NASB, KJV): The three "said to the king, 'Nebuchadnezzar, we do not need . . .'" Although this translation makes the three Jews sound disrespectful since proper protocol required that no one address the king without his title, it nonetheless follows the Masoretic accent that breaks the clauses (i.e., the *atnaḥ* under לְמַלְכָּא). The second way to break the clauses is after נְבוּכַדְנֶצַּר and then translate "to King Nebuchadnezzar," omitting the vocative from the speech of the three men (see, e.g., NET): The three said "to King Nebuchadnezzar, 'We do not need . . .'"[61] The way a translation divides these two clauses shapes the reader's perception of the Jews' response that they did not need to respond to the king concerning the matter (3:16b–c). Were they being bold and curt, or were they simply acknowledging the truth of the accusation and thus making no defense?

We have no comparative evidence to assess the three Jews' attitude toward gentile kings during their time of exile,[62] though Daniel's stance toward foreign monarchs throughout the book is generally one of deference and respect. The exception in Daniel's case is his interaction with Belshazzar, whose presumptuous arrogance earned him a tongue-lashing from the Judean exile.[63] While it is reasonable to assume that Shadrach, Meshach, and

---

58. Adele Berlin, *Poetics and Interpretation of Biblical Narrative* (Winona Lake, IN: Eisenbrauns, 1994), 23–24. By contrast, Nebuchadnezzar is a full-fledged or round character—that is, he acts as an individual, showing emotion and development.

59. See on 2:5 and 3:9 above.

60. Cook, *Aramaic Ezra and Daniel*, 11.

61. The NIV breaks the clauses against the Masoretic accents but then also preserves the לְ preposition "to," adding the pronoun "him" to smooth the translation: "replied to him, 'King Nebuchadnezzar . . .'"

62. The three men are present in the events of ch. 1, but the spotlight there is on Daniel.

63. See further on Dan 5.

Abednego would have shared Daniel's respectful attitude, it is possible that—given the portrayal of Nebuchadnezzar's overblown arrogance in this chapter—the narrator intends to portray the Jews as giving the king far less than what he demanded and received from everyone else in the narrative.

A series of discourse features in the rest of their speech may support the idea that Shadrach, Meshach, and Abednego's tone is more curt than courteous. First is the overspecification of the Jews' God in 3:17b. They specify their God with the semantically unnecessary relative clause דִּי־אֲנַחְנָא פָלְחִין, "whom we serve." This overspecification sets up the contrast with the king's gods, whom they emphatically do *not* serve (3:18c). The second relevant discourse feature is thematic address—specifically the two instances of the vocative מַלְכָּא, "O king" (3:17d, 18b). In both conditional statements of the Jews' response, the vocative appears where it is not required to identify the addressee. In these situations, the vocative draws attention to the speakers' characterization and perception of the person to whom they are speaking.[64] The first vocative falls in the midst of the statement "From the furnace of blazing fire and from your hand, O king, he may deliver" (3:17d)—recalling the king's arrogant challenge in 3:15i. The second vocative (3:18b) comes right before the Jews' refusal to serve Nebuchadnezzar's gods and pay homage to his image of gold (3:18c–e). The Jews acknowledge that Nebuchadnezzar is king, but his status as such is subordinate to the God of Shadrach, Meshach, and Abednego. Whether or not their God delivered them, he alone would have their allegiance and worship. The repeated use of the vocative מַלְכָּא, "O king," in the declaration of Shadrach, Meshach, and Abednego may be their way of highlighting the contrast between the human king (and his claim to power) and their God, to whom they will be faithful.

The third discourse feature that may support a curt response is the metacomment of 3:18b: יְדִיעַ לֶהֱוֵא־לָךְ, "let it be known to you." A metacomment is a speaker's pause in the flow of information to comment on what he or she is about to say. For example, statements like "I want you to know that . . ." or "Just for the record . . ." are not semantically necessary, but the speaker wants to emphasize the importance of what is about to be said.[65] What follows in Dan 3 is the Jews' affirmation that, even if their God does not meet the king's challenge and Nebuchadnezzar's boast of power appears to reflect truth, they still will not bow to the golden image. Their refusal ends up highlighting the impotence of the king: "Nebuchadnezzar literally has no power to enforce his command, to make the Jews behave like all the rest of his officials. He can kill the three Jews; but he cannot make them worship his god. Even if they should not be saved, in this matter they have more power than the mighty king of Babylon."[66] Not only do the three men have more power, but their God does as well, in that he has their faithfulness unto death.

The three men begin their response with the simple statement that they do not need to respond to the king concerning "this word" (3:16b), likely a reference to the rhetorical question Nebuchadnezzar had just posed: "Who is a god who will deliver you from my hand?" (3:15h–i). The statement that follows this opening has been controversial as long

---

64. Runge and Westbury, *LDHB: Introduction*, 2.3 Thematic Address.

65. Runge and Westbury, *LDHB: Introduction*, 1.3 Metacomments. For other Old Testament examples, see Moses's "See" in Exod 33:12 and "Hear" in Deut 6:4; and Joseph's oath, "by the life of Pharaoh," in Gen 42:15–16.

66. Newsom, *Daniel*, 110.

as Bible translators have encountered it.⁶⁷ Most translations reflect a pair of conditional statements that match Nebuchadnezzar's challenge (3:17 and 3:18; cf. 3:15a–d and 3:15e–g).⁶⁸ Probably the most popular of these translations is akin to those of the ESV, KJV, NASB: "If we are thrown into the blazing furnace . . . God . . . is able to deliver us."⁶⁹ However, scholars have long questioned this reading on grammatical grounds. A second translation that is more faithful to the grammar and syntax is that of the NRSV: "If our God . . . is able to deliver us . . ." (cf. JPS, NAB). The primary difference between these two renderings is the Jews' belief about whether their God was able to deliver them from the fiery furnace. In a third translation, the conditional statement hinges on whether the Jews' God exists: "If our God . . . exists, he is able . . ." (NET).⁷⁰ Many people find these latter two readings objectionable because they seem to create "a theological conundrum, whereby the friends in their speech entertain the possible non-existence of their God or his inability to deliver them."⁷¹

Cook offers another way to understand the grammar and syntax of 3:17–18 that is both faithful to the language and avoids sticky theological implications: "O Nebuchadnezzar, we have no need concerning this matter to respond to you whether our God whom we serve is able to deliver us; from the furnace of burning fire and from your hand, O king, he may deliver us. But (even) if not, let it be known to you, O king, that your gods we do not serve and to the statue of gold that you have erected we will not pay homage."⁷² In this translation, Shadrach, Meshach, and Abednego do not need to defend whether or not their God is able to deliver them (3:17a–c). Instead of entertaining "the king's implicit questioning of their God's ability," they "deftly shift the topic to their principled stand: whether or not our God saves us, we will not bow to your demand."⁷³ Their defiance is emphasized in the verbs of 3:18c and 3:18dβ, where, in 3:18c, the participle פָּלְחִין matches the other participial occurrences of פלח and סגד in the Chaldeans' accusation (3:12) and the king's query (3:14). In 3:18dβ, however, the speech employs an imperfect סגד instead of a participle (cf. 3:12, 14). The effect of this shift from a participle to an imperfect in the friends' final statement is global: they do not serve the king's gods now, nor will they ever.⁷⁴

While I am following Cook's translation here, in the past I have favored and am still open to the translation in which the three friends express un-

---

67. The uncertainty about translation of these verses arises because of an anomalous sentence structure in the Aramaic of v. 17.

68. Newsom summarizes this view: "Just as Nebuchadnezzar laid out the alternatives offered to the Jews as paired positive and negative conditional statements in v. 15 . . . so in vv. 17–18 their reply is phrased in paired positive and negative conditionals. . . . Just as Nebuchadnezzar did not pause for an answer after his question to them in v. 14 ("Is it true . . . ?"), but instead seeks the truth in their actions, so they declare that they have no need to answer his rhetorical question ("What god is there . . . ?") with words but will let subsequent events reply" (*Daniel*, 110).

69. Similarly, the Septuagint, the earliest translation of the Bible, translates v. 17a as a declaration of God's ability to save.

70. This is the view of Goldingay: "The three men speak as if their God's existence is an open question . . . , and thus as if their rescue is an open question. But the allowance is only made for the sake of argument; it is the point that Nebuchadnezzar has implicitly questioned (v. 15) and that events will have to establish. For themselves, the story assumes, the three have no doubt that their God can and will rescue them: v. 17 makes this conviction explicit. There is here no questioning of God's power or will separate from the questioning of his existence. If his existence is accepted, it is the existence of one who can and will rescue" (*Daniel*, 234).

71. John A. Cook, "Grammar and Theology in Daniel 3:16–18," *BBR* 28.3 (2018): 367–68.

72. Cook, "Grammar and Theology in Daniel 3:16–18," 377–78. Cook details the argument in his article.

73. Cook, "Grammar and Theology in Daniel 3:16–18," 377.

74. Cook, "Grammar and Theology in Daniel 3:16–18," 378.

certainty about the ability of their God to deliver them (e.g., NRSV).[75] Many translators and exegetes oppose this translation on theological, not grammatical, grounds—even the suggestion that God might not be able to deliver the three men makes people fidget—but we should not dismiss a reading *simply* because it makes us uncomfortable. The question in this translation is not whether the Jews' God was able to deliver, but whether the three men *believed* he was able—although the suggestion that Shadrach, Meshach, and Abednego were not sure God was able to deliver them makes some people just as uncomfortable. The three Jews facing death for their faith have long been paragons of both faith and faithfulness: they staunchly believed their God could rescue them from the king's hand, and if he chose not to, they still would not bow to any other god.

Yet in the context of Daniel and the larger context of the exilic period, is it possible that Shadrach, Meshach, and Abednego really were not sure that their God had the power to deliver them? The three men were standing before Nebuchadnezzar in exile precisely because their God had not delivered them from the king's hand earlier (Dan 1:1–2). We come to the text much later, and we are aware of the theology behind the exile: Israel's God did not lose to a more powerful god, as circumstances on the ground suggested; rather, he delivered his people into the hand of Nebuchadnezzar. But is it possible the three Jews in Dan 3 reflect the uncertainty of a captive people who had not been delivered by their God? A key theological question in the book of Daniel is God's sovereignty and control, and "if these devout youths are portrayed as publicly expressing skepticism about the God of Israel's omnipotence, then we, the readers, are certainly invited to question his powers to save them."[76] We then watch the text give resounding affirmation of God's power to rescue. Human doubt does not diminish God's power.

If the three men were in fact unsure about their God's ability to rescue them, then their response to Nebuchadnezzar would be all the more astounding: Whether our God will or even *can* deliver us, we will worship only him. We will not bow down. We will be faithful to the first two commandments: Have no other god before me and do not bow before carved images (Exod 20:3–6). Seow observes that the commandments were "predicated upon the saving acts of God already performed long ago (Exod 20:2; Deut 5:6);" thus faithfulness was simply "a response to grace already experienced."[77] It is no wonder that the king was impressed (Dan 3:28).

---

75. See Wendy L. Widder, *Daniel*, SOGBC 20 (Grand Rapids: Zondervan, 2016), 71–73.

76. Ariel A. Bloch, "Questioning God's Omnipotence in the Bible: A Linguistic Case Study," in *Semitic Studies in Honor of Wolf Leslau on the Occasion of His Eighty-Fifth Birthday November 14th, 1991*, Vol. 1, ed. A. S. Kaye (Wiesbaden: Harrassowitz, 1991): 174–88.

77. Seow, *Daniel*, 57–58.

4. Nebuchadnezzar's Second Display of Power (3:19a–20d)

Main Idea of the Passage

In Daniel 3:19–20 the king responds to the defiance of Shadrach, Meshach, and Abednego with a forceful display of his power.

Literary Context

This fourth section of ch. 3 contains the king's response to the Jews' refusal to serve his gods and pay homage to his golden image. In its broader literary context, the section serves at least two purposes. First, it adds to the portrayal of Nebuchadnezzar's inflated self-perception of his power by showing him recklessly flexing his muscles. Second, it magnifies the degree to which the king will be shown to be powerless.

> B. Narrative 2: God's Superior Power and His Servants' Faithfulness (3:1a–30)
> 1. Nebuchadnezzar's First Display of Power (3:1a–7d)
> 2. The Accusation against God's Servants (3:8a–12f)
> 3. The Confrontation between the King and God's Servants (3:13a–18e)
> → **4. Nebuchadnezzar's Second Display of Power (3:19a–20d)**
> 5. God's Power in the Fiery Furnace (3:21a–25g)
> 6. Nebuchadnezzar's Response to God's Superior Power (3:26a–30)

Translation and Exegetical Outline

(See page 168.)

Structure and Literary Form

The fourth section of the narrative that comprises ch. 3 (3:19–20) contains the king's harsh order in response to the defiance of the three Jews, and it consists of two subsections. The first describes the king's rage with two expressions: first, he

Daniel 3:19a–20d

19a	בֵּאדַיִן נְבוּכַדְנֶצַּר הִתְמְלִי חֱמָא	Then Nebuchadnezzar was filled with fury	4. Nebuchadnezzar's Second Display of Power (3:19a–20d)
19b	וּצְלֵם אַנְפּוֹהִי [אֶשְׁתַּנּוּ] (אֶשְׁתַּנִּו) עַל־שַׁדְרַךְ מֵישַׁךְ וַעֲבֵד נְגוֹ	and the image of his face was changed against Shadrach, Meshach, and Abednego.	a. The King's Rage (3:19a–b)
19c	עָנֵה ↓	↓ Responding,	b. The King's Command (3:19c–20d)
19d	וְאָמַר	he said[1]	(1) Concerning the Furnace (3:19c–f)
19e	לְמֵזֵא לְאַתּוּנָא חַד־שִׁבְעָה עַל ↑	↑ to heat the furnace seven times	
19f	דִּי חֲזֵה לְמֵזְיֵהּ׃	↑ more than was proper to heat it.	
20aα	וּלְגֻבְרִין גִּבָּרֵי־חַיִל ...	And to certain mighty men . . .	
20b	דִּי בְחַיְלֵהּ	↑ who were in his army	
20aβ	אֲמַר ...	. . . he said	(2) Concerning the Jews (3:20a–d)
20c	לְכַפָּתָה לְשַׁדְרַךְ מֵישַׁךְ וַעֲבֵד נְגוֹ ↑	↑ to bind Shadrach, Meshach, and Abednego	
20d	לְמִרְמֵא לְאַתּוּן נוּרָא יָקִדְתָּא׃ ↑	↑ to cast into the furnace of blazing fire.	

1. See commentary on 2:5.

was filled with fury (3:19a), and then the image of his face was changed (3:19b). The second subsection details the king's two commands to heat the furnace seven times hotter (3:19c–f) and to bind Shadrach, Meshach, and Abednego before casting them into the fire (3:20). The narrator simply reports the giving of these commands without recording the speech of the king.

Explanation of the Text

a. The King's Rage (3:19a–b)

The refusal of Shadrach, Meshach, and Abednego to bow before the golden image stoked the king's anger, which was already raging (3:19a; cf. 3:13a). The effect of his fury was evident on his face: צְלֵם אַנְפּוֹהִי אֶשְׁתַּנִּי, "the image of his face was changed" (3:19b), a narrative play on words that employs the word used eleven times elsewhere to refer to the king's statue—צְלֵם, "image" (3:1, 2, 3[2x], 5, 7, 10, 12, 14, 15, 18, 19). Coxon says the usage here creates a "subtly ironic effect."[78]

b. The King's Command (3:19c–20d)

In his flaming anger, the king issued a twofold order, which the narrator reports as indirect speech. First, concerning the furnace, Nebuchadnezzar ordered it heated seven times more than usual (3:19e–f). Obviously, this is hyperbole, the number seven indicating that the furnace is as hot as it can possibly be. The second part of his command was directed at a group of soldiers, whom Nebuchadnezzar tasked with binding the three Jews (3:20a–d). The narrator identifies the soldiers as "certain mighty men . . . who were in his army" (3:20a–b). The text could have simply reported that the king ordered the three Jews bound, without specifying to whom the order was directed—as the narrator did with the order to heat the furnace. However, by introducing the king's agents and noting their strength, the narrator lets Nebuchadnezzar make a show of his power against the three Jews and whatever weak God they might represent.

Both elements of the order were a flexing of muscle from a king irate at the refusal of three servants to acknowledge his power, and both were reckless acts that ultimately undermined his very purpose in using them. In just a few verses, Nebuchadnezzar's excessive heating of the furnace (any fire would be hot enough to accomplish the death sentence) will result in the death of his strongest men (3:22).[79]

---

78. Coxon, "The 'List' Genre and Narrative Style in the Court Tales of Daniel," 112.

79. As Cook notes, "the detailed description [of the king's mighty men] serves to underscore the significant loss of these men to the recklessly overheated furnace in the following verse" (*Aramaic Ezra and Daniel*, 183).

5. God's Power in the Fiery Furnace (3:21a–25g)

Main Idea of the Passage

In Daniel 3:21–25 the story of Shadrach, Meshach, and Abednego reaches its climax as the three men are delivered from the fiery furnace, while the king's strongest men are destroyed by it. God's presence protects his servants from the power of the king.

Literary Context

This fifth section of the ch. 3 narrative is the showdown between the muscle-flexing king of Babylon and the God of Israel. In its broader literary context, the section serves at least two purposes. First, it is the climax of the chapter: the three Jews face the consequences of their defiance against Nebuchadnezzar and his order to bow down to the golden statue, putting their God to the test against the gentile king and his gods. Second, it will prompt the king's acknowledgment in the next section of a power greater than his (3:28), and it will provide the rationale for his proclamation regarding the God of Shadrach, Meshach, and Abednego at the conclusion of the chapter (3:29).

> B. Narrative 2: God's Superior Power and His Servants' Faithfulness (3:1a–30)
>   1. Nebuchadnezzar's First Display of Power (3:1a–7d)
>   2. The Accusation against God's Servants (3:8a–12f)
>   3. The Confrontation between the King and God's Servants (3:13a–18e)
>   4. Nebuchadnezzar's Second Display of Power (3:19a–20d)
> ➡ **5. God's Power in the Fiery Furnace (3:21a–25g)**
>   6. Nebuchadnezzar's Response to God's Superior Power (3:26a–30)

Translation and Exegetical Outline

(See page 171.)

Daniel 3:21a–25g

	Aramaic	English	Outline
			5. God's Power in the Fiery Furnace (3:21a–25g)
			a. "Those Men" (3:21a–23)
21a	בֵּאדַיִן גֻּבְרַיָּא אִלֵּךְ כְּפִתוּ בְּסַרְבָּלֵיהוֹן (פַּטְּישֵׁיהוֹן) [פַּטְּשֵׁיהוֹן] וְכַרְבְּלָתְהוֹן וּלְבֻשֵׁיהוֹן	Then those men were bound in their coats, trousers, hats, and clothing	(1) The Jews: Bound and Cast In (3:21a–b)
21b	וּרְמִיו לְגוֹא־אַתּוּן נוּרָא יָקִדְתָּא׃	and they were cast into the midst of the furnace of blazing fire.	
22a	כָּל־קֳבֵל דְּנָה מִן־דִּי מִלַּת מַלְכָּא מַחְצְפָה	Because of this—because the command of the king was so harsh,	(2) The Soldiers: Death by Fire (3:22a–d)
22b	וְאַתּוּנָא אֵזֵה יַתִּירָא	and the furnace was heated excessively—	
22cα	גֻּבְרַיָּא אִלֵּךְ ...	those men...	
22d	דִּי הַסִּקוּ לְשַׁדְרַךְ מֵישַׁךְ וַעֲבֵד נְגוֹ	who carried up Shadrach, Meshach, and Abednego,	
22cβ	... קַטִּל הִמּוֹן שְׁבִיבָא דִּי נוּרָא׃	... the flame of the fire killed them.	
23	וְגֻבְרַיָּא אִלֵּךְ תְּלָתֵּהוֹן שַׁדְרַךְ מֵישַׁךְ וַעֲבֵד נְגוֹ נְפַלוּ לְגוֹא־אַתּוּן־נוּרָא יָקִדְתָּא מְכַפְּתִין׃	But those three men—Shadrach, Meshach, and Abednego—fell into the midst of the furnace of blazing fire bound.	(3) The Jews: Bound in the Fire (3:23)
24a	אֱדַיִן נְבוּכַדְנֶצַּר מַלְכָּא תְּוַהּ	Then Nebuchadnezzar the king was alarmed,	b. The King's Epiphany (3:24a–25g)
24b	וְקָם בְּהִתְבְּהָלָה	and he rose in haste.	(1) The King's Alarm (3:24a–b)
24c	עָנֵה →	Responding,	(2) The King's Question (3:24c–e)
24d	וְאָמַר לְהַדָּבְרוֹהִי	he said to his high officials,[1]	
24e	הֲלָא גֻבְרִין תְּלָתָא רְמֵינָא לְגוֹא־נוּרָא מְכַפְּתִין	"Did we not cast three men into the midst of the furnace bound?"	
24f	עָנַיִן →	Responding,	(3) The Officials' Response (3:24f–h)
24g	וְאָמְרִין לְמַלְכָּא	they said to the king,[2]	
24h	יַצִּיבָא מַלְכָּא׃	"Certainly, O king!"	
25a	עָנֵה →	Responding,	(4) The King's Response (3:25a–g)
25b	וְאָמַר	he said,[3]	
25c	הָא־אֲנָה חָזֵה גֻּבְרִין אַרְבְּעָה	"Look! I am seeing four men,	
25d	שְׁרַיִן	loosened,	
25e	מַהְלְכִין בְּגוֹא־נוּרָא	walking in the midst of the fire,	
25f	וַחֲבָל לָא־אִיתַי בְּהוֹן	and there is no injury on them.	
25g	וְרֵוֵהּ דִּי (רְבִיעָיָא) [רְבִיעָאָה] דָּמֵה לְבַר־אֱלָהִין׃	And the appearance of the fourth is like a son of the gods."	

1. See commentary on 2:5.
2. See commentary on 2:5.
3. See commentary on 2:5.

Structure and Literary Form

The fifth section of the narrative in ch. 3 records events that occurred in the fiery furnace (3:21–25). It contains two subsections: 3:21–23 and 24–25. The first subsection uses the far demonstrative אִלֵּךְ ("those") with גֻּבְרַיָּא ("men") three times, alternating the focus on the fates of the three Jews (3:21a, 23) and the soldiers carrying out the king's order (3:22cα). In the second subsection, the narrator uses reported speech in a conversation between the king and his officials to describe what the king sees in the fiery furnace (3:24–25). The dialogue is prompted by Nebuchadnezzar's alarm (3:24a–b) and begins with a question by the king to his officials: "Did we not cast three men into the midst of the furnace bound?" (3:24e). The officials respond in the affirmative: "Certainly, O king!" (3:24h). Nebuchadnezzar responds by describing his epiphany of four unbound and unharmed men walking around in the furnace (3:25).

Explanation of the Text

a. "Those Men" (3:21a–23)

The fifth section of ch. 3 opens with the statement "Then those men . . . " indicating what happened after the king issued his orders (3:19c–20d). The narrator structures the section with three uses of the far demonstrative "those men" (גֻּבְרַיָּא אִלֵּךְ), alternating between reporting the fates of the Jews and the king's mighty soldiers. In the first usage ("those men were bound . . . and they were cast into the midst of the furnace of blazing fire," 3:21a–b), the narrator reports that the king's orders were carried out. Shadrach, Meshach, and Abednego, גֻּבְרַיָּא אִלֵּךְ, were bound in a shroud of flammable material: their coats, trousers, hats, and clothing.[80]

Then the narrator suspends his reporting on the fate of the three Jews and shifts to the fate of the king's soldiers, "those men" (גֻּבְרַיָּא אִלֵּךְ, 3:22cα). Their fate was that the fire killed them when they carried out the king's orders. This second occurrence of the far demonstrative is part of the main clause that governs 3:22, but the clause itself (3:22cα) is preceded by two subordinate clauses (3:22a–b)—dependent clauses that provide the reason for the death of the king's soldiers: the king's harsh order (3:22a) to heat the furnace so excessively (3:22b). By prefacing the main clause with two explanatory clauses, the narrator makes it clear that the king himself was responsible for the death of his mighty men.

---

80. With respect to the vocabulary for Shadrach, Meshach, and Abednego's clothing, Coxon notes, "The precise meaning of these items is uncertain and this is reflected in the disparity in the ancient versions. The foreign origin (Persian?) of at least the first term and the precise cataloging which characterizes the formal lists of the court tales leave us in no doubt of the writer's antiquarian interests and inclination to provide an authentic setting to stories set in the Babylonian exile" (Coxon, "The 'List' Genre and Narrative Style in the Court Tales of Daniel," 104). As for what the furnace was like, we get little help from archaeology, though we know execution by fire occurred in the Assyrian, Babylonian, Persian, and Greek empires. The furnace

With a third and final use of the far demonstrative "those men," גֻּבְרַיָּא אִלֵּךְ (3:23a), the narrator returns to the fate of the bound Shadrach, Meshach, and Abednego and creates a contrast between their fate and that of the king's mighty men. While the soldiers were killed by the flames, the three Jews being bound fell into the midst of the furnace. Neither they nor their bonds were consumed by the flames that lapped up the lives of the king's soldiers. The king's show of power came to nothing except to highlight his own weakness. The king who had asked what god could deliver the three Jews from his hand had unwittingly used that same hand to destroy his own mighty men.

b. The King's Epiphany (3:24a–25g)

The second subsection describes what the king saw in the furnace by way of a conversation between Nebuchadnezzar and his officials. The conversation is initiated by the narrator's report that the king was alarmed (3:24a), a report that builds suspense by alerting us to the alarm before telling us what caused it.[81] The identification of the king as "Nebuchadnezzar the king" is another instance of overspecification in a chapter that uses the discourse device repeatedly to cast the Babylonian monarch in a negative light (see above on 3:2a, 2d, 3b, 5d, 7d, 9a);[82] he is a king with an exaggerated sense of himself and his power (see especially 3:15h–i and cf. 3:28c–e, 29e–g). In this instance, the king who thinks too much of his royal power is about to encounter a God with much more power than he has.

The dialogue that follows the report of the king's alarm contains three sections of reported speech, each framed with the typical speech frame of Daniel—namely, participles of ענה and אמר (3:24c–d, 24f–g, and 25a–b).[83]

In the first speech, the king asks how many men they cast into the fire: "Did we not cast three men into the midst of the furnace bound?" (3:24e). This was not a request for information or confirmation that his order was carried out as given. Rather, it is an expression of Nebuchadnezzar's surprise and perhaps an attempt to find an explanation for what alarms him (but has not been revealed to the reader yet). The narrator uses the query to build additional suspense about the cause of the king's alarm.

The second of the speeches is the response of the high officials to the king's query, and its frame includes overspecification of the addressee (לְמַלְכָּא, "to the king"); there is no textual need to clarify whom the high officials are addressing. This overspecification, combined with the unblinking agreement of the officials ("Certainly, O king!" 3:24h), may be another jab at the king and his sense of power by returning to the idea of his subjects' automatic obedience: whatever the king says, his subjects do; whatever the king thinks, his subjects affirm.

The third speech of the section is the king's response to his officials' affirmation (3:25). The king's speech opens with הָא, "Look!" an exclamation that functions as an attention-getting device. This speech also highlights the centrality of the king in the narrative since it contains the description of the chapter's main event told from his point of view and in his own words.[84] Additionally, in the next section, the theological response to the significance

---

of Dan 3 was obviously large enough for several people to move about. The fact that the Jews "fell" into the furnace suggests there was an opening at the top (v. 23a), but it apparently had a side window or entrance, since the king was watching the events inside.

81. Goldingay, *Daniel*, 229.
82. Runge and Westbury, *LDHB: Introduction*, 2.1 Overspecification.
83. See above on 2:5.
84. Lucas further notes the centrality of Nebuchadnezzar

of the main event will also be provided in the king's own words (3:28–29).[85]

In his response, Nebuchadnezzar provides the reason for his alarm and his question—namely, he sees four men walking in the middle of the fire, loosed from their bonds, and suffering no apparent injury. What is more, the unaccounted for fourth man looks "like a son of the gods" (3:25g). It is hard to know what is more startling to the king: that the three men were not dead or that there were four men alive in the furnace. The narrator does not say whether anyone else saw the fourth man, though it would be fitting if only the king saw the figure since he was the one who issued the challenge to Shadrach, Meshach, and Abednego about their God.[86]

Nebuchadnezzar describes the mysterious man's appearance as "like a son of the gods," but this was neither a confession of faith nor a theological statement about Israel's God. While some English translations say he saw a son (or Son) of God (see, e.g., NAB, KJV), the Aramaic phrase בַּר־אֱלָהִין can only mean "a son of [the] gods." Aramaic אֱלָהִין is not like Hebrew אֱלֹהִים, which can refer to a singular "God" (e.g., Gen 1:3; Exod 2:24) or plural "gods" (Gen 31:32; Deut 28:14), to inanimate objects (like Laban's idols in Gen 31), or to divine beings (as in Ps 82:6 and Isa 21:9). Later in Dan 3, it is clear that Nebuchadnezzar thought the fourth figure in the fire was an angelic messenger of the Jews' God (3:28).

Throughout the history of interpretation, many have considered the fourth man a preincarnate appearance of Christ.[87] While this is possible, neither Nebuchadnezzar nor the original author and audience would have thought this. The original audience of Daniel would likely have associated the mysterious fourth man in the furnace with the angel of YHWH, "the figure that often manifests divine power and presence to those for whom YHWH has a particular concern."[88] Other interpreters have understood the fourth figure to be an angel sent by God (but not the angel of YHWH), a view that aligns with Nebuchadnezzar's view (3:28). Although the narrator does not specify the identity of the fourth man, the significance of his presence does not depend on his exact identity. Whether the fourth figure was God himself or just his messenger, he represented God's presence and deliverance of his servants.

---

in the story by analyzing its characters using Adele Berlin's classification of characters in biblical narrative: agents, types, and full-fledged (*Poetics and Interpretation of Biblical Narrative*, 23–24). The Chaldeans and the fourth figure are agents, characters who serve a particular function in the narrative: the Chaldeans "bring the Jews' disobedience to the notice of the king," and the fourth figure brings "God's protection to the Jews." The Jews themselves and the king's officials are type characters, "typifying faithfulness to the God of Israel" and "typifying obedience to the king," respectively. Nebuchadnezzar alone is a full-fledged character, one who "speaks, acts and shows emotion" (*Daniel*, 87). The significance of this analysis is that it "brings out the fact that the real 'contest' in the story is not between the Jews and the king, or between the Jews and the Chaldeans. It is between Nebuchadnezzar and the God of Israel, who does not appear in the story as a character" (*Daniel*, 87).

85. Goldingay, *Daniel*, 229.
86. Hill, *Daniel*, 84.
87. See, e.g., church fathers Irenaeus (*Against Heresies* 4.20.11) and Hippolytus (*Scholia on Daniel* 3.92[25]) (both in *Ezekiel, Daniel*, ACCS:OTXIII, ed. by Kenneth Stevenson and Michael Glerup [Downers Grove, IL: InterVarsity Press, 2008], 182); Reformers Johann Wigand (*Brief Exposition of the Prophet Daniel*) and John Mayer (*Commentary upon All the Prophets*) (both in *Ezekiel, Daniel*, RCS:OT XII, ed. by Carl L. Beckwith [Downers Grove, IL: InterVarsity Press, 2012], 275–76).
88. See, e.g., Gen 16:7; 1 Kgs 19:5–8; 2 Kgs 19:35. Newsom, *Daniel*, 112. Newsom also notes, "The imagery of the fire that does not burn, however, most directly evokes the theophany of God to Moses in Exod 3:1–3, represented there also by the angel of YHWH."

6. Nebuchadnezzar's Response to God's Superior Power (3:26a–30)

Main Idea of the Passage

Having witnessed the deliverance of Shadrach, Meshach, and Abednego from death in the fiery furnace, Nebuchadnezzar acknowledges that their God has unrivaled power to deliver.

Literary Context

Daniel 3:26–30 is the last section of the narrative that comprises ch. 3. As such, it functions in at least two ways in its broader literary context. First, it brings the chapter's events to a conclusion. The climactic events of the preceding section (3:21–25) provide the primary context for the section: the Jews had been cast into the fire; the king's mightiest men had been destroyed by the same fire; and Nebuchadnezzar saw a fourth man—a divine being—in the furnace. His great show of power (excessively heating the furnace and dispatching his best soldiers) had fizzled into failure. In this section, the king responds to these events by acknowledging the superior power of the God of Shadrach, Meshach, and Abednego. A second function of the section is to make explicit the answer to the king's challenge in 3:15h–i, namely, "Who is a god who will deliver you from my hand?" The king answers his own question in his acknowledgment that the Most High God delivered his servants (3:28c–e).

> B. Narrative 2: God's Superior Power and His Servants' Faithfulness (3:1a–30)
>   1. Nebuchadnezzar's First Display of Power (3:1a–7d)
>   2. The Accusation against God's Servants (3:8a–12f)
>   3. The Confrontation between the King and God's Servants (3:13a–18e)
>   4. Nebuchadnezzar's Second Display of Power (3:19a–20d)
>   5. God's Power in the Fiery Furnace (3:21a–25g)
> ➡ **6. Nebuchadnezzar's Response to God's Superior Power (3:26a–30)**

Translation and Exegetical Outline

(See pages 177–78.)

Structure and Literary Form

The sixth and final section of the ch. 3 narrative (3:26–30) has four subsections: 3:26a–e, 26f–27f, 28a–29g, and 30. It consists of two reported speeches of the king: the first, an urgent order to Shadrach, Meshach, and Abednego to exit the furnace ("Come out and come here!" 3:26d–e); and the second, a lengthy declaration of the superiority of the God of the three Jews, praise of the three men for their faithfulness to their God, and a decree that no one speak ill of this newly discovered God (3:28c–29g). Between these reported speeches is a section reporting the effects of the fiery furnace: first, the three Jews walked out of it (3:26f) and, second, the officials assessed their condition—namely, they were unaffected by the fire in any way (3:27). The assessors include the earlier group of officials, listed here with slight variation from the earlier lists (3:27b; cf. 3:2b, 3a). The officials are assembling (מִתְכַּנְּשִׁין, 3:27a) for a second time in the narrative (cf. 3:2b, 3a), but this time they are witnesses to the power of the Jews' God instead of to the grandeur of Nebuchadnezzar's image. In the final subsection, the king rewards Shadrach, Meshach, and Abednego (3:30).

Explanation of the Text

a. The King's Summons (3:26a–e)

Having declared what he saw in the fire, Nebuchadnezzar approached the door of the furnace and called to the three Jews to come out. Presumably, he did not get very close to the door, given what happened to the soldiers tasked with throwing the men into the fire, and presumably, he also shouted his order since his distance and the noise of the fire would likely have required it.

His summons is set as direct speech (3:26b–c). He begins by calling the three men by name and identifying their master as someone other than himself. Calling them "servants of the Most High God" (3:26d) is overspecification: that is, it is a more specific description than context requires to identify the king's intended referent.[89] The purpose of this thematically loaded information is to cause us to think about the three men from Nebuchadnezzar's point of view after what he has just witnessed. He calls them by the Babylonian names he had assigned them when they were

---

89. Runge and Westbury, *LDHB: Introduction*, 2.1 Overspecification.

Daniel 3:26a–30

26a	בֵּאדַ֜יִן קְרֵ֣ב נְבוּכַדְנֶצַּ֗ר לִתְרַע֙ אַתּ֣וּן נוּרָ֣א יָקִֽדְתָּ֔א	Then Nebuchadnezzar approached the door of the furnace of blazing fire.	5. Nebuchadnezzar's Response to God's Superior Power (3:26a–30)
26b	עָנֵ֣ה →	→ Responding,	a. The King's Summons (3:26a–e)
26c	וְאָמַ֗ר	he said,[1]	
26d	(אֱלָהָא) שַׁדְרַ֨ךְ מֵישַׁ֜ךְ וַעֲבֵ֣ד נְגוֹ֩ עַבְד֨וֹהִי דִּֽי־אֱלָהָ֧א [עליא]	"Shadrach, Meshach, and Abednego, servants of the Most High God, come out	
26e	וֶאֱתֽוֹ	and come here!"	
26f	בֵּאדַ֣יִן נָֽפְקִ֗ין שַׁדְרַ֥ךְ מֵישַׁ֛ךְ וַעֲבֵ֥ד נְג֖וֹ מִן־גּ֥וֹא נוּרָֽא׃	Then Shadrach, Meshach, and Abednego were coming out from the midst of the fire.	b. The Effects of the Fire (3:26f–27f) (1) The Exit (3:26f)
27a	וּֽמִתְכַּנְּשִׁ֡ין →	→ Assembling,	
27b	אֲחַשְׁדַּרְפְּנַיָּ֡א סִגְנַיָּ֣א וּפַחֲוָתָא֩ וְהַדָּבְרֵ֨י מַלְכָּ֜א	the satraps, prefects, governors, and high officials of the king were seeing those men,	(2) The Witnesses (3:27a–b)
27c	חָזַ֣יִן לְגֻבְרַיָּ֣א אִלֵּ֗ךְ דִּי֩ לָֽא־שְׁלֵ֨ט נוּרָ֜א בְּגֶשְׁמְה֗וֹן	that the fire did not have power over their bodies,	(3) The Assessment (3:27c–f)
27d	וּשְׂעַ֤ר רֵֽאשְׁהוֹן֙ לָ֣א הִתְחָרַ֔ךְ	the hair of their heads was not singed,	
27e	וְסָרְבָּלֵיה֖וֹן לָ֣א שְׁנ֑וֹ	their coats were not affected,	
27f	וְרֵ֣יחַ נ֔וּר לָ֥א עֲדָ֖ת בְּהֽוֹן׃	and the smell of fire was not on them.	

Continued on next page.

---
1. See on 2:5 above.

178 Macro Unit 2: The Superiority of God and His Kingdom

Continued from previous page.

28a	↓ Responding,
28b	Nebuchadnezzar said,[2]
28c	"Blessed be the God of Shadrach, Meshach, and Abednego,
28d	who sent his angel
28e	and delivered his servants
28f	who trusted in him,
28g	and the command of the king violated,
28h	and gave their bodies,
28i	because they would not serve
28j	and would not worship any god except their God.
29a	By me a decree is made
29bα	that any people, nation, or language …
29c	who speaks negligence against the God of Shadrach, Meshach, and Abednego
29bβ	… will be dismembered,
29d	and his house will be made into a dung heap,
29e	because there is no other God
29f	who is able
29g	to deliver like this."
30	Then the king prospered Shadrach, Meshach, and Abednego in the province of Babylon.

c. The Royal Response (3:28a–29g)

  (1) A New Respect (3:28a–j)

  (2) A New Decree (3:29a–g)

d. The King's Reward (3:30)

2. See on 2:5 above.

new captives (see above on 1:6–7). Just as their theophoric Hebrew names praised the God of Israel and identified them as God's people, their new names were meant to praise Babylonian gods and signify their new identity as subjects of the Babylonian king. The names were also meant to symbolize their allegiance to Nebuchadnezzar and his gods. Nebuchadnezzar's use of their Babylonian names, followed by the appellation "servants of the Most High God" (3:26d), is an acknowledgment by the king that these three servants of his serve someone greater than he.

b. The Effects of the Fire (3:26f–27f)

The next subsection begins with the transitional בֵּאדַיִן, "then," and reports the response to the king's order: namely, Shadrach, Meshach, and Abednego were coming out of the furnace. They had been thrown into the fire bound, but with the bonds burned off, they walk out without any help. The narrator presents this action and the following action of the king's officials in a series of participles: נָפְקִין, "were coming out" (3:26f), מִתְכַּנְּשִׁין, "assembling" (3:27a), and חָזַיִן, "were seeing" (3:27b). The participles here, as in 3:3–4 above, reflect the "pluractional event" of multiple participles: the three Jews and the group of officials.[90]

For the second time in the narrative, the long roll call of officials assembles (מִתְכַּנְּשִׁין, 3:27a; cf. 3:3).[91] The narrative does not detail the whereabouts of these many officials during the chapter's events. The group last appeared in front of the statue (3:3); at what point they came to the furnace and where the furnace was in proximity to the statue and ceremony are not disclosed. In 3:24d the narrator does refer to the "high officials" who responded to the king's startled query about the number of men cast into the furnace. It may be that the term there was shorthand for all the officials, and the narrator did not list them because it served no particular purpose to do so. Here, however, the repetition of the list, in conjunction with the verb מִתְכַּנְּשִׁין in the prominent initial position, calls to mind the earlier occurrence in 3:3a. The first time these officials were assembling, it was a mechanistic response to the order of a power-hungry king (3:2). This time no one orders them to assemble; they gather as witnesses of God's power.

The dignitaries crowded around to see what the fire had done to "those men" (גֻּבְרַיָּא אִלֵּךְ, 3:27b; cf. 3:21a, 22cα, 23a). Answer? Nothing. They were alive (3:27c), and not even barely: their hair had not been singed (3:27d); their clothes were intact (3:27e); and they did not even smell like fire (3:27f).

d. The Royal Response (3:28a–29g)

The narrative nears its conclusion with a final speech by the king, a speech that provides in Nebuchadnezzar's own words the impact the Jews' God has had on him. As the only full-fledged character in the narrative, Nebuchadnezzar develops and changes, and his speech in response to the events of dedication day demonstrates how.[92] It also reveals how he has not changed.

The king's speech has two primary components. The first is his praise of the God of Shadrach, Meshach, and Abednego (3:28c–e); this praise leads to his commendation of the three Jews for their

---

90. See on 3:3–4 and 7 above.
91. This is the third occurrence of a list of officials, but the list in 3:2 is the report of whom the king summoned to the dedication ceremony. Only the lists in 3:3a and 3:27a share the passive (hithpaal) stem of כנש, "to assemble."
92. See above on 3:13 and nn58 and 84.

commitment to their God (3:28f–j). The second is the king's decree, made in light of the confession he has just made (3:29).

The king was clearly impressed by the God of Shadrach, Meshach, and Abednego. When the three Jews had defied his order, Nebuchadnezzar had condemned them with the words, "Who is a god who will deliver you from my hand?" (3:15h–i). It was, the king thought, a rhetorical question. There was no power great enough to rescue them from his fiery punishment. The three Jews could not have been clearer about their commitment to their God and their steadfast defiance of the king's order. Thus, when Nebuchadnezzar began his final speech, he started with accolades for the God of the three Jews, detailing what this God did that so impressed him: he sent his angel (3:28d), and he delivered his servants (3:28e).

It is worth noting that no one delivered the men from the fire; they were cast right into the midst of it (a point emphasized in 3:23, 24e, 25e, and 26f). However, they were delivered from the expected consequences of the fire—namely, death. It is also worth noting that it was not the angel (or fourth figure) who delivered the men;[93] God did. We might ask why the angel was there at all, if not to deliver. The first answer that probably comes to mind is that the angel represented God's presence with the men in their fiery trial; they were not alone. This may be true, but it is not obvious in the text. In the text, the angel is for the benefit of the king. He is the one who sees the fourth figure, and while it would be an argument from silence to say no one else (including Shadrach, Meshach, and Abednego) saw the miraculous figure, we should be careful how much we say about it. What we can say with confidence is that the narrator is not interested in who else—if anyone—witnessed the miracle. He relates both the scene in the fiery furnace and its interpretation from Nebuchadnezzar's point of view—and in words attributed to him. What the narrator cares about is the king. The primary purpose of the fourth man was to display the power of God to a power-flaunting king who mocked his existence and his ability to rescue his followers. The fourth man served another purpose for the king; his presence kept Nebuchadnezzar from thinking Shadrach, Meshach, and Abednego were gods themselves. The miraculous figure represented a divine presence to the king and provided the explanation for why three humans could be strolling around in the blazing furnace. The angel was necessary to show Nebuchadnezzar that the God of Shadrach, Meshach, and Abednego was the one with the power.

In the dependent clauses of 3:28f–h, all part of the דִּי that begins 3:28f, Nebuchadnezzar describes the devotion of Shadrach, Meshach, and Abednego: they trusted in their God (3:28f), defied the king (3:28g), and in so doing, they had signed their own death warrants (3:28h). They were willing to make this sacrifice because it was the only way they could avoid serving or worshiping a god (or king) besides their God (3:28i–j). The king was impressed by the dogged devotion of the three Jews to their God.

Nebuchadnezzar was impressed, but we should not overstate his position. In his praise of the God of Shadrach, Meshach, and Abednego, the polytheist Nebuchadnezzar was admitting the God of Israel into his pantheon as the god/God with unrivaled power to deliver (3:29e–g); he was the "Most High God" (3:26d). While the Babylonian king had ear-

---

93. Aramaic is characterized by liberal use of the pronoun דִּי, which often functions as a relative pronoun—e.g., "who," "which," "that," etc. If the narrator wanted to credit the angel with deliverance, I would expect דִּי instead of conjunctive וְ at the beginning of v. 28e. Both v. 28d and v. 28e are subordinate to the main clause in v. 28c. See Alger F. Johns, *A Short Grammar of Biblical Aramaic* (Berrien Springs: MI; Andrews University Press, 1972), 16.

lier made himself out to be chief among the gods (3:15), he appears at this point to have come down a notch in recognition that the God with power to deliver outranked him.

The subsection concludes with the king's decree about this newly discovered God, but the decree demonstrates that—although the king has made progress—he did not yet fully grasp the relationship between divine and human sovereignty. Newsom discusses the disturbing nature of his second decree, which emerges in comparison to the first decree: while he issued both decrees to his entire kingdom and both threatened those who disobeyed with "gruesome execution," the first decree was positive and the second was negative. In the first, he required worship of the image he set up, and in the second he prohibited blasphemy of Shadrach, Meshach, and Abednego's God. Newsom concludes:

> Both make the king the protector of the deity, thus confusing the issue of the nature, source, and uses of royal and divine power. Although Nebuchadnezzar answers his own earlier rhetorical question about the existence of a God who can save persons from his hand, the irony of his second command and the lack of understanding it reflects shows that the truth remains hidden from him.[94]

While he may have acknowledged the superior power of the Jews' God, Nebuchadnezzar still had further to go toward understanding the Most High God.

e. The King's Reward (3:30)

The last subsection of the sixth section begins with the transitional marker בֵּאדַיִן, "then" (3:30). After his declaration with respect to the God of Shadrach, Meshach, and Abednego (3:28c–29g), Nebuchadnezzar rewarded the three Jews. This is the second time in two chapters the king has rewarded the Jewish captives (cf. 2:49), though the reason for the king's action in ch. 2 is more obvious than in ch. 3. In ch. 2, Daniel helped the king by correctly interpreting his troubling dream, and then he asked the king to show favor to his friends. In ch. 3, those same friends have defied the king, though in doing so, they brought the Most High God to his attention. Perhaps he rewarded them as representatives of this greater God or for the chutzpah they demonstrated in their defiance of him.[95]

Canonical and Theological Significance

Who Is the God That Can Deliver You?

Daniel 3 is about idolatry, but in the discourse emphases of the chapter, it is about idolatry as it relates to the person and power of Nebuchadnezzar. He is the one who sets up the golden image (as we are repeatedly told). He is the one who demands allegiance. He is the one who threatens death for defiance. He is the one who orders the punishment. He is the one who witnesses the deliverance of Shadrach, Meshach,

---

94. Newsom, *Daniel*, 113.
95. Niditch and Doran note that court tales typically end with the king rewarding the successful courtier ("The Success Story of the Wise Courtier," 192).

and Abednego. He is the one who proclaims the superior power of their god. The chapter's revelation about God—namely, that his power is unrivaled—is told through Nebuchadnezzar's eyes and in his voice (3:24–25, 28–29). Whatever we say about idolatry should be said with Nebuchadnezzar in view.

Nebuchadnezzar is the quintessential gentile king in the Old Testament, receiving the most attention of any foreign monarch in the text.[96] He is a central character in the narrative of Daniel, and the prophet Jeremiah mentions him by name nearly forty times. As king of Babylon—the city that transcends its historical circumstances in the Bible and serves from start (Gen 11) to finish (Rev 18) as a metaphor "for world power in opposition to God—the empire where God's people live in exile"[97]—Nebuchadnezzar might well be considered the representative king and even god of this opposition.[98]

What is this opposition against God? In Dan 3, it is the pressure and even temptation to give allegiance to another king, to serve and worship another god, specifically, the king and gods of Babylon. In the Bible, the empire of exile for God's people was Babylon, which gave way to Persia, which gave way to Greece, which gave way to Rome.[99] Each of these empires had their kings and their gods, and full allegiance to one meant full allegiance to the other. The picture changes with the age of diaspora—the age in which we still live—where God's people are found in every nation of the world, in varying numbers and with varying degrees of welcome. We are not governed by one political entity, but we nonetheless face the pressure and even temptation to give allegiance to other kings, to serve and worship other gods. These kings and gods differ in their particulars, depending on our respective governments and cultures, but many "kings and gods" transcend political and cultural boundaries. We are all too familiar with the kings and gods of our exilic empire that easily gain mastery over us and threaten our full allegiance to the one God: money, power, sex, prestige, and happiness are some of the most powerful.

Nebuchadnezzar vies for the allegiance of his subjects in Dan 3 by making a spectacle of his greatness, and specifically of his great power. This is explicit in his challenge to Shadrach, Meshach, and Abednego when they refuse to bow before the golden image: "Who is a god who can deliver you from my hand?" (3:15). Nebuchadnezzar was referring to an immediate and very specific deliverance—namely, from

---

96. The pharaoh of the exodus receives considerable attention in the first part of Exodus, but unlike Nebuchadnezzar, none of the events described is told from his perspective. His appearance in the biblical text is predominantly limited to the book of Exodus, and he was not considered important enough even to name—a bothersome omission for scholars of Exodus.

97. "Babylon," in *Dictionary of Biblical Imagery*, ed. Leland Ryken, James C. Wilhoit, and Tremper Longman III (Downers Grove, IL: InterVarsity Press, 1998), 69.

98. See Lord of the King of Kings above (pp. 137–39, ch. 2), and see further on Dan 4, p. 236.

99. We could include Egypt in this list, although "exile" there predates the formation of Israel as a nation, and eleven of Jacob's sons moved there more or less voluntarily.

death in the fiery furnace—but in making this claim he set himself up as the highest power. No god had more power than he.

Nebuchadnezzar is not the first king in the canon to ask this question. Assyrian king Sennacherib had asked a similar rhetorical question a century or so earlier (701 BCE) when he had Judean king Hezekiah "locked up within Jerusalem, his royal city, like a bird in a cage."[100] As the besieged city neared starvation, Sennacherib's captain spoke for the Assyrian king and mocked the citizens of Jerusalem with the impotence of their own king and their God to defeat the mighty Sennacherib:

> This is what the king says: Do not let Hezekiah deceive you. He cannot deliver you from my hand. Do not let Hezekiah persuade you to trust in YHWH when he says, "YHWH will surely deliver us; this city will not be given into the hand of the king of Assyria." Do not listen to Hezekiah. This is what the king of Assyria says: Make peace with me and come out to me. Then each of you will eat fruit from your own vine and fig tree and drink water from your own cistern, until I come and take you to a land like your own—a land of grain and new wine, a land of bread and vineyards, a land of olive trees and honey. Choose life and not death! Do not listen to Hezekiah, for he is misleading you when he says, "YHWH will deliver us." Has the god of any nation ever delivered his land from the hand of the king of Assyria? Where are the gods of Hamath and Arpad? Where are the gods of Sepharvaim, Hena and Ivvah? Have they rescued Samaria from my hand? Who of all the gods of these countries has been able to save his land from me? How then can YHWH deliver Jerusalem from my hand? (2 Kgs 18:29–35; cf. Isa 36:18; 37:10–11).

The fact that the territorial gods of the ancient Near East had failed to deliver their respective peoples from Sennacherib and his god bolstered the king's certainty that his victory was secure. No god had been able to stand against him. Nebuchadnezzar, the reigning power of his day, likely had a similar belief. No god yet, including the God of Israel (as far as he knew), had been able to deliver people from his hand. Why should he think anything would be different in this case?

The poet of Ps 121 asks the gentile kings' question in a much different tone and with different words: "I will lift up my eyes to the hills—From whence comes my help?"[101] (Ps 121:1 NKJV). The hills were the places where ancient Near Eastern gods lived and where Israel's idolatrous neighbors worshiped their gods. They made

---

100. "Sennacherib's Siege of Jerusalem," trans. Mordechai Cogan (COS 2.119B:302–303).

101. There is some debate over the nature of the second clause in Ps 121:1, מֵאַיִן יָבֹא עֶזְרִי: is it interrogative ("From where does my help come?" e.g., NASB, ESV, NIV), relative ("the hills, from where my help comes," e.g., KJV), or an "indirect question" ("I look up to the mountains to see where my help is going to come from," e.g., Leslie C. Allen, *Psalms 101–150*, WBC 21 [Waco, TX, 1983], 150). I prefer the interrogative since the Hebrew word מֵאַיִן is interrogative, not relative, in function.

sacrifices to their gods in the hopes of gaining and keeping their favor. The gods made the rain fall, the sun shine, and the crops grow. The people depended on them for their lives and their livelihoods. The psalmist says, "I lift up my eyes to the hills—that place where the gods live. From where will my help come? Which of the gods is going to deliver me?" The rest of the psalm will answer this question, but we do well to dwell on the question in our own contexts before racing ahead to the answer.

Which god is going to save you? Few of us have foreign armies besieging us, but we are nonetheless looking for deliverance from any number of things: poverty, weakness, sickness, addiction, loneliness, unhappiness, futility, a bad relationship, a bad boss, a dissatisfying job, injustice, and on the list goes. Ultimately, we are all looking for deliverance from death, though we rarely put it so bluntly unless we are facing a dire medical diagnosis or live in obvious danger. But we all know, at least in our quiet moments, that we will die. It is the reality that drives the way we live, whether we realize it or not. Death may have the final word, but we will try to have all the words before that. Let's get the most out of life and hope for the best after that. Let's stay young (or at least look young); let's amass a fortune for the present and for a comfortable retirement; let's squeeze every ounce of pleasure out of life; let's change the world—or at least, leave a mark in our part of it. Which gods will make our one trip through life the best it can be? Which god can deliver us from the pitfalls and perils of life?

The empire where we live in exile is good at answering this question, offering gods to meet every need. Which god will save us from poverty?—a good education or a higher-paying job. Which god will save us from war?—a stronger military or diplomacy or peace treaties. Which god will save us from sickness?—vitamins or exercise or a better diet or medical technology. Which god will save us from futility?—a successful and satisfying career or community involvement or charitable giving. Which god will save us from unhappiness?—the right relationship or the right job or enough money to indulge in whatever pleasures we want. Which god will save us from loneliness?—sex or a spouse or children. Which god will save us from disappointment?—fun or food or drugs or alcohol.

We lift up our eyes to the hills all the time and wonder which god is going to help. We try an array of them on for size throughout life: careers, relationships, hobbies, possessions. These things are not intrinsically bad. Work was part of God's perfect creation, and a satisfying career is a gift. Relationships were designed by God, and they are rich blessings throughout life. Food and drink offer lifelong enjoyment of creative flavors that nourish us body and soul. Even most chemical compounds we call drugs can have an appropriate use. It is good for us to enjoy what God has made and what we have creatively developed, and it is right for us to find some measure of satisfaction in them. *They* are not the problem. We are. Our desperately wicked hearts, ever reaching for satisfaction outside God, are the problem. Our willingness to let God's good gifts become gods is the problem. They can never satisfy, because they were never meant to.

Where will we find real and lasting help? Nebuchadnezzar's question haunts all of us: who is a god who can deliver? In Dan 3, the king answers his own question after he sees the dramatic display of power in the fiery furnace (3:28–29): the God of Shadrach, Meshach, and Abednego—the Most High God—is the one who can deliver. He is one with unrivaled power. The psalmist also answers his own question: "From whence comes my help? My help comes from the LORD, who made heaven and earth" (Ps 121:1b–2 NKJV). He spends the rest of the psalm detailing the ways that YHWH helps.

God may not choose to display his power in our circumstances in the same stunning fashion of Dan 3, but his power is nonetheless unmatched. His is a power that upholds the universe because he made the universe. His is a power that extends beyond the grave because he defeated the grave. The Palm Sunday crowd shouted "Hosanna!" ("save us!"[102]) when Jesus—Immanuel, God with us—entered Jerusalem. By the following Sunday, that salvation was accomplished through his death, burial, and resurrection. One day—only God knows when—Jesus will destroy every ruler, power, and authority, and he will visibly reign forever on a new earth (1 Cor 15:20–28; Eph 1:16–23). Who is the god that can deliver us from any rival hand? That God.

Which God Will You Serve?

The question Nebuchadnezzar asked in Dan 3:15 is not the question Shadrach, Meshach, and Abednego answered in their solitary speech of the chapter (3:16–18). They were answering a question posed long before Nebuchadnezzar ever erected his golden image and even long before Babylon was a menace on the world stage. The question they were answering was asked by Moses at the foot of Sinai (Exod 19:1–7) and then again on the plains of Moab (Deut 30:11–20). It was asked by Joshua at Shechem (Josh 24:14–15) and by Samuel after the anointing of Saul at Gilgal (1 Sam 12:6–15). David on his deathbed asked it of Solomon (1 Kgs 2:1–4), and Elijah asked it atop Mount Carmel (1 Kgs 18:20–21). The prophets asked it as they chided, lambasted, and wept over God's wayward people (e.g., Jer 3:12–14; 4:1–4; Hos 14; Zech 1:2–4). Sometimes it was an explicit question, but more often, it was a question that lay at the heart of an invitation or a choice or an oracle. The question Shadrach,

---

102. "Hosanna" (Ὡσαννά, הוֹשִׁיעָה נָּא; see Matt 21:9 and Ps 118:25) technically means something like "Save! Please!" though by the time of the New Testament, the word seems to have morphed into a shout of joy or praise that belies its original meaning of desperation. So, while the Palm Sunday crowd may not have been thinking "Save us!" as they shouted, the Old Testament background of the word helps us understand why "hosanna" would have become associated with the anticipated Messiah—the one who would save them.

Meshach, and Abednego answered before Nebuchadnezzar that day was not "Which god can deliver you?" The question they answered was "Which god will you serve?"

Moses was the first to ask this question of the newly formed nation of Israel in the book of Exodus, and his rationale for what their answer should be was clear. Speaking on behalf of YHWH, Moses said, "You yourselves have seen what I did to Egypt, and how I carried you on eagles' wings and brought you to myself" (Exod 19:4). Which god/God to worship was an easy choice for those three-months-out-of-Egypt Israelites: "The people all responded together, 'We will do everything YHWH has said'" (Exod 19:8). What followed their hearty agreement were the Ten Commandments, which began with the reminder of the relationship between YHWH and Israel: "I am YHWH your God, who brought you out of Egypt, out of the land of slavery" (Exod 20:2). The first two stipulations of the covenant directly related to the nature of the relationship between YHWH and his people: because he had saved them, they were to have no other gods and they were not to make any kind of image to represent him (Exod 20:3–4).

The Israelites' initial enthusiasm to worship YHWH exclusively wore off quickly, and by the time Moses gave his last words to their children as they anticipated crossing the Jordan River into the promised land, he was prophesying a dismal future of idolatry and eventual exile. On the plains of Moab, he rehearsed Israel's history from forty years earlier, where he had witnessed the Sinai generation's freefall into unfaithfulness and idolatry with the golden calf. He pled with the second generation to guard themselves against such inclinations at all costs.

Moses began by reminding them of what they (by which he meant their ancestors) had seen and also *not* seen at Mount Sinai when they had encountered YHWH and received the Ten Commandments: "You came near and stood at the foot of the mountain while it blazed with fire to the very heavens, with black clouds and deep darkness. Then YHWH spoke to you out of the fire. You heard the sound of words but saw no form; there was only a voice" (Deut 4:11–12; cf. Exod 19:19–20; 20:18). The people heard YHWH's voice thundering from the mountain and they received his words inscribed on stone tablets, but they saw no physical form that represented him.

This formlessness is what drove Moses's argument against idolatry: "You saw no form of any kind the day YHWH spoke to you at Horeb out of the fire. Therefore watch yourselves very carefully, so that you do not become corrupt and make for yourselves an idol, an image of any shape, whether formed like a man or a woman" or an animal or bird or creeper or swimmer or celestial body—"do not be enticed into bowing down to them and worshiping things YHWH your God has apportioned to all the nations under heaven" (Deut 4:15–16, 19). Israel was unique among the nations of the world, and the Israelites' worship practice was unique among the religions of the world. They worshiped and served a God that could not be represented by anything he had created. He stood outside and above his creation and was not like it. Fashioning his form in the likeness of something he made would diminish his glory.

Moses reminded the Israelites that God had brought them out of "out of the iron-smelting furnace, out of Egypt" in order to make them his inheritance (Deut 4:20; cf. 1 Kgs 8:51; Jer 11:4). He implored the people to keep the covenant YHWH had made with them and make no idol of any kind because "YHWH your God is a consuming fire, a jealous God" (Deut 4:24). Then came the prophecy about idolatry and exile (Deut 4:25–28).[103] But all was not lost, even then. Moses assured the people that if they would repent and return to exclusive worship of YHWH in exile, he would remember his covenant with them and relent from destroying them because of his love for Abraham, Isaac, and Jacob (Deut 4:29–31).

The history of Israel bears out the sad fulfillment of Moses's prophecy. Idolatry was the besetting sin of God's people in the land of promise. Just like their Canaanite neighbors, the Israelites erected and bowed low before Asherah poles, Baals, and other idols of wood and stone. Before YHWH gave them into the hand of Nebuchadnezzar (Dan 1:2), he sent prophets to call them back to the covenant. One after another, the prophets asked the question: Which god will you serve? Time after time, the people responded by ignoring, deriding, or killing the prophets.

The reason for sole allegiance to YHWH was straightforward: YHWH had delivered the descendants of Abraham from bondage and made them his people. Also straightforward under the old covenant were the effects of obedience and disobedience: obedience brought abundant blessing in the land of promise, while disobedience brought famine, blight, pestilence, and ultimately the loss of the land.[104] Despite what YHWH had done for them and despite such a litany of clear incentives, the history of Israel chronicles how easy it was for YHWH's people to give their allegiance to other gods.

Shadrach, Meshach, and Abednego made their famous stand on the other side of the broken covenant: the disobedience of the nation had sent them into exile. These three men had no fields that needed rain, no crops that needed protection from pestilence. They were captives in another land. All they had was the command to

---

103. In a bit of biblical irony, Shadrach, Meshach, and Abednego obeyed the commandments not to worship any other god or bow to any idol and to be faithful instead to the God Moses had called a consuming fire (Deut 4:20), but the men paid for this obedience by being cast into a different kind of consuming fire. Shadrach, Meshach, and Abednego knew that the real fire to be feared was not death or foreign oppressors. The only fire worth fearing was the consuming fire of their God—the God who had delivered their ancestors from the furnace of Egyptian bondage.

104. We read the Old Testament wrongly if we read these covenant promises as promises to individuals. The covenant and its promises were made with the community of Israel; their corporate obedience/disobedience resulted in blessing/curses for the whole nation. We need only to read the case law in the Pentateuch to see that not everyone was "healthy, wealthy, and wise" (see, e.g., Lev 25; Deut 15; 24). The law protects the poor and downtrodden, which assumes there would be poor and downtrodden. Jesus himself refers to the ongoing presence of the poor (John 12:8).

give YHWH sole allegiance, to worship no other god. And that was enough. They obeyed because YHWH had told them to, and no matter what they might (or might not) gain from it, he would have their allegiance.

Whether the three men believed their God was able to deliver them may be ambiguous in the text (see above on Dan 3:16–18). The possibility of their uncertainty may make you uneasy, but consider why it makes you uncomfortable. Is it because Bible heroes should have stalwart faith, like Abraham about to sacrifice Isaac (Heb 11:17–19) or like the young David facing down the giant Goliath (1 Sam 17:45–47)? Is it because Bible heroes should be unwavering in their faithfulness, like tortured Hosea buying back his promiscuous wife (Hos 1) or like the disciple Stephen imploring God to forgive his murderers (Acts 7:60)? How could Bible heroes have waning faith or faltering devotion? Bible heroes should have steadfast faith and ardent faithfulness because we need to know it can be done; we need their examples to follow.

But is not faithfulness more difficult when our faith is small? Is it not harder to do the right thing when we cannot see how it makes any difference? Doing the right thing just because it is right is what Lucas calls a "truly ethical action": being "motivated by the intrinsic merit of the action, not by its positive or negative pay-off."[105] Whatever level of certainty Shadrach, Meshach, and Abednego had about their God's ability to deliver them, they gave him full allegiance. If it cost them their lives, they would not bow to any idol—just because it would be wrong to do so.

In our own new covenant context, we also have a straightforward reason for sole allegiance to YHWH: he has delivered us from bondage to sin and set us on the course of eternal life with him. Less immediate and concrete are the effects of obedience under the new covenant; we did not inherit the promise that obedience brings abundant material blessing while disobedience makes God's people subject to lost livelihoods and property.[106] In fact, the life and teachings of Jesus and the apostles demonstrate the difficult truth that steadfast obedience and sole allegiance are more likely to bring hardship, suffering, and even death (e.g., 1 Pet 4:12–14). The path of discipleship is difficult and often the rewards this side of heaven are few.

Why choose the hard road when our empires of exile offer an array of easier alternative routes? We choose it because the creator God alone is worthy of our allegiance and worship. According to Paul, everyone knows this, but—like generations of Israelites before us—we are prone to idolatry (Rom 1:18–25). We follow because he has saved us. We follow because his great and precious promises are ours—in this life and the life to come (2 Pet 1:3–4). We follow because, no matter what it may cost us, he alone has the words of eternal life; where else could we possibly go (John 6:68)?

---

105. Lucas, *Daniel*, 95.

106. The prosperity gospel misapplies God's promise of material blessing to Abraham in the Abrahamic covenant to the patriarch's spiritual children—Christians. For a quick summary of the theological missteps of the prosperity gospel, see David W. Jones, "Errors of the Prosperity Gospel," *The Gospel Coalition*, June 5, 2015, https://www.thegospelcoalition.org/article/5-errors-of-the-prosperity-gospel/.

Shadrach, Meshach, and Abednego did not answer the king's question because for them it was irrelevant. Their decision not to bow down was not motivated by the hope of deliverance. They answered a different question, and it is another question that we all answer—not just once, but every moment of every day. Which god will we follow? Which god will we serve no matter what? Which God has our allegiance because he alone is worthy?

The Folly of Idolatry

One of the obvious narrative features of Dan 3 is its repetition. Lists of officials are repeated, as are the instruments at the dedication ceremony; the trio of names "Shadrach, Meshach, and Abednego" is like a drumbeat through the chapter, and so is the king's mode of punishment ("the furnace of blazing fire"). But perhaps the most meaningful repetition is the phrase "the image which Nebuchadnezzar the king set up," which appears in some variation eleven times in the chapter (3:1, 2, 3[2x], 5, 7, 10, 12, 14, 15, 18).

As suggested in the commentary, one of the purposes of this repetition is to mock the proud Nebuchadnezzar and the image he set up.[107] While Nebuchadnezzar appears elsewhere in the Old Testament, he is never portrayed in the comedic way he is in the book of Daniel, and especially in ch. 3.[108] That the narrator pokes fun at Nebuchadnezzar for his idolatrous image should be no surprise; other biblical authors reserve some of their most biting language for the topic of idolatry. The prophet Isaiah turns his attention to the topic in Isa 44:9–20, where he mocks craftsmen who worship the same materials they use in their work. The blacksmith wears himself out forging his god out of the fire. The woodworker makes an idol out of wood from the forest—and then warms himself by a fire fueled by the rest of the log. Isaiah ridicules the foolishness of such behavior:

> The blacksmith takes a tool
>   and works with it in the coals;
> he shapes an idol with hammers,
>   he forges it with the might of his arm.
> He gets hungry and loses his strength;
>   he drinks no water and grows faint.
> The carpenter measures with a line
>   and makes an outline with a marker;

---

107. See Structure and Literary Form on 3:1–7 and n9.

108. For example, in Jer 25:9; 27:6; 43:10, Nebuchadnezzar is presented as God's servant. See Lord of the King of Kings above (pp. 137–39).

> he roughs it out with chisels
>> and marks it with compasses.
> He shapes it in human form,
>> human form in all its glory,
>> that it may dwell in a shrine.
> He cut down cedars,
>> or perhaps took a cypress or oak.
> He let it grow among the trees of the forest,
>> or planted a pine, and the rain made it grow.
> It is used as fuel for burning;
>> some of it he takes and warms himself,
>> he kindles a fire and bakes bread.
> But he also fashions a god and worships it;
>> he makes an idol and bows down to it.
> Half of the wood he burns in the fire;
>> over it he prepares his meal,
>> he roasts his meat and eats his fill.
> He also warms himself and says,
>> "Ah! I am warm; I see the fire."
> From the rest he makes a god, his idol;
>> he bows down to it and worships.
> He prays to it and says,
>> "Save me! You are my god!"
> They know nothing, they understand nothing;
>> their eyes are plastered over so they cannot see,
>> and their minds closed so they cannot understand.
> No one stops to think,
>> no one has the knowledge or understanding to say,
> "Half of it I used for fuel;
>> I even baked bread over its coals,
>> I roasted meat and I ate.
> Shall I make a detestable thing from what is left?
>> Shall I bow down to a block of wood?"
> Such a person feeds on ashes; a deluded heart misleads him;
>> he cannot save himself, or say,
>> "Is not this thing in my right hand a lie?" (Isa 44:12–20)

Isaiah's description of the woodworker making an image and then bowing before it in worship sounds similar to the series of events initiated by Nebuchadnezzar in Dan 3. Isaiah's woodworker then pleads with the image for deliverance, for "you are my god" (Isa 44:17). In Dan 3, Nebuchadnezzar threatens his officials that if they do not fall down and worship the image he has set up, no god will be able to deliver them.

Isaiah's purpose in highlighting the absurdity of idolatry was to praise the incomparability of Israel's God. Elsewhere in the "Book of Consolation" (Isa 40–66), the prophet had reminded the people that YHWH is not like the gods of the nations; those gods, made of silver and gold, need to be carried about or nailed to the floor to keep them upright (40:19–20; 41:7). The past and future are mysteries to them, whereas Israel's God knows and reveals secrets; he controls light and darkness; he bestows power and wisdom (42:16; 45:3; 44:7; 48:6). All the gods of the nations are helpless, but Israel can take comfort and find refuge in their incomparable God. Israel had a god—unlike any gods of the nations—who could deliver (42:18–43:13)—a truth played out in Dan 3. Isaiah assured the people that one day all gods and rulers will wither before the breath of YHWH (40:24), and other nations and kings would bow before his servants (49:7, 23; 60:10–14).

From beginning to end, the book of Daniel illustrates the superiority of Israel's God and his sovereign control over the events of history. The story of Nebuchadnezzar's golden image in Dan 3 is a head-on confrontation between the God of the captive Jews and the god of the most powerful king of the day. By chapter's end, he has proven his unsurpassed power to deliver. Isaiah's prophetic poetry about the incomparability of Israel's God was on display in the fiery furnace, and Isaiah's assessment of idolaters fits the Babylonian king who built an image that—had it been thrown into the furnace—could not have saved itself: "All who make idols are nothing, and the things they treasure are worthless. Those who would speak up for them are blind; they are ignorant, to their own shame. Who shapes a god and casts an idol, which can profit nothing?" (Isa 44:9–10).

Letting the Text Speak for Itself

Two principles for Christian living are often extracted from the miraculous events in Dan 3 and presented as God's promises to us. The first is that standing firm for God and trusting him will bring deliverance, and the second is that God is with us in the midst of whatever fire we may face. The first principle is erroneous, while the second is a biblical principle (and promise) but one that is only illustrated and not explicitly taught in Dan 3.[109] Careful interpretation should prevent both of these mistakes, and attention to discourse features helps us see more clearly what the passage is teaching.

---

109. This is often the case with biblical narrative, which seldom directly teaches doctrine. Rather, narrative illustrates truths taught propositionally elsewhere. See further Gordon D. Fee and Douglas Stuart, *How to Read the Bible for All Its Worth*, 3rd ed. (Grand Rapids: Zondervan, 2003). Fee and Stuart's ch. 5, "The Old Testament Narratives: Their Proper Use," is especially helpful for how to interpret and apply biblical narratives.

With respect to the idea that God will deliver us if we just stand firm and trust him, we need only to look elsewhere in the canon and in church history to refute this belief. The vast majority of the apostles suffered and died without deliverance, and Jesus himself hung dying, mocked for his apparent inability to save himself: "He saved others . . . but he can't save himself! He's the king of Israel! Let him come down now from the cross, and we will believe in him. He trusts in God. Let God rescue him now if he wants him, for he said, 'I am the Son of God'" (Matt 27:42–43). But no one came to Jesus's rescue. Church literature records a history of suffering and even death for the faithful[110]—a history that continues to be written today. We need only remember twenty-one men in orange jumpsuits lined up on a Mediterranean beach to realize that standing firm in the faith can still cost followers of God their lives. While our God is the one who can deliver, he often chooses not to.

The deliverance of Shadrach, Meshach, and Abednego describes what happened to those three men in their particular circumstances: they were faithful; God delivered them. Their faith and God's deliverance does not mean that if we are faithful in adversity, God will deliver us. He might choose to deliver us, but he might not.[111] God will act in accordance with his plan, which we are not usually privy to. Biblical narrative is *descriptive*, not *prescriptive*—that is, it describes what happened, not necessarily what *should* have happened or, more importantly, what *ought* to happen when we face analogous situations; it does not necessarily prescribe behavior for us.[112]

The second principle commonly taught from Dan 3 is that God is with us in the midst of whatever fire we may face. This is, in fact, a biblical principle, but it is not what is most significant about the presence of the fourth man in the fiery furnace. As with the first principle, we need to read the narrative descriptively, not prescriptively: God's presence was with the three men in the furnace; without further evidence,

---

110. Many of these stories are similar, perhaps patterned after the story of a second-century-BCE mother and her seven sons, who lived during Antiochus Epiphanes IV's reign of terror (see further on Dan 8 and 10–12). The martyr story is recorded in 2 Macc 7 (and embellished in 4 Macc 8), and although the details may be questionable, it is likely that the story derives from actual events. The mother and sons refused to eat swine's flesh, and one by one, Antiochus tortured them and then killed them in a frying pan. Each one stood firm, and each one died. The later story of Symphorosa and her seven sons, living under Roman emperor Hadrian (AD 117–138), tells of their refusal to sacrifice to idols and the similarly gruesome results (see Alban Butler, "Symphorosa and Her Seven Sons," in *The New Encyclopedia of Christian Martyrs*, comp. Mark Water [Alresford, Hampshire: Hunt, 2001], 117. Butler's original text is in *The Lives of the Saints* [Dublin, 1833], 2.90–91). Another story set during the reign of Marcus Aurelius (AD 161–180) tells of a third devout widow (Felicitas) and her seven sons. When Felicitas and her sons refused to sacrifice to idols, they were eventually scourged, clubbed to death, or beheaded (see Alban Butler, "Felicitas and Her Seven Sons," in *The New Encyclopedia of Christian Martyrs*, comp. Mark Water [Alresford, Hampshire: Hunt, 2001], 76. Butler's original text is in *The Lives of the Saints* [Dublin, 1833], 2.43–44. Note that this is not the Felicitas/Felicity that was martyred with Perpetua in turn-of-the-third-century Carthage.).

111. Of course, God has delivered every Christian from the power of sin and the second death, and so his people can endure suffering and hardship in this life because of the promise of the life to come (Rom 8:18). The point here is simply that God is in no way obligated to deliver his people from suffering in the here and now.

112. Fee and Stuart, *How to Read the Bible for All Its Worth*, 106.

we cannot say this means he will be with us in whatever trial we may face. If we want to teach the principle of God's presence in distress, Ps 23 is a good place to start. We will walk through dark valleys but need fear no evil because he is with us. Jesus's promise to be with his disciples "always, to the very end of the age" is our promise as we continue the Great Commission in their stead (Matt 28:20). These and other texts clearly teach that the follower of God need not fear adversity because God will be with us in every adversity. The fiery furnace in Dan 3 does not explicitly teach this principle, but it does illustrate it in a powerful way.[113]

We might ask then, if the primary purpose of the miracles in Dan 3 is not to assure us that God will deliver us from or be with us in adversity, what is their purpose? The narrator does not explicitly state their purpose, but as noted throughout the commentary above, he does shape the narrative in such a way as to focus attention on Nebuchadnezzar. He is the key character in the narrative. Significantly, he is the only one reported to have seen the fourth man, and the meaning of what he saw is given in his own words. In the discourse of the text, the presence of the fourth figure in the fire is for Nebuchadnezzar's benefit. God could have delivered the three men without sending his messenger to join them in the fire.[114] The primary purpose of the miracles—both the presence of the fourth man and the deliverance of Shadrach, Meshach, and Abednego from the fire—was to impress the gentile king Nebuchadnezzar with the superiority of Israel's God.

The idea that the miracles were often for the benefit of non-Israelite onlookers is a pattern in the Bible. In the cluster of miracles associated with the ten plagues and the exodus from Egypt, the text explicitly states one of their purposes: that Pharaoh and all Egypt would know that YHWH is superior to all other gods (see, e.g., Exod 7:5, 17; 8:18[22]; 14:4, 18). Elijah and Elisha's miracles demonstrated YHWH's superiority over gods in Canaan and among its neighbors (see, e.g., 1 Kgs 18:16–40; 2 Kgs 4:1–7, 4:38–5:27). When King Hezekiah implored YHWH to rescue Jerusalem from Assyrian King Sennacherib, his rationale was "so that all the kingdoms of the earth may know that you alone, YHWH, are God" (2 Kgs 19:19). In the New Testament, Jesus performed many miracles in the presence of and on behalf of outsiders (see, e.g., Matt 15:29–39; Mark 7:24–30; Luke 17:11–19). Craig Blomberg summarizes the purpose of miracles in the Bible: "Throughout the Bible, miracles consistently serve to point people to the one true God, ultimately revealed in Jesus Christ. Their primary purpose is not to meet human need, although that is an important spinoff

---

113. The deliverance from the fiery furnace also vividly illustrates Isa 43:1–2: "But now, this is what YHWH says—he who created you, Jacob, he who formed you, Israel: 'Do not fear, for I have redeemed you; I have summoned you by name; you are mine. When you pass through the waters, I will be with you; and when you pass through the rivers, they will not sweep over you. When you walk through the fire, you will not be burned; the flames will not set you ablaze."

114. See above on 3:28–29 and n93 on the source of the Jews' deliverance.

blessing. But they are first of all theocentric and Christocentric, demonstrating the God of Israel and of Jesus to be supreme over all rivals."[115]

The narrative of Dan 3 does not make this purpose as explicit as some other narratives do, but the discourse emphases lead to this conclusion. By the end of the chapter, Nebuchadnezzar has encountered the God of Shadrach, Meshach, and Abednego, and he acknowledges the superiority of their God over all others. His acknowledgment, however, is not complete; in Dan 4 the king will have an even closer encounter with the Most High through his miraculous acts.

---

115. Craig L. Blomberg, "Miracle," in *EDBT*, ed. Walter A. Elwell (Grand Rapids: Baker Books, 1996), 534.

Daniel 3:31a–4:34e[4:1a–37e]

C. Narrative 3: *A Humbled King and His Restored Power*

Main Idea of Narrative 3 (3:31a–4:34e[4:1a–37e])

Nebuchadnezzar recounts the events surrounding a second dream in which he gloried in God's gifts of dominion, power, glory, and honor, and the Most High humbled him. In response, Nebuchadnezzar acknowledged the eternity of God and the superiority of his eternal kingdom, and God restored him to greater power and glory.

Literary Context of Narrative 3 (Dan 3:31a–4:34e[4:1a–37e])

Daniel 4 is the third of six Aramaic chapters in the book, and it is third in a series of five consecutive narratives about encounters between the Judean exiles and gentile kings (chs. 2–6). Like ch. 2, ch. 4 recounts a disturbing dream of King Nebuchadnezzar and his subsequent need for someone to interpret its meaning. However, unlike ch. 2, the account of the dream in ch. 4 does not focus on the drama surrounding the king's need for a reliable interpreter. Also unlike ch. 2, in ch. 4 Nebuchadnezzar exhibits none of the paranoia and irrationality that figured so prominently into the earlier events (cf. Dan 2:1–16). This second dream will draw on imagery from the first dream and function as a follow-up to the lessons God conveyed to Nebuchadnezzar through the dream of the metallic statue.

As part of the chiasm of chs. 2–7, Dan 4 stands parallel with the account of Belshazzar's humbling in ch. 5. Together the two narratives stand at the heart of the chiastic structure, portraying what is likely the primary theme of the entire book of Daniel.[1] Both stories recount stories of proud human kings who encounter the authority of the God who bestowed authority on them, and each shows a different response to the reckoning. In the first account, the king responds by acknowledging the supreme authority of the Most High, and in the second, the king proves unaffected by God's claim to authority. The narratives in turn recount how God deals with each king in the aftermath of his response: the first he restores to power, while the second is cut down, his power irrevocably removed. The relationship between human kings and the divine king, human authority and divine authority, is a driving theme in the book of Daniel, and this relationship is nowhere more clearly on display than in chs. 4 and 5.

This third narrative is also the last of the book's stories in which King Nebuchadnezzar is an active character. As such, it provides the final look at the Babylonian king and invites consideration of his development as a character, as well as his role in the book as a whole.[2]

Daniel 4 is often classified as a court story and specifically a court contest,[3] though it shows the traits of the genre to a much lesser degree. Newsom notes, "The MT lightly shapes the narrative as a court contest by having the king summon the sages of Babylon. . . . That this is not the primary genre of the story is evident from the fact that Daniel vanishes from the story after giving his interpretation"[4]—that is, no reward is given to him for succeeding where the wise men of Babylon failed (as was true in ch. 2).

Literary Structure of Narrative 3 (3:31a–4:34e[4:1a–37e])

The narrative about Nebuchadnezzar's humbling has a unique structure, and while the commentary below discusses each section of the narrative in detail, an overview of the literary structure of the entire narrative is useful. The narrative is a combination of accounts told in first person and third person. It begins and ends with first-person accounts of King Nebuchadnezzar (3:31–4:15[4:1–18] and 4:31–34[34–37]). In these two sections the Babylonian king reflects on the events surrounding his dream of a magnificent tree. However, this flashback narrative of events is incomplete: the king reports the contents of his troubling dream (3:31–4:15[4:1–18]) and then he concludes with a doxology about the greatness of the Most High (4:31–34[34–37]), but he includes nothing of the dream's interpretation or its

---

1. See further the introduction for discussion of the chiastic structure and its significance for interpretation of the book.
2. See discussion on 4:34[37] below for more on the role of this narrative in the book of Daniel.
3. See further the Literary Context of the Macro Unit (pp. 79–80) and the introduction (p. 25).
4. Newsom, *Daniel*, 133.

fulfillment. The link between these first-person accounts of the dream at the beginning and the doxology at the end is found in the third-person narrative in the middle (4:16–30[19–33]). This third-person section of text includes Daniel's response to the king's report of his dream (4:16a–f[19a–f]), his repetition and the interpretation of the dream (4:16g–24[19g–27]), and the narrator's account of the dream's fulfillment (4:25–30[28–33]). The motivation for this narrative structure as well as its effect on the meaning of the narrative will be addressed below.

A second unique feature of the narrative is its multiple repetitions of the king's dream and its fulfillment. The events of the dream, interpretation, and fulfillment are told, in part, by three different voices in the narrative: the king's (4:7–14[10–17]), Daniel's (4:16–24[19–27]), and the narrator's (4:25–30[28–33]). This repetition invites comparison and contrast of the accounts, which in turn highlights points of significance for the narrator of the book.

A final item of note about the structure is the different versification in the Masoretic Text and in English translations. In English translations, the narrative about Nebuchadnezzar's humbling begins with his proclamation to all peoples, nations, and languages (4:1 in English Bibles, 3:31 in the MT). However, in the Masoretic Text, the narrative begins with the king's description of his flourishing and the troubling dream that disturbed his peace (4:4 in English translations, 4:1 in the MT). The history behind the development of alternate traditions is complex, but the versification that placed 3:31–33[4:1–3] at the end of the fiery furnace narrative rather than with the story of Nebuchadnezzar's humbling likely occurred in the 1200s, and it was probably motivated by the fact that other narratives in Daniel conclude with similar praise of the God of Heaven.[5]

> II. Macro Unit 2: The Superiority of God and His Kingdom (2:1a–7:28d)
>   A. Narrative 1: God's Superior Knowledge and His Eternal Kingdom (2:1a–49c)
>   B. Narrative 2: God's Superior Power and His Servants' Faithfulness (3:1a–30)
> → **C. Narrative 3: A Humbled King and His Restored Power (3:31a–4:34e[4:1a–37e])**
>   D. Narrative 4: A Humbled King and His Rescinded Power (5:1a–6:1[5:31])
>   E. Narrative 5: God's Superior Law and His Servant's Faithfulness (6:2a–29[1a–28])
>   F. Narrative 6: God's Superior King and Eternal Kingdom (7:1a–28d)

---

5. For example, chs. 2, 3, and esp. 6. Chapter divisions are usually credited to Archbishop of Canterbury Stephen Langton in the thirteenth century. Most modern Christian translations have rejected Langton's chapter division here, but the MT retains it. The bigger issue of variation in textual witnesses for Dan 4 is beyond the scope of this commentary, but see further Collins (*Daniel*, 2–12, 216–21) for detailed discussion about the history of the text. See also Montgomery, *Commentary on the Book of Daniel*, 223–24, 247–49.

1. Nebuchadnezzar's Reflection: *The Context* (3:31a–33d[4:1a–3d])

Main Idea of the Passage

Daniel 3:31a–33d[4:1a–3d] sets up Nebuchadnezzar's reflection about how the Most High God demonstrated the superiority of his power and his kingdom through signs and wonders that humbled the great king.

Literary Context

Daniel 3:31–33[4:1–3] opens the first-person narrative of Nebuchadnezzar's humbling, a lengthy two-part narrative that begins and ends the narrative (3:31–4:15[4:1–18] and 4:31–34[34–37]). As such it functions in at least three ways in its broader literary context. First, it sets the context for the king's reflection by identifying Nebuchadnezzar as the speaker and the people of his empire as the audience (3:31a–c[4:1a–c]). Second, it summarizes the significance of the reflection to follow—namely, the reflection will demonstrate the greatness of God and the eternality of his kingdom (3:32aα–33d[4:2aα–3d]). Finally, a third function of the section is that it forms a literary *inclusio* with the doxology at the end of the narrative (4:31c–34e[34c–37e]), and together they establish a key theme of the narrative: God's dominion surpasses that of any human king.

> C. Narrative 3: A Humbled King and His Restored Power (3:31a–4:34e[4:1a–37e])
> → **1. Nebuchadnezzar's Reflection: The Context (3:31a–33d[4:1a–3d])**
>   2. Nebuchadnezzar's Reflection: The Content (4:1a–15f[4a–18f])
>   3. The Prediction of the King's Humbling (4:16a–24d[19a–27d])
>   4. The King's Humbling (4:25–30f[28–33f])
>   5. Nebuchadnezzar's Reflection: The Conclusion (4:31a–34e[34a–37e])

Translation and Exegetical Outline

(See page 199.)

Daniel 3:31a–33d[4:1a–3d]

C. Narrative 3: A Humbled King and His Restored Power (Dan 3:31a–4:34e[4:1a–37e])

1. Nebuchadnezzar's Reflection: The Context (3:31a–33d[4:1a–3d])

   a. The King and His Audience (3:31a–c[4:1a–c])

   b. A Summary of the Reflection (3:32a–33d[4:2a–3d])

31[4:1]a		"Nebuchadnezzar the king to all peoples, nations, and languages,
31[4:1]b		which live in all the earth:
31[4:1]c		May your peace increase!
32[4:2]aα		… the signs and the wonders
32[4:2]b		which the Most High God did with me.
32[4:2]c		It seemed good to me
32[4:2]aβ		to declare …
33[4:3]a		How great are his signs!
33[4:3]b		And how mighty are his wonders!
33[4:3]c		His kingdom is an everlasting kingdom,
33[4:3]d		and his dominion is from generation to generation.

Structure and Literary Form

The third narrative of the book's Aramaic chiasm (chs. 2–7[6]) begins with a section that introduces a declaration King Nebuchadnezzar is making to "all people, nations, and languages ... in all the earth" (3:31–33[4:1–3]). The declaration that follows through much of the narrative is the king's reflection on events that happened to him at an unspecified time in the past.

In this initial section, Nebuchadnezzar sets the context for his declaration in two subsections: the first identifies the king and his audience (3:31[4:1]), and the second provides a summary statement of the king's declaration (3:32–33[4:2–3]). The first subsection (3:31[4:1]) has the form of a typical Aramaic epistolary greeting. It begins with the name of the sender and addressee (3:31a–b[4:1a–b]), and it continues with an initial greeting that includes the sender's desire for the well-being of the addressee ("May your peace increase!" 3:31c[4:1c]). The second subsection (3:32–33[4:2–3]) includes the king's purpose for his declaration ("It seemed good to me to declare ... , 3:32c–aβ[4:2c–aβ]), as well a summary of what is to follow—namely, a description of signs and wonders done by the Most High to demonstrate the everlasting nature of his kingdom to Nebuchadnezzar (3:32–33[4:2–3]).

The narrator casts this opening section (and the section that follows in 4:1–15[4–18]) as reported speech of the king, but without a quotative frame.[7] This unframed reported speech extends through 4:15[18] before giving way to the third-person narrative, and then it resumes in 4:31–34[34–37]. As an unframed quotation, it is indented in the darkened portion of the chart on p. 199. In my understanding of this reported speech, the first clause (3:31a[4:1a]) functions like a quotative frame since it is the king's identification of himself as the speaker. Thus, in the chart this clause is part of the reported speech (the darkened section), but it is the only clause set at the left margin; everything that follows it (i.e., the substance of what the king declared) depends on it and so is indented.

---

6. For the significance of this chiastic structure, see further the introduction (pp. 31–35).

7. Unframed reported speech is set to the left margin on the charts and is not indented as reported speech.

Explanation of the Text

a. The King and His Audience (3:31a–c[4:1a–c])

The initial clause of this narrative identifies the speaker of the proclamation that follows and the audience to whom it is addressed. It follows the traditional form of Aramaic letters from the time, and in the context of the king's confession to follow, the use of a royal letter format gives his words a special degree of authority as he acknowledges an authority higher than himself. The proclamation is made to "all people, nations, and languages . . . in all the earth" (3:31[4:1]a–b), an expansive audience that fits ancient Near Eastern royal ideology and casts Nebuchadnezzar as the "epitome of human kingship in [his] claim to universal rule."[8] Fewell notes that since Nebuchadnezzar simply identifies himself as "the king," without specifying "king of Babylon," "he implies that his kingship extends over all to whom he speaks—[namely, everyone in all the earth]. A ruler of the world commands attention. His communication is authoritative. The word of the king rules."[9]

b. A Summary of the Reflection (3:32a–33d[4:2a–3d])

After this greeting, four clauses provide the reason for this royal proclamation (3:32[4:2]), and the order of the information highlights what is most significant in the proclamation. The first clause (אָתַיָּא וְתִמְהַיָּא, "the signs and wonders," 3:32aα[4:2aα]) is actually the object of the last clause (לְהַחֲוָיָה, "to declare," 3:32aβ[4:2aβ]), and the second clause (דִּי עֲבַד עִמִּי אֱלָהָא עִלָּאָה, "which the Most High God did with me," 3:32b[4:2b]) is a relative clause describing the nature of the signs and wonders. The prominent placement of these two clauses before the sentence's main clause (שְׁפַר קָדָמַי, "it seemed good to me," 3:32c[4:2c]) and the infinitive complement that follows (לְהַחֲוָיָה, "to declare," 3:32aβ[4:2aβ]) bespeak their importance. Before it is anything else, this proclamation is about the signs and wonders the Most High did with Nebuchadnezzar.[10]

Nebuchadnezzar first referred to Israel's God as the Most High God in Dan 3:26 when he called Shadrach, Meshach, and Abednego out of the fiery furnace. In his acknowledgment there, the polytheist king was admitting the God of Israel into his pantheon as the god/God with unrivaled power to deliver (3:29e–g); he was the "Most High God" (3:26d). Earlier in the fiery furnace narrative, Nebuchadnezzar had made himself out to be chief among the gods (3:15), but after the miraculous deliverance of the three Jews, the Babylonian king recognized that the God with power to deliver outranked him. In the events of Dan 4, the Most High God steps directly into Nebuchadnezzar's world and performs "signs and wonders" in the king's own life.

---

8. Lucas, *Daniel*, 108.
9. Fewell, *Circle of Sovereignty*, 62.
10. Many scholars doubt the historicity of this chapter's events, and it is true that there is no known record of such a proclamation from Nebuchadnezzar outside the book of Daniel. However, this in itself is not reason enough to discount the veracity of the chapter's account. History has preserved limited information about Nebuchadnezzar's later years, and it would not be unexpected for such a humiliating account to be omitted from the royal annals. Longman notes that a "king's reign is not exhaustively documented and [this experience] is not the type of thing that Nebuchadnezzar may have wanted preserved for perpetuity in his royal inscriptions" (*Daniel*, 117). Archaeology has little to offer about such events without any written documentation.

The phrase "signs and wonders" is common in the Hebrew Bible, and it refers to miraculous acts God performed in order to reveal his power. At key periods in Israel's history, God was especially keen to demonstrate his power so that his own people and their foreign overlords would acknowledge his superiority to other gods and rulers. The exodus from Egypt is the event most frequently associated with "signs and wonders," as the God of Israel demonstrated his superior power over Pharaoh and the gods of Egypt (e.g., Exod 7:3; Deut 6:22; 7:19; 26:8; 34:11; Neh 9:10; Ps 135:9; Jer 32:20–21).[11] Its use here signals to knowledgeable readers that Israel's God is probably about to demonstrate his superiority over another gentile king.[12]

After the king's declaration of purpose, a cluster of four independent clauses expands on the nature of the signs and wonders and on the nature of God's kingdom in comparison to the kingdom of Nebuchadnezzar (3:33a–d[4:3a–d]). These clauses form a doxology that fits well the narrative's form as a royal proclamation. Ancient Near Eastern kings often used their proclamations as opportunities to praise their gods for showing them favor. The four clauses are all verbless with their topics in initial position; to get the discourse effect of this, we might translate, "His signs—how great! His wonders—how mighty![13] His kingdom—an everlasting kingdom! His dominion—from generation to generation!" The emphasis is on God's works and God's kingdom and, specifically, on their greatness and longevity. Newsom says the duration of the Most High's sovereignty is its distinct characteristic, noting that the terminology in Nebuchadnezzar's doxology derives from the psalmist's praise in Ps 145:13: "Your kingship is an eternal kingship, and your dominion endures through all generations." She concludes, "What distinguishes divine sovereignty from human sovereignty is its everlastingness."[14]

The narrator's choice to use first person for much of this chapter is noteworthy. This is the third of three chapters in the book which feature Nebuchadnezzar as a main character (chs. 2–4), and he also figures prominently into the events of ch. 1. The first two are primarily third-person accounts—that is, our view of Nebuchadnezzar so far has largely been filtered through the narrator's voice.[15] Why use first person here?[16] One reason may be that this narrative consists largely of a confession (3:32–33[4:2–3] and 4:31–32[34–35]) and a dream report (4:1–15[4–18]), two genres typically told in first person.[17] But the author of Daniel chose to place both of these in the form of an open letter to the empire and to let that letter

---

11. In the Bible false prophets, antichrists, and Satan also have the capacity to perform signs and wonders (e.g., Deut 13:2; Mark 13:22; 2 Thess 2:9).

12. The language of "signs and wonders" would not have resonated with the "people, nations, and languages" of Nebuchadnezzar's audience, but the Jewish diaspora audience of the book of Daniel would have made the connection and would have found comfort in the fact that their God was still "in the business of performing miracles for his people" (Hill, *Daniel*, 90).

13. The use of the adjectives רַבְרְבִין "great" (3:33a[4:3a]) and תַּקִּיפִין "mighty" (3:33b[4:3b]) foreshadows the appearance of the tree in the king's dream (4:8a–b[11a–b], 4:17c–d[20c–d]).

14. Newsom, *Daniel*, 135.

15. The king does speak in both chapters, and his speeches are important for our understanding of his character and motivation, but the chapters are structured as third-person stories with reported speech embedded.

16. A second and related question is, What is the effect of the first person here, now? If we reject the idea that a collection of stories has just been strung together to create the book of Daniel, and if we affirm the literary structure and design of the book, then this authorial decision is intentional. In the larger context of the Nebuchadnezzar stories (chs. 2–4), the Aramaic chiasm, and the book, how does this first-person chapter fit? What does it contribute? We will return to this question at the conclusion of the narrative (see on 4:34[37] below).

17. Goldingay, *Daniel*, 251.

stand alone in the chapter[18]—that is, there is no narrative framework to provide a historical context (e.g., a date formula).[19] It is simply the voice of Nebuchadnezzar.

Nebuchadnezzar's story is told in his own words because we are supposed to learn about him from it. If the narrator simply wanted us to know that Nebuchadnezzar was humbled and acknowledged the superiority of God, he could have narrated the events. Instead, he allows the king to speak and at great length. All speech in biblical narrative reflects and exposes the speaker: we learn about their character, their motivations, their thoughts, and their feelings from what they say. By crafting the account in Dan 4 as a first-person account by the king himself, the narrator invites us to listen to the king's words and consider what they tell us about him. In chs. 2 and 3, we heard stories about the king's encounters with Israel's God, and now we are finally hearing from him. Daniel 4 is Nebuchadnezzar's day in court. He speaks, and we have the opportunity to weigh his words and render a verdict on their validity.

But what is our standard for weighing his words? Part of the reason for the alternation between first and third person in the chapter is that we need a benchmark for assessing the validity of the king's words. To this point in the book, Nebuchadnezzar has not proven himself a very reasonable or rational voice; how are we to understand him here? The third-person section brings the voice of the omniscient and reliable narrator into this story and into the larger story cycle of Nebuchadnezzar at a critical place. Thus far in the cycle of Nebuchadnezzar stories, we have seen "Nebuchadnezzar's gradual and erratic awareness of the nature and power of the God of Daniel."[20] We have watched the Babylonian king move from ignorance about Daniel's God (1:17–20) to a recognition of him as "revealer of mysteries" (2:47), and then to the acknowledgment of his superior power (3:28–29). Yet, as Newsom notes, to this point in the cycle of stories, "it has not been clear that Nebuchadnezzar has actually grasped the full implications of his own statement that this deity must therefore be the 'Lord of kings' (2:47)."[21] This lack of clarity is what the balance of first-person and third-person narratives in ch. 4 addresses:

> Since Nebuchadnezzar's understanding in chs. 2 and 3 was demonstrably flawed, a wholly first-person narration in ch. 4 might leave the reader uncertain as to whether Nebuchadnezzar's account could be fully trusted. The third-person sections allow critical aspects of the meaning of Nebuchadnezzar's experience to be framed by . . . the anonymous narrator.[22]

---

18. This chapter (as is true of any biblical narrative) is not "pure history"—that is, it is not a transcript of an official Babylonian document. It is history told through literary, theological lenses. We do not have to assume that Nebuchadnezzar composed this first-person account as it appears in Dan 4. Rather, the author of Daniel composed the narrative in such a way as to capture the gist of the king's story in language that would make his theological points and resonate with the Jewish audience of the book. Did the king make a public acknowledgment of God's sovereignty because of the humbling events that happened to him? I think he did. Did he write Dan 4? I do not think we are required to think so. In his excellent *The Art of Biblical History*, V. Philips Long discusses the character of biblical historical narrative in terms of "pictures" versus "portraits" or representations of the events. What we have in the Bible are not "pictures" or "photos" of historical events; what we have are "portraits" or "representations" of them (Grand Rapids: Zondervan, 1994).

19. Note the narrative framework for Daniel's vision reports in chs. 7–10. The absence of a narrative framework here allows for the ambiguous relationship of 3:31–33[4:1–3] to what precedes (fiery furnace) and what follows (Nebuchadnezzar's tree dream). See Literary Structure of Narrative 3 above.

20. Newsom, *Daniel*, 133.

21. Newsom, *Daniel*, 133

22. Newsom, *Daniel*, 133. Others have noted that the section recounting the king's madness is told in third person,

The meaning, significance, and fulfillment of the dream are in the narrator's voice and in Daniel's voice (4:16–30[19–33]). Daniel's reported speech will reveal his character too, but we do not have to wonder whether he can be trusted since the book has presented him as God's faithful and trustworthy servant. It is the third-person section that allows us to assess the king's account.

2. Nebuchadnezzar's Reflection: *The Content* (4:1a–15f[4a–18f])

Main Idea of the Passage

In Daniel 4:1–15[4–18] Nebuchadnezzar reports in his own words the terrifying dream he had of the great tree, and in so doing, he reveals his perceptions of his own greatness and of Daniel's uniqueness.

Literary Context

Daniel 4:1–15[4–18] continues the first-person narrative of Nebuchadnezzar's humbling, a lengthy two-part narrative that begins and ends the entire narrative (3:31–4:15[4:1–18] and 4:31–34[34–37]; the intervening section, 4:16–30[19–33], is in the third-person voice of the narrator). As such it functions in at least two ways in its broader literary context. First, it contains the initial report of the king's dream, information that will be repeated with variation several times in the chapter. This initial telling creates a point of comparison and contrast with subsequent accounts in the chapter. A second function of the section is that, since this initial report is told in the king's words, it reveals his view of himself and his greatness, as well as his view of Daniel.

---

which makes good literary sense—that is, can someone with the mind of a beast really tell his own story? Further, if he had told his own story, could we trust his words? (As Fewell notes, "A madman is prone to make an unreliable narrator" [*Circle of Sovereignty*, 75]). Lucas also observes that the switch in person occurs at a critical place in the narrative: "Up to this point, Nebuchadnezzar appears as the one who is in control, seemingly of the world as well of his own fate. The beginning of the interpretation, signalled by Daniel's appalled reaction to the dream, is the beginning of the demonstration that in reality someone else, the Most High God, is in control both of the world and of Nebuchadnezzar's fate. So, at this point, Nebuchadnezzar loses 'control' of the narrative to an anonymous narrator" (*Daniel*, 104).

> C. Narrative 3: A Humbled King and His Restored Power (3:31a–4:34e[4:1a–37e])
>   1. Nebuchadnezzar's Reflection: The Context (3:31a–33d[4:1a–3d])
> → **2. Nebuchadnezzar's Reflection: The Content (4:1a–15f[4a–18f])**
>   3. The Prediction of the King's Humbling (4:16a–24d[19a–27d])
>   4. The King's Humbling (4:25–30f[28–33f])
>   5. Nebuchadnezzar's Reflection: The Conclusion (4:31a–34e[34a–37e])

Translation and Exegetical Outline

(See pages 206–8.)

Structure and Literary Form

The second section of the narrative of Dan 3:31–4:34[4:1–37] is Dan 4:1–15[4–18], and it continues the first-person report of Nebuchadnezzar as he reflects on the "signs and wonders which the Most High God" did for him (3:32aα[4:2aα] and 3:32b[4:2b]). The entire section is part of the unframed reported speech of Nebuchadnezzar that began in 3:31[4:1], but it also includes two embedded reported speeches with quotative frames.

Two subsections comprise the passage. In the first, the king provides the background for his frightening dream: at a time that he was "at ease . . . and flourishing" in his palace (4:1[4]), he had a disturbing dream that his experts were unable (or unwilling; see below) to interpret, so Daniel came before him (4:1–5[4–8]). The subsection concludes with a quotative frame (4:5d[8d]) that sets up the embedded reported speech in the subsection that follows. The second subsection (4:6–15[9–18]) is Nebuchadnezzar's report of his dream, spoken to Belteshazzar/Daniel. The dream report begins and ends with requests by the king that Belteshazzar/Daniel interpret the dream for him (4:6[9]; 4:15[18]). Both of these requests include the king's rationale for why Daniel was able to do what he was asking: "a spirit of the holy gods" was in him. Between these two requests is the recounting of the king's dream in two parts: the first (4:7–9[10–12]) is about the great tree Nebuchadnezzar saw, and the second (4:10–14[13–17]) is about the command of the watcher. Each of these parts begins with the king's statement "I was looking, and oh!" (וַאֲלוּ . . . חָזֵה הֲוֵית; 4:7b–c[10b–c]; cf. 4:10a–b[13a–b]). Embedded in the report about the watcher is a second reported speech with a quotative frame (4:11c–14g[14c–17g]; 4:11a–b[14a–b]); this embedded reported speech contains the order of the watcher.

Daniel 4:1a–15f[4a–18f]

2. Nebuchadnezzar's Reflection: The Content (4:1a–15f[4a–18f])

a. The King's Frightening Dream (4:1a–5d[4a–8d])

1[4]a I, Nebuchadnezzar, was at ease in my house,
1[4]b and [I was] flourishing in my palace.
2[5]a A dream I saw,
2[5]b and it was frightening me.
2[5]c And [I saw] fantasies upon my bed,
2[5]d and the visions of my head terrified me.
3[6]a I made a decree
3[6]b ↰ to bring before me all the wise men of Babylon,
3[6]c ↰ who could make known to me the interpretation of the dream.

b. The King's Dream Report (4:6a–15f[9a–18f])

(1) The King's Request (4:6a–f[9a–f])

4[7]a Then the magicians, enchanters, Chaldeans, and diviners were coming,
4[7]b and the dream I was saying before them,
4[7]c but its interpretation they were not making known to me.
5[8]a At last Daniel came before me
5[8]b ↰ (whose name is Belteshazzar, like the name of my god,
5[8]c and in whom is a spirit of the holy gods),
5[8]d and the dream I told him.
6[9]aα "Belteshazzar, chief of the magicians …
6[9]b ↰ who I know
6[9]c ↰ that a spirit of the holy gods is in you,
6[9]d and no mystery baffles you,
6[9]aβ … consider my dream
6[9]e ↰ that I saw,
6[9]f and say its interpretation.
7[10]a These were the visions of my head upon my bed:

(2) The King's Version of the Great Tree (4:7a–9f[10a–12f])

7[10]b I was looking,

7[10]c	and oh! A tree was in the middle of the earth,
7[10]d	and its height was great.
8[11]a	The tree grew great,
8[11]b	and it became strong.
8[11]c	Its height was reaching to the heavens,
8[11]d	and its visibility was [reaching] to the end of the whole earth.
9[12]a	Its foliage was beautiful,
9[12]b	and its fruit was abundant,
9[12]c	and food for all was on it.
9[12]d	Under it the beasts of the field were seeking shade,
9[12]e	and in its branches the birds of the heavens dwelled,
9[12]f	and from it all flesh was being sustained.
10[13]a	I was looking in the visions of my head upon my bed,
10[13]b	and oh! A watcher—that is, a holy one—was descending from the heavens.
11[14]a	He was calling out loudly,
11[14]b	and thus he was saying,
11[14]c	"Chop down the tree,
11[14]d	and cut off its branches!
11[14]e	Strip its foliage,
11[14]f	and scatter its fruit!
11[14]g	Let the beasts flee from under it,
11[14]h	and the birds from its branches.
12[15]a	But the stump of its roots leave in the ground, and with a band of iron and bronze in grass of the field.
12[15]b	And with the dew of the heavens let it become wet,
12[15]c	and with the beasts let its portion be with the grass of the ground.
13[16]a	Let its heart be changed from a man,
13[16]b	and let a beast's heart be given to him,
13[16]c	and let seven periods of time pass over him.

(3) The King's Version of the Watcher's Command (4:10a–14g[13a–17g])

Continued on next page.

---

1. Emending MT from חֶזְוֵי ("the visions of my dream"), which implies that Nebuchadnezzar wanted Daniel to tell him both his dream and the interpretation (as in Dan 2). Here, however, the king reports the dream himself.

Continued from previous page.

14[17]a	בִּגְזֵרַת עִירִין פִּתְגָמָא	By a decree of watchers is the message,
14[17]b	וּמֵאמַר קַדִּישִׁין שְׁאֵלְתָא	and a command of holy ones is the decision,
14[17]c	עַד־דִּבְרַת דִּי יִנְדְּעוּן חַיַּיָּא	in order that the living may know
14[17]d	דִּי־שַׁלִּיט עליא [עִלָּאָה] בְּמַלְכוּת אנושא [אֲנָשָׁא]	that the Most High is ruler over the kingdom of mankind,
14[17]e	וּלְמַן־דִּי יִצְבֵּא יִתְּנִנַּהּ	and to whomever he wishes, he gives it,
14[17]f	וּשְׁפַל אֲנָשִׁים יְקִים עליה [עֲלַהּ]׃	and the lowliest of men he sets over it."
15[18]a	דְּנָה חֶלְמָא חֲזֵית אֲנָה מַלְכָּא נְבוּכַדְנֶצַּר	This dream I, King Nebuchadnezzar, saw.
15[18]b	ואנתה [וְאַנְתְּ] בלטשאצר [בֵּלְטְשַׁאצַּר] פִּשְׁרֵא [פִּשְׁרָא] אֱמַר	Now you, Belteshazzar, say the interpretation.
15[18]c	כָּל־קֳבֵל דִּי כָּל־חַכִּימֵי מַלְכוּתִי לָא־יָכְלִין	As none of the wise men of my kingdom are able
15[18]d	פִּשְׁרָא לְהוֹדָעֻתַנִי	to make known the interpretation to me,
15[18]e	ואנתה [וְאַנְתְּ] כָּהֵל	but you are able,
15[18]f	דִּי רוּחַ־אֱלָהִין קַדִּישִׁין בָּךְ׃	for a spirit of the holy gods is in you."

(4) The King's Repeated Request (4:15a–f [18a–f])

The chart of this complex section uses indentation, shading, and differing borders to reflect the layers of embedded speech.

Explanation of the Text

a. The King's Frightening Dream (4:1a–5d[4a–8d])

The content of the king's reflection begins with "I, Nebuchadnezzar" (4:1[4]), an instance of overspecification since the reader already knows who is speaking.[23] The extra information here may serve as affirmation that what follows is a verifiable account of events. A comparable example might be the traditional opening statement of an individual's last will and testament: "I, John Doe, being of sound mind . . ." The title that accompanies most wills (e.g., "The Last Will and Testament of John Doe") renders such repetition unnecessary, but the overspecification functions as the testator's authentication of what follows.[24]

The account continues with a description of the king's circumstances at the time of the Most High's "signs and wonders": Nebuchadnezzar was "at ease . . . and flourishing" (4:1a–b[4a–b]). He was at the peak of his reign, contentedly prosperous. Then the text simply says חֲלֶם חֲזֵית, "A dream I saw" (4:2a[5a]), without a temporal marker or connector; a troubling dream intrudes into the narrative, much like it intruded into the king's comfortable existence. The dream was frightening and terrified Nebuchadnezzar (4:2b–d[5b–d]; cf. his first dream, which just troubled him [פעם, 2:1] and cost him sleep). The verbs are imperfects (. . . וִידַחֲלִנַּנִי, יְבַהֲלֻנַּנִי), translated here as ongoing events in the past (i.e., past progressive). Normally, we would expect a participle in such a context, but Cook notes that "the imperfect occurs in past contexts more frequently in this chapter than elsewhere in Daniel (e.g., 4:30–31, 33), suggesting the past imperfective interpretation is more likely here than elsewhere."[25]

The troubled king summoned the wise men of Babylon, and the events that follow his summoning are described with three participles: עָלִין, "were coming" (4:4a[7a]), אָמַר, "was saying" (4:4b[7b]), and מְהוֹדְעִין, "were making known" (4:4c[7c]). The use of participles here suggests "the pluractional event distributed across the multiple subjects entering and hearing the dream and failing to provide an interpretation."[26] The groups of wise men seem to arrive in succession, each group listening to the king's dream but each also being unable to tell him its meaning.[27]

---

23. Cook observes that this pattern is typical of West Semitic and Akkadian inscriptions (*Aramaic Ezra and Daniel*, 196; see n24 below), which means this overspecification may be part of the genre.

24. Cook translates, "I am Nebuchadnezzar; I was at ease . . ." rather than "I, Nebuchadnezzar, was at ease . . ." He notes that both patterns are found in West Semitic and Akkadian inscriptions, which Nebuchadnezzar's letter mimics. He opts for the former translation, noting that the pattern there is more typical of the beginning of inscriptions (cf. Eccl 1:12, "I am Qoheleth; I was king"). Of the account of Nebuchadnezzar's humbling, he further observes: "The account is subversively mimicking royal inscriptions, which often begin with the self-presentation and statement of how things were in the past, before they came to power and improved things. . . . By contrast, Nebuchadnezzar's encyclical testifies to his having been at ease and prosperous and then being debased by the 'most high God'" (*Aramaic Ezra and Daniel*, 195–97).

25. Cook, *Aramaic Ezra and Daniel*, 197.

26. Cook, *Aramaic Ezra and Daniel*, 199. See also on 3:4–5, 7, 26–27.

27. Cook observes, "The continued use of the participle . . . portrays successive failures (pluractionality) to explain the dream. The portrayal of the royal court is thus notably distinct

Then, "at last," עַד אָחֳרֵין (4:5a[8a]), Daniel came.²⁸ The king follows his statement about Daniel's arrival with an aside of two relative clauses (דִּי, "which/who," 4:5b[8b] and 4:5c[8c]) in which he describes Daniel. First, he notes that Daniel's name was Belteshazzar, like the name of the king's god (4:5b[8b]),²⁹ a reference that reminds the reader that the narrative is told from the king's point of view. In the second part of the aside, the king notes that Daniel possessed a spirit of the holy gods, a qualification that will be the rationale for why Daniel should be able to interpret the dream (see 4:6[9]). This recognition of Daniel's unique ability hearkens back to the events surrounding Nebuchadnezzar's dream in ch. 2 when his wise men protested that no one could reveal the king's dream "except the gods, whose dwelling place is not with flesh" (2:11). There the king learned that Daniel had access to supernatural knowledge that none of his royal experts had, and here he expects Daniel to be able to interpret his second dream because of it.

The king's connection of these two things—the name of his god and Daniel's unique ability—indicates that he considered Daniel's gift to be from the Babylonian god.³⁰ Even though these words describe events before his humbling, they are nonetheless spoken after it—and so they reflect Nebuchadnezzar's viewpoint at the time of the proclamation and indicate to the reader that the king "still really hasn't 'gotten it'"—he continues to refer to Daniel by his Babylonian name, connecting him and his ability to the king's native god.³¹ Despite the fact that in ch. 2, the king praised Daniel's God as the revealer of mysteries (2:47), by ch. 4, he has apparently forgotten all about Daniel's God and simply remembered Daniel's ability.

Throughout this section, words referring to the king's dream or its interpretation hold initial position in every clause where they occur (4:2a[5a], 2c[5c], 2d[5d], 3c[6c], 4b[7b], 4c[7c], 5d[8d]). The king's concern over his dream dominates the narrative. This is no surprise, given that this is the second time in the book that a disturbing dream has frightened him. In the first, he dreamed of a multilayered metallic statue—a magnificent structure that featured him as the head of gold. The dream foretold the ultimate destruction of human kingdoms, but for the young king, it held only the promise of splendor and success. By the time of his second dream in Dan 4, Nebuchadnezzar has achieved that splendor and success, but this troubling dream portends an ominous future.

---

from that in Daniel 2, in which the king gives a single threat to the entire group of counselors all at once" (*Aramaic Ezra and Daniel*, 199).

28. We might ask why Daniel was not with the rest of the wise men since he had shown superior ability after the king's first dream, and since he obviously had status among the wise men (i.e., the king calls him "chief of the magicians," 4:6aα[9aα]). Perhaps he was among the summoned, but for whatever reason, he arrived after they did. This delayed entrance fits the pattern of court stories, in which the hero comes at the end to save the day, and it also increases the drama: "A higher dramatic end is gained by having Dan. enter triumphantly *at last*, when his colleagues again have been nonplussed" (Montgomery, *Commentary on the Book of Daniel*, 225). The delay also sets Daniel apart from the rest of the wise men, perhaps to remind the reader of the difference between his colleagues, who used traditional dream interpretation techniques, and him—whose superior wisdom was a gift from his God (Longman, *Daniel*, 118). It is, of course, possible that Daniel *was* in the group summoned, and "at last" reflects that he was the first one able to give the interpretation. In the words of my editor, Lee Fields, "It is sort of like saying, 'I searched for my phone and it was in the last place I looked.' We know what this means; the phone was, of course, in the last place one looked but not necessarily literally in the last place that one might have looked. No one keeps looking after one finds it."

29. The etymology is false but it nonetheless "plays a thematic role in the story . . . since what Nebuchadnezzar will learn is that his kingship comes not from [his god] but from 'the Most High,' that is, the God of Israel" (Newsom, *Daniel*, 136).

30. Seow, *Daniel*, 66.

31. Longman, *Daniel*, 118.

The two accounts of Nebuchadnezzar's dreams have several features in common: the king has had a disturbing dream and his experts cannot help, but Daniel can. Both dreams foretell destruction or demise—whether that of human kingdoms or of an individual king. Both accounts also make similar use of suspense: the king's reactions to his dreams are described before we learn the dreams' contents; then the tension is heightened by the delay while an interpreter is sought.[32] Despite these similarities, the accounts are also very different. In ch. 4, the king reports the contents of his dream, and when his wise men do not interpret it, he simply turns to Daniel, who appears without fanfare. There is no raging paranoid king in ch. 4.

b. The King's Dream Report (4:6a–15f[9a–18f])

The king's report of his dream is set as reported speech, embedded in the larger reported speech of the first-person narrative in 3:31–4:15[4:1–18]. It begins with the vocative "Belteshazzar, chief of the magicians" (4:6aα[9aα]), which is followed by relative clauses (4:6b–d[9b–d]). The use of the vocative here is not necessary, since Nebuchadnezzar has already identified Belteshazzar/Daniel as the person to whom he is speaking (4:5a–b[8a–b]), and the information contained in the relative clause (i.e., that a spirit of the holy gods is in Daniel) has also already been provided (4:5c[8c]). Additionally, the king adds that because Belteshazzar/Daniel has a spirit of the holy gods, no mystery baffles him (4:6d[9d]). All this extra information characterizes Belteshazzar/Daniel based on Nebuchadnezzar's perception of him[33] and provides the rationale for the king's request that follows: "Consider my dream . . . and say its interpretation" (4:6aβ–f[9aβ–f]). At the conclusion of his dream report, the king will repeat this request as well as the reason he considers Belteshazzar/Daniel uniquely qualified to interpret the dream (4:15b–f[18b–f]).

The actual report of the dream begins in 4:7[10] and continues through 4:14[17]. It breaks into two distinct sections, each beginning with a statement including the expressions חָזֵה הֲוֵית . . . חֶזְוֵי רֵאשִׁי . . . וַאֲלוּ, "I was looking . . . the visions of my head . . . and oh!" (4:7a–c[10a–c]; 4:10a–b[13a–b]). The attention-getting וַאֲלוּ ("and oh!") breaks the flow of the discourse—much like saying "Listen up!" or "Look!"—and alerts the reader that something important or surprising follows.[34] What follows the first וַאֲלוּ is the king's description of the magnificent, beneficent tree he saw at the center of the earth (4:7–9[10–12]), and what follows the second is his description of the watcher's startling command (4:10–14[13–17]).

Nebuchadnezzar's description of the tree includes three extra clauses that Daniel does not repeat in his near verbatim retelling of the dream, hinting at the king's perception of what is important. First, he says the tree was "in the middle of the earth" (4:7c[10c]), and he follows this with a statement that the height of the tree was great (4:7d[10d]). At the conclusion of his description of the tree, Nebuchadnezzar includes a third statement that is absent in Daniel's retelling: "and from it all flesh was being sustained" (4:9f[12f]). These extra descriptions by the king may indicate his particular interest in the tree's magnitude and beneficence—imagery that clearly indicates his greatness.

---

32. Lucas, *Daniel*, 102. Lucas also notes that later in the chapter, Daniel's reaction to the dream, repetition of it, and then unsolicited admonition to the king will all cause further delay.

33. Runge and Westbury, *LDHB: Introduction*, 2.3 Thematic Address.

34. Runge and Westbury, *LDHB: Introduction*, 1.4 Attention-Getters.

The second section of the king's dream report, the watcher's command, includes another embedded speech—that of "a watcher—that is, a holy one" (4:10a–14[13a–17]), who "was descending from the heavens."[35] The king sets up the angel's orders with a redundant and descriptive speech frame, קָרֵא בְחַיִל וְכֵן אָמַר, "he was calling out loudly, and thus he was saying" (4:11a–b[14a–b]), likely an indication that he wanted to draw attention to the shocking nature of the speech that follows (note that the speech frame of this embedded speech in Daniel's retelling is simply וְאָמַר, "and saying," 4:20c[23c]).[36]

The angel barks out orders with respect to the tree, and Nebuchadnezzar reports the details of the angel's command with a series of staccato imperative, jussive, and verbless clauses (4:11c–13[14c–16]). In these commands, the angel orders the destruction of the tree, the scattering of its inhabitants, and the preservation of the stump, albeit as a beast, for "seven periods of time" (4:13c[16c]). The only remnant of the magnificent tree is the stump, which is left in the ground and bound with iron and bronze fetters.[37]

Midway through the angel's pronouncement, the imagery seamlessly shifts from trees to beasts and humans. With the beasts, the stump is to eat the grass of the ground. The human mind of the stump is to become the mind of a beast for seven periods of time.

The cosmic tree was a widespread motif in the ancient Near East. Given this and the relative clarity of the angel's command with respect to the tree in Nebuchadnezzar's dream, it stretches the imagination to think that Nebuchadnezzar did not understand the general meaning of his dream. This probably accounts for his lengthy reporting of the watcher's command (cf. Daniel's retelling in half as many clauses, 4:20[23]): as the one most affected by the watcher's words, Nebuchadnezzar had good reason to remember every vivid detail.

The angel's pronouncement concludes with a declaration of the command's certainty ("by a decree of watchers is the message, and a command of holy ones is the decision," 4:14a–b[17a–b]) and a statement of its three-fold purpose: recognition ("in order that the living may know," 4:14c[17c]) "that the Most High is ruler over the kingdom of mankind" (4:14d[17d]), that he gives the kingdom to whomever he wishes (4:14e–f[17e–f]), and that he sets the lowliest of men over it (4:14g[17g]). This purpose as stated by the angel in Nebuchadnezzar's dream report is also a good summary of the chapter's message.

The second section of this narrative in which Nebuchadnezzar reflects on the dream he had (4:1–15[4–18]) concludes much as it began, with the king making an "I, Nebuchadnezzar" statement (4:15a[18a]; cf. 4:1[4]), although in this second occurrence, the king adds his title: מַלְכָּא, "the king." In this case of overspecification, as with the earlier one, the extra information seems to be an affirmation that what has just been reported is a trustworthy account of events (see on 4:1[4] above). The inclusion of מַלְכָּא, "the king," in Nebuchadnezzar's self-identification also sets up a

---

35. The term "watcher" refers to a heavenly being and occurs in the Bible only here (4:10[13], 14[17], 20[23]), but it is common in postexilic Jewish literature. Some Second Temple literature uses the term to refer to fallen angels (e.g., 1 En. 1–36; the Testaments of the Twelve Patriarchs; Jubilees), but it is also used to refer to good angels who watch over God's people.

36. See on 2:5 above. See also Runge and Westbury, *LDHB: Introduction*, 1.5 Redundant Quotative Frames.

37. The purpose of the fetters on a tree stump and the significance of this imagery in the dream are lost to us since Daniel does not explain it in his interpretation and our knowledge of ancient Near Eastern arboriculture is limited. The fetters may indicate the protection of the stump or they may symbolize its captivity. We simply do not have enough information to know what purpose such fetters may have served.

contrast between himself and Daniel, identified in the next clause: "I, King Nebuchadnezzar . . . Now you, Belteshazzar . . . ," a reminder of the king's power over Daniel, a captive bearing the name of the king's god.

Then the king repeats his request to Belteshazzar/Daniel in much the same way he made it initially (4:15[18]; cf. 4:6[9]), forming an *inclusio* of the king's request around the dream report: he addresses Belteshazzar/Daniel by his Babylonian name (4:15b[18b]), requests that he interpret the dream (4:15b[18b]; cf. 4:6[9]), and repeats his qualifications to do so (4:15e–f[18e–f]; cf. 4:6b–d[9b–d]; see on 4:5[8] above). The structure of the second request differs from that of the first and helps focus attention on the king's perception of Daniel's uniqueness. In the first request, Nebuchadnezzar addressed Daniel, stated Daniel's qualification to interpret the dream, and then made his request. In the second, he addresses Daniel and makes his request, and then he explains Daniel's qualification by way of a contrast with his own wise men—i.e., they were unable to interpret the dream, but Daniel was able because a spirit of the holy gods was in him (4:15c–f[18c–f]). This contrast, along with the *inclusio* itself, highlights that what most impressed the king and convinced him Daniel was able to interpret his dream was Daniel's connection with the divine realm—something his own wise men did not have. While this narrative is first and foremost about the sovereignty of God over human rulers, a secondary theme is Daniel's access to the divine realm and his uniqueness among the wise men of Babylon.

The king's words also raise a question about the ability of his own wise men. One wonders whether they *could not* or *would not* interpret the dream. Everything in the narrative to this point has been relayed from Nebuchadnezzar's point of view, and what he has said is that they did not interpret it (4:4c[7c]) and that they could not interpret it (4:15c–d[18c–d]). Given the clarity of the imagery in the dream, we have to wonder if they grasped the dream's meaning but did not want to deliver such news to the king. It is possible that they needed another source of divination to confirm the meaning of the dream, and since the dream was not from one of their gods, they had no access to another means of divination.[38] But Daniel knew the message was from his God, and he did not need to confirm its meaning; he immediately understood the certainty and significance of the message.

3. The Prediction of the King's Humbling (4:16a–24d[19a–27d])

Main Idea of the Passage

Daniel 4:16–24[19–27] reveals the meaning of Nebuchadnezzar's dream, and it also reveals the concern and compassion that Daniel had for the king.

---

38. See on Dan 2:8–9.

Literary Context

Daniel 4:16a–24d[19a–27d] is the third section of the narrative that begins at 3:31a[4:1a] and extends through the end of ch. 4, and it opens the third-person portion of the chapter (4:16–30[19–33]). As such it functions in at least three ways in its broader literary context. First, it provides a second account of the king's dream, inviting the comparison and contrast with the king's account in the second section (4:6–15[9–18]). A second and related function is that, since the third-person account represents the authoritative voice of the narrator, it offers the means by which to weigh the king's words in his account. A final function of this section is that it serves as a follow-up to Daniel's interpretation of the king's first dream in ch. 2.

> C. Narrative 3: A Humbled King and His Restored Power (3:31a–4:34e[4:1a–37e])
> 1. Nebuchadnezzar's Reflection: The Context (3:31a–33d[4:1a–3d])
> 2. Nebuchadnezzar's Reflection: The Content (4:1a–15f[4a–18f])
> → 3. **The Prediction of the King's Humbling (4:16a–24d[19a–27d])**
> 4. The King's Humbling (4:25–30f[28–33f])
> 5. Nebuchadnezzar's Reflection: The Conclusion (4:31a–34e[34a–37e])

Translation and Exegetical Outline

(See pages 215–17.)

Structure and Literary Form

The third section of the narrative in ch. 4 is the beginning of the third-person narrative that breaks the first-person narrative of Nebuchadnezzar that has comprised the narrative to this point. The third-person narrative begins with this section (4:16–24[19–27]) and concludes at the end of the next section (4:25–30[28–33]). Together, these sections create the link between the two parts of Nebuchadnezzar's first-person narrative.

This first section begins with the transitional אֱדַיִן, "then" (4:16a[19a]) and includes two subsections. The first includes Daniel's shocked reaction to the king's dream report (4:16a–c[19a–c]) and the king's response in reported speech (4:16d–f[19d–f]). The second subsection is Daniel's interpretation of the dream, also set in

Daniel 4:16a–24d[19a–27d]

16a	אֱדַיִן דָּנִיֵּאל ... אֶשְׁתּוֹמַם כְּשָׁעָה חֲדָה	Then Daniel ... was appalled for a short time,	3. The Prediction of the King's Humbling (4:16a–24d[19a–27d])
16b	... דִּי־שְׁמֵהּ בֵּלְטְשַׁאצַּר ...	... whose name was Belteshazzar ...	a. Daniel's Response to the Dream (4:16a–f[19a–f])
16c	וְרַעְיֹנֹהִי יְבַהֲלֻנֵּהּ	and his thoughts were alarming him.	
16d	עָנֵה	Responding,	(1) Daniel's Shock (4:16a–c[19a–c])
16e	מַלְכָּא וְאָמַר	the king said,[1]	
16f	בֵּלְטְשַׁאצַּר חֶלְמָא וּפִשְׁרֵא אַל־יְבַהֲלָךְ	"Belteshazzar, do not let the dream or its interpretation alarm you."	(2) The King's Assurance (4:16d–f[19d–f])
16g	עָנֵה	Responding,	b. Daniel's Interpretation of the Dream (4:16g–24d[19g–27d])
16h	בֵלְטְשַׁאצַּר וְאָמַר	Belteshazzar said,[2]	(1) Daniel's Desire (4:16g–j[19g–j])
16i	(מָרִי) [מָרְאִי] חֶלְמָא (לְשָׂנְאָיִךְ) [לְשָׂנְאָךְ]	"My lord, may the dream be for those who hate you,	
16j	וּפִשְׁרֵהּ (לְעָרָיִךְ) [לְעָרָךְ]	and its interpretation for your adversaries.	
17a	אִילָנָא	The tree	(2) Daniel's Version of the Great Tree (4:17a–18e[20a–21e])
17b	דִּי חֲזַיְתָ	that you saw,	
17c	דִּי רְבָה	which grew great	
17d	וּתְקִף	and became strong,	
17e	וְרוּמֵהּ יִמְטֵא לִשְׁמַיָּא	and whose height reached to the heavens,	
17f	וַחֲזוֹתֵהּ לְכָל־אַרְעָא	and whose visibility [reached] to all the earth;	
18a	וְעָפְיֵהּ שַׁפִּיר	and whose foliage was beautiful,	
18b	וְאִנְבֵּהּ שַׂגִּיא	and whose fruit was abundant,	
18c	וּמָזוֹן לְכֹלָּא־בֵהּ	and on which was food for all;	
18d	תְּחֹתוֹהִי תְּדוּר חֵיוַת בָּרָא	under which dwelled the beasts of the field,	
18e	וּבְעַנְפוֹהִי יִשְׁכְּנָן צִפֲּרֵי שְׁמַיָּא	and in whose branches lived the birds of the heavens	

Continued on next page.

1. See on 2:5 in commentary.
2. See on 2:5 in commentary.

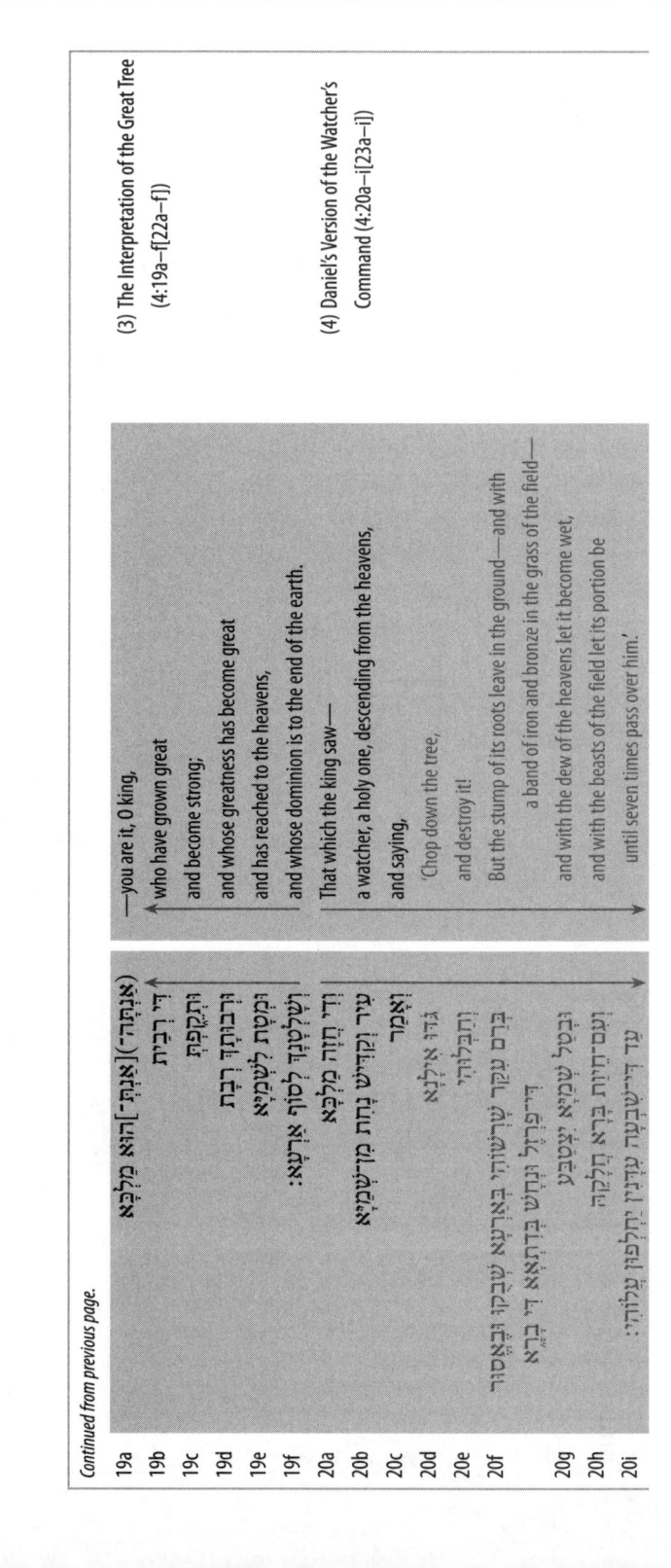

Continued from previous page.

19a	אנתה־הוא[־אנתה] מלכא	—you are it, O king,
19b	די רבית	who have grown great
19c	ותקפת	and become strong;
19d	ורבותך רבת	and whose greatness has become great
19e	ומטת לשמיא	and has reached to the heavens,
19f	ושלטנך לסוף ארעא׃	and whose dominion is to the end of the earth.
20a	ודי חזה מלכא	That which the king saw,
20b	עיר וקדיש נחת מן־שמיא	a watcher, a holy one, descending from the heavens,
20c	ואמר	and saying,
20d	גדו אילנא	'Chop down the tree,
20e	וחבלוהי	and destroy it!
20f	ברם עקר שרשוהי בארעא שבקו	But the stump of its roots leave in the ground—and with
20g	ובאסור די־פרזל ונחש בדתאא די ברא	a band of iron and bronze in the grass of the field—
20h	ובטל שמיא יצטבע	and with the dew of the heavens let it become wet,
20i	ועם־חיותא חלקה בעשב ארעא׃	and with the beasts of the field let its portion be until seven times pass over him.'

(3) The Interpretation of the Great Tree (4:19a–f[22a–f])

(4) Daniel's Version of the Watcher's Command (4:20a–i[23a–i])

21a	—this is the interpretation, O king,
21b	and it is the decree of the Most High
21c	that has come upon my lord, the king:
22a	You will be driven from mankind,
22b	and your dwelling place will be with the beasts of the field.
22c	You will be fed grass like cattle,
22d	and some of the dew of the heavens will be making you wet.
22e	Seven times will pass over you
22f	until you know
22g	that the Most High is ruler over the kingdom of mankind,
22h	and to whomever he wishes,
22i	he gives it.
23a	And as it was said
23b	to leave the stump of the tree's roots,
23c	your kingdom remains for you
23d	from when you acknowledge
23e	that heaven is sovereign.
24a	Therefore, O king, may my counsel be pleasing to you—
24b	break off your sins with righteousness,
24c	and your iniquities [break off] with showing mercy to the poor—
24d	perhaps there may be a lengthening of your prosperity."

(5) The Interpretation of the Watcher's Command (4:21a–23e[24a–26e])

(6) Daniel's Counsel (4:24a–d[27a–d])

reported speech (4:16g–24d[19g–27d]). The interpretation begins with an expression of Daniel's desire that the dream apply to someone else (4:16g–j[19g–j]) and continues with alternations between Daniel's description of the dream and its interpretation. First, he describes the great tree (4:17a–18e[20a–21e]) and interprets its meaning (4:19a–f[22a–f]), and then, after an introduction (4:20a–c[23a–c]), in another instance of embedded reported speech he describes the command of the watcher (4:20d–i[23d–i]) before interpreting its meaning (4:21a–23e[24a–26e]). Daniel's reported speech concludes with a word of counsel for the king (4:24a–d[27a–d]).

Explanation of the Text

a. Daniel's Response to the Dream (4:16a–f[19a–f])

The transitional אֱדַיִן, "then" (4:16a[19a]), opens the third-person narrative that will describe Daniel's reaction to the king's dream and then his retelling and interpretation of it. The narrative's shift to third person here, as already discussed (see on 3:32–33[4:2–3]), brings the voice of the omniscient and reliable narrator into this story and into the larger story cycle of Nebuchadnezzar at a critical place. It provides the standard against which we can weigh the king's words.

The narrator's reference to Daniel echoes the king's first reference to him: "whose name was Belteshazzar" (4:16b[19b]; cf. 4:5b[8b]), and twice more in this short section, Daniel is called "Belteshazzar" (4:16e–h[19e–h]). This use of Daniel's Babylonian name indicates that the narrative, though being told by the narrator, is still from Nebuchadnezzar's point of view. The chapter is cast as the king's account, and even in the third-person section, the narrator maintains the king's perspective.

Daniel's response to the king's dream was horror, and like the king, he was also terrified (יְבַהֲלֻנֵּהּ, 4:16c[19c]; cf. 4:2[5]). It has been suggested that Daniel's terror was at the prospect of delivering bad news to the king, but this seems unlikely, given that dreams were considered dangerous only as long as their meaning remained a mystery: "the interpreting [was] . . . a necessity, not performed primarily for the sake of establishing the content of the dream, but intended to rid the [dreamer] of the impact of the enigma."[39] But Daniel knew that no magic could negate the impact of the dream, and his reaction reflected the horror of what would befall the king (see below on 4:16g–j[19g–j]). Seeing Belteshazzar/Daniel's reaction, the king told him to let neither the dream nor its meaning alarm him, a reassurance that serves as an invitation for Daniel to speak, despite what he had to say.

b. Daniel's Interpretation of the Dream (4:16g–24d[19g–27d])

Daniel's interpretation begins with an expression of regret that these things had come upon the

---

39. Oppenheim, "The Interpretation of Dreams in the Ancient Near East," 219. See also Collins, *Daniel*, 228. Oppenheim is specifically referring to dreams in Sumer and Akkad, civilizations that predated Babylon; however, their influence on Babylon was great, so it is plausible that the same applies.

king. With the appropriate respect (מָרִי, "My lord," 4:16i[19i]), Daniel wishes the dream and its interpretation upon the king's enemies instead. This is a remarkable reaction by a captive to his overlord. The dream foretold the demise of the king who had taken Daniel captive and destroyed the holy city of Jerusalem. Secret satisfaction that the gentile king was finally getting what he deserved might be expected, but instead Daniel is overwhelmed and distressed. For the following analysis, please see fig. 2, pp. 220–23.

The interpretation that Daniel gives is interspersed with his retelling of the dream. He begins with "the tree" (4:17a[20a]), which is the "it" of a clause two verses later: "you are it, O king" (4:19a[22a]). Between these two clauses is Daniel's description of the tree, which has two occurrences of the relative דִּי. In 4:17b[20b], the דִּי relative clause identifies the tree as the one king saw, and the relative דִּי of 4:17c[20c] governs the descriptive clauses that comprise the rest of 4:17[20] and all of 4:18[21].[40]

Daniel's description of the tree echoes much of the king's earlier description. However, three omissions in Daniel's words may help us assess the king's words. First, Daniel omits the king's opening description that refers to the tree's central position in the earth and its great height (4:7c–d[10c–d]). Daniel's description affirms the tree's greatness, but his omission of these two clauses may indicate that while the king was indeed great, his self-perception was overblown. The third clause that Daniel does not include is the king's statement that all flesh was sustained by the tree (4:9f[12f]). He echoes the king's statement that "food for all" was on it (4:18c[21c]; cf. 4:9c[12c]), which implies that the king had the resources to care for all the inhabitants of his kingdom, but by omitting the second statement, Daniel implies that, despite his resources, the king did not take care of all his subjects.

Daniel's words also recall his interpretation of Nebuchadnezzar's first dream in Dan 2. In ch. 2, Nebuchadnezzar was the head of gold on the magnificent statue; he was the "king of kings," and God had given him "the kingdom, the power, and the strength, and the honor" so that he could be ruler over "the sons of man, the beast of the field, and the birds of heaven" (2:37–38). The similarities between the language of Daniel's interpretations in chs. 2 and 4 signal that the dreams are related. The young king of ch. 2 had become the head of gold, a towering and flourishing tree of life in the imagery of ch. 4. In ch. 2, Daniel said God gave Nebuchadnezzar dominion, power, strength, and honor, as well as the responsibility to care for all his subjects. In ch. 4, Daniel said Nebuchadnezzar had indeed cared for the subjects of his vast kingdom, but not to the extent he should have.[41] The dream of ch. 2 had predicted Nebuchadnezzar's glory, and the dream of ch. 4 announces its fulfillment. But it does more than that. The dream indicts the king for not learning the real message of his first dream: wisdom, power, dominion, and glory are God's alone, and he is the one who both gives them to humans and takes them away. It was the king's failure to acknowledge God as the supreme king that was his downfall.

The second part of the dream and interpretation begins in 4:20a[23a]. As before, Daniel recounts a portion of the dream and then gives its interpretation. In the complicated syntax of 4:20–21[23–24], 4:20a[23a] (וְדִי חֲזָה מַלְכָּא) is subordinate to 4:21a[24a] (דְּנָה פִּשְׁרָא מַלְכָּא), while the description in 4:20b–i[23b–i] is appositional to 4:20a[23a].

---

40. Cook, *Aramaic Ezra and Daniel*, 212–13.
41. This failure is also what lies behind Daniel's unsolicited counsel in 4:27[30].

Figure 2: Parallel Accounts in Daniel 3:31a–4:34e[4:1a–37e]

		Nebuchadnezzar's Account		Daniel's Account		Daniel's Interpretation		Fulfillment[a]	Fulfillment[b]
7a		אילנא די חזית די רבה ותקף	16i	[אנתה] [הוא] מלכא [די רבית]					
7b		ורומה ימטא	16j	[ותקפת] (ורבותך רבת) [ומטת]					
7c		לשמיא וחזותה לכל־ארעא	17a	רבה		רבה אילן [ארזא-נבוכדנצר]			
7d		ועפיה שפיר	17b	ותקף					
7e		ואנבה שגיא	17c	ורומה					
7f		ומזון לכלא־בה	17d	ימטא					
8a		תחתוהי תטלל חיות ברא	17e	לשמיא					
8b		ובענפוהי ידרון צפרי שמיא	17f	ושלטנך לסוף ארעא:					
8c		ומנה יתזין כל־בשרא:	18a	עפיה שפיר					
8d			18b	ואנבה שגיא					
9a		וארו עיר וקדיש מן־שמיא נחת	18c	ומזון לכלא־בה					
9b			18d	תחתוהי תדור חיות ברא					
9c			18e	ובענפוהי ישכנן צפרי שמיא:					
9d					21a				
9e					21b	מן (אנשא) [אנשין] טרדין	25		
							26		
							27a	וכלא מטא	
							27b	על־נבוכדנצר מלכא:	
							27c	לקצת ירחין תרי־עשר	
							27d	על־היכל מלכותא די בבל מהלך הוה: ענה מלכא ואמר: הלא דא־היא בבל רבתא די־אנה בניתה לבית מלכו בתקף חסני וליקר הדרי:	

Daniel 3:31a–4:34e[4:1a–37e]

Continued from previous page.

	Nebuchadnezzar's Account		Daniel's Interpretation		Fulfillment[a]		Fulfillment[b]
14a	מַלְכָּא נְבוּכַדְנֶצַּר						
14b	עֲנֵה מַלְכָּא וְאָמַר לְדָנִיֵּאל						
14c	בִּרְעוּת לִבְבָךְ [תֵּאמַר]	22f	בִּרְעוּת לִבְבָךְ				
14d	דִּי פִשְׁרֵהּ (אֲמַרְתָּ) [אֲמַרְתְּ]	22g	דִּי פִשְׁרֵהּ (אֲמַרְתָּ) [אֲמַרְתְּ]	29e	דִּי פִשְׁרֵהּ (אֲמַרְתָּ) [אֲמַרְתְּ]		
14e	לְהוֹדָעוּתַנִי	22h	לְהוֹדָעוּתַנִי	29f	לְהוֹדָעוּתַנִי		
14f	יָדַעְתָּ:	22i	יָדַעְתָּ:	29g	יָדַעְתָּ		
14g	אִילָנָא [דִי] חֲזַיְתָ	23a	דִּי מְטָא אִילָנָא	29h	יָדַעְתָּ:		
		23b	דִּי רְבָה וּתְקִף				
		23c	וְרוּמֵהּ יִמְטֵא לִשְׁמַיָּא				
		23d	וְשָׁלְטָנֵהּ לְסוֹף אַרְעָא:				
		24a	וְדִי חֲזָה מַלְכָּא				
		24b	עִיר וְקַדִּישׁ נָחִת מִן שְׁמַיָּא (וְאָמַר) [וְאָמְרִין]				
		24c	גֹּדּוּ אִילָנָא וְחַבְּלוּהִי				
		24d	בְּרַם עִקַּר שָׁרְשׁוֹהִי בְּאַרְעָא שְׁבֻקוּ				
31a	וְלִקְצָת יוֹמַיָּה						
31b	אֲנָה נְבוּכַדְנֶצַּר עַיְנַי לִשְׁמַיָּא נִטְלֵת						
31c	וּמַנְדְּעִי עֲלַי יְתוּב						
31d	(וּלְעִלָּאָה) [וּלְעִלָּיָא] בָּרְכֵת						
31e	וּלְחַי עָלְמָא שַׁבְּחֵת וְהַדְּרֵת						

								ונשתני:
31f								די מלכו תה עלם
31g								ושלטנה עם דר
32a								וכל־דארי ארעא
32b								(כלה) [כלא] כלא חשיבין וכמצבין עבד בחיל שמיא
32c								ודארי ארעא
32d								ולא איתי די־ימחא בידה
32e								ויאמר לה מה עבדת:
33a								בה־זמנא מנדעי יתוב עלי
33b								וליקר מלכותי הדרי וזוי יתוב עלי
33c								ולי הדברי ורברבני יבעון
33d								ועל־מלכותי התקנת
33e								ורבו יתירה הוספת לי:
34a								כען אנה נבכדנצר משבח ומרומם ומהדר למלך שמיא
34b								די כל־מעבדוהי קשט
34c								וארחתה דין
34d								ודי מהלכין בגוה
34e								יכל להשפלה:

It is easier to see if the order is reversed: "(4:21[24]) this is the interpretation ... (4:20[23]) of that which you saw." Cook notes that the length of the description in 4:20[23] accounts for its placement before the subject and predicate in 4:21[24].[42]

While his recounting of the tree portion of the dream generally echoed Nebuchadnezzar's report, Daniel's retelling of the watcher's activity is markedly shorter than the king's version. The king's quotative frame for the angel's embedded speech ("he was calling out loudly and thus he was saying," 4:11a–b[14a–b]) becomes simply וְאָמַר, "and [he was] saying" (4:20c[23c]), in Daniel's telling. The angel's command to destroy the tree takes six clauses for Nebuchadnezzar, while Daniel summarizes in two clauses (4:20d–e[23d–e]; see on 4:6–15[9–18] above). The king's lengthy description of the angel's appearance and orders is probably best explained by the fact that, as the one most affected by the events portrayed, the details were particularly vivid to him.

Daniel's condensed version may tell us more about him than about the king. We already know he is troubled by what will befall the king, and we also can see that the meaning of the dream is fairly transparent—Nebuchadnezzar probably had a good idea what was going to happen without the formal interpretation. Daniel may be summarizing the king's account in order to omit the gory details. This becomes more plausible when we consider Daniel's interpretation. He begins by affirming that what he is about to say is "the decree of the Most High" (4:21b[24b]) that has come upon "my lord, the king" (מָרִי מַלְכָּא; 4:21c[24c]). Then he summarizes the angel's commands about the tree's destruction, saying, "You will be driven from mankind" (4:22a[25a]). Three clauses detail the rest: the king would dwell with the beasts, be fed grass like cattle, and be wet with heaven's dew (4:22b–d[25b–d]).[43] What follows at this point in the king's report is omitted in Daniel's report: "let its heart be changed from a man, and let a beast's heart be given to him"

---

42. Cook, *Aramaic Ezra and Daniel*, 214.

43. Being driven from mankind may have meant that the king would be "ousted or deposed in some fashion by other members of the royal court as a result of his incompetence to govern" (Hill, *Daniel*, 95). The exact nature of this incompetence is much discussed, with most concluding it was a mental illness in which a person thinks he is an animal and so behaves like one (e.g., lycanthropy, boanthropy, zoanthropy). The Aramaic story of Ahikar contains a description like the one in Nebuchadnezzar's dream ("The hair on my head had grown to my shoulders, and my beard reached my breast; and my body was fouled with dust and my nails were grown like eagles"), as does the Mesopotamian Epic of Gilgamesh, where Gilgamesh was "hairy, unclothed, and eating grass before he became 'civilized' as a human being" (Lucas, "Daniel," 540). These similarities may mean Dan 4 intends to present Nebuchadnezzar "as an exile from civilized human society" (ibid.). Newsom further notes similarities with Mesopotamian symbolism related to demons and the dead, suggesting that the imagery of Nebuchadnezzar's period of punishment likens it to a time of death (*Daniel*, 148).

We have already noted (see p. 201 n10 above) that history has no record of this experience in Nebuchadnezzar's life, although there is some evidence that near the end of his life, he had some mental ailment: "A fragmentary cuneiform text seems to refer to some mental disorder afflicting Nebuchadnezzar and perhaps his neglecting and leaving Babylon, maybe putting his son Amēl-Marduk in charge for a while, and then of his repentance for neglect of the worship of the gods. Unfortunately, the text is too fragmentary for any firm conclusions to be drawn" (Lucas, "Daniel," 540–41). Scholars have long speculated that the account in Daniel really came from a later account about Babylonian king, Nabonidus, who spent ten years of his reign away from the throne. When a document called the "Prayer of Nabonidus" was discovered among the Dead Sea Scrolls and described the mental illness of Nabonidus, scholars appeared to have their smoking gun: the author of Daniel had adapted the story of Nabonidus to fit the Nebuchadnezzar story because it aligned with the purpose and context of the narrative. But there are significant differences between the two stories, including the kings' names, the nature of their illnesses, and the name

(4:13a–b[16a–b]). Daniel neither repeats this part in his recounting of the dream nor in its interpretation. When Daniel got to the worst part of the dream, he skipped it. Perhaps he knew the king had gotten the point. He did not need to repeat and explain the most painful detail. Daniel spared the king the last shred of his dignity—his humanity.

Daniel's interpretation concludes with the time frame ("Seven times will pass over you," 4:22e[25e]) and a restatement of the purpose of the dream first stated in the king's report (4:14c–g[17c–g]). Daniel adapts the king's version to personalize it; where the king had said "in order that the living may know" (4:14c[17c]), Daniel twice says "until/from when you know" (4:22f[25f], 23d[26d]). He also omits the last part of the purpose given in the king's telling: "and the lowliest of men he sets over it" (4:14g[17g]). As with his other omissions, this may be Daniel's sensitivity to or respect for the king: he does not refer to him as "the lowliest of men."

One final notable difference is the placement of Daniel's interpretation of the tree stump that remained when the tree was destroyed. In both the king's and Daniel's accounts of the dream, the angel's command to leave the stump occurs after the order to destroy and before the description of the king's beastlike existence (cf. 4:12a[15a] and 4:20f[23f]). But in Daniel's interpretation, the stump is saved for last (4:23[26]). Newsom comments on the significance: "Changing the order of the elements in the dream, Daniel reserves the image of the root stock until the end and disambiguates it as a sign of hope for restoration, dependent upon the king's recognition of the true source of sovereignty."[44] The presence of the stump indicated that the great king's empire would survive, but it would come at great personal cost.[45]

Daniel's interpretation concludes in 4:23[26], but then he draws an unsolicited conclusion for the king: . . . לָהֵן, "therefore . . ." (4:24a[27a]). In what follows, Daniel sounds like an Old Testament prophet, calling the king to repentance and reform. The reform is to do righteousness and mercy with respect to the poor (4:24b–c[27b–c])—indicating that Nebuchadnezzar had not done right by the poor in his kingdom (see on 4:18[21] above). The king had the resources and responsibility to care for all in his kingdom, and in the Old Testament, doing justice and taking action on behalf of the needy are royal obligations (Ps 72:2; Isa 11:4; Jer 22:15–16); even gentile kings "are called to be the means of God's caring kingship being implemented."[46] Daniel hoped that if the king took his counsel, his prosperous reign might continue (4:24d[27d]).

---

of the diviner/interpreter. Although some translations of the "Prayer of Nabonidus" identify the king's affliction as being made beastlike, the Qumran text is too fragmentary to make this definitive statement. Collins published a critical version of the text and notes that the fragmentary nature of the text makes the full account uncertain. Scholars have filled in the gaps, but Collins says, "Some reconstructions enhance the relationship between the two documents by filling lacunae in the scroll on the basis of Daniel" (*Daniel*, 218; see also 217n13). We know there are similar stories about Nebuchadnezzar and Nabonidus, but the exact nature of the relationship between them is not known.

44. Newsom, *Daniel*, 145.

45. Of the significance of the surviving stump in Daniel's interpretation (4:23[26]), Cook notes, "The expression appears to refer to the endurance of the kingdom during the king's absence. However, the following temporal מן־די ["from when," v. 23d[26d]] belies such an interpretation: it must refer to the '(re)establishing' of the kingdom with Nebuchadnezzar at its head" (*Aramaic Ezra and Daniel*, 217–18).

46. Goldingay, *Daniel*, 270.

4. The King's Humbling (4:25–30f[28–33f])

Main Idea of the Passage

Daniel 4:25–30[28–33] recounts the fulfillment of Nebuchadnezzar's dream about the destruction of the magnificent tree when he boasts of his great glory and success, gifts he had received from the Most High God.

Literary Context

Daniel 4:25–30[28–33] is the fourth section of the narrative that began at 3:31[4:1], and it concludes the third-person portion of the chapter (4:16–30[19–33]). It functions in at least two ways in its broader literary context. First, it provides the catalyst for the fulfillment of the king's dream. Nebuchadnezzar's act of hubris in 4:26–27[29–30] sets the decree of the Most High in motion. Second, it is the climax of the chapter in that it details the fulfillment of the dream and the judgment of the king.

> C. Narrative 3: A Humbled King and His Restored Power (3:31a–4:34e[4:1a–37e])
> 1. Nebuchadnezzar's Reflection: The Context (3:31a–33d[4:1a–3d])
> 2. Nebuchadnezzar's Reflection: The Content (4:1a–15f[4a–18f])
> 3. The Prediction of the King's Humbling (4:16a–24d[19a–27d])
> ➡ **4. The King's Humbling (4:25–30f[28–33f])**
> 5. Nebuchadnezzar's Reflection: The Conclusion (4:31a–34e[34a–37e])

Translation and Exegetical Outline

(See page 227.)

Structure and Literary Form

The fourth section (4:25–30[28–33]) of the narrative that began in 3:31[4:1] is the continuation of the third-person narrative that links the two parts of Nebuchadnezzar's first-person narrative. It has three subsections. In the first, the king demonstrates

Daniel 4:25–30f[28–33f]

25[28]	:אֲנָ֑ה עַל־נְבוּכַדְנֶצַּ֖ר מַלְכָּֽא	All this came upon Nebuchadnezzar the king.	4. The King's Humbling (4:25–30f[28–33f])
26[29]	לִקְצָ֥ת יַרְחִ֖ין תְּרֵֽי־עֲשַׂ֑ר עַל־הֵיכַ֛ל מַלְכוּתָ֥א דִּ֥י בָבֶ֖ל מְהַלֵּ֥ךְ הֲוָֽה׃	At the end of twelve months, he was walking on (the roof of) the palace of the kingdom of Babylon.	a. The King's Pride (4:25–27d [28–30d])
27[30]a	עָנֵ֤ה ↓	↓ Responding,[1]	
27[30]b	מַלְכָּא֙ וְאָמַ֔ר	the king said,	
27[30]c	הֲלָ֥א דָא־הִ֖יא בָּבֶ֣ל רַבְּתָ֑א	"Is this not Babylon the great,	
27[30]d	דִּֽי־אֲנָ֤ה בֱנַיְתַהּ֙ לְבֵ֣ית מַלְכ֔וּ בִּתְקַ֥ף חִסְנִ֖י וְלִיקָ֥ר הַדְרִֽי׃	↑ which I myself have built for a royal house, by the strength of my power and for the glory of my majesty?"	
28[31]a	ע֗וֹד מִלְּתָא֙ בְּפֻ֣ם מַלְכָּ֔א ↓	↓ While the word was in the mouth of the king,	
28[31]b	קָ֖ל מִן־שְׁמַיָּ֥א נְפַֽל	a voice came down from the heavens,	b. Heaven's Decree (4:28a–29h[31a–32h])
28[31]c	לָ֤ךְ אָֽמְרִין֙ נְבוּכַדְנֶצַּ֣ר מַלְכָּ֔א	"To you it is said, Nebuchadnezzar the king:	
28[31]d	מַלְכוּתָ֖ה עֲדָ֥ת מִנָּֽךְ׃	The kingdom has departed from you,	
29[32]a	וּמִן־אֲנָשָׁא֩ לָ֨ךְ טָֽרְדִ֜ין	and from mankind you are driven,	
29[32]b	וְֽעִם־חֵיוַ֧ת בָּרָ֣א מְדֹרָ֗ךְ	and with the beasts of the field is your dwelling.	
29[32]c	עִשְׂבָּ֤א כְתוֹרִין֙ לָ֣ךְ יְטַעֲמ֔וּן	You will be fed grass like cattle,	
29[32]d	וְשִׁבְעָ֥ה עִדָּנִ֖ין יַחְלְפ֣וּן עֲלָ֑ךְ	and seven times will pass over you	
29[32]e	עַ֣ד ↑ דִּֽי־תִנְדַּ֗ע	↑ until you acknowledge	
29[32]f	דִּֽי־שַׁלִּ֤יט עִלָּאָה֙ (עִלָּיָא֙) בְּמַלְכ֣וּת אֲנָשָׁ֔א	↑ that the Most High is ruler over the kingdom of mankind,	
29[32]g	וּלְמַן־דִּ֥י יִצְבֵּ֖א	and to whomever he wishes,	
29[32]h	יִתְּנִנַּֽהּ׃	he gives it."	
30[33]a	בַּהּ־שַׁעֲתָ֗א מִלְּתָא֮ סָ֣פַת עַל־נְבוּכַדְנֶצַּר֒ ↓	At that moment, the word about Nebuchadnezzar was fulfilled,	c. The King's Demise (4:30a–f[33a–f])
30[33]b	וּמִן־אֲנָשָׁ֣א טְרִ֔יד	and from mankind he was driven,	
30[33]c	וְעִשְׂבָּ֤א כְתוֹרִין֙ יֵאכֻ֔ל	and he was eating the grass like cattle,	
30[33]d	וּמִטַּ֥ל שְׁמַיָּ֖א גִּשְׁמֵ֣הּ יִצְטַבַּ֑ע	and some of the dew of the heavens was making his body wet,	
30[33]e	עַ֣ד דִּ֥י שַׂעְרֵ֛הּ כְּנִשְׁרִ֥ין רְבָ֖ה	↑ until his hair grew long like eagles'	
30[33]f	וְטִפְר֥וֹהִי כְצִפְּרִֽין׃	and his nails [grew] like birds.'	

---

1. See on 2:5 in the commentary.

his pride (4:25–27[28–30]). The narrator sets the context for the king's action and then uses reported speech to detail the king's act of hubris. The second subsection begins with a temporal reference ("While the word was in the mouth of the king," 4:28a[31a]). What follows this time frame is the reported speech of a voice from heaven announcing the fulfillment of Nebuchadnezzar's dream (4:28–29[31–32]). The third subsection begins with the temporal marker בַּהּ־שַׁעֲתָא, "at that moment" (4:30a[33a]), and the narrator's description of the dream's fulfillment follows (4:30[33]).

Explanation of the Text

a. The King's Pride (4:25–27d[28–30d])

After Daniel's interpretation of the dream and subsequent word of counsel to the king, the narrator continues the third-person section of the narrative with a summary statement of what follows ("All this came upon Nebuchadnezzar the king," 4:25[28]). Twelve months after Daniel's interpretation of the dream, the king was walking "on (the roof of) the palace of the kingdom of Babylon" (4:26[29]). The narrator offers no explanation for the inclusion of this time frame, but it may indicate that Nebuchadnezzar tried to reform his ways, as advised by Daniel, and so punishment was delayed.[47]

As Nebuchadnezzar walked atop the roof of his palace, he surveyed the great city beneath him. His response to what he saw is in his statement of 4:27c–d[30c–d].[48] The king calls Babylon בֵּית מַלְכוּ, "a royal house" (4:27c[30c]), the references to the "palace" and the king's "house" reminding the reader of the beginning of the king's account of events in 4:1[4], where he was at ease in his house and flourishing in his palace. In their first occurrence, the words described the king's situation—one of success, peace, and comfort. In their second occurrence here, they describe the king's perspective on his situation—namely, he was responsible for it. He lived in luxury and ease because he had earned it. He was a great king because he deserved it. He had built his "house"—an entire city, and we might assume an entire empire—by the "strength of my power and for the glory of my majesty" (4:27d[30d]).

In this chapter, Nebuchadnezzar experiences God's judgment for his pride. Rather than acknowledging God as the source of his power and the wealth that went along with it, he took the credit for everything he had become. While we are all guilty of this, the offense was amplified for Nebuchadnezzar because he was מַלְכָּא, "the king"—a point the narrator makes as he begins the story of the king's demise (4:25[28]) and then again when he reports the words of the "voice from heaven" ("To you it is said, Nebuchadnezzar the king," 4:28c[31c]). These dual instances of overspecification emphasize the king's office: as king, he was granted power by God for the purpose of doing justice and taking action on behalf of the needy (see above on 4:18[21], 24[27]).

---

47. Newsom notes that "just as Nebuchadnezzar in previous narratives both understands and fails to understand the significance of the divine revelations to him, his subsequent actions indicate that he has not grasped the full import of the dream" (*Daniel*, 145).

48. The quotative frame עֲנֵה מַלְכָּא וְאָמַר, translated here as "responding, the king said," reflects his response to the situation, not to someone else in conversation. See also on 2:5 and 2:20 above.

The repeated references to the king's residence and his situation (4:1[4], 26–27[29–30]) create a contrast between his comfortable life and the lives of his subjects suffering neglect and injustice. While he may have enjoyed great comfort, success, and wealth, inhabitants of his kingdom were oppressed and in great need—and he was responsible for it.

In 4:27[30] the narrator lets Nebuchadnezzar himself utter the words that led to his demise. The king asks a rhetorical question, in which he boasts of his greatness, in language that draws on the interpretation of his first dream, where Daniel said God had given him the kingdom, the power, and the strength, and the honor (Dan 2:37b; cf. 4:27d[30d]). Here in ch. 4, Nebuchadnezzar lays claim to everything God gave him, failing to learn the lesson of his earlier dream. The addition of אֲנָה in the king's words emphasize his pride: Babylon was the city which אֲנָה בֱנַיְתַהּ, "I myself have built" (4:27d[30d]). God's gifts became his source of pride.

b. Heaven's Decree (4:28a–29h[31a–32h])

Before the king could take another breath, his judgment was pronounced. In his dream, the king had reported seeing a "watcher—that is, a holy one" (עִיר וְקַדִּישׁ, 4:10b[13b]; cf. 4:20a–b[23a–b]) descend from heaven and then call out orders to destroy the tree, but in the enactment of the decree, only a voice (קָל) descends from heaven (4:28b[31b]). The narrator sets the decree itself as reported speech and in a much-abbreviated form of the watcher's speech as reported by the king and by Daniel (cf. 4:10–14[13–17] and 4:20[23]); it simply consists of what Daniel in his interpretation referred to as the "decree of the Most High" (4:21b[24b]). Daniel 4:28d[31d] captures all of the watcher's orders with respect to the tree: "The kingdom has departed from you." From that point, the decree closely follows Daniel's interpretation in 4:22[25],[49] although it says nothing about the preservation of Nebuchadnezzar's kingdom, as signified by the stump in the king's dream.

c. The King's Demise (4:30a–f[33a–f])

Following the decree, the narrator reports its fulfillment in 4:30[33]. A temporal clause (בַּהּ־שַׁעֲתָא, "at that moment") and a summary statement ("the word about Nebuchadnezzar was fulfilled") begin the fulfillment. The account of the fulfillment closely follows the account of the decree (see 4:28c–29h[31c–32h]), with one significant difference. Rather than reporting the length of time ("seven periods of time will pass over him/you," 4:13c[16c], 20i[23i], 22e[25e], 29d[32d]) as all the other accounts do, the fulfillment account illustrates the passage of time: the king's hair and nails would grow long like that of eagles and birds—not only would he live among the beasts, he would look like one of them.[50]

In the fulfillment of the decree, the greatest king of his day was transformed into a beastlike being for thinking himself to be a god. He had blurred the lines between divinity and humanity, and the Most High God judged him by blurring the lines between his humanity and sub-humanity.[51]

---

49. The only omission is Daniel's statement in 4:22d[25d], וּמִטַּל שְׁמַיָּא לָךְ מְצַבְּעִין, "and some of the dew of the heavens will be making you wet." See n50 below.

50. There are two small differences in the account of the dream's fulfillment. First, it omits "with the beasts of the field is your dwelling" (cf. 4:22b[25b], 29b[32b]), and second, it includes "some of the dew of the heavens will be making you wet" (cf. 4:12b[15b], 20g[23g], 22d[25d]). These two phrases have varied slightly throughout the accounts.

51. Fewell notes the poetic justice: "A man who thinks he is like a god must become like a beast to learn that he is only a human being" (*Circle of Sovereignty*, 72).

5. Nebuchadnezzar's Reflection: *The Conclusion* (4:31a–34e[34a–37e])

Main Idea of the Passage

Daniel 4:31–34[34–37] is the culmination of the signs and wonders done in Nebuchadnezzar's life, and the king honors the Most High God as sovereign and his kingdom as superior.

Literary Context

Daniel 4:31–34[34–37] concludes the first-person narrative of Nebuchadnezzar's humbling that comprises most of the narrative (3:31–4:15[4:1–18] and 4:31–34[34–37]), and it also is the final passage in the narrative. As such it functions in at least three ways in its broader literary context. First, it details the outcome and effect of the king's encounter with the Most High. Second, it includes a doxology praising the Most High that forms an *inclusio* with the doxology in the opening passage (3:31–33[4:1–3]) and so reaffirms the chapter's primary theme of God's superior nature and kingdom. Third, it offers the last words spoken in the book by Nebuchadnezzar, a character who has featured prominently in the previous four chapters. This final section (and the final narrative) invites the reader to consider the development of Nebuchadnezzar over the course of the chapter and the book.

> C. Narrative 3: A Humbled King and His Restored Power (3:31a–4:34e[4:1a–37e])
> 1. Nebuchadnezzar's Reflection: The Context (3:31a–33d[4:1a–3d])
> 2. Nebuchadnezzar's Reflection: The Content (4:1a–15f[4a–18f])
> 3. The Prediction of the King's Humbling (4:16a–24d[19a–27d])
> 4. The King's Humbling (4:25a–30f[28–33f])
> ➡ **5. Nebuchadnezzar's Reflection: The Conclusion (4:31a–34e[34a–37e])**

Translation and Exegetical Outline

(See page 231.)

Daniel 4:31a–34e[34a–37e]

31[34]a	אֱנָשׁ֖ה יוֹמַיָּא֩ אֲנָ֨ה נְבוּכַדְנֶצַּ֤ר עַיְנַי֙ לִשְׁמַיָּ֣א נִטְלֵ֔ת	"And at the end of the days, I, Nebuchadnezzar, lifted my eyes to the heavens.	5. Nebuchadnezzar's Reflection: The Conclusion (4:31a–34e[34a–37e])
31[34]b		And as my reason to me was returning,	a. The King's Acknowledgment (4:31a–32d[34a–35d])
31[34]c	וּמַנְדְּעִ֣י [וּמַנְדְּעִ֣י] (עֲלַ֣י) יְת֔וּב	the Most High I blessed,	
31[34]d	וּלְעִלָּאָה֙ בָּרְכֵ֔ת	and the one who lives forever I praised and honored,	
31[34]e	וּלְחַ֧י עָלְמָ֛א שַׁבְּחֵ֥ת וְהַדְּרֵ֖ת	whose dominion is an everlasting dominion,	
31[34]f	דִּ֤י שָׁלְטָנֵהּ֙ שָׁלְטָ֣ן עָלַ֔ם	and whose kingdom is from generation to generation.	
32[35]a	וּמַלְכוּתֵ֖הּ עִם־דָּ֥ר וְדָֽר׃	All the inhabitants of the earth are considered nothing,	
32[35]b	וְכָל־[דָּיְרֵ֤י] (דארי) אַרְעָא֙ כְּלָ֣א חֲשִׁיבִ֔ין	and according to his will he does with the host of the heavens and the inhabitants of the earth.	
32[35]c	וּֽכְמִצְבְּיֵ֗הּ עָבֵד֙ בְּחֵ֣יל שְׁמַיָּ֔א וְדָיְרֵ֖י אַרְעָ֑א	There is no one who can strike his hand and say to him,	
32[35]d	וְלָ֤א אִיתַי֙ דִּֽי־יְמַחֵ֣א בִידֵ֔הּ וְיֵ֥אמַר לֵ֖הּ מָ֥ה עֲבַֽדְתָּ׃	'What have you done?'	
33[36]a	בֵּהּ־זִמְנָ֞א מַנְדְּעִ֣י ׀ יְת֣וּב עֲלַ֗י	At the time that my reason was returning to me,	b. The King's Restoration (4:33a–e[36a–e])
33[36]b	וְלִיקַ֨ר מַלְכוּתִ֜י הַדְרִ֤י וְזִיוִי֙ יְת֣וּב עֲלַ֔י	and for the glory of my kingdom, my majesty and my splendor were returning to me,	
33[36]c	וְלִ֕י הַדָּבְרַ֥י וְרַבְרְבָנַ֖י יְבַעוֹ֑ן	and my counselors and my magistrates were seeking me;	
33[36]d	וְעַל־מַלְכוּתִ֣י הָתְקְנַ֔ת	over my kingdom I was established,	
33[36]e	וּרְב֥וּ יַתִּירָ֖ה ה֥וּסְפַת לִֽי׃	and surpassing greatness was added to me.	
34[37]a	כְּעַ֞ן אֲנָ֣ה נְבוּכַדְנֶצַּ֗ר מְשַׁבַּ֤ח וּמְרוֹמֵם֙ וּמְהַדַּר֙ לְמֶ֣לֶךְ שְׁמַיָּ֔א	Now I, Nebuchadnezzar, praise and exalt and glorify the king of the heavens,	c. The King's Final Word (4:34a–e[37a–e])
34[37]b	דִּ֤י כָל־מַעֲבָד֙וֹהִי֙ קְשֹׁ֔ט	whose every work is true,	
34[37]c	וְאֹרְחָתֵ֖הּ דִּ֑ין	and whose ways are just,	
34[37]d	וְדִי֙ מַהְלְכִ֣ין בְּגֵוָ֔ה יָכִ֖ל	and who the ones walking in pride is able	
34[37]e	לְהַשְׁפָּלָֽה׃	to humble."	

1. Emended from the MT הָתְקְנַת, "it was established," with most English translations.

Structure and Literary Form

The fifth and final section (4:31–34[34–37]) of the narrative in Dan 3:31a–4:34e[4:1a–37e] returns to the first-person reflection of Nebuchadnezzar that began in 3:31[4:1]. As a continuation of the unframed reported speech of 3:31–4:15[4:1–18]), it depends on the initial clause of the earlier section, which functioned as something of a quotative frame in context ("Nebuchadnezzar the king to all peoples . . . ," 3:31a[4:1a]; see above).

This concluding section has three subsections. The first begins with the temporal reference "and at the end of the days" (4:31a[34a]) and is the king's acknowledgment of the superiority of the Most High (4:31–32[34–35]). The second subsection also begins with a temporal reference—"at the time that" (4:33a[36a]), i.e., the earlier time of 4:31a[34a]—before its description of the king's restoration (4:33[36]). Both subsections refer to the same time period, but the first focuses on Nebuchadnezzar's praise of God, while the second focuses on the restoration of his kingdom and greatness. The final subsection, 4:34[37], consists of the book's final words from Nebuchadnezzar.

Explanation of the Text

a. The King's Acknowledgment (4:31a–32d[34a–35d])

The return in 4:31[34] to Nebuchadnezzar's first-person account begins with a temporal clause that sets the context: "At the end of the days, I, Nebuchadnezzar, lifted my eyes to the heavens." The time referenced is the time decreed for the king's judgment (4:13c[16c], 20i[23i], 22e[25e], 29d[32d], 30e–f[33e–f]). The overspecification of the king here (אֲנָה נְבוּכַדְנֶצַּר, "I, Nebuchadnezzar"), as earlier, is his affirmation that what is about to be recounted is a trustworthy report of events (see above on 4:1[4], 15[18]). The king reports that he lifted his eyes to heaven, an expression that suggests seeking God's aid (Pss 25:15; 121:1–2; 123:1–2; 141:8).[52] This action appears to be the trigger for what happens next[53]—namely, his reason returns. As his reason was returning,[54] he acknowledged God's sovereignty, an acknowledgment that was the outcome of the judgment he experienced.

The purpose of Nebuchadnezzar's judgment is clearly stated throughout the chapter, beginning with the king's report of his dream (4:14[17]); Dan-

---

52. Goldingay, *Daniel*, 263.
53. Newsom notes that this action is in line with Nebuchadnezzar's animalistic state: "He cannot speak, but he signals as an animal might, by directing his eyes to heaven. In response to this gesture of acknowledgment, his reason is restored" (*Daniel*, 148).
54. I read the imperfect verb יְתוּב in 4:31b[34b] as circumstantial: וּמַנְדְּעִי עֲלַי יְתוּב, "And as my reason to me was returning." See Li's discussion on the prefix conjugation in Dan 4:31–33[34–36] in *The Verbal System of the Aramaic of Daniel*, 106–8, and see below on 4:33[36].

iel repeats this purpose in his interpretation (4:22f-i[25f-i]), as does the voice from heaven in the dream's fulfillment (4:29e-h[32e-h]). The period of judgment would last "until you know that the Most High is ruler over the kingdom of mankind, and to whomever he wishes, he gives it."[55] Since the judgment has passed, the reader can assume the king now knows these things, and his words indicate that he does.

However, in a chapter full of repetition, we might wonder why the king does not say something like, "I praised and honored the Most High, who is ruler over the kingdom of mankind and gives it to whomever he wishes." Instead, he details the reason for his praise of the Most High—the everlasting nature of his person and his kingdom (4:31d-f[34d-f]) and for the power he wields (4:32[35]). The first set of statements by Nebuchadnezzar (i.e., about the eternality of God's kingdom) echoes his earlier words (3:33c-d[4:3c-d]), creating an *inclusio* that highlights a key theme of the chapter—the enduring (and thus superior) nature of God's kingdom in contrast with every human kingdom. Nebuchadnezzar's recognition of the nature of God's rule and kingdom grew out of his experience with his own finitude.

In his second set of statements, Nebuchadnezzar acknowledges God's sovereignty as it relates to his superior power (4:32[35]). All of the king's words are reminiscent of statements elsewhere in the Old Testament about God's power. His statement that "all the inhabitants of the earth are considered nothing" sounds like Isaiah: "Before him all the nations are as nothing; they are regarded by him as worthless and less than nothing" (Isa 40:17). His statement that "according to his will, he does with the host of the heavens and the inhabitants of the earth" sounds like the psalmists: "Our God is in heaven; he does whatever pleases him" (Ps 115:3); and "YHWH does whatever pleases him, in the heavens and on the earth, in the seas and all their depths" (Ps 135:6). His statement "There is no one who can strike his hand and say to him, 'What have you done?'" sounds like Job: "Who can say to [God], 'What are you doing?'" (Job 9:12) and "I know that you can do all things; no purpose of yours can be thwarted" (42:2). The narrator shapes Nebuchadnezzar's words in language that would resonate with the audience of the book of Daniel.[56]

b. The King's Restoration (4:33a-e[36a-e])

After his praise of the Most High, Nebuchadnezzar resumes talking about the time his reason was restored (בֵּהּ־זִמְנָא, 4:33a[36a]). The overspecification of the king in 4:34a[37a] (אֲנָה נְבוּכַדְנֶצַּר, "I, Nebuchadnezzar"), as earlier, is his affirmation that what is about to be recounted is a trustworthy report of events (see above on 4:1[4], 15[18]). He provides three circumstantial clauses that provide background for his main statement in 4:33d-e[36d-e] that his kingdom was reestablished and his greatness was even greater than before. First, his reason was returning; second, his majesty and splendor were returning to him; and third, his officials were seeking him out again.[57]

While the king may sound boastful here, his words are appropriate in the larger context of the chapter and the book. The book of Daniel explores the relationship between human kingship and divine kingship, and the greatness of Nebuchadnezzar is clearly cast as God's gift. In the interpretation

---

55. The king's version varies slightly. See above on 4:14[17].
56. We do not need to assume that the gentile king knew the sacred texts of his captives. See p. 203n18.

57. See 232n54 above for reading the imperfect verbs in 4:33[36] as circumstantial.

of the king's dream of ch. 2, Daniel said God had given Nebuchadnezzar "the kingdom, the power, and the strength, and the honor" (2:37). In the interpretation of the handwriting on the wall in ch. 5, Daniel will rehearse the greatness of Nebuchadnezzar for Belshazzar, saying God gave him "the kingdom and the greatness and the honor and the majesty" (5:18). Nebuchadnezzar's statement about his greatness, glory, and majesty in ch. 4 is tucked between his two statements acknowledging the greatness of God (4:31–32[34–35]; 4:34[37]). Nebuchadnezzar's problem was not that he thought his kingdom great and glorious; his problem was that he had taken credit for it rather than acknowledging that the Most High ruled over him and had given him dominion. The events of ch. 4 transformed the king's perspective on his place in the hierarchy of sovereignty.[58]

c. The King's Final Word (4:34a–e[37a–e])

With a final instance of overspecification (אֲנָה נְבוּכַדְנֶצַּר, "I, Nebuchadnezzar"), the king concludes his proclamation—affirming that what he is about to say is trustworthy (see above on 4:1[4], 15[18], 31[34]). In his closing words, Nebuchadnezzar again acknowledges God's sovereignty (4:34[37]), referring to Israel's God as the "king of the heavens," a title used only here in the Old Testament. In the context of Dan 4, this title is significant as the culmination of wordplay on the word שְׁמַיָּא, "the heavens," throughout the chapter. "Heaven" first described the tree's great height (4:8[11], 17[20], 19[22]) and its protection for the birds (4:9[12], 18[21]). It was also the source of the king's judgment (4:10[13], 20[23], 28[31]). Goldingay summarizes the effect of the wordplay:

The heavens to which he reached will supply his humble needs as it supplies those of the rest of creation (vv. 15, 22, 25, 33; 5:21). In the end he must look to the heavens as the real source of help rather than pretending to be self-sufficient; he must acknowledge that the heavens rule, and as a king on earth he must bow down to worship the King of the heavens who rules in the heavens as on the earth (vv. 26, 34, 35, 37).[59]

Nebuchadnezzar describes the king of heaven with a series of relative clauses. He is the king whose every work is true and every way just, and he is the king who is able to humble those walking in pride—a particularly poignant clause given the events of the chapter. This chapter has been about two sovereignties—human and divine—and the lesson learned by the king is that his rule was "utterly derivative, utterly contingent, and totally dependent upon the divine will."[60]

This is the final word from Nebuchadnezzar in the book after four chapters in which he has occupied center stage, chapters that have been carefully crafted and combined to provide a good look at the gentile king and to chronicle his gradual transformation "from a king who considers himself to be the most powerful figure in his kingdom to one who recognizes that his extraordinary greatness is but a gift from the Most High God."[61]

At the conclusion of this narrative, I return to an earlier discussion (see above on 3:31–32[4:1–2]) about the narrator's choice to use a first-person account of Nebuchadnezzar as a major component of this story. I discussed a motivation for the alternation between first and third person and suggested that the use of first person allows Nebuchadnezzar his "day in court," the opportunity to tell his own

---

58. See Lord of the King of Kings above (pp. 137–39)
59. Goldingay, *Daniel*, 261.
60. Towner, *Daniel*, 59–60.
61. Newsom, *Daniel*, 127.

story and be judged accordingly. A second and related issue that I turn to now is the effect of the first person here in the larger cycle of Nebuchadnezzar stories (chs. 1–4, esp. 2–4), the Aramaic chiasm (chs. 2–7), and the book as a whole. How does this first-person chapter fit, and what does it contribute?

First, what is the role of this chapter in the cycle of Nebuchadnezzar stories? In ch. 1, Nebuchadnezzar was responsible for the captivity and subsequent enculturation of Daniel and his friends. In ch. 2, he was a young king with a troubling dream about the future. The dream was a call for him to acknowledge the superiority of Israel's God and the derived nature of his own dominion and glory. We learn through Daniel's interpretation of the king's second dream (ch. 4) that he did not do this—he neither listened nor learned from God's indirect method of teaching him (i.e., through a dream). So God teaches him directly, bringing the mighty king to his knees in a most humiliating fashion. The placement of ch. 3 between these two related dream chapters illustrates the extent of the king's pride. In ch. 3, Nebuchadnezzar builds a garish golden statue on the narrative heels of dreaming about a magnificent gold-headed statue (see on 3:1) and shows himself to be egomaniacal, hot-headed, and overreactive. Chapter 3 is a grand display of the king's elevated view of himself—the problem that ch. 2's dream intended to head off, and the problem that ch. 4 addresses head on. The narrator uses ch. 3 to illustrate (and mock) the extent of Nebuchadnezzar's pride.

Second, what is the role of this chapter in the Aramaic chiasm of chs. 2–7? Though Nebuchadnezzar only appears as an active character in the first half of the chiasm, his presence lingers into the second half. In ch. 5, he is the foil for Belshazzar as Daniel indicts the blasphemous successor of Nebuchadnezzar for his failure to learn from the example of "his father" (see on ch. 5). In ch. 6, where Darius the Mede has Daniel thrown into the lions' den, the narrator concludes the story with a doxology that strongly echoes the doxologies of Dan 4.[62] In ch. 7, when a boastful little horn dominates Daniel's dream of four mutant beasts, the careful reader knows how to understand arrogant kingship and what to expect for such a king, based on the cycle of Nebuchadnezzar stories.

Third, what is the role of this chapter in the book of Daniel? In a book that showcases the sovereignty of God, one of the overriding themes is the relationship between divine and human kingship. All human dominion is derived dominion, but many kings fail to recognize the nature of their sovereignty and take undue credit for it. In this regard, Nebuchadnezzar is the quintessential gentile king and as such provides the paradigm by which to understand every other king in the book, beginning with Belshazzar. Nebuchadnezzar's encounter with God in ch. 4 portrays him at his worst and at his best. At his worst, he boasts of his greatness and fails to exercise justice and mercy on behalf of his subjects. At his best, he responds appropriately to God's judgment and experiences great restoration.

In ch. 4, the gentile king that dominates the narrative portion of the book is given nearly an entire chapter to speak, and what he says stands as a message to all. God is the one with an eternal kingdom and unsurpassed power, and he is the one who can humble those who fail to acknowledge him and their place in his kingdom.

---

62. Newsom, *Daniel*, 127.

Canonical and Theological Significance

Nebuchadnezzar's Humbling: The "Who," the "When," and Why It Matters

Nebuchadnezzar's dream of the great tree in Dan 4 is often interpreted as a lesson for the proud. This is a reasonable interpretation, given the obvious pride of the king and his closing confession that the Most High "the ones walking in pride is able to humble" (4:34[37]). But we might ask what purpose a lesson in pride might have had for the original audience of the book of Daniel. Diaspora Jews who were subject to the whims of proud gentile kings such as Nebuchadnezzar hardly seem like an audience in need of such a lesson. The Bible does have plenty to say about pride, but what is the significance of what this chapter says about the proud?

Certainly, the account of Nebuchadnezzar's humbling would have offered great comfort to the people of God, a powerless group that needed the reminder that their God appoints kings and sets up kingdoms, and he is also the one who brings them down (Dan 2:20–22). They needed the affirmation that, despite appearances to the contrary, their God was the one in control. He may not have acted in the ways and times they wanted, but nonetheless, he was at work (cf. Dan 1:2). God's rule is absolute, all human rule is relative, and all human rulers will give account for their actions. The king who devastated the lives of God's people and permanently altered their future received his due. His day of reckoning came.

This is comforting as far as it goes, but when we consider the account of Nebuchadnezzar's humbling in the context of the biblical canon, we discover a greater dynamic at play. Much of the significance of this chapter is found in the "who" and "when" questions: Who is being humbled, and when did it happen on the timeline of biblical history?

First—the "who." Nebuchadnezzar was the greatest king of Babylon, the city that stood for all that is proud, idolatrous, and opposed to God.[63] As king of Babylon, Nebuchadnezzar is the representative gentile king in the canon. In humbling *this* king, the king of kings (Ezek 26:7; Dan 2:37), Israel's God demonstrated to his people that he rules *all* kings and authorities. No king or power is greater than he.[64]

Second—the "when." In the flow of a book that explores the nature of the relationship between divine and human kingship, Dan 4 falls at the peak of Nebuchadnezzar's reign and chronicles a direct encounter between the greatest king of the day and the Most High God. In the larger story of the biblical canon, the book of Daniel falls "between the times"—the time when Israel was a nation with a land, king, and temple,

---

63. See 1 Pet 5:13; Rev 14:8; 16:19; 17:5; 18:2, 10, 21.

64. See Lord of the King of Kings above (pp. 137–39).

and the time of the inauguration of the messianic kingdom with the coming of Jesus. This book-long treatment of divine and human kingship, and specifically *gentile* kingship, comes at a pivotal time in Israel's history, and ch. 4 gives us a front-row seat when the mightiest king of his day was at his mightiest and God brought him to his knees.

The "in-between time" represented by the book of Daniel was a period of national calamity that put to the test what the people believed about their God—both what they believed about their status as his people and what they believed about his control of world events. They wondered about his plans for them, if he still had any, and they probably wondered how Nebuchadnezzar had ever defeated him.[65]

Israel was YHWH's chosen people, a "kingdom of priests" that he had delivered from Egyptian slavery (Exod 19:6). But Israel believed their God to be more than just *their* God. He was the God of all gods. His rule was not specific to their territory; rather, as creator of all, he was Lord of heaven and earth. Heaven was his throne and earth his footstool (Isa 66:1). At the right time in Israel's history, YHWH had ordained that human kings would also rule over his people, but he himself laid out instructions for what this kingship should like. Kings were to defend the cause of the poor and needy, treat the people fairly, and submit to the law of YHWH (Deut 17:14–20; Isa 11:4; Jer 22:15–16; Ps 72:2). Kings were YHWH's anointed ones, appointed to use their power and resources to tend his flock.

One by one, these anointed kings disappointed. Some reigned better than others, but all of them fell short of YHWH's ideal. They forsook the covenant; they exploited the people for their own gain; they sought security in wealth and military strength rather than in YHWH. In this rubble of royal failure, YHWH's prophets told of a coming king who would succeed where all other kings had failed. He would be David's descendant, but he would also be a divine descendant who would fulfill the promise of an eternal dynasty (2 Sam 7; Pss 89; 132:11–12; Isa 7:14; Ezek 36:24–28). In his kingdom, wars would cease, and peace and justice would reign in their stead (Isa 2:1–5; 11:1–10; Amos 9:11–15). This coming king would be *the* anointed one—Messiah—and the people, weary of miserable kings, longed for his arrival.

But when the nation was in its sixth-century-BCE death throes—a fine time for the Messiah to come to the rescue—the only king who showed up was Nebuchadnezzar, defeating their God, torching his temple and holy city, and taking his chosen people captive to a land of idolatry. Was not their God the God of all gods? How could they be in exile—a people without a land or king? Had YHWH abandoned his people to live under the rule of a king who knew nothing of their covenant with YHWH?[66]

---

65. The prophets, beginning with Moses, foretold the exile, but their audience was notoriously hardhearted and thus deaf to such warnings (e.g., Lev 26:14–33; Jer 9:12–15[13–16]). See on Dan 1:1–2 for the book's clear message that God's apparent defeat was no defeat at all.

66. The prophet Ezekiel answered these questions for the exilic people (see further on ch. 8, p. xxx) but given that his audience was stubborn and rebellious (see, e.g., Ezek 2:3–8; 3:4–9), it is no wonder they were in a crisis of faith.

They knew the truths set forth by their sacred texts—that their God was on the throne and that he ruled the earth—but when the earth was crumbling around them, these truths may have sounded more like platitudes, much like our attempts to "comfort" grieving people with the truth that God is working good through their tragedy. We may be speaking truth, but truth is not uniformly helpful: time and place matter.

What YHWH's people needed in their grief was to *see* their God demonstrating his rule and reign in all the earth. They needed to *see* that he was superior to their gentile overlords. It is this need that the book of Daniel addresses. For three chapters (Dan 1–3), the book recounts Nebuchadnezzar's indirect encounters with a superior God. First, he encountered the superior skills of the Judean exiles, favored by God (ch. 1); then he received the superior knowledge of Daniel's God (ch. 2); and finally, he saw the superior power of the God of Shadrach, Meshach, and Abednego (ch. 3). Nebuchadnezzar acknowledged the superiority of the Most High with respect to knowledge and power to deliver (Dan 2:47; 3:28–29), but his confessions were short lived. The significance of ch. 4 is that it chronicles in the king's own words how he came to understand the supremacy of the Most High; it details how the Most High directly confronted his pride; it demonstrates the rule of the Most High over the most powerful king of his day at the peak of his reign. God's superior kingship is on its best display in Dan 4, where the gentile king himself finally acknowledges his subordination to the Most High God after being brought from the peak of his glorious reign to the depths of subhumanity.

In his opening and closing doxologies, Nebuchadnezzar gives voice to the truths God's people needed to hear from an outsider with the power that Nebuchadnezzar had. Their God's kingdom is eternal. Their God's kingdom extends over the whole earth. It has no end in time or in space. Their God's kingdom would destroy and outlast all human kingdoms—even Nebuchadnezzar's. And the bedraggled people of God needed to hear—from the king himself—that he answered to this higher king.

Putting Government in Perspective

Most presidential campaigns in twenty-first-century America have been mud-slinging marathons. During an election season, I escaped the muck of campaign rhetoric by traveling halfway around the world to teach the book of Daniel to a small group of pastors in Myanmar. The men and women who attended my class endured with gentle spirits and good-humored perspectives the difficulties of living under a military government. They radiated sweet confidence in God's sovereignty over their country, a refreshing contrast to what was happening at home, where Americans across the political spectrum sneered and jeered at each other. Months later when the ballots had been cast, I scrolled through the predictable clash of responses in my

Facebook news feed: the new President-Elect was either the savior of the world or a sure sign of its soon demise.

The Bible speaks both directly and indirectly to the issue of human government, and the book of Daniel—especially chs. 2 and 4—makes a significant contribution to a biblical theology of government and how God's people should live "in exile"—that is, under the rule of those who may or may not acknowledge the Most High. The issues associated with political theology are complex and the views diverse,[67] but a few points of agreement across the diversity can be instructive.[68]

First, as both Dan 2 and 4 make explicit,[69] human rulers are set up by God and granted whatever degree of power they have. But God bestows power for a purpose—namely, to carry out justice, especially for those who need it most, and to "encourage and maintain what is beneficial and to discourage what is harmful and disruptive."[70] God also holds rulers accountable for how they fulfill their purpose. Nebuchadnezzar's great power was a divine gift, but he failed to acknowledge its source, and he failed to fulfill his responsibility as a ruler.

A second point of theological agreement about the nature of human government is that it is wholly related to the history of redemption: "Neither Pharaoh (Rom. 9:17) nor Herod nor Pontius Pilate (Acts 4:27) was beyond the scope of divine providence. Cyrus, the Persian ruler, is nothing less than the Lord's 'anointed' with a role in the redemption of the people of Israel (Isa. 45:1)"[71] Nebuchadnezzar, too, was the Lord's servant (Jer 25:9; 27:6; 43:10; see Lord of the King of Kings, pp. 137–39), and his actions furthered God's work in the world.

Third, human government is part of the "all things" that the New Testament says will be subject to Christ and have already been placed "under his feet" by God (1 Cor 15:24–28; Eph. 1:22). Christ is the one who will one day judge all nations—both their people and their governments—according to how they have welcomed the stranger, fed the hungry, and otherwise practiced justice (Matt 25:31–35).

Finally, God's people are obligated to pray for peaceful rule and to pray for their rulers (1 Tim 2:1–2). The divine origin and destiny of human governments should lead us to pray that "those in public service . . . may 'govern in peace,' and that through the faithful conduct of their duties the faithful may live serenely and

---

67. See further Jonathan Chaplin, "Political Theology," in *DTIB*, ed. Kevin J. Vanhoozer (Grand Rapids: Baker, 2005): 597–600; Jürgen Moltmann, "Political Theology," in *Global Dictionary of Theology*, ed. William A. Dyrness and Veli-Matti Kärkkäinen (Downers Grove, IL: InterVarsity Press, 2008): 669–72; Esther D. Reed, "Government," in *Dictionary of Scripture and Ethics*, ed. Joel B. Green (Grand Rapids: Baker Academic, 2011): 337–40; Stephen C. Mott and Mark A. Powell, "Government," in *The HarperCollins Bible Dictionary (Revised and Updated)*, 3rd ed., ed. Mark A. Powell (New York: HarperCollins, 2011): 345. For a full-length book that treats many similar topics, see Scott B. Rae, *Moral Choices: An Introduction to Ethics*, 4th ed. (Grand Rapids: Zondervan, 2018).

68. The points discussed are based on Reed, "Government," 340.

69. Daniel 2:21, 37–38; 4:14[17], 22[25], 29[32].

70. Mott and Powell, "Government," 345.

71. Reed, "Government," 340.

in holiness."[72] What is more, our prayers could lead human leaders to acknowledge, as Nebuchadnezzar finally did, that their power is derived and that God's rule surpasses their own. Nebuchadnezzar's confession is a foretaste of the day Paul speaks of in Phil 2:9–11, where "at the name of Jesus every knee [will] bow, in heaven and on earth and under the earth, and every tongue acknowledge that Jesus Christ is Lord, to the glory of God the Father." For now, the way is still open for human leaders to bend the knee voluntarily, but this will not always be. The day for repentance will end at some point in the future, and there will be no escape when Babylon the Great—not just its human representative—falls. Until that day, we heed Paul's admonition to pray for "kings and all those in authority" (1 Tim 2:1–2). We pray because God has appointed them, and we pray because the way is still open.

The perspective of the book of Daniel, generally, and Dan 4, specifically, that the Most High God is the one true king with the only eternal kingdom and that all human power is derived from and dependent on him is as relevant today as it was when Nebuchadnezzar learned it the hard way. Our God is the author, editor, and publisher of human history. Our thoughts about and reactions to our own leaders reflect the extent to which we believe this. Any disappointment or despair, hope or expectation, that we experience over the rise and fall of government leaders must be checked at the foot of the God who is on the throne. His plan will not be thwarted by a bad leader, nor will his kingdom come more quickly with a good one. If a government official or political party represents biblical values well, we should rejoice and pray that God will execute justice through them. If they poorly represent biblical values, we should take comfort in God's sovereignty and still pray that he executes justice through the governing administration. Our confidence belongs solely in the Most High and his eternal kingdom.

Humility: Resisting the "Dark Foil" and Respecting the Divine Image

While Dan 4 revolves around the pride of Nebuchadnezzar, the humility of Daniel is also on display. In his reaction to and interpretation of the king's dream, Daniel demonstrated humility when, ironically, a lesser man would probably have responded in kind: that is, with pride.

Pride can be an abstract offense (though crazy easy to recognize in others), but a fundamental characteristic of it is the failure to recognize who you are before God—that you are made in his image and that your very life is granted and sustained by him. When we do not recognize this, we take credit for who and what we are, and

---

72. Reed, "Government," 340. This prayer is based on the Divine Liturgy of John Chrysostom, widely used in orthodoxy since the fifth century.

we also consider others responsible for who and what they are—rather than seeing them as they really are—namely, the same as us: made in God's image and sustained by him.[73] We compare ourselves to others in any number of ways (e.g., bank accounts, makes and models of cars, education, achievements of children, number of weeds in the yard, etc.), and it is not hard to find ourselves superior. We use others' shortcomings or failures to bolster our own sense of superiority. Martin Luther describes "vainglory" or pride this way:

> It is the nature of vainglory to compare itself with those who are unlike itself, and from this comparison there follow contempt for one who is inferior and the sort of bladder that is inflated with one's own good qualities. For vainglory does not rejoice so much in the fact that it is or has something as in the fact that others are nothing or have nothing.[74]

In self-righteousness, we look down on others. Rather than considering their needs, as we would if we were demonstrating love, we rejoice because we have "such a dark foil for [ourselves]."[75]

If anyone had cause to look down on Nebuchadnezzar, Daniel did. He was an idolatrous king, but Daniel was a follower of the one true God. He had nearly killed Daniel, while Daniel had risked his own life to save his colleagues from the crazed king. He had destroyed the holy city, stripped the promised land of its resources, and demoted Daniel from a Judean aristocrat to a Babylonian captive, a "title" he likely held for the rest of his long life. If anyone had cause to rejoice over another person's misfortune, Daniel did. Nebuchadnezzar was the enemy of God's people, and he had irrevocably changed the course of Daniel's life.

But instead of regarding Nebuchadnezzar as a "dark foil" for himself, Daniel demonstrated love and so also humility. Two of his actions in Dan 4 indicate this. The first is his kneejerk response to the king's dream; he was appalled and terrified. He was grieved and distressed by what was going to happen to Nebuchadnezzar. We might have expected news of his enemy's humiliation to bring Daniel at least a little secret satisfaction. The king had, after all, brought it on himself.

In our fallenness, we like to see people get what they deserve—or at least what we think they deserve. Sometimes it is those who have wronged us (like Nebuchadnezzar

---

73. Obviously, we do bear great responsibility for who and what we are, but there is nothing in the exercise of that responsibility that increases our value or worth. We are still created and sustained by the hand of God, and any success or advantage we have is a gift from him.

74. Martin Luther, "Lectures on Galatians—1519," in *Lectures on Galatians, 1535: Chapters 5-6 and Lectures on Galatians, 1519: Chapters 1-6*, vol. 27 in Luther's Works, American Edition (St. Louis: Concordia, 1964), 385.

75. Paul Althaus, *The Theology of Martin Luther*, trans. Robert C. Schultz (Philadelphia: Fortress, 1966), 150.

had Daniel), but sometimes it goes far beyond that to include politicians with whom we disagree, the entitled rich and famous, too-big-for-their-britches athletes, or a coworker whose extra efforts make us look bad. We take perverse pleasure in the misfortune of our "enemies." But not Daniel. No matter how the king had wronged him, Daniel did not want to see the enactment of the Most High's decree. Regardless of who he was and what he had done, Nebuchadnezzar's suffering and misfortune was not a cause for Daniel to celebrate. And so it should be for us. Instead of secretly gloating over someone getting what's coming to them, we would do better to humbly acknowledge, "There, but for the grace of God, go I," and we might better pray, "God have mercy on their soul."

A second evidence of Daniel's humility is in his interpretation of the dream (see on 4:16g–24[19g–27] above). In his interpretation Daniel omitted the imagery of the king's mind being changed to that of a beast. He had divine sanction to tell the king he would lose his mind and in a most inglorious way—the imagery was part of the dream and fulfillment. But he left the words unsaid and so spared the king his last shred of dignity—his humanity.

It is remarkably easy in our thoughts and actions to deprive people of the dignity they deserve on the basis of their bearing the divine image. We dehumanize some people without realizing it and with others we are fully aware of what we are doing. Sometimes it happens when we think in terms of demographics or statistics, rather in terms of the living, breathing people that comprise those statistics. We buy cheap clothes, coffee, and canned tomatoes without a second thought about the factory or field laborers who work for nothing (and worse) so we can pay less at the checkout. Sometimes it happens when a stranger demonstrates the uncommonness of common sense, and we roll our eyes in disdain or make a snide remark. Sometimes it happens in the anonymity of the internet, where we use comment boxes to tear apart those who disagree with us. By what we think and say—or, in the case of buying cheap merchandise, what we *do not* stop to think—we deny people the dignity due every image-bearer. In so doing, we consider ourselves superior: my money is worth more than your time and effort; I would never do anything as stupid as *that*; I am too educated to believe *that*.

Few of us will actually commit the ultimate act of dehumanization—murder—and all of us think it deserves judgment. But after Jesus talks about murder in the Sermon on the Mount, he says plenty of "lesser offenses" are also worthy of judgment—offenses that sound a lot like the examples I gave above: "You have heard that it was said to the people long ago, 'You shall not murder, and anyone who murders will be subject to judgment.' But I tell you that anyone who is angry with his brother will be subject to judgment. Again, anyone who says to his brother, 'Raca,' is answerable to the Sanhedrin. But anyone who says, 'You fool!' will be in danger of the fire of hell" (Matt 5:21–22). According to Jesus, anger, contempt, and even abusive speech toward fellow followers of God ("brother") are "tantamount to a capital crime."[76] In the larger context of the Gospels, Jesus says loving God means loving people, no matter who they are or what they have going for them ("brother," neighbor, or enemy; Matt 5:43–48; Luke 10:25–37). The dignity of the divine image—no matter who is bearing it—demands love.

Nebuchadnezzar deserved everything he got, but Daniel grieved his judgment and dignified his humanity. There is deserved judgment ahead for those who have wronged us, those who flaunt their greatness, and those who live carelessly or callously—but it is God's to give. Our task is to reflect the image of the Son by loving God's image-bearers, no matter their shortcomings or offenses.

"The Kingdom of God Has Come Near" . . . "Your Kingdom Come"

The imagery of the great tree in the account of Nebuchadnezzar's humbling is significant. In ancient Near Eastern iconography, a massive flourishing tree such as the one Nebuchadnezzar saw in his dream often represented a cosmic tree of life that linked heaven and earth. Egyptian goddess Hathor is pictured as a tree whose height reached to heaven. In Babylonian mythology, an enormous tree reached both to the heavens above and the underworld below. Assyrian kings were often associated with a tree of life, serving as royal representatives of the gods and mediating the life, provision, and protection of the deity to their people.

Israel shared this imagery that associated mighty trees with kings. Sixth-century-BCE prophet Ezekiel told parables about towering trees to illustrate the great royal splendor of kings or nations—splendor that led to great pride and then to great destruction. In two of his parables, the trees represented the Davidic dynasty (Ezek 17:22–23; 19:10–14). In the first, a transplanted shoot grew into a "splendid cedar." The birds found shelter in the cedar that had replaced a once mighty tree, witnessing to the fact that "I YHWH bring down the tall tree and make the low tree grow tall" (17:24). In the second parable, the prophet says Jerusalem was once a flourishing vine "conspicuous for its height and for its many branches" (19:11), but it had been uprooted and stripped of its leaves and fruit and left to wither. In Ezekiel's third parable, an oracle against Egypt, the prophet used the example of once-mighty Assyria to warn a proud pharaoh of his coming judgment. Assyria had once been a towering cedar tree that reached into the clouds. It provided shade for the animals and a place for nesting birds, which represented the "great nations" that were the beneficiaries of Assyria's wealth and protection (Ezek 31:6). The shadow of the great tree fell over every great nation. But the magnificent tree grew proud, so God had

---

76. David L. Turner, *Matthew*, BECNT (Grand Rapids: Baker Academic, 2008), 169.

it destroyed. The birds and beasts that once found haven in it lived on its carcass of broken branches (31:13).

In the Old Testament, a tree that reached to the heavens and touched the sky was a metaphor for the pride of overreaching kings.[77] But these cosmic trees of the Old Testament are not the only way the Bible uses the imagery of flourishing trees. In the New Testament Jesus uses tree imagery to teach his disciples about the nature of the kingdom of God. He told them the kingdom was like a tiny mustard seed that grew into the largest of the garden plants. Much like the great tree of Nebuchadnezzar's dream, the tree of Jesus's parable provided shade for the birds and became a nesting place for them (Matt 13:32; Mark 4:32; Luke 13:19). The shared imagery between this parable and the Old Testament texts highlights the greatness and the extent of the kingdom of God.[78] Jesus told this and other parables to teach his disciples that, despite its small beginning, God's kingdom will achieve spectacular growth.

But in the here and now, the kingdom of God exists in a state of paradox. Jesus, and John the Baptist before him, inaugurated his earthly ministry with the words "the kingdom of God/heaven is come near" (Matt 3:2; 4:17; 10:7; Mark 1:15). In the Gospel of Luke, Jesus read from the scroll of Isaiah in the synagogue and announced that Isaiah's messianic words had been fulfilled: "The Spirit of the Lord is on me, because he has anointed me to proclaim good news to the poor. He has sent me to proclaim freedom for the prisoners and recovery of sight for the blind, to set the oppressed free, to proclaim the year of the Lord's favor" (Luke 4:18–19; cf. Isa 61:1–2). But elsewhere, Jesus taught his disciples to pray that the kingdom would come (Matt 6:10; Luke 11:2). Which is it? Is the kingdom here or should we pray for its coming? New Testament commentator R. T. France discusses the paradox:

> In such passages [as in the book of Daniel] God's kingship is stated as an eternal fact, but there are also a number of prophetic passages that, recognizing the extent of human rebellion against God's rule, look forward to a day when his kingship will be more effectively established. . . . Thus, when Jesus began his mission with the words "The kingdom of God has come near," he would be . . . heard as saying that the God whose sovereignty over his whole creation was a fundamental belief of Judaism was about to establish that sovereignty in a newly effective way; the king de jure was becoming the king de facto. . . . But there is still darkness as well as light, and God's

---

77. Trees are not the only thing in the Old Testament that reach to the heavens. The account of the tower of Babel in Gen 11 describes a group of people who built a tower that reached to the heavens in order to make a name for themselves. See further on "Shinar" at Dan 1:2.

78. France notes that it "reinforces the 'imperial' pretensions of the kingdom of God, which will take the place of the human empires of OT times," R. T. France, *The Gospel of Mark: A Commentary on the Greek Text*, NIGTC (Grand Rapids: Eerdmans, 2002), 217

people must go on praying 'Your kingdom come' until 'the kingdom of the world has become the kingdom of our Lord and of his Messiah' (Rev. 11:15 NRSV).[79]

France also notes that, above all, the kingdom is about God as king—not about an entity: "Thus, 'the kingdom of God has come near' means 'God is taking over as king,' and to 'enter the kingdom of God' is to come under his rule, to accept him as king."[80] The present reality is that God still allows people *not* to accept him as king, so his kingdom sometimes just looks like a defeated, powerless, motley crew of followers. Sometimes it looks like the kingdom of this world will win the day. But, as the author of Daniel made clear in ch. 1, what is real is not always obvious. Jesus's parables about the kingdom warn "against underestimating the significance of the proclamation of the kingdom of God, however unimpressive its initial impact may seem. What has begun in the Galilean ministry of Jesus will, by the power of God, one day prove to be of ultimate significance. If for the time being its power is hidden, it is not for that reason any less certain, and its growth will be spectacular."[81]

Someday, the "mustard seed kingdom" will be in full and glorious foliage. Christ's dominion, glory, power, and eternal kingship will be evident to all. Unlike the glorious kingdom of Nebuchadnezzar in Dan 4, this great kingdom will be ruled by a righteous and merciful king. The powerless, oppressed, and persecuted will find shalom. Unlike the sixth-century-BCE Babylonian kingdom of Nebuchadnezzar, the kingdom of Christ will have no end and no boundaries. It will fill the earth. Indeed, may your kingdom come!

---

79. R. T. France, "Kingdom of God," in *DTIB*, ed. Kevin J. Vanhoozer (Grand Rapids: Baker, 2005): 420–22.

80. France, "Kingdom of God," 420.

81. France, *Gospel of Mark*, 217.

Daniel 5:1a–6:1[5:31]

D. Narrative 4: *A Humbled King and His Rescinded Power*

Main Idea of Narrative 4 (5:1a–6:1[5:31])

Belshazzar, "son" of Nebuchadnezzar, encounters the God of Israel when he commandeers the Jerusalem temple vessels for his own common use. A divine, disembodied hand writes a cryptic message that Daniel reads and interprets, pronouncing judgment on the blasphemous king, who failed to learn humility from the example of his predecessor. That very night the Chaldean king dies and his kingdom passes to Darius the Mede, a demonstration of God's control over the course of history.

Literary Context of Narrative 4 (5:1a–6:1[5:31])

Daniel 5 is the fourth of six Aramaic chapters in the book, and it is fourth in a series of five consecutive narratives about encounters between the Judean exiles and gentile kings (chs. 2–6). Like ch. 4, ch. 5 recounts the humbling judgment of a proud gentile king, announced via a message that Babylonian experts could not interpret. The two chapters are similar in their general content, but they also are explicitly linked by the repeated references in ch. 5 to the events of ch. 4. The account of Belshazzar is cast as an extended comparison of the Babylonian king and his predecessor Nebuchadnezzar—specifically, the behavior of the former in light of the latter's response to the humbling events of ch. 4.

As part of the chiasm of chs. 2–7, Dan 5 stands parallel with the account of Nebuchadnezzar's humbling in ch. 4. Together these two accounts comprise the heart of the chiastic structure and so portray what is likely the primary theme of the structure and, arguably, of the entire book of Daniel.[1] Both chapters tell of arrogant human kings who encounter the authority of the God who gave them their power, and each chapter illustrates a different royal response to the reckoning. In ch. 4, Nebuchadnezzar acknowledges the supreme authority of the Most High, and in ch. 5, his successor Belshazzar is unfazed by God's claim to authority. The two narratives recount how God dealt with each king in light of their responses: he restored Nebuchadnezzar to power, and he destroyed Belshazzar. The relationship between human kings and the divine king, human authority and divine authority, is a driving theme of the book of Daniel, and this relationship is nowhere more clearly on display than in chs. 4 and 5.

In terms of the history conveyed by the book of Daniel and the "inexorable march of the four kingdoms"[2] presented in Nebuchadnezzar's statue dream (ch. 2) and Daniel's vision of the beasts (ch. 7), ch. 5 marks the transition of kingdoms from that of the Babylonians to that of the Medes. The events of ch. 5 clearly show that God is the one controlling the course of history with its rise and fall of empires.

As with the preceding narrative chapters, Dan 5 is often classified as a court story and specifically as a court contest.[3] King Belshazzar encounters a problem and summons his wise men to "unscrew the inscrutable," but they are unable. This prepares the way for Daniel, who succeeds where they failed and receives the reward of the king.

II. Macro Unit 2: The Superiority of God and His Kingdom (2:1a–7:28d)
  A. Narrative 1: God's Superior Knowledge and His Eternal Kingdom (2:1a–49c)
  B. Narrative 2: God's Superior Power and His Servants' Faithfulness (3:1a–30)
  C. Narrative 3: A Humbled King and His Restored Power (3:31a–4:34e[4:1a–37e])
  ➙ **D. Narrative 4: A Humbled King and His Rescinded Power (5:1a–6:1[5:31])**
  E. Narrative 5: God's Superior Law and His Servant's Faithfulness (6:2a–29[1a–28])
  F. Narrative 6: God's Superior King and Eternal Kingdom (7:1a–28d)

---

1. See further the introduction for discussion of the chiastic structure and its significance for interpretation of the book (pp. 31–35).

2. Pace, *Daniel*, 184.

3. See further the Literary Context of the Macro Unit (pp. 79–80) and the introduction (p. 25).

1. Belshazzar's Arrogant Offense (5:1a–4b)

Main Idea of the Passage

Daniel 5:1–4 displays the belligerent blasphemy of a new king who drank wine from YHWH's sacred temple vessels and praised idols at the same time.

Literary Context

Daniel 5:1–4 is the opening section of the narrative of Dan 5:1a–6:1[5:31]. As such, it functions in at least two ways in its broader literary context. First, it sets the immediate context for the events that follow by introducing the main character of Belshazzar and by describing his great feast. Second, it links the chapter to the previous four chapters of the book both explicitly and implicitly: (1) its repeated mention of the vessels taken from the Jerusalem temple specifically ties the chapter to the opening events of the book of Daniel (1:1–2; cf. 5:2–3); (2) its reference to "Nebuchadnezzar his father" links the chapter to Dan 1–4 generally since Nebuchadnezzar was a prominent character in all four chapters; (3) subtle similarities between the opening verses of Dan 5 and the account of Nebuchadnezzar's golden statue in Dan 3 indirectly link these two chapters. In all these references, whether overtly or obliquely, the narrator prepares the reader for an extended comparison of the book's two Babylonian kings, Nebuchadnezzar and Belshazzar.

> D. Narrative 4: A Humbled King and His Rescinded Power (5:1a–6:1[5:31])
> → **1. Belshazzar's Arrogant Offense (5:1a–4b)**
>   2. The Result of the Arrogant Offense (5:5a–8d)
>   3. The Queen's Words (5:9a–12d)
>   4. Belshazzar's Arrogant Words (5:13a–16i)
>   5. Daniel's Words to the Arrogant Belshazzar (5:17a–28b)
>   6. A Rescinded Power (5:29a–6:1[5:31])

Translation and Exegetical Outline

(See page 249.)

Daniel 5:1a–4b

			D. Narrative 4: A Humbled King and His Rescinded Power (5:1a–6:1[5:31])
			1. Belshazzar's Arrogant Offense (5:1a–4b)
			a. The Setting of the Offense (5:1a–b)
1a	בֵּלְשַׁאצַּר מַלְכָּא עֲבַד לְחֶם רַב לְרַבְרְבָנוֹהִי אֲלַף	Belshazzar the king made a great feast for a thousand of his noblemen,	
1b	וְלָקֳבֵל אַלְפָּא חַמְרָא שָׁתֵה׃	and in front of the thousand, he was drinking wine.	
			b. The King's Order (5:2a–e)
2a	בֵּלְשַׁאצַּר אֲמַר בִּטְעֵם חַמְרָא	Belshazzar said, with the taste of the wine,	
2b	לְהַיְתָיָה לְמָאנֵי דַּהֲבָא וְכַסְפָּא	to bring the vessels of gold and silver	
2c	דִּי הַנְפֵּק נְבוּכַדְנֶצַּר אֲבוּהִי מִן־הֵיכְלָא	that Nebuchadnezzar his father had taken from the temple	
2d	דִּי בִירוּשְׁלֶם	that was in Jerusalem,	
2e	וְיִשְׁתּוֹן בְּהוֹן מַלְכָּא וְרַבְרְבָנוֹהִי שֵׁגְלָתֵהּ וּלְחֵנָתֵהּ׃	so the king and his noblemen, his wives and his concubines, could drink with them.	
			c. The King's Blasphemy (5:3a–4b)
3a	בֵּאדַיִן הַיְתִיו מָאנֵי דַהֲבָא	Then they brought the vessels of gold	
3b	דִּי הַנְפִּקוּ מִן־הֵיכְלָא	that had been taken from the temple	
3c	דִּי־בֵית אֱלָהָא	which was the house of God	
3d	דִּי בִירוּשְׁלֶם	which was in Jerusalem,	
3e	וְאִשְׁתִּיו בְּהוֹן מַלְכָּא וְרַבְרְבָנוֹהִי שֵׁגְלָתֵהּ וּלְחֵנָתֵהּ׃	and the king and his noblemen, his wives and his concubines, drank with them.	
4a	אִשְׁתִּיו חַמְרָא	They drank the wine,	
4b	וְשַׁבַּחוּ לֵאלָהֵי דַּהֲבָא וְכַסְפָּא נְחָשָׁא פַרְזְלָא אָעָא וְאַבְנָא׃	and they praised the gods of gold and silver, bronze, iron, wood, and stone.	

Structure and Literary Form

The fourth narrative of the book's Aramaic chiasm (chs. 2–7[4]) begins with a section that details an arrogant and blasphemous offense by a heretofore unknown king, Belshazzar (5:1–4). Three subsections comprise this initial section: 5:1, 2, and 3–4.

The first subsection consists of two independent clauses that establish the setting of the blasphemous offense and the circumstances that initiated it: the setting is "a great feast," which Belshazzar hosted for a thousand of his noblemen (5:1a), and the circumstances that may have impelled the king's offense were that he "was drinking wine" (5:1b).

The second subsection (5:2) consists of a main clause in which the king issues an order (אֲמַר, 5:2a), an infinitive complement clause that contains the king's order ("to bring the vessels of gold and silver," 5:2b), and a pair of relative clauses that further describe the vessels called for by the king (5:2c–d)—namely, they were the vessels taken from the Jerusalem temple by "Nebuchadnezzar his father." The final clause in the second subsection provides the purpose for Belshazzar's order: so the king and his guests "could drink with them" (5:2e).

The third subsection of the initial section (5:3–4) begins with the report that the king's order was carried out (5:3), and it then details the blasphemous outcome of these actions: "they praised the gods of gold and silver, bronze, iron, wood, and stone" (5:4).

Explanation of the Text

a. The Setting of the Offense (5:1a–b)

The previous chapter, the account of Nebuchadnezzar's humbling, ended with the great king's acknowledgment that the "king of the heavens" was sovereign over all, including him. Chapter 5 begins with a topical frame to introduce a new character—בֵּלְשַׁאצַּר מַלְכָּא, "Belshazzar the king"—but provides no explanation of what happened to the king who dominated the book for four chapters. Furthermore, the chapter moves on to this new king without explaining who he is or what his relationship to Nebuchadnezzar is. Instead, the narrator focuses on what is important for the scene to follow: this king hosted a great feast, and he was drinking wine "in front of the thousand"—perhaps at an elevated table facing them (5:1b).[5]

We can easily imagine what this party of a thousand people imbibing alcohol from a bottomless keg looked like. The guests were likely drunk, and

---

4. For discussion regarding the significance of this chiastic structure, see further the introduction (pp. 31–35).

5. Goldingay, *Daniel*, 278. It is unlikely that Belshazzar was drinking *with* his guests (e.g., NIV), which would be highly unusual. Seated conspicuously in front of his guests, the king may very well have been making a display of himself. Seow says he was "showing off" (*Daniel*, 78).

many commentators dating back to Jerome think Belshazzar was, too.[6] The later mention of Belshazzar's wives and concubines adds to the picture and probably suggests debauchery (cf. 5:2e and 3e).[7] Goldingay says the scene "can be read as one of ostentation, decadence, carousing, coarseness, wantonness, and self-indulgence."[8] The narrator does not reveal the occasion for this feast, just as he does not explain who this new king is (yet).[9] In the immediate context of ch. 5, the only information necessary to set the context for the chapter's events is that Belshazzar was drinking wine in front of a large audience.

However, the narrator's purpose in 5:1 may be greater than simply setting the immediate context for the chapter's events. Fewell notes that Dan 5:1 bears several similarities to Dan 3:1 and suggests that the narrator may be intentionally linking the two chapters. Both chapters begin abruptly, with no temporal clause (as in chs. 1 and 2) and no orientation to the narrator or the narrative (as in ch. 4). Both opening verses begin with similar vocabulary and grammar: "Belshazzar the king made..." (בֵּלְשַׁאצַּר מַלְכָּא עֲבַד) and "Nebuchadnezzar the king made..." (נְבוּכַדְנֶצַּר מַלְכָּא עֲבַד). From there, both sentences "develop a description of excess"—Nebuchadnezzar builds a disproportionately large statue, and Belshazzar hosts a feast for a thousand guests.[10] What these structural similarities may mean is that the narrator has shaped ch. 5 to invite the comparison of the two kings and their actions, a subtle invitation that becomes more pronounced as the chapter develops.

b. The King's Order (5:2a–e)

In the main clause of subsection 5:2, Belshazzar gives an order בִּטְעֵם חַמְרָא, "with the taste of the wine" (5:2a)—a possible reference to the king's drunkenness. The order itself is in 5:2b ("to bring the vessels..."), and the purpose of the order is in 5:2e: Belshazzar gave orders to bring the vessels so he, his guests, and his harem could drink from them.

Which vessels these are is detailed in the relative clauses of 5:2c–d. These were the vessels Nebuchadnezzar had taken (הַנְפֵּק, 5:2c) from the Jerusalem temple (cf. Dan 1:1–2). When the great king had plundered the temple of Israel's God, he transferred its sacred vessels to the temple of his god in Babylon. In so doing, Nebuchadnezzar honored his god by giving him what was considered rightfully his as the victorious god.[11] The vessels became the possession of the Babylonian god (or so everyone thought), and no one had any right to use them.

Belshazzar's use of these sacred vessels for nonsacred use was "an outrage even by pagan standards,"[12] and while drunkenness may have been a factor in his action, it was not the only one.

---

6. The oldest Greek translation of Daniel has a preface at the beginning of ch. 5 that includes the following: "On that day, Baltasar [Belshazzar], puffed up from the wine and boasting, praised all the molten and graven gods in his drink" (Collins, *Daniel*, 237).

7. Seow, *Daniel*, 78.

8. Goldingay, *Daniel*, 295.

9. The narrator never reveals the occasion for Belshazzar's feast. Such banquets are widely attested in Persian times (cf. Xerxes's banquet in Esth 1), and they undoubtedly occurred during Babylonian times as well. Since the chapter ends with the fall of Babylon, a historical event dating to mid-October of 539 BCE, a few possibilities have been proposed: (1) it was a New Year's festival of the moon god Sîn, which occurred during the first part of October; (2) Belshazzar was throwing himself a coronation feast, given the defeat of his father Nabonidus to Cyrus fifty miles away at Opis; (3) Belshazzar knew Persia was knocking at the door, so he threw a party as a morale booster, a distraction from the inevitable, or a final fling in the face of death.

10. For additional similarities between the two chapters, see further below.

11. See on Dan 1:1–2 above.

12. Collins, *Daniel*, 245.

Such an act of impiety was neither random nor impulsive. As Longman notes, Belshazzar must have "had a particular propaganda purpose in mind,"[13] and Seow thinks the king intentionally made the "desecration of the vessels an item on the evening's program . . . something to go with the tasting of the wine."[14] Yet aside from the presence of the wine, the narrator does not explicitly say what may have prompted Belshazzar's action or what he may have intended to accomplish by it. Why was he even thinking about the sacred vessels of the defeated god of a disgraced people from decades earlier?

To this point in the narrative, all we know about Belshazzar is his name, title, and present circumstances: he is a king who is hosting a massive banquet and quite possibly making a scene of himself drinking in front of his guests. Over the course of the chapter, the narrator will give us hints about *who* this king is and *why* he may have done this. The first such hint is tucked in the relative clause that describes the vessels: they were the vessels taken (הַנְפֵּק) by "Nebuchadnezzar his father" (5:2c). Throughout the chapter, the father-son relationship of Nebuchadnezzar and Belshazzar will be one of the narrator's major emphases. The queen, Belshazzar, and Daniel will all refer to this relationship (5:11, 13, 18, 22). The significance of Belshazzar's blasphemous actions is related to his role as the son of Nebuchadnezzar.[15]

c. The King's Blasphemy (5:3a–4b)

While Dan 5:2 reports Belshazzar's order from the king's point of view, Dan 5:3 reports its execution from the narrator's point of view. This report includes two main clauses: they brought the vessels (5:3a), and the king, his guests, and his harem drank from them (5:3e). Tucked between these two main clauses are three relative clauses that describe the vessels for the second time in as many verses (cf. 5:2c–d). Two of the clauses are repetitive (5:3b and 5:3d; cf. 5:2c–d), and the third expands the description of the temple which previously housed the vessels: it was the בֵּית אֱלָהָא, "house of God" (5:3c).

The effects of this overspecification and expansion are twofold. First, the repetition itself highlights the significance of the vessels. Far removed from time and place, we cannot grasp the significance of the temple vessels to Daniel's audience, but for

---

13. Longman, *Daniel*, 137.
14. Seow, *Daniel*, 78.
15. Biologically speaking, Belshazzar was not the son of Nebuchadnezzar. It is possible but unsubstantiated that Belshazzar's biological father, Nabonidus, married a daughter of Nebuchadnezzar, in which case Belshazzar would have been Nebuchadnezzar's grandson (see Alan R. Millard, "Daniel in Babylon: An Accurate Record?" in *Do Historical Matters Matter to Faith? A Critical Appraisal of Modern and Postmodern Approaches to History*, ed. James K. Hoffmeier and Dennis R. Magary [Wheaton, IL: Crossway, 2012], 269–80). Belshazzar was the oldest son of Nabonidus, the last king of Babylon who spent much of his seventeen-year reign (556–539 BCE) at an oasis in north Arabian Teima. (An inscription entitled "Nabonidus and His God" says Nabonidus was in Teima for ten years. Piecing together other ancient documents, scholars think he was at the oasis as early as his third or fourth year on the throne [553/552 BCE] and returned to Babylon ca. 543.) While Nabonidus was away, Belshazzar attended matters in Babylon and so was effectively the king. Nabonidus himself was not a legitimate successor of Nebuchadnezzar but had been part of the overthrow of Nebuchadnezzar's grandson Labashi-Marduk in 556 BCE. Thus, although Nabonidus and Belshazzar were successors of Nebuchadnezzar, neither was related to him nor was a legitimate successor. However, none of this matters in terms of the use of father-son language for Nebuchadnezzar and Belshazzar in Dan 5. Such familial terms are used in Semitic languages to refer to royal successors, no matter how they came to the throne. The Black Obelisk of Shalmaneser III gives a similar example of this father-son construct. Shalmaneser was the Assyrian king who defeated Israelite King Jehu, a success he touts on the Black Obelisk as he refers to tribute received from "Jehu, son of Omri." Yet the narrative in 2 Kgs 9–10 indicates that Jehu was not related to Omri; he was a usurper who destroyed the Omride dynasty on his bloody way to the throne ("Black Obelisk," trans. by K. Lawson Younger, Jr. [*COS* 2.113F:270]).

exilic Jews, the sacred vessels were the only tangible remains of Israel's relationship with their covenant God. Near the time of Jerusalem's fall, false prophets had assured the people that, although Nebuchadnezzar was destroying their holy city and temple, YHWH would return the vessels to the temple within two years (Jer 28:3). Jeremiah, however, had prophesied that the sacred vessels would remain in Babylon and the rest of the temple valuables would be taken as well (Jer 27:16–22). But Jeremiah also assured the people that the vessels would be safe in Babylon until YHWH returned them home. Bound up in the temple vessels was the people's hope that God would remember and restore them.[16]

A second effect of the overspecification and expansion of the description of the temple vessels is that the reader is reminded whose vessels these were. In the first description, the order given from Belshazzar's point of view, the vessels were those which "Nebuchadnezzar his father" had taken (הַנְפֵּק) from the temple (5:2c). In the second description, the execution of the order from the narrator's point of view, the vessels are simply those "that had been taken from the temple" (הַנְפִּקוּ, 5:3b), with no mention of Nebuchadnezzar. Further, the vessels were from the temple, which was the "house of God" (5:3c). Belshazzar may have thought "his father" had taken the vessels and so demonstrated control over them, but the narrator adjusts the perspective from one of agency (Nebuchadnezzar took the vessels) to one of allowance (the vessels were taken) from the house of God.[17] This adjustment "lessens Nebuchadnezzar's importance and underscores the rightful sovereignty of God."[18] The events of the chapter will show that, despite being the "defeated" God, the God from whose house the sacred vessels had been taken was still very much in charge of them.

In these differing descriptions of the vessels may also be the narrator's hint as to why Belshazzar was thinking about these particular vessels. Belshazzar does not care about Jerusalem, the temple, or the Jews; what he *does* care about is that these were the vessels "Nebuchadnezzar his father" had taken. Fewell argues that the vessels from the Jerusalem temple represent what the book of Daniel portrays as Nebuchadnezzar's greatest achievement—the capture of Jerusalem and its temple ("despite the fact that he does not know how this success came about"[19]).[20] As the "son" who has accomplished nothing, Belshazzar has to compete with the reputation of his successful "father" as he tries

---

16. The importance of the vessels is evident in the 2 Kings account of Nebuchadnezzar's destruction of the temple (chs. 24-25). The narrator tracks the whereabouts of the vessels, making it clear to his exilic audience that many vessels survived the destruction. In the postexilic book of 2 Chronicles, the retelling of the same events gives even greater attention to the vessels. On the differences between the 2 Kings and 2 Chronicles accounts, Kalimi and Purvis note that, for the Chronicler, "the vessels were more important than anything else—the queen, the officials, the other captives, and the treasures" (Isaac Kalimi and James D. Purvis, "King Jehoiachin and the Vessels of the Lord's House in Biblical Literature," *CBQ* 56 [1994], 452). This meticulous attention paid to the vessels shows their significance to the postexilic audience, the people that God had remembered and restored. In Ezra's account of the return to Jerusalem after exile, 5,400 vessels that returned with the exiles are itemized and inventoried (Ezra 1:7–10).

17. Both verbs are *haphel*, but the second is in the impersonal third-person plural, "they took the vessels"—typically translated as passive, "the vessels were taken."

18. Pace, *Daniel*, 164.

19. Fewell is referring to the fact that Dan 1:1-2 reveals to the reader that the Lord *gave* (נתן) Nebuchadnezzar the Judean king and the temple vessels: "To Nebuchadnezzar, the vessels symbolize his success and, implicitly, the success of his god. He does not realize, as does the reader, that that vessels are a *gift* from the god to whom they belong" (*Circle of Sovereignty*, 85).

20. Fewell acknowledges that "this conquest assumes such importance by default—it is the only one mentioned. Nonetheless, it is, for the narrator, Nebuchadnezzar's most noteworthy achievement" (*Circle of Sovereignty*, 85).

to gain credibility in the eyes of his subjects. The significance of the vessels for Belshazzar then is that they represent a way he can feasibly "outdo his father"—namely, by taking his accomplishments and values lightly. Belshazzar sends for the temple vessels because they represent his father's greatest deed. Fewell concludes:

> He belittles his father's achievement by using the vessels as if they were ordinary things. He discredits his father's values by demonstrating that what his father considered sacred is not sacred to him. And he shows himself to be more courageous than his father by doing something his father would never do—drinking from a vessel dedicated to a god. And let us not forget, that although the vessels are from the house of God in Jerusalem, they have since been dedicated to *Nebuchadnezzar's* god. By drinking from these vessels, Belshazzar is saying, like Rehoboam, Solomon's son, in 1 Kings 12:10, "My little finger is thicker than my father's loins."[21]

The importance of the temple vessels for Belshazzar was that "Nebuchadnezzar his father" had taken them. For the narrator, however, the importance of the vessels was that they were from "the house of God" in Jerusalem.

The final verse in this section elaborates on what happened when Belshazzar's order was carried out. The assembly drank the wine, but they also praised gods of "gold and silver, bronze, iron, wood, and stone" (5:4b). The sacrilege of using the sacred vessels for nonsacred use was compounded by idolatry. Listing materials that made up the gods is common in anti-idolatry texts (cf. Deut 4:28; 29:16[17]; Isa 2:20; 30:22; 31:7; 44:9–20; Jer 10:3–5; Hos 8:4; Pss 115:4–7; 135:15) and "is often used in conjunction with the claim that the statues cannot see or hear or eat or smell and thus evidently have no power when compared to the living God, a point that will be made in Dan 5:23."[22] The effect of this rhetoric in 5:4b is that the reader has "no doubt that Belshazzar's praise of these gods, which is carried out in the very act of desecrating the sacred vessels of the Most High God, will be exposed as deadly folly."[23]

The section that began with strong parallels to the beginning of Dan 3 continues to show commonalities with the earlier chapter. In ch. 3, Nebuchadnezzar demanded that a line-up of political officials assemble for the dedication of the statue, and the narrator repeated the instructions word-for-word in his report that the king's command was fulfilled (3:2–3); similarly, Belshazzar orders that the vessels from the Jerusalem temple be brought so he and his guests can drink from them, and the narrator again repeats word-for-word the carrying out of the command (5:2–3). Finally, at this point in both chapters, the assembled groups pay homage to idols (3:4–7; 5:4).[24] Fewell summarizes the significance of these similarities:

> Hence, as we begin our reading, two characters and their actions are paired: Belshazzar and Nebuchadnezzar. Both are kings. Both "make" grand things. Both invite a multitude of subjects to admire and/or participate in these things. The story's second sentence gives us important information that formally links the two kings.... Thus we learn that the two kings are not simply being paired; they fall into a chronological pattern. One comes after the other. One knows of the other and imitates. A son models his father.[25]

---

21. Fewell, *Circle of Sovereignty*, 85.
22. Newsom, *Daniel*, 168.
23. Newsom, *Daniel*, 168.
24. Fewell, *Circle of Sovereignty*, 82.
25. Fewell, *Circle of Sovereignty*, 82.

In this case, each king appears to be showcasing his power and either testing or trying to gain his subjects' allegiance. In ch. 3, the events revolve around the statue, which is clearly the focus of the chapter ("the image, which Nebuchadnezzar the king had set up," see 3:2, 3, 5, 7, 10, 12, 14, 15, 18). The great king made a grand display of his power in the massive statue and commanded his subjects' obedience on threat of death. By contrast, the focus of ch. 5 is Belshazzar himself. He brings attention to himself by drinking wine "in front of the thousand," and everyone at the feast is described by their relationship to the king—they are *his* lords, *his* wives, *his* concubines.[26] In terms of power and greatness, Belshazzar has nothing to his credit. History barely knows him, and he is a blip even in the story of the Bible. Unlike "his father," Belshazzar has done nothing to command the respect of his subjects, so he buys their loyalty with food, wine, and entertainment by giving a feast to celebrate himself.[27]

These opening verses of ch. 5 subtly set up a contrast between the great king Nebuchadnezzar and "his son" Belshazzar. Daniel will bring this contrast front and center in his speech later in the chapter (5:17–28).

2. The Result of the Arrogant Offense (5:5a–8d)

Main Idea of the Passage

Daniel 5:5–8 details what resulted from Belshazzar's arrogant offense: a disembodied hand appeared and wrote on the palace wall, terrifying the king and signifying God's control over the house of Belshazzar.

Literary Context

Daniel 5:5–8 is the second section of the narrative that comprises ch. 5. It follows the opening section of the chapter in which Belshazzar hosted a great feast and called for the vessels from the Jerusalem temple in order to drink from them (5:1–4). In its broader literary context, this section functions in at least four ways. First, it introduces the conflict that drives the plot: Belshazzar receives a distressing divine revelation that his experts cannot interpret. A second function of the section is that its portrayal of the wise men's inability to read or interpret the writing sets up Daniel's entrance later in the chapter. Third, the similarities of this section's events with those of Nebuchadnezzar in earlier chapters (i.e., both kings receive troubling revelations that their experts prove unable to interpret) develop the chapter's extended compari-

---

26. Fewell, *Circle of Sovereignty*, 83.   27. Fewell, *Circle of Sovereignty*, 83.

son of Belshazzar and "his father." Finally, in its description of the hand writing on the wall, this second section subtly extends the temple theme begun in the first section, where Belshazzar called for vessels from the Jerusalem temple.

> D. Narrative 4: A Humbled King and His Rescinded Power (5:1a–6:1[5:31])
>   1. Belshazzar's Arrogant Offense (5:1a–4b)
> ➤ **2. The Result of the Arrogant Offense (5:5a–8d)**
>   3. The Queen's Words (5:9a–12d)
>   4. Belshazzar's Arrogant Words (5:13a–16i)
>   5. Daniel's Words to the Arrogant Belshazzar (5:17a–28b)
>   6. A Rescinded Power (5:29a–6:1[5:31])

Translation and Exegetical Outline

(See page 257.)

Structure and Literary Form

The second section of the narrative in Dan 5 (5:5–8) begins with a temporal clause, . . . בַּהּ־שַׁעֲתָה, "at that moment . . ." (5:5a), and consists of three subsections: 5:5, 6–7, and 8. The first reports the appearance and writing of the hand/fingers in two clauses—a perfect verb in the first (נְפַקָה, "came forth, appeared," 5:5a) and a participle in the second (וְכָתְבָן, "were writing," 5:5b)—and it also reports that the king was watching the hand as it wrote (חָזֵה, 5:5c).

The second subsection is the king's reaction to what he witnessed and consists of two parts: his physical response (5:6) and his call for help (5:7). The first clause of this subsection begins with the transitional אֱדַיִן, "then," and then the noun מַלְכָּא, "the king," without a verb—a left dislocation structure that introduces the topic of the four clauses that follow: all these things happened to the king. This structure sets information outside the syntax of the four independent clauses in 5:6 and allows the narrator to emphasize the topic without increasing the complexity of the main clause. All four independent clauses describe the king's reaction with a suffixed noun ("his countenance," 5:6a; "his thoughts," 5:6b; "the joints of his loins," 5:6c; "his knees," 5:6d) followed by a verb ("changed," 5:6a; "were alarming him," 5:6b; "were loosening, 5:6c; "were knocking," 5:6d). The second part of the subsection, 5:7, consists of the narrator's report that the king called for help (5:7a–b) and the reported speech of the

Daniel 5:1a–6:1[5:31]

Daniel 5:5a–8d

			2. The Result of the Arrogant Offense (5:5a–8d)
			a. The Hand Writing on the Wall (5:5a–d)
5a	בַּהּ־שַׁעֲתָ֗ה [נְפַ֙קוּ֙] (נְפַ֙קָה֙) אֶצְבְּעָ֔ן דִּ֥י יַד־אֱנָ֖שׁ	At that moment, fingers of a human hand appeared,	
5b	וְכָֽתְבָן֙ לָקֳבֵ֣ל נֶבְרַשְׁתָּ֔א עַל־גִּירָ֕א דִּֽי־כְתַ֥ל הֵיכְלָ֖א דִּ֣י מַלְכָּ֑א	and they were writing opposite the lampstand on the plaster of the wall of the palace of the king.	
5c	וּמַלְכָּ֣א חָזֵ֔ה פַּ֥ס יְדָ֖ה	The king was watching the back of the hand	
5d	דִּ֥י כָתְבָֽה׃	↑ which was writing.	
			b. The King's Reaction (5:6a–7i)
			(1) The King's Physical Response (5:6a–d)
6a	אֱדַ֤יִן מַלְכָּא֙ זִיוֹ֣הִי שְׁנ֔וֹהִי	Then the king—his countenance changed,	
6b	וְרַעְיֹנֹ֖הִי יְבַהֲלוּנֵּ֑הּ	and his thoughts were alarming him,	
6c	וְקִטְרֵ֤י חַרְצֵהּ֙ מִשְׁתָּרַ֔יִן	and the joints of his loins were loosening,	
6d	וְאַ֨רְכֻבָּתֵ֔הּ דָּ֥א לְדָ֖א נָֽקְשָֽׁן׃	and his knees were knocking together.	
			(2) The King's Call for Help (5:7a–i)
7a	קָרֵ֤א מַלְכָּא֙ בְּחַ֔יִל	The king was calling loudly	
7b	לְהֶֽעָלָה֙ לְאָ֣שְׁפַיָּ֔א [כַּשְׂדָּיֵא֙] (כַּשְׂדָּאֵי֙) וְגָזְרַיָּ֑א	↑ to bring the conjurers, the Chaldeans, and the diviners.	
7c	עָנֵ֨ה	↓ Responding,[2]	
7d	מַלְכָּ֜א וְאָמַ֣ר ׀ לְחַכִּימֵ֣י בָבֶ֗ל	the king said to the wise men of Babylon,	
7eα	דִּ֣י כָל־אֱנָ֡שׁ …	"Any man …	
7f	דִּֽי־יִקְרֵ֞ה כְּתָבָ֤ה דְנָה֙	↳ who reads this writing	
7g	וּפִשְׁרֵהּ֙ יְחַוִּנַּ֔נִי	and makes known its interpretation to me	
7eβ	אַרְגְּוָנָ֣א יִלְבַּ֗שׁ	… will be clothed with purple,	
7h	[וְהַֽמְנִיכָ֤א] (וְהַֽמּוֹנְכָ֤א) דִֽי־דַהֲבָא֙ עַֽל־צַוְּארֵ֔הּ	and a necklace of gold will be around his neck,	
7i	וְתַלְתִּ֥י בְמַלְכוּתָ֖א יִשְׁלַֽט׃	and he will have power as third in the kingdom."	
			c. The Wise Men's Inability to Help (5:8a–d)
8a	אֱדַ֙יִן֙ [עָלִּ֔ין] (עָלֲלִ֔ין) כֹּ֖ל חַכִּימֵ֣י מַלְכָּ֑א	Then all the wise men of the king were coming in,	
8b	וְלָֽא־כָהֲלִ֗ין	but they were not able	
8c	כְּתָבָ֤א לְמִקְרֵא֙	↰ to read the writing	
8d	(וּפִשְׁרֵהּ֙) [וּפִשְׁרָא֙] לְהוֹדָעָ֥ה לְמַלְכָּֽא׃	or make its interpretation known to the king.	

1. Emended from וְהַמְנִיכָא. See *BHS* apparatus.
2. See on 2:5 in the commentary.

king to the wise men (5:7c–i). The king's speech begins with a topical frame, a specific frame of reference that applies to the clauses that follow.[28] In this case, the topical frame is found in 5:7eα–g ("Any man who reads this writing and makes known its interpretation to me"), and it identifies the recipient of the king's three rewards in clauses 5:7eβ–i.

The third subsection is the narrator's report that the wise men came but were unable to do either of the things the king requested: read the writing or interpret it (5:8).

Explanation of the Text

a. The Hand Writing on the Wall (5:5a–d)

As Belshazzar and his guests used YHWH's temple vessels to praise idols, fingers of a human hand appeared writing on the wall. The text does not say whose fingers they might be or what they represent, but the narrator has worked several hints into the text that give the careful reader a good idea of what is going on.

The first hint is the temporal phrase that begins the section: בַּהּ־שַׁעֲתָה, "at that moment" (5:5a), is a phrase that recalls 4:30[33], where the voice from heaven announced judgment בַּהּ־שַׁעֲתָה, "at that moment," on Nebuchadnezzar as he engaged in idolatrous self-praise. The reader might suspect that here in Dan 5, Belshazzar's judgment has been similarly declared.

A second hint is the verb that describes the appearance of the hand: נְפַקָה, "appeared" or "came forth" (5:5a). This verb has already been used twice in the chapter to refer to the taking or the "bringing forth" of the vessels from the Jerusalem temple (5:2c, 3b). The wordplay signals to the reader "that the mysterious hand is a direct response to Belshazzar's blasphemy."[29]

A third hint is the detail that "fingers . . . were writing" (5:5a–b). In the chapter's three references to the hand, the fingers are only mentioned here (cf. 5:5c, 24a). The reader suspects these fingers belong to God, whose finger(s) also appear in Exod 8:15[19] during the ten plagues, in Exod 31:18 and Deut 9:10 with respect to the Ten Commandments, and in Ps 8:4[3], where the psalmist praises God for creation, "the work of your fingers." Of these occurrences, only two associate God's finger with writing: when "the finger of God" writes the two stone tablets for Moses on Mount Sinai (cf. Exod 32:16; 34:1).[30] In the Dan 5:5 statement that fingers were writing on the wall, the narrator hints that God is behind this writing and perhaps suggests that the writing is related to the covenant he has with his people.

A fourth hint about what is happening in this text is in the description of where the fingers were writing: "opposite the lampstand on the plaster of the wall of the palace of the king" (לָקֳבֵל נֶבְרַשְׁתָּא עַל־גִּירָא דִּי־כְתַל הֵיכְלָא דִּי מַלְכָּא, 5:5b). This is a lot of

---

28. Runge and Westbury, *LDHB: Introduction*, 5.1 Topical Frames.

29. Newsom, *Daniel*, 169. Newsom is summarizing the argument by Bill T. Arnold, "Wordplay and Narrative Techniques in Daniel 5 and 6," *JBL* 112/3 (1993): 479–85.

30. In light of these Old Testament texts, it is interesting to consider the only other instance in the Bible of God's "finger" writing: Jesus's writing in the dirt in the account of the woman taken in adultery (John 8:6).

description if the narrator simply wanted to say the hand was writing on the wall. Most commentators associate the mention of the lampstand with the visibility of the writing—namely, it was clear for all (or just Belshazzar; see below) to see.[31] This observation is probably true, but it seems the narrator may be doing more by mentioning the lampstand and its proximity to the writing. In this context, where God's vessels are being used, the narrator is suggesting God's presence—specifically, his sanctuary. In the Hebrew Bible, references to lamps and lampstands occur most frequently with respect to the tabernacle and the temple and more particularly to the central sanctuary, the holy place (e.g., Exod 25:31–40; 27:20; 1 Kgs 7:49; 1 Chr 28:15). In fact, nearly all references to literal lamps are to lamps in the central sanctuary.[32] In the holy place of the tabernacle, a lampstand was one of three pieces of furniture: an incense altar, the table of presence, and the lampstand.[33] In the nearly four dozen Pentateuchal references that detail the instructions for and construction of the lampstand for the tabernacle, two are concerned with its placement in the holy place. It was to stand "in front of" or "opposite"[34] the table of the presence that held the bread of the presence (Exod 26:35; 40:24).[35]

We already know that the temple in Jerusalem lies below the surface of events in Dan 5. The narrator has taken pains to emphasize the temple vessels and the temple itself (5:2c–d, 3b–d). The narrator has also specified that Belshazzar and his guests drank specifically from the *gold* vessels (5:3a; cf. "gold and silver" of 5:2b), which would have been vessels of the central sanctuary.[36] Into this context, the narrator sets a lampstand "opposite" the fingers (of God) writing on the wall. The narrator seems to be showing that God is in this place.

But what is "this place," and, more importantly, what is God doing there? The narrator gives his final hint at what is really happening in this scene in the overspecification that the writing was on the wall of הֵיכְלָא דִּי מַלְכָּא, "the palace of the king" (5:5b). This information is not necessary in terms of simply understanding where the writing was; the reader already knows the setting is Belshazzar's feast, presumably in his palace. The significance of this information is the contrast it creates with two earlier uses of הֵיכְלָא, "the palace." In 5:2c and 5:3b, הֵיכְלָא referred to the temple, first, that it was in Jerusalem and, second, that it was the "house of God." The vessels came from God's הֵיכְלָא; God has come to Belshazzar's הֵיכְלָא.

---

31. E.g., Lucas, *Daniel*, 129; Pace, *Daniel*, 166; Longman, *Daniel*, 138. The reference to the plaster may substantiate this, since we know from archaeological reports that the walls of the Babylonian throne room were covered with white gypsum. The white background and the lamp would have made both the hand and the writing stand out (Miller, *Daniel*, 155).

32. The exceptions are 2 Kgs 8:19 and Dan 5:5. "Lamp, Lampstand," in *Dictionary of Biblical Imagery*, ed. Leland Ryken, James C. Wilhoit, and Tremper Longman III (Downers Grove, IL: InterVarsity Press, 1998), 486.

33. In Solomon's temple centuries later, the holy place had ten lampstands and ten tables of presence (1 Kgs 7:49; 1 Chr 9:32; 2 Chr 4:7, 19).

34. The preposition "in front of, before" in Biblical Hebrew is נֹכַח (which does not have a cognate in BA), and the noun "lampstand" is מְנוֹרָה, a noun that exists in Aramaic but does not occur in Biblical Aramaic. While my proposal would be stronger if מְנוֹרָה were used in Dan 5, the rest of the narrative hints of God's presence at Belshazzar's feast make it plausible.

35. The table of presence held twelve loaves of bread arranged in two stacks of six. Every Sabbath the priests replaced the bread (Lev 24:5–9). The table was a sign for YHWH and for Israel, reminding YHWH of his obligations to sustain Israel and Israel of its obligation to keep the covenant (J. Kelly, "Bread of the Presence," in *The Lexham Bible Dictionary* (Bellingham, WA: Lexham, 2016), https://ref.ly/logosres/lbd?hw=Bread+of+the+Presence).

36. All the furniture and vessels of the central sanctuary (holy place, holy of holies) were made of gold. Silver and bronze were used in the curtained courtyard surrounding the tabernacle itself.

Greg Goswell argues that the temple is one of the major themes in the entire book, and its desecration by foreign rulers represents the main challenge to God's kingship within history: "Such interference with the temple is a direct challenge to God's rule and appears to call into question the reality of his rule."[37] Belshazzar may not have physically entered the Jerusalem temple, but he brought it to his doorstep when he commandeered the vessels of God's הֵיכְלָא for his own use. In so doing, he invaded territory that was not his and so challenged God's rule (whether he meant to or not[38]). God responded to the challenge, invading Belshazzar's הֵיכְלָא. The presence of God's gold vessels, the mention of the lampstand opposite the writing, and the fingers (of God) writing on the wall all suggest the presence of God, invading the "palace of the king." This may have been Belshazzar's home turf, but the God of Israel has taken control of it. Further, he has come to pass judgment—a judgment that would lead to the overthrow of Belshazzar's kingdom and the eventual restoration of God's vessels and God's covenant people.

In 5:5c, the narrator says the king was watching the hand as it was writing, and as was true when Nebuchadnezzar saw the fourth man in the fiery furnace,[39] it is not clear whether anyone else saw the hand or the writing. Segal argues that Belshazzar alone saw what happened, "which explains why the Babylonian wise men were unsuccessful in their attempts to read and interpret the writing"—namely, they could not *see* it to *read* it.[40]

b. The King's Reaction (5:6a–7i)

In response to seeing a disembodied hand writing on the wall of his palace, Belshazzar came undone. The narrator reports his physical response with four descriptions, prefaced by a noun (מַלְכָּא, "the king," 5:6a) that stands outside the syntax of the sentence and sets the topic of the next four independent clauses: all these things happened to the king. The four clauses share a similar structure and together describe from top to bottom what happened to Belshazzar. His "countenance changed" (זִיוֹהִי שְׁנוֹהִי, 5:6a), and "his thoughts were alarming him" (רַעְיֹנֹהִי יְבַהֲלוּנֵּהּ, 5:6b). Additionally, "the joints of his loins were loosening" (קִטְרֵי חַרְצֵהּ מִשְׁתָּרַיִן, 5:6c), a possible reference to the loss of control of his sphincter muscles—and thus, his bodily functions.[41] Finally, "his knees were knocking together" (5:6d). The God of Israel has invaded Belshazzar's home turf, and any bravado the king had when he called for the sacred vessels dissolves. He utterly loses control.

The first two responses (alarming thoughts and changed countenance) are repeated later (5:9b, 10e–f), and in the references to the "thoughts" of the king causing his fear, Segal finds support for the idea that only Belshazzar saw the hand and the writing:

---

37. Greg Goswell, "The Temple Theme in the Book of Daniel," *JETS* 55.3 (2012), 520.

38. Belshazzar's interest in the vessels was not that they belonged to God, but that they were the ones taken by "his father Nebuchadnezzar."

39. See on Dan 3:24–25.

40. Michael Segal, "Rereading the Writing on the Wall (Daniel 5)," *ZAW* 125.1 (2013), 175. He argues that Daniel's ability later to read the writing and interpret it makes a strong parallel with Dan 2, where the king demanded that his wise men read his mind (where the dream was) and interpret it.

41. Al Wolters details the argument that the king became incontinent in "Untying the King's Knots: Physiology and Wordplay in Daniel 5," *JBL* 110.1 (1991): 117–22. However, Newsom contends that the chapter "does not have the bawdy style that fits such a narrative detail" (*Daniel*, 170). In his revised edition, Goldingay allows that "there is perhaps some humor in the description of Belshazzar's reaction to the portent, if it refers to his losing control of his bodily functions" (*Daniel*, 288–89), a modification from his earlier conclusion that there is "nothing humorous about the description of Belshazzar's reaction to the portent. It is a deadly serious comprehensive description of the physical manifestation of terror . . . the appropriate response to the prospect of divine judgment" (*Daniel* [1989], 109).

The narrator in this tale twice refers to the "thoughts" of the king as the cause of his fear (vv. 6, 10). An identical term is found elsewhere in Daniel in reference to knowledge found in the mind of an individual (2,29–30; 4,16; 7,28), and in two of these instances, there is specific reference to the fear that these thoughts cause the one who received them, either through direct revelation or a dream (4,16; 7,28; cf. also 4,2; 7,15). It thus supports the suggestion here that the [sic] only Belshazzar was privy to this divine communication, since he alone knew what was in his own head.[42]

Belshazzar then קְרָא . . . בְּחַיִל, "was calling loudly" or "with strength" for his experts (5:7a; cf. 3:4; 4:11[14])—that is, he shouted or screamed. The king made them an offer, set in reported speech by the narrator, providing the reader with a window into the king's mind.[43] What the king's speech reveals is his weakness. Consider his response alongside the response of "his father" when he too faced troubling revelations (chs. 2 and 4). Of Nebuchadnezzar in chs. 2 and 4, Fewell observes that while Nebuchadnezzar was also afraid and troubled, he never allowed his fear to be seen in public view; when he needed his wise men, he commanded or issued a decree that they come (2:2; 4:3[6]). Despite his "state of anxiety, he acts authoritatively. . . . He promises [his sages in ch. 2] reward for success, but only after he has threatened death for failure. He is an uncompromising king who uses his power as he wills."[44]

By contrast, of Belshazzar Fewell observes that he "loses his composure. He shows all the signs of being overcome by what he has just witnessed." He wants to appear powerful but instead shows himself weak, crying loudly for his wise men to brought (5:7) and responding in panic. When the wise men do come, "Belshazzar . . . promises only reward, and rather excessive reward at that, to any sage who can explain the writing to him (5:7). . . . He acts with decidedly less assurance than does King Nebuchadnezzar."[45] The narrator portrays neither king positively in their reactions to divine revelation, but the contrast between the two highlights Belshazzar's weakness.[46]

c. The Wise Men's Inability to Help (5:8a–d)

As expected, the wise men are unable to do what the king needs. They could neither read nor interpret the writing—though the narrator does not explain why. Segal thinks it was because they could not see it: "There was no special code or symbols, nor did they have difficulty reading an unvocalized text—they were well-trained wise men! Rather, they could not read it simply because it was revealed only to the king."[47] Regardless, the wise men's inability sets the stage for Daniel, who—on account of the divine wisdom given him—will both read the inscription and reveal its meaning.

---

42. Segal, "Rereading the Writing on the Wall (Daniel 5)," 167.
43. See ch. 1, n40xx.
44. Fewell, *Circle of Sovereignty*, 87.
45. Fewell, *Circle of Sovereignty*, 87.
46. Newsom, *Daniel*, 172.
47. Segal, "Rereading the Writing on the Wall (Daniel 5)," 168. If the inscription was visible, it is not clear what made it so baffling. Some think the message was written in code, abbreviations, or a peculiar script, but the most common view is that the inscription was entirely consonantal (as was true of all Aramaic of the time). Being able to read a vowelless text in your first language is relatively simple: consider the consonantal sentence "Jn rd th bk," which could be either "Jon/Jane read the book" or "rode the bike." If the consonants are not separated by space, the task is more difficult: "Jnrdthbk." A famous painting by Rembrandt, *Belshazzar's Feast*, reflects

3. The Queen's Words (5:9a–12d)

Main Idea of the Passage

In Daniel 5:9–12 the queen mother presents Belshazzar with the solution to his knotty problem by recounting the extraordinary ability of the man Daniel, Nebuchadnezzar's chief magician.

Literary Context

Daniel 5:9–12 is the third section of the narrative of 5:1a–6:1[5:31]. It follows the narrator's report of the king's increased terror at his wise men's inability to read or interpret the writing on the wall (5:5–8). It functions in at least four ways in its broader literary context. First, it introduces the queen, who presents the king with the answer to his problem and so sets the stage for resolution of the conflict in the narrative. Second, through the words of the queen, the narrator continues the contrast between the kings Nebuchadnezzar and Belshazzar. The queen's words also provide a backdrop for interpreting Belshazzar's words in the narrative's fourth section. And finally, this third section introduces Daniel into the narrative by his reputation; he enters the narrative as an active character in the next section.

> D. Narrative 4: A Humbled King and His Rescinded Power (5:1a–6:1[5:31])
>   1. Belshazzar's Arrogant Offense (5:1a–4b)
>   2. The Result of the Arrogant Offense (5:5a–8d)
> → **3. The Queen's Words (5:9a–12d)**
>   4. Belshazzar's Arrogant Words (5:13a–16i)
>   5. Daniel's Words to the Arrogant Belshazzar (5:17a–28b)
>   6. A Rescinded Power (5:29a–6:1[5:31])

---

another possible difficulty—namely, using the letters from the illustration above, the words appear vertically:
JRTB
NDHK

In terms of the inscription in Dan 5, Daniel's eventual reading does not make a sentence. Rather, it is simply three words of measurement, like "grams, kilograms, tons." It still needs interpretation. See further below on 5:25–28.

Translation and Exegetical Outline

(See page 264.)

Structure and Literary Form

The third section of the narrative in Dan 5 (5:9–12) introduces a new character into the narrative—the queen. The section primarily consists of her response to Belshazzar's growing alarm over the writing on the wall and the inability of his wise men to read and interpret the writing.

The section begins with the transitional אֱדַיִן, "then," and has three subsections: 5:9, 10, and 11–12. In the first subsection (5:9), the narrator reports the increased alarm (5:9a) of the king and its effect on his expression (5:9b), and he also reports the confusion of the king's noblemen (5:9c), characters absent in the narrative since the report in 5:4 of their drinking from the temple vessels.

The second subsection begins simply with "the queen" (5:10a), followed by a reason/result clause explaining her sudden presence in the narrative: "because of the words of the king and his noblemen." This subsection continues with the queen's admonition to Belshazzar (5:10d–f), set as reported speech. Her admonition corresponds to the narrator's report of Belshazzar's growing alarm: he should not let his thoughts alarm him (5:10e; cf. 5:9a) or let his countenance be changed (5:10f; cf. 5:9b). In the third subsection (5:11–12), she describes an extraordinary man in the administration of מַלְכָּא נְבֻכַדְנֶצַּר אֲבוּךְ, "King Nebuchadnezzar, your father" (5:11d). She details the exceptional nature of this man's abilities, and then she offers the king her solution to his problem: "Now let Daniel be called" (5:12c).

Explanation of the Text

a. The King's Increased Alarm (5:9a–c)

The third section of the Dan 5 narrative begins with the transitional אֱדַיִן, "then," and describes events that followed those of the previous section—specifically, the wise men's inability to help the king (5:8). Its description of what happened begins with the overspecification of מַלְכָּא בֵלְשַׁאצַּר, "King Belshazzar" (5:9a). There is no need for the narrator to clarify which king the text is referring to since the preceding verse ended with the wise men's inability to make the interpretation known לְמַלְכָּא, "to the king" (5:8d). Further, this is the only place in the chapter where Belshazzar is referred to this way.[48]

---

48. Compare "Belshazzar the (Chaldean) king" (vv. 1a, 30a); "Belshazzar" (vv. 2a, 22a, 29a); and most commonly, "the king" or "O king" (vv. 2e, 3e, 5b–c, 6a, 7a, 7d, 8a, 8d, 10a, 10d, 13a, 13c, 17b, 17e, 18).

Daniel 5:9a–12d

9a	אֱדַיִן מַלְכָּא בֵלְשַׁאצַּר שַׂגִּיא מִתְבָּהַל	Then King Belshazzar was greatly alarmed,	3. The Queen's Words (5:9a–12d)
9b	וְזִיוֹהִי שָׁנַיִן עֲלוֹהִי	and his countenance was changing,	a. The King's Increased Alarm (5:9a–c)
9c	וְרַבְרְבָנוֹהִי מִשְׁתַּבְּשִׁין׃	and his noblemen were becoming perplexed.	
10a	מַלְכְּתָא לָקֳבֵל מִלֵּי מַלְכָּא וְרַבְרְבָנוֹהִי לְבֵית מִשְׁתְּיָא [עַלַּת] (עללת)	The queen, because of the words of the king and his noblemen, came to the banquet house.	b. The Queen's Admonition (5:10a–f)
10b	עֲנָת →	→ Responding,[1]	
10c	מַלְכְּתָא וַאֲמֶרֶת	the queen said,	
10d	מַלְכָּא לְעָלְמִין חֱיִי	"O king, live forever.	
10e	אַל־יְבַהֲלוּךְ רַעְיוֹנָךְ	Do not let your thoughts alarm you,	
10f	וְזִיוָיךְ אַל־יִשְׁתַּנּוֹ׃	and do not let your countenance be changed.	
11a	אִיתַי גְּבַר בְּמַלְכוּתָךְ	There is a man in your kingdom	c. The Queen's Solution (5:11a–12d)
11b	דִּי רוּחַ אֱלָהִין קַדִּישִׁין בֵּהּ	who has a spirit of the holy gods in him.	
11c	וּבְיוֹמֵי אֲבוּךְ נַהִירוּ וְשָׂכְלְתָנוּ וְחָכְמָה כְּחָכְמַת־אֱלָהִין הִשְׁתְּכַחַת בֵּהּ	In the days of your father, illumination, insight, and wisdom like the wisdom of the gods were found in him.	
11d	וּמַלְכָּא נְבֻכַדְנֶצַּר אֲבוּךְ רַב חַרְטֻמִּין אָשְׁפִין כַּשְׂדָּאִין גָּזְרִין הֲקִימֵהּ אֲבוּךְ מַלְכָּא׃	King Nebuchadnezzar, your father, appointed him chief of the magicians, conjurers, Chaldeans, and diviners—your father, the king.	
12a	כָּל־קֳבֵל דִּי רוּחַ יַתִּירָה וּמַנְדַּע וְשָׂכְלְתָנוּ מְפַשַּׁר חֶלְמִין וַאֲחַוָיַת אֲחִידָן וּמְשָׁרֵא קִטְרִין הִשְׁתְּכַחַת בֵּהּ בְּדָנִיֵּאל	Because an extraordinary spirit and knowledge, and insight for interpreting dreams, declaring riddles, and 'untying knots' were found in this Daniel,	
12b	דִּי־מַלְכָּא שָׂם־שְׁמֵהּ בֵּלְטְשַׁאצַּר	for whom the king appointed the name 'Belteshazzar,'	
12c	כְּעַן דָּנִיֵּאל יִתְקְרֵי	now let Daniel be called,	
12d	וּפִשְׁרָה יְהַחֲוֵה׃	that the interpretation he might declare."	

1. See on 2:5 in the commentary.

In this same section, Nebuchadnezzar is also referred to by his title for the only time in the chapter: מַלְכָּא נְבֻכַדְנֶצַּר, "King Nebuchadnezzar" (5:11d).[49] Such overly specific references are often "thematically loaded" and prompt the reader "to think about a certain person or setting based on what the writer seeks to accomplish. The redefinition may highlight a change in the center of attention."[50] In this case, the narrator may be centering attention on the comparison between the two kings. To this point in the narrative, the narrator has been preparing the reader for an extended comparison of the two monarchs. In the first section (5:1–4), he established the relationship between them, and he subtly linked Belshazzar's great feast in ch. 5 to Nebuchadnezzar's great statue in ch. 3 through similar sentence structures and vocabulary (see on 5:1–4 above). In the second section (5:5–8), similarities between the two kings' encounters with divinely sourced mysteries invited comparison (see on 5:5–8 above). Beginning in this third section, the comparison becomes more pronounced.

The three participial clauses of 5:9 convey the circumstances behind the queen's entrance in 5:10 (עֲלַת, peal perfect).[51] The use of participles suggests the pluractional nature of the events—that is, several things are happening to different people at the same time.[52] First, the king's physical reaction to the apparition of the hand and the writing intensify. He is now *greatly* (שַׂגִּיא) alarmed (מִתְבָּהַל, 5:9a; cf. 5:6b), and his countenance changes again (זִיוֹהִי שָׁנַיִן, 5:9b; cf. 5:6a). Second, his noblemen were becoming perplexed (מִשְׁתַּבְּשִׁין, 5:9c). The narrator did not mention any reaction by the noblemen to the initial appearance of the hand, and the comment here lends support to the notion that only the king saw the hand and the writing. Segal argues that the narrator's silence on the reaction of the noblemen to the writing and his explicit statement that they were perplexed by the king's fear is precisely because they were "not privy to the terrifying sight." It is their lack of awareness to the writing that makes them "unable to read the entire situation, perplexed and confused at the king's behavior."[53]

The king's intensified fear and the noblemen's confusion launch a series of three speeches in the narrative. The queen makes the first speech to Belshazzar, while the second and third are a dialogue between the king and Daniel. Scholars differ in their understanding of the tone of the speeches. Some hear a compassionate, motherly queen, while others "detect irritation in her voice."[54] Some hear Belshazzar's words to Daniel as "gracious speech"[55] given "with the greatest courtesy,"[56] while others pick up a "condescending attitude"[57] in a speech that is "a complex mixture of skepticism, challenge, desperation, and resentment."[58] While the ambiguity in the text and lack of consensus about the dynamics between the characters caution us against holding any particular view too tenaciously, discourse features of the text as discussed in what follows make some readings more likely than others.

---

49. Compare "the king" (vv. 11d, 12b, 13f) and variations that include "father" (vv. 2c, 11c–d, 13f, 18).
50. Runge and Westbury, *LDHB: Introduction*, 2.1 Overspecification.
51. Li, *The Verbal System of the Aramaic of Daniel*, 47.
52. See Cook, *Aramaic Ezra and Daniel*, 10.
53. Segal, "Rereading the Writing on the Wall (Daniel 5)," 169.
54. Longman, *Daniel*, 140.
55. Collins, *Daniel*, 249.
56. Norman W. Porteous, *Daniel: A Commentary*, OTL (Philadelphia: Westminster, 1976), 80.
57. Longman, *Daniel*, 140.
58. Fewell, *Circle of Sovereignty*, 94.

b. The Queen's Admonition (5:10a–f)

The queen enters the narrative in 5:10 in a clause-initial topical frame to introduce a new character (cf. 5:1a). What follows her introduction is a reason/result clause that explains her presence: she came because of the commotion in the banquet hall. The narrator offers no description of her, why she was not already at the banquet,[59] or whether she saw the hand or the inscription. Instead, she immediately begins speaking; the narrator's use of reported speech for the queen's words gives a window into her thoughts, interests, and motivations.

The queen begins with the expected protocol: "O king, live forever" (5:10d). Then she responds to the king's reactions as reported by the narrator: his alarm and his changed countenance (5:10e–f; cf. 5:9a–b). She tells him to not be alarmed or let his countenance be changed, words that suggest comfort. However, Fewell says her language is really double-edged: "While on the one hand, her words *speak* a message of comfort, on the other hand, her words *function* to bring attention to the king's discomfort. If any of those present have missed the king's display of fear, she makes sure they now take note of it."[60]

c. The Queen's Solution (5:11a–12d)

The queen offers her solution to Belshazzar's problem, beginning in 5:11. She responds to the third element reported by the narrator (the noblemen's perplexity, 5:9c), recounting her memory of "a man in your kingdom," who may be able to help the king (5:12d). The queen first describes this man with a relative clause that explains what makes him unique: he has "a spirit of the holy gods in him" (5:11b). By this, she meant that Daniel had access to supernatural knowledge that none of the other royal experts had.[61] In 5:11c she describes Daniel further by recalling the days of "your father," when wisdom akin to the gods' wisdom, illumination, and insight were found in this particular man. The queen's words suggest that Belshazzar does not know about Daniel.

What the queen says next, however, lessens the likelihood that Belshazzar was ignorant about Daniel. After just referring to "your father" (5:11c), she explains the place of this particular man in the days of "your father"—namely, he was appointed chief of the wise men (5:11d). This statement is framed by two overly specific references to Belshazzar's "father." First, the queen calls him מַלְכָּא נְבֻכַדְנֶצַּר אֲבוּךְ, "King Nebuchadnezzar, your father," in her explanation that Nebuchadnezzar had appointed him chief of the wise men, and then she repeats אֲבוּךְ מַלְכָּא, "your father, the king" (5:11d). Several English versions omit this second reference (e.g., NIV, NET, NRSV, NJPS) because, although present in the Aramaic, it sounds redundant and is missing in the Greek text of Theodotion and in the Syriac. It may sound redundant and even awkward, but this does not necessarily mean the second occurrence is an error.[62] Its very redundancy may contribute to its discourse purpose. The KJV gets at the effect of the repetition: "whom the king Nebuchadnezzar thy father, the king, *I say*, thy father, made master of the magicians, astrologers, Chaldeans, *and*

---

59. Belshazzar's wives were already present at the banquet, so this unnamed queen may have been his mother, the queen mother—an important figure in ancient Near Eastern cultures (cf. 1 Kgs 15:13; Jer 13:18). She would have had a degree of authority over Belshazzar and was free to enter the king's presence unbidden.

60. Fewell, *Circle of Sovereignty*, 88.
61. See on Dan 4:5–6[8–9], 15[18].
62. The apparatus of *BHS* notes the omission in Theodotion and the Syriac and says it should be deleted. Commentators, like English versions, are divided.

soothsayers." The queen's repetition emphasizes the relationship between Nebuchadnezzar and Belshazzar, a relationship that may well explain Belshazzar's behavior in this chapter (see on 5:1–4).

It is hard to believe that Belshazzar would not know about someone as important as Nebuchadnezzar's gifted chief magician. What seems more likely is that Belshazzar had chosen to ignore Daniel *because* of his importance to "his father."[63] His later words, as well as Daniel's, will confirm this. In light of this, there may very well be a sarcastic bite in the queen's repetition of "your father": "If you were worthy to sit on your father's throne, I would not need to tell you this."[64]

The queen's explanation for why Nebuchadnezzar had promoted this man builds on much of what she has already said (5:12a; cf. 5:11b–c): his extraordinary spirit and insight enabled him to interpret dreams, declare riddles, and "untie knots" (מִשָׁרֵא קִטְרִין). This last description is a delicious wordplay on the narrator's description of what had happened when Belshazzar saw the hand writing on the wall: the king whose "knots" had been "loosened" (קִטְרֵי חַרְצֵהּ מִשְׁתָּרַיִן, 5:6c; see above) needed the help of this man who was able to loosen or "untie knots." The queen meant that this man could solve difficult problems, but she may also have been making a jab at the king. At the very least, the narrator uses the wordplay to make her words sound derisive.

The queen finally names the man she has been praising: all these abilities were found בֵּהּ בְּדָנִיֵּאל, "in this Daniel" ("in him, in Daniel," 5:12a). By using Daniel's Hebrew name, she may have indicated to Belshazzar that this man was one of the Judean exiles, though this does not seem important to her as it will to Belshazzar later (5:13d–f). She clarifies in the next clause that this man was the one Nebuchadnezzar had named Belteshazzar (5:12b), an aside perhaps intended to ensure that the king knew which man she was talking about. But given the remarkable similarity between the names "Belshazzar" and "Belteshazzar," her comment may have been another jab at the king whose character could not have been more different than Daniel's.[65]

In all the queen's accolades, Fewell again notes the double-edged nature of her language, that it "*does* more than it *says*." While her words themselves communicate Daniel's credibility—that is, she is recommending him to Belshazzar on the basis of his service to Nebuchadnezzar—her use of the phrase "your father, the king" also communicates "two kinds of hierarchy": those of fathers commanding the respect of their sons and kings commanding the respect of their subjects. Her reference to Nebuchadnezzar (rather than Belshazzar) as "the king" undermines Belshazzar's claim to the title—"that is to say, we might well hear her words implying that Nebuchadnezzar was a real king while Belshazzar has yet to prove himself." When the queen then tells Belshazzar that Nebuchadnezzar gave Daniel the name Belteshazzar and she quotes Nebuchadnezzar's own words about "a spirit

---

63. Goldingay says there could be three explanations for why Daniel had not been called with the rest of the wise men: the first is historical (Daniel was probably 85 by this point), the second is psychological (Belshazzar knew what kind of message Daniel would give), and the third is rhetorical (in court tales, the successful interpreter only appears after the others have failed) (*Daniel*, 290). Also cf. Dan 8:27, where, in his report of a vision that occurred in the third year of Belshazzar (Dan 8:1), Daniel says he arose and "did the work of the king"—i.e., he was employed in some way by Belshazzar.

64. Longman says the queen "chides Belshazzar for his panic, unbefitting a king, and for his ignorance of Daniel, who had played an important role in Nebuchadnezzar's court" (*Daniel*, 139).

65. "Daniel . . . has a Babylonian name that differs from that of the king by only one additional medial syllable. Yet the two are so different in character and faith" (Pace, *Daniel*, 171). Anyone who has taught the book of Daniel knows the confusion these names cause among students.

of the holy gods" being in Daniel (cf. 4:5[8], 6[9], 15[18]), she is not only "informing Belshazzar that Daniel was highly regarded during the reign of Nebuchadnezzar" but she is "communicat[ing] Nebuchadnezzar's attitude toward Daniel. Indeed, she is the voice, and perhaps not such a welcome voice, of the dead king Nebuchadnezzar."[66]

In the queen's entrance to the narrative in 5:10, the narrator skipped past explaining what she knew and how she learned it. We do not know whether she saw the hand or the writing—and she mentions neither in her speech—but her concluding words in 5:12c–d indicate that somewhere between the commotion that drew her (5:9) and her speech, she learned what was causing the uproar. Whether or not she could see the writing, she knew the wise men had been called in for an interpretation of some sort but had proven inadequate. Her solution for Belshazzar's problem was that he call Daniel, who would declare the interpretation (5:12d).

By this point in the narrative, the reader is justified in thinking that Belshazzar knows who Daniel is but has chosen not to summon him—perhaps because his father had favored the Judean exile, and he wanted to distinguish himself from his great father. But the queen is forcing his hand. Seow explains:

> [T]he queen mother, who has come barging into his party, places him in an awkward position. In front of his thousand nobles, his consorts, and his concubines, she goes on and on about this wonderful fellow whom Nebuchadnezzar had promoted, this brilliant person who has a reputation for all kinds of special gifts, including the ability to "loosen knots." She tells Belshazzar to let Daniel be brought forth to give his interpretation (5:12). Belshazzar now has no choice but to summon Daniel.[67]

When Daniel arrives, the king will reveal more of his character in the way he interacts with his father's chief magician.

4. Belshazzar's Arrogant Words (5:13a–16i)

Main Idea of the Passage

Daniel 5:13–16 makes explicit Belshazzar's disregard and disdain for Daniel, whom he nonetheless needs to understand the writing on the wall.

Literary Context

Daniel 5:13–16 is the fourth section of the narrative in 5:1a–6:1[5:31]. It follows the queen's recommendation that the king call Daniel to give an interpretation (5:9–12), and it precedes Daniel's speech to the king (5:17–28). As such, it functions

---

66. Fewell, *Circle of Sovereignty*, 89.

67. Seow, *Daniel*, 81.

in at least two ways in its literary context. First, as an extended speech by Belshazzar, it further reveals the king's thoughts, motivations, and character. Since Belshazzar's words are directed to Daniel, they specifically reveal his attitude toward his father's chief magician. Second, in the development of the plot, Belshazzar's words provide the immediate context for Daniel's response in the following section.

> D. Narrative 4: A Humbled King and His Rescinded Power (5:1a–6:1[5:31])
> 1. Belshazzar's Arrogant Offense (5:1a–4b)
> 2. The Result of the Arrogant Offense (5:5a–8d)
> 3. The Queen's Words (5:9a–12d)
> → **4. Belshazzar's Arrogant Words (5:13a–16i)**
> 5. Daniel's Words to the Arrogant Belshazzar (5:17a–28b)
> 6. A Rescinded Power (5:29a–6:1[5:31])

Translation and Exegetical Outline

(See pages 270.)

Structure and Literary Form

The fourth section of the narrative in Dan 5 (5:13–16) is Belshazzar's response to the queen's suggested solution in the previous section (5:9–12). It consists of three subsections (5:13–14, 15, and 16), and most of it is set as reported speech.

The first subsection begins with the narrator's report that Daniel was brought before the king (5:13a). It continues with Belshazzar's question to Daniel (5:13d–14c), which the narrator has set as direct speech. Belshazzar's introductory words include both a question (. . . אַנְתְּ־הוּא דָנִיֵּאל, "Are you that Daniel . . . ," 5:13d) and a statement that implies why the king has summoned Daniel ("I have heard about you . . . ," 5:14a). Each is followed by a pair of relative clauses that expand on the question (5:13e–f) and the statement (5:14b–c).

In the second subsection, a continuation of the king's reported speech, Belshazzar explains his problem. The main clause states that the wise men were brought before the king (5:15a), and two dependent clauses identify the task they were given: "that they might read this writing" (5:15b) and "make known to me its interpretation" (5:15c). A second independent clause (5:15d) with an infinitive complement clause (5:15e) gives the outcome: "but they are not able . . ."

Daniel 5:13a–16i

13a	Then Daniel was brought in before the king.	4. Belshazzar's Arrogant Words (5:13a–16i)
13b	Responding,[1]	a. The King's Question (5:13a–14c)
13c	the king said to Daniel,	
13d	"Are you that Daniel,	
13e	who is one of the sons of the exile of Judah,	
13f	which my father the king brought from Judah?	
14a	I have heard about you	
14b	that a spirit of the gods is in you,	
14c	and illumination, insight, and great wisdom are found in you.	
15a	Just now the wise men and conjurers were brought before me	b. The King's Problem (5:15a–e)
15b	that they might read this writing	
15c	and make known to me its interpretation.	
15d	But they are not able	
15e	to make known the interpretation of the words.	
16a	But I myself have heard about you,	c. The King's Challenge (5:16a–i)
16b	that you are able	
16c	to interpret interpretations	
16d	and to loosen knots.	
16e	So, if you are able	
16f	to read the writing	
16g	and make its interpretation known to me,	
16h	you will be clothed with purple,	
16i	and a necklace of gold will be around your neck, and you will have power as third in the kingdom."	

1. See on 2:5 in the commentary.

The third subsection contains the king's challenge to Daniel, beginning with a second statement about what he had heard concerning him (5:16a–c; cf. 5:14) and concluding with a conditional statement (5:16d–i): "if you are able" to interpret the writing (5:16d–f), then rewards await (5:16g–i).

Explanation of the Text

a. The King's Question (5:13a–14c)

In response to the queen's advice in the preceding section, Daniel is brought before the king. Although the queen referred to him in her speech, 5:13a marks his physical presence in the narrative. The narrator reports that he is brought before the king, rather than saying Belshazzar summoned him as he did the wise men earlier (5:7a; cf. 2:2a; 4:3[6]). Daniel is before him, whether Belshazzar wanted him or not, and now he has no choice but to talk to him.

For the second time in the narrative, the narrator sets a character's words in reported speech, and in this important section, the narrator will reveal a great deal about Belshazzar's character in his own words.

The king begins with a telling question: אַנְתְּ־הוּא דָנִיֵּאל דִּי . . . We could translate this clause several ways to get at the king's meaning: "Are you *that* Daniel who . . ."; "are *you* Daniel who . . ."; or even "Are you the Daniel who . . ."[68] The relative clauses that follow identify what Belshazzar considers to be Daniel's most defining characteristic. Given the king's predicament and what the queen has said about Daniel, we might expect the king to say, "Are you that Daniel who can solve difficult problems?" or "Are you the Daniel who was my father's chief magician because of your extraordinary ability?" Instead Belshazzar asks if he is one of the exiles from Judah (5:13e). This clause alone would be sufficient to identify Daniel as a foreign slave (which seems to be part of Belshazzar's purpose), but Belshazzar continues: "which my father the king brought from Judah?" (5:13f).

The queen had not described Daniel in this way,[69] further support for the idea that Belshazzar did know about Daniel but had chosen not to summon him when the inscription appeared. There are at least two reasons for Belshazzar to ask this question in which he bypasses all of Daniel's achievements and focuses instead on a decades-old event. First, he wanted to make a statement of his superiority to the man "his father" had so highly esteemed by reminding him that he was just a Jewish slave. Second, the fill-in son-of-a-usurper king wanted to make a statement about his own status relative to "his father's." Fewell explains:

> Belshazzar has overtly shunned Daniel because Daniel is a symbol of his father's regime. First of all, Daniel, being an exile, falls into the same category as do the temple vessels. They were brought from Judah by Nebuchadnezzar, the king, the father. Daniel, like the vessels, symbolizes the success of Nebuchadnezzar, a success that Belshazzar would

---

68. The king's words could also be translated as a statement: "You are that Daniel who . . ."
69. She had used Daniel's theophoric name (*Danî-'El* means "God is my judge." Theophoric names included the name of a god, which may have tipped off the king that Daniel was an exile from Judah. However, this was not important to her, as her speech clearly reveals.

like to belittle. Secondly, Daniel was respected and admired by Nebuchadnezzar's administration. What Belshazzar has attempted to show with the vessels, he has also attempted to show with Daniel: What was important to his father is not important to him.[70]

The king has shown his hand. What the narrator has hinted at all along, the king confirms in his own words: his real problem is how he perceives himself with respect to "his father." His actions first with respect to the temple vessels and now with respect to Daniel were calculated to show his superiority to his father.

But Belshazzar needs Daniel, whether he likes it or not. If his problem is to be solved, he is stuck with his father's chief of magicians. So he begrudgingly says only what he must—reporting Daniel's abilities as hearsay: "I have heard about you . . ." (5:14a). His report includes two things that the queen had said. First, Daniel had in him a spirit of the gods (5:14b; cf. 5:11b in which the queen mother specifies that he has "a spirit of the *holy* gods"), and second, illumination, insight, and great wisdom[71] were found in him (5:14c; cf. 5:11c).

b. The King's Problem (5:15a–e)

The king then spells out his problem. The wise men had just been brought in to read and interpret the writing. The king calls it "this writing," כְּתָבָה דְנָה, perhaps pointing to the inscription on the wall. The narrator still does not tell us whether anyone else can see the writing. The king reports only that the wise men were not able to declare the interpretation. If they had not even been able to see it, one wonders if they would have admitted it to the king.

c. The King's Challenge (5:16a–i)

After telling Daniel the problem, the king returns to his hearsay report in 5:16, adding וַאֲנָה ("but I myself . . .") and including two additional elements of the queen's report: he heard that Daniel was able "to interpret interpretations" and "to loosen knots" (5:16b–c; cf. 5:12a). On either side of explaining his problem (5:15), Belshazzar reports pieces of what he has heard about Daniel. Everything he has said is from the queen's report, but he omits one key piece of information. In 5:11d, the queen had said that "King Nebuchadnezzar, your father," had appointed Daniel chief of the magicians, and then she repeated "your father, the king" (see on 5:11 above). In her effusive praise of Daniel's extraordinary abilities, the queen had included his promotion by Nebuchadnezzar. However, nowhere does Belshazzar acknowledge Daniel's rank as his father's chief magician. He neither endorses Daniel's abilities nor recognizes his rise to high rank. What Belshazzar cares about is that Daniel was a slave taken captive from Judah by his father.

He then makes the same offer to Daniel that he made to his wise men—though here it is expressed as a conditional offer: "if you are able . . ." (5:16d–i; cf. 5:7eα–i). Unlike his father, who had expressed confidence in Daniel's ability to interpret his dream (cf. 4:6[9], 15[18]), Belshazzar only reports what he has heard and challenges Daniel to prove the report correct.[72]

---

70. Fewell, *Circle of Sovereignty*, 124.

71. Where Belshazzar says "great wisdom," the queen had said "wisdom like the wisdom of the gods" (5:11c).

72. Lacocque calls the king's promise of reward "one more attempt to bribe the 'divine' and to change a 'fate' which he intuits as being fatal for him." He compares it to "Balak's pathetic and vain efforts to reorient Balaam's prophecy in a favourable direction (Num. 23–24)" (André Lacocque, *The Book of Daniel*, trans. by David Pellauer [London: SPCK, 1979], 101.

Belshazzar's attitude toward Daniel emerged in his opening words to "one of the sons of the exile of Judah" (5:13). Highlighting Daniel's status as a Jewish slave and never acknowledging his earned role as Nebuchadnezzar's chief magician, Belshazzar demonstrated his disregard and even disdain for his father's esteemed servant. But Belshazzar needs Daniel. He needs to know what the inscription says; he just does not want Daniel to be the one to tell him. "He is desperate, he is vulnerable, and he resents having to depend upon Daniel, the man who most represents his father's power and success."[73] When Daniel speaks in the next section, he will indict Belshazzar for his disregard and disdain—but not for the disregard and disdain he has for Daniel.

5. Daniel's Words to the Arrogant Belshazzar (5:17a–28b)

Main Idea of the Passage

Daniel 5:17–28 discloses the inscription on the wall as well as its interpretation that foretold Belshazzar's demise. It also reveals the reason the hand appeared and wrote on the wall at all.

Literary Context

Daniel 5:17–28 is the fifth section of the ch. 5 narrative. It follows Belshazzar's speech to Daniel and contains his response to the king's actions and attitude. In its broader literary context, this section functions in at least four ways. First, it is the climax of the plotline in the chapter, since it finally reveals what the hand wrote on the wall and what the inscription meant. Second, in Daniel's review of Nebuchadnezzar's greatness and Belshazzar's failure to learn from the great king's example, it provides a fuller picture of Belshazzar's offense before God as well as the reason behind the appearance of the hand. Third, Daniel's explicit connection of the two kings' behavior is the culmination of the chapter's extended comparison of Nebuchadnezzar and Belshazzar. Finally, it provides the theological interpretation of the historical events that occur in the final subsection (5:29–6:1[5:31]).

---

73. Fewell, *Circle of Sovereignty*, 94.

> D. Narrative 4: A Humbled King and His Rescinded Power (5:1a–6:1[5:31])
>   1. Belshazzar's Arrogant Offense (5:1a–4b)
>   2. The Result of the Arrogant Offense (5:5a–8d)
>   3. The Queen's Words (5:9a–12d)
>   4. Belshazzar's Arrogant Words (5:13a–16i)
> → **5. Daniel's Words to the Arrogant Belshazzar (5:17a–28b)**
>   6. A Rescinded Power (5:29a–6:1[5:31])

Translation and Exegetical Outline

(See pages 275–76.)

Structure and Literary Form

The fifth section of the narrative in Dan 5:1a–6:1[5:31] is the longest (5:17–28) and is almost entirely comprised of reported speech as Daniel responds to Belshazzar's question and challenge in the previous section (5:13–16). It consists of four subsections: 5:17, 18–21, 22–23, and 24–28.

The first subsection (5:17) contains Daniel's refusal of Belshazzar's reward and his subsequent consent to read the writing. It begins with the transitional בֵּאדַיִן, "then," followed by the speech frame for Daniel's reported speech that makes up the rest of the section (5:17–28). Two independent clauses comprise both Daniel's refusal (5:17c–d) and his consent (5:17e–f).

In the second subsection (5:18–21), Daniel gives Belshazzar a history lesson about "Nebuchadnezzar your father" (5:18). In the first part of this lesson, Daniel rehearses Nebuchadnezzar's greatness, given to him by the Most High God (5:18–19). In a series of four statements, he focuses especially on Nebuchadnezzar's greatness in terms of his power to do whatever he wished with "whom he wished" (5:19c, 19e, 19g, 19i). In the second part of the history lesson, Daniel recounts the story of Nebuchadnezzar's humbling (5:20–21; cf. Dan 4), concluding with the purpose of the humbling as stated throughout Dan 4: "until he acknowledged that the Most High God is ruler over the kingdom of man and whomever he wishes, he establishes over it" (5:21f–i; cf. 4:14c–g[17c–g], 22f–i[25f–i], 29e–h[32e–h]).

The third subsection is Daniel's indictment of Belshazzar for his own arrogance (5:22–23). It begins with words of contrast and emphasis as Daniel makes clear why he reviewed the story of Nebuchadnezzar: "but you, his son, Belshazzar, did not

Daniel 5:17a–28b

5. Daniel's Words to the Arrogant Belshazzar (5:17a–28b)

a. Daniel's Refusal and Consent (5:17a–f)

17a	בֵּאדַ֖יִן עָנֵ֣ה דָנִיֵּ֔אל	↓ Then responding,
17b	וְאָמַ֖ר קֳדָ֥ם מַלְכָּֽא	Daniel said before the king,
17c	מַתְּנָתָךְ֙ לָ֣ךְ לֶֽהֶוְיָ֔ן	"Let your gifts be for yourself,
17d	וּנְבָ֥זְבְּיָתָ֖ךְ לְאָחֳרָ֣ן הַ֑ב	and give your rewards to another.
17e	בְּרַ֗ם כְּתָבָא֙ אֶקְרֵ֣א לְמַלְכָּ֔א	Nevertheless, I will read the writing to the king,
17f	וּפִשְׁרָ֖א אֲהוֹדְעִנֵּֽהּ׃	and I will make known the interpretation to him.

b. Daniel's History Lesson (5:18–21h)

(1) Nebuchadnezzar's Greatness (5:18–19j)

18	[אַ֖נְתְּ] (אַ֣נְתָּה) מַלְכָּ֑א אֱלָהָא֙ עִלָּאָ֔ה מַלְכוּתָ֤א וּרְבוּתָא֙ וִיקָרָ֣א וְהַדְרָ֔א יְהַ֖ב לִנְבֻכַדְנֶצַּ֥ר אֲבֽוּךְ׃	As for you, O king—the Most High God gave the kingdom and the greatness and the honor and the majesty to Nebuchadnezzar your father.
19a	וּמִן־רְבוּתָא֙ דִּ֣י יְהַב־לֵ֔הּ	↓ Because of the greatness which he gave him,
19b	כֹּ֣ל עַֽמְמַיָּ֗א אֻמַיָּא֙ וְלִשָּׁ֣נַיָּ֔א הֲו֛וֹ [זָאֲעִ֥ין] (זָיְעִ֥ין) וְדָחֲלִ֖ין מִן־קֳדָמ֑וֹהִי	all peoples, nations, and languages were trembling and in fear before him;
19c	דִּֽי־הֲוָ֤ה צָבֵא֙ הֲוָ֣א קָטֵ֔ל	↓ whom he wished he killed;
19d	וְדִֽי־הֲוָ֥ה צָבֵ֖א הֲוָ֥ה מַחֵֽא	→ and whom he wished he let live;
19e	וְדִֽי־הֲוָ֤ה צָבֵא֙ הֲוָ֣ה מָרִ֔ים	→ and whom he wished he exalted;
19f	וְדִֽי־הֲוָ֥ה צָבֵ֖א הֲוָ֥ה מַשְׁפִּֽיל׃	→ and whom he wished he humiliated.
20a	וּכְדִי֙ רִ֣ם לִבְבֵ֔הּ	And when his heart was lifted up,
20b	וְרוּחֵ֖הּ תִּקְפַ֣ת לַהֲזָדָ֑ה	and his spirit hardened so that he acted proudly,
20c	הָנְחַת֙ מִן־כָּרְסֵ֣א מַלְכוּתֵ֔הּ	he was deposed from the throne of his kingdom,
20d	וִֽיקָרָ֖ה הֶעְדִּ֥יוּ מִנֵּֽהּ׃	and the glory was taken from him.
21a	וּמִן־בְּנֵי֩ אֲנָשָׁ֨א טְרִ֜יד	From the sons of man he was driven,
21b	וְלִבְבֵ֣הּ ׀ עִם־חֵיוְתָ֣א [שַׁוִּ֗י] (שַׁוִּ֗יו)	and his heart was like the beasts,
21c	וְעִם־עֲרָֽדַיָּא֙ מְדוֹרֵ֔הּ	and his dwelling was with wild donkeys,
21d	עִשְׂבָּ֤א כְתוֹרִין֙ יְטַ֣עֲמוּנֵּ֔הּ	and grass was fed to him like cattle.

(2) Nebuchadnezzar's Pride and Punishment (5:20a–21i)

Continued on next page.

Continued from previous page.

21e	וּמִטַּל שְׁמַיָּא גִּשְׁמֵהּ יִצְטַבַּע	And from the dew of heaven his body was wet	
21f	↑ עַד דִּי־יְדַע	↑ until he acknowledged	
21g	דִּי־שַׁלִּיט אֱלָהָא [עִלָּאָה] (עִלָּיָא) בְּמַלְכוּת אֲנָשָׁא	↑ that the Most High God is ruler over the kingdom of man	
21h	↓ וּלְמַן־דִּי יִצְבֵּה	↓ and whomever he wishes,	
21i	יְהָקֵים [עֲלַהּ] (עֲלַיהּ):	he establishes over it.	
22a	וְאַנְתְּ בְּרֵהּ בֵּלְשַׁאצַּר לָא הַשְׁפֵּלְתְּ לִבְבָךְ	But you, his son, Belshazzar, did not humble your heart,	c. Daniel's Indictment (5:22a–23i)
22b	↑ כָּל־קֳבֵל דִּי כָל־דְּנָה יְדַעְתָּ:	↑ even though you knew all this.	
23a	וְעַל מָרֵא־שְׁמַיָּא הִתְרוֹמַמְתָּ	But over the Lord of heaven you exalted yourself,	
23b	וּלְמָאנַיָּא דִי־בַיְתֵהּ הַיְתִיו [קָדָמָךְ] (קָדָמָיִךְ)	and over the vessels of his house they have brought before you.	
23c	וְאַנְתְּ [וְרַבְרְבָנָיִךְ] (וְרַבְרְבָנָךְ) שֵׁגְלָתָךְ וּלְחֵנָתָךְ חַמְרָא שָׁתַיִן בְּהוֹן	And you and your noblemen, your wives and concubines, are drinking wine with them.	
23dα	וְלֵאלָהֵי כַסְפָּא־וְדַהֲבָא נְחָשָׁא פַרְזְלָא אָעָא וְאַבְנָא ...	And the gods of silver and gold, bronze, iron, wood and stone …	
23e	דִּי לָא־חָזַיִן	which do not see,	
23f	וְלָא־שָׁמְעִין	and do not hear,	
23g	וְלָא יָדְעִין	and do not know,	
23dβ	... שַׁבַּחְתָּ	… you praised.	
23hα	וְלֵאלָהָא ...	But the God …	
23i	דִּי־נִשְׁמְתָךְ בִּידֵהּ וְכָל־אֹרְחָתָךְ לֵהּ	↑ in whose hand is your life and all your ways,	
23hβ	... לָא הַדַּרְתָּ:	… him you have not honored.	
24a	בֵּאדַיִן מִן־קֳדָמוֹהִי שְׁלִיחַ פַּסָּא דִי־יְדָא	Then from him the back of the hand was sent,	d. The Inscription (5:24a–28b)
24b	וּכְתָבָא דְנָה רְשִׁים:	and this writing was written.	(1) The Writing (5:24a–25c)
25a	וּדְנָה כְתָבָא	This is the writing	
25b	↑ דִּי רְשִׁים	↑ that was written:	
25c	מְנֵא מְנֵא תְּקֵל וּפַרְסִין:	*Mene, mene, tekel, upharsin.*	
26a	דְּנָה פְּשַׁר־מִלְּתָא	This is the interpretation of the message:	(2) The Interpretation (5:26a–28b)
26b	מְנֵא מְנָה־אֱלָהָא מַלְכוּתָךְ	*Mene*: God has numbered your kingdom,	
26c	וְהַשְׁלְמַהּ:	and brought an end to it.	
27a	תְּקֵל תְּקִילְתָּה בְמֹאזַנְיָא	*Tekel*: You have been weighed on the balances	
27b	וְהִשְׁתְּכַחַתְּ חַסִּיר:	and you have been found lacking.	
28a	פְּרֵס פְּרִיסַת מַלְכוּתָךְ	*Peres*: 'Your kingdom has been divided	
28b	וִיהִיבַת לְמָדַי וּפָרָס:	and given to the Medes and Persians."	

humble your heart, even though you knew all this" (5:22a–b). It continues with the specific offenses that resulted from Belshazzar's pride—namely, drinking from the vessels from the house of "the Lord of heaven" (5:23a); praising worthless material gods (5:23dα–dβ); and failing to honor the God "in whose hand is your life and all your ways" (5:23i).

In the fourth subsection, Daniel finally turns his attention to the inscription on the wall (5:24–28). He first reads the three words of the writing (5:24–25), and then he interprets each in a two-clause statement containing an action and a result of that action (5:26b–c; 5:27a–b; 5:28a–b).

Explanation of the Text

a. Daniel's Refusal and Consent (5:17a–f)

Daniel is the third and final character to speak in a chapter largely made up of speeches (5:7c–i, 10b–12, 13b–16, 17–28). His response to Belshazzar begins with the transitional בֵּאדַיִן, "then," followed by, first, his refusal of the king's reward and, second, his consent to read and interpret the writing anyway. Both independent clauses of his refusal begin with topical frames: מַתְּנָתָךְ, "your gifts," and נְבִזְבְּיָתָךְ, "your rewards" (5:17c–d). Similarly, both independent clauses of his consent begin with topical frames: כְּתָבָא, "the writing," and פִּשְׁרָא, "the interpretation" (5:17e–f). Topical frames, fronted thematic elements, establish specific frames of reference for the clauses that follow.[74] Often they introduce new information, but in the four clauses of 5:17c–f, none of the items is new information. In this context, the fronting of the nouns—along with the second-person pronominal suffixes in Daniel's refusal ("your," 5:17c–d), the first-person verbs in his consent ("I," 5:17e–f), and the contrastive בְּרַם, "nevertheless," that joins the two sections—seems intended to contrast Belshazzar and Daniel and create distance between them. We might paraphrase Daniel: "Keep your stuff. Do whatever you want with it. *I* don't want it. But I'll read the writing anyway." Daniel will read the writing, but not for any reward or because of any respect or concern he has for the king.[75]

Daniel's response to Belshazzar is usually interpreted as a terse rejection and even a rebuff of the king. Given Belshazzar's attitude toward Daniel and Daniel's God, this reaction is understandable. Daniel had shown great respect for Belshazzar's "father," but he wants little to do with this king who has, it appears, wanted nothing to do with him.

b. Daniel's History Lesson (5:18–21i)

Daniel consents to reading and interpreting the writing, but as with Nebuchadnezzar earlier, he has other things to say to the Babylonian king first (see on 2:27–30). He will not get to the writing itself

---

74. Runge and Westbury, *LDHB: Introduction*, 5.1 Topical Frames.

75. Others have noted that Daniel's rejection of Belshazzar's reward is important in the narrative because it guarantees that the message he delivers is in no way motivated by a price tag (cf. Balaam and Balak in Num 22–24 and Elisha and Naaman in 2 Kgs 5). Daniel's refusal to accept gifts also maintained his credibility as a true prophet (Mic 3:5, 11). See, e.g., Seow, *Daniel*, 81–82.

until 5:24. Before then, he gives Belshazzar a history lesson about "Nebuchadnezzar your father" (5:18) that sets up his indictment of the great king's "son" in the next section (5:22–23). In these two subsections, Daniel exploits the father-son relationship between the two kings in order to demonstrate Belshazzar's inferiority and even unworthiness to sit on Nebuchadnezzar's throne.

Daniel's history lesson begins in 5:18 with אַנְתְּ מַלְכָּא, "As for you, O king," an opening that leads us (and Belshazzar) to expect Daniel will be talking about Belshazzar or the writing in what follows (cf. 2:29, 31, 37; 4:19[22], 21[24]). But Daniel has other things in mind. He begins as expected, saying that "the Most High God gave the kingdom and the greatness and the honor and the majesty"—by the time Daniel had said all this, no doubt Belshazzar was gloating in his greatness. But Daniel delivers the blow with the last two words: "to Nebuchadnezzar your father." The narrator uses word order to build suspense and ultimately intensify the sting of Daniel's words: vocative ("You, O king")–subject ("the Most High God")–direct object ("the kingdom and the greatness and the honor and the majesty")–verb ("gave")–prepositional phrase/indirect object ("to Nebuchadnezzar your father").[76] Daniel's reference to "Nebuchadnezzar your father" is another instance in this chapter of overspecification and returns to the chapter's comparison of the "father" and the "son."

The next clause in Daniel's speech ("Because of the greatness which he gave him," 5:19a) is a dependent clause that explains what Daniel will say in the main clause of 5:19b that follows—the reason all peoples, nations, and languages feared Nebuchadnezzar (5:19b) was because God had given him such greatness. But this dependent clause has two additional effects in its context. First, its repetition of what Daniel has just said in 5:18 about Nebuchadnezzar's greatness adds insult to injury by reaffirming what a great king Nebuchadnezzar was (and implying that Belshazzar is not). Second, it reinforces the source of Nebuchadnezzar's greatness: he was great because the Most High God saw fit to make him so.

Daniel continues his description of Nebuchadnezzar's greatness by illustrating precisely what made Nebuchadnezzar's subjects regard the great king with fear and trembling. In four statements (5:19c–d, e–f, g–h, i–j), he describes how Nebuchadnezzar did whatever he pleased with whomever he pleased. The narrator begins each of Daniel's statements with the direct object דִּי־הֲוָה ... צָבֵא, "whom he wished . . ." (5:19c, 19e, 19g, 19i). The fourfold repetitive effect of this is to highlight Nebuchadnezzar's power over his subjects: no one was out of his reach. Whomever he wished to do anything to, he could and did. He killed at will, and he spared at will. He exalted people at will, and he humiliated people at will.

These are indeed indications of Nebuchadnezzar's greatness and power, but they also hint at the offense that was his downfall. The language of determining life and death, exalting and bringing low, is typically reserved for God in the Bible (Deut 32:39; 1 Sam 2:6–7; Ps 75:8[9]; Dan 2:21; 4:14[17]). While Nebuchadnezzar's acts of killing, sparing, exalting, and humbling were not explicitly part of his damning offense in ch. 4, in these acts he embodied attributes that belong to God. By describing Nebuchadnezzar in such language, Daniel underlined the ambiguity of the king's position.[77]

---

76. Fewell notes that "Daniel stings Belshazzar in his most sensitive spot. What the young king has desired most—power, prestige, authority—has not been attributed to him, but to the man whose memory he has tried to defeat—his father" (*Circle of Sovereignty*, 95).

77. Goldingay, *Daniel*, 298.

Nebuchadnezzar had great power and splendor, but both were derived—a point Daniel makes in 5:18—and the possession of such greatness is a temptation. Goldingay explains: "There is a link and a contrast between Nebuchadnezzar's great power and his great fall. It was his area of strength that became his area of vulnerability. His power became his weakness."[78] The king had challenged the sovereignty of God and so "was punished in order that all might *know* that the Most High is sovereign over the kingdom of mortals (see Dan. 4:17)."[79]

In most English translations, Nebuchadnezzar's offense is not raised until 5:20, where the initial וּכְדִי, *waw* conjunction on the temporal "when," is most commonly translated "but when" (e.g., NIV, NASB, ESV, KJV, NRSV), signifying a contrast with what has just been said. A better translation may be "and when," since it captures the idea that what happens in 5:20 is an outgrowth or continuation of the offenses from 5:19.[80] With such unfettered power, Nebuchadnezzar began to think of his greatness as his own accomplishment, an offense that reached its full measure on the roof of his palace as he surveyed "Babylon the great, which I myself have built for a royal house, by the strength of my power and for the glory of my majesty" (4:27[30]).

In what follows (5:20–21), Daniel recounts the story of Nebuchadnezzar's humbling, echoing many elements of ch. 4. Much like the original account, Daniel's retelling is largely in the passive or stative: the king was deposed from his throne; his glory was taken from him; he was driven from humankind; grass was fed to him; his heart was like the animals; his dwelling was with donkeys; his body was wet from the dew of heaven. Daniel concludes with the purpose of this humbling, echoing a refrain from Dan 4: "until he acknowledged that the Most High God is ruler over the kingdom of man and whomever he wishes, he establishes over it" (5:21f–i; cf. 4:14c–g[17c–g], 22f–i[25f–i], 29e–h[32e–h]).

While Daniel's ch. 5 recounting of Nebuchadnezzar's humbling has many similarities to the account in ch. 4, it does not include the earlier chapter's focus on the divine source of the events. From the opening verses of ch. 4, where Nebuchadnezzar declares that the Most High God did signs and wonders for him (3:31–33[4:1–3]), to its closing frame, where he blesses the Most High and praises the king of heaven "who the ones walking in pride is able to humble" (4:31–34[34–37]), the divine origin and nature of the chapter's events are obvious. In between the king's doxologies is his account of a dream he knew to be from the divine realm, requiring someone with a "spirit of the holy gods" to interpret it (4:5–6[8–9], 15[18]). In the dream itself, a holy one comes down from heaven (4:10[13], 20[23]; cf. 4:28[31]), and in Daniel's interpretation, he explicitly tells Nebuchadnezzar that his judgment is a decree of the Most High (4:21[24]). The divine hand in the events of Nebuchadnezzar's humbling permeates the entire chapter.

In ch. 5, while the reader knows God was responsible for Nebuchadnezzar's demise, his presence in the retold events is subtle. Rather than being explicitly identified as the agent, the Most High's involvement is implied by the way in which Daniel tells the story. He begins by twice saying that Nebuchadnezzar's greatness was given to him by the Most High God (5:18, 19a), and he concludes with the purpose of the great king's humbling: his acknowledgment that "the Most High God is ruler over the kingdom of man and whomever he wishes,

---

78. Goldingay, *Daniel*, 298.
79. Seow, *Daniel*, 82.

80. See also the NET Bible.

he establishes over it" (5:21f–i). Between these two mentions of the Most High God, Daniel describes the king's unrivaled power (5:19), which led to his great pride (5:20a–b), which brought about his great humiliation (5:20c–e). In similar statements at the beginning and the end, the king who had done whatever he wanted to whomever he wished (דִּי־הֲוָה צָבֵא, 5:19c, 19e, 19g, 19i) was brought low until he acknowledged that the Most High establishes whomever he wishes (לְמַן־דִּי יִצְבֵּה, 5:21h–i) as ruler over the kingdom of man. Nebuchadnezzar finally understood that his power was derived. His greatness was superseded by the one who gave him his greatness, the one who truly rules over the kingdom of man.

Chapter 5 is Belshazzar's encounter with this same God, whose presence in the account has been subtle (see above on Dan 5:2–5). But what has been subtle so far is about to become explicit as Daniel turns to his indictment of Belshazzar for his offenses against the Most High God.

c. Daniel's Indictment (5:22a–23i)

Daniel's speech turns on his second use of אַנְתְּ, "you" (5:22a). The first time he directly addressed the king with a vocative אַנְתְּ מַלְכָּא, "As for you, O king" (5:18), he went on to not to praise the king seated in front of him, but his predecessor. This time, he will go on to indict the king in front of him for failing to learn from that predecessor. The *waw* conjunction on the pronoun sets up the contrast: וְאַנְתְּ, "but you," and the subsequent overspecification of "his son, Belshazzar," confirms that a contrast between the father and the son is about to follow.

Daniel's purpose in reviewing the story of Nebuchadnezzar becomes clear at this point. Belshazzar knew "all this" (כָּל־דְּנָה) about his father, but he still did not humble his heart. He knew his father's heart had grown proud (5:20a), but he still refused to humble his own heart (5:22a). Instead he did exactly the opposite, exalting himself over the Lord of heaven that his father had finally exalted (4:34[37]). The evidence of this egregious pride was having the vessels of his (i.e., the Lord's) house (בַּיְתֵהּ) brought so that he and his guests could drink wine with them (5:23b–c; cf. 5:2–3).

Daniel continues his indictment by setting up another contrast in 5:23 that grows out of Belshazzar's use of the temple vessels. He contrasts Belshazzar's action toward the gods of silver and gold, bronze, iron, wood and stone, and his action toward Lord of heaven. The two parts of the contrast follow the same syntax: a topical frame containing the direct object, namely, the gods/God (5:23dα, 23hα); relative clauses describing attributes of the respective deities (. . . דִּי, 5:23e–g, 23i); and the main clause describing Belshazzar's actions with respect to the deities (5:23dβ, 23hβ).

As with the use of the topical frames in Daniel's refusal and consent (see on 5:17 above), the purpose of the fronted elements here (the gods/God) is not to introduce new topics, since the respective deities are already known in the narrative. The purpose is rather to draw attention to the shift in topic and sharpen the contrast Daniel is making between the gods Belshazzar praised and the God he has not honored (5:23dβ, 23hβ). The narrator uses a series of relative clauses to make the contrast plain. The gods Belshazzar praised do not see, do not hear, do not know (5:23e–g; cf. Deut 4:28; Pss 115:4–7; 135:15–18; Isa 40:18–20). The God that Belshazzar has not honored (note the emphatic לֵהּ at the beginning of the main clause in 5:23hβ—"*him* you have not honored") is the one who holds the king's life and all his ways in his hand (5:23i). The king has worshiped gods with no life in them, while he has scorned the God who holds his life. The contrast could not be any sharper.

Daniel's history lesson about Nebuchadnezzar created the context for his indictment of Belshazzar, who had learned nothing from the example of his predecessor. Rather, he scorned his father's example and then some, exalting himself against the Lord of heaven. The language of exalting oneself against God is similar to what Isaiah and others say in their descriptions of proud kings (e.g., Isa 14:12–20; cf. 2 Kgs 19:28). More importantly, in the context of Daniel it is language that looks ahead to what will be said later of the little horn and "the king" in Daniel's visions (8:11, 25; 11:36)—visions that, not coincidentally, take place during the reign of Belshazzar. Belshazzar is the book's first glimpse at a blasphemous king who defies the Lord of heaven.

d. The Inscription (5:24a–28b)

Daniel is finally ready to do what he was brought before Belshazzar to do: read the writing and interpret it. The new subsection begins with transitional בֵּאדַיִן, "then" (5:24a), as Daniel connects his history lesson and indictment of Belshazzar to the phenomenon of the hand: מִן־קֳדָמוֹהִי, "from him"—the pronominal suffix "him" referring back to the God that Belshazzar did not honor—"the back of the hand was sent" (5:24a). Daniel's delay in reading and interpreting the writing allowed him to "provide a detailed interpretation of the life of Belshazzar, one that, in fact, gives a fuller understanding of what the cryptic words on the wall mean."[81]

The narrator's description of the "back of the hand" matches his description of what the king originally saw (5:5c; cf. 5:5a), the only other time the hand is mentioned. The narrator has never said whether anyone else in attendance at the banquet saw it. Nor does he say whether the hand was still visible to the king at his point, or if it disappeared when the inscription was finished. He also does not say whether Daniel sees the hand; if it was visible to him, we might expect him to say "this hand," like he says "this writing" in the next clause (5:24b), rather than referring simply to "the hand." The narrator also does not report that anyone told Daniel about the hand—the focus of the narrative has been on the writing. In terms of the narrative then, Daniel has knowledge he could only have because of his extraordinary ability on account of "a spirit of the gods" being in him (5:11–12, 14, 16a–c).[82]

Both 5:23 and 5:24 refer to the hand that wrote on the wall. Lucas observes that "In a sense, [the hand] is a manifestation of the 'hand of God', the very hand that has hold of Belshazzar's 'breath' (i.e., 'life')."[83] Scattered throughout the book of Daniel are references to God's hand (2:45; 4:32[35]; 8:25; 9:15), and its presence in the story of Belshazzar's humbling fits well with its use elsewhere in the Old Testament to symbolize God's power and his victory over his enemies (e.g., Exod 7:4–5; 15:6; Judg 2:15; Isa 14:27).

Daniel prefaces his reading of the inscription with "This is the writing that was written" (5:25a–b), a forward-pointing reference that creates additional anticipation and attracts extra attention to what he is about to say—much like "Get this!" or "Here's the deal" do in English.[84] The inscription itself is four words: מְנֵא מְנֵא תְּקֵל וּפַרְסִין, "mene,

---

81. Pace, *Daniel*, 174.

82. Fewell notes additional information that Daniel has without being explicitly told in the narrative: "His indictment reveals that he, too, knows many things that he has not been told. Belshazzar has not told him any of the events that have led up to the writing. He has not mentioned the vessels, the drinking, or the worship of idols. He has not even told Daniel about the hand" (*Circle of Sovereignty*, 97).

83. Lucas, *Daniel*, 139.

84. Runge and Westbury, *LDHB: Introduction*, 1.2 Forward-pointing Reference and Target.

mene, tekel, upharsin" (5:25c).[85] The consonantal letters of the words could have been vocalized a number of ways, but Daniel reads them according to the simplest nominal pattern in Aramaic, each word referring to a standard of weights and measures: the mina, the shekel, and parsin (the plural of *peres*, which means "half"). A mina is worth sixty shekels (Ezek 45:12), and parsin likely refers to half-shekels.[86] Thus the inscription reads, "A mina, a shekel, and [two] half-shekels."

These words do not form even a sentence, much less present an obvious interpretation. But Daniel continues, prefacing his interpretation with another forward-pointing reference: "This is the interpretation of the message" (5:26a). What follows is an interpretation of the three different words, based on a different vocalization pattern of the consonants. Daniel read three nouns (mina, shekel, parsin), but his interpretation is based on three verb forms (מְנָה, תְּקִילְתְּ, פְּרִיסַת). Specifically, he interprets the consonants as passive participles that mean, respectively, numbered, weighed, and divided. Daniel interpreted the writing using wordplay, "loosening the knots" of the riddle.[87] Towner explains the wordplay:

> The solution contained in the text is based upon folk etymologies of the three words, each turning on a pun. The three nouns listed in verse 25 are treated as three passive verbs by Daniel in verse 26–28: MENE is related to the verb *m-n-h*, "numbered"; TEKEL is related to the verb *t-q-l*, "weighed"; and PERES is construed as the verb *p-r-s*, "divided." Belshazzar's days are numbered; his rule has been weighed and found wanting and his kingdom will be divided two ways, half to the Medes and half to the Persians (the word *peres*, Persia, is itself another pun on the word *p-r-s*).[88]

But what is the significance of *these* words and their meaning in *this* context? Nebuchadnezzar had dreamed of a magnificent statue and then a magnificent tree—imagery that portrayed the greatness and also the vulnerability of human kingdoms. How do the imagery of coins and verbs of assessment and evaluation fit in the context of Belshazzar's feast? Fewell argues that the words and imagery suggest that the issue is one of value: "indeed, the problem of value has been the crux of the story."[89] In Belshazzar's actions and in Daniel's speech, the narrator portrays a Belshazzar who had not valued the example of his father, the vessels of the Jerusalem temple, his father's chief magician, or the God his father learned to exalt. Rather, he valued his own reputation; he valued gods who could not see, hear, or know.[90]

In the closing words of Daniel's long speech, God is finally an explicit agent—the one who numbered Belshazzar's kingdom and brought an end to it. The king had been weighed on the scales and found wanting. His kingdom would be divided (or broken) and given over to the Medes and Persians.

---

85. The inscription in the MT has four words, with repetition of מְנֵא that is not represented in Theodotion, the Old Greek, or the Vulgate. This fact, combined with the fact that Daniel only interprets one מְנֵא, prompts some to omit the duplicate מְנֵא on the basis of dittography. Others consider the more difficult reading of the MT to be original and explain the discrepancy in various ways. Newsom notes that if both words are retained, the first should be interpreted as a passive participle, "counted as a mina" (*Daniel*, 161; Newsom is following Eissfeldt, who first proposed this solution [Otto Eissfeldt, "Die Menetekel-Inschrift und ihre Deutung," *ZAW* 63 [1951]:105–14]).

86. The identification of the three nouns as terms for weights is credited to C. Clermont-Ganneau, "Mané, Thécel, Parès, et le Festin de Balthasar," *JA* 8 (1886), 36–37.

87. For an interesting proposal about the riddle, see Wolters, "Untying the King's Knots." He suggests three levels of meaning and significance for the three words.

88. Towner, *Daniel*, 76.

89. Fewell, *Circle of Sovereignty*, 100.

90. Fewell, *Circle of Sovereignty*, 100.

6. A Rescinded Power (5:29a–6:1[5:31])

Main Idea of the Passage

Daniel 5:29–6:1[5:31]) reports the fulfillment of God's judgment on Belshazzar, according to the writing on the wall, and announces the transition from the Babylonian Empire to the Median Empire—also in accordance with God's plan.

Literary Context

Daniel 5:29a–6:1[5:31]) is the final section of the Dan 5 narrative, and as such, it functions in at least three ways in its broader literary context. First, its enactment of the judgment pronounced in the writing on the wall brings the chapter's events to their fulfillment and conclusion. Second, in Belshazzar's response to Daniel's interpretation, the narrator concludes his comparison of Nebuchadnezzar and Belshazzar—"father" and "son." Finally, its report of the transition of the Chaldean kingdom to Darius the Mede moves the book into the second empire of the four described in Nebuchadnezzar's statue dream.

> D. Narrative 4: A Humbled King and His Rescinded Power (5:1a–6:1[5:31])
>   1. Belshazzar's Arrogant Offense (5:1a–4b)
>   2. The Result of the Arrogant Offense (5:5a–8d)
>   3. The Queen's Words (5:9a–12d)
>   4. Belshazzar's Arrogant Words (5:13a–16i)
>   5. Daniel's Words to the Arrogant Belshazzar (5:17a–28b)
> ➡ 6. **A Rescinded Power (5:29a–6:1[5:31])**

Translation and Exegetical Outline

(See page 284.)

Daniel 5:29a–6:1[5:31]

29a	בֵּאדַ֣יִן ׀ אֲמַ֣ר בֵּלְשַׁאצַּ֗ר	Then Belshazzar said [gave orders],
29b	וְהַלְבִּ֤ישׁוּ לְדָֽנִיֵּאל֙ אַרְגְּוָנָ֔א	and Daniel was clothed with purple,
29c	(וְהַמְנִיכָ֥א) [וְהַֽמְנִכָ֥א] דִֽי־דַהֲבָ֖א עַֽל־צַוְּארֵ֑הּ	and a necklace of gold was around his neck,
29d	וְהַכְרִ֣זֽוּ עֲל֔וֹהִי	and a proclamation was made about him
29e	דִּֽי־לֶהֱוֵ֥א שַׁלִּ֛יט תַּלְתָּ֖א בְּמַלְכוּתָֽא׃	that he was the third ruler in the kingdom.
30	בֵּ֚הּ בְּלֵ֣ילְיָ֔א קְטִ֕יל בֵּלְאשַׁצַּ֖ר מַלְכָּ֥א (כַשְׂדָּאָֽה) [כַשְׂדָּיָֽא]׃	On that very night Belshazzar the Chaldean king was killed,
6:1[5:31]	וְדָרְיָ֙וֶשׁ֙ (מָדָאָ֔ה) [מָֽדָיָ֔א] קַבֵּ֖ל מַלְכוּתָ֑א כְּבַ֖ר שְׁנִ֥ין שִׁתִּ֥ין וְתַרְתֵּֽין׃	and Darius the Mede received the kingdom at about the age of sixty-two.

6. A Rescinded Power (5:29a–6:1[5:31])

   a. The King's Reward (5:29a–e)

   b. The King's Judgment (5:30–6:1[5:31])

Structure and Literary Form

The sixth and final section of the narrative in Dan 5 (5:29a–6:1[5:31]) returns to the narrator's voice. It begins with בֵּאדַיִן, "then" (5:29a), and recounts in two subsections the events that transpired after Daniel read and interpreted the writing on the wall. In the first subsection (5:29), Belshazzar commands (אֲמַר, 5:29a) that Daniel receive the three promised rewards for interpreting the writing (5:29b–e; cf. 5:7d–h and 5:16d–i). In the second subsection, Belshazzar is judged according to the interpretation of the writing, and the kingdom passes to the Darius the Mede (5:30–6:1[5:31]).

Explanation of the Text

a. The King's Reward (5:29a–e)

In response to Daniel's interpretation of the writing, Belshazzar rewards him as promised (cf. 5:16), but even here, the narrator reflects Belshazzar's distance from his father's chief magician. The king gives orders (אֲמַר, 5:29a), and "Daniel was clothed with purple . . . and a proclamation was made about him" (הַלְבִּישׁוּ . . . הַכְרִזוּ, impersonal plurals usually translated as passives; 5:29b–d). When Nebuchadnezzar rewarded Daniel for interpreting his dream in ch. 2, he fell over himself in praise of Daniel, and he rewarded him greatly (2:46, 48). Even in his rewarding of Daniel, Belshazzar does not involve himself with the man his father so highly esteemed.

Also unlike his predecessor, Belshazzar has no words of praise for the God who sent the message (cf. 2:47). Nor does he have any words of confession (cf. 4:31–34[34–37]). While arguments from silence should be made cautiously, Seow's observation that Belshazzar's response suggests that he "has, indeed, learned nothing from the experience of his 'father'"[91] fits the narrator's portrayal of Belshazzar throughout the chapter.

Daniel accepts rewards he earlier refused, and while the narrator does not explain this, the rewards were irrelevant given the meaning of the writing on the wall.

b. The King's Judgment (5:30–6:1[5:31])

The last two clauses of the narrative report the fulfillment of the inscription.[92] First, the narrator notes the timing of the events: בֵּהּ בְּלֵילְיָא, "on that very night" (5:30), a detail which means all the events of ch. 5 took place on a single night. This is another contrast in a chapter of contrasts between father and son: the humbling of Nebuchadnezzar seems to have transpired over the course of eight years from the time of his troubling dream.

---

91. Seow, *Daniel*, 83.
92. The MT concludes the account of Belshazzar with his death in 5:30. The report that Darius received the kingdom is part of the following account involving Darius and Daniel (6:1[5:31]). But the connective *waw* between the two clauses seems to link them more in accord with English versions that conclude the account of Belshazzar with the transfer of the kingdom to Darius. Regardless, the two chapters are closely related since the introduction of Darius in 6:1[5:31] is the background for 6:2[1] and following.

The narrator's report of the king's judgment and the transfer of kingdoms is in passive voice: Belshazzar was killed (קְטִיל, 5:30), and Darius received the kingdom (קַבֵּל, 6:1[5:31], active in form but passive in meaning). Who killed Belshazzar is not important, and how or from whom Darius received the kingdom is not important. As Goldingay notes, "The historical and human factors that brought this revolution, and the means by which it was effected, are again ignored.... Certainly the sovereign purpose of God in the event is alone of interest in this story."[93]

The sovereign purpose of God is also behind the narrator's references to the two kings: "Belshazzar the Chaldean king" and "Darius the Mede." This is the first time the narrator has called Belshazzar this, and the purpose of the change in reference is to highlight the transfer of kingdoms from Chaldea/Babylon to Media. The raising up and taking down of kings is a theme of the book of Daniel, explicitly raised in ch. 2 when Nebuchadnezzar's dream involved four human kingdoms. In that dream, the first kingdom was Babylon, which gave way to a second, inferior kingdom—that of Media.[94] The fall of Babylon to the Medes was a fulfillment of prophecies by Isaiah and Jeremiah (Isa 13:17; 21:2; Jer 51:11, 28), and the narrator of Daniel is careful to make the connection by calling Belshazzar "the Chaldean king" and noting his successor was Darius "the Mede."[95] The narrator will bring Cyrus the Persian back into the narrative in 6:29[28] and 10:1 (cf. 1:21), and the Greek Alexander the Great is the Greek king of Dan 8:21. The four-kingdom schema of history in Daniel is similar to one known from extrabiblical literature of the ancient Near East: Assyria, Media, Persia, Greece.[96] In the theology of

---

93. Goldingay, *Daniel*, 301.

94. This is the Greek view of the kingdoms: Babylon, Media, Persia, Greece. See on chs. 2, 7, and 8 and esp. IN DEPTH: The Identities of the Kingdoms (pp. 115–17).

95. The identity of Darius the Mede is a long-standing historical difficulty in the book of Daniel. While Persia had several kings named Darius, dating from 522 BCE, there is no extrabiblical record of a Median Darius. The reference to Darius the Mede in Dan 5 is commonly considered the error of a late author who pulled the name from Persian records without realizing the problem. However, the narrator's repeated reference to Darius as a Mede throughout the book makes this argument suspect (6:1[5:31]; 9:1; 11:1)—not to mention the low view of the author it represents.

One suggestion for the identity of Darius is that he was appointed by Cyrus to rule over Babylon, and he simply remains unknown so far in ancient records. The passive language of 6:1[5:31] ("Darius... received the kingdom") and Dan 9:1 (Darius "was made ruler") may support this, but since extant records indicate Cyrus's appointees and their chronologies, it is hard to find room in the historical record for an unknown official appointed by him.

Another plausible explanation for the identity of Darius the Mede comes out of Dan 6:29[28], where the narrator summarizes Daniel's service in the foreign court before moving into the apocalyptic half of the book. Most English translations render this verse along the lines of "Daniel prospered during the reign of Darius and the reign of Cyrus the Persian" (cf. NIV, ESV), understanding Darius and Cyrus to be two distinct people. But in another legitimate reading of the Aramaic syntax, Darius and Cyrus are the same person. In this reading, the *waw* on וּבְמַלְכוּת in Dan 6:29[28] is explicative: "Daniel prospered during the reign of Darius, that is, the reign of Cyrus the Persian." (See 1 Chr 5:26 for a similar construction in Hebrew [i.e., "Pul" is Tiglath-Pilesar]. This argument is found in D. J. Wiseman, "Some Historical Problems in the Book of Daniel," in *Notes on Some Problems in the Book of Daniel* [London: Tyndale Press, 1965], 12–13. In the Aramaic of the book of Daniel, a *waw*-explicative construction is found in 4:10[13], where "a watcher—that is, a holy one—was descending from the heavens.") As to how Cyrus and Darius could be the same person, Cyrus's mother was a Mede and his father a Persian, making him both Median and Persian. Admittedly, this does not explain the significance of the name "Darius," though it is possible "Darius" functioned as a title, like "Caesar."

But what would be the motivation for calling the same person by two separate names and titles in the same book? The best explanation may be that it served the narrator's purposes to demonstrate the fulfillment of prophecy that Babylon would fall to the Medes—history was moving exactly as God had said. Additionally, the four-kingdom schema of Assyria/Babylon–Media–Persia–Greece fits well within its broader ancient Near Eastern context (see n96 below).

96. While the four-kingdom schema of ancient Near Eastern literature appears to omit Babylon, the Babylon of the book of Daniel is properly known as the "Neo-Babylonian" Empire

the book Daniel, God controls this history and its rise and fall of kingdoms. Thus, when the narrator of Daniel reports that Darius the Mede received the kingdom of Belshazzar the Chaldean, world history was moving exactly as expected and according to the divine plan.

A final detail seems to give further support to the narrator's message that God was working his plan through history. The narrator notes that Darius was "about the age of sixty-two" (כְּבַר שְׁנִין שִׁתִּין וְתַרְתֵּין) when he received the kingdom, a curious detail that could just indicate his advanced age (for that day) and thus the brevity of his rule before the narrative moves on to Cyrus.[97] But why not use the round number sixty, which is more appropriate with "about" (כְּ)? The narrator needs to make a point about the very specific number sixty-two, and since Darius is close enough to that age, he can. In a chapter of riddles, this may be one more to drive home the point: the weights of the inscription—a mina, a shekel, and (two) half-shekels—have a value of sixty shekels, one shekel, and one shekel; sixty-two shekels in sum. Thus, "the years attributed to Darius 'sum up' another aspect of the omen's meaning: he is the person who brings its fulfillment upon Belshazzar"[98]—or, in the passive voice of the narrative, he is the actual person through whom its fulfillment is brought upon Belshazzar. God's plan is present even in the smallest of historical details.

Canonical and Theological Significance

"Visiting" the Temple Vessels

Belshazzar's offense in ch. 5 revolves around his use of the vessels from the temple in Jerusalem. It is hard for us to appreciate the significance of the temple vessels for the people of God—especially for those in exile or diaspora during the days when there was no temple. As noted above (see on 5:3–4), the temple vessels represented the people's hope that God would remember and restore them.

The Old Testament reflects the importance of these vessels in its detailed account of their construction for the wilderness tabernacle (Exod 25–31; 35–40) and then in its later description of the vessels for Solomon's temple (1 Kgs 7–8).[99] This focused interest in the vessels resumes in the account of Israel's history leading up to and immediately following the years of exile. The author of Israel's history in 2 Kings

---

and in ancient literature is treated as a continuation of the Assyrian Empire (see John H. Walton, "The Four Kingdoms of Daniel," *JETS* 29/1 [1986], 34).

97. See, e.g., Newsom, *Daniel*, 179.

98. Goldingay, *Daniel*, 294. This proposition assumes a Babylonian mina (sixty shekels) and not a mina worth fifty shekels, as attested in Assyria and Ugarit (e.g., Collins, *Daniel*, 242).

99. P. R. Ackroyd notes that "it is not simply the fact that these descriptions are preserved which is important. It is the extent and the detail of them. It is a very substantial part of Exodus which is devoted to the tabernacle, and not only that, but virtually the entire material appears twice, once as command to do and once as description of what is done. It is a substantial part of the descriptions in 1 Kings which is devoted to the equipment of the temple, even though this is a relatively small part of the whole work in which it belongs; the same is true for 2 Chronicles, though to this we should really add the large preparatory sections in 1 Chronicles" ("The Temple Vessels—A Continuity Theme," *Studies in the Religion of Ancient Israel*, VTSup 23 [Leiden: Brill, 1972], 169–70).

keeps careful record of their whereabouts during the tumultuous years of Babylonian siege and then destruction of the holy city (2 Kgs 23:29–24:17), and the Chronicler similarly tracks the vessels from the time of King Jehoiakim through the fall of Jerusalem under Zedekiah (2 Chr 36:5–21). The postexilic book of Ezra picks up the fate of the vessels after the exile, portraying a "full reversal"[100] of their earlier loss by providing an inventory of the implements released by Cyrus and given into the hands of those returning to the land of Israel (Ezra 1:5–11).

Between these references fall the decades of exile and the book of Daniel, which itself begins with a reference to the vessels even before it mentions the four captives from Jerusalem (Dan 1:2; cf. 1:3–6). The narrator notes that the vessels, given to Nebuchadnezzar by their owner, were put in the treasury of the Babylonian king's god in Shinar. Jeremiah had said this would happen: all the vessels would be taken to Babylon and kept there עַד־יוֹם פָּקְדִי אֹתָם, "until the day I visit them" (Jer 27:22). The verb פקד is difficult to translate here. Most English translations say "visit," but that word carries a different sense today than it did in earlier days of English. Others try to get at the sense a little better by translating "come for them" (NIV), "show consideration for them" (NET), and "give attention to them" (NRSV). Regardless of the word's exact sense, when God did "visit" the vessels, Jeremiah said he would also הַעֲלִיתִים, "bring them up," and הֲשִׁיבֹתִים אֶל־הַמָּקוֹם הַזֶּה, "restore them to this place."[101] Jeremiah did not specify when this "day of visitation" might be, but elsewhere he prophesied a timeline of seventy years for the exile. At that time, YHWH would "punish[102] the king of Babylon and his nation, the land of the Babylonians, for their guilt," and he would "make it desolate forever" (Jer 25:12). YHWH's instrument of judgment would be the Medes (Jer 51:11).

Jeremiah's prophecies help us connect the dots of the events happening in Dan 5. First, the temple vessels take center stage, both in terms of their role in the narrative and the emphasis the narrator puts on them (see above on 5:2–3, 23). Second, God invades Belshazzar's home turf, showing his presence and power over the king's territory (see above on 5:2–5). Third, the Babylonian king is judged and subsequently killed (5:30). Finally, the kingdom passes to its Median successor (6:1[5:31]).

Seventy years, more or less, were up on the night of Belshazzar's feast. When the king commandeered the temple vessels for his own profane use, God paid him (and them) a visit; he took notice of the vessels and paid attention to them. Then he meted out punishment to the Babylonians and their leader. Nebuchadnezzar's "son" died, and the nation of Babylon passed away with him. In the aftermath of Belshazzar's death and the fall of Babylon, Persian Cyrus issued his famous decree

---

100. Ackroyd, "The Temple Vessels—A Continuity Theme," 178.

101. A similar promise is made two chapters later of the people (Jer 29:10).

102. The word translated "punish" here is also the verb פקד, which has varied uses.

that allowed captive peoples to return to their homelands—with temple plunder and spare cash, compliments of the king. The events of Dan 5 mark the turning point between Jeremiah's prophecies of doom and his prophecies of restoration. Thanks to the blasphemous Belshazzar, the vessels and the people were about to return home. Through the prophecies of Jeremiah and their fulfillment in Daniel, God demonstrated his control over the course of history.

The Shadow and Reality of Babylon's Fall

In the book's first mention of the temple vessels (see on Dan 1:2 above), the narrator of Daniel noted that they were transferred to the treasury of Nebuchadnezzar's god in Shinar, an infrequently used name for Babylon that occurs nowhere else in Daniel. By referring to Nebuchadnezzar's home as "Shinar" in the opening verses of the book, the narrator called to mind the most notable occurrence of "Shinar" in the Bible—in the Gen 11:1–9 account of the tower of Babel, the birth of Babylon in the biblical text—and so invited readers to consider what follows in light of what happened there.

Five chapters later, the narrator recounts the demise of Babylon, and we might expect such a momentous event to receive significant attention in the biblical narrative. After all, this is the nation that took God's people captive and ravished their homeland. But the defeat of the great Babylon could not be told more succinctly or in a more detached manner. Aside from Belshazzar's feast, for which we do not even know the occasion, there are no historical circumstances described. There is no mention of the Persian army. There is not a whiff of military action. Belshazzar is simply killed, and Darius the Mede receives the kingdom (5:30–6:1[5:31]). While the defeat of Nebuchadnezzar's great empire is the outcome of the events of Dan 5, it is not the focus of the chapter. The details of Babylon's demise are not important.

Perhaps the demise of sixth-century-BCE Babylon is understated because "Babylon" has not yet fallen. In the biblical text, the city/empire is a symbol of the quintessentially sinful city, a metaphor "for world power in opposition to God—the empire where God's people live in exile."[103] While the historical city may fade from the biblical story in Dan 5, the metaphorical city lives on. The apostle Peter uses it as a code word for Rome (1 Pet 5:13), and it comes roaring back in the book of Revelation as a symbol for the whole wicked world that opposes God and oppresses Christ's church (Rev 14:8; 16:19; 17:5; 18:2, 10, 21).

Although the demise of historical Babylon *was* a big deal for God's people in exile,

---

103. "Babylon," in *Dictionary of Biblical Imagery*, ed. Leland Ryken, James C. Wilhoit, and Tremper Longman III (Downers Grove, IL: InterVarsity Press, 1998), 69. See Lord of the King of Kings above (pp. 137–39) and Who Is the God That Can Deliver You above (pp. 181–85).

it did not launch the glorious restoration the prophets had foretold. That day still awaited—as Daniel will learn during his first year under the new regime (Dan 9:1). In his vision of ch. 9, he will be stunned by the revelation that seventy years of exile may have been nearing an end, but "exile" and even greater evil would continue far into the future.[104] Victory was assured, but the road would be long and more difficult than anyone had imagined. The defeat of sixth-century-BCE Babylon was only a shadow of a greater defeat still longed for.

Between the shadow and its reality, the indestructible and eternal kingdom of God spoken about in the book of Daniel broke into the world (Dan 2:44; 4:31[34]; 6:27[26]). It began in the womb of an unmarried teenager and took shape among fishermen, tax collectors, and prostitutes. But such small and unimpressive beginnings belied its hope for survival; it endures to this day and its future is bright. The carpenter's son who inaugurated this mustard-seed kingdom (Matt 13:31; Mark 4:31; Luke 13:19) in first-century Palestine will return in great glory one day to destroy all other rulers and powers. He will present this great kingdom in all its fullness to God (1 Cor 15:23–25). We long for the day when his kingdom comes.

Bothering with Belshazzar

The fall of the great Babylon is almost a footnote in Dan 5, where the greater interest by far is the judgment of the unworthy and blasphemous successor of Nebuchadnezzar. But why such interest in a historically inconsequential king—the stand-in-son of a usurper barely known in the historical record and barely appearing in the Bible?

Belshazzar is important because, while Nebuchadnezzar is portrayed as the prototypical gentile king in the Old Testament and the king in Daniel who responds properly to God's incursions into his life,[105] his "son" Belshazzar is portrayed by the book of Daniel as the prototypical enemy of God. He is the pattern for later (and worse) enemies of God in the book and perhaps even in the canon.

The narrator laid the foundation for this portrayal of Belshazzar in the same verse that set up the consideration of Babylon's death in light of its birth—Dan 1:2. While the narrator's usage of the rare word "Shinar" looked backward to the events at the tower of Babel, his mention of the temple vessels looked forward to the actions of Belshazzar in Dan 5. In the book of Daniel, the temple vessels are only mentioned in Dan 1:2, where they are taken from Jerusalem to Shinar by Nebuchadnezzar, and then again in the events of ch. 5, where they are brought to the feast and desecrated by Belshazzar's order. In these two royal acts with respect to the temple vessels, the

---

104. See on Dan 9:24–27.

105. See on 2:47; 3:28; and ch. 4.

narrator sets up his comparison of kings Nebuchadnezzar and Belshazzar, a dominating theme of ch. 5.

For four chapters, the reader watches Nebuchadnezzar encounter and then respond to the God of Israel. He is a powerful, hot-headed, and egomaniacal king, but he ultimately acknowledges the derived nature of his kingship and his dependence on the Most High God. We know from elsewhere in the Old Testament that, although a foreign king, he is God's chosen servant.[106] For all his stumbling along the way in the book of Daniel, Nebuchadnezzar at the end of ch. 4 stands as the example for how gentile kings ought to respond to God.

By contrast, it is clear from Belshazzar's brief appearance in the book of Daniel that he did not follow the example of his predecessor. He utterly disregarded it. The illustration par excellence of this is his treatment of the temple vessels, and this may very well be why the narrator uses the vessels as his first link between the two kings. Nebuchadnezzar had transferred the vessels from the home of their God to the treasury of his god—an act the Jews would certainly have considered defiling, but it was an act that nonetheless fit within Nebuchadnezzar's polytheistic ancient Near Eastern framework of showing honor to the god deserving of honor. It appeared that Nebuchadnezzar's god had defeated the God of Israel, so the sacred vessels were due him. The king treated them with the respect appropriate for sacred vessels. But Belshazzar took these vessels from their sacred place and used them for his own purposes.[107]

Belshazzar's attitude and offense toward Israel's God were egregious, but in the narrative of Daniel, they are but faint shadows of the evil that lay ahead. He is the book's first look at a king who shakes his fist at God and launches an assault against him.[108] His pride, blasphemy, and assault against God's holy things will look like child's play when his defiant successors in chs. 7–12 come on the scene. Belshazzar is the prototypical royal enemy of God.

In the chiastic structure of the Aramaic chapters in Daniel, chs. 4 and 5 lay at its heart: side-by-side chapters that show two gentile kings at their arrogant worst. An explicit comparison is made between the two, and at the end of the respective chapters, the first king is given "surpassing greatness" (Dan 4:33[36]), while the second is weighed on the balances and found lacking (Dan 5:27). Two gentile kings. Two responses to the authority of the Most High God. The first demonstrates a response worth following, and when the second fails to follow it, his example sets the narrative pattern for greater arrogance and evil to come in the book.

---

106. See Lord of the King of Kings above (pp. 137–39).

107. Obviously, for the author of Daniel, it is of utmost importance that these vessels belonged to the God of Israel and therein lay the offense; but in terms of Belshazzar's context, it would not have mattered *which* god possessed them. They were not his to use.

108. As discussed earlier, Belshazzar was not launching an intentional assault against the God of Israel. His interest in the vessels was related to Nebuchadnezzar. See p. 260n38 above.

Seeing Our Own Blasphemy and Sacrilege

The terms "blasphemy" and "sacrilege" are often used interchangeably, and while the two concepts are closely related, the former deals specifically with our treatment of God while the latter involves our treatment of sacred things—that is, anything that has been consecrated to God for his use. Belshazzar's blasphemous disdain for the God who held his life and breath was made evident by his sacrilegious (and idolatrous) use of the Jerusalem temple vessels. No one has any trouble seeing blasphemy and sacrilege among Belshazzar's offenses.

Similarly, no one has trouble seeing blasphemy and sacrilege in news headlines. When Morgan Freeman responds to an interviewer asking if he is a God-fearing man, "I don't fear anything. I'm God," we easily recognize the blasphemy.[109] When the punk rock group Pussy Riot offers a profane "prayer" of political protest in Moscow's Cathedral of Christ the Savior in 2012, we easily see the sacrilege.

We have much greater difficulty seeing blasphemy and sacrilege in some of our own actions. Many of us probably do not give much thought to the possibility that we might be treating God and what rightfully belongs to him inappropriately. We go to church, read our Bibles, sing worship songs, and even put money in the offering. We would not dream of swearing with God's name, and we certainly would not deface church property in any way. But blasphemy and sacrilege are bigger than that.

Blasphemy, most simply, is failing to take God seriously and honor him for who he has revealed himself to be. We can do this in both our words and our actions. In our speech, we violate the third commandment's prohibition against taking "the Lord's name in vain" (Exod 20:7, KJV). Certainly, this means we should not swear using God's name, but the NIV's "You shall not misuse the name of YHWH your God" helps capture the bigger meaning. What is forbidden is the use of God's name in any way that does not properly reflect his character or person. God gave his name to his people to use freely in their speech to and of him, but we should never use it for idle, frivolous, or insincere purposes.[110] God is holy. God's name is holy. When we are careless with it, we blaspheme him. We are careless with it when we text "OMG" or say "Jeez." We are careless with it when we give God names others than those he has revealed to us. Whenever and however we use his name, we should do so with an awareness of his person and character.

---

109. Freeman's words came during a series of 2011–2012 interviews related to a television science series hosted by the iconic actor. In the series, Freeman asked material and philosophical questions about the universe and also about God's existence. See Ravelle Mohammed, "Morgan Freeman Tells Piers Morgan: 'I Am God,'" *The Christian Post*, Sept 26, 2011 (http://global.christianpost.com/news/morgan-freeman-tells-piers-morgan-i-am-god-56510).

110. S. R. Driver, *The Book of Exodus in the Revised Version with Introduction and Notes* (Cambridge: Cambridge University Press, 1911), 196.

In our actions we blaspheme when we exercise "practical atheism," living as if God does not exist, as if we are the ones in control of our lives (Dan 5:23). We blaspheme when we disregard God's self-revelation in the Bible. Whenever we hear and understand the word, we must choose what to do: accept or dismiss God's call to belief or action. We blaspheme when we pick and choose what we like or believe from the Bible. We blaspheme by making God into an image that is more "acceptable" to us and the world around us, rather than submitting to him as he has revealed himself.

As for sacrilege, it was easy for the Old Testament Israelites to distinguish between the common and the sacred and treat each as appropriate. Sacred things were set apart for God and were reserved for use in the holy spaces of the tabernacle or temple. The boundaries of the sacred precincts made a clear diving line. But Jesus's death on the cross revolutionized the idea of sacred and common. The curtain of the temple tore from top to bottom; the division between sacred and common dissolved. But instead of *nothing* being sacred anymore, *everything* is sacred. Every part of creation—the environment, our neighbors—was reclaimed for God in Christ's redemptive act. The earth is indeed the Lord's and everything in it. How do we live and breathe in sacred space that is all around us?

Living as Students of the Divine Teacher

Since ch. 5 offers an extended comparison of Belshazzar and his predecessor Nebuchadnezzar, and since chs. 4 and 5 each portrays an account of a gentile king humbled by God, we would do well to consider the different responses God had to the pride of each king. He punishes both, but one is ultimately restored to his throne while the other is killed within hours of the pronounced judgment.

At first glance, Belshazzar's immediate and irreversible judgment may appear drastic and unfair. He has one really bad night, and God metes out severe judgment. Furthermore, God's representative Daniel shows him no sympathy and offers him no explicit chance at repentance.[111]

Compare this with Nebuchadnezzar, whose offenses span four chapters and probably decades. He engages in and orders obvious idolatry, and he tries to kill God's followers (ch. 3). He does not listen to the implicit warnings against pride in his dream of ch. 2, and in ch. 4 he claims all the credit for his great power and his life achievements. His boastful words trigger God's judgment in ch. 4, but not before Daniel pleads with him to repent and perhaps stay the judgment. When Nebuchadnezzar eventually did repent, God restored his power and greatness.

---

111. Some commentators think Daniel's words to Belshazzar had an implicit invitation to repent (e.g., Goldingay, *Daniel*, 298). Most, however, consider his words to be "more like that of a prophet delivering a word of judgment than like that of a sage" (Newsom, *Daniel*, 173). Cf. Elijah before Ahab in 1 Kgs 21:20–24 and Nathan before David in 2 Sam 12:1–14.

Were Belshazzar's acts of blasphemy and sacrilege worse than any of Nebuchadnezzar's offenses? Doubtful. We learn from Daniel's speech to the blasphemous king that his main problem was his refusal to learn from the example of his predecessor (5:22). He knew everything that had happened to Nebuchadnezzar and why—and he ignored its implications for his own life. Nebuchadnezzar may have been a slow learner, but his "son" was unteachable. The great king showed himself to be receptive to Daniel and the uniqueness of his God (2:47–49; 4:5–6[8–9], 15[18], 31–34[34–37]; cf. 3:26, 28–29), while Belshazzar disrespected Daniel and blasphemed his God.

God announced Belshazzar's judgment by way of the handwriting on the wall and then sent Daniel to pronounce the king's doom for his belligerence and blasphemy. Unlike Daniel, this is not our task when confronted with the sins of others. We are not privy to their hearts and so do not know when people may be irretrievably unteachable. We do not know how the Spirit might be at work. We do not know God's timing or modes of judgment. We must, as Longman says, "offer words of life, not condemnation. We are to play the role of Daniel before Nebuchadnezzar, not Daniel before Belshazzar."[112]

Furthermore, we do not always know our *own* hearts very well, and so do not know if God might find *us* unteachable. Learning the way of faith is like most kinds of learning—seldom a straight line of success. Usually it entails steps forward and steps backwards or sideways. We wander. We fall. We kick and scream sometimes. But over time, we show progress. And if we do not, we might rightly wonder about the condition of our heart. Rather than holding fast to the "eternal security" we believe came with a prayer we once prayed, we would do better to examine our hearts closely and consider how we respond to God's word. Theologian Mike Wittmer says it well:

> I'm attracted to the comfort that comes from knowing my salvation is secure. As Luther said, if salvation was in my hands I am sure I would drop it. I prefer the term "perseverance of the saints" to "total security," for the former implies there is work for me to do. I can't kick back, sin as I please, and still take comfort that I am "totally secure." My perseverance rests in God's hands, yet it requires effort on my part. Paul grounded my effort in God's power when he encouraged believers to "work out your salvation with fear and trembling, for it is God who works in you to will and to act according to his good purpose" (Philippians 2:12–13).
>
> One helpful answer on the question of perseverance comes from my New Testament colleague David Turner. When asked if he thought it was possible to lose our salvation, he replied, "Let's not find out." Why do we even care to know where God draws the line? Let's not make our final judgment a toss-up, an excruciatingly close

---

112. Longman, *Daniel*, 151.

call for God to make, but let's live such godly, grace-fueled lives that the question becomes moot.[113]

God has revealed himself to be a willing teacher, creating the conditions in which learning can occur. He wants people to know who he is, and he is willing to give mulligans when we have trouble learning. Consider the pharaoh of the exodus. He did not "know YHWH" (Exod 5:2), but God graciously gave him numerous opportunities to learn who he was and to submit to him. He refused. You might protest that he had no choice in the matter since God hardened his heart (e.g., Exod 4:21; 9:12). Yet the text also clearly says Pharaoh hardened his own heart (e.g., Exod 7:13; 8:15[19]). Was God involved? Yes. Was Pharaoh culpable? Yes. The interplay of divine sovereignty and human responsibility is a mystery, but this much is clear: God willingly teaches, but he does not force people to learn (is this even possible?). He can force people to comply, if he so chooses, but this is not the same as learning. We freely choose whether to learn or not. May we delight the divine teacher with our eager obedience.

---

113. Michael E. Wittmer, *Despite Doubt: Embracing a Confident Faith* (Grand Rapids: Discovery House, 2013), 160.

Daniel 6:2a–29[1a–28]

E. Narrative 5: *God's Superior Law and His Servant's Faithfulness*

Main Idea of Narrative 5 (6:2a–29[1a–28])

When Darius, successor of Belshazzar, intends to appoint Daniel as a senior administrator in his government, an unsavory group of officials conspires to ruin him, "one of the exiles of Judah" (6:14c[13c]). They convince the unsuspecting king to sign a law that forces Daniel to choose between the law of his God and the law of the land. Daniel chooses faithfulness to his God, as they knew he would, and Darius is compelled to condemn his exemplary servant to the lions' den. Early the next morning Darius witnesses the deliverance of the God of Israel when Daniel emerges from the den unscathed. The gentile king responds by declaring the greatness of Daniel's God and his eternal kingdom.

Literary Context of Narrative 5 (Dan 6:2a–29[1a–28])

Daniel 6 is the fifth of six Aramaic chapters in the book and the last in a series of five consecutive narratives about encounters between the Judean exiles and gentile kings (chs. 2–6). It is also the last of the narrative chapters in the book before the second half of the book shifts to apocalyptic literature.

Chapter 6 follows the death of Belshazzar and the transfer of his Babylonian kingdom to Darius the Mede (5:30–6:1[5:31]), and at the end of ch. 6, the narrator notes Daniel's success during the reign of Cyrus the Persian (6:29[28]). Thus the chapter's events fall between the kingdoms of Babylon and Persia and so mark the second kingdom of Nebuchadnezzar's statue dream of ch. 2 (and Daniel's vision of the four beasts in ch. 7): Babylon, Media, Persia.[1]

As part of the chiasm of chs. 2–7, Dan 6 stands parallel with the account of Shadrach, Meshach, and Abednego and the fiery furnace in ch. 3,[2] and the chapters have many similarities. Both involve the challenge of a foreign king to participate in idolatry, and both feature animosity from colleagues. In both accounts, failure to engage in idolatry carries the threat of death, and in both chapters, God's servants remain faithful despite this threat. Both accounts demonstrate God's miraculous deliverance of his servants and foreign kings rendering praise to the God of Israel after witnessing these rescues from death. Finally, in both accounts, the faithful servants are restored or promoted to places of greater honor in the administration.

However, there are also significant differences between the parallel chapters. In the fiery furnace account, God's servants refuse to participate in idolatrous religious practices, but in the lions' den account, God's servant refuses to refrain from the proper worship of God.[3] For the three Judean exiles civil disobedience was public; for Daniel, it was in a private place (and yet observable by the public). Thus, the two accounts "complement and supplement one another. Together they make the point that people of faith in different times and places are regularly challenged to live out their faith convictions despite the risks and dangers in their particular circumstances."[4]

Daniel 6 is also the final chapter of narrative in the book before the book gives way to Daniel's apocalyptic visions in chs. 7–12. In this context, Darius's doxology at the conclusion of the narrative is particularly significant as it weaves together themes of God's sovereignty from the earlier narratives. One key purpose of this cumulative praise is to prepare the reader for what lay ahead—namely, the horrors of Daniel's visions. Darius's resounding praise of Daniel's God recalls the many ways God demonstrated his superior power and authority over the gentile kings of exile. As the people face even greater exile and suffering ahead, they can cling to the truth that their God alone has the everlasting authority, power, and glory. They can endure suffering and remain faithful to their God—just as Daniel did—because they serve the superior king whose kingdom surpasses all human kingdoms.

As with the other narrative chapters in Daniel, ch. 6 is commonly classified as a court story, and specifically as a court conflict (cf. ch. 3).[5] Daniel found favor with the foreign king and was about to be promoted in the kingdom, so his rivals looked for an opportunity to bring him down. In the end, Daniel is vindicated and prospers even more.

---

1. This is the Greek view of the kingdoms. See The Identities of the Kingdoms above (pp. 115–17).
2. See the introduction, pp. 31–35, for discussion of the chiastic structure and its significance for interpretation of the book.
3. Longman, *Daniel*, 159.
4. Seow, *Daniel*, 87.
5. See Literary Context of the Macro Unit (pp. 79–80) and the introduction (p. 25).

> II. Macro Unit 2: The Superiority of God and His Kingdom (2:1a–7:28d)
>   A. Narrative 1: God's Superior Knowledge and His Eternal Kingdom (2:1a–49c)
>   B. Narrative 2: God's Superior Power and His Servants' Faithfulness (3:1a–30)
>   C. Narrative 3: A Humbled King and His Restored Power (3:31a–4:34e[4:1a–37e])
>   D. Narrative 4: A Humbled King and His Rescinded Power (5:1a–6:1[5:31])
> ➡ **E. Narrative 5: God's Superior Law and His Servant's Faithfulness (6:2a–29[1a–28])**
>   F. Narrative 6: God's Superior King and Eternal Kingdom (7:1a–28d)

1. God's Servant in Darius's Service (6:2a–5f[1a–4f])

Main Idea of the Passage

Daniel 6:2–5[1–4] describes Darius's appointment of administrators over his domain and establishes the centrality of Daniel in the narrative, highlighting his example of faithfulness. It also introduces Daniel's conspiratorial colleagues and their intent to discredit him.

Literary Context

Daniel 6:2–5[1–4] is the opening section of the narrative that comprises ch. 6. As such, it functions in at least four ways in its broader literary context. First, it sets the context for the events that follow by introducing the main characters of Darius, the satraps and overseers, and Daniel, and by setting up the conflict that will drive the plot. Second, it links the chapter to the previous chapter by continuing the narrative of Darius the Mede, first mentioned in the closing verse of the ch. 5 narrative.[6] An additional link to ch. 5 is the description of Daniel as having "an extraordinary spirit" (6:4[3]); the queen had described him to Belshazzar in the same way (5:12). Third, the similarity of the section's opening clause (שְׁפַר קֳדָם דָּרְיָוֶשׁ, "It seemed good to Darius") to an opening clause of the ch. 4 narrative (שְׁפַר קָדָמַי, "It seemed good to me," 3:32[4:2]) links Darius's action in the opening events of ch. 6 to the account of

---

6. The English and Hebrew texts differ slightly in their chapter division between chs. 5 and 6. While the MT begins ch. 6 with the announcement of Darius as king (6:1[5:31]), the English concludes the Belshazzar account with the introduction of Darius. I am following the English preference.

Nebuchadnezzar's humbling. Finally, this opening section sets up two wordplays in the narrative and introduces key themes of the narrative in its use of the words בעא/בעה, "to seek," and שכח, "to find."

> E. Narrative 5: God's Superior Law and His Servant's Faithfulness (6:2a–29[1a–28])
> **1. God's Servant in Darius's Service (6:2a–5f[1a–4f])**
> 2. The Establishment of an Inferior Human Law (6:6a–10[5a–9])
> 3. Daniel's Faithfulness to God's Law (6:11a–15f[10a–14f])
> 4. The Enforcement of an Inferior Law (6:16a–19d[15a–18d])
> 5. The Triumph of Daniel's God (6:20a–25g[19a–24g])
> 6. The Superior God and His Faithful Servant (6:26a–29[25a–28])

Translation and Exegetical Outline

(See page 300.)

Structure and Literary Form

The fifth narrative of the book's Aramaic chiasm (chs. 2–7[7]) begins with a section that describes the administration of Darius and Daniel's place in it (6:2–5[1–4]). Three subsections comprise this initial section: 6:2–3[1–2], 4[3], and 5[4].

In the first subsection (6:2–3[1–2]), the narrator describes how Darius established a bureaucratic structure to protect his interests (6:3d[2d]): 120 administrators (אֲחַשְׁדַּרְפְּנַיָּא, "satraps") were appointed over the kingdom, and they were to report to three overseers (סָרְכִין), of which Daniel was one. The second subsection (6:4[3]) begins with the transitional marker אֱדַיִן, "then," and includes the narrator's report of Daniel's extraordinary performance as one of the overseers and Darius's intent to promote him on account of it. The third subsection (6:5[4]) similarly begins with the transitional אֱדַיִן, "then," and describes the conspiratorial machinations of the satraps and remaining overseers against Daniel: they "began seeking a cause," הֲווֹ בָעַיִן עִלָּה, against him. The narrator notes the futility of these efforts given Daniel's trustworthiness (מְהֵימַן; 6:5c–f[4c–f]).

---

[7]. For the significance of this chiastic structure, see further the introduction (pp. 31–35).

Daniel 6:2a–5f[1a–4f]

E. Narrative 5: God's Superior Law and His Servant's Faithfulness (6:2a–29[1a–28])

1. God's Servant in Darius's Service (6:2a–5f[1a–4f])

   a. Darius's Administration (6:2a–3d[1a–2d])

2[1]a	שְׁפַר קֳדָם דָּרְיָוֶשׁ	It seemed good to Darius
2[1]b	וַהֲקִים עַל־מַלְכוּתָא לַאֲחַשְׁדַּרְפְּנַיָּא מְאָה וְעֶשְׂרִין	to establish over the kingdom 120 satraps
2[1]c	דִּי לֶהֱוֹן בְּכָל־מַלְכוּתָא	who would be in all the kingdom.
3[2]a	וְעֵלָּא מִנְּהוֹן סָרְכִין תְּלָתָא	And over them were three overseers
3[2]b	דִּי דָנִיֵּאל חַד־מִנְּהוֹן	(which Daniel was one of them)
3[2]c	דִּי לֶהֱוֹן אֲחַשְׁדַּרְפְּנַיָּא אִלֵּין יָהֲבִין לְהוֹן טַעְמָא	to whom these satraps were to give account,
3[2]d	וּמַלְכָּא לָא־לֶהֱוֵא נָזִק	and the king would not suffer harm.

   b. Daniel's Exemplary Service (6:4a–d[3a–d])

4[3]a	אֱדַיִן דָּנִיֵּאל דְּנָה הֲוָא מִתְנַצַּח עַל־סָרְכַיָּא וַאֲחַשְׁדַּרְפְּנַיָּא	Then this Daniel was distinguishing himself among the overseers and satraps,
4[3]b	כָּל־קֳבֵל דִּי רוּחַ יַתִּירָא בֵּהּ	Because an extraordinary spirit was in him,
4[3]c	וּמַלְכָּא עֲשִׁית	the king was intending
4[3]d	לַהֲקָמוּתֵהּ עַל־כָּל־מַלְכוּתָא	to set him over all the kingdom.

   c. The Emergence of Conspirators (6:5a–f[4a–f])

5[4]a	אֱדַיִן סָרְכַיָּא וַאֲחַשְׁדַּרְפְּנַיָּא הֲווֹ בָעַיִן עִלָּה	Then the overseers and satraps began seeking a cause
5[4]b	לְהַשְׁכָּחָה לְדָנִיֵּאל מִצַּד מַלְכוּתָא	to find against Daniel concerning the kingdom,
5[4]c	וְכָל־עִלָּה וּשְׁחִיתָה לָא־יָכְלִין	but no cause or corruption were they able
5[4]d	לְהַשְׁכָּחָה	to find.
5[4]e	כָּל־קֳבֵל דִּי־מְהֵימַן הוּא	Because he was trustworthy,
5[4]f	וְכָל־שָׁלוּ וּשְׁחִיתָה לָא הִשְׁתְּכַחַת עֲלוֹהִי	no negligence or corruption did they find concerning him.

Explanation of the Text

a. Darius's Administration (6:2a–3d[1a–2d])

After the demise of Belshazzar and the Babylonian Empire with him in Dan 5, Dan 6 recounts events that happened early in the reign of Darius the Mede, who was introduced in the narrative at the end of ch. 5 as Belshazzar's successor. The first two clauses of 6:2[1] are both independent clauses ("It seemed good to Darius" and "to establish . . ." [woodenly, "and he established"]), but as Cook notes, the semantic subject of 6:2a[1a] is 2b[1b]—that is, establishing satraps over the kingdom seemed to good Darius.[8] The relative clause that follows clarifies the extent of these appointments as "in all the kingdom" (6:2c[1c]). Darius appointed 120 officials who would tend to his interests throughout the kingdom.

The opening clause of the narrative, "it seemed good to Darius" (שְׁפַר קֳדָם דָּרְיָוֶשׁ, 6:2a[1a]), is an unusual comment by the narrator. We might have expected him simply to say, "Darius established 120 satraps over the kingdom," much like Nebuchadnezzar "laid siege" to Jerusalem (1:1) and "made an image of gold" (3:1) or like Belshazzar "made a great feast" (5:1). That it seemed like a good idea to Darius seems obvious and irrelevant. But in the greater context of the book of Daniel, the narrator may be making a connection with an earlier occurrence of this expression. In the ch. 4 account of Nebuchadnezzar's humbling, the king began his proclamation about the signs and wonders the Most High God had done for him by saying, "It seemed good to me to declare" them (שְׁפַר קָדָמַי לְהַחֲוָיָה, 3:32[4:2]).[9] Of this connection, Fewell suggests the narrator means for the reign of Darius to represent "a return to the latter days of Nebuchadnezzar": "In chapter 4, 'it seemed good' to Nebuchadnezzar to render authority to the Most High. In chapter 6, 'it seems good' to Darius to render authority to other people, in particular, to Daniel."[10] She goes on to suggest a more substantial similarity between the stories: "Both stories depict the relationship between sage and sovereign to be one of amiability and cooperation, unlike the stories in chapters 3 and 5 in which the relationship between sage and sovereign is not without friction and opposition."[11]

Further description of Darius's administration follows in several clauses. The verbless clause of 6:3a[2a] says the satraps were overseen by three supervisors. A parenthetical relative clause then notes that Daniel was one of these three supervisors (6:3b[2b]). The next relative clause returns to the topic of the overseers generally, noting that the satraps were to answer to them (6:3c[2c]). The final clause provides the purpose of this organizational structure: protecting the king's interests (6:3d[2d]).

In these two opening verses (6:2–3[1–2]) the narrator introduces the main characters: Darius, who is apparently vulnerable to loss at the hands of

---

8. "Semantically, the subject of שׁפר is the והקים clause, but an infinitive predicate or די would be required to mark the latter clause as the syntactic subject (cf. 3:32). As it stands, the two verbs form a sort of hendiadys, whereby the clauses are coordinate ("pleased Darius and he appointed") but must be interpreted as a main clause and complementary clause, respectively" (Cook, *Aramaic Ezra and Daniel*, 252–53).

9. Later in the same chapter, when Daniel pleads with Nebuchadnezzar to repent, he uses the imperfect form of the same verbal root: (עֲלָיִךְ) [עֲלָךְ] מִלְכִּי יִשְׁפַּר, "may my counsel be pleasing to you" (4:24[27]).

10. Fewell, *Circle of Sovereignty*, 108.

11. Ibid.

his employees and has taken measures to prevent it; the appointed satraps and overseers, who manage the king's domain and the satraps, respectively; and Daniel, who is one of the three overseers. The narrator's second reference to the satraps in 6:3c[2c] as "these satraps," אֲחַשְׁדַּרְפְּנַיָּא אִלֵּין, is a use of the near demonstrative ("these") that marks the satraps as thematically central to the story.[12] Later, the satraps and the overseers together will be referred to as "these overseers and satraps" (6:7a[6a]).

With the information of these first two verses, the reader might reasonably expect that the plot of the chapter will revolve around Daniel and the activity of unscrupulous satraps who want to take advantage of the king. The chapter will prove this partially true, but not in the way the reader expects.

b. Daniel's Exemplary Service (6:4a–d[3a–d])

In the second subsection (6:4[3]), the narrator focuses on Daniel, whom he refers to as דָּנִיֵּאל דְּנָה, "this Daniel" (6:4a[3a]). The use of the near demonstrative "this" with respect to Daniel, as with the satraps above, indicates Daniel's central importance to the story.[13] This observation may seem obvious and unnecessary since he is a named character in a book that bears his name, but Dan 6 is the only chapter in the book that refers to Daniel this way—and it does so three times (6:4[3], 6[5], 29[28]).[14] While one of these three occurrences is in reported speech of the conspirators and so has a different pragmatic effect (see below on 6:6[5]), two of the occurrences are by the narrator. Daniel may be a main character throughout the book, but he is not always thematically central. This chapter, in addition to its other interests, is about Daniel.[15]

The narrator describes Daniel's performance as one of the administrators—he "was distinguishing himself" (6:4a[3a]). Then he notes the king's intention to promote Daniel (6:4c[3c]) on account of the extraordinary spirit that was in him (6:4b[3b]). This description echoes the queen's words about Daniel before Belshazzar; Nebuchadnezzar had promoted Daniel to chief magician "because an extraordinary spirit and knowledge, and insight for interpreting dreams, declaring riddles, and untying knots were found" in him (see on 5:12 above). Like Nebuchadnezzar before him, Darius intended to promote Daniel because of his exemplary performance and extraordinary spirit.

c. The Emergence of Conspirators (6:5a–f[4a–f])

Darius may have appreciated Daniel and his extraordinary ability, but the remaining overseers and the satraps did not. Their response to the king's

---

12. While near and far demonstratives are most commonly used to make a distinction between characters or entities based on distance (e.g., "this house" is closer to the speaker than "that house"), they can also be used when spatial distance is not in view to "express a thematic distinction as though it were a spatial one" (Runge, *Discourse Grammar of the Greek New Testament*, 365). The near demonstratives ("this", "these") are used to signify characters or entities that are central to the story (thematic), while the far demonstratives ("that", "those") are used to indicate elements that are not central (athematic). Runge's grammar specifically refers to the Greek NT, and he notes that this kind of thematic usage of demonstratives is not used much in English but is common in the Greek NT. In *Lexham Discourse of the Hebrew Bible*, he similarly notes the thematic usage of demonstratives in Hebrew (and, presumably, in Aramaic as well) (Runge and Westbury, *LDHB*, 2.5 Near and Far Distinctions).

13. See on 6:3[2] and n12 above.

14. English translations (including mine) of Dan 5:12, where the queen speaks of Daniel, typically read "this Daniel," but there "this" does not represent the demonstrative דְּנָה. See on 5:12 above.

15. Like every story in the Bible, this narrative is primarily God's self-revelation: we learn what God is like from everything recorded in Scripture.

intent to promote Daniel over them is the focus of the third subsection (6:5[4]). In the initial clause (6:5a[4a]) and its infinitive complement clause (6:5b[4b]), the group "began seeking . . . to find" (הֲווֹ בָעַיִן . . . לְהַשְׁכָּחָה) a reason to implicate Daniel in wrongdoing. The rest of the subsection describes their inability to do so.

In his description of the conspirators' activity, the narrator sets up a wordplay with two key words in the narrative: בעה/בעא, "to seek," and שכח, "to find." In 6:5–6[4–5], the narrator uses a high concentration of these two verbs. Arnold argues that the repetition here and in the rest of the chapter creates a contrast between Daniel's character and that of his enemies.[16] The conspirators "seek" to "find" a cause against Daniel (6:5a–b[4a–b] but are not able to "find" (6:5d[4d], 5f[4f]) anything because of his character. They recognize that they will not be able to "find" anything against him unless they "find" it with respect to the law of his God (6:6b–c[5b–c]). This will prompt them to propose a law that anyone who "seeks" a petition from anyone other than Darius be punished (6:8e[7e]). They will then "find" Daniel "seeking" his God (6:12b–c[11b–c]) and report his "seeking" to the king (6:13e[12e], 14e[13e]). When Daniel is delivered from the lions, he will say his God "found" him innocent (6:23d[22d]). The narrator then reports that no harm was "found" on him because he trusted in God (6:24f[23f]). Arnold summarizes the effect of this wordplay:

> In Daniel 6, *bĕʿāʾ* and *šĕkaḥ* denote the insidious hatred of Daniel's enemies in their attempt to gain favor politically. Both parties, Daniel and his enemies, are seeking something. His enemies are seeking security by finding fault in Daniel, but Daniel is seeking God, where he will find security as a by-product. This becomes a central motif in the chapter. . . .
>
> The irony here is that his enemies think they have found Daniel's weakness, but the narrator knows they have actually found his greatest strength. Indeed, it is his devotion to God that delivers him from the lions.[17]

The narrator does not specify how many of the other officials were involved in these efforts, allowing the reader to assume that a mob of 122 colleagues is ganging up against Daniel. The conspirators themselves will give this impression in 6:8[7], when they tell Darius that כֹּל, "all," of his officials agreed about the proposed law. Later details of the narrative will make this unlikely (i.e., the logistics of throwing 122 men and their families into the lions' den; 6:25[24])[18], but the hyperbolic effect at this point is that *everyone*, save Darius, was against Daniel. (One of the many ironies in the narrative is that it is Darius himself who puts Daniel in harm's way.)

The conspirators tried to find something in Daniel's professional life that they could use as grounds for complaint, some reason Darius should not promote him. But the narrator emphatically notes the futility of these efforts. First, he says they were not able to find (לָא־יָכְלִין לְהַשְׁכָּחָה, 6:5c–d[4c–d]) any ground for complaint nor any corruption against him, and then he says they did not find (לָא הִשְׁתְּכַחַת, 6:5f[4f]) any negligence or corruption. Tucked between these two statements is the explanation for their failure to find cause against Daniel: מְהֵימַן הוּא, "he was trustworthy" (6:5e[4e]).

---

16. Arnold, "Wordplay and Narrative Techniques in Daniel 5 and 6," 483.

17. Arnold, "Wordplay and Narrative Techniques in Daniel 5 and 6," 485.

18. Wills notes that if the entire mob were thrown in, "surely they died of suffocation and not from the hungry lions" Lawrence M. Wills, *The Jew in the Court of a Foreign King: Ancient Jewish Court Legends*, HDR 26 [Minneapolis: Fortress, 1990], 138n12. See on v. 25[24] below.

His character was impeccable. The reader is reminded that this chapter is about Daniel.

The narrator does not say explicitly why the satraps and overseers had it out for Daniel, though their later reference to him as "one of the exiles of Judah" suggests ethnic prejudice (6:14c[13c]; cf. 3:12 and 5:13). Additionally, the narrator's emphasis on Daniel's integrity and the efforts of his colleagues to undermine him imply that they were not nearly so honorable; with Daniel in charge, their attempts to take advantage of the king would likely be thwarted.

The reader's initial expectation that the chapter's plot would revolve around Daniel and the activity of unscrupulous satraps who want to take advantage of the king has taken a twist. The officials *do* want to take advantage of the king, but Daniel is in the way; therein lies the plot.

2. The Establishment of an Inferior Human Law (6:6a–10[5a–9])

Main Idea of the Passage

Daniel 6:6–10[5–9] recounts the conspirators' acknowledgment that finding fault with Daniel would require a law that conflicted with his religious practice. They propose such a law to the unsuspecting King Darius, and he subsequently establishes a prohibition against praying to anyone but the king for thirty days.

Literary Context

Daniel 6:6–10[5–9] is the second section of the narrative that comprises ch. 6. It follows the opening section of the chapter that introduced the main characters and set up the conflict of the plot. In its broader literary context, this section functions in at least four ways. First, it focuses the conflict on Daniel's religious practice (דָּת אֱלָהֵהּ, "the law of his God). This law will stand in juxtaposition to the law the conspirators propose. Thus, a second function of this section is establishing the contrast of two immutable laws. A third function of this section is further developing the themes of seeking (בעה/בעא) and finding (שכח) that entered the narrative in the first section (6:5–6[4–5]). A final literary function is introducing the weakness of King Darius, particularly with respect to his manipulative administrators.

> E. Narrative 5: God's Superior Law and His Servant's Faithfulness (6:2a–29[1a–28])
>   1. God's Servant in Darius's Service (6:2a–5f[1a–4f])
>   2. **The Establishment of an Inferior Human Law (6:6a–10[5a–9])**
>   3. Daniel's Faithfulness to God's Law (6:11a–15f[10a–14f])
>   4. The Enforcement of an Inferior Law (6:16a–19d[15a–18d])
>   5. The Triumph of Daniel's God (6:20a–25g[19a–24g])
>   6. The Superior God and His Faithful Servant (6:26a–29[25a–28])

Translation and Exegetical Outline

(See page 306.)

Structure and Literary Form

The second section of the narrative in Dan 6 (6:6–10[5–9]) describes the conspiracy of the satraps and overseers, who manufacture a law that they know Daniel will not keep. The section consists of three subsections: 6:6[5], 7–9[6–8], and 10[9].

The first subsection begins with the transitional marker אֱדַיִן, "then," and is reported speech of the conspirators amongst themselves (6:6[5]), as they acknowledge what the narrator has already reported: namely, there is no legitimate ground for finding fault with Daniel (cf. 6:5c–f[4c–f]). The second subsection also begins with אֱדַיִן, "then," and is also largely comprised of reported speech of the conspirators—this time to the king (6:7–9[6–8]). In their speech, the conspirators propose a new law (6:7c–8d[6c–7d]) and urge the king to establish it (6:9[8]).

The third subsection (6:10[9]) begins with כָּל־קֳבֵל דְּנָה, "therefore," and reports that King Darius signed the document. This statement functions as a hinge between section 2 of the narrative (i.e., The Establishment of an Inferior Human Law; 6:6–10[5–9]) and section 3 (i.e., Daniel's Faithfulness to God's Law; 6:11–15[10–14]): the result of the conspirators' proposal was that Darius did what they wanted him to do, but his action is then the cause of Daniel's action (see further below on section 3).

Daniel 6:6a–10[5a–9]

6[5]a		Then those men were saying,
6[5]b		"We will not find against this Daniel any cause
6[5]c		↑ unless we find (it) against him with respect to the law of his God."
7[6]a		Then these overseers and satraps came by collusion to the king,
7[6]b		and were saying thus to him,
7[6]c		"O Darius the king, live forever.
8[7]a		All the overseers of the kingdom, the prefects and the satraps, the counselors
		and the governors have consulted together
8[7]b		to establish a statute of the king
8[7]c		and to enforce a prohibition
8[7]dα		that anyone …
8[7]e		↑ who seeks a petition from any god or man except you for thirty days,
8[7]dβ		… will be thrown to the den of lions.
9[8]a		Now, O king, you should establish the prohibition
9[8]b		and sign the document,
9[8]c		↑ which cannot be changed, according to the law of the Medes and Persians
9[8]d		↑ which cannot be annulled."
10[9]		Therefore, King Darius signed the document, that is, the prohibition.

2. The Establishment of an Inferior Human Law (6:6a–10[5a–9])
   a. The Conspirators' Problem (6:6a–c[5a–c])
   b. The Conspirators' Proposal (6:7a–9d[6a–8d])
   c. The King's Establishment of the Law (6:10[9])

Explanation of the Text

a. The Conspirators' Problem (6:6a–c[5a–c])

The narrator has already reported the conspirators' inability to find any grounds for complaint against Daniel because of his character (6:5c–f[4c–f]). In this section, he uses reported speech to let the conspirators themselves voice their problem, allowing the reader a window into their thoughts, interests, and motivations.[19] This is the conspirators' first reported speech in a chapter driven by their speech (6:6[5], 7–9[6–8], 13[12], 14[13], 16[15]).

In the quotative frame for this first speech, the narrator uses the far demonstrative to refer to the group of conspirators: גֻּבְרַיָּא אִלֵּךְ, "those men" (6:6a[5a]).[20] The conspirators have already been established as central (thematic) to the story (see on 6:3c[2c] above), which means the "correct" demonstrative to use in 6:6a[5a] is the near demonstrative אִלֵּין, "these" (cf. 6:3c[2c], 7a[6a]), since the far demonstrative typically indicates elements that are not central (athematic) to the story. However, the narrator uses the "incorrect" (far) demonstrative to create distance between the men and Daniel; as one of the three overseers, Daniel was technically part of the group called "overseers and satraps," but the story has turned so that there are really two distinct entities in the king's employ—Daniel and everyone else.[21]

Another noteworthy use of the demonstrative occurs in the next clause (6:6b[5b]), where the conspirators admit the futility of their search for cause against דָּנִיֵּאל דְּנָה, "this Daniel." Since Daniel is well known to everyone in the conversation, there is no need to clarify which Daniel is meant. As with the narrator's use of the far demonstrative in 6:6a[5a], the conspirators' use of the near demonstrative also "has the effect of distancing the speaker[s] from the known entity" and even expressing "a sense of alienation or disgust."[22]

Given their failure to find any legitimate grounds for complaint against Daniel, the conspirators realize they will have to invent a crime for him to commit. Knowing Daniel's commitment to his God—either from their search for incriminating evidence or, more likely, from their observation of Daniel—the conspirators knew their only chance of getting him to break a law was to create a conflict between a law of the land and the law of his God (דָּת אֱלָהֵהּ, 6:6c[5c][23]). This reference to "the law of his God" (6:6c[5c]) sets up a key theme and tension

---

19. See on 4:1–5[4–8], pp. 209–11.
20. Note that most English translations use the near demonstrative here ("these men"), but the Aramaic word is אִלֵּךְ, "those." BDB makes no distinction in its glosses for אִלֵּךְ and אֵל/אִלֵּין—both are glossed as "these." However, HALOT and many Aramaic grammars distinguish between אִלֵּךְ, "those," and אֵל/אִלֵּין, "these."
21. See Andreas Schuele, *An Introduction to Biblical Aramaic* (Louisville: Westminster John Knox), 33: "The 'those'-type pronouns indicate spatial and sometimes also emotional distance."
22. Runge, *Discourse Grammar of the Greek New Testament,*

372. Runge discusses the use of near and far demonstratives to express contempt in the context of reported speech in the NT, but his application seems to fit here as well. See Runge, *Discourse Grammar of the Greek New Testament,* 371–74.
23. The best understanding of "law" here is probably "religious practice," since there is no biblical command for Daniel's routine of praying three times a day, much less in front of an open Jerusalem-facing window. On the other hand, there was a law against worshiping anyone except the LORD (Exod 20:3–7), and this would have included praying.

of the narrative. In the prohibition that the conspirators will convince Darius to sign, they will pit the דָּת־מָדַי וּפָרַס, "law of the Medes and Persians" (6:9[8], 13[12], 16[15]), against the דָּת אֱלָהֵהּ, "the law of God." Daniel will have to violate one of these two unchangeable laws, and the conspirators bank their success on Daniel's reputation.[24] They devise a law that will twist Daniel's commitment to his God into something the king will be forced to treat as a threat to state security.[25]

b. The Conspirators' Proposal (6:7a–9d[6a–8d])

In the second subsection the conspirators make their proposal for a new law to Darius. The narrator sets their proposal as reported speech—the longest in the narrative with the exception of Darius's closing proclamation (6:26–28[25–27]). Here the narrator calls the conspirators "these overseers and satraps" (6:7a[6a]), another use of the near demonstrative that may refocus the conspirators as central to the narrative (see on 6:3c[2c] above).[26] Indeed, their actions and speech drive the narrative.

The narrator says the group הַרְגִּשׁוּ to the king; הַרְגִּשׁוּ (רְגַשׁ) is a famously difficult word to translate (cf. 6:7[6], 12[11], 16[15]). "Came by collusion" is the NET rendering of the verb and the one adopted here because it seems to best capture the idea of gathering together with conspiratorial purposes.[27]

The conspirators' opening words follow the expected protocol: "O Darius the king, live forever" (6:7c[6c]), but then they gang up on the king. The reader knows the conspirators are satraps and overseers (6:5a[4a], 7a[6a]), but in their opening words, they exaggerate the situation, telling the king that everyone in his employ decided together that the king needed to establish this law: "All the overseers of the kingdom, the prefects and the satraps, the counselors and the governors" (6:8a[7a]). The effect of this in the narrative is twofold. First, it may indicate why Darius, who is portrayed as passive and easily manipulated throughout the narrative, so willingly agreed: he lacked the support to disagree with his administrators if everyone agreed. Second, it sets Daniel apart; everyone was against him. Even Darius will find himself unwittingly (and unwillingly) against Daniel.

Together, the group had decided the king should do two things: establish a royal statute and see that it was enforced (6:8b–c[7b–c]). In this speech, they accomplish the first of these (6:10[9]); in a later speech, they will accomplish the second (6:16c–17c[15c–16c]). The contents of this proposed statute are in the relative clauses of 6:8d–e[7d–e]. Anyone who יִבְעֵה בָעוּ, "seeks a petition," from "any god or man" except Darius would be thrown to the lions.[28] The conspirators conclude

---

24. Daniel will ultimately claim he broke neither law (6:22–23[21–22]).
25. Pace, *Daniel*, 201.
26. The narrator refers to the group of conspirators as "these overseers and satraps" (6:7a[6a]) and "those men" (6:6a[5a], 12a[11a], 16a[15a], 25b[24b]). See commentary on each.
27. Cf. "conspired and went" (NRSV), "assembled together" (KJV), "went as a group" (NIV), and "came by agreement" (NASB/ESV). BDB suggests "to come thronging," but as the NET Bible observes in its notes on Dan 6:7[6], "it is unlikely that subordinates would enter a royal court in such a reckless fashion." At least in Dan 6, the word refers a group acting in agreement "in the pursuit of a duplicitous goal, namely the entrapment of Daniel" (NET Bible Notes, Dan 6:7[6]). Most commentators agree that word suggests conspiracy, agitation, and the intent to stir up trouble. The Hebrew equivalent, *rāgaš*, appears in Ps 2:1. See Hill, *Daniel*, 119, for further discussion.
28. The exact nature of the proposed law is not as straightforward as it may appear for at least two reasons: the nature of Medo-Persian religion (Zoroastrianism) and the context of

their proposal by urging the king to "establish the prohibition and sign the document" (6:9a–b[8a–b]).

The vocative מַלְכָּא, "O king" (6:8e[7e], 9a[8a]), occurs twice in the reported speech of the conspirators, and neither is required by court protocol, as in 7c[6c], or to identify the addressee. The second occurrence seems intended to "add prominence to something . . . important that follows"[29]—namely, "the ask" of the conspirators; they have proposed the law, and now they ask the king to do it.[30] The use of the vocative creates a pause before this shift. However, the first vocative falls in the middle of the conspirators' description of the proposed law (6:8e[7e]). The pragmatic effect in this usage may

---

Dan 6. With respect to Medo-Persian religion, the law conflicts with what we know about Zoroastrian religious practice. While in its pure form, Zoroastrianism was monolatrous in its worship of Ahura Mazda, in actuality, most people practiced a syncretistic form of the religion and worshiped multiple deities. Since ancients believed every god to have a degree of power, it was important to maintain the favor of all of them. For Darius to prohibit prayer to other gods would be to risk the wrath of the snubbed gods. Additionally, it would be "unenforceable and politically suicidal [for Darius], for he would be prohibiting the religious practice of every Iranian" (John Walton, "The Decree of Darius the Mede in Daniel 6," *JETS* 31 [1988], 282). Furthermore, Mesopotamian kings—unlike Egyptian kings—did not deify themselves, so it would be odd for Darius to require that people pray to him, though, as Young observes, "Who is to say that an oriental despot, yielding to the subtle flattery of such a proposal, might not, in a weak moment, have agreed to it? This is not the first time in history that men have acted foolishly and entered upon an ill-considered plan of action, only to regret it later" (*The Prophecy of Daniel*, 133). Montgomery notes the rhetorical effect of Darius's "divinity": "The king with despotic power and his formal claims to divine rights was the symbol and summation of the denial of the true God. Hence monarchs like Nebuchadnezzar and Darius, who otherwise are sympathetically treated, appear as the incarnation of all the forces arrayed against God" (*Commentary on the Book of Daniel*, 268–69). Another difficulty with the law proposed in Dan 6 is that the Persians did not require captive people to adopt their religious practice (consider the 539 BCE decree of Cyrus, which encouraged and funded the return of captives to their lands to reestablish their national religions).

With respect to the context of Dan 6, the decree fits uneasily in the unfolding events of the chapter. When Daniel is found guilty, Darius is dismayed. One wonders how he would not have known the deep religious convictions of the man he wanted to make second-in-command, and his own words about Daniel's commitment reveal that he *did* know (vv. 17[16], 21[20]). When Daniel eventually emerges unscathed from the lions' den, he claims his innocence before the king (v. 23[22]); would he say such a thing if he had blatantly defied the king's order? (Compare the bold defiance of Shadrach, Meshach, and Abednego in 3:16–18.) It seems that whatever Darius decreed, he did not realize Daniel would turn up guilty for praying to his God.

John Walton has proposed that the decree of Dan 6 had to do with an insiders' conflict between Persians who advocated a strict version of Zoroastrianism and those who were happy with the syncretistic version. Daniel's conspirators made the case that if Darius was "the only legitimate mediator for prayers for a period of thirty days a stand could be made for the worship of Ahura Mazda according to the pure teachings of [Zoroaster]" (Walton, "The Decree of Darius the Mede in Daniel 6," 285). In this case, Darius would have been acting as a priest of Ahura Mazda, not as a god himself. While enacting a thirty-day law would not eliminate widespread syncretistic worship, it would nonetheless make a strong political statement in favor of orthodox Zoroastrianism. What would have motivated Darius to make this statement may have more to do with the power play that seems to be at work between him and his officials ("everyone," 6:8a[7a]). If his entire administration wanted the decree, Darius lacked means to oppose it.

All of this returns us to the question of Daniel's guilt in Dan 6. As a foreign captive, Daniel would have been free to worship his own God and not adhere to the Persian cult. However, the conspirators could have argued that if Darius was going to promote Daniel to second-in-command, he should be expected to demonstrate total allegiance by keeping the letter of the law, foreigner or not. In this case, Daniel would not have been technically guilty of breaking the law, but Darius would have had no choice but to bow to his officials' demands.

Walton's hypothesis is attractive, though he admits the lack of evidence makes it tenuous. Another factor to consider is that although Daniel later said he was innocent (v. 23[22]), he also seemed to know where his actions could lead (v. 11[10]) and thus that he could be perceived as guilty.

29. Runge and Westbury, *LDHB*, 2.4 Thematic Address.
30. "Ask" is a generous word for what was probably happening. In a scenario where "all" his officials have decided this is a good idea, Darius likely had little choice but to comply. Throughout the narrative, the conspirators are portrayed as the ones with the power, while Darius comes across as weak and ineffective.

be flattery: "Any ingrate who prays a prayer to any god or man except you, O king (because you alone are worthy of such devotion), will be thrown to the lions (where they deserve to be)."[31]

The immutability of the law is also noted twice in this reported speech of the conspirators. The first mention is in the relative clause of 6:9c[8c], which describes the signed royal document of 6:9b[8b]; it could not be changed, because apparently the law of the Medes and Persians dictated that such a royal prohibition could not be changed. The second occurrence is in the relative clause of 6:9d[8d], which describes the law of the Medes and Persians; it also could not be changed.[32] The conspirators' proposed law was doubly secure.

The strength of the conspirators' law contributes to a larger theme of the chapter—namely, who really is sovereign. Who has the greatest right to rule? The conspirators tout the irrevocability of their law, but it was a decree that ultimately came to nothing—at least, for Daniel. Even with such great power, the law could not accomplish its intended purpose, and banking on it cost the conspirators their lives. By contrast, Daniel remained faithful to the law of his God, the one with real power and total sovereignty.

c. The King's Establishment of the Law (6:10[9])

The narrator reports the conspirators' success in 6:10[9]. King Darius "signed the document, that is, the prohibition." Just as the conspirators had appealed to דָּרְיָוֶשׁ מַלְכָּא, "Darius the king," in their opening words to the king, so מַלְכָּא דָּרְיָוֶשׁ, "King Darius," responded. They needed the royal representative to enact their law, and he did.

The conspirators had asked the king to establish (תְּקִים, 6:9a[8a]) the prohibition and then sign the document, but the narrator simply reports that he signed the document (רְשַׁם כְּתָבָא, 6:10[9]). The implication is that Darius signed a document placed in front of him—the statute that all his officials had predetermined for him (6:8a–c[7a–c]). For it to be a royal statute (קְיָם מַלְכָּא, 6:8b[7b]), it had to have the signature of the king.

Darius's response to this proposal is telling. In the narrator's recounting of the events, the king asks no questions, poses no challenges, makes no verbal response at all. He simply signs it because they "asked" him to.[33] The law may be strong, but the king behind it is weak—a portrayal that the story will reinforce as it unfolds.

---

31. It is also possible that this vocative carries the derision of the officials, who know the king will do it because he really has no choice. His signature is just a required formality for the law they are enacting.

32. The idea of an unchangeable Medo-Persian law also appears in the book of Esther (1:19; 8:8) but is not clearly documented in extrabiblical sources.

33. Longman observes that Darius's earlier establishment of administrators may also help explain his willingness to agree to the conspirators' proposal: he had pushed "the governance of Babylonia in the direction of decentralization, which may help explain his later quick acceptance of the proposal to make him the chief mediator of prayer. In other words, this suggestion assures him of his continued central place in the government while at the same time delegating authority to others" (*Daniel*, 159).

3. Daniel's Faithfulness to God's Law (6:11a–15f[10a–14f])

Main Idea of the Passage

In Daniel 6:11–15[10–14], Daniel proves faithful to God's law despite what he knew it would cost. His response to the law prohibiting prayer to anyone but the king is to continue his practice of praying to his God. When his enemies report the offense to Darius, the king responds with surprise, distress, and concerted effort to change the immutable law that has trapped him.

Literary Context

Daniel 6:11–15[10–14] is the third section of the narrative that comprises ch. 6 and follows the narrator's report that King Darius signed the proposed prohibition into law (6:10[9]). It functions in at least four ways in its broader literary context. First, it continues the narrative's focus on Daniel and his example of faithfulness by detailing his response to the newly signed law. Second, it develops the contrast between the two immutable laws in the chapter—the law of Daniel's God and the law of Darius and the Medes and Persians; the law of God prompts Daniel's unwavering commitment, while Darius's law causes the king's frantic attempts to undo it. A third and related function of the section is to contrast Daniel the captive and Darius the king. The section opens and closes with their respective responses to the new law: despite the prohibition, Daniel is free and unfazed, while Darius is trapped and frenzied because of it. A final literary function of this section is to continue the portrayal of a weak King Darius. While the previous section demonstrated his weakness with respect to his administrators, this section shows him to be powerless in the face of a law he established.

> E. Narrative 5: God's Superior Law and His Servant's Faithfulness (6:2a–29[1–28])
> 1. God's Servant in Darius's Service (6:2a–5f[1a–4f])
> 2. The Establishment of an Inferior Human Law (6:6a–10[5a–9])
> → **3. Daniel's Faithfulness to God's Law (6:11a–15f[10a–14f])**
> 4. The Enforcement of an Inferior Law (6:16a–19d[15a–18d])
> 5. The Triumph of Daniel's God (6:20a–25g[19a–24g])
> 6. The Superior God and His Faithful Servant (6:26a–29[25a–28])

Translation and Exegetical Outline

(See pages 313–14.)

Structure and Literary Form

The third section of the narrative in ch. 6 (6:11–15[10–14]) describes Daniel's response to the law signed by Darius and the actions of both the conspirators and the king in the aftermath of Daniel's action. It consists of three subsections: 6:11–12[10–11], 13–14[12–13], and 15[14].

The first subsection (6:11–12[10–11]) recounts Daniel's immediate response to the law—namely, maintaining his habit of praying three times a day at his Jerusalem-facing window (6:11[10]). It then describes the success of the conspirators and their manufactured law—that is, finding something against Daniel with respect to the law of his God (6:12[11]; cf. 6:6c[5c]).

The second subsection (6:13–14[12–13]) begins with the transitional marker אֱדַיִן, "then," and is made up of dialogue between the conspirators and the king. Having caught Daniel in violation of the new law, the conspirators now catch the king by surprise. In their first reported speech of the subsection (6:13a–dβ[12a–dβ]), they repeat the king's law back to him in the form of a question. In the reported speech of the king's response (6:13f–i[12f–i]), the king answers their question with emphatic affirmation of the law. In the conspirators' response to the king (6:14[13]), they accuse Daniel of violating the king's law.

The third subsection (6:15[14]) also begins with אֱדַיִן, "then," and it recounts the king's dismay at the news (6:15aα–b[14aα–b]) and his subsequent efforts to undo what he had unwittingly done (6:15c–f[14c–f]).

Daniel 6:11a–15f[10a–14f]

			3. Daniel's Faithfulness to God's Law (6:11a–15f[10a–14f])
			a. Daniel's Response to the Inferior Law (6:11a–12d[10a–11d])
11[10]aα	וְדָנִיֵּאל ...	But Daniel ...	(1) Daniel's Habit (6:11a–i[10a–i])
11[10]b	כְּדִי יְדַע	when he knew	
11[10]c	דִּי־רְשִׁים כְּתָבָא	that the document had been signed	
11[10]aβ	עַל לְבַיְתֵהּ ...	... went to his house.	
11[10]e	וְכַוִּין פְּתִיחָן לֵהּ בְּעִלִּיתֵהּ נֶגֶד יְרוּשְׁלֶם	His windows were opened in his upper chamber facing Jerusalem,	
11[10]f	וְזִמְנִין תְּלָתָה בְיוֹמָא הוּא בָּרֵךְ עַל־בִּרְכוֹהִי	and three times a day he would kneel on his knees,	
11[10]g	וּמְצַלֵּא	praying	
11[10]h	וּמוֹדֵא קֳדָם אֱלָהֵהּ	and praising before his God,	
11[10]i	כָּל־קֳבֵל דִּי־הֲוָא עָבֵד מִן־קַדְמַת דְּנָה׃	as he had been doing before this.	
12[11]a	אֱדַיִן גֻּבְרַיָּא אִלֵּךְ הַרְגִּשׁוּ	Then those men came by collusion,	(2) The Conspirators' Success (6:12a–d[11a–d])
12[11]b	וְהַשְׁכַּחוּ לְדָנִיֵּאל	and they found Daniel	
12[11]c	בָּעֵא	seeking	
12[11]d	וּמִתְחַנַּן קֳדָם אֱלָהֵהּ׃	and imploring before his God.	
13[12]a	בֵּאדַיִן קְרִיבוּ	Then they approached [the king],	b. The Conspirators' Prey (6:13a–14e[12a–13e])
13[12]b	וְאָמְרִין קֳדָם־מַלְכָּא עַל־אֱסָר מַלְכָּא	and they were saying before the king concerning the prohibition of the king,	(1) A Leading Question (6:13a–e[12a–e])
13[12]c	הֲלָא אֱסָר רְשַׁמְתָּ ...	"Did you not write a prohibition	
13[12]dα	דִּי כָל־אֱנָשׁ ...	that any man ...	
13[12]e	דִּי־יִבְעֵה בָעוּ מִן־כָּל־אֱלָהּ וֶאֱנָשׁ עַד־יוֹמִין תְּלָתִין לָהֵן מִנָּךְ מַלְכָּא	who seeks from any god or man except you for thirty days, O king,	
13[12]dβ	יִתְרְמֵא לְגֹב אַרְיָוָתָא׃	... will be thrown into the den of lions?"	

Continued on next page.

	Continued from previous page.		
13[12]f	עָנֵה ↓	↓ Responding,[1]	
13[12]g	וְאָמַר מַלְכָּא	the king said,	(2) A Royal Affirmation (6:13f–i[12f–i])
13[12]h	יַצִּיבָא מִלְּתָא כְדָת־מָדַי וּפָרַס	"The matter is certain, according to the law of the Medes and Persians,	
		← which cannot be annulled."	
13[12]i	דִּי־לָא תֶעְדֵּא׃		
14[13]a	בֵּאדַיִן עֲנוֹ וְאָמְרִין קֳדָם מַלְכָּא	Then they answered, saying before the king,	(3) An Unexpected Blow (6:14a–e[13a–e])
14[13]bα	דִּי דָנִיֵּאל ←	"Daniel...	
14[13]bβ	דִּי מִן־בְּנֵי גָלוּתָא (דִּי) [מִן] יְהוּד ←	↑ who is one of the exiles of Judah	
14[13]c	לָא־שָׂם עֲלָךְ ←	...does not pay heed to you, O king, or to the prohibition	
14[13]d	מַלְכָּא טְעֵם ←	↑ which you signed.	
14[13]e	וְעַל־אֱסָרָא דִּי רְשַׁמְתָּ׃	But three times in a day he makes his petition."	
15[14]aα	וְזִמְנִין תְּלָתָה בְּיוֹמָא בָּעֵא בָּעוּתֵהּ׃	Then the king,...	c. The King's Response to the Inferior Law (6:15a–f[14a–f])
15[14]b	אֱדַיִן מַלְכָּא ←	↑ when he heard the word,	
15[14]aβ	כְּדִי מִלְּתָא שְׁמַע ...	...was very distressed,	
15[14]c	שַׂגִּיא בְּאֵשׁ עֲלוֹהִי ←	and set [his] mind upon Daniel	
15[14]d	וְעַל דָּנִיֵּאל שָׂם בָּל ←	↑ to deliver him.	
15[14]e	לְשֵׁיזָבוּתֵהּ ←	Until the sun went down, he was struggling	
15[14]f	וְעַד מֶעָלֵי שִׁמְשָׁא הֲוָה מִשְׁתַּדַּר לְהַצָּלוּתֵהּ׃	↑ to rescue him.	

1. See on 2:5 in the commentary.

Explanation of the Text

a. Daniel's Response to the Inferior Law (6:11a–12d[10a–11d])

The previous subsection ended with the result of the conspirators' proposal: Darius signed the document (6:10[9]). But the king's action is also the reason for what happened next: Daniel went home and prayed (6:11[10]). The temporal clause כְּדִי יְדַע, "when he knew" (6:11b[10b]), indicates this cause-and-effect relationship between the actions of Darius and Daniel.

The narrator begins the subsection with וְדָנִיֵּאל, "but Daniel" (6:11aα[10aα]), followed by the temporal clause כְּדִי יְדַע דִּי־רְשִׁים כְּתָבָא ("when he knew that the document had been signed," 6:11b–c[10b–c]), before providing the predicate for which "Daniel" is the subject: עַל לְבַיְתֵהּ ("went to his house," 6:11aβ[10aβ]). This structure and order of the clauses places the emphasis on Daniel, a reminder that the chapter is about him.

The detailed description of Daniel's practice of prayer in 6:11[10] is presented in such a way as to make readers feel like they are following Daniel through his routine: first he learns about the document, and then he goes to his house; he goes upstairs where he has windows opened toward Jerusalem; he kneels down at the window to pray and praise. Then he goes about his business, but returns to the window again and again.

This detailed description also provides a wealth of information for the careful reader. This information is in the participial clauses of 6:11e–i[10e–i], a shift from the perfect verbs of 6:11b–aβ[10b–aβ] that signals a shift from foregrounded action to background information. (The foregrounded action continues in 6:12[11] with the return to perfect verbs.) In the first descriptive clause (6:11e[10e]), the narrator comments about the layout of Daniel's house: its second floor has windows opened toward Jerusalem. There is no explicit claim that this is where Daniel prayed, but by including the information here, the narrator expects that the reader will conclude that he does. This information accomplishes several things in the narrative. First, Daniel praying at an open upstairs window indicates the high visibility of his routine to everyone—most of all, to the conspirators. Daniel did not have a prayer closet; he had an upstairs prayer window. This suggests that the conspirators already knew about Daniel's practice and had likely seen him praying there before they concocted their law. His habit of praying at the open window gave them the "crime" Daniel would commit. Undoubtedly, Daniel knew this. He also knew, then, that if he closed the window or prayed in a downstairs room to avoid detection, he would have compromised his commitment to his God; the conspirators may well have concluded that he violated the law of his God, because, for all they knew, the law of his God required that he pray at an open window.[34]

A second thing that the Jerusalem-facing window accomplishes in the narrative is that it suggests the content of Daniel's prayer. Praying toward Jerusalem is imagery from Solomon's prayer of dedication of the newly built temple in 1 Kings. In the tenth-century-BCE king's great dedicatory prayer,

---

34. Goldingay observes that "when prayer is fashionable, it is time to pray in secret (Matt 6:5–6), but when prayer is under pressure, to pray in secret is to give the appearance of fearing the king more than God: one must 'render to Caesar, but also render to God' (Matt 22:21; cf. Act 4:18–20; 5:29)" (*Daniel*, 319).

he pleaded with YHWH to hear his people's prayers when—someday in their rebellious future—they prayed from lands of exile toward the city of Jerusalem and the temple of YHWH (1 Kgs 8:29–30, 35, 38, 42, 44, 48[35]). Solomon implored YHWH to hear and forgive his wayward people. He asked YHWH to cause their captors to show mercy to his people (1 Kgs 8:50). Solomon's prayer in the background of Daniel's routine hints about what the specifics of Daniel's prayer may have been: praise of YHWH's greatness, confession of sin, pleas for restoration, and even a request for mercy in the face of what he knew lay ahead.[36]

From this statement about Daniel's open window, the narrator returns to Daniel's actions of prayer in 6:11f-h[10f-h]. Three times a day Daniel knelt on his knees.[37] Daniel is one of only three Old Testament figures reported to have knelt in prayer.[38] The first is Solomon in his prayer of dedication of the temple (1Kgs 8:54; 2 Chr 6:13). Daniel is the second, and postexilic Ezra is the third in his great prayer of confession for the nation's sin (Ezra 9:5). Both Solomon and Ezra knelt with outstretched arms (1 Kgs 8:54; 2 Chr. 6:13; Ezra 9:5),

and the content of their prayers is similar: Solomon implored YHWH to forgive the people when they confessed their sin in lands of exile; Ezra confessed the people's sin and pleaded for mercy when exile was over. Ezra's confession is portrayed by the Chronicler as the fulfillment of Solomon's prayer of dedication from centuries earlier. While Daniel is not said to be confessing sin and the words of his prayer are not included, his kneeling posture combined with his Jerusalem-facing window suggests a narrative link to the prayers of Solomon and Ezra.[39]

While kneeling, Daniel was praying and praising (מְצַלֵּא וּמוֹדֵא, 6:11g–h[10g–h]). Although the conspirators will find Daniel "seeking ... before his God" (בָּעֵא ... קֳדָם אֱלָהֵהּ, 6:12b–d[11b–d])—the action prohibited by their concocted law—the narrator does not report that Daniel did what was prohibited (6:12–14[11–13]). The satraps and overseers will find exactly what they need to find to condemn Daniel, but the narrator presents an innocent Daniel.[40]

This lengthy description of Daniel's response to the signed document in 6:11[10] is another reminder that the chapter is about him. The nar-

---

35. Cf. 2 Chr 6:20–21, 26, 29, 34, 38.

36. Given Solomon's prayer that the people's captors show them mercy, it is probably not coincidental that in the rest of Dan 6, the narrator takes pains to show how Daniel's captor Darius showed great compassion toward him.

37. Scripture does not mandate the number of times per day someone should pray (except for Paul's admonition to "pray continually," 1 Thess 5:17). In the Old Testament, three times a day is suggested by Ps 55:17, while Ps 119:164 refers to praise seven times a day. In 1 Chr 23:30 are the morning and evening prayers of the Levites. See further Collins (*Daniel*, 268–69), who thinks Daniel's practice at least reflects a custom of the eastern diaspora.

38. Psalm 95:6, the only other Old Testament reference to kneeling before God, seems to describe a posture of worship instead of prayer specifically. Goldingay notes that standing is the regular posture throughout the Bible for prayer (e.g., 1 Chr 23:30; Neh 9; Matt 6:5; Mark 11:25; Luke 18:11, 13); "Daniel's kneeling, which implies prostration, indicates a marked self-lowering, which elsewhere suggests circumstances of particular solemnity or need (1 Kgs 8:54; Ezra 9:5; Luke 22:41; Acts 7:60; 9:40; 20:36; 21:5)" (*Daniel*, 316).

39. Solomon asked YHWH to hear his people when they made supplication (HtD of חנן; see, e.g., 1 Kgs 8:47, 49), and the conspirators find Daniel making supplication (Aramaic HtD of חנן; Dan 6:12[11]). Admittedly, my case for a connection between Ezra, Solomon, and Daniel would be stronger if the narrator's report in 6:11[10] said Daniel "confessed" instead of or in addition to his "praying and giving thanks" (מְצַלֵּא וּמוֹדֵא). The NJPS and James Montgomery both translate מוֹדֵא as "confessing," not "thanking." Montgomery's translation appears to be influenced by Dan 9:4, where Daniel is clearly confessing (וָאֶתְוַדֶּה) (*Commentary on the Book of Daniel*, 274). See Goswell, "The Temple Theme in the Book of Daniel" (p. 513), who argues that Daniel's prayer in ch. 6 "is the same type of prayer" as his prayer in ch. 9.

40. Daniel also claims innocence (6:23[22]).

rator does not simply report that Daniel prayed: he details the location where he prayed, the time that he prayed, and the general content of what he prayed. This extensive detail indicates the importance of Daniel's routine in his own life and also in the events of Dan 6. Despite what it would cost him, Daniel carried on as if nothing had changed because, for him, nothing had changed. His God was still on the throne, so three times a day he knelt toward Jerusalem in prayer and thanks. He prayed to the God whose house lay in ruins in Jerusalem. Like Shadrach, Meshach, and Abednego before him, Daniel cast himself at the mercy of a God who may or may not deliver him.[41] The narrator portrays him as a faithful Jew, keeping the covenant and "praying without ceasing" to the God of a broken covenant, and so provides an example for diaspora Jews to follow. His eventual deliverance from death would also have assured them that sometimes God does choose to deliver.[42]

The narrator reports that "those men" (גֻּבְרַיָּא אִלֵּךְ, 6:12a[11a]) colluded together again (cf. 6:7a[6a], 16a[15a]) and "found" (הַשְׁכַּחוּ) Daniel doing exactly what they intended to find him doing and exactly what the law prohibited: "seeking before his God" (בָּעֵא . . . קֳדָם אֱלָהֵהּ, 6:12b–d[11b–d]).[43]

b. The Conspirators' Prey (6:13a–14e[12a–13e])

Having found what they needed, the conspirators "drew near" or "approached" the king (קְרִיבוּ, 6:13a[12a]). In the quotative frame for the conspirators' speech to the king (6:13b[12b]), the narrator notes that they speak "concerning the prohibition of the king," an unnecessary clarification in terms of the narrative: the reader knows full well why the conspirators are speaking to the king. The effect of this otherwise unnecessary phrase is that it keeps the king's law at the center of the chapter's events. Eleven references to this inferior law appear in the chapter,[44] and three additional references associate it with the law of the Medes and Persians (6:9c–d[8c–d], 13h–i[12h–i], 16d[15d]). The events of the narrative revolve around the royal prohibition that puts Daniel in conflict with God's law.

On this second visit to the king, the conspirators dispense with any royal protocol (i.e., "O king, live forever;" cf. the conspirators in 6:7c[6c] and Daniel in 6:22[21]; see also 2:4; 3:9; 5:10).[45] They begin with a leading question that will put Darius right where they want him: "Did you not write a prohibition . . ." (. . . הֲלָא אֱסָר רְשַׁמְתָּ, 6:13c[12c]). The king will have no choice but to answer in the affirmative, walking right into the conspirators' trap.

Darius's response (6:13f–i[12f–i]) is his only reported speech to the conspirators in the entire narrative.[46] He responds by giving triple affirmation to their question: (1) "the matter is certain," (2) "according to the law of the Medes and Persians," and (3) "which cannot be annulled" (6:13h–i[12h–i]). The king's words parrot the conspirators' original description of the document the king was to sign (6:9c–d[8c–d]): he had done exactly what they wanted him to do—both in his signing of the document and now in his owning it.

---

41. See discussion on 3:16–18 above.

42. The declaration of Shadrach, Meshach, and Abednego cautions against promising that God will deliver his followers from trials (3:17–18). However, there remains the promise of his ultimate deliverance (12:1–3), a hope that would have resonated with Daniel's diaspora audience.

43. See on 6:5–6[4–5] above for discussion of "seeking" and "finding" in the narrative of ch. 6.

44. קָיָם (vv. 8b[7b], 16dα[15dα]), אֱסָר (vv. 9a[8a], 10[9], 13b[12b], 13c[12c], 14bβ[13bβ], 16dα[15dα]), כְּתָבָא (vv. 9b[8b], 10[9], 11c[10c]).

45. The Greek and Syriac omit the phrase עַל־אֱסָר, which would allow מַלְכָּא to function as a vocative. See Newsom, *Daniel*, 189.

46. Cf. the conspirators' reported speech in all three of their encounters with the king (vv. 7–9[6–8], 13–14[12–13], 16[15]).

In the speech frame for the conspirators' reply, the narrator sets up their blow. The multiverb frame of ענה + אמר in 6:14[13] is one of five exceptions to the format of the typical speech frame in Daniel, in which both ענה and אמר are participles. Here, ענה is a perfect, while אמר is a participle. As noted by Cook, the use of this divergent speech frame seems to correlate with "a salient and dispreferred response." Here (as in 3:9) the frame sets up the charges against Daniel, which is "both a dispreferred response in the king's eyes and salient inasmuch as the charges drive the whole storyline."[47]

The conspirators' first word after Darius's resounding affirmation of his law was, no doubt, calculated for effect: דָּנִיֵּאל, "Daniel" (6:14bα[13bα]). From this first word, the conspirators go on to cast Daniel in the worst possible light. Miller describes their strategy in terms of Daniel's identity and his actions. First, the conspirators call Daniel "one of the exiles of Judah," emphasizing "that Daniel was not truly one of them." The conspirators had no reason to mention Daniel's status from decades earlier "other than to humiliate him and make him seem more likely to be disloyal."[48] With respect to Daniel's actions, the conspirators accuse Daniel of disrespect, "not merely of the king's law ("the decree") but of the king himself." By declaring that Daniel "does not pay heed" to the king, they make it clear to Darius that Daniel does not consider him significant. Additionally, the conspirators emphasize to the king that he personally had signed the decree, further proof of Daniel's disregard for Darius and his authority. The conspirators conclude their calculated report against Daniel by noting that "not only had Daniel disobeyed the king and broken the law, but he did it three times every day ("prays three times a day"). It was not a mere lapse on Daniel's part."[49]

Like the enemies of Shadrach, Meshach, and Abednego, the conspirators of Dan 6 insinuated that the king had in his employ "a dangerous subversive . . . and thus a threat to the stability of the kingdom."[50] Not only did the immutability of the law mean he had no choice but to enforce it, the conspirators imply it was also in Darius's best interest to do so.

c. The King's Response to the Inferior Law (6:15a–f[14a–f])

Darius never saw it coming. Playing right into the conspirators' hands, he found himself trapped by his own words and his own law. The narrator describes Darius's immediate response to the conspirators' report in a main clause (6:15a[14a]) and a subordinate temporal clause (6:15b[14b]). The main clause occurs in two parts, with the subject (מַלְכָּא, "the king") and the predicate (שַׂגִּיא בְּאֵשׁ עֲלוֹהִי, "was very distressed") separated by the subordinate temporal clause כְּדִי מִלְּתָא שְׁמַע ("when he heard the word"). This syntactic structure has two effects. First, the prominent position of מַלְכָּא focuses the reader's attention on the king and his response to the conspirators' report. He is greatly distressed and determined to deliver Daniel. In the two clauses that follow (6:15e–f[14e–f]) the narrator emphasizes the king's efforts: the temporal frame ("until the sun went down") and the verb

---

47. Cook, *Aramaic Ezra and Daniel*, 11. See further the commentary on 2:7, 10; 3:16.

48. Cf. Belshazzar's similar reference to Daniel (5:13) and also the accusers' reference to Shadrach, Meshach, and Abednego as Jews (3:12).

49. Miller, *Daniel*, 184.

50. Hill, *Daniel*, 121.

("he was struggling") suggest the king was doing everything he could to prevent giving Daniel to the lions.

A second effect of the syntactic structure of 6:15a–b[14a–b] is in its relationship to an earlier occurrence of a similar structure. In 6:11a–c[10a–c], the narrator had described Daniel's response when he knew the document had been signed. There the description began with the subject וְדָנִיֵּאל, "but Daniel" (6:11aα[10aα]), followed by the subordinate temporal clause "when he knew that the document had been signed" (כְּדִי יְדַע דִּי־רְשִׁים כְּתָבָא, 6:11b–c[10b–c]), and then the predicate of the main clause: "went to his house" (עַל לְבַיְתֵהּ, 6:11aβ[10aβ]). The similarity of these structures and their contexts—namely, recounting responses of Daniel and Darius—creates a contrast between the captive and the king. When Daniel knew he had been targeted by the law, he went home and did what he always did. He exerted no effort to save himself. There is no hint of distress or panic. There is, in fact, no emotion in the narrator's report of Daniel's response. He simply followed his routine. By contrast, when Darius realized that Daniel had been targeted, he was distraught and determined to spare Daniel, and then he spent the entire day struggling to save him. Daniel may have been targeted by the king's law, but Darius is the one who found himself trapped by it. Daniel's faithfulness to a higher law left him unfazed by the collusion of his enemies and the commotion of his king.

Darius's daylong efforts come to nothing, as the next section will make clear. Longman notes the irony of the situation: "the law cannot even be repealed by the king himself. A law that has as its ostensible purpose the intention to set the king up as an ultimate authority actually imprisons him to its own authority."[51] Daniel will not be saved by Darius's efforts to undo a bad law; he will be saved by the God whose good law he faithfully kept.

4. The Enforcement of an Inferior Law (6:16a–19d[15a–18d])

Main Idea of the Passage

Daniel 6:16–19[15–18] recounts the apparent triumph of the conspirators as Darius is forced to have Daniel cast into the lions' den for violating the prohibition against praying to anyone but the king. The king expresses hope that Daniel's God will deliver him and then spends a sleepless night worrying about the fate of his extraordinary servant.

---

51. Longman, *Daniel*, 166.

Literary Context

Daniel 6:16–19[15–18] is the fourth section of the narrative in ch. 6. It follows the report of Daniel's faithfulness and Darius's distress over the consequences of the new law. As such, it functions in at least four ways in its literary context. First, the section furthers the plot by showing the result of Daniel's civil disobedience—namely, he was thrown into the lions' den by Darius's order. Second, it escalates the suspense of the narrative to its highest point by reporting the execution of Daniel's punishment without describing its expected outcome; Daniel is left in the lions' den while the narrative follows the distressed king back to the palace. In this second description of the king's distress (cf. 6:15[14]), the section also continues the chapter's portrayal of a powerless Darius who was unable to change his own law and then spent the night worrying about the fate of Daniel. Finally, the section sets up the climax of the plot in Darius's expressed hope that God would deliver Daniel from the lions.

> E. Narrative 5: God's Superior Law and His Servant's Faithfulness (6:2a–29[1–28])
> 1. God's Servant in Darius's Service (6:2a–5f[1a–4f])
> 2. The Establishment of an Inferior Human Law (6:6a–10[5a–9])
> 3. Daniel's Faithfulness to God's Law (6:11a–15f[10a–14f])
> → **4. The Enforcement of an Inferior Law (6:16a–19d[15a–18d])**
> 5. The Triumph of Daniel's God (6:20a–25g[19a–24g])
> 6. The Superior God and His Faithful Servant (6:26a–29[25a–28])

Translation and Exegetical Outline

(See page 321.)

Structure and Literary Form

The fourth section of the narrative in Dan 6 (6:16–19[15–18]) recounts the enforcement of Darius's new law in three subsections: 6:16[15], 17–18[16–17], and 19[18].

The first subsection begins with the transitional בֵּאדַיִן, "then," and consists largely of reported speech as the conspirators prod Darius to enforce the law that Daniel violated (6:16[15]). The second subsection similarly begins with בֵּאדַיִן, "then," and

Daniel 6:16a–19d[15a–18d]

16[15]a	אֱדַיִן גֻּבְרַיָּא אִלֵּךְ הַרְגִּשׁוּ עַל־מַלְכָּא	Then those men came by collusion to the king,	4. The Enforcement of an Inferior Law (6:16a–19d[15a–18d])
16[15]b	וְאָמְרִין לְמַלְכָּא	and they were saying to the king,	a. The Conspirators' Prodding (6:16a–e[15a–e])
16[15]c	דַּע מַלְכָּא	"Know, O king,	
16[15]dα	דִּי־דָת לְמָדַי וּפָרַס דִּי־כָל־אֱסָר ...	that a law of the Medes and Persians is that any prohibition or statute ...	
16[15]e	וּקְיָם דִּי־מַלְכָּא יְהָקֵים	which the king establishes	
16[15]dβ	לָא לְהַשְׁנָיָה׃	... cannot be changed."	
			b. The King's Orders (6:17a–18d[16a–17d])
17[16]a	בֵּאדַיִן מַלְכָּא אֲמַר	Then the king gave the order,	(1) Daniel in the Lions' Den (6:17a–c[16a–c])
17[16]b	וְהַיְתִיו לְדָנִיֵּאל	and they brought Daniel,	
17[16]c	וּרְמוֹ לְגֻבָּא דִּי אַרְיָוָתָא	and they threw (him) to the den of lions.	
17[16]d	עָנֵה	→ Responding,[1]	(2) The King's Desire (6:17d–h[16d–h])
17[16]e	מַלְכָּא וְאָמַר לְדָנִיֵּאל	the king said to Daniel,	
17[16]f	אֱלָהָךְ	↑ "Your God,	
17[16]g	דִּי אַנְתָּה [אַנְתְּ] (פָּלַח) פָלַח־לֵהּ בִּתְדִירָא	↑ whom you serve continually—	
17[16]h	הוּא יְשֵׁיזְבִנָּךְ׃	may he deliver you."	
18[17]a	וְהֵיתָיִת אֶבֶן חֲדָה	A stone was brought,	(3) The Stone and the Seal (6:18a–d[17a–d])
18[17]b	וְשֻׂמַת עַל־פֻּם גֻּבָּא	and it was set over the mouth of the den.	
18[17]c	וְחַתְמַהּ מַלְכָּא בְּעִזְקְתֵהּ וּבְעִזְקָת רַבְרְבָנוֹהִי	And the king sealed it with his signet ring and with the signet ring of his noblemen,	
18[17]d	דִּי לָא־תִשְׁנֵא צְבוּ בְּדָנִיֵּאל׃	so that nothing concerning Daniel would be changed.	
19[18]a	אֱדַיִן אֲזַל מַלְכָּא לְהֵיכְלֵהּ	Then the king went to his palace.	c. The King's Long Night (6:19a–d[18a–d])
19[18]b	וּבָת טְוָת	He passed the night without food,	
19[18]c	וְדַחֲוָן לָא־הַנְעֵל קָדָמוֹהִי	and he did not summon entertainment for himself.	
19[18]d	וְשִׁנְתֵּהּ נַדַּת עֲלוֹהִי׃	His sleep fled from him.	

1. See on 2:5 in the commentary.

details the king's orders that Daniel be thrown into the lions' den (6:17a–c[16a–c]); his reported speech to Daniel, expressing his hope that Daniel's God would deliver him (6:17d–h[16d–h]); and further activity with respect to the den—the placement of a stone marked by the king's seal to ensure that there would be neither escape nor rescue for Daniel (6:18[17]). The third subsection (6:19[18]) begins with the transitional אֱדַיִן, "then," and includes the narrator's report that the king returned to his palace and spent a long, sleepless night.

Explanation of the Text

a. The Conspirators' Prodding (6:16a–e[15a–e])

The conspirators return to the king after his day of struggling to save Daniel (6:15[14]). The narrator again refers to them as "those men," גֻּבְרַיָּא אִלֵּךְ (see also 6:6a[5a], 12a[11a], 25b[24b]). By this point in the narrative, it is clear that this is the narrator's name for the conspirators. It reflects their opposition to Daniel and the narrator's disdain for them.[52] They again הַרְגִּשׁוּ, "come by collusion" (6:16a[15a]; cf. 6:7a[6a] and 6:12a[11a]), as they make their final move to destroy Daniel.

The narrator uses reported speech to recount their interaction with the king. The chapter has been dominated by the speech of the conspirators, who clearly have control over the actions of the king. To this point in the narrative, Darius has spoken once (6:13f–i[12f–i]).

On this third visit, the conspirators again dispense with royal protocol (see on 6:7c[6c] and 6:13[12] above). In their first encounter, they maintained proper protocol for addressing the king as they laid their trap for Daniel (and for Darius). They began their second encounter with a question that led the king right into their trap:

"Did you not write a prohibition . . . ?" In this third encounter, the conspirators begin with an imperative: "Know, O king . . ." (דַּע מַלְכָּא, 6:16c[15c]). In this progression from proper protocol to leading question to imperative verb in the conspirators' reported speech, the narrator demonstrates the group's increasing control over the king.

The speech of the conspirators is masterful manipulation. Without actually commanding the king, they nonetheless tell him exactly what to do. They begin with the vocative מַלְכָּא, "O king" (6:16c[15c])—a title that is not required to identify the addressee since the narrator has already said the conspirators came "to the king" (6:16a[15a]) and said "to the king" (6:16b[15b]). Here it serves the purpose of adding prominence to what they are about to say.[53] They follow this with mention of the law of the Medes and Persians, the third time this famed law has been brought into the narrative (cf. 6:9c[8c] and 6:13h[12h]). The effect of its mention here is its sheer weight: what the conspirators are about to say has the authority of the empire behind it. Then they refer in the abstract to "any prohibition or statute which the king establishes" (6:16dα–e[15dα–e]). Finally, they get to the bottom line—such a law cannot be changed (6:16dβ[15dβ]).

---

52. See on 6:6[5].

53. Runge and Westbury, *LDHB*, 2.4 Thematic Address.

Without referring directly to the law at issue, the transgression of Daniel, or the daylong efforts of the king to save him, the conspirators have made their point clear: A king ("O king") in the Medo-Persian Empire had established a law, and he had better keep it. The impotence of Darius is clear. He is utterly powerless before "those men," and his weakness puts Daniel in peril. Pace summarizes:

> [Darius's] impotence vis-à-vis his courtiers leaves Daniel completely unprotected and in danger of losing his life.... Darius never challenges Daniel's accusers concerning their pretexts, even though he has several opportunities to do so. Furthermore, the king fails to challenge the law that a decree cannot be changed, nor does he offer another law to supersede it. This incompetence of the king is contrasted with the dominance of his officials, which cannot be underestimated.[54]

In the narrative of Dan 6, the weakness of King Darius of the Medo-Persian Empire and the destructive law he established stand in contrast to the power of Daniel's God and the life-giving nature of his law for his faithful followers.

b. The King's Orders (6:17a–18d[16a–17d])

As in the first interaction between the conspirators and the king (6:7–10[6–9]), there is no reported speech of the king in response to the conspirators. As before, he simply complies—there he signed the infamous document into law (6:10[9]), and here he gives the order that condemns Daniel to the lions' den (6:17a–c[16a–c]).

Then in reported speech, the king addresses Daniel. The king begins his speech with "your God" (6:17f[16f]; see also 6:21eα[20eα]), the fourth reference to Israel's God in the chapter. The first was by the conspirators in their recognition that Daniel's crime would need to relate to the "law of his God" (6:6c[5c]), and twice the narrator referred to "his God" (6:11h[10h] and 6:12h[11h]). Later Daniel will refer to "my God" (6:23a[22a]). The changing pronouns throughout reflect changing points of view in the narrative: the conspirators', the narrator's, Darius's, and eventually Daniel's. It is this God Darius will also call "the living God" (6:21eα[20eα] and 6:27c[26c]) and "the God of Daniel" (6:27b[26b]).

The main clause of Darius's reported speech is 6:17h[16h]: "may he deliver you," with the pronoun's antecedent in Darius's opening word אֱלָהָךְ, "Your God," and its overspecifying relative clause: "whom you serve continually" (6:17f-g[16f-g]). This placement of the antecedent outside the syntax of the main clause and in initial position makes it prominent. Furthermore, the king's description of Daniel's God in 6:17g[16g] is not needed to identify him, and so its presence here has twofold significance. First, as reported speech, it gives a window into the king's thoughts, and second, as overspecification, it is thematically loaded, prompting the reader to think about the referent in a specific way—in this case, as the recipient of Daniel's continual service.[55] With respect to being reported speech, the relative clause indicates that Darius knew of Daniel's faithfulness to his God and affirmed it. Whether the king realized before signing the new law that it targeted that service remains

---

54. Pace, *Daniel*, 196.
55. Runge and Westbury, *LDHB: Introduction*, 2.1 Overspecification.

a question—but at the very least, he wants Daniel to know he recognizes his service to his God. As overspecification, Darius's description of Daniel's God actually focuses on *Daniel*—and specifically on his faithfulness. As already noted (see above on 6:4–5[3–4]), this chapter is very much about Daniel and his example of steadfast service.

Translations of the main clause (6:17h[16h]) with the imperfective/future (i.e., "he will deliver you;" e.g., KJV, NASB, NET, NJPS) attribute to the king a belief not supported by the rest of the narrative. His sleepless night, rush to the den in the morning, and anxious cry to Daniel all indicate that he may have hoped for deliverance, but he did not have confidence in it. The jussive is contextually better: "may he deliver you" (e.g., ESV, NIV). The king may not have been able to deliver Daniel (לְשֵׁיזָבוּתֵהּ, 6:15d[14d]), but he desperately hoped Daniel's God could (יְשֵׁיזְבִנָּךְ, 6:17h[16h]).

With Daniel in the lions' den and Darius hoping the best for him, precautions were taken to prevent tampering with Daniel's situation. The text does not say, as it did with the orders to throw Daniel in the den, that the king ordered these precautions—just that they were done. It is possible that the king's order included all precautions, but the text leaves room for more collusion by the conspirators who wanted to guarantee nothing undid the law and, more importantly, its consequences for Daniel. A stone was brought and set over the mouth of the den. The king then sealed the den with his signet ring, as well as with his noblemen's signet ring—an extra guarantee, perhaps, that the king himself would not undo the deed and then reseal the den under cover of darkness. Nothing would be changed.

The narrator's statement of purpose, "so that nothing concerning Daniel would be changed" (6:18d[17d]), has significance beyond the literal sealing of the den. Daniel himself has not changed in the narrative; the law designed to destroy him did not alter his routine. He remained steadfast in his commitment to the law of his God. Furthermore, as the king will discover the next morning, nothing concerning Daniel changed: he was still alive after a night with the lions. His God saw to that.

c. The King's Long Night (6:19a–d[18a–d])

The narrator then reports in a main clause that the king went to his palace, where he spent a long, sleepless night. The details of the king's night are independent but circumstantial clauses, providing background information about the events (or non-events) of his night (6:19b–d[18b–d]). He did not eat. Many translations say he fasted (e.g., NASB, ESV, KJV), which is possible—but the Aramaic simply says he "passed the night hungrily" (cf. "without eating," NIV, NET), and it is possible that he simply had no appetite given his deep distress. No entertainment was brought to relax him. He spent the night wide awake and worried about Daniel's fate—a concern the reader shares since the narrator increased suspense by following Darius to his palace instead of following Daniel into the lions' den.[56]

---

56. Newsom, *Daniel*, 198.

5. The Triumph of Daniel's God (6:20a–25g[19a–24g])

Main Idea of the Passage

Daniel 6:20–25[19–24] reveals the triumph of Daniel's God as the living God, the one who is able to deliver his faithful servant from the jaws of the hungry lions because of his trust in God. Daniel's innocence before God and king is proclaimed, and Darius punishes the conspirators.

Literary Context

Daniel 6:20–25[19–24] is the fifth section of the ch. 6 narrative. It follows the recounting of Darius's sleepless night of worry while Daniel was in the lions' den. In its broader literary context, this section functions in at least four ways. First, it is the climax of the chapter's plotline since it discloses what happened to Daniel after he was cast into the lions' den. It is also the culmination of the chapter's description of Daniel's faithfulness; he credits his deliverance to his innocence before God and Darius, and the narrator adds that Daniel was unharmed because of his trust in God. Third, the section brings full circle the chapter's wordplay and thematic use of the verb שׁכח, "to find," in its description of Daniel's innocence. Finally, it also includes some of the chapter's denouement in its detailing of what happened to Daniel's enemies in the aftermath of his deliverance.

> E. Narrative 5: God's Superior Law and His Servant's Faithfulness (6:2a–29[1a–28])
> 1. God's Servant in Darius's Service (6:2a–5f[1a–4f])
> 2. The Establishment of an Inferior Human Law (6:6a–10[5a–9])
> 3. Daniel's Faithfulness to God's Law (6:11a–15f[10a–14f])
> 4. The Enforcement of an Inferior Law (6:16a–19d[15a–18d])
> → **5. The Triumph of Daniel's God (6:20a–25g[19a–24g])**
> 6. The Superior God and His Faithful Servant (6:26a–29[25a–28])

Translation and Exegetical Outline

(See pages 326–27.)

Daniel 6:20a–25g[19a–24g]

20[19]a	בֵּאדַ֙יִן֙ מַלְכָּ֔א בִּשְׁפַּרְפָּרָ֖א יְק֣וּם בְּנָגְהָ֑א	→ Then arising at daybreak, at dawn,	5. The Triumph of Daniel's God (6:20a–25g[19a–24g])
20[19]b	וּבְהִ֨תְבְּהָלָ֔ה לְגֻבָּ֥א דִֽי־אַרְיָוָתָ֖א אֲזַֽל׃	the king went with haste to the lions' den.	a. The King's Urgent Question (6:20a–21g [19a–20g])
21[20]a	→ וּכְמִקְרְבֵ֣הּ לְגֻבָּ֔א	→ As he drew near to the den,	
21[20]b	לְדָ֣נִיֵּ֔אל בְּקָ֥ל עֲצִ֖יב זְעִ֑ק	he cried out to Daniel with a troubled voice.	
21[20]c	→ עָנֵ֤ה	→ Responding,	
21[20]d	מַלְכָּא֙ וְאָמַ֣ר לְדָנִיֵּ֔אל	the king said to Daniel,	
21[20]eα	דָּֽנִיֵּאל֙ עֲבֵ֣ד אֱלָהָ֣א חַיָּ֔א ...	"Daniel, servant of the living God, ...	
21[20]f	↑ אֱלָהָ֗ךְ דִּ֣י אַ֤נְתְּ (אַנְתָּה) פָּֽלַֽח־לֵהּ֙ בִּתְדִירָ֔א	↑ has your God, whom you serve continually	
21[20]eβ	הַיְכִ֥ל לְשֵׁיזָבוּתָ֖ךְ ...	... been able	
21[20]g	↑ מִן־אַרְיָוָתָֽא׃	↑ to deliver you from the lions?"	
22[21]a	אֱדַ֙יִן֙ דָּנִיֵּ֔אל עִם־מַלְכָּ֖א מַלִּ֑ל	Then Daniel with the king spoke,	
22[21]b	מַלְכָּ֖א לְעָלְמִ֥ין חֱיִֽי׃	"O king, live forever!	b. God's Deliverance of His Faithful Servant (6:22a–23e[21a–22e])
23[22]a	אֱלָהִ֗י שְׁלַ֤ח מַלְאֲכֵהּ֙	My God sent his angel,	
23[22]b	וּֽסֲגַ֖ר פֻּ֣ם אַרְיָוָתָ֑א	and he shut the mouth of the lions,	
23[22]c	וְלָ֣א חַבְּל֔וּנִי	and they did not harm me.	
23[22]d	כָּל־קֳבֵ֗ל דִּ֤י קָֽדָמ֙וֹהִי֙ זָכוּ֙ הִשְׁתְּכַ֣חַת לִ֔י	→ Inasmuch as before him I was found to be innocent,	
23[22]e	וְאַ֤ף (קָֽדָמָךְ) מַלְכָּ֔א חֲבוּלָ֖ה לָ֥א עַבְדֵֽת׃	so also before you, O king, I have not done harm."	

c. The King's New Orders (6:24a–25g[23a–24g])

(1) Orders Concerning Daniel (6:24a–f[23a–f])

24[23]a	בֵּאדַ֣יִן מַלְכָּ֔א שַׂגִּ֥יא טְאֵ֖ב עֲלֹ֑והִי	Then the king was exceedingly glad concerning him,
24[23]b	וּלְדָנִיֵּ֕אל אֲמַ֖ר	and he gave the order concerning Daniel
24[23]c	לְהַנְסָקָ֣ה מִן־גֻּבָּ֑א	to bring up from the den.
24[23]d	וְהֻסַּ֤ק דָּֽנִיֵּאל֙ מִן־גֻּבָּ֔א	So Daniel was brought up from the den,
24[23]e	וְכָל־חֲבָ֖ל לָא־הִשְׁתְּכַ֣ח בֵּ֑הּ	and no harm was found on him,
24[23]f	דִּ֥י הֵימִ֖ן בֵּאלָהֵֽהּ׃	who had trusted in his God.
25[24]a	וַאֲמַ֣ר מַלְכָּ֗א	The king gave the order
25[24]b	וְהַיְתִ֞יו גֻּבְרַיָּ֤א אִלֵּךְ֙	and they brought those men
25[24]c	דִּֽי־אֲכַ֤לוּ קַרְצֹ֙והִי֙ דִּ֣י דָֽנִיֵּ֔אל	who accused Daniel,
25[24]d	וּלְג֤וֹב אַרְיָוָתָא֙ רְמ֔וֹ אִנּ֖וּן בְּנֵיהֹ֥ון וּנְשֵׁיהֹ֑ון	and they threw them, their sons, and their wives to the lions' den.
25[24]e	וְלָֽא־מְט֞וֹ לְאַרְעִ֣ית גֻּבָּ֗א	They did not reach the bottom of the den
25[24]f	עַ֣ד דִּֽי־שְׁלִ֤טֽוּ בְהֹון֙ אַרְיָ֣וָתָ֔א	before the lions overpowered them
25[24]g	וְכָל־גַּרְמֵיהֹ֖ון הַדִּֽקוּ׃	and crushed all their bones.

(2) Orders Concerning the Conspirators (6:25a–g[24a–g])

1. See on 2:5 in the commentary.

Structure and Literary Form

The fifth section of the narrative in ch. 6 (6:20–25[19–24]) describes the triumph of Daniel's God in three subsections: 6:20–21[19–20]), 22–23[21–22], and 24–25[23–24].

In the first subsection (6:20–21[19–20]), which begins with the transitional marker בֵּאדַיִן, "then," the narrator describes the king hurrying to the den at first light and, in reported speech, his cry to Daniel about whether his God had delivered him. The second subsection (6:22–23[21–22]) also begins with the transitional אֱדַיִן, "then," and is the reported speech of Daniel in response to the king. The third subsection begins with בֵּאדַיִן, "then," and reports the king's relief (6:24a[23a]) and his issuance of two sets of orders in light of the events at the lions' den: first, he orders Daniel brought up from the den, and when he emerges, no harm is found on him (6:24b–f[23b–f]); then he orders the conspirators thrown into the den, where they are destroyed before reaching the bottom (6:25[24]).

Explanation of the Text

a. The King's Urgent Question (6:20a–21g[19a–20g])

The fifth section of the narrative begins with a clause that is both temporal and repetitive in its reference to time: "arising at daybreak, at dawn" (בִּשְׁפַּרְפָּרָא יְקוּם בְּנָגְהָא, 6:20a[19a]).[57] The narrator's repetition highlights the emotional state of the king. He has spent a sleepless night worried about Daniel, and as soon as it was light enough to find his way to the den of lions, he did. The main clause in 6:20b[19b] adds to the portrayal of his emotional state: he went "with haste." The king cannot get there fast enough.

The next main clause and its subordinate clause only add to this depiction of the king's desperation. Before he even gets to the den ("as he drew near to the den," 6:21a[20a]), he cries out (זְעִק) in a troubled voice (בְּקָל עֲצִיב) to Daniel. The narrator is providing a lot of detail in order to depict the king's desperate emotional state. He is distraught and worried. While the narrative is about Daniel (see above on 6:4–5[3–4] and 6:11[10]), it is also about Darius—and specifically his concern for Daniel (cf. 6:15[16] and 6:19[18]).

The king's words to Daniel are a near repetition of his words to Daniel the night before (6:21e–g[20e–g]; cf. 6:17f–h[16f–h]). There he had expressed his desire, his hope, that Daniel's God might deliver him. Here he asks whether Daniel's God has been able to deliver him. It is possible that Darius's belief, slight though it was, that Daniel

---

57. Translators deal differently with the imperfect + perfect verb combination (יְקוּם . . . אֲזַל) in 6:20a–b[19a–b]. My understanding here is based on Li, *The Verbal System of the Aramaic of Daniel*, 106. Also, although "king" is in the first clause (6:20a[19a]), in my translation it is in the second clause (6:20b[19b]) for ease of reading.

might be alive aligns with an ancient Near Eastern custom of allowing the gods to determine one's guilt or innocence. People accused of wrongdoing underwent "an ordeal," and if the tortuous experience killed them, they were guilty. If they survived, then the gods had found them innocent and so spared their lives. (Daniel himself will declare that his God found him innocent and so sent his angel to spare his life; 6:22–23[21–22].) But if this were the case, we might have expected Darius to ask a question that better reflects his statement from the night before. There he had said, "May he [your God] deliver you" (הוּא יְשֵׁיזְבִנָּךְ, 6:17f–h[16f–h]). The logical follow-up question in the morning would be "Did your God deliver you?" But this is not what Darius asks. He asks if Daniel's God had been *able* to deliver him—that is, did he have the power to deliver him from what was certain death? Darius's question recalls Nebuchadnezzar's challenge to Shadrach, Meshach, and Abednego in ch. 3: "Who is a god who will deliver you from my hand?" (3:15). Nebuchadnezzar had scorned the idea that any god could deliver someone from his power; Darius clung to the hope that Daniel's God could.

The first word Darius shouts into the lions' den is "Daniel!" He then calls Daniel "servant of the living God" (6:21eα[20eα]). Neither of these vocatives is required by the narrative; the narrator has already said the king is addressing Daniel (6:21c[20c]). The purpose of both, then, is to provide important information about how Darius regards Daniel.[58] With respect to calling him "Daniel," Darius is the first (and only) king in the book to address the captive by his Hebrew name. Daniel had long ago been renamed (1:7), and although Nebuchadnezzar—the one who likely ordered the new name—knew his Hebrew name and referred to him using it, he only ever directly addresses him in the narrative as "Belteshazzar" (see 4:5–6[8–9], 15–16[18–19]; cf. 5:13). Perhaps the name "Belteshazzar" fell away with the death of Nebuchadnezzar (or the fall of his kingdom decades later), but Darius's use of Daniel's Hebrew name nonetheless suggests a warmth toward and acceptance of the man who worshiped his foreign (to Darius) God so faithfully.

In terms of calling him "servant of the living God," Darius shows a respect for Daniel's God before he even knows whether Daniel is alive. This is remarkable for several reasons. Nebuchadnezzar had said some praiseworthy things about Israel's God—but only *after* he witnessed his wisdom (2:47), power (3:28–29), and ability to humble the proud (3:32–33[4:2–3]; 4:31–34[34–37]). By contrast, Darius utters a powerful epithet for Israel's God that is well known in the Old Testament but is only ever spoken by his followers: "the living God."[59] Goldingay explains the significance of the name: "This rich OT title for God suggests not merely that God is alive rather than dead but that he is active and powerful, awesome and almighty, involved in bringing judgment and blessing. The title is appealed to when human beings are inclined to slight him or to doubt him in situations of pressure and weakness."[60] In using this title, Darius proclaims Daniel's God as the true God, in contrast to the lifeless idols of the nations—a remarkable statement on the lips of a gentile king. Darius's use of this thematically loaded title also hints at what's to come in the narrative. Goldingay says it "builds

---

58. Runge and Westbury, *LDHB: Introduction*, 2.3 Thematic Address.

59. See, e.g., Deut 5:26 (Moses); Josh 3:10 (Joshua); 1 Sam 17:26 (David); and 2 Kgs 19:16 (Hezekiah).

60. Goldingay, *Daniel*, 322.

up our expectation regarding what we are about to discover."[61]

In the next clause (6:21f[20f]) Darius again overspecifies Daniel's God as the one he serves continually (see on 6:17[16] above). In the estimation of Darius, Daniel's defining characteristic is that he serves his God faithfully, another reminder that Daniel and his example are central to the chapter.

b. God's Deliverance of His Faithful Servant (6:22a–23e[21a–22e])

Daniel calls back to the king in his only reported speech of the entire narrative. He begins with proper royal protocol, "O king, live forever!" (6:22[21]), the only time in the book that a Judean addresses a king in this way. He reports that his God (6:23a[22a]) sent his angel who shut the lions' mouth (פֻּם, 6:23b[22b]). The conspirators had seen to it that the mouth (פֻּם) of the den had been sealed, guaranteeing that "nothing concerning Daniel would be changed" (6:18b–d[17b–d]), but what the conspirators had no control over was the mouth of the lions. Ironically the conspirators' attempt to see that nothing concerning Daniel would be changed is exactly what happened: *nothing* had changed. Daniel had spent the night confined to the den with the hungry lions. Daniel still served his God faithfully. He was still alive. He was not even harmed—that is, nothing on his body had even changed. Darius probably went ahead with his promotion as planned. Nothing had changed.

Daniel reports that the lions had not harmed him (חַבְּלוּנִי, 6:23c[22c]). Then he claims both his innocence before God (6:23d[22d]) and before Darius; just as the lions had not harmed him, he had not done harm (חֲבוּלָה, 6:23e[22e]) to the king. Longman notes the irony: "the administrators who urged the king to create this law were actually disloyal to Darius, working against his own desires and intentions, whereas Daniel, who finds himself under the judgment of the law, is actually the most true of his subordinates."[62]

No more is said in the narrative of the angel sent by God to shut the lions' mouths. Whether it was the angel of YHWH or a messenger angel we do not know, but like the fourth figure in the furnace with Shadrach, Meshach, and Abednego, this figure's presence makes clear that God was present with his faithful servant in distress.

c. The King's New Orders (6:24a–25g[23a–24g])

Again the narrator reports the king's emotions. In contrast to his great distress earlier (שַׂגִּיא בְּאֵשׁ, 6:15aβ[14aβ]), he now has great gladness on account of Daniel (שַׂגִּיא טְאֵב, 6:24a[23a]). Then he issues two new sets of orders. The first concerns Daniel (6:24b–c[23b–c]), and the second concerns the conspirators, "those men" (גֻּבְרַיָּא אִלֵּךְ, 6:25a–d[24a–d]; see on 6:6a[5a], 12a[11a], 16a[15a]).

With respect to Daniel, Darius orders him brought up from the den. The orders are followed (6:24d[23d]), and like Shadrach, Meshach, and Abednego before him, Daniel comes out unscathed (כָּל־חֲבָל לָא־הִשְׁתְּכַח בֵּהּ, "no harm was found on him," 6:24e[23e]; cf. 3:26–27). This is the last occurrence of the verbal root שׁכח, "to find," in the narrative.

---

61. Ibid.

62. Longman, *Daniel*, 166.

"Finding" has been a key theme in the narrative beginning in 6:5[4], where the conspirators attempt to find (לְהַשְׁכָּחָה [2x], הַשְׁתְּכַחַת) fault with Daniel in his professional capacities. When they deem this impossible, they decide they must find (הַשְׁכַּחְנָה) his fault related to the law of his God (6:6[5]). After they concoct the law and coerce the king into signing it, they find (הַשְׁכַּחוּ) exactly what they need to in Daniel's routine (6:12[11]). But at the end of the ordeal, Daniel is found (הִשְׁתְּכַחַת) innocent by God (6:23d[22d]), and no harm is found (הִשְׁתְּכַח) on him (6:24e[23e]).[63] Although his enemies did everything to malign his character and destroy his body, they failed. Just as he was found innocent, he is now found unmarred. He is whole in body and character.

Then the narrator further describes Daniel as one "who had trusted in his God" (דִּי הֵימִן בֵּאלָהֵהּ, 6:24f[23f]). This too brings full circle a key theme of the chapter—name, the integrity and faithfulness of Daniel. The conspirators had been thwarted in their original plans to find fault with Daniel because "he was trustworthy" (מְהֵימַן הוּא, 6:5[4]), and here he trusted in his God and was delivered. We should not infer from this that trusting in God leads to deliverance from deadly circumstances. God is never obligated to rescue us. For his own purposes he did spare Daniel from the lions and Shadrach, Meshach, and Abednego from the furnace. But he did not have to. Seow notes that these stories "are not meant to be read as tales that assure one of God's deliverance in times of trial, for in each case the faithful are not delivered from their trials, and the response of the human heroes of these stories is never contingent upon any assurance of divine salvation."[64] In this chapter, the statement about Daniel's trust in God is another reminder that Daniel is central to the chapter. This chapter is about Daniel's faithfulness.

The king's second set of orders was that "those men" (גֻּבְרַיָּא אִלֵּךְ, 6:25a–d[24a–d]) who accused[65] Daniel be brought and cast into the den of lions. The entire lot of them,[66] along with their children and wives, was thrown to the lions, who were so vicious that they destroyed the conspirators before they ever hit the bottom.[67] John Calvin says this gruesome detail points to the greatness of God's salvation: "For if any one should say that the lions were satisfied, or there was any other reason why Daniel was not destroyed, why, when he was withdrawn, did such great madness immediately impel those beasts to tear and devour."[68]

---

63. On the wordplay and use of בעה/בעא, "to seek," and שׁכח, "to find" in the narrative of ch. 6, see above on 6:5[4].

64. Seow, *Daniel*, 87.

65. The Aramaic describing the conspirators' action here is the same as in ch. 3: אֲכַלוּ קַרְצוֹהִי, "they ate the pieces" of Daniel. See on Dan 3:8 above.

66. The sheer number of people involved here suggests that the group of conspirators did not include all 122 satraps and administrators. It would be difficult to cast such a mob into the lions' den. The actual group that had it out for Daniel was probably relatively small (note that the group in the Greek includes two officials and their wives and children). But allowing the reader to assume all the overseers and satraps conspired against Daniel contributes to the narrator's portrayal that *everyone* was against Daniel and his God.

67. The thought of punishing women and children is repugnant to us, but ancient customs such as this emphasized corporate responsibility. Compare the account of Achan in Josh 7.

68. Calvin, *Daniel*, 386.

6. The Superior God and His Faithful Servant (6:26a–29[25a–28])

Main Idea of the Passage

In Daniel 6:26–29[25–28]) Darius issues a second written document, this time extolling the superiority of Daniel's God for his indestructible kingdom and his unsurpassed power to deliver. Daniel continues to succeed in the royal court of Media and Persia.

Literary Context

Daniel 6:26–29[25–28]) is the final section of the Dan 6 narrative, and as such, it functions in at least four ways in its broader literary context. First, it presents the rest of the chapter's denouement (see on 6:20–25[19–24] above) in Darius's proclamation of praise for Daniel's God and the narrator's closing statement about Daniel's continued success. Second, as the second document associated with Darius in the chapter, it creates a contrast between his earlier inferior law and his declaration here. A third function of the section is to set up a comparison and contrast between Darius and his proclamation and the earlier proclamation of Nebuchadnezzar in the aftermath of his humbling (3:32–33[4:2–3]). Finally, the doxological content of Darius's proclamation draws together prominent themes from the book's narrative chapters in order to prepare the reader for what follows in the apocalyptic chapters.

> E. Narrative 5: God's Superior Law and His Servant's Faithfulness (6:2a–29[1a–28])
>   1. God's Servant in Darius's Service (6:2a–5f[1a–4f])
>   2. The Establishment of an Inferior Human Law (6:6a–10[5a–9])
>   3. Daniel's Faithfulness to God's Law (6:11a–15f[10a–14f])
>   4. The Enforcement of an Inferior Law (6:16a–19d[15a–18d])
>   5. The Triumph of Daniel's God (6:20a–25g[19a–24g])
>   ➡ **6. The Superior God and His Faithful Servant (6:26a–29[25a–28])**

Translation and Exegetical Outline

(See page 334.)

Structure and Literary Form

The sixth and final section of the narrative in ch. 6 (6:26–29[25–28]) emphasizes the superiority of Daniel's God and the success of his servant Daniel. It consists of two subsections: 6:26–28[25–27] and 6:29[28]. The first begins with the transitional בֵּאדַיִן, "then," and consists of the narrator's statement that Darius issued a proclamation to his subjects (6:26a–b[25a–b]) and the reported speech of the king himself, recounting the greatness and superiority of Daniel's God, who rescued Daniel from the lions (6:26c–28d[25c–27d]). The second subsection is the narrator's statement that Daniel prospered in his continued service to the royal court (6:29[28]).

Explanation of the Text

a. The Decree of Darius (6:26a–28d[25a–27d])

The final section concludes the narrative with a decree from Darius. In his decree Darius extols the person and work of Daniel's God, a doxology that the narrator uses to weave together several thematic threads about God's interaction with gentile kings from the narrative chapters.

The narrator changes his reference for Darius, calling him דָּרְיָוֶשׁ מַלְכָּא, "Darius the king" (6:26a[25a]), for the only time in the chapter.[69] This changed reference may be less about recharacterizing an established character or highlighting thematically important information (as changed references typically are[70]) and more about connecting this section with an earlier narrative in the book: namely, Nebuchadnezzar's declaration about the greatness of the Most High in light of the signs and wonders he had done in Nebuchadnezzar's life (3:31–4:34[4:1–37]). Except for the addition of the verb כְּתַב, "[he] wrote," in ch. 6, Nebuchadnezzar's opening words (3:31[4:1]) and Darius's are the same:

- Dan 3:31[4:1] reads נְבוּכַדְנֶצַּר מַלְכָּא לְכָל־עַמְמַיָּא אֻמַּיָּא וְלִשָּׁנַיָּא דִּי־דָיְרִין בְּכָל־אַרְעָא שְׁלָמְכוֹן יִשְׂגֵּא, "Nebuchadnezzar the king to all peoples, nations, and languages, which live in all the earth: May your peace increase!"

---

69. See on 6:10[9] above.
70. Runge and Westbury, *LDHB: Glossary*, 2.6 Changed Reference.

Daniel 6:26a–29[25a–28]

26[25]a		Then Darius the king wrote to all peoples, nations, and languages,
26[25]b		← which were living in all the land:
26[25]c		"May your peace abound!
27[26]a		By me a decree is made
27[26]b		that in the whole dominion of my kingdom they must tremble and fear before the God of Daniel—
27[26]c		who is the living and enduring God forever,
27[26]d		and whose kingdom will not be destroyed,
27[26]e		and whose dominion is until the end.
28[27]a		He delivers,
28[27]b		and he rescues,
28[27]c		and he does signs and wonders in the heavens and on the earth—
28[27]d		← who has delivered Daniel from the power of the lions."
29[30]		Then this Daniel prospered in the reign of Darius, that is, in the reign of Cyrus the Persian.

6. The Superior God and His Faithful Servant (6:26a–29[25a–28])
   a. The Decree of Darius (6:26a–28d[25a–27d])

   b. The Success of Daniel (6:29[28])

- Dan 6:26[25] reads דָּרְיָ֣וֶשׁ מַלְכָּ֗א כְּתַב֙ לְכָֽל־עַֽמְמַיָּ֣א אֻמַּיָּ֤א וְלִשָּֽׁנַיָּא֙ דִּֽי־דָיְרִ֣ין בְּכָל־אַרְעָ֔א שְׁלָמְכ֖וֹן יִשְׂגֵּֽא "Darius the king wrote to all peoples, nations, and languages, which were living in all the land: May your peace abound!"

What would be the purpose of connecting these two accounts? While both gentile kings witness amazing acts of Israel's God and both respond appropriately, Darius's response goes beyond that of his predecessor. When Nebuchadnezzar had witnessed God's superior wisdom (ch. 2) and then his deliverance of his faithful servants from the fiery furnace (ch. 3), he acknowledged God's wisdom and power in each circumstance, but his most fervent expression of the greatness of the Most High only came after God humbled him in dramatic fashion (ch. 4). By contrast, Darius witnessed God's deliverance of his faithful servant from the lions' den and praised him for his surpassing greatness and sovereignty; he needed no humbling hand of God in his life to render the praise due the Most High.

As noted, Nebuchadnezzar's opening words there (3:31[4:1]) and Darius's here are the same except for the addition of the verb כְּתַב, "[he] wrote," in the ch. 6 version. Elsewhere in ch. 6, this root occurs in nominal form three times: כְּתָבָא, "document." It is the document the conspirators want Darius to sign (6:9[8]), which he does (6:10[9]), and when Daniel hears of it (6:11[10]), he goes to his house and prays. A verb was not needed in the narrative of ch. 4 since Nebuchadnezzar was recounting his proclamation in the first person, and his format follows that of Aramaic letters, while the narrator introduces Darius's proclamation in the third person. However, the verb choice of כתב seems intentional in a chapter consumed with a כְּתָבָא signed by the same king who issues another piece of writing at chapter's end.[71] In this second document, Darius will make an amazing declaration about the God whose law far surpassed his.

The king's decree is a tapestry of themes from earlier chapters, woven together to display God's sole claim to sovereignty.[72] In Nebuchadnezzar's statue dream of ch. 2, the indestructible kingdom of God first entered the narrative (cf. 6:27d[26d]). God's enduring dominion is also a key theme of ch. 2, as the rock crushed the magnificent statue representing human kingdoms (cf. 6:27e[26e]). In the aftermath of his second dream in ch. 4, Nebuchadnezzar praised the Most High for his eternal dominion as he proclaimed the signs and wonders he had done for the Babylonian king (cf. 6:27c[26c]; 6:28c[27c]). In the events of ch. 3, God's ability to rescue and deliver is central (cf. 6:28[27]).

The narrator's primary purpose in drawing together all these themes is not to summarize what has come before. Rather, *by* summarizing the themes and so recalling all the ways God demonstrated his sovereignty among gentile kings—both hostile and amicable—the narrator prepares the reader for what follows in the book: the horrors of the apocalyptic visions Daniel receives. While the time is right chronologically in the book for exile to end and restoration to begin, the remaining chapters will instead reveal a greater exile and more suffering to come. At this point in the book—that

---

71. Other choices for verbs include רשם ("to inscribe or sign," as in 6:9–10[8–9], 13–14[12–13]), שלח ("to send," as in 3:2), or שִׂים טְעֵם ("make a decree," as in 3:29 and 6:27a[26a]).

72. We do not need to assume that Darius had access to any texts that eventually became the book of Daniel, nor that he was familiar with his predecessor's encounters with the Most High. Rather, the narrator of Daniel crafts this doxology much as he did Nebuchadnezzar's proclamation in ch. 4 to capture the gist of the king's words in language that would make his theological points. See further on 3:32–33[4:2–3] above, and especially n18 there.

is, the conclusion of the narrative portion—Darius's doxology functions as the lifeline into the rest of the book. With these truths about the living God's eternal, indestructible kingdom firmly embedded, the inhabitants (nay, eventual possessors! See on 7:18 and 22 below) of his kingdom can read on with confidence that their God alone has the authority, power, and ultimate glory.

b. The Success of Daniel (6:29[28])

The narrative ends with a statement about the success of "this Daniel" in the reign of Darius. The use of the near demonstrative ("this") here is the narrator's second for Daniel (see on 6:4a[3a] above).[73] As with the earlier use, the near demonstrative indicates Daniel's central importance to the story.[74] It is one final reminder that the chapter, in addition to its other emphases, is about him.

As at the end of ch. 5, where the narrator marked the transfer of kingdoms from Babylon to Media, he marks at the end of ch. 6 the "transfer" from Darius (the Mede) to Cyrus the Persian. While Darius and Cyrus may well be the same person,[75] the kingdoms of Media and Persia are what is really important in the narrative. God is the one who raises up kings and takes them down, and according to the four-kingdom schema of history in Daniel, Persia follows Media—thus the mention of Cyrus the Persian on the heels of Daniel's service to Darius the Mede. In the theology of the book, God controls history's rise and fall of kingdoms, and at the end of ch. 6, the narrator reminds the reader that history marches on, exactly as expected and according to the divine plan.

This note about the reign of Cyrus also forms an *inclusio* with the first mention of Cyrus in the book in 1:21. Between these two references to Cyrus, the narrator of the book recounts God's interaction with three different gentile kings of the exile: Nebuchadnezzar, Belshazzar, and Darius. While Daniel's decades of service in the foreign court would have involved at least half a dozen foreign kings, the narrator is only interested in these three. Each responded differently to Daniel and to the God of Israel, but Baldwin observes that, for all their foibles, none of them persecuted God's followers in the ways Antiochus IV Epiphanes, a main character in Daniel's apocalyptic visions, would do centuries later. She notes that in these six narrative chapters, "persecution is not the point. . . . The episodes chosen demonstrate that the world's great empires, and the kings who represent them, are all subject to the God of the exiles from Judah, who made Himself known outside the land of promise as well as within it."[76] Persecution will intensify in the apocalyptic chapters, but God's people can trust—as Daniel did in the face of death—in their God. They can endure faithfully because their God is the superior king, and his kingdom alone is eternal.

---

73. The conspirators also refer to Daniel as דָּנִיֵּאל דְּנָה (v. 6b[5b]), but the near demonstrative functions differently there. See on 6:6[5] above.

74. See on 6:3[2] and n12 there.

75. See on 6:1[5:31] above for the discussion of 6:28[27] and its contribution to our understanding of the identities of Darius the Mede and Cyrus the Persian

76. Joyce G. Baldwin, *Daniel*, TOTC 21 (Downers Grove, IL: InterVarsity Press, 1978), 119.

Canonical and Theological Significance

The Value and the Valuing of Prayer

One of the main interests of Dan 6 is Daniel himself—his faithfulness to the law of God. The narrator draws attention to Daniel throughout the chapter by using the near demonstrative "this" (i.e., "this Daniel;" see on 6:4[3] and 6:29[28]), detailing his routine of prayer (see on 6:11[10]), and even through the speech of the king (see on 6:17[16] and 6:21[20]).[77] While Daniel is a main character in nearly every chapter of the book, it is only here that the narrative puts such great attention on him and his example. This chapter, among other things, is about Daniel. But what is the purpose of this emphasis both in the context of the narrative and as we consider its application to Daniel's original audience and every audience since?

First, in the narrative itself, it suggests the source of Daniel's strength. In a chapter characterized by frantic motion—the scurrying about of the conspirators and the frenzied state of Darius—Daniel is unfazed. He learns of the signed document, and he goes home and prays in front of his open window. There is no record of his thoughts or emotions when he is condemned and cast to the lions. There is no description of his thoughts or emotions the next morning. There is no description of Daniel's state of mind *anywhere*. He prays—as he always did—and then he credits God with his deliverance because of his innocence. One effect of this in the narrative is that Daniel's habit of prayer appears to be the source of his calm. He trusted in God—what fuss was there to be made about any of his circumstances?[78]

Many of us know people whose lives testify to the consistency and depth of their practice of prayer. One of those people in my life was Judy, the mother of one of my best friends. Judy once told me that whenever she prayed for her own daughters, she also prayed for me. I do not remember ever asking Judy to pray for me; she had just decided she would. I do not know what she prayed—though I could venture a few guesses—nor do I know how God answered those prayers. But isn't that the way of prayer? We pray, with varying degrees of faith, that God will do what is good and best, but we often never see what that looks like. Surely he is working in ways we do not know, but perhaps more often that work is in *us*. This was true for Judy, who spent the last few years of her life in a dark place of mental illness. Yet, even there—perhaps *especially* there—her ongoing conversation with God was the deep river that sustained her. Like Daniel, she would have faced lions rather than give

---

77. See also on 6:5[4] and 6:24[23].

78. In ch. 6 Daniel is what Berlin would call a type character—a flat character in literary terms because he shows no emotion or character development. His character is "built around a single quality or trait," in this case, his faithfulness to the law of his God (*Poetics and Interpretation of Biblical Narrative*, 23–24). See also on the characters of Nebuchadnezzar and Shadrach, Meshach, and Abednego in ch. 3.

up praying, and just as Daniel was not alone with the lions, Judy was not alone in those final years of darkness. Her years of disciplined prayer were the lifeline to her sustaining strength.

A second purpose for the narrator's focus on Daniel in the narrative is to set him up as an example—first, for his original audience, namely, Jews of the diaspora. His example of faithfulness encouraged them to be similarly faithful to God as they lived in foreign, idolatrous places.[79] His courage under trial and even his willingness to die challenged them to persevere through their own circumstances. But Daniel's example of faithful prayer and his commitment to God also challenge followers of God in every age and place, including us. Daniel valued his commitment to God and the place of prayer in that commitment so much that he was willing to die for it. I am convicted by this. When I consider how little it takes for me not to pray in a given day, how easy it is to hurry into my day without pausing to seek out the true source of wisdom and power (Dan 2–3) and gain the needed perspective prayer gives, I can only confess that I do not value prayer like Daniel did.

I do not value prayer like my friend Verna does either. As I write this, Verna is celebrating her ninetieth birthday, but she has more life in her than most people do. As a member of my home church for nearly seven decades, Verna has been part of my life's landscape for as long as I can remember, but we did not become particularly important to each other until late in 2002 when a mutual friend from church died. Eunice Evans was a prim and proper Southern gal-grown-old with a giggle and a smile that lit up the church lobby. She was also the first of my senior friends. We enjoyed a friendship that I, as a twenty-something then, did not know enough to seek out—after all, what did she and I have in common? But she had lived long enough to know better, and so introduced me to a new kind of friendship and a new generation of friends. For reasons I will never know, Eunice loved me enough to include me on one of her special and exclusive prayer lists.

When Eunice was in the slow process of dying from cancer, Verna helped care for her. Somewhere during those difficult weeks, Verna became concerned about Eunice's special prayer list—and what those so dear to Eunice would lose when she died. Prompted by the Spirit, Verna adopted Eunice's special list—and she prayed for me every day after that. She journeyed with me from afar as I plodded through graduate school degrees and then as I moved back and forth across the country in a season of career angst. We barely crossed paths after Eunice died, but Verna's daily prayers kept her close to my heart. Her prayers, generously and lovingly given "for no good reason," are testimony to the value she places on talking with God about what concerns us—or, in her case, what concerned someone else years ago.

---

79. See "History of Reception, by Brennan W. Breed," in Newsom, *Daniel*, 202–10, and especially 204–7, for specific ways Dan 6 has influenced the religious practice of both Jews and Christians.

Like Daniel, Verna's example of steadfast, unmovable prayer encourages me, and I am sure God changed things in my life along the way because she prayed. Like Daniel, her example also challenges and convicts me. She stepped into the deep river of prayer that moves from generation to generation—that *changes* generation after generation—and she stayed there. Day after day, year after year, Verna prayed. May I find the courage and commitment to do half as much.

The Life-Giving Law of God

The account in Dan 6 sets up a contrast between competing laws: the law of Daniel's God and the law designed to destroy Daniel—the law signed by Darius and governed by the immutable law of the Medes and Persians. Daniel has to choose which law to obey, but there is never a doubt in anyone's mind what he will choose.

The conspirators believed they had trapped Daniel with the law prohibiting prayer to anyone but Darius, but Daniel is the one who shows the greatest freedom of anyone in the narrative. The conspirators spend the chapter scurrying about in their determination to bring Daniel down, and ultimately they lose their lives on account of the law they concocted. Darius is trapped by his administrators and then labors in desperation to get out from under the bondage of his own law. Daniel, however, goes about his business as usual and may very well have spent that fateful night in the lions' den sleeping with a lion's belly for a pillow. Daniel is free, and Daniel thrives, despite the danger on every side (cf. Ps 3).

The דָּת, "law," that Daniel obeyed should not be understood as the Mosaic law specifically or any other official Jewish law of the time. Rather, the דָּת אֱלָהֵהּ, "law of his God," is best understood as Daniel's religious practice, the habits that kept him focused on the God of his people, YHWH. Obviously, Daniel's practice included prayer, but we also know that he spent time reading and reflecting on the words of YHWH spoken through Jeremiah (Dan 9:2).

The narrator does not explicitly tell us *why* Daniel did this, nor does he allow Daniel to voice the reasons for his dissenting action in Dan 6—as Luke does in Acts 5 when Peter and the apostles refuse to stop teaching in the name of Jesus ("We must obey God rather than human beings!" Acts 5:29); or as the narrator of Gen 39 does when Joseph refuses Potiphar's wife ("How then could I do such a wicked thing and sin against God?" Gen 39:9); or even as the narrator of Daniel does when Shadrach, Meshach, and Abednego defy the king with their declaration of allegiance to the God who may or may not save them (Dan 3:16–18). Daniel says very little in this chapter, and his emotions are never described by the narrator.[80] While Daniel is indeed a

---

80. For Daniel's only reported speech, see above on 6:22–23 [21–22]. By contrast, the speech and emotions of the conspirators and of Darius are of great interest to the narrator, and through both he allows the reader to see the thoughts and

central interest of the chapter,[81] the narrator is less interested in Daniel as a *person* than in Daniel as an *example*—and specifically as an example of faithfulness to God and the effects of such faithfulness. Rather than *telling* us what Daniel thought of the law and the consequences of his disobedience, the narrator *shows* us the results of Daniel's faithful obedience: freedom and life.

But that is what obedience to God always brings. *True* freedom and *everlasting* life. Since the giving of the first "law" from God—"You are free to eat from any tree in the garden; but you must not eat from the tree of the knowledge of good and evil, for when you eat from it you will certainly die" (Gen 2:16–17)—obedience has been the path to freedom and life. Disobedience, the path more often taken, has always been the path to bondage and death. As the creator of human beings, God knows what makes us flourish, and he provided the guidelines to make it possible. Choosing the right "law" leads to freedom and life.

We should not think that this means obeying God leads to an easy life or deliverance from whatever distresses or oppresses us—although the prosperity gospel gains many followers on the basis of this wrong belief. Whether we consciously adhere to the "health and wealth" gospel or not, many of us still assume things should go well for people who confess Jesus as Lord and try to live like he is. We see the examples of Daniel and his three friends, who, the Bible makes a point to say, were faithful to God, who then delivered them from death. Isn't there page after page in the Bible that supports the idea that God blesses those who are faithful?

Yes—but we need to read the Bible (and especially the Old Testament) more carefully before we assume such a pattern applies to us. Much of the belief that God prospers faithful followers derives from misinterpreting the Old Testament. The old covenant between God and national Israel *did* include the promise that keeping Torah would result in the blessing of rain and fertile crops, while breaking the covenant would result in drought, blight, pestilence, and threats to safety. But this promise of material blessing was part of the old covenant. Under the new covenant, the promise of eschatological salvation supersedes any promise of "health and wealth" in the present. Will God bless us if we obey him? Yes—but we might have to wait to enjoy that blessing.

Most of us would have to admit, if we are honest, that we believe if we are "good Christians," God will make it worth our while in the present.[82] We probably also

---

motivations of the gentile characters. See on vv. 6[5], 7–9[6–8], 13–14[12–13], 15[14], 16[15], 17[16], 19–21[18–20], 24a[23a], 26–28[25–27].

81. See above on vv. 4[3], 5[4], 11[10]), 17[16], 21[20], 24[23], 29[28]; see also The Value and the Valuing of Prayer (pp. 337–39).

82. Job's friends illustrate this belief in reverse: if you sin, then God will curse you. Because Job appeared to be cursed, he had obviously sinned grossly.

then believe that when things do not go as hoped or expected, God is just testing our patience and endurance—he surely has something better (as we define it) for us. Eventually, he will come through for us and bless us with what we really want. It will all be worth the wait.

I heard this bad theology often in my single twenties when well-meaning friends promised me that God had someone wonderful for me. I heard it again in my career-challenged forties when loving friends assured me that God had the perfect job for my training, gifts, and passions. They assumed that since I was doing my best to follow God, he would fulfill my desires.

As it turned out, in his lavish grace God *did* bring me a wonderful husband in his own sweet (and I do mean that) time. Not unexpectedly, some friends commented how wonderful it was that God had "rewarded" me after so long, as if I somehow earned a prize. I did not, and he has not. I did not somehow deserve to get married because I did something good, nor did my life need to go this way for God to be considered faithful. Godly people remain single, despite their deepest desires. Faithful God-followers find themselves unemployed or underemployed. Devoted Christians lose their health and wealth. People who love God lose their spouses to death or divorce as often as those who do not care a whit about obeying God. Committed Christian parents watch their children walk away from the faith, never to return. Nowhere in the Bible are we authorized to promise suffering people that God must have something "better" when life disappoints or devastates us.

The truth is that sometimes the life of obedience leads in quite the opposite direction than our "happiness" or comfort. Just ask Job. Or Paul. Or even Daniel. Faithful followers of Jesus Christ will suffer in this life, and some much more than others. But the gospel redeems all things—even suffering. In ways we cannot begin to fathom, God can bring beauty and benefit out of suffering. He probably will not do it in ways we might define as "better"—like a coveted job or a clean bill of health—but God is nonetheless working a greater plan that transcends our individual circumstances. Suffering is a training ground for his children (Heb 12:5–13); suffering is a way he demonstrates his grace to us (2 Chr 32:24–26, 31); suffering is a means by which he can display his power to the world (John 9:1–3; 2 Cor 12:7–10).[83]

Prior to authoring two books about grace, Jerry Sittser lost his family in a tragic accident. He writes about the concept of living "happily ever after":

> Eventually, we will live happily ever after, but only when the redemptive story ends, which seems a long way off. In the meantime, you and I are somewhere in the middle

---

83. We do sometimes bring suffering on ourselves (e.g., Prov 1:31; 1 Cor 11:30; Jas 5:15–16), and some suffering is simply part of living in a fallen world—no one is exempt (Gen 3:16–19; Isa 33:24).

of the story, as if stuck in the chaos and messiness of a half-finished home improvement project. We might have one chapter left in our story, or we might have fifty. We could experience more of the same for years to come, or we could be on the verge of a change so dramatic that if we knew about it we would faint with fear or wonder, or perhaps both. We could be entering the happiest phase of our lives, or the saddest. We simply don't know and can't know.[84]

We cannot predict the future, much less control it. What we can do is what Daniel did. Be faithful to the דָּת אֱלָהּ, "law of God." Maintain the habits of talking and listening to God. Be steadfast, no matter what. Believe that trusting in God leads to everlasting life and live in the freedom of obedience to the God who makes it possible.[85]

Suffering for Something

Much of the suffering we endure in life results from living in a fallen world. Often we can find no one to blame for it except, if we dare, God. In his inscrutable providence, he allows disappointment, disaster, and premature death. Being committed to him in the midst of such pain can test our faithfulness.

But a great deal suffering in the world is inflicted by others. Worse, much of this pain comes to people who are simply trying to do what is right before God, and worst, it comes *because* they are simply trying to do what is right. This was certainly the case for Daniel and for Joseph before him. Joseph refused to give in to the advances of Potiphar's wily wife on the grounds that he could not sin against his master and against God (Gen 39:9). The scorned woman then falsely accused him before her husband, and Joseph was sent to prison. Daniel refused to compromise his commitment to God when his colleagues plotted against him, and it landed him in the lions' den. Both men were going about their business with excellence and integrity (Gen 39:2–6; Dan 6:4–6[3–5]), and then one day, doing what was right before God nearly cost them everything. Although the text of Dan 3 does not emphasize the excellence and integrity of Shadrach, Meshach, and Abednego, the three men also nearly lost their lives for doing what was right before God.

The suffering of the four Judean captives in Babylon differed from Joseph's situa-

---

84. Jerry Sittser, *A Grace Revealed* (Grand Rapids: Zondervan, 2012), 260.

85. Towner's words about Daniel's faithfulness and taking the long view of God's deliverance are apt: "Viewed from the perspective of God's coming victory, all faithfulness whatever, and all the good that has ever been wrought, are vindicated. In this light, the salvation of good and trusting Daniel from the lions' den is an anticipation of the rescue from destruction by God's own transcendent power of God's people. . . . Daniel is . . . a man of the present age, like ourselves, who by trust and steadfastness gives a hint of the way in which believers can deport themselves now even as they draw strength from the certainty of God's coming great victory" (*Daniel*, 86).

tion in at least one significant way: Daniel and his three friends were forced to violate the law of the state in their commitment to do what was right. Nebuchadnezzar had issued an order that everyone at the ceremony bow before his golden image; if they refused, they would be thrown into the fiery furnace (Dan 3:4–6). Darius's law stipulated that anyone who prayed to a god or man other than the king would be thrown into the lions' den (Dan 6:8–10[7–9]). Maintaining their commitment to God put the four men in positions where they had to disobey the law of the land or compromise their commitment to God.

Countless followers of God have faced this same choice throughout the centuries, and certainly it still faces Christians in many parts of the world today. This is not yet the case where I live, but if some people have their way, religious freedom in America and in the West more broadly will be severely restricted. As culture becomes increasingly secular, pluralistic, and tolerant, hostility toward Christians will grow because, although a pluralist culture claims that all beliefs are legitimate, it does not really mean it. Ironically, the one thing that pluralists cannot tolerate is *in*tolerance or exclusivity, and Christianity's claims that Christ is the only way of salvation and that the Bible reveals God's absolute truth are decidedly exclusive. We cannot help but be "intolerant" of other belief systems.[86] As such, we can be perceived as dangerous, a threat to the prevailing way of life and to other people's freedom.

Consider the story of Barronelle Stutzman, a Washington state florist who was going about her business of arranging flowers with excellence and integrity, when one day doing what she believed to be right before God cost her greatly.[87] When long-time gay customer Rob Ingersoll asked her to do flowers for his wedding, Stutzman says she "walked him to a private part of my shop, took his hand in mine, told him why I couldn't do what he asked, and referred him to three other florists who I knew would do a good job. Rob said that he understood, and we hugged before he left."[88]

If not for social media, Rob and his partner may well have found a florist for their special occasion and then returned to Stutzman's shop for business after their wedding. But when Rob's partner posted something on Facebook about Stutzman's decision, the hate mail, nasty phone calls, and even death threats started rolling in.[89]

---

86. How we express this "intolerance," however, is critical and a topic worth considering in its own right and in light of the life and ministry of Jesus.

87. Stutzman's case was settled in November 2021 after nearly a decade of wrangling. I say she "was doing what she believed to be right before God" rather than "what was right before God" because not all Christians take the same position on how business owners ought to interact with issues such as Mrs. Stutzman faced. She acted according to her conscience and convictions before God.

88. Barronelle Stutzman, "Washington state florist: My life has been turned upside down because of my religious beliefs," Fox News, Published 29 June 2018, http://www.foxnews.com/opinion/2018/06/29/washington-state-florist-my-life-has-been-turned-upside-down-because-my-religious-beliefs.html.

89. "Barronelle awaits outcome of cake artist's Supreme Court case," Alliance Defending Freedom, (no date): http://www.adflegal.org/freedom-in-america.

The "news" made its way to the Washington attorney general, who decided to make an example of Stutzman. According to Stutzman, he

> has relentlessly—and on his own initiative—come after me in ways he's never come after anyone else. . . .
>
> The attorney general doesn't just want to punish me in my role as a business owner. He's sued me in my "personal capacity," meaning that my husband and I are now at risk of losing everything we own.[90]

Stutzman and others like her who obey what they believe the Bible teaches will continue to be the target of legal suits against Christians as Western culture moves farther away from Christianity. More Christians will face the difficult decision of how to live faithfully before God in a culture and under a government that considers them dangerous to freedom. More Christians will face the choice of whether to disobey their government or their God.

The truth is, Christians *are* dangerous. We profess a gospel message that, if taken seriously, *does* undermine belief systems, challenge status quos, and revolutionize values. The gospel has a long history of shaking things up. But "gospel" means good news—and the groaning of creation under the weight of sin means that "shaking things up" is exactly what God's creation wants and needs. Any "danger" we represent is really redemption at work, changing lives and furthering the everlasting kingdom of God in *his* world. Thank God for the "danger" of the gospel! May his people around the world be faithful to it, no matter the cost.

From the Pit to the Passion to the Promise

There are several intertextual connections between Daniel and Joseph, most notably in ch. 2,[91] and even in Dan 6 there is an obvious connection between the two Old Testament figures. Joseph is the victim of a plot when he refuses to do the wrong thrown at him in the person of Potiphar's wife, and his commitment to do what was right lands him in prison. Daniel is the victim of a plot because of his integrity and exemplary character, and his commitment to do what was right lands him in the lions' den.

But there is another less obvious link between Joseph and Daniel that also includes Jeremiah and culminates in Jesus, and it has to do with being unjustly and even maliciously thrown into a pit that would lead to certain death.

---

90. Barronelle Stutzman, "Washington state florist: My life has been turned upside down because of my religious beliefs."
91. See IN DEPTH: A Theological Paradigm for God's Work among the Nations: The Court Stories of Daniel (Dan 2) and Joseph (Gen 41) in Canonical Context above (pp. 123–37).

For Joseph, it came at the hands of his jealous brothers. Sent by father Jacob to check on his shepherding brothers, Joseph wandered unawares into the trap they laid for him when they saw him approaching. Their plan was to throw him into a cistern to die and then report to their father that a wild animal had killed him (Gen 37:18–20). When Joseph arrived, they took (לקח) him and threw (שלך) him into the cistern (Gen 37:23–24). The narrator of Genesis adds this descriptive note: "The cistern was empty; there was no water in it" (Gen 37:24). That it was empty meant Joseph would not drown, but left in a wilderness pit, he most certainly would die. With Joseph in the pit, his brothers sat down to eat, and Reuben waited for the right time to rescue his brother (Gen 37:22, 25). It never came.

For Jeremiah, the pit came at the hands of King Zedekiah's officials, who convinced a weak Zedekiah to authorize their action. In the waning days of Jerusalem and Judah, the prophet had warned of pursuing alliance with Egypt against Babylon, telling the people instead to surrender to Babylon. YHWH had said the city would be handed over to Nebuchadnezzar, so the people should accept that this was coming and go to Babylon willingly. If they stayed put, they would die by sword, famine, or plague (Jer 38:2–3). Zedekiah's officials, however, were pro-Egyptian, embracing the false hope offered by other prophets, so they told the king that Jeremiah was discouraging the soldiers and the people; he did not want their good but their ruin (Jer 38:4). Zedekiah had already rescued Jeremiah from death once (37:20–21), but he—like Darius—was ultimately powerless before his officials: "'He is in your hands. . . . The king can do nothing to oppose you'" (Jer 38:5). The officials took (לקח) Jeremiah and threw (שלך) him into a cistern, lowering him down by ropes. The narrator notes that the cistern "had no water in it, only mud,"[92] and then he adds, "Jeremiah sank down into the mud" (Jer 38:6).[93] In its near verbatim echo of Joseph's situation in Genesis, Jeremiah's situation is nonetheless more dire. His cistern may not have had water, but it did have mud, into which he sank. And unlike the would-be rescuer, Reuben, in Genesis, we know of no one looking for an opportunity to rescue Jeremiah.[94]

---

92. "A cistern of this description is what we might expect in July, the month the city was taken (39:2). The water had been used up, and under normal circumstances the cistern would not begin to fill up again until the winter rains came, which would be about November" (Jack R. Lundbom, *Jeremiah 37–52: A New Translation with Introduction and Commentary*, AB 21/3 [New York: Doubleday, 2004], 68).

93. Besides signaling Jeremiah's certain (and probably soon) death, the detail of him sinking in the mud (יטבע . . . בטיט) echoes imagery of lament psalms (e.g., Ps 69:15[14]) and psalms of thanksgiving for deliverance (i.e., Ps 40:3[2]). The narrator use of the word "mud" (טיט) to describe Jeremiah's situation is the only occurrence of this word in the prose (nonpoetic, nonprophetic/poetic) of the MT, making it "likely that the description of Jeremiah has drawn on the image of the psalmist falsely accused by treacherous enemies" (Mary C. Callaway, "Telling the Truth and Telling Stories," *USQR* 44 [1991]: 258).

94. The prophet is ultimately rescued by Ebed-Melech, but he does not enter the narrative until after Jeremiah is in the cistern and he hears word of it. For a more detailed analysis of the narrative surrounding Jeremiah's imprisonment, see Wendy L. Widder, "Thematic Correspondences between the Zedekiah Texts of Jeremiah (Jer 21–24; 37–38)," *OTE* 26/2 (2013): 491–503.

For Daniel, the pit came at the hands of Darius's officials, who manipulated the king into signing a cooked-up law that Daniel would have to violate. When he did, he was thrown into the den of hungry lions by order of the king, and the den was sealed to prevent any would-be rescuer from delivering Daniel. Death seemed certain and immediate.

Each of these victims of injustice prefigures a greater injustice, a greater suffering, a deeper pit, and a greater victory. Daniel's story, especially, provides the closest parallel for the passion of Jesus, and the Gospel writers themselves seem to draw from the Daniel narrative in their accounts of Jesus's entombment and resurrection.[95] The account in Dan 6 begins with the report of a conspiracy and betrayal by Daniel's colleagues. When the satraps and overseers realize they will find no legitimate cause against Daniel, they create a conflict between the law of his God and the law of the state. Before Daniel was "caught" in his crime, he spent time praying and thanking God, just as he always did. The king sympathized with Daniel and sought his release until he was forced by his own law to condemn the accused. Daniel was thrown to certain death and his would-be tomb was covered with a stone and sealed to prevent tampering. Early the next morning, however, he emerged unharmed from the den, saved and vindicated by the power of God.

By comparison, Jesus's passion in Matthew's account begins with Jesus's announcement that he would be betrayed (Matt 26:2; cf. Mark 8:31), a report of a conspiracy among the religious leaders (Matt 26:3–5; cf. Mark 14:1; Luke 22:2; John 11:47–53), and Judas's decision to betray Jesus (Matt 26:14–16; cf. Mark 14:10; Luke 22:4–6). The conspirators realize they will have to manufacture a reason to have him killed, so they report his "treasonous" claim to be king of the Jews (Matt 27:11; cf. Mark 15:2; Luke 23:1–3; John 19:19). Before being taken by the soldiers, Jesus spent time praying, as he often did (Matt 26:36–55; cf. Mark 14:32; Luke 22:39–45; John 18:1–2). The next day he stood before a sympathetic Pilate, who protested that the "criminal" was innocent (Matt 26:23; cf. Mark 15:14; Luke 23:4; John 18:38). Under pressure from the crowd, however, he "honored the law that allow[ed] him to release to the crowd the one condemned man" they demanded (Matt 26:24; cf. Mark 15:15; Luke 23:18–25; John 18:39–40).[96] After his execution, Jesus was placed in a tomb covered with a stone and then sealed to prevent tampering (Matt 27:60, 64–66; cf. Mark 15:46). Early the next morning, he emerged from the tomb alive, raised to life and vindicated by the power of God (Matt 28:1; cf. Mark 16:2; Luke 24:1; John 20:1).

Jesus's suffering was greater—the greatest possible, in fact[97]—and he *did* die on

---

95. See Towner (*Daniel*, 84) for the parallels discussed here.
96. Towner, *Daniel*, 84.
97. Many other innocent people have faced horrible torture and gruesome deaths, but only the perfect Jesus experienced the full mental, emotional, and spiritual anguish of separation from God.

account of it, unlike Daniel, Jeremiah, or Joseph. Like Daniel, he too had trusted God, but it did not lead to deliverance *from* death. It led to once-for-all victory *over* death—by means of the very death he suffered. The story of Daniel and the lions' den was a foretaste of Jesus's future victory over all foes, even death itself. When Jesus rose, he guaranteed that we too will rise. Daniel may have modeled how to live as a faithful follower, but Jesus, the greater Daniel, makes that living possible, meaningful, and everlasting.

Daniel 7:1a–28d

F. Narrative 6: *God's Superior King and Eternal Kingdom*

Main Idea of Narrative 6 (7:1a–28d)

During the reign of a blasphemous king, Daniel reports a troubling vision in which he sees four mutant beasts arising out of a tumultuous sea, the divine throne room with the Ancient of Days upon his throne, and one like a son of man receiving the eternal kingdom. He sees a panoply of ten horns on the fourth beast, and then an eleventh "little horn" growing among them. This little horn challenges the Most High and oppresses his holy ones, but ultimately it suffers judgment and defeat, while the holy ones inherit the eternal kingdom. God's eternal kingdom triumphs in the face of great opposition.

Literary Context of Narrative 6 (Dan 7:1a–28d)

Daniel 7 is the last of the six Aramaic chapters in the book (chs. 2–7), and it follows the series of five narratives about encounters between the Judean exiles and gentile kings (chs. 2–6). Daniel 7 is also the first of the apocalyptic chapters that comprise the rest of the book and the first of four visions that Daniel receives (chs. 7, 8, 9, 10–12).[1] While the chronology of the narrative chapters ended with the reign of Darius the Mede in 6:29[28] (with reference to Cyrus the Persian), chapter 7 moves back to the reign of Belshazzar, the king of Dan 5, and so disrupts the chronology of the book.

As part of the chiasm of chs. 2–7, Dan 7 stands parallel with the account of

---

1. See further the introduction for a discussion of apocalyptic literature and its role in the book of Daniel (pp. 24–27).

Nebuchadnezzar's dream of the magnificent metallic statue in ch. 2,[2] and the chapters have significant similarities. Both include troubling dreams that require interpretive help. Both revelations involve four earthly kingdoms and a fifth eternal and divine kingdom that destroys and surpasses all human kingdoms. Both reveal a fourth kingdom with "ironlike strength (פרזל) and crushing power (דקק)" that nonetheless suffers from division and conflict.[3] There are, however, also significant differences between the parallel chapters. Chapter 2 relates a dream received by a gentile king, while ch. 7 recounts a vision received by Daniel himself. In ch. 2 Daniel was able to interpret the king's dream, while he does not understand the meaning of his own vision in ch. 7. Nebuchadnezzar's dream is concerned with the kingdoms themselves, while Daniel's vision reveals suffering for his people. Together the chapters offer a cosmic view of God's eternal kingdom.

Daniel 7 is the heart and hinge of the book of Daniel. It shares the Aramaic language of the narratives in chs. 2–6, but it shares the apocalyptic genre of chs. 8–12. It stands parallel to the dream of ch. 2, but it sets up the framework for understanding the visions of chs. 8–12. Chapter 7 prevents a tidy division of the book into two genres or two languages, and instead links the narrative and apocalyptic chapters together.[4] Appropriately, its message that God's eternal kingdom will triumph in the face of great opposition is also central to the book whose primary message is that God's kingdom will endure. In its conveyance of this message, Daniel's vision showcases the tumultuous relationship between human kingdoms and the divine kingdom. It also offers one of the Bible's clearest pictures of the triumph of God's superior king and his everlasting kingdom. These dual portrayals span the biblical canon in their significance: the motifs of a chaotic sea, beasts, and a humanlike figure receiving the right to rule reach back to the Genesis account of creation, and the appearance of "one like a son of man" reaches forward to the Gospels and on to Revelation, where "one like a son of man" stands at the center of John's apocalyptic vision.[5] The terror and the grandeur of Daniel's vision provide the perspective needed for God's people to face intense suffering and to endure until God's eternal kingdom triumphs.

As apocalyptic literature, the symbolic visions of Dan 7–8, especially, share many literary features with the New Testament book of Revelation. As such, Ralph Korner's study of the literary structure of Revelation provides helpful terminology for considering the structure of these two visions, with some application to the visions in Dan 9–12 as well.[6] Korner identifies several literary conventions that organize a given

---

2. See further the introduction for a discussion of the chiastic structure and its significance for interpretation of the book (pp. 31–35).

3. Goldingay, *Daniel*, 353–54.

4. For more detailed discussion of these issues, see the introduction, pp. 31–35.

5. See further below, From Creation to Forever: Humanity as God Intended, pp. 393–400.

6. Ralph J. Korner, "'And I Saw . . .' An Apocalyptic Literary Convention for Structural Identification in the Apocalypse," *NovT* 42.2 (April, 2000): 160–83.

vision report—what he calls a "vision episode." The first is a "space/time referent," a statement that explains "the date in the Seer's life and/or the location, or state, of the Seer's physical body at the time of the vision's initiation and/or conclusion. In other words, it emphasizes the 'where' and/or the 'when'" of the vision.[7] In Daniel's visions, these statements occur at 7:1, 8:1, 9:1, and 10:1–5.[8]

The second literary convention that organizes a vision report is the use of formulaic statements such as "after these things I saw" and "I saw" and "behold"[9] to indicate major and minor elements within the vision report. Within an entire "vision episode" (i.e., Dan 7 and Dan 8) are major visions and minor visions: "vision block" describes the major sections, while "individual vision" describes the minor sections. In Daniel's vision of ch. 7, the major and minor elements are introduced by variations of the statement . . . חָזֵה הֲוֵית, "I was looking . . ." (e.g., 7:2, 4, 5, 6, 7).

The most complex variation of the "I was looking" statement in Dan 7 is חָזֵה הֲוֵית בְּחֶזְוֵי עִם־לֵילְיָא [בְּחֶזְוֵי לֵילְיָא] . . . וַאֲרוּ, "I was looking in my vision in the night [or "in the visions of the night"] . . . and oh!" (7:2c–d, 7a–b, 13a–b), and the pronounced complexity of this statement provides the boundaries for the three major sections (vision blocks) of the ch. 7 vision report: 7:1–6 (including the space/time referent of 7:1), 7–12, and 13–28. Within the vision blocks initiated by this complex statement are occurrences of the less complex variations of the "I was looking . . ." statement: . . . חָזֵה הֲוֵית, "I was looking . . ." (7:4c, 9a, 11a, 11c, cf. 21a), חָזֵה הֲוֵית וַאֲרוּ, "I was looking, and oh!" (7:6a–b), and simply וַאֲרוּ or וַאֲלוּ, "and oh!" (7:5a, 8b, 8d). Each of these variations introduces another element of the vision—such as the transformation of the lion-like creature (7:4c–g), the destruction of the fourth beast and outcome for the other three beasts (7:11d–12b), and the little horn's war against the holy ones (7:21–22). These lesser elements are identified as "individual visions."

In the discussion that follows, we will use the expression "vision episode" interchangeably with "vision report" to refer to Daniel's two visions in their entirety (chs. 7, 8), the expression "vision block" to refer to the major sections of each report, and "individual vision" to refer to the minor elements within each major section.

---

7. Korner, "'And I Saw . . .'," 162.

8. Korner's emphasis is on the book of Revelation, though he includes illustrations from the book of Daniel. His analysis and terminology are useful, though we differ in our understanding of its particular application to Daniel's visions. See further Korner, "'And I Saw . . .'," 170–71.

9. Korner's "behold" represents ἰδού in Greek. The corresponding Hebrew and Aramaic words in the book of Daniel are אֲלוּ, הִנֵּה, and אֲרוּ. With a few exceptions, I have translated these forms as "oh!" See the discussion of הִנֵּה at Dan. 8:3 (p. 412).

II. Macro Unit 2: The Superiority of God and His Kingdom (2:1a–7:28d)
   A. Narrative 1: God's Superior Knowledge and His Eternal Kingdom (2:1a–49c)
   B. Narrative 2: God's Superior Power and His Servants' Faithfulness (3:1a–30)
   C. Narrative 3: A Humbled King and His Restored Power (3:31a–4:34e[4:1a–37e])
   D. Narrative 4: A Humbled King and His Rescinded Power (5:1a–6:1[5:31])
   E. Narrative 5: God's Superior Law and His Servant's Faithfulness (6:2a–29[1a–28])
   F. **Narrative 6: God's Superior King and Eternal Kingdom (7:1a–28d)**

1. Vision Block 1: *The Three Beasts* (7:1a–6e)

Main Idea of the Passage

Daniel 7:1–6 introduces the setting of Daniel's first vision and includes the beginning section of his vision report, where he sees three beasts emerging from a churning sea: a lion-eagle creature, a bear-like beast, and a leopard-like beast with four heads and four wings.

Literary Context

Daniel 7:1–6 is the first and shortest of the three vision blocks that comprise the vision report of ch. 7.[10] As such, it functions in at least four ways in its broader literary context. First, its space/time referent provides the immediate context for Daniel's first vision. Second, its use of a date formula that recalls Belshazzar's reign evokes a foreboding sense of what is to come. A third function is introducing the initial beasts that create the context for the emergence of the fourth beast, different from them all, in the next vision block. Finally, the recounting of the transformation of the first beast into a humanlike figure in this opening vision block lays the foundation for a comparison with the humanlike figure that appears in the final vision block.

---

10. See Literary Context of Narrative 6 (Dan 7:1–28) above (pp. 348–50).

> F. Narrative 6: God's Superior King and Eternal Kingdom (7:1a–28d)
> 1. **Vision Block 1: The Three Beasts (7:1a–6e)**
> 2. Vision Block 2: The Fourth Beast (7:7a–12b)
> 3. Vision Block 3: One Like a Son of Man (7:13a–28d)

Translation and Exegetical Outline

(See pages 353–54.)

Structure and Literary Form

The sixth and final narrative of the book's Aramaic chiasm (chs. 2–7[11]) begins with the first of three vision blocks. The section includes the setting and initial elements of a troubling vision Daniel received during the reign of Belshazzar (7:1–6). It has five subsections: 7:1, 2–4b, 4c–g, 5, and 6.

The first subsection (7:1) is in the third-person voice of the narrator and establishes the time and place of the vision's occurrence. It is the only portion of the section (and the narrative) that is told from the narrator's point of view; the rest of chapter is set as the reported speech of Daniel who recounts in first person the vision he saw.

The remaining four subsections of this initial vision block are individual visions. Each begins with a variation of the formulaic חָזֵה הֲוֵית, "I was looking," statement.[12] The first subsection (7:2–4b) begins with the complex statement, חָזֵה הֲוֵית בְּחֶזְוַי עִם־לֵילְיָא, "I was looking in my vision in the night" (7:2c), signaling the beginning of the vision block as well as the first element of the vision. Daniel reports seeing four beasts arising from a tumultuous sea, the first of which was a hybrid lion-eagle. In the second individual vision (7:4c–g), Daniel reports the transformation of the lion-like creature (כְּאַרְיֵה, 7:4) to a creature with human characteristics. In the third individual vision (7:5), Daniel describes the second beast he saw, a creature resembling a bear (דָּמְיָה לְדֹב, 7:5). In the fourth individual vision, Daniel witnessed a third beast coming out of the sea—a leopard-like creature (כִּנְמַר, 7:6).

---

11. For the significance of this chiastic structure, see further the introduction (pp. 31–35).

12. See Literary Context of Narrative 6 (Dan 7:1–28) above (pp. 348–50).

Daniel 7:1a–6e

1a	בִּשְׁנַת חֲדָה לְבֵלְאשַׁצַּר מֶלֶךְ בָּבֶל →	↓	In the first year of Belshazzar, king of Babylon,
1b	דָּנִיֵּאל חֵלֶם חֲזָה וְחֶזְוֵי רֵאשֵׁהּ עַל־מִשְׁכְּבֵהּ		Daniel saw a dream and visions of his head upon his bed.
1c	בֵּאדַיִן חֶלְמָא כְתַב		Then the dream he wrote down;
1d	רֵאשׁ מִלִּין אֲמַר׃		the beginning of the account he said.
2a	עָנֵה →	↓	Responding,
2b	דָנִיֵּאל וְאָמַר		Daniel said,[1]
2c	חָזֵה הֲוֵית בְּחֶזְוִי עִם־לֵילְיָא		"I was looking in my vision in the night,
2d	וַאֲרוּ אַרְבַּע רוּחֵי שְׁמַיָּא מְגִיחָן לְיַמָּא רַבָּא׃		and oh! The four winds of heaven were stirring up the great sea.
3a	וְאַרְבַּע חֵיוָן רַבְרְבָן סָלְקָן מִן־יַמָּא		Four great beasts were coming up from the sea,
3b	שָׁנְיָן דָּא מִן־דָּא׃	↑	each different from the other.
4a	קַדְמָיְתָא כְאַרְיֵה		The first one was like a lion,
4b	וְגַפִּין דִּי־נְשַׁר לַהּ		but it had wings of an eagle.
4c	חָזֵה הֲוֵית		I was looking
4d	עַד דִּי־מְרִיטוּ גַפַּיהּ	←	until its wings were plucked,
4e	וּנְטִילַת מִן־אַרְעָא		and it was lifted from the ground,
4f	וְעַל־רַגְלַיִן כֶּאֱנָשׁ הֳקִימַת		and it was set upon its feet like a man.
4g	וּלְבַב אֱנָשׁ יְהִיב לַהּ׃		And a human heart was given to it.

F. Narrative 6: God's Superior King and Eternal Kingdom (7:1a–28d)

 1. Vision Block 1: The Three Beasts (7:1a–6e)

  a. The Setting of the Vision (7:1a–d)

  b. Individual Vision: Beasts Arising from the Tumultuous Sea and the First Beast (7:2a–4b)

  c. Individual Vision: The Transformation of the Lion-like Beast (7:4c–g)

Continued on next page.

---

1. See commentary on 2:5.

Continued from previous page.

5a	וַאֲרוּ חֵיוָה אָחֳרִי תִנְיָנָה דָּמְיָה לְדֹב	And oh!—another beast, a second one, resembling a bear,	d. Individual Vision: The Second Beast, Resembling a Bear (7:5a–f)
5b	וְלִשְׂטַר־חַד הֳקִמַת	but to one side it was raised up.	
5c	וּתְלָת עִלְעִין בְּפֻמַּהּ בֵּין [שִׁנַּיהּ] (שִׁנַּהּ)	And three ribs were in its mouth, between its teeth.	
5d	וְכֵן אָמְרִין לַהּ	And thus they said to it,	
5e	קוּמִי	'Arise!	
5f	אֲכֻלִי בְּשַׂר שַׂגִּיא׃	Eat much meat!'	
6a	בָּאתַר דְּנָה חָזֵה הֲוֵית	After this, I was looking,	e. Individual Vision: The Third Beast, Like a Leopard (7:6a–e)
6b	וַאֲרוּ אָחֳרִי כִּנְמַר	and oh!— another, like a leopard!	
6c	וְלַהּ גַּפִּין אַרְבַּע דִּי־עוֹף עַל־[גַּבַּיהּ] (גַּבַּהּ)	But it had four wings of a bird on its back,	
6d	וְאַרְבְּעָה רֵאשִׁין לְחֵיוְתָא	and the beast had four heads,	
6e	וְשָׁלְטָן יְהִיב לַהּ׃	and dominion was given to it.	

Individual Vision	Verse	Table 7.1. Vision Block 1 (Dan 7:1–6) Vision Block 1—The Three Beasts (7:1–6)
1	2	*I was looking in my vision in the night,* *and oh!* The four winds of heaven were stirring up the great sea. Four great beasts were coming up from the sea, each different from the other. The first one was like a lion, but it had wings of an eagle.

2	4c	*I was looking*
		     until its wings were plucked,
		     and it was lifted from the ground,
		     and it was set upon its feet like a man.
		 And a human heart was given to it.

3	5	*And oh!*—another beast, a second one, resembling a bear,
		 but to one side it was raised up.
		 And three ribs were in its mouth, between its teeth.
		 And thus they said to it,
		     "Arise!
		     Eat much meat!"

4	6	After this, I was looking, *and oh!*— another, like a leopard! But it had four wings of a bird on its back, and the beast had four heads, and dominion was given to it.

Explanation of the Text

a. The Setting of the Vision (7:1a–d)

The vision of Daniel 7 opens with a date formula, what Korner calls the space/time referent of an apocalyptic vision: it provides the when and/or where of the seer's vision.[13] In this case, the "when" is "in the first year of Belshazzar, king of Babylon" (7:1a), and the "where" is Daniel's bed in Babylon (7:1b). This date formula disrupts the chronology of the book, which had advanced to the reign of Belshazzar's successor, Darius the Mede (6:1[5:31]). If taken literally, the reference to Belshazzar's first

---

13. Korner, "'And I Saw . . .'," 162.

year is 553 BCE,[14] though it is also possible that Goldingay's comment on Dan 1:1–2 about the use of "first" and "third" could apply here—namely, "first" may be a more concrete way of saying "at the beginning" of a king's reign (while "third" may then mean "not long after the beginning"; cf. 8:1).[15]

To this point in the book, date formulae have been infrequent,[16] but in the apocalyptic chapters, they appear in connection with all four of Daniel's visions (7:1; 8:1; 9:1; 10:1). These formulae are part of a more general characteristic of apocalyptic literature—namely, setting first-person vision reports in a third-person narrative framework.[17] A discourse effect of these chronological references is that they link the two halves of the book, intertwining the apocalyptic visions with the events and chronology of the narrative chapters, where each of the kings in the date formulae is introduced.[18] In the two later visions (9:22d–27d and chs. 10–12), the historical context provided by each date formula is also a meaningful part of understanding the purpose of each vision.[19] In the first two visions (chs. 7 and 8), however, the historical context of Belshazzar's reign is less about understanding the visions themselves and their purpose than it is about evoking an emotional expectation for the visions. This fits well with the nature of the apocalyptic genre, where extensive symbolism is employed to create an overall impression, not provide extensive details about the course of future events.

The timing of Daniel's visions during the reign of Belshazzar is significant because the story of the Babylonian king's disdain for God's sacred vessels offered the book's first glimpse of a blasphemous, arrogant king shaking his fist at Israel's God. In Daniel's apocalyptic visions, he will see God's people encountering gentile kings whose defiant blasphemy makes Belshazzar look almost saintly; Lucas calls Belshazzar a "pale foreshadowing" of the later kings of Daniel's visions.[20] The association with Belshazzar may also be a subtle reminder of the end of Daniel's tenure under Nebuchadnezzar, the king whose last appearance in the book was in ch. 4, where he acknowledged the sovereignty of the Most High God and where he demonstrated an affable and even warm relationship with Daniel, servant of the Most High. Chapter 5 continued the favorable portrayal of Nebuchadnezzar in its contrast of him with "his son," the blasphemous Belshazzar, who scorned the God of Israel and his servant Daniel. Daniel's interaction with Belshazzar may be limited to one chapter, but its dark overtones portend future hostility between God's people and their gentile overlords—a theme that will dominate the apocalyptic visions of chs. 7–12.[21]

---

14. The dating of Belshazzar's reign is contingent on when his father, Nabonidus, made him coregent; see on Dan 5:2, esp. n15.

15. Goldingay, *Daniel*, 152–53. See the commentary on Dan 1:1–2.

16. See on Dan 1:1 and 2:1 above.

17. See further John J. Collins, "Introduction: Towards the Morphology of a Genre," *Semeia* 14 (1979), 9: "There is always a narrative framework in which the manner of revelation is described. This always involves an otherworldly mediator and a human recipient—it is never simply a direct oracular utterance by either heavenly being or human. The content always involves both an eschatological salvation which is temporally future and present otherworldly realities. The eschatological salvation is always definitive in character and is marked by some form of personal afterlife." See also the introduction, pp. 24–27.

18. Belshazzar in ch. 5; Darius the Mede in ch. 6; Cyrus the Persian in Dan 1:21.

19. The revelation of the Seventy Weeks in Dan 9 occurs when the seventy years of Babylonian exile should be drawing to a conclusion, and the vision of Dan 10–12 occurs after the return and restoration might reasonably be underway. See further on these chapters below.

20. Lucas, *Daniel*, 222.

21. Newsom also notes, "Belshazzar's first year . . . marks a regnal transition, and such a time may be symbolically suited for a vision report that looks forward to the ultimate transfer of sovereignty. Moreover, Belshazzar is the only king

The narrator shifts from the narrative note of time and place to the account of the dream itself. The transitional בֵּאדַיִן, "then," marks the shift, and the real focus of the chapter—that is, the dream—is signaled by the placement of חֶלְמָא, "the dream," before the verb (כְּתַב, 7:1c). The narrator notes that Daniel saw the dream and then wrote it down, a common characteristic of apocalyptic literature. The practice of documenting a prophecy is known in non-apocalyptic literature as well, the act of writing both preserving the words for others to read and allowing them to test the veracity of the prophetic elements. Sometimes the act of writing the prophecy also triggered its fulfillment (e.g., Isa 8:1, 16; Jer 30:2; Ezek 43:11).

In the last clause of 7:1 is the awkward statement רֵאשׁ מִלִּין אֲמַר, which translates woodenly as "head of words he said" and usually appears in English translations as something like "he spoke the sum/substance of the matter" (e.g., ESV, NIV, NASB). The translation here ("the beginning of the account he said") follows Cook, who observes that "at some textual level, this expression acts as a bookend with עַד־כָּה סוֹפָא דִי־מִלְּתָא 'until thus (is) the end of the matter' in verse 28. . . . As such, the clause must be understood as signaling the beginning of Daniel's account, albeit redundantly with the following."[22]

b. Individual Vision: Beasts Arising from the Tumultuous Sea and the First Beast (7:2a–4b)

As noted above, Daniel's report itself is organized by the repetition of variations of the statement חָזֵה הֲוֵית, "I was looking."[23] This expression is common in apocalyptic literature, where seers are reporting what they saw. The macrostructure of Daniel's report is that it consists of three vision blocks, each initiated by the most complex variation of the "I was looking" statement: "I was looking in my vision in the night [or "in the visions of the night"] . . . and oh!" (חָזֵה הֲוֵית בְּחֶזְוַי עִם־לֵילְיָא [בְּחֶזְוֵי לֵילְיָא] . . . וַאֲרוּ, 7:2c-d, 7a-b, 13a-b).

In addition to signaling the beginning of a vision block, this "I was looking" statement also identifies the first element of the vision block. The first element Daniel sees is the four winds of heaven stirring up the great sea, from which four different beasts were emerging. The first of these was a lion-like creature with eagle's wings (7:2c–4b).

Four is a number that can express totality, and that certainly is the case in 7:2c when Daniel refers to "the four winds of heaven."[24] He simply means that wind was swirling from every direction and stirring up the sea. The "great sea" in the Bible often refers to the Mediterranean Sea (e.g., Num 34:6; Josh 1:4), but here it is more likely a reference to the great mythological sea of primeval chaos. In the mythology of the ancient world, the raging waters of the sea were a perpetual threat to the order of creation. The waters threatened to undo the created order and return the world to its primordial chaotic state. Only the strength of gods could defeat and restrain such a powerful foe. Daniel would have been familiar with the Babylonian myth Enuma Elish, where the god Marduk waged war against the sea goddess, Tiamat, and he may also have been familiar with Ugaritic mythology in which the cloud-riding god, Baal, defeated the sea god, Yamm, to win the right to rule over the gods. Everywhere in the ancient world, imagery of the

---

in the narrative cycle who is destroyed for his arrogant impiety by the command of God. Thus his own narrative foreshadows the judgment enacted against the fourth beast in ch. 7" (*Daniel*, 220).

22. Cook, *Aramaic Ezra and Daniel*, 280.
23. See Literary Context of Narrative 6 (Dan 7:1–28) above, pp. 348–50.
24. Cf. Jer 15:3; 49:36; Dan 11:4; Zech 2:10[6].

vast sea forebode nothing good—symbolism that is very much at play in Daniel's vision as well (cf. Isa 17:12–13).

From the tumultuous waters, Daniel saw four great beasts arise. Whether the creatures rose concurrently or consecutively is not entirely clear at this point in the vision. Daniel's vision on the whole will unfold one element at a time—that is, as he sees it, he says it. While it is possible that all four arose at roughly the same time, several features of the report make it more likely that the vision progressed from one beast to the next: (1) the use of an "I was looking" statement to preface the description of each one (7:2c–d, 4c, 6a, 7a); (2) the inclusion of temporal indicators before Daniel's description of the second and third beasts (בָּאתַר דְּנָה, "after this," 7:6a, 7a); and (3) the use of ordinal numbers (קַדְמָיְתָא, "the first one," 7:4a; תִּנְיָנָה, "a second one," 7:5a; רְבִיעָאָה, "a fourth," 7:7b).

What, then, would be the purpose of saying at the outset that four beasts were rising (סָלְקָן, *peal* active participle, 7:3a) from the sea? The statement may simply serve as a summary of what is to follow, but more likely, since Daniel otherwise reports elements as they unfold, the purpose is one of effect. The effect of reporting that *four* creatures were arising from the sea, which was stirred by the *four* winds of heaven, is one of totality: while these four beasts do refer to four kingdoms (according to the interpretation Daniel later receives; 7:17), they also refer to the totality of human kingdoms. The significance of the vision transcends its closest historical referents and encompasses all of human history.[25]

Daniel then notes that each beast was different from the others (7:3b), and his first individual vision concludes with his description of the first beast: it was like a lion, but it had an eagle's wings (7:4a–b). It was like something he recognized, but not quite—a pattern that holds for his descriptions of the first three beasts.[26] Lions in the world of the Bible represent the mightiest of the beasts (e.g., Prov 30:30), while eagles typically represent speed. Jeremiah uses the imagery of both creatures to describe Nebuchadnezzar (Jer 49:19, 22).

c. Individual Vision: The Transformation of the Lion-like Beast (7:4c–g)

The second individual vision is prefaced with חָזֵה הֲוֵית, "I was looking" (7:4c), and it consists of four clauses governed by עַד דִּי, "until," in 7:4d. The clauses describe the transformation of the the lion-like creature into a creature more human than animal: it stands on two feet and has a human heart. This transformation is effected upon the creature, as evidenced by the four consecutive passive verbs describing the metamorphosis: its wings "were plucked" (מְרִיטוּ, *peil* perfect; 7:4d); the creature "was lifted" from the ground where it had stood on four lion legs (נְטִילַת, *peil* perfect; 7:4e); then it "was set" on its feet like a man (הֳקִימַת, *huphal* perfect; 7:4f); and finally, a human heart "was given" to it (יְהִיב, *peil* perfect; 7:4g). The transformation from beast to biped with a human mind makes this first "beast" into "a truly astounding creature: a lion with wings that then walks and talks/thinks like a human."[27]

---

25. Goldingay says, "*Four* winds and *four* creatures suggest the world-encompassing totality of divine power and disorderly energy (cf. the fourfold stream of Gen 2:10)" (*Daniel*, 386).

26. Lucas highlights this in his translation: the first beast was "like a lion, *but* it had eagle's wings;" the second "resembled a bear, *but* it was raised up on one side;" the third was "like a leopard, *but* it had four bird's wings on its back [and] four heads" (*Daniel*, 158, emphasis mine).

27. Cook, *Aramaic Ezra and Daniel*, 282.

The lion-like beast is unique among the three beasts of this first vision block in that two individual visions relate to it. First is the vision of its initial appearance (7:4a–b), and second is the vision of the beast's transformation from a lion-like beast into a humanlike figure (7:4c–g). The length and descriptive detail of this second element and the fact that it stands as a separate vision indicate the significance of the transformation in which a beast becomes more human than animal. We will return to this issue below (see on 7:17).

There is a long interpretive tradition for the identity of each beast in Daniel's vision, but rather than engaging these traditions as the beasts appear, I will follow the discourse of the chapter and reserve interpretation until the point at which Daniel himself receives it (see below on 7:15–20 and 7:23–27).[28]

d. Individual Vision: The Second Beast, Resembling a Bear (7:5a–f)

The third individual vision that is a component of the first vision block begins with the attention-getting word וַאֲרוּ, "and oh!" (7:5a). Daniel describes the second creature, saying it resembled a bear, but it was raised up on one side. The significance of this cockeyed posture may be that the creature, with three ribs already in its teeth, was "pausing to devour a mouthful before springing again on its prey,"[29] though Cook notes that, given the previous description of the lion with the unexpected presence of wings, this "raised up on one side" description of the second beast "is a startling feature of the beast that otherwise resembles a bear."[30]

The ribs are evidence of the beast's recent exploits, but the creature is nonetheless ordered to get up and eat much meat (קוּמִי אֲכֻלִי בְּשַׂר שַׂגִּיא, 7:5e–f). Since these imperative verbs are directed at an animal of prey that presumably would not need to be commanded to do what it instinctively does, they are probably better understood as a granting of permission to satisfy the creature's appetite.[31] The second beast does not act of its own accord; it is given permission to act. As in the transformation of the lion-like creature, there is an outside force controlling this beast (see on 7:4c–g).

e. Individual Vision: The Third Beast, Like a Leopard (7:6a–e)

The last element of the opening vision block in Dan 7 begins with בָּאתַר דְּנָה חָזֵה הֲוֵית וַאֲרוּ, "After this, I was looking, and oh!" (7:6a–b). Daniel reports that the next creature was "like a leopard" (כִּנְמַר, 7:6b), except it had four wings and four heads. This ghoulish beast was given (יְהִיב, 7:6e) dominion, another element in the vision's theme of divine control (cf. on 7:4c–g and 7:5). The exilic prophet Ezekiel had also seen four-faced, four-winged creatures in his vision of YHWH's divine throne chariot (Ezek 1), but by contrast, the creatures there carried YHWH's throne, the symbol of his authority; the hybrid creature of Daniel's vision was granted authority of its own.

Much like the ominous churning sea of Daniel's vision, these three mutant creatures forebode nothing good. While Israelite law rendered such hybrid creatures unclean and off-limits (Lev 11; Deut 14),

---

28. In this regard, I appreciate Baldwin's comment: "In eagerness to identify the beasts it is important not to miss the emotional reactions these fierce symbols arouse.... The reader is meant to register terror before these fearsome beasts, especially in view of their supernatural features, and not regard them merely as signs, satisfactorily interpreted by reason alone" (*Daniel*, 138–39).

29. Montgomery, *Commentary on the Book of Daniel*, 288.

30. Cook, *Aramaic Ezra and Daniel*, 283.

31. Li, *The Verbal System of the Aramaic of Daniel*, 130.

Babylonian tradition considered the birth of an anomalous animal to be an omen. Such omens could be good or bad, but given what Daniel has seen to this point, he certainly expected nothing good to come of what he was witnessing.[32] And things were about to get worse.

2. Vision Block 2: *The Fourth Beast* (7:7a–12b)

Main Idea of the Passage

In Daniel 7:7–12, Daniel's vision of beasts continues when he sees a fourth beast, unlike the previous three, arise from the sea. He also receives a glimpse into a divine court scene, and then he witnesses the subsequent judgment of the beasts.

Literary Context

Daniel 7:7–12 is the second section and the second vision block of the narrative that comprises ch. 7. It follows the opening vision block in which Daniel reported seeing four beasts emerge from the sea, and it functions in at least three ways in its broader literary context. First, it concludes Daniel's description of the four beasts reported in the first vision block, where he only actually described the first three. Second, this section indicates the significance of the fourth beast as it devotes greater detail to the description of the beast and the emergence of a little horn on its head; in so doing, the section highlights the differences between the fourth beast and the first three beasts. A third function of the section is that it puts the beasts (and especially the fourth beast) in proper perspective as it culminates with a vision of the divine throne room, where one with power over the beasts issues judgment that is carried out.

---

32. Ancient Mesopotamians believed that the birth of an abnormal animal was an omen or a message from the gods. Omens could be good or bad, and it was up to diviners to interpret the significance of a malformation by means of long-established interpretive traditions, such as the *Shumma izbu* collection of texts. These texts detailed the significance of each abnormality. Examples of good and bad omens, respectively, are "if a ewe gives birth to a lion and it has two horns on the right—the prince will take the land of his enemy," and "if a ram has (only) one horn inserted into his forehead like a peg—its owner will be killed by force" (Nicla De Zorzi, "The Omen Series Šumma Izbu: Internal Structure and Hermeneutic Strategies," *Kaskal* 8 [2011], 55). Goldingay notes that some details of an omen were not interpreted, and some aspects of an interpretation did not correspond to specific aspects of the omen; this will also prove true with Daniel's vision and its angelic interpretation (*Daniel*, 345–46).

F. Narrative 6: God's Superior King and Eternal Kingdom (7:1a–28d)
  1. Vision Block 1: The Three Beasts (7:1a–6e)
  2. **Vision Block 2: The Fourth Beast (7:7a–12b)**
  3. Vision Block 3: One Like a Son of Man (7:13a–28d)

Translation and Exegetical Outline

(See pages 362–63.)

Structure and Literary Form

The second section of the narrative in Dan 7 (7:7–12) continues the first-person report of Daniel's vision. It is the second of three vision blocks that comprise the entire vision episode of ch. 7 (7:1–6, 7–12, and 13–28), and it consists of five subsections (7:7, 8a–c, 8d–e, 9–10, and 11–12). Each subsection is an individual vision that begins with a variation of the formulaic statement חָזֵה הֲוֵית, "I was looking," or וַאֲלוּ, "and oh!"[33]

The first subsection (7:7) begins with the similar language as that of the first vision block—the complex statement: "After this, I was looking in the visions of the night" (בָּאתַר דְּנָה חָזֵה הֲוֵית בְּחֶזְוֵי לֵילְיָא, 7:7a; cf. 7:2c), signaling the beginning of the vision block as well as its first element: the appearance of the fourth beast (חֵיוָה רְבִיעָאָה, 7:7b). In the second individual vision, Daniel sees a little horn (קֶרֶן אָחֳרִי זְעֵירָה), the eleventh to appear on the fearsome beast (7:8a–b). In the third individual vision in 7:8d–e, Daniel realizes that the little horn has human eyes and a boastful mouth. In the fourth individual vision, the scene shifts to a heavenly throne room, where Daniel sees thrones being set up (7:9–10). Finally, in the fifth individual vision, the scene returns to the beasts, and Daniel witnesses their judgment (7:11–12).

---

33. See Literary Context of Narrative 6 (Dan 7:1–28) above (pp. 348–50)

Daniel 7:7a–12b

7a		After this I was looking in the visions of the night,	2. Vision Block 2: The Fourth Beast (7:7a–12b)
7b		and oh!—a fourth beast, dreadful and terrifying and exceedingly strong!	a. Individual Vision: The Beast Unlike the Others (7:7a–i)
7c		It had great teeth of iron.	
7d		It was eating,	
7e		and it was crushing,	
7f		and it was trampling the rest with its feet.	
7g		And it was different from all the beasts	
7h		that were before it.	
7i		It had ten horns.	
8a		I was considering the horns,	
8b		and oh! Another horn, a little one, came up among them.	b. Individual Vision: A Little Horn (7:8a–c)
8c		And three of the former horns were uprooted before it.	
8d		And oh! Eyes like the eyes of a man were on this horn,	c. Individual Vision: The Little Horn's Eyes and Mouth (7:8d–e)
8e		and a mouth speaking great things.	
9a		I was looking,	d. Individual Vision: The Divine Throne Room (7:9a–10f)
9b		until thrones were set up,	
9c		and an Ancient of Days sat.	
9d		His garment was white like snow,	
9e		and the hair on his head was white like wool.	

9f	כָּרְסְיֵהּ שְׁבִיבִין דִּי־נוּר	His throne had flames of fire;
9g	גַּלְגִּלּוֹהִי נוּר דָּלִק׃	its wheels were burning fire.
10a	נְהַר דִּי־נוּר נָגֵד	A river of fire was gushing
10b	וְנָפֵק מִן־קֳדָמוֹהִי	and coming out from before him.
10c	אֶלֶף [אַלְפִין] (אַלְפַיָּא) יְשַׁמְּשׁוּנֵּהּ	A thousand of thousands were attending him,
10d	וְרִבּוֹ [רִבְבָן] (רִבְבָתָא) קָדָמוֹהִי יְקוּמוּן	and a myriad of myriads was standing before him.
10e	דִּינָא יְתִב	The court sat,
10f	וְסִפְרִין פְּתִיחוּ׃	and books were opened.
11a	חָזֵה הֲוֵית	I was looking
11b	בֵּאדַיִן מִן־קָל מִלַּיָּא רַבְרְבָתָא דִּי קַרְנָא מְמַלֱּלָה	then from (the time of) the sound of the great words that the horn was speaking,
11c	חָזֵה הֲוֵית	I was looking
11d	עַד דִּי קְטִילַת חֵיוְתָא	until the beast was killed,
11e	וְהוּבַד גִּשְׁמַהּ	and its body was destroyed,
11f	וִיהִיבַת לִיקֵדַת אֶשָּׁא׃	and it was given to the burning of the fire.
12a	וּשְׁאָר חֵיוָתָא הֶעְדִּיו שָׁלְטָנְהוֹן	As for the rest of the beasts, their dominion was taken away,
12b	וְאַרְכָה בְחַיִּין יְהִיבַת לְהוֹן עַד־זְמַן וְעִדָּן׃	but a prolonging in life was given to them until a season and a time.

e. Individual Vision: The Fate of the Four Beasts (7:11a–12b)

Table 7.2. Vision Block 2 (Dan 7:7–12)		
Individual Vision	**Verse**	**Vision Block 2—The Fourth Beast (7:7–12)**
1	7	*After this I was looking in the visions of the night,* *and oh!*—a fourth beast, dreadful and terrifying and exceedingly strong! It had great teeth of iron. It was eating, and it was crushing, and it was trampling the rest with its feet. And it was different from all the beasts that were before it. It had ten horns.
2	8a 8b	*I was considering the horns,* *and oh!* Another horn, a little one, came up among them. And three of the former horns were uprooted before it.
3	8d	*And oh!* Eyes like the eyes of a man were on this horn, and a mouth speaking great things.

4	9	*I was looking,*
		   until thrones were set up,
		   and an Ancient of Days sat.
		 His garment was white like snow,
		 and the hair on his head was white like wool.
		 His throne had flames of fire;
		 its wheels were burning fire.
		 A river of fire was gushing
		 and coming out from before him.
		 A thousand of thousands were attending him,
		 and a myriad of myriads was standing before him.
		 The court sat,
		 and books were opened.

5a	11a	*I was looking* then from (the time of) the sound of the great words that the horn was speaking,

5b	11c	*I was looking*
		   until the beast was killed,
		     and its body was destroyed,
		     and it was given to the burning of the fire.
		 As for the rest of the beasts, their dominion was taken away,
		 but a prolonging in life was given to them until a season and a time.

Explanation of the Text

a. Individual Vision: The Beast Unlike the Others (7:7a–i)

The second vision block begins with "I was looking in the visions of the night, and oh!" (חָזֵה הֲוֵית בְּחֶזְוֵי לֵילְיָא וַאֲרוּ, 7:7a–b), the most complex variation of the "I was looking" statement (see also 7:2c–d, 13a–b). This statement also identifies the first element of the vision block, "a fourth beast" (7:7b).

Daniel's description of this final beast differs from those of the other three. He described the first three beasts by way of comparison with other animals. They all resembled something he knew—a lion, a bear, and a leopard (7:4a, 5a, 6b). Daniel does not, however, compare the fourth beast to any other animals. The beast was, apparently, not like any creature he had ever seen and so defied comparison.[34] Instead he describes it with a series of adjectives: "dreadful and terrifying and exceedingly strong" (דְּחִילָה וְאֵימְתָנִי וְתַקִּיפָא יַתִּירָא, 7:7b).[35] This description probably fails to have its intended effect on us because contemporary usage of the words "dreadful" and "terrifying" is often relatively benign. We use "dreadful" to describe things that are extremely unpleasant (e.g., a dreadful meal), poorly executed (e.g., a dreadful performance), or shocking (e.g., dreadful behavior). We rarely use it in its sense of "inspiring dread" or "causing great and oppressive fear."[36] The word "terrifying" fares only slightly better. Daniel was filled with great dread, oppressive fear, and unmitigated terror at the sight of the fourth beast.

The two words "dreadful" and "terrifying" together in Daniel's description function as a hendiadys—that is, a "two for one" figure of speech in which two related words (usually joined by "and") communicate a single idea. Perhaps the most famous English example of hendiadys is Shakespeare's phrase "sound and fury" in Macbeth, when the Scottish lord says of life, "It is a tale told by an idiot, full of sound and fury, signifying nothing."[37] He could have said life is full of a "furious sound," but the use of a hendiadys creates a more striking image. In Dan 7, the "dreadful and terrifying" fourth beast filled Daniel with the worst imaginable fear and horror. It was a monster like no other.[38]

The description of the fourth beast as "exceedingly strong" (תַּקִּיפָא יַתִּירָא) calls to mind the fourth kingdom of Nebuchadnezzar's statue dream in Dan 2. That last kingdom, represented by iron legs and iron-clay feet, was said to be "strong like iron" (תַּקִּיפָה כְּפַרְזְלָא, 2:40; cf. 2:42). This correspondence

---

34. This comparative language is common in apocalyptic literature, where the seer is often witnessing otherworldly things and struggles to find adequate words to convey the divine world. Consider how often Ezekiel, in his attempt to describe the divine throne chariot in Ezek 1, says something was "like" (כְּ) something else (see Ezek 1:4, 7[2x], 13, 14, 16[2x], 22, 24[3x], 26[2x], 27[2x], 28).

35. דְּחִילָה is a passive participle functioning adjectivally.

36. See "dreadful" in *Merriam-Webster's Collegiate Dictionary*, Tenth Edition (Springfield, MA: Merriam-Webster, 1993) or online: https://www.merriam-webster.com/dictionary/dreadful.

37. *The Tragedy of Macbeth*, ed. G. Blakemore Evans (Dallas: Houghton Mifflin, 1974), 5.5.26–28. Biblical examples of hendiadys include the "hope and future" YHWH planned to give his people (Jer 29:11), meaning they had a hopeful future. "Justice and righteousness" is another common biblical pairing and means "righteous justice."

38. Eugene Peterson's translation captures some of these ideas: "This [beast] was a grisly horror—hideous. It had huge iron teeth. It crunched and swallowed its victims. Anything left over, it trampled into the ground. It was different from the other animals—this one was a real monster" (Dan 7:7, MSG).

of Daniel's vision to the earlier dream of Nebuchadnezzar continues in his description of the fourth beast as he reports some of its specific features. He describes the beast's teeth, a prominent feature on account of their size (רַבְרְבָן, "great," 7:7c) and their substance (פַּרְזֶל, "iron," 7:7c).³⁹ Cook observes that the placement of the adjective רַבְרְבָן, "great," so far from the noun it describes "underscor[es] the enormity of the teeth from reasonable expectations."⁴⁰ The teeth also stand out because of what the beast was doing with them: eating and crushing (אָכְלָה וּמַדֱּקָה, 7:7d–e). Then with its feet, it was trampling (רָפְסָה, 7:7f) whatever was left of its prey. The strength (תַּקִּיפָא יַתִּירָא), substance (פַּרְזֶל), and vicious trampling with its feet (בְּרַגְלַהּ רָפְסָה) everything in its path all recall the fourth kingdom of Nebuchadnezzar's dream: the kingdom with iron-clay feet (רַגְלוֹהִי, 2:33; cf. 2:34, 41–42) was strong as iron (תַּקִּיפָה כְּפַרְזְלָא, 2:40), and like iron, it crushed (מְהַדֵּק, 2:40) everything.⁴¹

Daniel then notes that this beast was different (מְשַׁנְיָה, 7:7g) from the three that came before it, highlighting the beast by the use of the otherwise unnecessary subject pronoun הִיא, "it." At the beginning of his vision report, he had said the four beasts were all different (7:3b), and his description of each beast bore this out. Restating it here with respect to the fourth beast implies a greater difference than just the appearance of this beast; this beast was different on account of what it *did*—and, in fact, that it "did" anything. It is the only one of the four beasts that Daniel describes with active verbs (אָכְלָה וּמַדֱּקָה . . . רָפְסָה, 7:7d–f). The first three beasts were all acted upon by an unseen agent: the lion was transformed into a humanlike figure; the bear was granted permission to satisfy its appetite; the leopard was given dominion. By contrast, nothing is done *to* this final beast (yet); rather, it is the one *doing*.⁴² Goldingay comments, "The first three animals were under control. The fourth decides for itself what to do. It was brought into being by God, but it overreaches itself."⁴³

In the immediate context of Daniel's vision, the use of passive verbs to describe the beasts suggests the divine hand behind their activity.⁴⁴ The larger context of the Old Testament prophets also leads in this direction. In an oracle of the eighth-century-BCE prophet Hosea against the apostate Israel, YHWH threatened to fight against his own people like a lion, a leopard, a bear, and an unidentified wild beast (Hos 13:7–8). Just as the divine hand was behind the beasts of Hosea's vision, so it is behind the beasts in Daniel's vision. These beasts will, to varying degrees, cause hardship for God's people, but like YHWH's "servant"

---

39. The NET Bible notes that שִׁנַּיִן, the Aramaic word for "teeth," is the dual form rather than plural and suggests it means the beast had two rows of teeth.

40. Cook, *Aramaic Ezra and Daniel*, 285.

41. Consider how the crushing (דקק) also works the other way in Nebuchadnezzar's dream: the iron may have crushed everything, but then the stone crushed the iron-clay feet (2:34–35, 44–45). (Note that in ch. 2, I translated דקק as "shatter" rather than "crush," because the English verb "shatter" better fits the context there.)

42. Of the fourth beast's difference, Newsom notes: "What is most important in the description . . . is the shift from the divine control over the first three beasts, represented through the use of the divine passive and direct command—and the fact that this different beast acts autonomously, signified by active verbs: eating and crushing and trampling" (*Daniel*, 225).

43. Goldingay, *Daniel*, 391.

44. Ultimately the fourth beast will also be subject to the divine hand; see on v. 11.

Nebuchadnezzar (Jer 25:9; 27:6; 43:10), they too are God's instruments.[45] Newsom comments that the "intertextual echo again suggests that the events of history are in some way expressions of YHWH's intentionality."[46]

Daniel's only other description of the physical appearance of the fourth beast is in 7:7i: "It had ten horns." In the Old Testament, the imagery of a "horn" often conveys power. With a panoply of ten horns ("five times the natural two"[47]), the fourth beast has extraordinary power. This description sets up the next vision element.

b. Individual Vision: A Little Horn (7:8a–c)

While Daniel was considering the beast's array of horns, he had another individual vision. It is a short vision, but its importance is indicated by the fact that it stands as a separate individual vision, prefaced with an "I was looking" statement (the attention-getting וַאֲלוּ, "and oh!" 7:8b). It is tied to the end of the previous vision by "I was considering the horns" (מִשְׂתַּכַּל הֲוֵית בְּקַרְנַיָּא, 7:8a); the ten horns are integral to the new visionary element. What Daniel sees is "another horn" (קֶרֶן אָחֳרִי), more specifically, "a little one" (זְעֵירָה), coming up among the other ten (7:8b).

The eleventh horn may have been small, but it was mighty; its emergence results in the uprooting of three other horns (7:8c), while the remaining seven effectively disappear from the scene. The late-coming little horn dominates all that follows with respect to the fourth beast.

c. Individual Vision: The Little Horn's Eyes and Mouth (7:8d–e)

The importance of the little horn is amplified by the use of another visionary element to describe it: a second attention-getting וַאֲלוּ, "and oh!" (7:8d), prefaces the description of the little horn's appearance. It had "eyes like the eyes of a man" and it had "a mouth speaking great things" (7:8d). Eyes and speech throughout the Old Testament often indicate character (e.g., Prov 6:16–19; cf. Isa 2:11),[48] making it significant that the only descriptors of this horn besides its small size are that it has human eyes and an arrogant mouth. Hill notes that "although no particular bent of character is explicitly attributed to the small horn, the description seems to anticipate the arrogance, irreverence, and wickedness" that will characterize it.[49]

d. Individual Vision: The Divine Throne Room (7:9a–10f)

The scene unfolding before Daniel continues with a fourth individual vision beginning in 7:9a with the statement חָזֵה הֲוֵית, "I was looking." From the terrifying fourth beast and the boastful little horn (7:7b–8), Daniel's vision shifts to a throne room where multiple thrones were being set up (7:9b) and "an Ancient of Days sat" (עַתִּיק יוֹמִין יְתִב, 7:9c)—both clauses governed by the עַד דִּי, "until," of 7:9b.

There is no indication in the vision that Daniel's location has changed, though the information in

---

45. Assyria (Isa 10:5), Cyrus (Isa 44:28), and the Chaldeans (Hab 1:5–11) are also called YHWH's "servants."
46. Newsom, *Daniel*, 223.
47. Baldwin, *Daniel*, 140.
48. Lucas, *Daniel*, 180.
49. Hill, *Daniel*, 136.

7:9b–c indicates that Daniel is seeing the throne room of the divine council, the heavenly host that administers cosmic affairs under YHWH (e.g., Deut 32:8–9; Pss 82:1; 89:6–8[5–7]).[50] The divine council would normally be found in the heavenly realm, but as Goldingay observes, the court meets on earth when YHWH is engaged in judgment (Dan 7:9–11; see Jer 49:38; Joel 4[3]:1–2, 12; Zech 14:1–5; Pss 50; 96:10–13[51]).[52]

At the center of this scene is "an Ancient of Days" (7:9c), and most of what follows in this fourth individual vision is description of him (7:9d–10d). The title "Ancient of Days" in the canon occurs only in Dan 7, where it appears three times (cf. 7:13, 22).[53] In this first occurrence, it is indefinite: "an Ancient of Days." Once the character has been established in the account, Daniel refers to him as "the Ancient of Days" (7:13, 22). The title highlights the longevity and authority of the one on the throne, in contrast with the beasts and their dominion, which will shortly come to an end (7:11; cf. 7:17–18).

Daniel's description of the Ancient of Days is set in poetry, a feature that makes the entire section stand out and highlights its significance in the chapter. Four pairs of parallel lines describe his resplendent appearance (7:9d–e), his fiery throne (7:9f–g), the gushing river of fire (7:10a–b), and his innumerable attendants (7:10c–d). Keeping the one on the throne as the focus, the imagery moves through the scene—from his clothes, to his hair, to his throne and its wheels, to the river flowing "from before him" (מִן־קֳדָמוֹהִי, 7:10b), to the multitudes in his service. This scene is all about him.

The fiery language in this vision is evocative of other Old Testament theophanies. Moses saw a burning bush in the desert of Horeb/Sinai when YHWH appeared to him and commissioned him to bring the Israelites out of Egypt (Exod 3:2); the Israelites later saw fire atop the same mountain when YHWH was making his covenant with them (Exod 19:18), and they traveled to the promised land following YHWH's pillar of fire (Exod 13:21). Most similarly is Ezekiel's vision of the divine throne chariot, in which he saw a flaming throne with wheels of burning fire (Ezek 1).

Fire also represents YHWH's judgment. In the

---

50. The divine council was part of every Mesopotamian religion, including Israel. This tiered council consisted of divine beings with various responsibilities. The Ugaritic divine council provides a useful point of comparison for understanding Israel's divine council: the top tier god in Ugarit was the gray-bearded El. The royal family of gods comprised the second tier. The most notable member of the royal family was El's son Baal, the storm god and "Rider of the Clouds" who served under El as vice-regent. The third tier of the council consisted of craftsmen gods, while the fourth tier was servants. (For more on the divine council in the ancient Near East and Israel, see Michael S. Heiser, "Divine Council," *DOTWPW*; ed. Tremper Longman III and Peter Enns [Downers Grove, IL: InterVarsity Press, 2008]: 112–16. See also Heiser's website: www.thedivine-council.com.)

The Israelite divine council resembled that of Ugarit with "a hierarchy of an upper tier of beings (those seated in council), a servant class of heavenly beings, and a vice-regent who [is] given authority over the earth and, by extension, over all the sons of God who were thought to rule the earth in light of Ps 82:1, 6, and Deut 4:19–20; 32:8–9" (Michael S. Heiser, "The Divine Council in Late Canonical and Non-Canonical Second Temple Jewish Literature" [PhD diss., University of Wisconsin-Madison, 2004], 157). At the head of the council was YHWH, and below him in the second tier were the "sons of God." Angels comprised the servant or messenger third tier, and Israel does not appear to have had a tier of "craftsmen gods." It is in the vice-regent position that the Israelite council was distinct from that of Ugarit and all other concepts of the divine council. It is this important distinction that Daniel's vision will highlight.

51. See also 1 En. 1:3–9; 25:3; 90:20–27.

52. Goldingay, *Daniel*, 361. Newsom adds that "the background for the imagery is the practice of victorious kings or generals to sit in the gate and receive their troops or judge the defeated rebels" as in 2 Sam 19:9[8], Jer 39:3, and Ps 122:5 (*Daniel*, 228).

53. God's eternality, however, is a topic throughout the Old Testament (e.g., he is the "everlasting king" [Jer 10:10], the "eternal father" [Isa 9:6], and the "eternal God" [Gen 21:33; Ps 90:2; Isa 40:28]).

Psalms, "fire goes before him and consumes his foes on every side" (Ps 97:3) and "devours before him" when he comes to judge his people (Ps 50:3). In Lev 10, Aaron's sons Nadab and Abihu offer an "unauthorized fire" before YHWH and are subsequently consumed by a fire that comes out from his presence. The river of fire gushing out from before YHWH's throne in Daniel's vision is one of judgment (7:11).

This description of YHWH, like other apocalyptic descriptions of God, is what Newsom calls "audacious" and intended to "overwhelm the senses in such a way that the transcendent mystery of the divine is preserved."[54] His hair and clothing are white, and his throne is fiery. Fire gushes out from his presence. He is attended by innumerable beings. Of this imagery here and elsewhere in apocalyptic literature, Newsom notes that "the awe-inspiring wholly otherness of the divine being is suggested imagistically through the motifs of whiteness for the Deity and fire for his throne." The primary emphasis of apocalyptic authors is on "shining brightness" as characteristic of divine beings, perhaps to emphasize the difference between the divine and the "fleshly and opaque" nature of humans. Deity is of a substance "more akin to light and fire."[55] Newsom explains the significance of this difference generally and in particular with respect to Daniel's vision of the throne room:

Since fire is deadly to humans, the association of the divine presence with fire underscores its transcendent otherness. The overwhelming sublimity of the divine presence is completed with a reference to the thousands and myriads of angelic figures who stand in attendance and serve him.... The image serves to suggest the unlimited power and splendor of the divine court.[56]

The throne room scene culminates in the convening of the court: it sat and books were opened (7:10e–f). While the Bible mentions several kinds of books,[57] the vision's portrayal of the fate of the four beasts in the next individual vision suggests these books contained the grounds for judgment.

e. Individual Vision: The Fate of the Four Beasts (7:11a–12b)

The final individual vision of the second vision block has a twofold "I was looking" statement (7:11a and 7:11c). The first gives the temporal context (7:11a–b), and the second is the content of the visionary element (7:11c–12)—that is, what Daniel saw. The first "I was looking" statement reaches back to the earlier visions of the little horn's boastful speaking (7:8) and links it to the judgment Daniel witnesses in this vision (7:11c–12). The syntax is difficult and awkward,[58] but it "coordinate[s]

---

54. Newsom, *Daniel*, 229. Newsom is contrasting physical descriptions of God in the Hebrew Bible generally (which are very rare) with the way in which apocalyptic literature describes God.

55. Newsom, *Daniel*, 229–30. Of the shining brightness of "white," she notes similar imagery in the Gospels (Matt 28:3; Mark 9:2–3). Cf. also Isa 45:7 and Jas 1:17.

56. Newsom, *Daniel*, 230–31.

57. Kinds of books in the Bible include a record of decreed destinies (Ps 139:16), a remembrance of sufferings and deeds (Ps 56:8–9; Isa 65:6), and a "book of life" (Ps 69:29[28]; cf. Exod 32:32–33). Later chapters of Daniel also refer to written records of God's purposes for history (8:26; 9:24; 10:21; 12:4, 9).

58. The translation of v. 11 is difficult on account of v. 11b: בֵּאדַיִן מִן־קָל מִלַּיָּא רַבְרְבָתָא, "then from the sound of the great words...." The word בֵּאדַיִן, "then," is usually a discourse marker that begins a new section of narrative, but here it stands after the verbal clause of v. 11a. Because of this unusual and difficult syntax, many commentators delete the first חָזֵה הֲוֵית, "I was looking" (v. 11a). However, given insufficient textual grounds to delete it, I follow those who retain it (e.g., Goldingay [*Daniel*, 333–36], Newsom [*Daniel*, 213–14], and Montgomery [*Commentary on the Book of Daniel*, 301–2]).

Daniel's perception of two scenes taking place concurrently."⁵⁹

This final vision of the second vision block contains a string of passive verbs in clauses all governed by the עַד דִּי, "until," of 7:11d: the fourth beast "was killed" (קְטִילַת, 7:11d); its body "was destroyed" (הוּבַד, 7:11e); it "was given" to the fire (יְהִיבַת, 7:11f). Then Daniel notes that the other three beasts had their dominion "taken away" (הֶעְדִּיו, 7:12a),⁶⁰ but an extension of life "was given" to them (יְהִיבַת, 7:12b). The reader knows that YHWH is the agent behind all this activity, but as was the case earlier in the vision (i.e., 7:4d–g, 5d–f, 6e), his sovereignty is subtle; Newsom comments, "The reader sees, but not everything."⁶¹

The topic of three clauses, the fourth beast and its destruction are the focus of this individual vision (7:11d–f). The other three beasts lose their power but have their lives prolonged. While the exact meaning of this judgment is unclear, at the very least it reiterates the fact that the horrible fourth beast was different from the others; appropriately, its judgment is different and much worse.⁶²

3. Vision Block 3: *One Like a Son of Man* (7:13a–28d)

Main Idea of the Passage

In Daniel 7:13–28 Daniel's vision continues, and he sees one "like a son of man" receiving the eternal kingdom and the worship of all people, nations, and languages. He reports his alarm at the vision he saw, and he learns from an unnamed interpreter what the vision meant. Then the vision of the four beasts concludes with Daniel's recounting of his troubled reaction to it.

Literary Context

Daniel 7:13–28 is the third and final section of the narrative that comprises ch. 7. The longest of the vision blocks, it is the climax and conclusion of Daniel's first vision. As the climax, it presents the fifth figure of Daniel's vision—the humanlike figure that contrasts with the beasts and receives a kingdom that surpasses theirs.

---

59. Newsom, *Daniel*, 232.

60. הֶעְדִּיו is a 3mp *haphel*, a grammatically active verb functioning as an impersonal (or divine) passive here. Biblical Aramaic uses this construction frequently—that is, expressing a passive by way of an impersonal or indefinite subject with an active verb. See Johns, *A Short Grammar of Biblical Aramaic*, 26. When the agent is understood to be YHWH, the label "divine passive" is often used.

61. Newsom, *Daniel*, 232.

62. Lucas says the difference reflects the discriminating and just nature of YHWH's judgment: "The fourth beast was *different* from the others and so was dealt with differently, as its greater offences deserved" (*Daniel*, 183).

Through a divine interpreter, it also provides the interpretation of the vision that Daniel saw, an interpretation that assured the victory of the eternal kingdom against the warring eleventh horn of the fourth beast. In the conclusion of the vision report, the section leaves the reader with a Daniel deeply troubled by what he had witnessed. This section also brings the Aramaic portion of the book of Daniel to a close.

> F. Narrative 6: God's Superior King and Eternal Kingdom (7:1a–28d)
>   1. Vision Block 1: The Three Beasts (7:1a–6e)
>   2. Vision Block 2: The Fourth Beast (7:7a–12b)
>   **3. Vision Block 3: One Like a Son of Man (7:13a–28d)**

Translation and Exegetical Outline

(See pages 372–74.)

Structure and Literary Form

The third section in ch. 7 (7:13–28) continues and concludes Daniel's first-person report of his vision of the beasts and the heavenly throne room. This final vision block consists of five subsections (7:13–14, 15–20, 21–22, 23–27, and 28) that include two individual visions (7:13–14 and 7:21–22), two interpretive interludes (7:15–20 and 7:23–27), and Daniel's concluding thoughts (7:28).

In the first subsection (7:13–14), Daniel's vision returns to the divine throne room, where he witnesses the arrival of "one like a son of man" (כְּבַר אֱנָשׁ, 7:13b), who receives the eternal kingdom and the worship of all peoples, nations, and languages (7:13–14). In the second subsection (7:15–20), the first interpretive interlude, Daniel recounts his emotional reaction to what he had been seeing—distress and alarm (יְבַהֲלֻנַּנִי, אֶתְכְּרִיַּת; 7:15). He then reports that he approached "one of those standing by" to ask about the vision (7:16a–b). In an embedded reported speech, the interpreter provides Daniel with information about the four beasts (7:17) and the eternal kingdom (7:18). Then Daniel inquires about the fourth beast in particular (7:19b), the ten horns (7:20a), and the eleventh horn (7:20c–d).

The third subsection (7:21–22) is another individual vision in which Daniel witnesses more of the little horn's activity (7:21b), particularly with respect to the "holy ones" (קַדִּישִׁין, 7:21b), while the fourth subsection (7:23–27) is another interpretive interlude in which Daniel learns the meaning of the fourth beast (7:23), the ten horns

Daniel 7:13a–28d

3. Vision Block 3: One Like a Son of Man (7:13a–28d)

a. Individual Vision: Coming with the Clouds and Receiving the Eternal Kingdom (7:13a–14f)

13a	חָזֵה הֲוֵית בְּחֶזְוֵי לֵילְיָא	I was looking in the visions of the night,
13b	וַאֲרוּ עִם־עֲנָנֵי שְׁמַיָּא כְּבַר אֱנָשׁ אָתֵה הֲוָה	and oh! With the clouds of heaven one like a son of man was coming.
13c	וְעַד־עַתִּיק יוֹמַיָּא מְטָה	He came up to the Ancient of Days,
13d	וּקְדָמוֹהִי הַקְרְבוּהִי׃	and they presented him before him.
14a	וְלֵהּ יְהִיב שָׁלְטָן וִיקָר וּמַלְכוּ	And to him was given dominion and glory and a kingdom,
14b	וְכֹל עַמְמַיָּא אֻמַּיָּא וְלִשָּׁנַיָּא לֵהּ יִפְלְחוּן	and all peoples, nations, and languages will serve him.
14c	שָׁלְטָנֵהּ שָׁלְטָן עָלַם	His dominion is an eternal dominion
14d	דִּי־לָא יֶעְדֵּה	↑ that will not pass away,
14e	וּמַלְכוּתֵהּ	and his kingdom (is one)
14f	דִּי־לָא תִתְחַבַּל׃	↑ that will not be destroyed.

b. Interpretive Interlude 1 (7:15a–20h)

(1) Daniel's Distress and Query (7:15a–16b)

15a	אֶתְכְּרִיַּת רוּחִי אֲנָה דָנִיֵּאל בְּגוֹא נִדְנֶה	My spirit was distressed—I, Daniel—within me,
15b	וְחֶזְוֵי רֵאשִׁי יְבַהֲלֻנַּנִי׃	and the visions of my head were alarming me.
16a	קִרְבֵת עַל־חַד מִן־קָאֲמַיָּא	I approached one of those standing by,
16b	וְיַצִּיבָא אֶבְעֵא־מִנֵּהּ עַל־כָּל־דְּנָה	and I sought from him the truth concerning all this.
16c	וַאֲמַר־לִי	He spoke to me,
16d	וּפְשַׁר מִלַּיָּא יְהוֹדְעִנַּנִי׃	↑ so that he might make known to me the interpretation of the matter.

(2) Four Human Kings and the Eternal Kingdom (7:16c–18b)

17aα	אִלֵּין חֵיוָתָא רַבְרְבָתָא	'These great beasts, …
17b	דִּי אִנִּין אַרְבַּע	↑ which they are four,
17aβ	… אַרְבְּעָה מַלְכִין	… are four kings.
17c	יְקוּמוּן מִן־אַרְעָא׃	They will arise from the earth,
18a	וִיקַבְּלוּן מַלְכוּתָא קַדִּישֵׁי עֶלְיוֹנִין	but the holy ones of the Most High will receive the kingdom,
18b	וְיַחְסְנוּן מַלְכוּתָא עַד־עָלְמָא וְעַד עָלַם עָלְמַיָּא׃	and they will possess the kingdom forever and forever and ever.'

(3) Daniel's Inquiry about the Fourth Beast (7:19a–20h)

19a	אֱדַיִן צְבִית לְיַצָּבָא	Then I desired
19b	עַל־חֵיוְתָא רְבִיעָיְתָא	↑ to make certain concerning the fourth beast,
19c	דִּי־הֲוָת שָׁנְיָה מִן־כָּלְּהֵין [כֻּלְּהוֹן]	↑ which was different from all of them—
19d	דְּחִילָה יַתִּירָה	(it was) exceedingly dreadful;

	English	Section
19e	Its teeth were of iron,	
19f	and its claws were of bronze.	
19g	It was eating,	
19h	and crushing,	
19i	and trampling the rest under its feet	
20a	—and concerning the ten horns,	
20b	which were on its head.	
20c	And [concerning] the other	
20d	which came up	
20e	and three fell before it.	
20f	And as for that horn—it had eyes	c. Individual Vision: The Little Horn and the Holy Ones (7:21a–22d)
20g	and a mouth speaking great things.	
20h	And its appearance was larger than its associate(s).	
21a	I was looking,	
21b	and that horn was making war with the holy ones,	
21c	and it was overcoming them	
22a	until the Ancient of Days came,	
22b	and judgment was given for the holy ones of the Most High.	
22c	And the time came,	
22d	and the holy ones took possession of the kingdom.	
23a	Thus he said,	d. Interpretive Interlude 2: The Fourth Beast and the Horns (7:23a–27b)
23b	'The fourth beast will be a fourth kingdom on the earth	(1) The Fourth Kingdom (7:23a–f)
23c	that will be different from all kingdoms,	
23d	and will devour all the earth,	
23e	and will trample it down,	
23f	and will crush it.	

Continued on next page.

Continued from previous page.

	Aramaic	English	Outline
24a		As for the ten horns—from this kingdom ten kings will arise,	(2) The Ten Horns (7:24a)
24b		and another will arise after them.	(3) The Little Horn (7:24b–26d)
24c		He will be different from the previous ones.	
24d		He will subdue three kings,	
25a		and he will speak words against the Most High,	
25b		and he will wear out the holy ones of the Most High.	
25c		And he will intend	
25d		↑ to change times set by law.[1]	
25e		They will be given into his hand until a time, times, and half a time.	
26a		The court will sit,	
26b		and his dominion they will take away,	
26c		↑ in order to destroy	
26d		and abolish until the end.	
27a		And the kingdom, the dominion, and the greatness of the kingdoms under all the heavens will be given to the people of the holy ones of the Most High.	(4) The Victory of the Eternal Kingdom (7:27a–b)
27b		Their kingdom is an everlasting kingdom,	
27c		and all dominions will serve and obey them.'	
28a		At this point was the end of the account.	e. Daniel's Conclusion (7:28a–d)
28b		As for me, Daniel, my thoughts were greatly alarming me,	
28c		and my countenance was changing upon me.	
28d		But I kept the matter in my heart."	

1. The translation here is similar to that of Goldingay's "to change times set by edict." He reads "times and law" as hendiadys, "a frequent device in ch. 7" (*Daniel*, 334, 338n25.b–b).

(7:24a), and the little horn (7:24b–26). The interpreter concludes with details about the triumph of the everlasting kingdom (7:27). In the fifth and final subsection, Daniel concludes his vision report by saying that his thoughts were deeply troubling to him (7:28).

Table 7.3. Vision Block 3 (Dan 7:13–28)		
Individual Vision	**Verse**	**Vision Block 3—One Like a Son of Man (7:13–28)**
1	13	*I was looking in the visions of the night,*
		and oh! With the clouds of heaven one like a son of man was coming.
		He came up to the Ancient of Days,
		and they presented him before him.
		And to him was given dominion and glory and a kingdom,
		and all peoples, nations, and languages will serve him.
		His dominion is an eternal dominion
		that will not pass away,
		and his kingdom (is one)
		that will not be destroyed.
		INTERPRETIVE INTERLUDE 1 (7:15–20)
	15	MY SPIRIT WAS DISTRESSED—I, DANIEL—WITHIN ME,
		AND THE VISIONS OF MY HEAD WERE ALARMING ME.
	16	I APPROACHED ONE OF THOSE STANDING BY,
		AND I SOUGHT FROM HIM THE TRUTH CONCERNING ALL THIS.
		HE SPOKE TO ME,
		SO THAT HE MIGHT MAKE KNOWN TO ME THE INTERPRETATION OF THE MATTER.
	17	"THESE GREAT BEASTS, . . .
		WHICH THEY ARE FOUR,
		. . . ARE FOUR KINGS.
		THEY WILL ARISE FROM THE EARTH,
	18	BUT THE HOLY ONES OF THE MOST HIGH WILL RECEIVE THE KINGDOM,
		AND THEY WILL POSSESS THE KINGDOM FOREVER AND FOREVER AND EVER."
	19	THEN I DESIRED
		TO MAKE CERTAIN CONCERNING THE FOURTH BEAST,
		WHICH WAS DIFFERENT FROM ALL OF THEM—

Continued on next page.

Continued from previous page.

	20	(IT WAS) EXCEEDINGLY DREADFUL;
		 ITS TEETH WERE OF IRON,
		 AND ITS CLAWS WERE OF BRONZE.
		 IT WAS EATING,
		 AND CRUSHING
		 AND TRAMPLING THE REST UNDER ITS FEET
		 —AND CONCERNING THE TEN HORNS,
		   WHICH WERE ON ITS HEAD.
		 AND [CONCERNING] THE OTHER
		   WHICH CAME UP
		   AND THREE FELL BEFORE IT.
		 AND AS FOR THAT HORN—IT HAD EYES
		   AND A MOUTH SPEAKING GREAT THINGS.
		 AND ITS APPEARANCE WAS LARGER THAN ITS ASSOCIATE(S).

2	21	*I was looking,*
		 and that horn was making war with the holy ones,
		 and it was overcoming them
		   until the Ancient of Days came,
		     and judgment was given for the holy ones of the Most High.
		 And the time came,
		 and the holy ones took possession of the kingdom.

		INTERPRETATIVE INTERLUDE 2 (7:23–27)

	23	THUS HE SAID,
		 -
		 "THE FOURTH BEAST WILL BE A FOURTH KINGDOM ON THE EARTH
		   THAT WILL BE DIFFERENT FROM ALL KINGDOMS
		   AND WILL DEVOUR ALL THE EARTH,
		   AND WILL TRAMPLE IT DOWN,
		   AND WILL CRUSH IT.

	24	AS FOR THE TEN HORNS—FROM THIS KINGDOM TEN KINGS WILL ARISE, AND ANOTHER WILL ARISE AFTER THEM. HE WILL BE DIFFERENT FROM THE PREVIOUS ONES. HE WILL SUBDUE THREE KINGS,
	25	AND HE WILL SPEAK WORDS AGAINST THE MOST HIGH, AND HE WILL WEAR OUT THE HOLY ONES OF THE MOST HIGH.

	26	AND HE WILL INTEND
		    TO CHANGE TIMES AND LAWS
		THEY WILL BE GIVEN INTO HIS HAND UNTIL A TIME, TIMES, AND HALF A TIME.
		THE COURT WILL SIT,
		AND HIS DOMINION THEY WILL TAKE AWAY,
		    IN ORDER TO DESTROY
		    AND ABOLISH UNTIL THE END.

	27	AND THE KINGDOM, THE DOMINION, AND THE GREATNESS OF THE KINGDOMS UNDER ALL THE HEAVENS WILL BE GIVEN TO THE PEOPLE OF THE HOLY ONES OF THE MOST HIGH. THEIR KINGDOM IS AN EVERLASTING KINGDOM, AND ALL DOMINIONS WILL SERVE AND OBEY THEM."
	28	DANIEL'S CONCLUSION (7:28) AT THIS POINT WAS THE END OF THE ACCOUNT. AS FOR ME, DANIEL, MY THOUGHTS WERE GREATLY ALARMING ME, AND MY COUNTENANCE WAS CHANGING UPON ME. BUT I KEPT THE MATTER IN MY HEART.

		Abbreviated Version of Vision Block 3
Individual Vision	**Verse**	**Vision Block 3—One Like a Son of Man (7:13–28)**

1	13	*I was looking in the visions of the night,*
		and oh! With the clouds of heaven one like a son of man was coming.
		He came up to the Ancient of Days,
		and they presented him before him.
		And to him was given dominion and glory and a kingdom,
		    and all peoples, nations, and languages will serve him.
		His dominion is an eternal dominion
		    that will not pass away,
		and his kingdom [is one]
		    that will not be destroyed.
		
		INTERPRETATIVE INTERLUDE 1 (7:15–20)

Continued on next page.

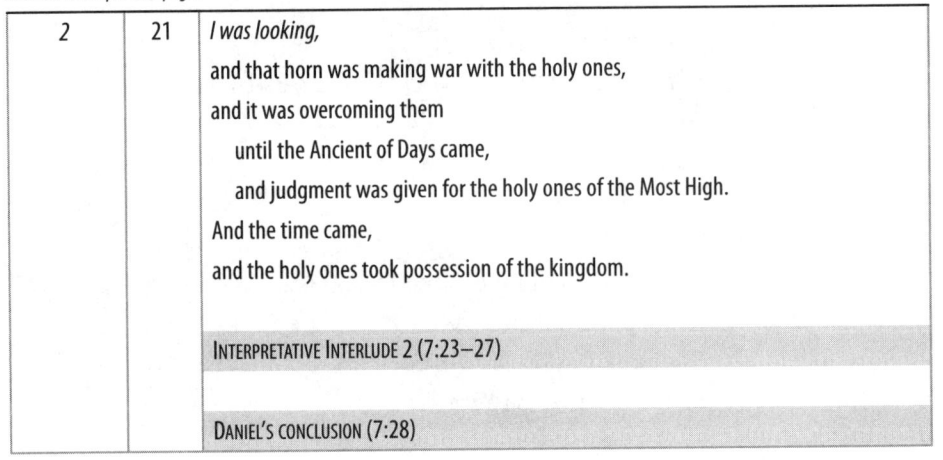

2	21	I was looking,
		and that horn was making war with the holy ones,
		and it was overcoming them
		until the Ancient of Days came,
		and judgment was given for the holy ones of the Most High.
		And the time came,
		and the holy ones took possession of the kingdom.
		INTERPRETATIVE INTERLUDE 2 (7:23–27)
		DANIEL'S CONCLUSION (7:28)

Explanation of the Text

a. Individual Vision: Coming with the Clouds and Receiving the Eternal Kingdom (7:13a–14f)

The final vision block is the longest of the three vision blocks and begins with חָזֵה הֲוֵית בְּחֶזְוֵי לֵילְיָא וַאֲרוּ, "I was looking in the visions of the night, and oh!" (7:13a–b), the most complex variation of the "I was looking" statement (see also 7:2c–d, 7a–b). This statement also identifies the first element of the vision block: the coming of "one like a son of man" (כְּבַר אֱנָשׁ) "with the clouds of heaven" (7:13b).

Daniel's description of this fifth distinct being contrasts with the description of the previous four in several ways. The first contrast is in location: the first four beings arose from a tumultuous sea (7:2–3), but the fifth comes with the clouds of heaven (7:13b). The placement of the prepositional phrase "with the clouds of heaven" (עִם־עֲנָנֵי שְׁמַיָּא) in clause-initial position sharpens the contrast between the beasts that arose from the sea and this final figure whose origin is in the heavenly sphere. The second contrast between the four creatures and the fifth figure is in their nature: the first four were said to be beasts (7:3a) and three of them were compared with recognizable beasts (7:4–6, 7, 11–12), while the fifth is compared to a human. This human likeness stands in sharp contrast to the grotesque, other worldly beasts that arose from the sea. The third contrast between the beasts and the "one like a son of man" is in activity: the first three beings were described with passive verbs (7:4d–g, 5b, 6e, 12a–b) or as subject to an outside agent (7:5d–f), and the fourth was described with active verbs (until its destruction; 7:7d–f, 11d–f), but the fifth is described with a balance of active and passive verbs: מְטָה, "he came" (7:13c); הַקְרְבוּהִי, "they presented him" (3mp *haphel* perfect, a "divine passive," 7:13d); יְהִיב, "was given" (7:14a).

The imagery of clouds in this scene is significant. While עָנָן (Aramaic עֲנָן), "cloud," in the Hebrew Bible can refer to the meteorological phenomenon (e.g., Gen 9:13–14; Job 26:8; Ezek 1:28), more often it is used in figurative language (e.g., a metaphor for impermanence in Hos 6:4, for immensity in Ezek 38:9, and for impenetrability in

Lam 3:44). But by far, its most frequent association is with theophanies—that is, appearances of God. Fifty-eight of the eighty-seven occurrences of עָנָן appear in the context of God's presence.[63] The Pentateuch, especially, speaks of visible manifestations of YHWH's glory in the cloud atop Sinai and over the tent of meeting (e.g., Exod 24:16; 40:34–35), and his presence in the pillar of cloud guides the people through the wilderness (e.g., Num 14:14; Deut 31:15). Later texts about the temple also refer to the cloud (1 Kgs 8:11; Ezek 10:4).

But it is not just the presence of clouds in Dan 7 that is significant—we already know YHWH (the Ancient of Days) is present in the throne room (see above on 7:9–10). What is particularly significant about the clouds in Dan 7 is that someone is coming on/with them (7:13b). Those of us outside Daniel's context may well picture someone floating into the throne room on a billowy heap of clouds,[64] but this is probably not what Daniel would have seen. In Daniel's ancient Near Eastern context, he would have seen someone riding the clouds like a chariot. The Old Testament speaks of YHWH riding his cloud chariot through the heavens (Ps 104:3; cf. Ps 68:5[4] where the rider imagery is present without specifying the clouds), and the prophets speak of YHWH riding a cloud in judgment (Isa 19:1; cf. Jer 4:13; Nah 1:3). In the wider Canaanite world, the storm god, Baal, was the Rider of the Clouds who controlled weather and thus agricultural fertility. Armed with a bolt of lightning, he bestowed rain on faithful worshipers. In Ugarit, a fifteenth-century-BCE city-state on the Syrian coast north of Israel, Baal was the divine hero who had defeated Yamm in the sea god's attempt to become god over the pantheon. Baal's victory won him kingship among the gods, and he served as vice-regent under his father, the high god El, an aged wise figure who presided over the world and was attended by a divine council.

Do not miss what is happening in Daniel's vision. There is a fiery scene surrounding YHWH, seated on the throne, *and* there is a cloud with someone riding on it. In the Old Testament, YHWH *is* the one who rides the clouds. In this single vision, there are two YHWH figures: the Ancient of Days YHWH on the throne and the cloud-riding YHWH receiving the eternal right to rule. Daniel was seeing *two* powers in heaven—the one on the throne and a vice-regent, sharing YHWH's essence and receiving everlasting dominion and power.

Daniel's vision of the throne room provides a stunning portrayal of the divine council in Israelite theology, as well as highlighting its most significant difference from other divine councils of the ancient Near East. In the Canaanite divine council, the Rider of the Clouds was El's vice-regent and received the eternal right to rule when he defeated Yamm. But Baal was a different god than El. In the Israelite divine council, however, the vice-regent position "was not filled by another god, but by Yahweh himself in another form. This 'hypostasis' of Yahweh was the same essence as Yahweh but a distinct, second person."[65] Israel's divine council was headed by YHWH (El/Elohim), but its vice-regent shared the essence of YHWH. This has pro-

---

63. Mark D. Futato, "עָנָן," *NIDOTTE* 3:465–66.

64. The imagery in *my* head of someone coming "on/with the clouds" relates to the second coming of Christ, since Jesus himself draws on the imagery of Dan 7 (see Matt 24:30; 26:64; Mark 13:26; 14:62; cf. 1 Thess 4:17; Rev 1:7; 14:14–16). My mental picture of this event before I immersed myself in the Old Testament was of a shining Jesus in a white billowy robe descending—floating, really—in a heap of clouds down to the earth. More likely, the imagery entails Jesus riding the clouds as a warrior.

65. Heiser, "Divine Council," 114. Heiser observes that this hypostasis is most evident in the Name theology of the Old Testament and in the "angel of YHWH."

found implications for understanding monotheism according to the Old Testament. Israel's divine council had a "second person" sharing YHWH's essence—exactly what was needed to understand Jesus's claim to be one with the Father in the New Testament.[66]

The humanlike figure was formally presented to the Ancient of Days (7:13d), and "to him" (לֵהּ) was given dominion and a glorious kingdom (7:14a). The placement of לֵהּ, "to him," in clause-initial position is significant in light of how the previous vision block ended—that is, with dominion being taken away from the beasts (7:12a). Now it is given to the cloud-riding humanlike figure—forever. It will never pass away or be destroyed, as all others will.

The "one like a son of man" will ultimately receive the service[67] of "all peoples, nations, and languages," a list that calls to mind the worshipers of Nebuchadnezzar's statue in ch. 3 (3:4, 7) and the recipients of Nebuchadnezzar's and Darius's proclamations in chs. 4 and 6 (3:31[4:1]; 6:26[25]; cf. 5:19). That this kingdom is eternal also echoes earlier references in the book (2:44; 3:33[4:3]; 4:31[34]); the bestowal of this kingdom on the cloud-rider is the book's culminating perspective on "kingdoms"—all others will pass away or be destroyed, but this one will last forever.[68]

b. Interpretive Interlude 1 (7:15a–20h)

Daniel's emotional response to what he had seen was distress (אֶתְכְּרִיַּת, 7:15a), and the inclusion of the phrase אֲנָה דָנִיֵּאל, "I, Daniel," in the report of his response draws attention to the fact that the one who had interpreted troubling dreams for others was himself troubled by a vision (cf. 2:1; 4:1[4]). Cook paraphrases the effect: "even I, Daniel, was disturbed in my spirit (by this vision)."[69] His active response to what he had just seen was to approach "one of those standing by" (7:16a). The identity of this figure is not provided, but given what Daniel has just seen, it is likely he approached one of the attendants at the throne of the Ancient of Days (7:10c–d). A supernatural interpreter is a feature of apocalyptic literature, and typically the task falls to a heavenly attendant.[70]

Daniel's actual question to the interpreter is not included, but the interpreter's answer is embedded as reported speech (7:17–18). The initial answer to Daniel's query is little more than a tantalizing summary: the four beasts are four kings, arising from the earth; the eternal kingdom will be received by the holy ones of the Most High, and they will possess it forever.

The interpreter begins by identifying "these great beasts" (7:17aα) as four kings (7:17aβ). An im-

---

66. The Jews' understanding of monotheism developed during the Second Temple period, but how that happened goes beyond the scope of this study. For more information and full bibliographies, see resources already cited on the divine council, and especially see p. 368n50.

67. The NIV translates פלח as "worship" in 7:14, where others say "serve" (e.g., ESV, NASB). While the Aramaic word can refer to service or worship given to humans or to gods, outside Dan 7 the recipient is always divine (3:12, 14, 17–18, 28; 6:17[16], 21[20]; Ezra 7:24). In Dan 7, the difficulty is that the same word is used in v. 27, where the "holy ones" are the recipients.

68. The vision later says the kingdom is received by the "holy ones of the Most High" (v. 18) and the "people of the holy ones of the Most High" (v. 27). The relationships between the son of man figure and these other groups has been discussed extensively without reaching consensus. The debate includes theories on the identity of "one like a son of man" and the ancient Near Eastern background of the imagery. For this discussion, see Goldingay (*Daniel*, 364–70) and the excursus in Collins (*Daniel*, 304–10). At the very least, we can say that the son of man figure symbolized or represented the saints in some way, though it need not have been a one-to-one correspondence. See further below on vv. 18 and 27.

69. Cook, *Aramaic Ezra and Daniel*, 293.

70. See, e.g., Zech 1 and the book of Revelation; Cook, *Aramaic Ezra and Daniel*, 294.

mediate question with respect to this interpretation is whether the number "four" is symbolic. Earlier in the vision, when the "four winds of heaven" stirred up the sea (7:2), "four" was symbolic for the totality of the wind: it was swirling from every direction. Do the four beasts here represent the totality of human kings or do they represent four specific kings? Perhaps, as Baldwin suggests, both are true, and perhaps the redundancy of the number "four" in 7:17b (דִּי אִנּוּן אַרְבְּעָה, "which they are four") points in this direction.

In this first vision, the interpreter offers no definitive identification of the kings or kingdoms,[71] as he will in subsequent visions (i.e., 8:20–21; 11:2). Instead, we have only what is of greatest interest to the interpreter: "the transfer of sovereignty from the four earthly kingdoms to 'the holy ones of the Most High.'"[72] While we assume the details of Daniel's vision are meaningful, the scant information provided cautions us against assigning too much significance to secondary issues in the text.[73] The text's focus should be our focus.

The interpreter says these four kings will arise from the earth (7:17c), whereas in the vision itself the beasts were said to arise from the sea (7:3). These are not contradictory statements, but rather they express different theological emphases. In 7:3, the sea represented chaos and forces opposed to the creator God; in 7:17, the point is that the kings/kingdoms are of a human, earthly origin, in contrast to the heavenly kingdom of the son of man figure.[74]

Verse 18 provides the contrast to the kingdoms of these "four grotesque and vicious beasts" that represent earthly kings—"*but* the holy ones of the Most High will receive the kingdom."[75] The assurance of the interpreter is that ultimately, the only enduring kingdom will belong to the "holy ones of the Most High" (קַדִּישֵׁי עֶלְיוֹנִין).[76] The longevity of their possession is also of great importance in the text: it is "forever and forever and ever" (עַד־עָלְמָא וְעַד עָלַם עָלְמַיָּא, 7:18b). This threefold repetition "underscores the unending perpetuity" of the holy ones' possession of the kingdom.[77]

While the interpretation itself includes no specific information about the lion-like creature, the text's earlier emphasis on the first beast and especially on its transformation invites further discussion at this point (see above on 7:4). There is consensus among interpreters that the lion-eagle beast represents Nebuchadnezzar,[78] and the description of the beast's removal of wings, elevation upon two feet, and human mind seems to capture well the description of the great king's humbling and restoration in Dan 4.[79] In the context of Daniel's vision, the significance of this transformation

---

71. The switch between "kings" and "kingdoms" is fluid in this chapter and also in ch. 2. A king represents a kingdom.
72. Newsom, *Daniel*, 237.
73. See IN DEPTH: The Identities of the Kingdoms, Take 2 below.
74. Lucas, *Daniel*, 187–88.
75. Cook, *Aramaic Ezra and Daniel*, 296.
76. The holy ones of the Most High (קַדִּישֵׁי עֶלְיוֹנִין) are best understood as heavenly beings (cf. 4:10[13], 14[17], 20[23]), a view "especially supported by the designation in 7:27 of the עַם קַדִּישֵׁי עֶלְיוֹנִין 'the people of the holy ones of the Most High,' which clearly distinguishes between the 'people' and the 'holy ones'" (Cook, *Aramaic Ezra and Daniel*, 296). Understanding heavenly beings as recipients of the eternal kingdom in Dan 7 (see also v. 22) also coheres with the Gospel writers' references to the "Son of Man" coming "with the (holy) angels" (Matt 16:27; 25:31; Mark 8:38; Luke 9:26).
77. Cook, *Aramaic Ezra and Daniel*, 297.
78. See further IN DEPTH: The Identities of the Kingdoms, Take 2 below.
79. Commentators interpret the description of the lion's transformation in opposite ways. Some see only judgment in the lion's loss of strength and ferocity as it becomes humanlike, while others see judgment and restoration in the imagery (as I do).

from beast to humanlike biped lies in the vision's contrast between the beastly, earthly kingdoms doomed to destruction and the superior heavenly kingdom given to the humanlike figure. Of the four beasts, only the first one is metamorphosed into a being more man than beast. Nebuchadnezzar's transformation from king to beast and back again in ch. 4 was propelled by how he responded to the royal power granted him by the Most High: when he failed to acknowledge the superior sovereignty of the Most High, he became beastlike; when he acknowledged the Most High as ruler over all human kings and kingdoms, he became a greater version of the human he had been before (4:33[36]). The matrix of images associated with Nebuchadnezzar in the book of Daniel suggests that human rulers are most human when they rule in humble recognition of their place in God's hierarchy.[80] Goldingay observes that God appointed this creature "to a humanlike position of honor, authority, responsibility, and care for the world (cf. 2:38; 4:20–22[17–19]). It is given a role in the world with a significance like that of a *symbolic* human figure."[81]

Returning to the scant summary of the interpretation in Dan 7, Daniel (like most readers today) was not satisfied with what he learned, and so he requested more information—and specifically about the fourth beast, its ten horns, and the little eleventh horn. Whereas he had originally asked the interpreter "concerning all this" (עַל־כָּל־דְּנָה, 7:16b), where "this" referred to his entire vision, here his query is largely repetitious of his account of the vision itself (7:19-20; cf. 7:7-8). The effect of this repetition, when Daniel could have simply said (as I just did) that he wanted to know more about the fourth beast, the ten horns, and the little horn, is twofold. First, it reinforces Daniel's horror at what he saw in the fourth beast and its stages of development. Second, it sets up what he is about to report in 7:21–22—namely, a further individual vision involving the little horn (קַרְנָא דִכֵּן, "that horn," 7:21b).

The two descriptions have a few differences. Daniel's original description began with details about the activity of the fearsome fourth beast (eating, crushing, and trampling; 7:7d-f) and concluded with the summary that the fourth beast was different from the rest (7:7g-h). In his query, however, he begins by identifying the fourth beast as the one that was different from the rest (7:19c) and then describes the activity that made it so (eating, crushing, and trampling; 7:19g-i). His original description mentioned the great iron teeth (7:7c), while his query adds that the beast also had bronze claws (7:19f). Newsom notes that since the beast's activities include an action with the teeth and an action with the feet, "the addition of a note about the appearance of the feet complements the detail about the iron teeth."[82] His original description of the eleventh horn included that it was little (7:8b), but his query notes that its appearance was larger than the others (7:20h)—probably suggesting "its dynamic and aggressive nature."[83]

c. Individual Vision: The Little Horn and the Holy Ones (7:21a–22d)

Before the interpreter could respond, Daniel recounts another element of his vision, beginning in 7:21. This individual vision begins with the formulaic statement חָזֵה הֲוֵית, "I was looking" (7:21a), and in it Daniel sees the eleventh little horn, called

---

80. See From Creation to Forever: Humanity as God Intended below, pp. 393–400.
81. Goldingay, *Daniel*, 358.
82. Newsom, *Daniel*, 238.
83. Newsom, *Daniel*, 238.

"that horn" (קַרְנָא דִכֵּן)—here, a reference back to his description in 7:20c–h. The horn was making war with the "holy ones" and gaining the upper hand over them "until" (עַד דִּי, 7:22a) the Ancient of Days came and judgment was pronounced in favor of the holy ones (7:22b).

What Daniel witnesses is a scene that appears to fit between 7:8 and 7:9 of his earlier vision involving the little horn. There, the little horn spoke "great things" (רַבְרְבָן, 7:8e), and here it oppresses the holy ones with great success. What appears to save the holy ones from defeat is the coming of the Ancient of Days and the subsequent passing of judgment, as described in the throne room scene of 7:9–10. But the actual enactment of the pronounced judgment seems to be delayed. Verse 22c begins "and the time came," and then the holy ones took possession of the kingdom (7:22d). "Time" is a recurring idea in the book of Daniel, where God is the one who controls the times—raising up rulers for a time and taking them down again (2:21; 4:29[32], 31[34]); here, when the time has come, the holy ones take possession of the kingdom.

d. Interpretive Interlude 2: The Fourth Beast and the Horns (7:23a–27c)

After Daniel's vision of 7:21–22, the angelic interpreter continued speaking, giving Daniel additional information about the fourth beast in 7:23. He first repeats that it represents a kingdom (cf. 7:17), specifying that it is a fourth kingdom. As with the number "four" in 7:17b, the ordinal "fourth" is semantically unnecessary here and likely hints at the symbolic nature of the number. In his commentary on the apocalyptic book of Revelation, Beale notes that four is "a number of completeness, especially connoting something of universal or worldwide scope."[84] It is "the number of cosmic completeness."[85] In Daniel's vision, this fourth beast/kingdom does have a historical referent (see IN DEPTH: The Identities of the Kingdoms, Take 2 below), but it also goes beyond that. This beastly kingdom represents the worst of human kingdoms; its horror is the culmination of all that opposes God.[86]

In 7:23 the interpreter describes the activity of the fourth beast in a description that echoes the two earlier descriptions by Daniel (cf. 7:7, 19). He first notes its difference from "all kingdoms" (7:23c), not simply the ones that came before it (cf. 7:7g–h, 19c, 24c)—another textual hint at the universal scope and significance of this final kingdom. Similarly, the beast devours "all the earth" (7:23d).

In 7:24 the interpreter addresses the meaning of the beast's horns. He first identifies the ten horns as ten kings arising from the fourth kingdom. The use of the number "ten" again raises the question of numerical symbolism since "ten" appears frequently in apocalyptic literature, where authors commonly divide history into ten periods of time.[87] As noted earlier (see on 7:7 above), the imagery of a "horn" conveys power, so this beast—with five times the number of horns that are natural for a beast—has extraordinary power.

The interpreter then turns his attention to the

---

84. G. K. Beale, *The Book of Revelation: A Commentary on the Greek Text*, NIGTC (Grand Rapids; Carlisle, Cumbria: Eerdmans; Paternoster Press, 1999), 59.

85. Beale, *The Book of Revelation*, 60.

86. Mowinckel says, "The fourth unites in itself all the power and cruelty of its predecessors" (S. Mowinckel, *He That Cometh*, trans. G. W. Anderson [Nashville: Abingdon, n.d.], 349).

87. Collins, *Daniel*, 321. See IN DEPTH: The Identities of the Kingdoms, Take 2 below for theories on the identity of the ten kingdoms.

eleventh king—"another one" (אָחֳרָן, 7:24b). He does not directly refer to the appearance of the horn that represented this king (i.e., its eyes, mouth, and size; cf. 7:8b, 8d–e, and 20f–h), but simply summarizes the king's uniqueness by saying he would be different from the earlier ones (הוּא יִשְׁנֵא מִן־קַדְמָיֵא, 7:24c)—using the overt subject pronoun הוּא to focus attention on this king. This king would subdue three kings, represented by the three uprooted horns (7:8c) that fell before it (7:20e) in Daniel's vision. This king would speak words against the Most High—the interpretation of the "great things" spoken by the mouth of the little horn in Daniel's vision (7:8e, 20g). The interpreter offers no explanation of the human eyes on the little horn, and it may simply be that the eyes suggest the "arrogance, irreverence, and wickedness"[88] of the little horn in its challenge of the Most High and its oppression of "the holy ones of the Most High" (7:25a–b; cf. Isa 5:15; Ps 18:28[27]; Prov 21:4).

At this point, the question about the identity of these holy ones again arises. As noted earlier, the holy ones in Daniel (as elsewhere in the Old Testament) are best understood as heavenly beings,[89] and there is good reason to see heavenly beings here as well. Although most of the Bible addresses life on earth, there are a few glimpses of life in the heavenly realm, and from this "pulling back of the curtain," we learn that what happens in the earthly realm mirrors what is happening in the heavenly realm.[90] Earthly conflicts can have significance beyond this terrestrial planet. In the conclusion of the book of Daniel, the narrator says the "wise will shine . . . like the stars" (12:3 NIV), an apocalyptic idiom for "fellowship with the angels. There is, therefore, a synergism between the faithful Israelites on earth and their angelic counterparts in heaven."[91]

If the eleventh king (and whatever divine beings he represented) was wearing out the holy ones of the Most High, he was heavily oppressing "their people" on earth (cf. 27a). In his vision, Daniel had seen the little horn overcoming the holy ones, imagery that is probably behind the interpreter's statement that the holy ones would be given into the eleventh king's hand "until a time, times, and half a time" (7:25e; cf. 21c). The significance of this enigmatic phrase is that the time allotted for the king's power was appointed and under divine control. Although the eleventh king would have considerable success, there was a limit; his oppression would not go on forever.[92]

Daniel had seen the little horn overcoming the holy ones "until" (עַד דִּי, 7:22a) the Ancient of Days came and judgment was given in favor of the holy ones, but he saw nothing of what that judgment looked like in terms of the little horn. In the interpreter's explanation, the court will remove the eleventh king's dominion in order to destroy and abolish it for all time.

With all that is evil about beastly rule done away with forever, the everlasting kingdom is given to "the people of the holy ones of the Most High" (7:27a). This is the book's final word on the everlasting kingdom.[93] Come what may in chs. 8–12, the people of this kingdom can cling to the promise

---

88. Hill, *Daniel*, 136. See on 7:8 above.
89. See on 7:18 and p. 381n76 above.
90. The second half of the book of Daniel contains several such references (8:10; 10:13–11:1).
91. Collins, *Daniel*, 318.
92. The expression is commonly understood to refer to a period of three and a half years, but עִדָּן does not mean "a year." Seow calls it "somewhat of a stretch" to think "that 'a time and times, and a portion of time' means 'a year, two years, and half a year'" (*Daniel*, 112). More important is its contrast with the everlasting nature of the divine kingdom (v. 27).
93. The eternal kingdom is a dominant theme of the first half of Daniel, but this is the last time in the book that it is mentioned (2:44; 3:33[4:3]; 4:31[34]; 6:27[26]).

that only the kingdom of the "one like a son of man," the "holy ones of the Most High," and the "people of the holy ones of the Most High" will endure forever and forever and ever (7:13–14, 22d, 27).

The interpreter's explanation concludes in 7:27, with much left unsaid about the vision's meaning; yet the interpreter also provided details not present in the imagery Daniel reported seeing. As Goldingay observes of the vision and its interpretation, "There is more symbolism than interpretation and more interpretation than symbolism; each stands on its own as a revelation."[94]

e. Daniel's Conclusion (7:28a–d)

Daniel concludes his vision report in 7:28a with the statement "at this point was the end of the account" (עַד־כָּה סוֹפָא דִי־מִלְּתָא). This statement has its corollary in 7:1d, "the beginning of the account he said" (רֵאשׁ מִלִּין אֲמַר), and the two statements bookend the vision report. Daniel again emphasizes the troubling effect of what he has seen by including the phrase "as for me, Daniel" (אֲנָה דָנִיֵּאל, 7:28b; cf. 7:15). The one who had interpreted dreams that troubled and alarmed others was himself alarmed by a vision (cf. 4:2[5]; 5:6, 9), and his face paled (cf. 5:6, 9).

While Daniel's vision portended worse times ahead for his people than their present exilic reality, the vision also offered comfort for God's people. First, from the portrayal of the little horn warring against the holy ones of the Most High, their situation took on cosmic significance; their struggle was greater than they knew, but it was one over which their God had complete control. Second, the struggle of the holy ones on their behalf reminded the people that they did not fight alone. Finally, God's kingdom would ultimately triumph. In Seow's words of summary, "Nothing less than world order is at stake, and 'the holy ones of the Most High'—both the celestial and the terrestrial—are together the champions fighting on the side of all that is good."[95]

Daniel's vision of the beasts in ch. 7 complements and supplements Nebuchadnezzar's dream of the statue in ch. 2, and particularly with respect to the fourth kingdom. Together, the chapters provide a full perspective on the realities of human sovereignty. Gooding summarizes:

> The pairing of these two chapters ... seems to be aimed at calling attention to the fact that there are two different ways of looking at, and estimating the character of, Gentile imperial rule, its strengths and its weaknesses. ... Gentile governments are from one point of view manlike, humane, majestic, but plagued with the weakness of incoherence, and at the same time ... from another point of view [they] are basically amoral, self-seeking, cruelly destructive, animal-like power-blocs.[96]

The combination of the chapters affirms that, regardless of the human government, the Most High God is sovereign over all. His rule is cosmic. He controls the circumstances and the times. His kingdom will eventually surpass and destroy all human kingdoms, and his people will possess that kingdom forever.

Chapter 7 leaves many unanswered questions, some of which will be answered in the visions of chs. 8 and 10–12. But not all questions will be resolved. As is the nature of apocalyptic literature,

---

94. Goldingay, *Daniel*, 351. See also Lucas, *Daniel*, 165–66.
95. Seow, *Daniel*, 111.
96. Gooding, "The Literary Structure of the Book of Daniel and Its Implications," 60–61.

the imagery "speak[s] truly and accurately, but not precisely. We often do not know where the analogy stops. In this way, images preserve mystery about ideas that are ultimately beyond our comprehension."[97] But despite the remaining mystery, the message of Dan 7 is clear: God's faithful may suffer great oppression, but he will not abandon them and they will one day share in his eternal kingdom.

> ### IN DEPTH: The Identities of the Kingdoms, Take 2[98]
>
> The angel's interpretation of Daniel's vision of the beasts in Dan 7 is little more than a summary, but all interpreters assume the symbolism is meaningful and do their best to fill in the gaps. As a starting point, most believe that the four kingdoms of Dan 7 and Dan 2 align with each other. Most also take a position on the identity of all four kingdoms (despite meager textual information about the second and third kingdoms[99]). As discussed in the commentary on ch. 2, two main interpretations dominate: the "Greek view" and the "Roman view," so named for their identification of the fourth kingdom. These interpretations are summarized in table 7.4 alongside the corresponding components of each chapter:
>
> **Table 7.4. The Identities of the Kingdoms in Daniel 2 and 7**
>
> | Chapter 2 | Chapter 7 | Roman view | Greek view |
> |---|---|---|---|
> | Gold head | Lion with wings | Babylon | Babylon/Nebuchadnezzar |
> | Silver torso | Bear with ribs | Medo-Persia | Media |
> | Bronze midsection | Leopard with four heads/wings | Greece | Persia |
> | Iron legs | Fourth beast/ten horns/little horn | Rome/revived or extended old Roman empire/antichrist | Greece/Seleucid kings/ Antiochus IV Epiphanes |
> | Rock | One like son of man/saints of the Most High | God's kingdom | God's kingdom |
>
> Some details of Daniel's vision present extensive difficulties for both views, but interpreters generally fall along party lines: traditionalists hold the Roman view and nontraditionalists the Greek. There are nonetheless strong arguments in favor of the Greek view,[100] and in what follows, the Greek view is presented.

---

97. Longman, *Daniel*, 178.
98. See IN DEPTH: The Identities of the Kingdoms, pp. 115–17.
99. Of the little information about the second and third kingdoms, Goldingay says it indicates that "the four-empire scheme as a whole is more important than the identification of its parts" (*Daniel*, 374).
100. For an in-depth discussion on the Greek view by evan-

With respect to the first kingdom, nearly all interpreters, regardless of their view on the fourth kingdom, agree on the identity of the first beast, the lion with eagle's wings. It corresponds to the gold head of the statue in Nebuchadnezzar's dream of ch. 2, where Daniel explicitly identified Nebuchadnezzar as the head of gold.[101]

The second beast, the raised-up bear with three ribs in its mouth, symbolizes the kingdom of Media under the reign of its last king, Astyages, and specifically his reign after the death of Babylonian Nebuchadnezzar in 562 BCE. While its significance as an empire in its own right is often lost in the wake of Persia,[102] Media was quite powerful. Lucas summarizes: "Throughout the lifetime of the Neo-Babylonian Empire Media could be seen as at least its equal in power, and a potential rival. . . . Following Nebuchadnezzar's death, whilst Babylon was weakened by court intrigues, Media could be seen as the major power in the eastern Mediterranean world—until Cyrus rebelled and brought the Persians to the fore."[103] It is also significant in the Bible as the empire that would destroy Babylon (5:27–29).[104] That the beastly bear of Daniel's vision was ordered to arise and eat itself full may represent an exhortation to attack Babylon (cf. Jer 51:11).

The third beast of Daniel's vision was a leopard with four heads and four wings. It symbolizes the Persian Empire, beginning with Cyrus, who overthrew Median Astyages and established the joint kingdom of Medo-Persia in 550 BCE. The leopard's four heads and four wings represent totality and may indicate that it looked everywhere for its prey (i.e., the four heads[105]) and exhibited astounding speed (i.e., the four wings[106]).

The fourth beast of Daniel's vision, the beast unlike anything Daniel recognized, symbolizes the Greek Empire. This beast was noteworthy for its difference from all the other beasts and for its destructive activity. The Greek Empire under

---

gelical authors, see Robert J. M. Gurney, "The Four Kingdoms of Daniel 2 and 7," *Themelios* 2.2 (1977): 39–45; Walton, "The Four Kingdoms of Daniel," 25–36. Walton's article is a response to and interaction with Gurney's article.

101. See on 7:17–18 above.

102. The Greeks, who ultimately brought down the Persian Empire, considered the Medes to be the predecessors of the Persians. When Cyrus first arrived at the Aegean with the Persian army, Persia itself was still relatively unknown.

103. Ernest C. Lucas, "The Origin of Daniel's Four Empires Scheme Re-examined," *TynBul* 40 (1989), 193.

104. For further discussion of Jer 51:27–29, see Walton, "The Four Kingdoms of Daniel," 30.

105. Some advocates of the Greek view consider the four heads representative of the first four Persian kings (Dan 11:2) or the four directions of Cyrus's empire. Those holding the Roman view say the leopard's four heads symbolize the four generals who divided up Alexander the Great's empire.

106. The prophet Isaiah may hint at the speed with which Cyrus conquered the ancient world in Isa 41:3 (אֹרַח בְּרַגְלָיו לֹא יָבוֹא). While the NIV translates, "by a path his feet have not traveled before," some understand the phrase to refer to Cyrus's speed (see, e.g., NET; Montgomery, *Commentary on the Book of Daniel*, 289; Christopher R. North, *The Second Isaiah: Introduction, Translation and Commentary to Chapters XL–LV* [Oxford: Clarendon Press, 1964], 94).

famed Alexander the Great was fundamentally different from those that preceded it because it was western and not eastern,[107] unlike its Roman successor, which was very much a continuation of Greece and its Hellenistic culture.

As for the ten horns on the fourth beast, if the number "ten" is literal, the ten horns may have represented ten sovereign states that had grown out of Alexander the Great's empire by the second century BCE.[108] If the number "ten" is symbolic, the horns may have represented Seleucid kings from Seleucus I (305–281 BCE) to Antiochus IV Epiphanes (175–164 BCE), the little horn of chs. 7 and 8.[109] What is meant by the little horn's uprooting of three horns is uncertain, but I favor the view expressed by Collins:

> When Antiochus III died, Epiphanes was only fourth in line for the throne, being preceded by his brother Seleucus IV and the latter's sons, Antiochus and Demetrius. [Antiochus IV was directly responsible for the death of only one of these three.] From the viewpoint of a Jewish writer, however, the appropriate attribution of guilt may not have been apparent, only that Epiphanes in fact came to the throne because all three were somehow out of the way.[110]

This understanding of the three horns may help explain the use of the number "ten": "If Seleucus IV and his two sons, then, count as the last three kings, Alexander and the first six Seleucids make up ten in all," and Antiochus IV Epiphanes makes eleven.[111]

The eleventh king's oppression of the "holy ones" and his intention "to change times set by law" refers to Antiochus's outlawing of Jewish religious practices such as sacrifice, Sabbath, and circumcision and to his sanctioned massacre of Jews who refused to comply.[112] This horrific oppression lasted from 167 to 164 BCE, just over three years, an oft accepted meaning of the "time, times, and half a time" in 7:25.

---

107. Lacocque notes that Alexander brought "a wholly different civilization" to the ancient Near East; "Alexander's conquests were without parallel in ancient history. They really did break up the Asiatic cultures, replacing them with Greek culture." Lacocque's "replacing" would include the forced Hellenization that the second-century-BCE Jews of Palestine experienced at the hands of Antiochus IV Epiphanes (*The Book of Daniel*, 140–41). While Lacocque makes the point, his implication that the Greeks imposed a new top-down culture on conquered territories overstates the situation. Hellenism was a mixture of Greek values that emerged in conquered territories from the ground up and predominantly through the Greek school in Hellenistic cities—the gymnasium. A Greek education was the ticket to citizenship.

108. See Walton, "The Four Kingdoms of Daniel," 31–34, 36.

109. For this period as treated in Daniel, see the commentary on Dan 8–11.

110. Collins, *Daniel*, 321.

111. Ibid.

112. See further on chs. 8–12, and 1 Macc 1:20–64. The Roman view considers the little horn in ch. 7 a representation of the antichrist, whose three-and-a-half-year oppression refers to great tribulation for believers before the second advent (see further, e.g., Miller, *Daniel*, 212–17).

The kingdoms of Daniel's vision of the beasts in ch. 7 also correspond to kingdoms of his vision of the ram and goat in ch. 8. The primary point of disagreement between interpreters specifically is the "little horn" of both visions. These little horns have significant similarities, and it makes the best textual sense to say they share a historical referent. Chapter 8's angelic interpreter identifies the goat as the Greek Empire, the empire from which the little horn emerges. This strongly suggests that the beast on which the little horn grows in Dan 7 is also the Greek Empire. In this reading, the sequence of empires is then Nebuchadnezzar's Babylon, Media, Persia, and Greece (i.e., the Greek view of the kingdoms' identity).

Regardless of whether one adopts the Greek or Roman view of the four kingdoms, it is important to keep in mind that the symbols are not ciphers; there is not a straightforward "this is that" correspondence. Rather, each set of images would have evoked a host of culturally specific ideas, images, and values. In the end, the primary message of both Dan 2 and 7 stands: all human kingdoms will be destroyed and surpassed by the everlasting kingdom of God, where his people will reign forever with him.

One of the arguments against the Greek view of the kingdoms is that Antiochus's death should have been followed by the inbreaking of God's kingdom and a present reality with God's people ruling over an everlasting kingdom (7:26–27). Instead, there is a gap between the second-century-BCE defeat of the little horn and the incarnation. However, both views have to work with gaps in their chronology of events, and both can fit within what we know biblical prophecy to be like—namely, telescopic. Klein, Blomberg, and Hubbard explain: "From Denver, the Rocky Mountains appear as a series of distant peaks close together, though in reality the peaks are many miles from each other. Similarly, the prophets saw the future as a single succession of events (i.e., the view of distant 'peaks' from Denver), but the NT shows that, in fact, large time gaps intervene between them."[113] While the "one like a son of man" in Dan 7 ultimately represents Jesus, there is still distance between the initial and the full establishment of his kingdom—i.e., his first and his second comings.

Whether the Greek or Roman view makes the best sense of the vision's details, the chapter's representation of historical events does not affect its future significance. Antiochus launched his assault against God and his people in the

---

113. William W. Klein, Craig L. Blomberg, and Robert L. Hubbard, Jr., *Introduction to Biblical Interpretation*, revised and updated (Nashville: Nelson, 2004), 376.

> second century BCE and then died, but the pattern of his behavior lives on as a paradigm for defiance against God and oppression of his people. In the book of Daniel, this paradigm began with Belshazzar, the blasphemous "son" of Nebuchadnezzar. As the book progresses, the pattern intensifies: Belshazzar was bad, but Antiochus would be worse. There are enough eschatological hints in the remainder of the book to let us say, "Antiochus was worse, but the worst is yet to come." The rest of the canon, not to mention world history, affirms the validity of this intensifying pattern. The New Testament man of lawlessness (2 Thess 2:3) and the apostle John's reference to many antichrists (1 John 2:18) are echoes of Antiochus IV and Belshazzar before him. While there may yet be "a specific worldwide figure who will accompany the final events of the end . . . , the ambiguity of the New Testament texts themselves [should lead to caution] and lack of dogmatic certainty."[114] Such caution is especially necessary when it comes to interpreting the imagery of apocalyptic literature. Thankfully, the primary message of Daniel's vision in ch. 7 is clear: God's faithful may suffer great oppression, but he will not abandon them, and they will one day share in his eternal kingdom.

Canonical and Theological Significance

Keeping the Unseen in View

One of the primary themes of the Bible is the sovereignty of God, a theme that entails his kingship. An assertion of this kingship "presupposes, of course, a realm over which he has dominion and a narrative explaining or recounting the implementation of his relationship to it."[115] The realm is the cosmos and the narrative begins in Gen 1 with the transcendent, all-powerful God creating the heavens and earth. From these first pages of the Bible, the story of God's kingship is primarily played out on the stage of human history, but it is clear that his sovereignty encompasses the entire cosmos (e.g., "Heaven is my throne, and the earth is my footstool," Isa 66:1).

In much of the biblical story, the vocabulary of God's sovereignty and kingship is not explicit. Goldingay notes that while "it has been said that kingship is a root metaphor for understanding Yhwh, . . . if this is so, the plant keeps its roots beneath

---

114. Fee and Stuart, *How to Read the Bible for All Its Worth*, 264.

115. Eugene H. Merrill, *Everlasting Dominion: A Theology of the Old Testament* (Nashville: Broadman & Holman, 2006), 646.

the surface and waits a long time before thrusting its head above ground."[116] Nonetheless, the centrality of the idea is evident throughout, and specifically in repeated use of "Lord" to refer to God/YHWH—more than 400 times in the Old Testament alone: "As Lord, he is the sovereign one, the creator of all, the one who deserves praise and obedience."[117]

This oft implicit central idea of the biblical story is explicit in the book of Daniel, where the endurance of God's kingdom is the driving theme of the book. The narrator of chs. 1–6 weaves the theme of God's sovereignty into a series of stories that recount specific situations in which God demonstrated his superiority over any challenger. This focus begins in the opening verses of the book, where "the Lord gave into [Nebuchadnezzar's] hand Jehoiakim, king of Judah, and some of the vessels of the house of God" (Dan 1:2), and it is a key theme in every narrative story that follows. God revealed his superior knowledge to Nebuchadnezzar through a dream only Daniel could interpret (ch. 2); he displayed his superior power over Nebuchadnezzar when he delivered Shadrach, Meshach, and Abednego from death by fiery furnace (ch. 3); he humbled the greatest king of the day at the peak of his power (ch. 4); he humbled and destroyed a blasphemous king (ch. 5); he revealed his superior law when Daniel defied the immutable law of the Medes and Persians (ch. 6). The truth of God's sovereignty is driven home in chapter after chapter with concrete displays of God's ability to triumph in a variety of adverse circumstances.

But sometimes we need more than just seeing God act on someone else's behalf. When a friend finally lands just the right job, we may well rejoice with him, but we may also think, "I'm glad God worked that out for you, but I don't see a promise that he'll do the same for me." When a praying acquaintance's cancer goes into remission, we are thankful for her sake, but we might also say (to ourselves), "Sure, God *can* do what I need him to do, but will he?" When a missionary recounts stories of God's miraculous activity against demonic forces, we are glad to be in God's camp, but we might also wonder, "When is God going to do something miraculous for me?" The truth is that he may not. He may never give you the perfect job, a clean bill of health, or miraculous deliverance from whatever darkness you are facing.

Sometimes seeing that God is *able* to triumph over whatever ails or oppresses us

---

116. He further notes that the first application of the Hebrew word מָלַךְ, "to reign," to YHWH does not appear until Exod 15:18, and the noun מֶלֶךְ, "king," first applied to YHWH is in Num 23:21 (John Goldingay, *Old Testament Theology, Volume 2: Israel's Faith* [Downers Grove, IL: InterVarsity Press, 2006], 59–61).

117. Thomas R. Schreiner, *The King in His Beauty: A Biblical Theology of the Old and New Testaments* (Grand Rapids: Baker Academic, 2013), xiii. I concur with Schreiner's conclusion, though he gets there by saying, "The focus on God as King is evident in the regular refrain found in Scripture, particularly the OT, where God is identified as the Lord. . . . In other words, saying that the theme of Scripture is God's kingship is verified and confirmed by the constant refrain that God is the Lord." If the "refrain" he is referring to is אֲנִי יהוה, "I am YHWH," this is problematic since the divine name is used—not אָדוֹן, "lord/Lord." Furthermore, the purpose of this statement is not to declare YHWH's kingship over the cosmos, but rather to remind Israel that he was *their* God—the one who brought them out of Egypt (the statement occurs more than 150 times).

is not enough. Sometimes we need to see more than the particulars. We need to see the transcendent, cosmic nature of God's rule. We need to be reminded that, even when life falls apart never to be put back together this side of heaven, God is ever and always on the throne.

This is the territory of the apocalyptic literature of Dan 7. The stories of Dan 1–6 schooled their audience in God's ability to work through the particulars, his ability to triumph over any challenger. Make no mistake—that the Most High God is living and active on the stage of history is important[118]—but sometimes just knowing the particulars is not enough. The only way God's people would find the strength to endure the apocalyptic horrors to come was by catching a glimpse of the transcendent nature of God's rule and clinging to the truth that his sovereignty is bigger than whatever ailed or oppressed them. Daniel 7 is that glimpse. Together with Nebuchadnezzar's dream of the statue in ch. 2, ch. 7 offers a cosmic perspective on God's kingdom that transcends all earthly particulars. Together, the chapters portray the nature of human and divine kingdoms, as well as the relationship between the two.

The most important aspect of this relationship as portrayed in Dan 7 is that, though there are "beastly rulers," there is always, in the words of contemporary songwriters Keith and Kristyn Getty, a higher throne.[119] Daniel's vision of that throne puts human power in perspective. This is true of other Old Testament visions of YHWH's throne as well. When the eighth-century-BCE prophet Isaiah "saw YHWH, high and exalted, seated on a throne," the train of his robe filling the temple, King Uzziah had just died after a reign that lasted fifty-two years—surely an unsettling event for the people of Judah (Isa 6:1). When Daniel's exilic counterpart, Ezekiel, saw a vision of YHWH's fiery throne chariot, the exile in Babylon was underway and the holy city in Jerusalem was on the eve of its destruction under King Zedekiah, the fourth-in-line successor of Josiah who proved no more like the good king than his three predecessors.[120] Whether a human throne is vacant, occupied by a rebellious king, or, as in Daniel's vision, occupied by a tyrant, a glimpse of the Ancient of Days on the highest throne relativizes human power. Just as he raises kings up, he also takes them down (Dan 2:21). All human thrones are subject to the Ancient of Days, and one day he will judge them.

---

118. God's acts in history are critical for both Judaism and Christianity. His foundational act in the Old Testament was delivering Israel from bondage in Egypt; his repeated calls to obedience often began with the reminder, "I am YHWH who brought you out of Egypt." God's foundational act in the New Testament is the resurrection; Paul summarizes its importance when he says, "If only for this life we have hope in Christ, we are of all people most to be pitied" (1 Cor 15:19). Because God's acts in the past are foundational to faith, their historicity matters.

119. Keith and Kristyn Getty, "There Is a Higher Throne," (Thankyou Music, 2003).

120. The dating in Ezek 1:1 is difficult, but many scholars date Ezekiel's vision to 593 BCE. See, e.g., Block, *The Book of Ezekiel: Chapters 1–24*, 80–83; Walther Zimmerli, *Ezekiel 1*, trans. Ronald E. Clements, Hermeneia (Philadelphia: Fortress, 1979), 112–15.

Until that day, God's people cling to the unseen reality that the all good, all wise, wholly just, and completely righteous king is on the throne. Without the truth of this unseen reality, the world order can appear to be in jeopardy and God's people could rightfully fear extinction. What is more, without the truth of this transcendent dimension, life can sometimes "seem at best 'a tale / Told by an idiot, full of sound and fury, / Signifying nothing' (Shakespeare, *Macbeth*, V.5) or at worst, 'solitary, poor, nasty, brutish, and short' (Thomas Hobbs, *Leviathan* 1.13). Faced with suffering, injustice and oppression, and with no deliverance or remedy at hand, hope has to lie in the belief that there is more to reality than is apparent."[121] But, as Lucas further notes, this truth in itself may not be particularly encouraging or comforting. We also need the truth "that there is a throne occupied by a righteous Judge, who will act to deliver the faithful from their oppressors." The book of Revelation, the Christian apocalypse, goes even further,

> because on the throne is "a lamb standing as though it had been slain" (Rev. 5:6) so that the throne is "the throne of God and of the Lamb" (Rev. 22:1). Thus, on the throne there is One who has shared the experience of being trampled on by the beasts but has remained faithful. His vindication by resurrection and enthronement gives the specifically Christian ground of hope.[122]

Daniel's vision assures us that before that fiery highest throne, all lesser thrones are but flickers of heat and light—mere fireflies. The kings of the nations may rage against YHWH and his anointed (Ps 2), but YHWH will have the final word (cf. Ps 110).

From Creation to Forever: Humanity as God Intended

When "one like a son of man" arrived at the throne of the Ancient of Days, Daniel's vision reached its climax: this was the figure that stood in contrast to the terrible beasts from the sea, and this was the figure that would inherit the eternal, indomitable kingdom of the Most High. But whom did this figure represent? And what is the significance of its being a human figure?

Christian theology, with good support from the New Testament portion of the biblical canon, came to understand the "one like a son of man" as a representation of Jesus, but Daniel's original audience would have had different ideas. Because of their ancient Near Eastern context and also because of their familiarity with the Old Testament texts, Daniel's earliest audiences would most likely have had creation on their minds. From the opening vision of a churning sea and powerful beasts

---

121. Lucas, *Daniel*, 199.   122. Ibid., 199–200.

to the humanlike figure receiving dominion, they would have been thinking about YHWH's sovereignty and humanity's unique mandate, as described in the first chapters of the Bible.

The Genesis account of creation shares similarities with other ancient Near Eastern creation stories, but with notable differences. Throughout the ancient world, creation stories were centered around a chaotic cosmic sea and battles between the gods for the right to rule. In the Babylonian Enuma Elish, the god Marduk waged war against the sea goddess, Tiamat, and her army of ghoulish beasts. The victor would hold the "tablet of destinies," which gave its possessor the right to rule the world. In the Ugaritic creation myth, the god Baal defeated the sea god, Yamm, to win the right to rule among the gods. While the Genesis account does not depict YHWH engaged in a struggle to bring order to the cosmos, the imagery in Gen 1 of darkness, the deep, and the wind seems intended to evoke the worldview behind those myths and then challenge it with God's transcendent power: he dispelled chaos at creation with simply the power of his word (Gen 1:1–10). While the Israelites would have considered the sea dangerous, it was not a threat to their God, whose powerful rebuke could make the waters flee (Ps 104:7).[123]

Imagery of watery chaos and monstrous beasts is employed in other Old Testament texts that proclaim YHWH's power as the creator who subdued the sea and defeated its monsters. In Ps 74, the psalmist implores YHWH to defend the cause of his people on the basis of his past record: he "broke the heads of the monster in the waters" and he "crushed the heads of Leviathan and gave it as food to the creatures of the desert" (Ps 74:13–14; cf. also Job 7:12; 26:12–13; 41; Leviathan, a well-known sea creature in ancient Near Eastern myths, symbolized the destructive waters of the primeval sea and thus the chaotic forces that threatened the created order). Other psalmists declare YHWH's victory over chaos at creation and also in history—specifically in the exodus from Egypt (see, e.g., Pss 77:17–21; 89:11–12[10–11]; cf. Isa 51:9–10). Similar imagery is used to praise YHWH for his kingship: because of his power over the tumultuous waters, he is enthroned in heaven (see, e.g., Pss 29 and 93).

This same kind of power also lies behind the prophet Isaiah's declaration of YHWH's future deliverance: "In that day, YHWH will punish with his sword—his fierce, great and powerful sword—Leviathan the gliding serpent, Leviathan the coiling serpent; he will slay the monster of the sea" (Isa 27:1). Imagery of raging waters and monstrous creatures carries over into the New Testament's apocalypse, where beasts emerge from the sea (Rev 13).[124] That Daniel saw a churning sea and monstrous beasts in his vision is surely suggestive of creation and who has the right to rule.

---

123. Cf. Jesus's rebuke of the wind and waves in the Gospels (Mark 4:39–41; Luke 8:24; cf. Mark 6:51).

124. While most people have no trouble seeing that Daniel's vision lay behind John's, some fail to consider the cultural milieu that lay behind Daniel's vision—ancient Near Eastern imagery about creation and which god wins the right to rule.

It is significant, then, in light of Daniel's Israelite theology of creation, that an outside force was acting on this sea—that is, the four winds of heaven were stirring it up (7:2). Newsom explains, "The sea is not represented as *itself* roiling or surging in an aggressive fashion. Here the sea is being *acted upon* by the winds . . . an allusion to Gen 1:2, in which a divine wind sweeps over the surface of the cosmic waters."[125] In Daniel's vision, the divine hand is at work for those who have eyes to see, and what the divine hand is at work doing is raising up kings/kingdoms.[126] YHWH is not only the creator of the natural world, he is the creator of history. What arises out of the sea in Daniel's vision is the political history of four gentile nations, imagery that echoes Gen 1:2 and so suggests that even this process is under God's control.[127] This is the God who controls history and the entire cosmos. But beyond echoing the Israelite creation account of Gen 1, Daniel's vision also calls to mind the chaotic sea of ancient Near Eastern combat myths, "indicat[ing] that there is something inherently unruly and dangerous in the Gentile kingdoms, which will ultimately have to be dealt with by force."[128]

While the use of beasts to represent kingdoms is not in itself negative,[129] in Daniel's vision where creation lies in the background, the imagery of beasts stands in contrast to the humanlike figure who appears before the Ancient of Days. In the Genesis account of creation, humans are created in the image and likeness of God, and they are given dominion over all the other creatures (Gen 1:26–28; cf. Ps 8). Beale summarizes the human mandate that included this dominion:

> Just as God . . . subdued the chaos, ruled over it and further created and filled the earth with all kinds of animate life, so Adam and Eve . . . were to reflect God's activities in Genesis 1 by fulfilling the commission to "subdue" and "rule over all the earth" and to "be fruitful and multiply" (Gen 1:26, 28).[130]

But the problem that drives the biblical narrative is that Adam and Eve—and all their successors—failed to fulfill this creation mandate; their rebellion and the

---

125. Newsom, *Daniel*, 221.

126. The use of passive verbs throughout Daniel's vision to describe the beasts and their activity is further evidence of the divine hand at work. See on 7:4–6, 12 above.

127. Newsom, *Daniel*, 221.

128. Ibid.

129. In his final blessing of his sons and the future tribes of Israel they represented, Jacob described many of them with animal imagery: Issachar was a "rawboned donkey" (Gen 49:14), Dan was a "viper along the path" (Gen 49:17), Naphtali was a "doe set free that bears beautiful fawns" (Gen 49:21), Benjamin was a "ravenous wolf" (Gen 49:27), and Judah a lion's cub (49:9). Cf. also Moses's final blessing of the tribes of Israel in Deut 33. Centuries later, the prophet Ezekiel relates a parable of two eagles, each representing a king of Babylon and of Egypt (Ezek 17).

130. G. K. Beale, *The Temple and the Church's Mission: A Biblical Theology of the Dwelling Place of God*, NSBT 17 (Leicester: Apollos, 2004), 83. Beale's larger argument entails the role of the Old Testament tabernacle and temple as symbols of a future reality when God's presence is no longer limited to the holy of holies but extends throughout the whole cosmos. His discussion of the "son of man" thus occurs in the context of "temple" but is relevant here given the interwoven themes of temple and creation in the Bible.

scourge of sin prevented them from representing and reflecting the glory of the divine king in their rule of the earth. On page after page, in chapter after chapter, the Bible recounts how God raised up "other Adam-like figures" to do what Adam himself had failed to do, but they too failed.[131]

Into this history of human failure comes Daniel's vision of the "one like a son of man" receiving everlasting dominion over the "beasts." What Daniel sees is nothing less than the fulfillment of the creation mandate for humanity to co-rule the earth with God. Finally, the human race will function as God intended from the beginning, bearing his image and reflecting glory as it rules the earth.[132] The human figure at the center of Daniel's vision is a "Last Adam" figure—the one who would finally and forever fulfill God's plans for humanity.[133]

But this is only part of the story—the Old Testament part. Whatever the Old Testament and ancient Near Eastern nuances of imagery behind the "one like a son of man" were, there is no doubt that the New Testament finds the expression significant and applicable to Jesus. It is an expression used more than any other by Jesus in the Gospels to refer to himself.[134] There is considerable scholarly debate over what Jesus meant by his use of the expression, but most scholars at least agree that the expression derives from Daniel's vision in ch. 7.

While בֶּן אָדָם (Hebrew) and בַּר אֱנָשׁ (Aramaic), "a son of man," in the Old Testament were simply ways of saying "a human being,"[135] by the time of the New Testament, the expression had morphed into a title: "the Son of Man." How this development happened from the closing of the Old Testament canon to Jesus's first-century-AD context goes beyond the scope of this study, but we can ask four questions to help us better understand the significance of Jesus's use of the title: (1) What did title mean

---

131. Beale describes how the creation mandate (what he calls the "commission") passed to Noah, Abraham, Isaac, Jacob, and even to the nation of Israel (*The Temple and the Church's Mission*, 95). Of Israel, he says, "it is not an overstatement to say that Israel was conceived of as a 'corporate Adam'. The nation's task was to do what Adam had first been commissioned to do. Israel failed even as had Adam. And like Adam, Israel was also cast out of their 'garden land' into exile. Though a remnant of Israel returned from exile, her failure to carry out the Adamic task continued until the beginning of the first century AD" (pp. 120–21).

132. In this context of image-bearing, Lucas notes the particular significance of the contrast between beasts and the "one like a son of man" in Daniel's vision: "It is when humans *image* God that they have the right to rule as his vice-regents. When they try *to be* God they both forfeit that right and mar the image that distinguishes them from the animals. As a result, they become 'bestial' to some degree. That the kingdom is given to a human figure, rather than to an animal one, asserts that when God acts to deliver his people and establish his kingdom he is consummating the purpose behind the creation of the cosmos" (*Daniel*, 200).

133. Beale, *The Temple and the Church's Mission*, 93–94.

134. The crowd in John 12:34 uses it in reference to Jesus's claims about himself. Outside the Gospels, it occurs only three times with reference to Jesus: Acts 7:56; Rev 1:13; 14:14. (The expression also appears in the citation of Ps 8:5[4] in Heb 2:6, where it is a reference to humans.)

135. Turner says the expression "most often describes frail, finite humanity in contrast to the awesomeness of God" (*Matthew*, 36). Most of the more than 100 Old Testament occurrences are in Ezekiel, where YHWH calls the prophet "son of man" rather than by his name—perhaps "emphasiz[ing] the distance between God and the human" (Block, *The Book of Ezekiel: Chapters 1–24*, 30). See also Num 23:19 and Ps 8:5[4].

to Jesus's audience? (2) How did Jesus use the title? (3) What did Jesus mean by it?[136] and (4) Why did Jesus use this title for himself more often than any other?

The answer to the first question is that, although there are many unknowns about the Jewish concept of "the Son of Man" by the time Jesus arrived on the scene, it seems at least certain that for first-century Jews, it was "a messianic title for a pre-existent heavenly being who comes to earth with the glorious Kingdom of God."[137]

The second question, how Jesus used the title, has three answers. First, he used it to refer to his earthly ministry. For example, he said the Son of Man had the authority to forgive sins (Matt 9:6; Mark 2:10; Luke 5:24); he claimed that the Son of Man was Lord of the Sabbath (Matt 12:8; Mark 2:27; Luke 6:5); he said the Son of Man came to seek and save the lost (Luke 19:10). Jesus also used the title to teach his disciples about his coming passion: he would suffer (Matt 17:12; Mark 8:31); he would be betrayed (Matt 26:45); he would die and be buried for three days (Mark 10:45; Luke 11:30); he would rise again (Matt 19:9; Luke 18:31). The final way Jesus used the Son of Man title was to teach his followers about his glorious eschatological return: he would come with the clouds of heaven (Matt 26:64); he would return at an unexpected hour (Luke 12:40); he would sit on his glorious throne (Matt 19:28).[138]

Considering all of these uses together helps provides an answer to the third question—what did Jesus mean by his use of the title? Ladd says Jesus used this title because it both made "an exalted claim" and also allowed Jesus "to fill the term with new meaning."[139] Jesus accomplished this by combining the roles of the "Son of Man" and the Suffering Servant. In the former title, "Jesus laid claim to heavenly dignity and probably to pre-existence itself and claimed to be the one who would one day inaugurate the glorious Kingdom." However, as Ladd observes, accomplishing this meant the Son of Man would have to become the Suffering Servant and submit to death. Ladd summarizes the significance of Jesus's use of the title "Son of Man":

> Jesus will be the heavenly, glorious Son of Man coming with the clouds to judge people and to bring the glorious Kingdom. However, in advance of this apocalyptic manifestation as the Son of Man, Jesus is the Son of Man living among them incog-

---

136. This is, of course, a much-debated question. The answer offered here is that of New Testament theologian George Eldon Ladd in *A Theology of the New Testament*, rev. ed. (Grand Rapids: Eerdmans, 1993).

137. See Ladd, *A Theology of the New Testament*, 147.

138. The influence of the book of Daniel on Jesus's understanding of the kingdom of God and his role in it is discussed by New Testament scholar Craig A. Evans, who identifies "at least seven telling indications of Daniel's influence in Jesus's understanding of the kingdom of God," several of which lie outside the purview of Dan 7: "(1) the emphatic qualification that the awaited kingdom is God's kingdom; (2) the language of imminence; (3) the kingdom as 'mystery'; (4) the stone that crushes; (5) the saying about what is 'not made with hands'; (6) promises to the disciples' and (7) the 'abomination of desolation.'" For fuller discussion of each element, see pp. 510–23 in "Daniel in the New Testament: Visions of God's Kingdom," in *The Book of Daniel: Composition and Reception*, vol. 2, ed. John J. Collins and Peter W. Flint (Leiden: Brill, 2001): 490–527.

139. Ladd, *A Theology of the New Testament*, 156.

nito, whose ministry is not to reign in glory but in humiliation to suffer and to die for them. The future, heavenly Son of Man is already present among women and men but in a form they hardly expected. There is indeed a messianic secret.[140]

With respect to the subjective fourth question—why was "the Son of Man" Jesus's favorite title for himself?—we can only speculate. Why did he send his audience repeatedly back to the imagery of Dan 7? I suggest two possible reasons. First, Jesus knew himself to be the "Last Adam," the human who would finally accomplish God's purposes for the human race as laid out at creation, the human in Daniel's vision who would rule God's everlasting kingdom forever. Jesus's repeated use of the title "the Son of Man"—and all he meant by it (see above)—drove home this truth. Furthermore, as he makes clear in the Great Commission, Jesus would enable his followers to fulfill God's purposes as well. Beale describes how Jesus invokes Dan 7 in the Great Commission to accomplish this:

> The New Testament pictures Christ and the church as finally having done what Adam, Noah, and Israel had failed to do in extending the temple of God's presence throughout the world. . . . This is why Matthew 28:18 portrays Jesus as the Son of Man saying, "All authority has been given to Me in heaven and on earth." This is an allusion to the prophecy of Daniel 7:13–14, where it is said of the "Son of Man", "authority was given to him, and all the nations of the earth . . . [were] serving him". . . . On the basis of this authority, Jesus then gives the well-known commission "therefore, as you go, disciple all the nations . . . and, behold, *I am with you* all the days until the end of the age". . . . His presence will enable them to fulfil "the great commission" to rule over and fill the earth with God's presence, which Adam, Noah and Israel had failed to carry out.
>
> In this respect . . . Jesus is a Last Adam figure, and this is partly why he implicitly identifies himself with Daniel's "Son of Man" in issuing the universal commission to his followers: he is the "son of Adam," the equivalent to Daniel's "Son of Man," finally accomplishing what the first Adam should have and what Daniel predicts the messianic end-time Adam would do.[141]

Perhaps a second reason "the Son of Man" was Jesus's favorite title is because it is in Daniel's vision of ch. 7 that we find the clearest Old Testament picture of the divine council and in it, Jesus's relationship to YHWH—probably the truth about him that his listeners had the hardest time grasping and accepting. In Daniel's vision of the Israelite divine council, YHWH sat at the head of the council but shared his

---

140. Ibid.

141. Beale, *The Temple and the Church's Mission*, 169.

essence with a second power that was a distinct figure,[142] to whom he gave everlasting dominion and power. This portrayal of the divine council shows that Old Testament "monotheism" had room for a "second person." Perhaps sending his listeners back to the vision of Dan 7 was Jesus's repeated invitation for people to recognize him as that second person, to understand and believe that he was one with the Father (see the discussion above, pp. 378–80).[143]

We know that at least Jesus's educated audience understood what he was doing in claiming to be "the Son of Man." We know this because they charged him with blasphemy when he used the title at his trial. Jesus told the Sanhedrin, "In the future you will see the Son of Man sitting at the right hand of the Mighty One and coming on the clouds of heaven" (Matt 26:64; cf. Mark 14:62; Luke 22:69), a clear reference to Dan 7:13, and they all heard him claim to share the essence of the Father,[144] the one who would ultimately exalt him and give him the everlasting kingdom. It was not a claim they could—or would—tolerate; they demanded his death.

The title "the Son of Man" is also in the book of Revelation (1:13; 14:14), just one of many allusions to Daniel's vision.[145] We need not consider the many interpretive approaches to the book of Revelation here to agree that the imagery of Dan 7 is relevant for our understanding of both advents of Christ and the future reward for God's faithful. At his first advent, Jesus announced that the kingdom of God was at hand. He taught people what this kingdom was, and he guided them to an understanding that he was its king. Upon his postresurrection ascension to heaven, Jesus was seated at the right hand of the Father, where he remains to this day as our advocate. On some glorious day, his second advent will bring the culmination of his kingdom to earth. Until then, we live in the "underground resistance" begun by Jesus's ascension; theologian Michael Horton explains:

> Christ's ascent has opened up a hole in these last days of our present history, through which the Spirit descends, dispensing the spoils of Christ's victory. Because of the ascension, there is now present—even in this passing evil age—a new order at work,

---

142. Any discussion of the nature of the Trinity ventures into a field of heretical landmines. Jesus will identify himself as the great "I Am," which means he too is YHWH of the Old Testament; that is, "YHWH" is not simply God the Father, but all of the Godhead in singular reference. What we can say (without falling into heresy) is that there is an internal complexity within God that was not altogether apparent in the Old Testament. Jesus can be both distinguished from God and also identified as God.

143. Jewish friends would disagree, as attested by what is known as the "two powers in heaven" heresy. See Alan F. Segal, *Two Powers in Heaven: Early Rabbinic Reports about Christianity and Gnosticism* (Leiden: Brill, 2002), for the history of "the thorny problem" of the "son of man" title in the interpretive tradition.

144. The language of "essence" is loaded with later patristic theological value, but for our purposes, it means that the New Testament religious leaders understood Jesus to be claiming a specialized and exclusive relationship with God that put him on a par with him; Jesus was claiming an ontological share in the identity of Israel's God.

145. For example, the four winds (Rev 7:1); the lion, bear, and leopard (13:2); the ten-horned beast (12:3; 13:1); the reigning holy ones (20:4; 22:5).

an underground resistance to the principalities and powers of sin and death. Though we are still living in this present evil age, the powers of the age to come are breaking in upon us in the Spirit through preaching and sacrament (He 6:4–5). Because Jesus Christ is Lord, we are made alive by the Spirit, drawn away from our alliance with death, and made cosufferers as well as coheirs with Jesus Christ. It is the ascension that both grounds the struggle of the church militant and guarantees that one day it will share fully in the triumph of its King.[146]

The significance of "the one like a son of man" in Daniel's vision reaches from Genesis to Revelation. As Jesus fulfilled God's purposes for humanity, he also empowers his church to do the same—in this life and in the life to come.

Living Beyond Babylon

Daniel had glimpsed the grandeur of God's eternal glory and the promise of vindication for God's people, but he was nonetheless profoundly troubled by what he saw in his vision. Perhaps part of the reason for his distress was that the vision revealed that exile was not the worst God's people would experience. To this point in the history and theology of the nation that had lived in national covenant with YHWH, exile *was* the worst possible scenario. Exile meant a broken covenant with YHWH: they were not living in the promised land, worshiping at YHWH's temple, or paying taxes to a Davidic king. God's chosen people were scattered to the four winds, and the covenant was null and void. The dire nature of their situation is metaphorically illustrated in the vision of dry bones that Daniel's contemporary Ezekiel saw—only a resurrection would do (Ezek 37:1–14). Those educated enough to be familiar with the writings of the prophets may well have anticipated a future restoration, but it is hard to know how much the rank and file knew of the prophets' words. Even Daniel, a member of the educated Judean elite, seems to have discovered for himself what the prophet Jeremiah had said about the length of exile and responded with the appropriate confession of sin (see on Dan 9:1).

Daniel's life unfolded in the midst of YHWH's long-threatened punishment of his disobedient people. Yet Daniel's visions in Dan 7–12 revealed incredible suffering ahead for God's *faithful* people; no wonder he was appalled.

Part of Daniel's difficulty grasping what he saw was that it entailed a new definition of exile. To this point in his understanding, "exile" meant the loss of relationship with YHWH and absence from the land he promised on account of national unfaithfulness. But while his visions portray the end of exile as he understood it, they

---

146. Michael Horton, *Pilgrim Theology: Core Doctrines for Christian Disciples* (Grand Rapids, Zondervan: 2011, 2012), 227.

also reveal the beginning of a greater exile. Exile in Babylon would end, evident in his visions by the presence of YHWH's people back in their land, but suffering that included assaults on the holy temple and city as well as against "the people of the holy ones of the Most High" lay ahead.[147] "Exile" was the new normal for the faithful people of God. Exile still meant living under foreign and often evil rule, but now it would happen *because* of obedience to covenant ideals. Exile meant living with impaired conditions for justice and righteousness—wherever in the world God's people found themselves.[148] Those disobedient to God's covenant ideals would actually find themselves quite at home in "exile," while those who sought to remain faithful would often be at odds with the prevailing culture.

It is in this redefinition of exile that *we* find our place in the book of Daniel. As followers of Jesus, the Son of Man, we live without a national covenant that entails a piece of real estate or a national identity. We live in exile—citizens of an everlasting kingdom. We are subject to a higher throne—a throne that will often bring us into conflict with lesser thrones.[149] That conflict will look different for God's followers around the globe. Apocalyptic horror may not loom large in my present circumstances, but it does for a myriad of saints living elsewhere. Many of the faithful pay a steep price for standing with the Son of Man. Should the culmination of God's eternal kingdom tarry, many more of us may come know the reality of oppression and suffering. When it does, the message of Dan 7 that YHWH is on the throne, our victory is assured, and he will judge the oppressors will be the hope we need to persevere until God's eternal kingdom fills the earth. We can endure whatever befalls us because the best is yet to come.

---

147. These assaults become more pronounced in the visions of chs. 8–12, but the idea is introduced in the oppression of the holy ones in ch. 7.

148. I am indebted to George Athas for this idea.

149. For provocative thoughts about how "to strategize what the radical gospel of Christian community means in this particular neighborhood of Babylon (Nineveh, Rome, Antioch, London, Los Angeles . . .), and in this particular year of its reign over humanity," see Daniel L. Smith-Christopher, *A Biblical Theology of Exile*, OBT (Minneapolis: Augsburg Fortress, 2002) (quote from p. 194).

MACRO UNIT 3

Daniel 8:1a–12:13c

Encouragement until God's Eternal Kingdom Comes

Main Idea of the Macro Unit

The third macro unit of the book of Daniel consists of the final five chapters (chs. 8–12), where the book returns to Hebrew after six chapters of Aramaic (chs. 2–7). These chapters include three visions that Daniel received, each involving events that would transpire after the Jews returned to the land of Palestine in the postexilic period. The primary focus of the chapters is the destruction of the sanctuary and the oppression of God's people under the second-century-BCE Seleucid king Antiochus IV Epiphanes. While these events are the nearest historical referent for the circumstances portrayed in Daniel's visions, they also represent a pattern of oppressors and oppression that would continue throughout the history of God's people. Taken as a whole, the visions provide glimpses of great suffering but also offer the comfort of God's sovereignty and the promise of future reward for God's people who remain faithful.

Literary Context of the Macro Unit

There are three macro units in the book of Daniel: ch. 1, chs. 2–7, and chs. 8–12. The first functions as a prologue for the book, and the second develops themes that prepare the way for the third. The second macro unit, a chiasm of six chapters, focused on the dynamic between divine and human kingship and also illustrated how God's followers can live faithfully under foreign rulers. These themes carry into the apocalyptic visions of chs. 8–12, which are primarily concerned with the intense suffering God's people face under gentile kings, and especially under Seleucid king Antiochus IV Epiphanes in the second century BCE. These sufferings would surpass their suffering in exile, and their ability to influence their rulers for good (as Daniel and his friends do in the first half of the book) diminishes: the faithful can only endure and look forward to their everlasting reward while anticipating God's judgment on their oppressors.

The three visions of chs. 8–12 are varied in nature. The first (ch. 8) is a vision in which Daniel is transported in some sense to the location of the vision. It bears many similarities to the vision he saw in ch. 7 (Aramaic), and the two are intended to be read in tandem. The second (ch. 9) is less a vision than a revelation that Daniel receives from Gabriel after reflecting and praying over the words of Jeremiah the prophet. The final vision (chs. 10–12) is also a verbal revelation received from a divine messenger.

I. Macro Unit 1: God's Kingdom in Exile: The Conflict Begins (1:1a–21)
II. Macro Unit 2: The Superiority of God and His Kingdom (2:1a–7:28d)
➡ **III. Macro Unit 3: Encouragement until God's Eternal Kingdom Comes (8:1a–12:13c)**
    A. Narrative 1: God's Leash on Evil (8:1a–27f)
    B. Narrative 2: Repentance and God's Promise of Restoration (9:1a–27d)
    C. Narrative 3: The Ultimate Conflict and God's Final Victory (10:1a–12:13c)

Daniel 8:1a–27f

A. Narrative 1: *God's Leash on Evil*

Main Idea of Narrative 1 (8:1a–27f)

Daniel reports a second troubling vision, this one involving a powerful ram being challenged and overtaken by a raging goat with a large single horn. The goat's horn is broken, four other horns take its place, and an extremely powerful smaller horn grows from one of them. This smaller horn assaults the host of heaven and its commander. The angel Gabriel tells Daniel the meaning of the vision, but Daniel remains troubled by what he had seen.

Literary Context of Narrative 1 (Dan 8:1a–27f)

In Daniel's second vision report of ch. 8, he recounts the vision entirely in first person, in contrast to his vision in ch. 7, which was introduced by a third-person narrator (7:1). This second vision has many similarities to the earlier vision, and its reference to the vision appearing "after the one that appeared to me previously" (8:1) indicates that the two visions are to be read in tandem.

There are several similarities as well as differences between the two visions. Both occurred during the reign of Belshazzar, and both recount dreams that troubled and confused Daniel—even after they were interpreted for him. Both visions involve animals and horns representing kings or kingdoms, and both describe the persecution of God's people—most particularly by a smaller horn that arose out of one of the bigger horns. Both also recount the eventual defeat of the oppressors. The most notable difference between the two visions is the shift in language from Aramaic back to Hebrew in ch. 8. The reason for the return to Hebrew is not contextually obvious, but it may coincide with a shift in scope and focus that begins in ch. 8 and continues through the rest of the book: that is, while the vision of four beasts in ch. 7 encompassed four world empires and the totality of human history, the vision of ch. 8 only includes two beasts. Chapter 7 and the narrative chapters before it were largely concerned with the universal rule of Israel's God as demonstrated through the experiences of the Jews in exile. By contrast, the visions of chs. 8–12 focus on events that would transpire after the Jews had returned to their land—events that specifically involved God's sanctuary.[1]

Since ch. 8 is apocalyptic literature, the discussion that follows will incorporate Korner's language as used in the commentary on Dan 7.[2] However, while all four of Daniel's visions are apocalyptic in nature, each of them is unique: Dan 7 is the report of a symbolic vision, has an angelic interpreter, includes a third-person narrator who introduces the report, and is written in Aramaic; Dan 8 is the report of a symbolic vision, has an angelic interpreter, does not include a third-person narrator, and is written in Hebrew; Dan 9 is a verbal revelation transmitted to Daniel by an angel and without a symbolic vision associated with it; Dan 10–12 includes a vision of divine beings and a revelation transmitted by an angel without a symbolic vision associated with it. This diversity of form requires an individualized approach to the structure of each vision.

In the approach to the vision of Dan 8, we again will use the language of "vision block" to refer to the large segments that comprise the vision report and "individual vision" to refer to each element of the vision blocks. The vision report in Dan 8 includes nine individual visions, each introduced by a verb of observation (ראה, "to look, see" [8:2a, 2e, 3b, 4a, 7a]; שמע, "to hear" [8:13a, 16a]); or a combination of הִנֵּה with an orienting statement of perception (וַאֲנִי הָיִיתִי מֵבִין וְהִנֵּה, "I was considering, and oh!" [8:5a–b]; וָאֲבַקְשָׁה בִינָה וְהִנֵּה, "I sought understanding. And oh!" [8:15b–c]).[3] These nine individual visions fall into three vision blocks: 8:1–4, 5–14, and 15–27. Each properly begins with a preliminary orienting statement followed by וְהִנֵּה: וָאֶרְאֶה וְהִנֵּה, "I looked—and oh!" (8:3b–c); וַאֲנִי הָיִיתִי מֵבִין וְהִנֵּה, "I was considering, and oh!" (8:5a–b); and וָאֲבַקְשָׁה בִינָה וְהִנֵּה, "I sought understanding. And oh!" (8:15b). While the first vision block begins properly in 8:3a–b, for the sake of simplicity I have included in it Daniel's first-person space/time referent in 8:1–2, including its

---

1. Seow proposes that the reason for the return to Hebrew is wrapped up in the shift in scope and focus: "Perhaps the very subject matter, namely, the survival of the Jewish people and their faith in the face of such humiliation, inspired the linguistic shift from Aramaic, still the lingua franca of the Eastern Mediterranean world, to the rejuvenated national language of the Jewish people" (*Daniel*, 117).

2. Korner, "'And I Saw . . . ,'" 160–83. See Literary Context of Narrative 6 (Dan 7:1–28) above, pp. 348–50.

3. See on 8:3 below for a discussion of הִנֵּה.

two individual visions (8:2a–d, 2e–f).[4] With this in mind, the vision report begins in 8:1, but the vision itself begins with the statement וָאֶשָּׂא עֵינַי, "I lifted my eyes" (8:3a; cf. Ezek 8:5; Zech 2:5[1]; 5:1, 9; 6:1).

> III. Macro Unit 3: Encouragement until God's Eternal Kingdom Comes (8:1a–12:13c)
> → A. **Narrative 1: God's Leash on Evil (8:1a–27f)**
> B. Narrative 2: Repentance and God's Promise of Restoration (9:1a–27d)
> C. Narrative 3: The Ultimate Conflict and God's Final Victory (10:1a–12:13c)

1. Vision Block 1: *The Two-Horned Ram* (8:1a–4e)

Main Idea of the Passage

Daniel 8:1–4 introduces the time and location of Daniel's second vision and recounts his vision in Susa of the two-horned ram that had extraordinary power. No other beast was able to challenge it or even help any who fell before it.

Literary Context

Daniel 8:1–4 is the first and shortest of three vision blocks that comprise the vision report of ch. 8. As such, it functions in at least five ways in its broader literary context. First, its space/time referent provides the immediate context for Daniel's vision. Second, as was true in the vision of Dan 7, its use of a date formula that recalls Belshazzar's reign (בִּשְׁנַת שָׁלוֹשׁ לְמַלְכוּת בֵּלְאשַׁצַּר הַמֶּלֶךְ, 8:1) evokes a foreboding sense of what is to come. A third function is connecting this second vision to the first one Daniel received in ch. 7 so that the two are considered together. Two final functions of the opening vision block are to introduce the character of the two-horned ram and, through it, to establish a pattern of behavior for the rest of the characters in the vision.

---

4. Note that the third vision block includes Daniel's conclusion (v. 27), which is also not properly part of the vision.

> A. Narrative 1: God's Leash on Evil (8:1a–27f)
>   1. **Vision Block 1: The Two-Horned Ram (8:1a–4e)**
>   2. Vision Block 2: The Billy Goat of the Goats (8:5a–14b)
>   3. Vision Block 3: The Interpretation of the Vision of the Evenings and the Mornings (8:15a–27f)

Translation and Exegetical Outline

(See page 409.)

Structure and Literary Form

The vision report of Dan 8 begins with the first of three vision blocks that comprise Daniel's report. This opening vision block has four subsections: 8:1, 2, 3, and 4.

The first two subsections (8:1 and 2) include the space/time referent of Daniel's vision. In the first (8:1), Daniel establishes himself as the one speaking and provides the timing of the vision—i.e., "in the third year of the reign of Belshazzar the king." In the second (8:2), he details the location of the vision in two individual visions, each beginning with the statement "I looked in the vision" (וָאֶרְאֶה בֶּחָזוֹן, 8:2a, 2e): Daniel reports that he was "in Susa the citadel" (8:2c–d) and specifically, "along the canal of Ulai" (8:2f).

The third subsection (8:3) marks the beginning of what he witnessed in his vision with the statement וָאֶשָּׂא עֵינַי, "I lifted my eyes" (8:3a), followed by וָאֶרְאֶה וְהִנֵּה, "and I looked—and oh!" (8:3b–c), to indicate the beginning of the first vision block (cf. 8:5a–b, 15a–c). The report of a ram with two horns follows (8:3c–g). The fourth subsection (8:4) is the last individual vision of the first vision block and begins with רָאִיתִי, "I saw" (8:4a), to report the activity of the two-horned ram.

Since the entire narrative is Daniel's first-person report of his vision, it is all set as reported speech (shaded on the charts).

Daniel 8:1a–4e

III. Encouragement Until God's Eternal Kingdom Comes (8:1a–12:13c)
A. Narrative 1: God's Leash on Evil (Dan 8:1a–27f)
1. Vision Block 1: The Two-Horned Ram (8:1a–4e)
a. The Timing of the Vision (8:1a–c)

1a	"In the third year of the reign of Belshazzar the king,
1b	a vision appeared to me — I, Daniel —
1c	after the one that appeared to me previously.

b. The Location of the Vision (8:2a–f)
(1) Individual Vision: In Susa the Citadel (8:2a–d)

2a	And I looked in the vision,
2b	and while I was looking,
2c	I was in Susa the citadel,
2d	which is in Elam the province.

(2) Individual Vision: Along the Ulai Canal (8:2e–f)

2e	I looked in the vision,
2f	and myself was along the canal of Ulai.

c. Individual Vision: The Appearance of a Two-Horned Ram (8:3a–g)

3a	I lifted my eyes,
3b	and I looked —
3c	and oh! A single ram was standing in front of the canal.
3d	It had two horns.
3e	The horns were long,
3f	but one was longer than the other,
3g	and the longer one was coming up later.

d. Individual Vision: The Action of the Two-Horned Ram (8:4a–e)

4a	I saw the ram charging westward and northward and southward,
4b	and no animal could stand before it;
4c	and there was none who could deliver from its hand.
4d	It did as it pleased,
4e	and it magnified itself.

		Table 8.1. Vision Block 1 (Dan 8:1–4)
Individual Vision	**Verse**	**Vision Block 1—The Two-Horned Ram (8:1–4)**
	1	In the third year of the reign of Belshazzar the king,
		a vision appeared to me—I, Daniel—
		after the one that appeared to me previously.
1	2	And I looked in the vision,
		and while I was looking,
		I was in Susa the citadel,
		which is in Elam the province.
2		*I looked in the vision,*
		and I myself was along the canal of Ulai.
	3	I lifted my eyes,
3		and I looked—
		and oh! A single ram was standing in front of the canal.
		It had two horns.
		The horns were long,
		but one was longer than the other,
		and the longer one was coming up later.
4	4	*I saw* the ram charging westward and northward and southward,
		and no animal could stand before it;
		and there was none who could deliver from its hand.
		It did as it pleased,
		and it magnified itself.

Explanation of the Text

a. The Timing of the Vision (8:1a–c)

The vision of Dan 8 opens with a date formula, the space/time referent of an apocalyptic vision that provides the when and/or where of the seer's vision.[5] In this case, the "when" is "in the third year of the reign of Belshazzar the king" (8:1a). This date formula follows the disrupted chronology of ch. 7 (see on 7:1). As noted there, reference to Belshazzar's "third year" might be a more concrete way of saying "not long after the beginning" of his reign. If taken literally, the reference to his third year is 550 BCE, about the time Persian Cyrus established the Medo-Persian Empire after achieving

---

5. Korner, "'And I Saw . . . ,'" 162.

independence from Media—events that led to the end of Babylonian world dominance and Israel's enforced exile.[6]

As discussed earlier (see on 7:1), date formulae are infrequent in the non-apocalyptic chapters of Daniel (chs. 1–6), but all four of Daniel's visions in the second half of the book have dates associated with them (7:1; 8:1; 9:1; 10:1). One effect of these chronological markers is that they connect the apocalyptic visions to the events and chronology of the narrative chapters. In the case of Daniel's visions in chs. 7 and 8, the significance of their connection to Belshazzar's reign is that he is the book's prototype for a blasphemous, arrogant king who shakes his fist at Israel's God. The apocalyptic visions that Daniel sees will reveal gentile kings who follow in Belshazzar's footsteps—and then some. While Daniel's interaction with Belshazzar in the book of Daniel is limited to one chapter, the dark overtones of the events in ch. 5 foreshadow future hostility between God's people and their gentile overlords.

The main clause of the opening verse is 8:1b, "a vision appeared to me—I, Daniel" (חָזוֹן נִרְאָה אֵלַי אֲנִי דָנִיֵּאל), letting the reader know that Daniel is the narrator for the chapter. Unlike the vision report in ch. 7, which the third-person narrator introduced, this report is introduced by the one who saw the vision (cf. 7:1; 9:1; 10:1).[7]

A second note about the "when" of this vision follows the main clause; the vision is said to have occurred "after the one that appeared to me previously" (8:1c). Given the date formulae in both chs. 7 and 8, this information is redundant, and its purpose is likely to link the two visions together and invite the reader to consider them in light of each other.[8]

b. The Location of the Vision (8:2a–f)

As noted above,[9] Daniel's vision report is introduced by the statement in 8:3a, "I lifted my eyes" (וָאֶשָּׂא עֵינַי) and consists of three vision blocks, each properly beginning with a preliminary orienting statement followed by וְהִנֵּה, "and oh!" The first vision block thus begins in 8:3b–c with וָאֶרְאֶה וְהִנֵּה, "and I looked—and oh!" However, the space/time referent for the vision (8:1–2) includes two visionary elements that stand outside the vision Daniel sees and establish the location of the vision.

The "where" of this vision is told over the course of the six clauses that comprise the two visionary elements of 8:2. The first visionary element is introduced in 8:2a (וָאֶרְאֶה בֶחָזוֹן, "And I looked in the vision") and then includes a second semantically unnecessary statement about "looking" in 8:2b (the infinitive construct בִּרְאֹתִי, "while I was looking") before Daniel details his location in two clauses: the main clause of 8:2c ("I was in Susa the citadel") and the relative clause of 8:2d ("which is in Elam the province"). The second visionary element is introduced in 8:2e with the same introductory formula (וָאֶרְאֶה בֶחָזוֹן, "I looked in the vision"), which sets up the main clause further detailing Daniel's location: "and I myself was along the canal of Ulai" (8:2f). This final clause includes a grammatically unnecessary first-person subject pronoun, emphasizing the speaker as the subject of the statement.

---

6. For the relevance of this date with respect to the vision, see on 8:2 below.

7. Date formulae, when included, are part of the more general characteristic of apocalyptic literature in which visions are set in a narrative framework. See above on Dan 7:1 and the introduction, pp. 24–27.

8. See further Literary Context of Narrative 1 (Dan 8:1a–27f) for the similarities and differences between the two visions.

9. See Literary Context of Narrative 6 (Dan 7:1a–28d) above.

This lengthy "where" information, with its emphasis on looking and Daniel's presence, functions like a video camera panning over a location, coming into focus, zooming in, and then refocusing. It is as if Daniel is looking through the lens, and as the camera pans over Elam, he sees himself in the citadel city of Susa. He keeps looking as the camera zooms in and focuses, allowing him to realize he is along the Ulai Canal.

The significance of Susa as the location of Daniel's vision is that it corresponds to the content of the vision itself. Susa lay 220 miles east of Babylon in what would become the mighty Persian Empire, and the ram that appears in the vision represents the Medo-Persian Empire.[10] As Babylon faded and fell from world dominance, its eastern neighbor would rise and ultimately be challenged by the western empire of Greece, represented by the goat in Daniel's vision. Thus, in the conflict between the ram and goat, Daniel was seeing future events in which Babylon would have no part. Accordingly, in his vision he is transported out of Babylon.[11]

c. Individual Vision: The Appearance of a Two-Horned Ram (8:3a–g)

The vision itself begins in 8:3a with the statement וָאֶשָּׂא עֵינַי, "I lifted my eyes," followed by וָאֶרְאֶה וְהִנֵּה, "and I looked—and oh!" (8:3b–c), signaling the first vision block (cf. 8:5a–b, 15a–c). The attention-getting הִנֵּה, "oh!" is common in Biblical Hebrew, and its use in vision reports typically expresses the speaker's surprise at what he is seeing.[12] Daniel did not expect to see a lone ram along the banks of the citadel's waterway. He reports that the ram had two horns, long horns. However, one of the horns was longer than the other. The active participle עֹלָה, "was coming up," may indicate that Daniel watched as the second horn grew longer (8:3g). Rams are used symbolically for leaders or rulers, and horns indicate power (e.g., Jer 48:25; Lam 2:3; Ezek 34:17; see also Exod 15:15, "leaders ['rams'] of Moab;" Ezek 17:13, "leading men ['rams'] of the land").

d. Individual Vision: The Action of the Two-Horned Ram (8:4a–e)

After observing the appearance of the ram, Daniel has another individual vision in which he watches the activity of the two-horned ram. This last visionary element of the first vision block begins with רָאִיתִי, "I saw" (8:4a). He watches the ram charge in three directions—toward the west, the north, and the south. While the word translated "charged" (מְנַגֵּחַ) may simply mean that the ram's

---

10. At the time of Daniel's vision, Susa was part of the Elam province in Media. Assyrian Asshurbanipal had conquered Elam and destroyed Susa in the mid-seventh century BCE, and in the third year of Babylonian Belshazzar, Susa was a relatively insignificant location. It remained that way until 521 BCE when Darius I rebuilt the city as a fortress city that functioned as the administrative capital of Persia and the royal winter palace. The Ulai Canal—"Eulaeus" in later classical sources—was a large, artificial canal that ran near the city (Collins, *Daniel*, 329).

11. Daniel was apparently awake during this vision—and not dreaming in bed as he was in ch. 7. It is possible, of course, that he was physically there—whether in an administrative function or having been physically transported by the Spirit. However, it is more likely that, like Ezekiel before him (Ezek 8:1–3; 11:1; 37:1) and the apostle John after him (Rev 4:1–2; 17:3), he was experiencing an altered state of consciousness.

12. This is the case in Dan 8:3, 5, and 15. For the use in 8:19, see further below. See the comprehensive study of הִנֵּה by Cynthia L. Miller-Naudé and C. H. J. van der Merwe, "הִנֵּה and Mirativity in Biblical Hebrew," *HS* 52 (2011): 53–81.

aggression made its challengers scatter in fear (cf. Deut 33:17; Ezek 34:21; Ps 44:6[5]), it seems more likely in context that the ram ran at its challengers and gored them (cf. Exod 21:28–29, 31–32, 36; 1 Kgs 22:11; 2 Chr 18:10). Daniel says nothing of these challengers or the details of the ram's assaults, but what he does say suggests that he watched an army of challengers try to stand against the ram and fail: "no animal could stand before it" (8:4b). He adds, "and there was none who could deliver from its hand" (8:4c). Perhaps Daniel saw some animals try to help others or perhaps none dared. Daniel does not describe the competitors or the conflicts because they do not matter; what matters is that this ram aggressively subdued every animal around. There was no escape.

The summary of all this activity is in 8:4d–e: the ram did whatever it wanted and magnified itself. The *waw* + perfect forms that begin 8:4d and 8:4e (וְהִגְדִּיל, וְעָשָׂה) suggest the habitual nature of the activity: we might say, "It kept on doing whatever it wanted and it made itself greater and greater." The expression "magnify (oneself)" is used positively of God himself in the Bible (e.g., 2 Sam 7:26; Ps 138:2), but when used of humans, it is often negative, suggesting arrogance (e.g., Job 19:5; Ps 35:26; Lam 1:9)—a behavior we have come to expect of the beasts in Daniel's visions (cf. 7:8, 20, 25).

In this description of the ram's activity, Daniel introduces key words and phrases that will continue through the rest of this vision report and appear again in his final vision. A variation of the phrase "no animal could stand before it" (8:4b) reappears in the description of the goat in 8:7e–f. That "there was none who could deliver from its hand" (8:4c) is echoed in 8:7i. The statement that the ram "magnified itself" (הִגְדִּיל, 8:4e) will also be said of the goat (8:8a), the little horn (8:8, 9, 10, 11, 25), and the king in Dan 11:36–37. That the ram "did as it pleased" (עָשָׂה כִרְצֹנוֹ, 8:4d) will be said of kings in Daniel's final vision (11:3, 16, 36). This repetition establishes themes of power and conflict that become a pattern of behavior in the ram's successors, where the power and the conflict become exponentially greater.

2. Vision Block 2: *The Billy Goat of the Goats* (8:5a–14b)

Main Idea of the Passage

In Daniel 8:5–14, Daniel's vision continues as he sees a single-horned goat crossing the landscape to charge at the ram, with the result that it breaks its horns, knocks it to the ground, and tramples it. The goat magnifies itself greatly before its single horn is broken and four horns take its place. From one of them a smaller horn emerges, rises to greatness, and launches an assault against the host of heaven, its commander, and his sanctuary. The holy ones in Daniel's vision say the destruction wrought by the smaller horn will last 2,300 evenings and mornings.

Literary Context

Daniel 8:5–14 is the second vision block of the narrative that comprises ch. 8. It follows the opening vision block in which Daniel established the time and place of his vision and detailed his vision of an indomitable ram, and it functions in at least four ways in its broader literary context. First, it introduces the character of the goat, along with the four horns that eventually grow on it and the smaller horn that emerges from one of them. Second, it signals the importance of that smaller horn by the length of description devoted to it. Third, it reinforces the themes of power and greatness introduced by the ram in the first vision block, and finally, it introduces the most important idea of the vision—namely, there would be an appointed end to the horrors portrayed in the vision.

> A. Narrative 1: God's Leash on Evil (8:1a–27f)
> 1. Vision Block 1: The Two-Horned Ram (8:1a–4e)
> → **2. Vision Block 2: The Billy Goat of the Goats (8:5a–14b)**
> 3. Vision Block 3: The Interpretation of the Vision of the Evenings and the Mornings (8:15a–27f)

Translation and Exegetical Outline

(See pages 415–16.)

Structure and Literary Form

The second section of the narrative in Dan 8 (8:5–14) continues the first-person report of Daniel's troubling vision of the ram and goat. It is the second of three vision blocks that comprise the entire vision episode of ch. 8 (8:1–4, 5–14, and 15–27), and it consists of three subsections (8:5–6, 7–12, and 13–14). Each subsection is an individual vision.

The first subsection (8:5–6) begins the second vision block with language similar to the language that initiated the first vision block—a combination of הִנֵּה with an orienting statement of perception: "I was considering, and oh!" (וַאֲנִי הָיִיתִי מֵבִין וְהִנֵּה, 8:5a; cf. 8:3b–c, 15a–c). This statement also introduces the first individual vision of the block—the appearance of a one-horned goat.

Daniel 8:5a–14b

	Hebrew	English	Outline
			2. Vision Block 2: The Billy Goat of the Goats (8:5a–14b)
			a. Individual Vision: The Appearance of the Billy Goat (8:5a–6c)
5a	וַאֲנִי ׀ הָיִיתִי מֵבִין	I was considering,	
5b	וְהִנֵּה צְפִיר־הָעִזִּים בָּא מִן־הַמַּעֲרָב עַל־פְּנֵי כָל־הָאָרֶץ	and oh! A billy goat of the goats was coming from the west across the face of all the earth,	
5c	וְאֵין נוֹגֵעַ בָּאָרֶץ	and nothing was touching the ground.	
5d	וְהַצָּפִיר קֶרֶן חָזוּת בֵּין עֵינָיו׃	The billy goat had a prominent horn between his eyes.	
6a	וַיָּבֹא עַד־הָאַיִל בַּעַל הַקְּרָנַיִם	He came up to the ram that had two horns,	
6b	אֲשֶׁר רָאִיתִי עֹמֵד לִפְנֵי הָאֻבָל	which I saw standing before the canal,	
6c	וַיָּרָץ אֵלָיו בַּחֲמַת כֹּחוֹ׃	and he ran toward it in his raging strength.	
			b. Individual Vision: The Rampage of the Billy Goat (8:7a–12d)
			(1) The Destruction of the Ram (8:7a–i)
7a	וּרְאִיתִיו מַגִּיעַ אֵצֶל הָאַיִל	I saw him reach the side of the ram,	
7b	וַיִּתְמַרְמַר אֵלָיו	and he was enraged at it.	
7c	וַיַּךְ אֶת־הָאַיִל	He struck the ram,	
7d	וַיְשַׁבֵּר אֶת־שְׁתֵּי קְרָנָיו	and he broke its two horns.	
7e	וְלֹא־הָיָה כֹחַ בָּאַיִל	There was no power in the ram	
7f	לַעֲמֹד לְפָנָיו	to stand against him.	
7g	וַיַּשְׁלִיכֵהוּ אַרְצָה	He threw it to the ground	
7h	וַיִּרְמְסֵהוּ	and trampled it.	
7i	וְלֹא־הָיָה מַצִּיל לָאַיִל מִיָּדוֹ׃	And no one delivered the ram from his hand.	
			(2) The Broken Horn and Four New Horns (8:8a–d)
8a	וּצְפִיר הָעִזִּים הִגְדִּיל עַד־מְאֹד	The billy goat of the goats magnified himself exceedingly,	
8b	וּכְעָצְמוֹ	but when he was strong,	
8c	נִשְׁבְּרָה הַקֶּרֶן הַגְּדוֹלָה	the great horn was broken,	
8d	וַתַּעֲלֶנָה חָזוּת אַרְבַּע תַּחְתֶּיהָ לְאַרְבַּע רוּחוֹת הַשָּׁמָיִם׃	and four prominent ones came up in its place to the four winds of heaven.	

Continued on next page.

Continued from previous page.

9a		From one of them went out a smaller horn,	(3) The Smaller Horn (8:9a–12d)
9b		and it grew exceedingly great to the south and to the east and to the Beautiful.	
10a		It grew as far as the host of heaven,	
10b		and it caused some of the host and some of the stars to fall to the earth,	
10c		and it trampled them.	
11a		Even to the commander of the host it magnified itself,	
11b		and from him was taken away 'the continual,'	
11c		and the place of his sanctuary was thrown down.	
12a		And the host was being given over, alongside 'the continual,' on account of transgression,	
12b		and it was casting truth to the ground.	
12c		It did,	
12d		and it was successful.	
13a		I heard a holy one speaking,	c. Individual Vision: The Dialogue of the Holy Ones (8:13a–14b)
13b		and another holy one said to that one, the one speaking,	(1) The Question (8:13a–e)
13c		'How long is the vision—	
13d		"the continual" and the transgression that desolates,	
13e		the giving over of both a sacred place and a host for trampling?'	
14a		And he said to me,	(2) The Answer (8:14a–b)
14b		'Until 2,300 evenings and mornings, then a sacred place will be put right.'	

The second subsection (8:7–12) is an individual vision introduced with a verb of observation: "I saw him" (וּרְאִיתִיו, 8:7a). This individual vision reports the rampage of the one-horned goat—its destruction of the two-horned ram (8:7), its broken horn and the four that replace it (8:8), and the emergence of a smaller horn and its subsequent assaults on the heavenly host and its commander (8:9–12).

The third subsection (8:13–14) is an individual vision introduced with another verb of observation: "I heard" (וָאֶשְׁמְעָה, 8:13a), and it initiates the report of a dialogue between two holy ones. The dialogue includes a question by one holy one: "how long . . ." (. . . עַד־מָתַי, 8:13c–e) and the answer addressed to Daniel by another holy one (8:14).

		Table 8.2. Vision Block 2 (Dan 8:5–14)
Individual Vision	**Verse**	**Vision Block 2—The Billy Goat of the Goats (8:5–14)**
1	5	*I was considering,* *and oh!* A billy goat of the goats was coming from the west across the face of all the earth, and nothing was touching the ground. The billy goat had a prominent horn between his eyes.
	6	He came up to the ram that had two horns, which I saw standing before the canal, and he ran toward it in his raging strength.
2	7	*I saw* him reach the side of the ram, and he was enraged at it. He struck the ram, and he broke its two horns. There was no power in the ram to stand against him. He threw it to the ground and trampled it. And no one delivered the ram from his hand.
	8	The billy goat of the goats magnified himself exceedingly, but when he was strong, the great horn was broken, and four prominent ones came up in its place to the four winds of heaven.
	9	From one of them went out a smaller horn, and it grew exceedingly great to the south and to the east and to the Beautiful.

Continued on next page.

Continued from previous page.

	10	It grew as far as the host of heaven,
		and it caused some of the host and some of the stars to fall to the earth,
		and it trampled them.
	11	Even to the commander of the host it magnified itself,
		and from him was taken away "the continual,"
		and the place of his sanctuary was thrown down.
	12	And the host was being given over, alongside "the continual," on account of transgression,
		and it was casting truth to the ground.
		It did,
		and it was successful.
3	13	*I heard* a holy one speaking,
		and another holy one said to that one, the one speaking,
		"How long is the vision—
		'the continual' and the transgression that desolates,
		the giving over of both a sacred place and a host for trampling?"
	14	And he said to me,
		"Until 2,300 evenings and mornings, then a sacred place will be put right."

Explanation of the Text

a. Individual Vision: The Appearance of the Billy Goat (8:5a–6c)

The second vision block begins with an orienting statement of perception: וַאֲנִי הָיִיתִי מֵבִין, "I was considering" (8:5a; cf. 8:3b, 15b), and וְהִנֵּה, "and oh!" (8:5b; cf. 8:3c, 15c). This statement also introduces the first individual vision of the block—the unexpected appearance of a one-horned goat from the west (see on 8:3 above). Daniel watched as the goat was coming (ptc. בָּא) into view from far away ("across the face of all the earth," 8:5b). Its incredible speed covering that distance is evident from the statement "and nothing was touching the ground" (8:5c). We might say the goat "flew" across the earth. The goat had one large horn (קֶרֶן חָזוּת, "horn of vision," 8:5d) between its eyes.

Two *wayyiqtol* clauses conclude Daniel's description of the goat's appearance on the scene. It came (וַיָּבֹא, 8:6a) up to the two-horned ram Daniel already described, and it ran (וַיָּרָץ, 8:6c) toward the ram in furious strength.

b. Individual Vision: The Rampage of the Billy Goat (8:7a–12d)

Daniel's vision continues with another individual vision indicated by "I saw" (וּרְאִיתִיו, 8:7a), in which he witnesses the rampage of the goat against the ram. A series of *wayyiqtols* recounts the rampage: וַיִּתְמַרְמַר, "he was enraged" at the ram (8:7b); וַיַּךְ, "he struck" it (8:7c); וַיְשַׁבֵּר, "he broke" the ram's two horns (8:7d); וַיַּשְׁלִיכֵהוּ, "he threw it" to the ground (8:7g); and וַיִּרְמְסֵהוּ, "he trampled it" (8:7h). The goat's success at throwing the ram to the ground and trampling it was possible because the ram had no power to stand against him (8:7e–f)—just as other beasts had been unable to stand against the ram (8:4b). Again, Daniel notes the absence of a deliverer (8:7i); just as there had been no one to deliver from the ram's power (8:4c), so there was no one to deliver the ram from the raging goat.

With the ram destroyed, there was nothing in the goat's way. In language that echoes the ram's earlier activity, the goat "magnified himself" (הִגְדִּיל), but he did so even more than the ram had (מְאֹד, "exceedingly," 8:8a). However, when he was strong (כְּעָצְמוֹ)—perhaps at the pinnacle of his strength—the single great horn was broken (נִשְׁבְּרָה, 8:8c). Unlike the broken horns of the ram, for which the goat was the agent of action (8:7d), no agent is identified for the goat's broken horn. In place of the one great horn came up four great horns "to the four winds of heaven" (8:8d)—that is, they extended in all directions. The vision spends no more time on these four great horns but moves quickly to "a smaller horn" (קֶרֶן־אַחַת מִצְּעִירָה) that went out from one of the four horns (8:9a). The rest of the vision of the billy goat is consumed by the activity of this smaller horn (8:9–12). As the longest part of this vision, the rise and reign of the smaller horn is clearly "the destination of the vision."[13]

Another series of *wayyiqtol* clauses describes the exploits of the smaller horn (cf. those of the goat described in 8:6–7): וַתִּגְדַּל־יֶתֶר, "it grew exceedingly great" in three directions (8:9b); וַתִּגְדַּל, "it grew" as far as the host of heaven (8:10a); וַתַּפֵּל, "it caused to fall" some of the host and the stars (8:10b); and וַתִּרְמְסֵם, "it trampled them" (8:10c).

With respect to the "exceedingly great" growth of the smaller horn, it seems likely that—since a single horn cannot go in three directions at once (unlike the four horns that spread to the four winds of heaven)—Daniel watched as the smaller horn grew to extraordinary proportions first to the south, then to the east, and then finally toward "the Beautiful," a reference to the land of Israel and to Jerusalem, specifically.[14] In its growth toward the Beautiful, the smaller horn also grew upward—as far as the host of heaven (8:10), causing some of the host and some of the stars to fall to earth (נפל, 8:10b). The smaller horn then trampled them (רמס, 8:10c)—just as the goat had thrown the ram to the ground (שלך, 8:7g) and trampled it (רמס, 8:7h).[15]

Then in 8:11–12 the vision recounts the most egregious exploits of the smaller horn,[16] introducing them with the preposition עַד to describe the extraordinary extent of the smaller horn's aggression: it magnified itself (הִגְדִּיל) "even to" the commander of the host (8:11a).[17] Twice already the verb גדל has been used to describe the smaller horn's growth; in 8:9–10 the *qal* reports the expansion of the smaller horn southward, eastward, westward (toward the Beautiful), and upward (8:9b, 10a). Here in 8:11,

---

13. Wells and Sumner, *Esther and Daniel*, 176.

14. Jerusalem was "the Beautiful" (or the "the Beautiful Land") because YHWH had chosen to dwell there (cf. 11:16, 41; Jer 3:19; Ezek 20:6).

15. While the "host of heaven" in the Old Testament typically refers to celestial beings or their visible manifestations, stars, here it seems to refer to the heavenly assembly that served before YHWH's throne and fought on Israel's behalf (Josh 5:14; 1 Kgs 22:19).

16. Semantic obscurities and grammatical difficulties make 8:11–12 quite difficult. Porteous observes, "Although it is in general quite certain what the author is talking about, it is quite impossible to be sure of all the details" (*Daniel*, 125).

17. Most scholars agree that "the commander of the heavenly host" is a reference to God himself.

however, the shift to the *hiphil* echoes what has already been said of the both the ram and the goat (8:4, 8; cf. 7:8, 11, 20): they all magnified themselves, the *hiphil* highlighting the hubris that accompanied their rises to power (see also on 8:4, 8 above).

In this self-exaltation of the smaller horn, two things happened with respect to the commander of the host. The first is that "from him was taken away 'the continual'"[18] (וּמִמֶּנּוּ הוּרַם הַתָּמִיד, 8:11b).[19] The order of elements in this clause (8:11b) is notable: it begins with the prepositional phrase וּמִמֶּנּוּ, "and from him," followed by the verb הוּרַם, "was taken away," and then it concludes with the subject in final position (הַתָּמִיד, "the continual"). The prepositional phrase, "and from him," in initial position emphasizes the significance of who suffered this loss: it was *from him*—the commander of the host!—that "the continual" was taken away. The second thing that happened with respect to the commander of the host is that "the place of his sanctuary was thrown down" (וְהֻשְׁלַךְ מְכוֹן מִקְדָּשׁוֹ, 8:11c). This clause begins with a *waw* + perfect *hophal* (וְהֻשְׁלַךְ), "a simple (con)sequential situation" in which the previous clause provides the logical basis or cause for what is said here:[20] that is, removing the daily sacrifice, the practice that represented the entire temple ritual (Exod 29:38–42; Num 28:2–8) effectively destroyed the sanctuary.

The success of the smaller horn continues in 8:12, where the host was being given over along with "the continual."[21] All these things happened "on account of transgression" (בְּפֶשַׁע, 8:12a), though it is not clear whose transgression is meant. If it is the transgression of "the host," the offenders would be celestial beings (or their earthly counterparts among God's people).[22] In this case, being given over to the small horn was punishment for the host. However, if the transgression is that of the smaller horn and, specifically, his assault against the commander of the host, then the commander's host suffers not for its own offenses but because the smaller horn was allowed great success—at the expense of the commander and his host.

While the smaller horn seems to have unfettered power, there are subtle hints that someone else is allowing his success. His greatest achievements—taking away "the continual" from the commander, throwing down his sanctuary, and taking control of the host—are recounted with passive verbs: הוּרַם, הֻשְׁלַךְ, תִּנָּתֵן (8:11b, 11c, 12a). The smaller horn may have had great power, but he is not the grammatical agent of these actions. This subtle grammatical shift makes someone else the agent. The smaller horn may have magnified himself to be equal with the commander of the host, but he did not reach the pinnacle of his power on his own merits; someone else allowed it. Someone else allowed him to inflict devastating loss on the commander and assault his host.

The smaller horn's agency resumes in 8:12b, where תַּשְׁלֵךְ אֱמֶת אַרְצָה, "it was casting truth to the ground."[23] The final two clauses of 8:12 summarize the activity of the smaller horn and also echo the

---

18. Scholars largely agree that הַתָּמִיד, translated here as "the continual," is a reference to the daily sacrifice in the temple. The sacrifice itself is commanded in Exod 29:38–42 and Num 28:2–8, where it was to be offered תָּמִיד, "continuously." The word used by itself to represent the daily offering is unique to the book of Daniel (see also Dan 11:31; 12:11), though it later becomes the standard way to refer to the daily sacrifice (Newsom, *Daniel*, 265).

19. This reflects the *qere* הוּרַם, the *hophal* of רוּם.

20. *IBHS*, 32.2.3c.

21. The verbs in 8:12a–b are imperfect (וְתַשְׁלֵךְ, תִּנָּתֵן), but the context does not support translating them as future tense. I have translated them to reflect the progressive/imperfective nature of the conjugation.

22. Given the cosmic perspective of Daniel's visions and the blurring of lines that occurs between the celestial and terrestrial realms, this is a reasonable understanding: mutiny among divine beings would also be reflected on earth (and vice versa).

23. On וְתַשְׁלֵךְ, see p. n21 above.

earlier description of the ram (8:4d–e). It did and it succeeded (וְעָשְׂתָה וְהִצְלִיחָה). As was true of the ram, so is true of the smaller horn. The *waw* + perfect forms in 8:12c and 8:12d suggest the habitual nature of the activity: "It kept on doing and it made itself greater and greater." In this case, the verb עָשָׂה, "to do," has no object (cf. וְעָשָׂה כִרְצֹנוֹ, "it did as it pleased," 8:4d), the gap perhaps inviting the reader to fill in the blank: it did [anything and everything it wanted to do]. There were no apparent limits to the power of the smaller horn.

The actions of the three key players (the ram, the goat, the smaller horn) in Daniel's vision are similarly described, with one significant difference. Of both the ram and the goat, Daniel reported that there was no one to deliver from their hand (מַצִּיל, 8:4c, 7i). Their powers were so great that no challenger could stand against them (8:4b, 7e–f). Since the exploits of the smaller horn exceed those of its predecessors, it would follow that there was no one able to deliver from its hand either. Yet the vision includes no such statement. While arguments from silence are by nature tenuous, an implication of this silence may be that there *was* someone able to deliver from the smaller horn's power—though, as the vision reveals, he stays his hand.[24]

c. Individual Vision: The Dialogue of the Holy Ones (8:13a–14b)

The second vision block (8:5–14) concludes with a third individual vision in which Daniel overhears a conversation between two holy ones (8:13–14). The vision begins with the verb of observation "I heard" (וָאֶשְׁמְעָה, 8:13a) and continues with two embedded reports of speech (8:13c–e and 14b) that include a question by one holy one and an answer by another.

To this point in the vision, Daniel has only reported what he has been seeing, and he has not reported seeing any holy ones. Yet suddenly, he reports hearing one speak, though he does not report what was being said (8:13a). Newsom says the effect of this "to suggest that Daniel's attention has been so focused on what he is seeing that he only gradually becomes aware of a conversation that has been going on between two angelic beings, who, like Daniel, have been witnessing the vision."[25] Daniel then hears a second holy one call to the first. In the language of lament, the holy one asks, "How long?" (עַד־מָתַי, 8:13c). How long would the events of the vision last—the removal of the daily sacrifice (8:13d; cf. 8:11b, 12a), the desolating transgression (8:12a), the giving over of the holy place (8:11c) and the host to be trampled (8:10c, 12a)?

Daniel reports that the answer to this question was addressed "to me" (8:14a),[26] presumably by the first holy one (הַמְדַבֵּר, "the one speaking," 8:13b): 2,300 evenings and mornings, and then a sacred place would be put right.[27] No further response is offered, and the second vision block concludes, leaving Daniel in need of interpretation, which he seeks in the third vision block (8:15–27).

---

24. This is not to suggest that the one able to deliver from the smaller horn's hand would not have been able to deliver from the ram or goat. At issue with the smaller horn is its unchallenged assault against the commander of the host, his sanctuary, and his host, none of which was in view with the rampages of the ram and the goat or of particular significance to a Jewish audience far removed from the events.

25. Newsom, *Daniel*, 266.

26. The LXX and Vulgate read "to him" (אליו); cf. NRSV.

27. Later in the text, the interpreting angel does not explain this part of the vision. The commentaries offer three explanations: (1) 2,300 is the number of evening and morning sacrifices that would have occurred in the temple, an equivalent of 1,150 days or a little more than three years, roughly equivalent to what some understand the "times, time, and half a time" of the oppression by the little horn of ch. 7 (see on 7:25 above)

3. Vision Block 3: *The Interpretation of the Vision of the Evenings and the Mornings* (8:15a–27f)

Main Idea of the Passage

In Daniel 8:15–27 Daniel seeks to understand the vision of the ram, the goat, and the smaller horn, and Gabriel is directed to explain it to him. Gabriel first strengthens him to hear the interpretation and then recounts the meaning of the vision. When Gabriel finishes, Daniel is sick and appalled by what he had seen, and he does not understand it.

Literary Context

Daniel 8:15–27 is the third and final section of the narrative that comprises ch. 8. It follows the vision block in which Daniel witnessed the rampage of the goat against the once indomitable ram and heard holy ones converse about the length of the vision's horror (8:5–14). It functions in at least three ways in its broader literary context. First, it provides the interpretation of what Daniel has witnessed in the first two vision blocks. Second, the emphases of this interpretation highlight what is most important about the vision. Finally, it brings the vision report and chapter to a conclusion with Daniel's report of his reaction to what he had seen.

> A. Narrative 1: God's Leash on Evil (8:1a–27f)
>   1. Vision Block 1: The Two-Horned Ram (8:1a–4e)
>   2. Vision Block 2: The Billy Goat of the Goats (8:5a–14b)
> → **3. Vision Block 3: The Interpretation of the Vision of the Evenings and the Mornings (8:15a–27f)**

(see, e.g., Baldwin, *Daniel*, 158, and Montgomery, *Commentary on the Book of Daniel*, 343); (2) since "evening [and] morning" is a common way of referring to a single day (see, e.g., Gen 1), 2,300 represents six years and four months, which is just shy of seven years, a period of completeness (see, e.g., Miller, *Daniel*, 229, and cf. Goldingay, *Daniel*, 425–26); (3) the number is symbolic and does not need to fit a calendrical interpretation (see Goldingay's discussion, *Daniel*, 425–26). The point seems to be that, whatever the exact time, the sanctuary would be restored.

Translation and Exegetical Outline

(See pages 424–25.)

Structure and Literary Form

The third section of the narrative in Dan 8 (8:15–27) continues and concludes Daniel's first-person report of his visions of the ram, the goat, and the smaller horn. It is the third and longest vision block in the entire vision episode of ch. 8 (8:1–4, 5–14, and 15–27), and it consists of three subsections (8:15, 16–26, and 27). The first two subsections are individual visions, while the third is Daniel's conclusion to the vision report.

The first subsection (8:15) begins with a temporal clause that establishes the timing of the final vision block (8:15a): "And so it was that when I, Daniel, saw the vision." Then language similar to what initiated the first two vision blocks introduces the content of this vision block: a combination of הִנֵּה with an orienting statement of perception (וָאֲבַקְשָׁה בִינָה וְהִנֵּה, "I sought understanding. And oh!" 8:15b–c; cf. 8:3b–c, 5a–b). This statement also introduces the first individual vision of the block—the appearance of a humanlike figure.

The second subsection (8:16–26) is an individual vision introduced with a verb of observation: "I heard" (וָאֶשְׁמַע, 8:16a). This individual vision reports Gabriel's interpretation of the vision, and it includes three sections: the order to Gabriel to interpret the dream (8:16), the preparation of Daniel to receive the interpretation (8:17–18), and the lengthy interpretation of the vision itself (8:19–26).

The third subsection (8:27) lies outside the proper report of the vision and is Daniel's conclusion to his report. In it, he describes his response to what he had seen.

Daniel 8:15a–27f

			3. Vision Block 3: The Interpretation of the Vision of the Evenings and the Mornings (8:15a–27f)
			a. Individual Vision: One with the Appearance of a Man (8:15a–c)
15a		↓ And so it was that when I, Daniel, saw the vision,	
15b		I sought understanding.	
15c		And oh! Standing in front of me was one with the appearance of a man.	
			b. Individual Vision: The Interpretation (8:16a–26e)
			(1) The Order to Gabriel to Interpret (8:16a–d)
16a		I heard the voice of a man between the Ulai.	
16b		He called,	
16c		and he said,	
16d		'Gabriel, explain the vision to this man.'	
			(2) The Preparation to Receive the Interpretation (8:17a–18d)
17a		And he came near where I was standing.	
17b		↓ And when he came,	
17c		I was terrified,	
17d		and I fell on my face.	
17e		He said to me,	
17f		'Understand, son of man,	
17g		↑ that the vision is for an end time.'	
18a		↓ As he spoke with me,	
18b		I fell into a deep sleep, my face to the ground.	
18c		He touched me,	
18d		and he set me upright where I was standing.	
			(3) The Interpretation of the Vision (8:19a–26e)
			(a) A Summary (8:19a–d)
19a		He said,	
19b		'Look, I am letting you know	
19c		↑ what will be at the end of the indignation,	
19d		↑ because at an appointed time will be an end.	
			(b) The Two-Horned Ram (8:20a–b)
20aα		The ram ...	
20b		↑ which you saw with the two horns	
20aβ		... represents the kings of Media and Persia.	

21a	And the shaggy goat is the king of Greece.	(c) The Shaggy Goat (8:21a–c)
21b	↓ As for the great horn which was between his eyes—	
21c	it is the first king.	
22a	↓ As for the broken one and the four that rose in its place—	(d) The Four Horns (8:22a–c)
22b	four kingdoms will arise from a nation,	
22c	↑ but not with its power.	
23a	In the latter part of their rule when the transgressors have reached full measure,	(e) The Smaller Horn (8:23a–25e)
23b	a king will arise—fierce of face and who understands riddles.	
24a	His power will be mighty,	
24b	↑ but not with his own power.	
24c	He will destroy extraordinarily.	
24d	He will be successful,	
24e	and he will do.	
24f	He will destroy mighty men and a holy people.	
25a	By his shrewdness, he will cause deceit to succeed by his hand.	
25b	In his own mind, he will make himself great.	
25c	He will destroy many at ease,	
25d	and against the prince of princes he will stand.	
25e	But without human hand, he will be shattered.	
26a	The vision of the evenings and the mornings,	(f) The Vision of the Evenings and the Mornings (8:26a–e)
26b	↑ which has been said—	
26c	it is true.	
26d	But as for you, seal up the vision,	
26e	↓ for it belongs to many days.'	
27a	But I, Daniel, was undone,	c. The Conclusion of the Vision Report (8:27a–f)
27b	and I was sick for days.	
27c	Then I arose,	
27d	and I did the work of the king.	
27e	I was appalled about the vision,	
27f	but there was no one to explain."	

		Table 8.3. Vision Block 3 (Dan 8:15–27)
Individual Vision	**Verse**	**Vision Block 3—The Interpretation of the Vision of the Evenings and the Mornings (8:15–27)**
	15	And so it was that when I, Daniel, saw the vision,
1		*I sought* understanding.
		And oh! Standing in front of me was one with the appearance of a man.
2	16	*I heard* the voice of a man between the Ulai,
		He called,
		and he said,
		"Gabriel, explain the vision to this man."
	17	And he came near where I was standing.
		And when he came,
		I was terrified,
		and I fell on my face.
		He said to me,
		"Understand, son of man,
		that the vision is for an end time."
	18	As he spoke with me,
		I fell into a deep sleep, my face to the ground.
		He touched me,
		and he set me upright where I was standing.
	19	He said,
		"Look, I am letting you know
		what will be at the end of the indignation,
		because at an appointed time will be an end.
	20	The ram . . .
		which you saw that had two horns
		. . . represents the kings of Media and Persia.
	21	And the shaggy goat is the king of Greece.
		As for the great horn which was between his eyes—
		it is the first king.
	22	As for the broken one and the four that rose in its place—
		four kingdoms will arise from a nation,
		but not with its power.
	23	In the latter part of their rule when the transgressors have reached full measure,
		a king will arise—fierce of face and who understands riddles.

	24	His power will be mighty,
		but not with his own power.
		He will destroy extraordinarily.
		He will be successful,
		and he will do.
		He will destroy mighty men and a holy people.
	25	By his shrewdness, he will cause deceit to succeed by his hand.
		In his own mind, he will make himself great.
		He will destroy many at ease,
		and against the prince of princes he will stand.
		But without human hand, he will be shattered.
	26	The vision of the evenings and the mornings,
		which has been said—
		it is true.
		But as for you, seal up the vision,
		for it belongs to many days."
	27	But I, Daniel, was undone,
		and I was sick for days.
		Then I arose,
		and I did the work of the king.
		I was appalled about the vision,
		but there was no one to explain.

Explanation of the Text

a. Individual Vision: One with the Appearance of a Man (8:15a–c)

The final vision block is prefaced with a temporal clause ("And so it was that when I, Daniel, saw the vision," 8:15a) that both reestablishes Daniel as the speaker after the embedded speech of the two holy ones (8:13c–e and 14b) and functions as a break between the vision and its interpretation, itself a visionary experience.

A combination of הִנֵּה and an orienting statement of perception (וָאֲבַקְשָׁה בִינָה וְהִנֵּה, "I sought understanding. And oh!" 8:15b–c [cf. 8:3b–c; 8:5a–b]) follows the temporal clause of 8:15a and introduces the first individual vision of the third vision block—the appearance of a humanlike figure (כְּמַרְאֵה־גָבֶר, 8:15c). Daniel is surprised (הִנֵּה) by the appearance of this figure (cf. 8:3, 5). In the earlier vision of ch. 7, Daniel approached "one of those standing by" (7:16a) and inquired about the meaning of the vision. The "one standing by" then provided him with an initial interpretation (7:17–18). In this vision report, Daniel simply says he "sought understanding" (8:15b), without specifying how he did this. It seems likely that he asked the holy one who had just spoken to him (8:14), or maybe he approached another holy one and asked. Perhaps he does not report this since none of the holy ones in the vision to this point is the one who eventually helps him. An entirely new figure appears (הִנֵּה, "oh!"), and this is the one who will tell him what the vision means. Note that Daniel describes this new humanlike figure with the word גֶּבֶר rather than the more common אָדָם, an appropriate introduction to the "man" whose name, Daniel will learn, is גַּבְרִיאֵל, "Gabriel" (8:16d; cf. 9:21).

b. Individual Vision: The Interpretation (8:16a–26e)

After the humanlike figure appears in front of him (8:15c), Daniel has a second individual vision, signaled by the verb of observation "I heard" (וָאֶשְׁמַע, 8:16a). This individual vision comprises the remainder of Daniel's vision report (8:19–26), and it includes the interpretation of the vision after a series of events sets the stage for the interpretation (8:17–18).

With the humanlike figure standing some distance in front of him (cf. 8:17a), Daniel hears a human voice coming from the direction of the Ulai Canal. He does not, apparently, see a figure to go with the voice. The content of what that voice said is in an embedded speech report: "Gabriel, explain the vision to this man" (8:16d). Daniel had sought understanding (בִּינָה, 8:15b), and it is being provided (הָבֵן, 8:16d). Gabriel is one of only two named angels in the Bible, appearing twice in Daniel (8:16; 9:21) and twice in the infancy narrative of Luke (Luke 1:19; 1:26).[28] In each appearance, he relays messages from God.

While the text of Dan 8 never discloses the source of the voice commanding Gabriel to explain the vision, the fact that it is someone with authority over Gabriel suggests it may be the voice of God himself. God's audible voice in the Bible is often described as thunderous and terrifying (e.g., Deut 4:33; 1 Sam 7:10; Ps 29:3; Ezek 1:24), but at other times, it seems to be a normal human voice as, apparently, here (e.g., Num 7:89; 1 Kgs 19:13). Daniel will be terrified as this scene unfolds, but it is the approach of Gabriel that triggers his fear, not the voice (8:17).

Gabriel came near to where Daniel was standing, and Daniel fell to his face in terror (8:17d). Gabriel spoke to the prostrate Daniel, his words embedded in another report of direct speech (8:17f–g). He addresses Daniel as בֶּן־אָדָם, "son of man" (8:17f; cf. Ezek 2:1, 3), and explains (הָבֵן) that that vision belongs to "an end time" (עֵת־קֵץ). In most English translations, this sounds like the end of human history (i.e., "the time of the end"), but neither the text nor the context of Dan 8 supports this idea. The vision is for *an* end time, not *the* end time; "end" here simply means the end of *something*. What Daniel has witnessed relates to the end of a particular time; Gabriel will specify *which* end time later (8:19).

Still face down on the ground, Daniel fell into a deep asleep as Gabriel spoke (נִרְדַּמְתִּי, 8:18a–b). The verb רדם is related to a noun used to refer to a deep sleep brought on by YHWH (תַּרְדֵּמָה, e.g., Gen 2:21; 1 Sam 26:12; Isa 29:10; cf. Gen 15:21; Job 4:13), and that is likely the case here since it is hard to imagine a terror-stricken Daniel dropping off into a sound sleep. Gabriel touched him (8:18c), raised him to his feet (8:18d), and spoke to him again (8:19a).

All of these preliminaries to the actual revelation

---

28. The only other named angel in the Bible is Michael (Dan 10:13, 21; 12:1; Jude 1:9; Rev 12:7). Second Temple Jewish literature includes many more (e.g., Raphael, Uriel, Phanuel, Sariel; see, e.g., Tobit, 1 Enoch, and 4 Esdras).

may suggest both its importance and the difficulty Daniel will have taking it in:[29] the appearance of Gabriel to interpret the vision, when a unnamed interpreter explained the earlier vision (7:16, 23); the voice from the Ulai commanding Gabriel to explain the vision, when previously Daniel inquired directly about the meaning of what he had seen (7:16, 19); the details of Daniel's position (i.e., falling on his face, in a deep sleep on the ground, upright); and the ministrations of Gabriel (i.e., touching Daniel and setting him on his feet). What Daniel is about to hear will have an even greater effect on him than the earlier vision (cf. Dan 8:27 and 7:28).[30]

Gabriel's interpretation begins in 8:19b with הִנְנִי, "Look, I . . ." This use of הִנֵּה differs from the other occurrences in the chapter (8:3c, 5b, 15c), where it expresses Daniel's surprise at what he saw. Here the word points out information that Daniel needs to keep in mind as the speech progresses[31]—namely, that what Gabriel is telling Daniel relates to "what will be at the end of the indignation" (8:19c). Gabriel supports this statement in the next clause: "because at an appointed time will be an end" (8:19d). The indignation *will* end, but it will end at an appointed time.

Why does Daniel need to keep this particular information in mind? Because it will prove to be the comfort of the vision and its interpretation. Thus far in the discourse of this vision report, there have been five embedded reports of direct speech related to what Daniel saw in the vision (8:13c–e, 14b, 16d, 17f–g, and 19b–d). All but the command to Gabriel to explain the vision (8:16d) have addressed the duration of the events represented by the vision.

In the first, a holy one specifically asked "How long . . . ?" (עַד־מָתַי, 8:13c), and the response in the second embedded speech was specific: "Until 2,300 evenings and mornings . . ." (8:14b). In Gabriel's initial statement to Daniel, he told him that the vision was for "an end time" (8:17f–g), and when he spoke again, he said he was telling Daniel what would be "at the end of the indignation, because at an appointed time will be an end" (8:19c–d). Before any details of the vision are explained, the point is repeatedly made that what Daniel has seen will have an appointed end. This unmistakable emphasis draws attention to the most important element of the interpretation: the horrors will end, and they will end at an appointed time. Someone has appointed the end of the horrors and will see that it comes to pass. As the rest of the interpretation will make clear, this is the primary comfort of the vision.

From these initial words, Gabriel begins to interpret the various elements of the vision: the ram in 8:20 (cf. 8:3–4); the goat and its great horn in 8:21 (cf. 8:5–7); the four horns in 8:22 (cf. 8:8); the smaller horn in 8:23–25 (cf. 8:9–12). Gabriel's interpretation provides remarkable specificity for some elements of the vision, while leaving others unexplained.[32] The ram with the two horns represented the kings of Media and Persia (8:20). Unexplained by Gabriel is why one horn of the ram's two horns was longer, why the longer one came up after the shorter one, and everything about the ram's behavior: what the charging signified, why it did not butt eastward, who tried standing before it, what it was pleased to do, and how it magnified itself.

The shaggy goat represented the king of Greece

---

29. This will be even more the case in the final revelation of Dan 10–12.

30. See further on Dan 8:27; cf. Dan 7:28.

31. Miller-Naudé and van der Merwe, "הִנֵּה and Mirativity in Biblical Hebrew," 54.

32. Such specificity has resulted in near consensus among interpreters, a sweet reprieve in the interpretive challenges of the book of Daniel!

(8:21a), and the prominent horn between the goat's eyes was the "first king" of Greece. Gabriel's interpretation does not explain the goat's eastward race across the earth, its approach to the ram, its charging in furious strength, its rage at the ram, striking the ram, breaking its horns, the ram's helplessness before the goat, throwing the goat to the ground and trampling it, the absence of any one able to deliver the ram, and how the goat magnified itself.

The broken horn giving way to four horns represented four kingdoms arising from one empire, though they would have less power than the single horn/king had had: "but not with its power" (וְלֹא בְכֹחוֹ). By itself, this statement with respect to the power of the four kingdoms is irrelevant, since neither the vision nor the interpretation is interested in the four horns beyond the explanation they provide for the emergence of the smaller horn. The relevance of the statement will only come into view when the clause is echoed in the description of the new king's power in 8:24a–b: "His power will be mighty, *but not with his own power*" (וְעָצַם כֹּחוֹ וְלֹא בְכֹחוֹ). The two statements are identical (וְלֹא בְכֹחוֹ, 8:22c, 24b), but their meaning and significance are not. While the power of the four kings is relativized by the power of the single horn/king from which they came, the power of the new king is not relativized by that of any other human king. In fact, from the description of his actions, this king will appear to have unfettered human power. Rather, the relativization of his power is as subtle as the passive verbs that described elements of the smaller horn's activity in the vision report (8:11b–12a). He indeed will exercise great power, but someone else is empowering him and thus enabling his great success. This will be the context in which to understand the description of the new king's rise to unprecedented heights.

The timing of the new king's arrival on the world scene is in the twofold temporal clause of 8:23a. It would be "in the latter part of their [i.e., the four kingdoms] rule," and it would occur "when the transgressors have reached full measure" (כְּהָתֵם הַפֹּשְׁעִים).[33] This is the third and final use of the verbal root פשע, "to transgress," in ch. 8 (8:12, 13, 23; cf. also Dan 9:24). In 8:12a, it was the reason behind the giving over of the host and "the continual" (בְּפֶשַׁע); in 8:13d, it was what caused the desolation (הַפֶּשַׁע); and here in 8:23b its use describes those whose completed transgressions marked the rise of the new king (הַפֹּשְׁעִים). While much about the use of פשע in Dan 8 is debated, it at least is clear in the vision and interpretation that the transgressors and their transgressions lay behind the rampage of the new king.[34]

Before describing any of this king's exploits, Gabriel characterizes the king himself. He would be "fierce of face" (עַז־פָּנִים) and one "who understand riddles" (מֵבִין חִידוֹת, 8:23b), language that is reminiscent of Proverbs. In Prov 1:6 understanding

---

33. Some English translations (e.g., NET, NRSV) and many commentators (e.g., Collins, *Daniel*, 339; cf. Newsom, *Daniel*, 253) emend the MT's כְּהָתֵם הַפֹּשְׁעִים, "when the transgressors have reached full measure," to כְּהָתֵם הַפְּשָׁעִים, "when the transgressions have reached full measure" (cf. LXX, Syriac, Vulgate). An appeal to Gen 15:16 (and 2 Macc 6:14) is made for the idea of transgressions being filled up, but the language there is different, and the MT makes good sense as it is.

34. Whose rebellion lay behind the Antiochene persecution has no easy answer. Was it the transgression of Antiochus himself or that of apostate Jews in the Second Temple period? The primary motivation for understanding it to be Antiochus's transgression is that the book of Daniel seems to portray the Jews as being sinned against rather than sinning (see, e.g., Longman, *Daniel*, 204; Goldingay, *Daniel*, 423, 430–31; Pace, *Daniel*, 275). Also in support of this view is the statement in 8:23 that the transgressors/transgressions had reached their full measure (see p. n33 above).

However, the situation described in Dan 8 is not analogous to the situation in Gen 15:16 (and 2 Macc 6:14), where God was waiting for the full measure of gentile rebellion so that he could punish *them*, not afflict his own (innocent) people. Furthermore, that Antiochus's transgressions were behind the persecution seems so obvious as to be superfluous. It is true that

riddles is a positive trait that characterizes the wise. Collins notes that for an ancient Near Eastern king to be described this way was generally commendable: "Mastery of riddles was normally considered a good thing.... Such wisdom was a traditional attribute of monarchy (or at least of royal propaganda) all over the ancient Near East."[35] However, this king would also be "fierce of face," or of a "brazen face," a description suggestive of the adulteress woman in Prov 7. Dressed like a prostitute, she had a "brazen face" (הֵעֵזָה פָנֶיהָ, Prov 7:13) and grabbed and kissed a naïve lad, who foolishly wandered near her house. With a silken tongue (Prov 7:5, 21; cf. 2:16; 5:3; 6:24), she lured him to her house, "a highway to the grave" (7:27). Instead of recognizing her for what she was, the lad listened to her "like a deer stepping into a noose" (7:22). In characterizing the smaller horn/king as "fierce of face" and "understanding riddles," Gabriel implies that he will appear to be wise, but ultimately his wisdom will show itself to be brazenly perverse.[36]

Only with these telltale descriptive elements in place—the king's wily character (8:23b) and expansive power that is not his (8:24a–b)—is Gabriel ready to describe his actions, because only in this context can his actions be correctly understood.

Gabriel begins with a summary of the significance of the smaller horn's actions (8:9b–12d) in 8:24c–e. In the vision, the smaller horn was said to grow great toward the south, east, and Beautiful. He grew as far as the host of heaven, causing some of them to fall along with some of the stars to the earth, where he trampled them. Then he advanced as far as the commander of the host. "The continual" was taken from the commander, his sanctuary was thrown down, and the host and "the continual" were given over to the smaller horn. It cast truth to the ground; it did, and it was successful. All of these details of the vision itself are summarized in Gabriel's explanation that the king would destroy extraordinarily (נִפְלָאוֹת יַשְׁחִית), be successful (הִצְלִיחַ), and do (עָשָׂה)—presumably whatever he wanted to do.

In this great power that was not his, the king would destroy mighty men and a holy people (8:24f). In his wiliness, he would deceive with great success (8:25a). He would delude himself about his own greatness (8:25b),[37] destroy many "at ease" (8:25c), and even stand against the prince of princes (8:25d)—though Gabriel does not say that he would succeed in this final stand. Rather, he says the king would be shattered "without human hand" (בְּאֶפֶס יָד, 8:25e). Newsom notes the "stunning reversal" of this statement:

To this point in both the vision and in the interpretation, Dan 8 has described Antiochus for verse upon verse almost wholly in terms of his strength and success against both earthly and heavenly

---

Daniel's visions generally portray the Jews as the ones wronged, but the book also makes a distinction between Jews who were wise, righteous, and resisted Antiochus, and Jews who were insincere, unrighteous, and violated the covenant (11:32–35; 12:1–3). It is possible that the vision of chapter 8 hints at this division among God's people without explicitly blaming them for the persecution. In this case, God used Antiochus to chasten and purify his own people—perhaps another reason Daniel was so appalled by what he had seen. This interpretation also fits the perspective of 1–2 Maccabees, where Jews who support Antiochus's Hellenistic reforms are condemned (1 Macc 1:11–15, 43; 2 Macc 7:18). (See, e.g., Porteous, *Daniel*, 126; Young, *The Prophecy of Daniel*, 179; Miller, *Daniel*, 234.)

35. Collins, *Daniel*, 339. Collins notes that Solomon provides the obvious illustration of such a king.

36. Collins, *Daniel*, 340. Susan Niditch notes that "cleverness or wisdom used for evil purposes and physical power or strength are also the characteristics of the character-type of the tyrant" in ancient literature (*The Symbolic Vision in Biblical Tradition*, HSM 30 [Chico, CA: Scholars Press, 1980], 230).

37. Newsom observes, "Ironically, [Antiochus] is not only someone who deceives others; he also deceives himself. The outcome of this inflated self-perception is that he will stand against the Prince of princes, meaning God" (*Daniel*, 272).

opponents. In a stunning reversal, his demise is communicated in only three Hebrew words: *ûbĕʾepes yād yiššābēr*, "but he will be broken, and not by hands." The rhetorical economy of the text deflates Antiochus's massive pretensions.[38]

The destruction of the smaller horn was not part of the vision. The ram had been trampled by the more powerful goat, and the goat had been eclipsed by the emergence of the smaller horn, but the vision of the smaller horn's activities ended with the statement that "it did, and it was successful" (8:12c–d)—leaving the impression that nothing could stop the smaller horn. Its unfettered power took it as far as the commander of the host—and, it appeared, beyond. This unfettered power hangs over the vision report like a dark cloud until the very end of Gabriel's interpretation, when Daniel (and the reader) finally hears that the small-horn king would be shattered.[39] Despite all the displays of great power (that was not his), the king whose success seemed to know no limits was shattered.

The revelation of the king's destruction is the conclusion of Gabriel's interpretation. He then assures Daniel that "the vision of the evenings and the mornings" (מַרְאֵה הָעֶרֶב וְהַבֹּקֶר, 8:26a) is true (8:26c). Commentators and Bible translations that include headings usually refer to Dan 8 as "the vision of the ram and the goat," and while this title may help us remember the content of the vision, it does not focus on what matters most in the vision. The ram and the goat simply pave the way for the main character—the smaller horn. But Gabriel does not call this "the vision of the smaller horn." Rather, he calls it "the vision of the evenings and the mornings," bringing to mind the earlier use of "evening and morning" in the vision, where the holy one had assured Daniel that the horrors portrayed in the vision would last 2,300 "evenings and mornings" and then the sacred place would be restored (8:14b). Gabriel's name for the vision is a final reminder in a chapter full of reminders that, while the evil would be unimaginable, it was on a leash. What Daniel had witnessed was horrifying, but it would not last forever. When its "evenings and mornings" were completed, there would be restoration.

Daniel was then instructed to seal up the vision "for it belongs to many days" (8:26d–e). At the time of this vision—namely, the third year of Belshazzar—Jerusalem and Solomon's temple still lay in ruins from Nebuchadnezzar's 587 BCE assault. The vision of the evenings and the mornings portrayed a *new* desolation of a *new* temple—events for which Daniel had no point of reference.

| Table 8.4. The Greek View of the Kingdoms in Daniel 2, 7, and 8 ||||
Historical Referent	**Chapter 2**	**Chapter 7**	**Chapter 8**
Babylon/Nebuchadnezzar	Gold head	Lion	—
Media	Silver torso	Bear	Ram (one horn Media; one horn Persia)
Persia	Bronze midsection	Leopard	
Greece/Seleucid kings ↪Antiochus IV Epiphanes	Iron legs	Fourth beast/ten horns ↪Little horn	Goat ↪Little horn
God's kingdom	Rock	One like son of man/saints of the Most High	

---

38. Newsom, *Daniel*, 272.
39. Goldingay says the symbolic part of the vision "terminates at a surprising point and leaves us in suspense" until "the climactic line of the interpretive vision in v. 25" (*Daniel*, 414).

Historical Referent	Chapter 2	Chapter 7	Chapter 8
Babylon/Nebuchadnezzar	Gold head	Lion	—
Medo-Persia	Silver torso	Bear	Ram (one horn Media; one horn Persia)
Greece ↳Antiochus IV Epiphanes	Bronze midsection	Leopard	Goat ↳Little horn
Rome/revived or extended old Roman empire ↳Antichrist	Iron legs	Fourth beast/ten horns ↳Little horn	—
God's kingdom	Rock	One like son of man/saints of the Most High	—

Table 8.5. The Roman View of the Kingdoms in Daniel 2, 7, and 8

c. The Conclusion of the Vision Report (8:27a–f)

Daniel again concludes his vision report in 8:27 by emphasizing the troubling effect of what he had seen. At the conclusion of his first vision report, he had said he was greatly alarmed, and his face paled at what he had seen (7:28). Things are worse this time. He was undone and was sick for days before returning to the work of the king.[40] Even then, though, he continued to be appalled by the vision, but there was no one to explain.

Daniel does not explain why his reaction to this vision was more severe, but we can venture a guess. The vision of Dan 7 had revealed immense suffering to come, but it had also promised a glorious future for faithful saints.[41] The vision of Dan 8, however, settles on the suffering, its primary comfort being that the suffering will come to an appointed end. A secondary comfort of the vision of the evenings and the mornings is that the commander of the host himself suffers alongside his host—a foreshadowing glimpse of the God who would incarnationally enter into the suffering of his people and suffer a greater loss than any they had ever known.

---

40. Goldingay comments, "Awareness of where history is going puts you into a complicated position. It indeed gives you confidence where you might otherwise have been overcome by worry: you know that a supernatural hand has already broken all evil power and that the risks you have to live with can be lived with. But you may also be awed and troubled, by having been put in touch with heavenly realities, by the knowledge of what the future may bring to you and to other people. And at the same time you have to get on with the job of living" (*Daniel*, 222).

41. Contrasting Daniel's reaction to the dreams and visions of Dan 4, Dan 7, and Dan 8, Newsom writes, "In 4:19 (16) Daniel reacted with distress and alarm to Nebuchadnezzar's dream report, not because it eluded him but precisely because he understood what it entailed. In 7:28 Daniel similarly reports being disturbed and even physically affected by the vision. In ch. 7, however, the dream vision is not for the king but for Daniel's knowledge, and so he does not share it with anyone. Yet there is no indication that he fails to grasp the import of what he has seen. The situation is different in ch. 8. The mental and physical distress Daniel experiences is even more pronounced and leads to his psychological isolation. . . . Daniel's distress is unrelieved because he does not understand what has been revealed" (*Daniel*, 272–73).

IN DEPTH: The History in the Vision of the Evenings and the Mornings

Gabriel's interpretation focuses on what is most important about the vision—and so should the reader. We have done that in the commentary on ch. 8. However, unlike ch. 7, which Goldingay compares to "an impressionist painting open to several interpretations," the vision of ch. 8 is like "a political cartoon with the names of the characters incorporated to make sure the reader understands it."[42] And like a political cartoon, the vision evokes an array of images and ideas not explicit in the drawing itself. In light of this, the following interpretation of the vision is based on the historical record as it corresponds to Gabriel's specifications.

The two-horned ram represents Cyrus, whose rise to world prominence began in a relatively small vassal state of the Median Empire—Persia. Eventually Cyrus rebelled, defeating Median king Astyages and merging the once formidable Median Empire into a joint Medo-Persian Empire (550 BCE).[43] Over the coming years, the Medo-Persian ram expanded to the west (Babylonia, Syria, and Asia Minor), to the north (Armenia, Scythia, and the Caspian Sea region), and to the south (Egypt and Ethiopia). The Medo-Persians also went east into India, imagery not included in exploits of the ram in Daniel's vision—perhaps because the Jewish diaspora did not include India,[44] or because Medo-Persia *was* "the east" to the Jews (cf. Isa 41:2),[45] and so expansion to the east was not of importance or interest to Daniel's audience.[46]

The one-horned goat in the vision represents Alexander the Great (born 356 BCE), son of Philip II of Macedon. Philip had transformed the backwater Balkan kingdom of Macedon into a force to be reckoned with when he conquered neighboring Greek city states. He dreamed of the defeat of Persia and world domination, but when he was assassinated in 336 BCE, his twenty-year-old son inherited the kingdom. Within five years, Alexander had conquered

---

42. Goldingay, *Daniel*, 410. He concludes his comparison, "As exercises in theology and communication, the two visions thereby complement each other. Chapter 7 is deep, allusive, imaginative; ch. 8 is sober, explicit, concrete."

43. Proponents of the Roman view of Daniel's four empires consider the two-horned ram to be evidence that Media and Persia are also a single entity (i.e., Medo-Persia) in the statue dream of ch. 2 (i.e., the silver torso) and among the four beasts of ch. 7 (i.e., the bear) (see, e.g., Young, *The Prophecy of Daniel*, 167). However, ch. 8 is not part of the chiasm in which chs. 2 and 7 correspond to each other, so it need not follow their pattern. Furthermore, ch. 8 narrows the perspective of chs. 2 and 7, so it might be expected that it would simplify the entities represented while still reflecting the historical reality of separate kingdoms. See tables 8.4 and 8.5.

44. Louis F. Hartman and Alexander A. DiLella, *The Book of Daniel* (AB 23; Garden City, NY: Doubleday, 1978), 234.

45. See, e.g., Lacocque, *The Book of Daniel*, 160, and Montgomery, *Commentary on the Book of Daniel*, 328. As Goldingay notes: "from a Judean perspective [Cyrus] is already the ruler of the east (Isa 41:2)" (*Daniel*, 420).

46. See, e.g., Porteous, *Daniel*, 122.

Persia and ruled an empire that stretched from Greece to India.[47] His stint as king of the world came to an abrupt end when he succumbed to illness and died in 323 BCE at the age of thirty-two. Alexander had no viable heir, leaving his empire to be divided among a quartet of squabbling generals—the broken horn and "the four that rose in its place ... but not with its power" (8:22). The Diadochi, the "successors,"[48] were four generals who were each prominent in their own right,[49] but Daniel's vision skips past their achievements and 150 years of history in order to focus on the eighth ruler of the Syrian Seleucid dynasty, the smaller horn of Daniel's vision. Nearly all scholars identify this as Antiochus IV Epiphanes (r. 175–164 BCE), "one of [history's] truly flamboyant characters," who named himself "Epiphanes"—"God Manifest"—and minted his face on coins that should have borne Zeus's face.[50]

Antiochus was a wily ruler, maneuvering his way to the Seleucid throne in place of his nephew and the rightful heir, Demetrius. As king, he made military incursions to the south (Egypt; 1 Macc 1:16–20), the east (Parthia; 1 Macc 3:27–37; 6:1–4), and "the Beautiful Land," which was the recipient of his great hostility during the latter part of Antiochus's reign. His persecution of the Jews and their way of life, as well as his assaults on the Jerusalem temple, was motivated by at least three factors.[51] First, he had inherited a massive debt from his predecessors, and he looked to the temple treasury, taxes, and even bribes

---

47. Newsom notes, "Ancient readers would have had no trouble recognizing the he-goat with a single conspicuous horn as a symbol for the Macedonian army and its king, Alexander the Great. Not only the direction (from the west) but also the reference to the goat's speed would be markers for Alexander's swift destruction of the Persian Empire, which made a profound impact on the ancient world (cf. 1 Macc 1:2–4)" (*Daniel*, 262). Those who hold the Roman view of the kingdoms in ch. 7 consider the speed of the goat evidence of its correspondence with the third beast (i.e., the four-winged leopard) of ch. 7: "Both figures denote the rapid conquests of Alexander's forces as he moved throughout the earth. This is another indication that the leopard in chap. 7 signifies Greece not Persia" (Miller, *Daniel*, 223n17).

48. Alexander's son and would-be heir (Alexander IV) was born months after Alexander's death, though Alexander also had a reputed illegitimate son (Heracles) who was quite young at the time of Alexander's death.

49. Macedonia went to Cassander; Thrace and Asia Minor to Lysimachus; Babylon and Syria to Seleucus; and Egypt to Ptolemy. The identification and even number of these generals vary slightly among scholars, but the four named here would have been of greatest interest to Daniel's audience. Furthermore, as Newsom observes, "The author of Dan 8 is less interested in the specifics of political history ... than he is in the symbolism. The four kings/kingdoms represent a totality, as they are oriented to the 'four winds of heaven' (cf. 7:2; more generally, the 'four kingdoms' of 2:37–40 and 7:3–7 are also a way of representing the totality and unity of Gentile imperial rule)" (*Daniel*, 262).

50. Tomasino, *Judaism Before Jesus*, 128. Tomasino's book is one of the best resources I have found for understanding the events surrounding the reign of Antiochus IV. A fictionalized account of the time period is deSilva's *Day of Atonement: A Novel of the Maccabean Revolt*.

51. As noted in the commentary on 8:10, the reference to the host being thrown down and trampled by the smaller horn is best understood as a reference to angels. Obviously, Antiochus IV did not pull angels or stars out of heaven; he persecuted Jewish people. This blurring of lines between the celestial and terrestrial realms is consistent with portrayals elsewhere in Daniel of the cosmic nature of life (see, e.g., Dan 7:18, 27; 10:12–11:1). An assault on God's people was an assault on the heavenly forces and God himself.

to bring down the debt. Second, Judea itself was a tinderbox, with some Jews wanting to adopt Hellenistic ways, while others were determined to maintain their cultural and religious distinctives. Antiochus encouraged the proliferation of Hellenism, and progressive Jews who wanted reform were easy prey for his smooth talk, currying his favor with bribes. Conservative Jews, however, wanted nothing to do with any "reform" that threatened their Jewish identity.[52] Third, Antiochus had been humiliated in an Egyptian campaign in 168 BCE, and he took out his anger on Judaism and Jews, an enemy he could defeat. Prior to this, he had killed Jews and plundered the temple, but in the aftermath of his Egyptian humiliation, he made Judaism a crime (167 BCE). He had the Jerusalem temple turned into a pagan shrine, while having Jerusalemites massacred and the city itself set ablaze. Gentile priests offered pigs and other unclean animals as sacrifices to Zeus.[53] Festivals, Sabbath, and circumcision were outlawed. Torah scrolls were torched,[54] and their owners were killed (see 1 Macc 1:20–57). Rather than worship Zeus, many Jews chose martyrdom (e.g., 2 Macc 7). If the 2,300 evenings and mornings of the vision (8:14b) represent a specific time frame, there are two options: first, 2,300 is roughly six years and represents a period of intense persecution beginning with the assassination of Jewish high priest Onias III in 170 BCE and ending with the rededication of the Jerusalem temple after the Maccabean revolt (164 BCE); second, the 2,300 represents half as many days, and the beginning of the persecution is dated to Antiochus's defeat in Egypt (167 BCE).[55] In historical terms, Gabriel's interpretation of the king's

---

52. See further 1 Macc 1–2 for a glimpse of the cultural divide that had developed in Judea by the time of Antiochus IV.

53. The vision's statement that the smaller horn threw down the "place of his sanctuary" (8:11c) sounds like utter destruction of the temple, though Newsom notes that the verb שלך "can be used metaphorically as meaning to abandon or to treat with contempt (cf. Neh 9:26)" (*Daniel*, 265). While Antiochus IV did not literally destroy the temple, his desecration of it rendered it unfit for use (1 Macc 1:54–55, 59; 4:41–44). The temple lay desolate and overgrown with weeds until 164 BCE, when a group of observant Jews led by a priest named Mattathias and his five sons revolted against Antiochus (the Maccabean revolt) and ultimately retook Jerusalem from the Seleucid forces. The temple was cleansed, sacrifice was reestablished, and the temple was rededicated—an occasion celebrated by the Festival of Lights (Hanukkah) every December.

54. Many commentators think this action is the likely referent for "and it was casting truth to the ground" (וְתַשְׁלֵךְ אֱמֶת אַרְצָה, 8:12), though Newsom (following Dieter Bauer, *Das Buch Daniel*, NSKAT 22 [Stuttgart: Katholisches Bibelwerk, 1996], 171) thinks it more likely that אֱמֶת "means something like 'world-order,' which [Bauer] associates with the 'times and seasons' of 2:21 and the 'times set by decree' of 7:25.... Thus *'ĕmet* seems to refer to the course of human history as determined by God and to the proper relation of divine to human sovereignty, which is the central topic of concern in both parts of the book of Daniel. Although the issue is framed more dualistically in some of the writings from Qumran, in the Two Spirits Treatise (1QS 3.13–4.26), the contrast between truth and deceit is the contrast between that which God loves and that which God abhors (1QA 3.18–19; 3.26–4.1), as it is manifested in the predetermined course of events in the world. The power of deceit is represented as acting aggressively against those associated with light and truth and righteousness. This is also what the little horn attempts to do in casting truth to the ground" (*Daniel*, 266).

55. See p. 421n27 above.

> destruction "without human hand" (8:25; cf. the NIV's "not by human power") probably refers to the fact that Antiochus IV died by accident or illness, not by enemy hand in battle. In theological terms, however, the point of Gabriel's words is that Antiochus's days were in God's hand, and when God decreed it, the oppressor would be shattered.

Canonical and Theological Significance

The Little Horn in the Big Story

The smaller horn of Daniel's vision of the evenings and mornings (ch. 8) has many similarities with the little horn of his vision of the four beasts and the divine throne room (ch. 7). In both visions, the small horns represent secondary growth. The horn of ch. 7 grows up in a panoply of ten larger horns, while the horn of ch. 8 grows out of one horn in a quartet of larger horns. In both visions, these secondary horns start small but then grow disproportionately large. The horns of both visions are characterized by their arrogance, blasphemy, and opposition against what is God's—whether his holy ones (ch. 7) or his sanctuary (ch. 8). Both little horns experience extraordinary success but are also restrained by an unseen hand, and in both visions the little horns are ultimately destroyed.

These similarities suggest that both horns have the same historical referent—namely, Antiochus IV Epiphanes.[56] The vision of ch. 8 narrows the cosmic scope of ch. 7 from four empires that, at one level, represented all of human history to two explicitly named empires.[57] The two remaining visions of the book will continue this pattern of increased specificity and sharpened focus, adding to what precedes,

---

56. This correlates with the Greek view of the four empires (see further IN DEPTH: The Identities of the Kingdoms, pp. 115–17, and IN DEPTH: The Identities of the Kingdoms, Take 2, pp. 386–90). Those who take the Roman view of the four empires consider the two horns to have different referents; the little horn of ch. 7 represents the antichrist, and that of ch. 8 represents Antiochus. The Roman view focuses on the differences between the two little horns: (1) the little horn in ch. 7 is an eleventh horn that uproots three horns, while the horn of ch. 8 is a fifth horn that grows from one of the other horns, displacing none; (2) the little horn in in ch. 7 assaults holy ones, but the horn of ch. 8 attacks the holy place; (3) the oppression in ch. 7 lasts for "a time, times, and half a time" (7:25) while the oppression in ch. 8 lasts for 2,300 evenings and mornings (8:14). (See Baldwin, *Daniel*, 162, and Young, *The Prophecy of Daniel*, 276, for further discussion of the differences.) These differences are legitimate, but they do not thereby require different referents. Rather, they may reflect different symbolic perspectives on the same set of circumstances, like a kaleidoscope displays differing colors and shapes with each twist of the hand.

57. See p. 434n43 above.

and together the visions of Dan 7–12 portray a single, particularly horrific period in Jewish history: the Antiochene persecution of the second-century BCE. Chapter 7 provided a glimpse of the entire cosmos and even world history, and as ch. 8 narrowed that focus, it also brought the all-important Jerusalem and the temple into view. Chapter 9 will focus entirely on Jerusalem and the temple, and chs. 10–12 will incorporate the second-century-BCE backdrop of events in Syria-Palestine into the larger picture of Antiochus IV's reign. The Antiochene persecution is the primary event of Daniel's visions, and the arrogant Antiochus IV is their central historical character.

But this does not mean the relevance of the visions ended with the historical events surrounding the persecution unleashed by Antiochus IV. While the immediate focus of Daniel's visions may have been the Antiochene persecution, their message and their comfort are part of a bigger story in the book of Daniel and in the Bible itself. In the book of Daniel, the kind of arrogant king represented by the little horns of Daniel's two initial visions first appears in the story of Belshazzar in ch. 5. Belshazzar is the prototype of a king in opposition to God. As noted above (see on 7:1), the setting of Daniel's first two visions—in which the character of Antiochus IV Epiphanes makes his initial symbolic appearance—during the reign of Belshazzar is significant because the story of his disdain for God's sacred vessels were the book's first glimpse of a blasphemous arrogant king who flagrantly opposed Israel's God. Daniel's apocalyptic visions portray gentile kings whose defiant blasphemy show that Belshazzar was but a "pale foreshadowing" of what was to come.[58] Belshazzar was bad, but his successors (Antiochus IV, in particular) would be worse. The dark overtones of Dan 5 portended future hostility between God's people and their gentile overlords—a driving theme of Daniel's visions.

This pattern of casting one character in light of a previous character is what scholars commonly refer to as typology. Neither Antiochus IV Epiphanes nor Belshazzar is the first king in the Bible to defy God in such egregious ways. They fall in a long line of kings going back to Adam, "the representative and deputy of God" in the garden[59]—that is, the "king" of the garden. In his lament against the king of Tyre in Ezek 28, Ezekiel portrays the Tyrian king's splendor in language that takes the reader back to creation when God anointed Adam as his agent to tend the garden:

> You were the seal of perfection,
> > full of wisdom and perfect in beauty.
> You were in Eden,

---

58. Lucas, *Daniel*, 222.

59. Block, *The Book of Ezekiel: Chapters 25–48*, 111.

the garden of God;
every precious stone adorned you:
 carnelian, chrysolite and emerald,
 topaz, onyx and jasper,
 lapis lazuli, turquoise and beryl.
Your settings and mountings were made of gold;
 on the day you were created they were prepared.
You were anointed as a guardian cherub,
 for so I ordained you.
You were on the holy mount of God;
 you walked among the fiery stones. (Ezek 28:12–14)

Ezekiel continues his lament with motifs from the garden, using Adam's pride and the fall as his framework for denouncing the king of Tyre:

You were blameless in your ways
 from the day you were created
 till wickedness was found in you.
Through your widespread trade
 you were filled with violence,
 and you sinned.
So I drove you in disgrace from the mount of God,
 and I expelled you, guardian cherub,
 from among the fiery stones.
Your heart became proud
 on account of your beauty,
and you corrupted your wisdom
 because of your splendor.
So I threw you to the earth;
 I made a spectacle of you before kings.
By your many sins and dishonest trade
 you have desecrated your sanctuaries.
So I made a fire come out from you,
 and it consumed you,
and I reduced you to ashes on the ground
 in the sight of all who were watching.
All the nations who knew you
 are appalled at you;
you have come to a horrible end
 and will be no more. (Ezek 28:15–19)

The eighth-century-BCE prophet Isaiah similarly taunts the proud and oppressive king of Babylon who had struck down nations in angry aggression. Isaiah's sardonic description of the great king's demise as he is met in the underworld by his powerful predecessors gives a window into what happens to kings who fit this "type":

> How the oppressor has come to an end!
>> How his fury has ended! . . .
> The realm of the dead below is all astir
>> to meet you at your coming;
> it rouses the spirits of the departed to greet you—
>> all those who were leaders in the world;
> it makes them rise from their thrones—
>> all those who were kings over the nations.
> They will all respond,
>> they will say to you,
> "You also have become weak, as we are;
>> you have become like us."
> All your pomp has been brought down to the grave,
>> along with the noise of your harps;
> maggots are spread out beneath you
>> and worms cover you. (Isa 14:4, 9–11)

Isaiah's dirge continues with a description of the rest of the shame and disgrace that would come to the one who had achieved such greatness among earthly kings:

> How you have fallen from heaven,
>> morning star, son of the dawn!
> You have been cast down to the earth,
>> you who once laid low the nations!
> You said in your heart,
>> "I will ascend to the heavens;
> I will raise my throne
>> above the stars of God;
> I will sit enthroned on the mount of assembly,
>> on the utmost heights of Mount Zaphon.
> I will ascend above the tops of the clouds;
>> I will make myself like the Most High."
> But you are brought down to the realm of the dead,
>> to the depths of the pit.

> Those who see you stare at you,
> > they ponder your fate:
> "Is this the man who shook the earth
> > and made kingdoms tremble,
> the man who made the world a wilderness,
> > who overthrew its cities
> > > and would not let his captives go home?"
>
> All the kings of the nations lie in state,
> > each in his own tomb.
> But you are cast out of your tomb
> > like a rejected branch;
> you are covered with the slain,
> > with those pierced by the sword,
> > > those who descend to the stones of the pit.
> Like a corpse trampled underfoot,
> > you will not join them in burial,
> for you have destroyed your land
> > and killed your people.
>
> Let the offspring of the wicked
> > never be mentioned again. (Isa 14:12–20)

Because the one who had been so great set out to be even greater and enthrone himself above the stars of God, he would be cast to the depths in utter ignominy.

Both Belshazzar and the little horn of Daniel's visions fit the Old Testament type of a king who fails to acknowledge his God-given appointment to power and flaunts his own greatness instead.[60] While the visions' depictions of the little horn's demise are quite restrained by comparison to Isaiah's and Ezekiel's, the fact that the little horn fits the type hints at the destruction that awaits the pompous king represented by the horn: His delusions of greatness would result in his being cast to the depths as a mere man, disgraced in death. Those who looked on would wonder what they had been afraid of.[61]

---

60. Nebuchadnezzar breaks this pattern, as illustrated by the narrative chapters that trace his pride, judgment, and eventual voluntary acknowledgment of God's sovereignty. By the time he exits the book of Daniel, Nebuchadnezzar has become the prototype for what a gentile king *ought* to be, while his "son" becomes the prototype for gentile kings in opposition to God.

61. Newsom identifies four recurring elements in the type of an "arrogant king who opposes the God of Israel by oppressing his people . . . : (1) the king's initially near godlike domination of the situation; (2) his unbridled arrogance; (3) his ignorance of the fact that his success has actually been determined by God; (4) his downfall and humiliation" (*Daniel*, 271). Newsom is specifically referring to Antiochus IV as being the type that subsequent kings would resemble, but her list fits the larger Old Testament portrait of such kings.

This "type" of king does not end with Daniel's depiction of the little horn, nor does the type of suffering inflicted by such a ruler. In his Olivet Discourse, Jesus speaks of future suffering and ultimate victory, drawing specifically on imagery of Dan 7 and Dan 9 (Matt 24:1–51; Mark 13:1–37; Luke 21:5–36). Paul spends half a chapter warning the Thessalonians about "the man of lawlessness," one who "will oppose and will exalt himself over everything that is called God or is worshiped, so that he sets himself up in God's temple, proclaiming himself to be God" (2 Thess 2:4). Revelation's portrayal of a final ruler in opposition to God is the culmination of this type (see, esp., the beast from the sea in Rev 13 and 17), a figure Christian history has named the antichrist.[62] Each earlier arrogant king points to this ultimate and exponentially worse ruler.

Daniel 8 reveals Antiochus IV Epiphanes as one of these earlier arrogant kings, whose success seemed to know no bounds and whose advances into God's territory shock. The comfort of Daniel's second vision is scant—it simply assures that God has evil on a leash, so there is a determined end to the suffering. But in the larger context of the book of Daniel and the biblical canon there is great comfort for those who suffer under rulers who fit the type and especially for those who will suffer under the oppression of the last blasphemous king. Just as the demise of historical Babylon came about because God judged a blasphemous king who flagrantly opposed the Most High God (Dan 5), so will the ultimate demise of Babylon the Great come when God judges the worst of blasphemous rulers who flagrantly oppose the Most High God (Rev 18). His victory is assured. Evil will be destroyed, and suffering will cease. Forever.

Learning to Lament

The storyline of the Bible plays out on the muddy stage of planet earth, where all kinds of bad things happen to good people. The rich get richer, and the poor go hungry. The powerful make the rules, and the vulnerable endure the consequences. The wicked prosper, and the godly suffer.

If these scenarios comprised the entire storyline of the Bible, people of the book would be, to paraphrase Paul, the most miserable (1 Cor 15:19). But even though story after story traipses through this kind of muck, these stories are not *the* story. They are not what theologians like to call "the metanarrative," the grand story of the Bible. That story is one of hope, one of promise, one of expectation that God is bringing everything to a glorious end that is really just the beginning.

---

62. The word *antichrist* only appears four times in the Bible and not in Revelation, where the depiction of the coming opponent is particularly startling (1 John 2:18, 22; 4:3; 2 John 7).

This hope glimmers in stories like the one recounted in 2 Kgs 18–19, where the besieged Jerusalemites watched in wonder as the Assyrian army headed for home, leaving 185,000 inexplicably dead in the camp. This hope shines through the song of Hannah in 1 Sam 2, where the torment of the barren woman turned to joy with the dedication of her son to YHWH's service: "for I delight in your deliverance ... He raises the poor from the dust and lifts the needy from the ash heap" (1 Sam 2:1, 8). This hope is what drove the Shunammite woman to plead that the prophet Elisha come to the bedside of her dead son, whom he then restored to her alive (2 Kgs 4:8–37). This is the hope that rings through psalm after psalm that cries out for deliverance (e.g., Pss 123, 126, 137) and those that praise YHWH for his great acts of salvation (e.g., Pss 18, 21, 39).

Throughout the metanarrative is the hope, not the wishful thinking but the confident expectation, that God will act on behalf of the weak, the oppressed, and the disenfranchised. The expectation that God will right all wrongs, vindicating those who suffer unjustly and judging those who oppress. The Old Testament prophets proclaimed this kind of hope—first warning the people of judgment for their own sin, urging repentance, and then assuring the people that God would restore them to a glorious future. Judgment, repentance, restoration: God would make the old new.

But for some stories in the Bible, there is no hope of restoration. Things had gone so far wrong, there was no making right. The world was so bad there was no fixing it. The only hope was a fresh start—destruction of the old and a brand-new beginning. This is the world of apocalyptic literature, the literature of suffering people whose only hope was cataclysmic divine intervention. God needed to show up, annihilate evil, and reward the righteous, wiping the cosmic slate clean. Salvation is only possible in the new world of the eschatological future. The comfort of apocalyptic literature is that God is in control, suffering will not last forever, and at the right time, God will bring judgment and reward.

These are the themes of Dan 7, where the judgment of the beasts stands alongside the splendor of the divine throne and the holy ones' inheritance of the eternal kingdom. These are the themes of the climactic book of Revelation, where the scene of the heavenly throne and the Lion-Lamb with the scroll sets the context for seven seals of judgment, and where the resplendent New Jerusalem finally fills the earth.

Daniel 8 is apocalyptic literature, but its comfort does not get that far. There is no flaming throne, no son of man receiving the eternal kingdom, no inheritance for God's people, no New Jerusalem. There is not any clear sign of judgment for the oppressors, much less any hint of reward for the righteous. There is no long view in Dan 8, as in Dan 7 and Revelation. Rather, Dan 8 parks in the present. It settles on the theme of suffering. Its primary comfort is that suffering will not last forever, because at the appointed time, God will end the suffering.

We do not like to live in the world of Dan 8. And for many of us the kind of political suffering that spawned apocalyptic literature is far removed from our experiences—at least, for now. But may we never forget this is not true for millions of believers worldwide who pray for relief and rescue, fully aware that it will take cataclysmic divine intervention to fix all that is wrong in the world. While many of us may not understand that kind of suffering, most of us do understand other kinds of suffering that accompany living in a fallen world: poverty, disease, broken relationships, abuse, discrimination, death. Most of us have endured or are enduring a degree of suffering, and if we have not, we will. And a whole lot of this suffering will not have a happy ending until the other side of the apocalypse.

Daniel struggled to understand the suffering he witnessed—why would the commander of the host *allow* the small horn to trample some of his host, throw down his sanctuary, and cast truth to the ground (Dan 8:10–12). Why did God allow such a successful assault to be launched against himself and his own territory? Why didn't he intervene? We still struggle to understand suffering. Why does God allow such excruciating pain, in whatever form it takes, to ravage our lives?[63]

The presence of evil in the God-created, God-sustained world is a perennial question, and not one I am looking to answer or even address here. Rather, I am interested in the question asked by the holy one of Daniel's vision: "How long . . . ?" (Dan 8:13). This is the language of lament, echoed in psalm after psalm by God's people struggling to understand their suffering and God's apparent silence. How long, O YHWH? Will you forget me forever? How long will you look on? How long, O YHWH? Will you be angry forever? How long, O YHWH? Will you hide yourself forever? How long, O YHWH, will the wicked be jubilant? How long must your servant wait?[64] These are the questions suffering people ask when they see no end to their circumstances. These are the questions suffering people who feel abandoned by God ask. In Dan 8, it was the question asked by a holy one who watched the incomprehensible triumph of evil and saw no divine intervention.

This is the language of lament. If we are honest, most of us would have to admit we do not know this language very well. We may be well acquainted with suffering, but few people are well acquainted with lamenting. Let me explain. Suffering is the pain. Lament is the response. Suffering is what happens to us. Lament is what we do with it—or in it. The conditioned response of most people to suffering, whether their own or someone else's, is to get through it—as quickly as possible. Find the bright side. Change the topic. Go shopping. Check off the stages of grief. Start a new life.

None of this is lament, and all of it ignores that suffering has any value. What is more, it ignores the fact that not all suffering will end this side of the New Jerusa-

---

63. For thoughtful discussions on suffering, see, e.g., D. A. Carson, *How Long, O Lord?: Reflections on Suffering and Evil* (Grand Rapids: Baker Academic, 2006); and Philip Yancey, *Disappointment with God: Three Questions No One Asks Aloud* (Grand Rapids: Zondervan, 1997).

64. Pss 13:3[2]; 35:17; 79:5; 89:47[46]; 94:3; 119:84.

lem. Lament acknowledges both. We would do well—for ourselves and for those we love—to learn how to lament.

Pastor Mark Vroegop learned how to lament after his wife delivered their fourth child, a stillborn daughter, at full term. Although he was a long-time student of the Bible, lament was new for him. In it, he found a gut-level-honest voice for his pain—a "minor-key language" for suffering. Lament became a guide, teacher, and solace as he and his wife navigated the wilderness of grief:[65] "[Lament] gives you permission to vocalize your pain as it moves you toward God-centered worship and trust. Lament is how you live between the poles of a hard life and trusting in God's sovereignty."[66]

As the means by which we can bring our pain and our sorrow to God, lament enables us to process our pain and to avoid having our spiritual lives dominated by silence, bitterness, and even anger. Lament also enables us to help others in their sorrow. Without knowing how to lament, "we'll offer trite solutions, unhelpful comments, or impatient responses." Lament is distinctively Christian[67] and what Vroegop calls "a gift [and] a neglected dimension of the Christian life for many twenty-first-century Christians."[68] We desperately need it—and so does our world:

> A broken world and an increasingly hostile culture make contemporary Christianity unbalanced and limited in the hope we offer if we neglect this minor-key song. We need to recover the ancient practice of lament and the grace that comes through it. Christianity suffers when lament is missing.... There is deep mercy under dark clouds when we discover the grace of lament.[69]

Songs of lament comprise the largest category of psalms,[70] and they demonstrate a fairly consistent pattern that can help us learn to lament for ourselves. Vroegop describes four elements of the pattern: (1) turn to God in prayer; (2) bring complaints to him; (3) ask boldly; and (4) choose to trust.[71] In what follows, I only summarize Vroegop's guide to lament, "prayer in pain that leads to trust."[72]

(1) Lament begins when we turn to God in prayer from the depths of our pain. This kind of messy, confused prayer is far better than giving God the silent

---

65. Mark Vroegop, *Dark Clouds, Deep Mercy: Discovering the Grace of Lament* (Wheaton: Crossway, 2019), 17–18.
66. Vroegop, *Dark Clouds, Deep Mercy*, 21.
67. "To cry is human, but to lament is Christian" (Vroegop, *Dark Clouds, Deep Mercy*, 26).
68. Vroegop, *Dark Clouds, Deep Mercy*, 21.
69. Vroegop, *Dark Clouds, Deep Mercy*, 21–22.
70. The total number of lament psalms varies, depending on the classification criteria used. But most scholars count at least 60 lament psalms among the 150 songs in the Psalter.
71. Vroegop's book has three parts. The first is a study of four psalms of lament (Pss 77, 10, 22, 13), and from them he shows how to lament. Part 2 is a study of Lamentations with a focus on what can be learned from lament, and part 3 is a practical exploration of how to live with lament—both personally and corporately.
72. Vroegop, *Dark Clouds, Deep Mercy*, 28.

treatment—what Vroegop considers a sign of unbelief, the "the hopeless resignation that God doesn't care, he doesn't hear, and nothing is ever going to change."[73] Lament gives voice to our hurts and confusion, our questions and doubts. Lament is a prayer of faith whereby we take our pain to the cross, the proof that God is for us and not against us.

(2) Lament invites us to complain. We can find complaining throughout the Bible: prophets complain, psalmists complain, Job complained. What complaining is *not* is "vent[ing] self-centered rage at God when life has not turned out like you planned."[74] What complaining *is* is making a case against God when he appears to have forgotten his word or when he seems to be acting out of character. Complaining is throwing God's promises and God's character back at him, reminding him of who he is and what he is capable of doing. It is not that God has actually forgotten these things, but when it sure feels to us like he has, we should complain about it. Vroegop say biblical complaint offers the alternative to anger or denial, the places suffering people often land. In godly complaint we express to God our disappointment with life and with him, and the basis of these expressions is who we believe God to be and what we believe he can do—beliefs derived from God's self-revelation. Stacey Gleddiesmith defines this aspect of lament: "A lament honestly and specifically names a situation or circumstance that is painful, wrong, or unjust—in other words, a circumstance that does not align with God's character and therefore does not make sense within God's kingdom."[75]

(3) Lament involves boldly asking God to act according to his character. The lament psalms are full of bold requests: "Do something, Lord, please!" (e.g., Ps 3), "Let justice be done!" (e.g., Ps 83), "Keep your promises!" (e.g., Ps 25), "Listen to me! Answer me!" (e.g., Ps 28), "Vindicate me!" (e.g., Ps 35).

These "requests" sound more like commands because the confidence the psalmists have in who God is and what he has done compels them to be so bold, to speak with such authority. But Vroegop observes that requests like these do something more:

> Boldly asking God for help based upon who he is and what he's promised eclipses the complaints. I say "eclipses" for a reason. It captures the fact that *why* questions are not always answered before we move into requests. Just as one heavenly body moves into the shadow of another during an eclipse, so too the *why* questions and the *who* questions coexist, but not equally. Who God is becomes the more prominent reality while not removing the lingering questions. As we make our bold requests, "Why is this happening?" moves into the shadow of "Who is God?"

---

73. Vroegop, *Dark Clouds, Deep Mercy*, 32.
74. Vroegop, *Dark Clouds, Deep Mercy*, 43.
75. Stacey Gleddiesmith, "My God, My God, Why? Understanding the Lament Psalms," *Reformed Worship*, June 2010, https://www.reformedworship.org/article/june-2010/my-god-my-god-why (cited in Vroegop, *Dark Clouds, Deep Mercy*, 44).

That's why we need to ask boldly.[76]

(4) Perhaps the most important step in lamenting is this last one—choosing to trust. Trust in what we know to be true, no matter what life looks like. Trust in God's steadfast love—and focus on remembering how he has demonstrated that love in the past. Trust that God is working out his purposes, even though we cannot imagine what they might be. Vroegop defines this trust as "active patience":

> Now do not make the mistake of thinking that trust is something you decide once and for all as you are walking through pain. It's not as if you pray one lament prayer, and you never need to lament again. Life isn't that simple. Grief is not that tame. Instead, we must enter into lament over and over so that it can keep leading us to trust.
>
> In this respect, lament allows us to embrace an endurance that is not passive. Lament helps us to practice active patience. Trust looks like talking to God, sharing our complaints, seeking God's help, and then recommitting ourselves to believe in who God is and what he has done—even as the trial continues. Lament is how we endure. It is how we trust. It is how we wait. Rebekah Eklund provides this helpful summary: "The prayer of lament rejoices in God's saving actions in the now and hopes urgently for God's saving actions in the future, the 'not yet' of the eschatological timeline. . . . Those who lament stand on the boundary between the old age and the new and hope for things unseen."[77]

Trust is the destination of lament, and trust also leads us to the place of expressing belief in the goodness of God and faith in what he is doing. It leads us to worship—and maybe here is where we begin to understand why psalms of lament make up so much of Israel's song book, Israel's worship manual. Life *is* hard, but lamenting through the hard times leads us to worship.[78]

Daniel 8 asks the question of lament—a question that reverberates through the biblical canon and culminates on that dark Friday when the sky went dark and the earth shook. When it looked for all the world that God had lost. As after-the-fact readers, we know where the story is going. We know Sunday is coming, and while Jesus's followers *should* have known, they did not. For Jesus's followers, Friday gave way to Saturday long before Sunday came. Of that day after, the Gospels only say the tomb was sealed and guarded (Matt 27:62–66) and that Jesus's followers kept

---

76. Vroegop, *Dark Clouds, Deep Mercy*, 57–58.

77. Vroegop, *Dark Clouds, Deep Mercy*, 74, citing Rebekah Ann Eklund, "Lord, Teach Us How to Grieve: Jesus's Laments and Christian Hope," (ThD diss., Duke Divinity School, 2012), 276. He notes that his expression "active patience" is an adaptation of what Eklund calls "nonpassive patience."

78. Musician and author Michael Card says, "All true songs of worship are born in the wilderness of suffering," *A Sacred Sorrow: Reaching Out to God in the Lost Language of Lament* (Colorado Springs: NavPress, 2005), 63.

the Sabbath (Luke 23:56). But it must have been a dreadful, dark Saturday in which sorrows like sea billows rolled. All hope was gone. For Jesus's followers, there was only lament, no making things right this side of the New Jerusalem.

We are right to cling to the comfort of resurrection, the promise of renewal, and the fulfillment of a new creation. But in our expectation, let us not hurry past the deep suffering of Friday and the despair of Saturday. When we live in the space where it seems God is silent, where it seems that God does not care, let us lament. Let us endure the darkness, knowing that the fullness of resurrection Sunday awaits.[79]

The Presence of God, the People of God

In Daniel's vision of the evenings and the mornings, the upstart little horn launched a remarkably successful assault against what was precious to God and even against his divine throne. The commander of the host suffered great loss. And even though the text hints that someone else was allowing the little horn such great success (see on 8:11–12, 22–24 above), what happened should nonetheless give us pause.

It is a stunning thought that God allowed evil to have such free reign in his own territory, but Dan 8 is not the first time we see this in the Old Testament. God allowed similar devastating assaults against himself twice before the fated depiction of the Second Temple's destruction that Daniel witnessed. The first time is recounted in 1 Sam 4, where the Israelites went out to fight their perennial enemy, the Philistines. YHWH's people were defeated that day, and as the leaders of the people reflected on why YHWH allowed such a thing, they formulated the battle plan for the next day: take the ark of YHWH's covenant, the symbol of YHWH's throne and his presence on earth, into battle with them. They dispatched some men to Shiloh to retrieve the ark from the tabernacle, "so that he may go with us and save us from the hand of our enemies" (1 Sam 4:3). The ark was their secret weapon against the Philistines. Victory was assured.

When the ark arrived in the Israelite camp, the people broke into cheers that shook the nerve of the Philistines, who were afraid of the Israelites' "mighty gods . . . who struck the Egyptians with all kinds of plagues in the wilderness" (1 Sam 4:8).

---

79. Another kind of lament in Scripture is when *God* laments. The words "how long" are repeatedly heard from God in the biblical narrative. In the years of Israel's wilderness wanderings, YHWH expressed exasperation with his people's lack of faith, their grumbling, and their refusal to keep his laws (Exod 16:28; Num 14:11, 27). During the period of the kingdoms, he lamented through the prophet Elijah the people's waffling allegiance between YHWH and Baal (1 Kgs 18:21). When the Pharaoh of the exodus refused to humble himself after seven decimating plagues, YHWH lamented (Exod 10:3). In the Gospels, God-Incarnate lamented the unwillingness or the inability of the Jews (Matt 23:37) or even of his own disciples to believe (Matt 17:17; Mark 9:19; Luke 9:41). These laments reveal God's longsuffering with human rebellion, both that of his people and that of those still outside the fold (2 Pet 3:9). While we are right to learn the biblical language of lament as described above, we should also be careful to examine ourselves for sin that might trigger *God's* lament—and perhaps his discipline (Heb 12:5–12).

Nonetheless, they rallied themselves to fight for their lives against the odds, and to everyone's surprise (except the owner of the ark), Israel was defeated, and the ark was captured. When the old Israelite priest Eli heard the news, he fell off his chair and died. When Eli's daughter-in-law heard the news, she went into labor and delivered a son she named Ichabod: "The Glory has departed from Israel" (1 Sam 4:21). Both Eli and his daughter-in-law had also lost loved ones in the battle, but it was the loss of the ark that particularly devastated them.

Five hundred years later, the Judahites showed a similar attitude toward the temple that their forefathers had shown toward the ark. As the forces of Nebuchadnezzar bore down on Jerusalem, God's people shrugged at the threat. They were safe because the temple of YHWH was in Jerusalem. The Most High God was on *their* side. No one was going to defeat them. The prophet Jeremiah confronted the sinful, complacent people with YHWH's message as they came to worship in the temple:

> Hear the word of YHWH, all you people of Judah who come through these gates to worship YHWH . . .: Reform your ways and your actions, and I will let you live in this place. Do not trust in deceptive words and say, "This is the temple of YHWH, the temple of YHWH, the temple of YHWH!" . . . You are trusting in deceptive words that are worthless. Will you steal and murder, commit adultery and perjury, burn incense to Baal and follow other gods you have not known, and then come and stand before me in this house, which bears my Name, and say, "We are safe"—safe to do all these detestable things? Has this house, which bears my Name, become a den of robbers to you? (Jer 7:2–11)

When Nebuchadnezzar destroyed that temple of YHWH in 586 BCE, the people were shaken to their core. The loss of the ark had been devastating, but within seven months, the crisis had passed.[80] The loss of the temple was more devastating, and it dragged on for seventy years.[81]

Walter Brueggemann's reflections on the loss of the ark could also be applied to the loss of the temple: "It is a moment of loss that defies theological coherence, a loss underneath all losses. The loss invites the unthinkable, that YHWH could not manage, did not prevail, was not strong enough, did not care enough, could not cope."[82]

That may have been how it looked "on the ground," but the reader knows that behind each loss was Israel's sin. The vision of Dan 8 shows a similar loss—the dese-

---

80. The rest of the story is that the Philistines quickly discovered that they actually had no control whatsoever over the Israelite God they had apparently defeated by capturing the ark, and after seven months of YHWH's hand being heavy upon them (1 Sam 5:7, 11), the Philistines could not get rid of the ark fast enough.

81. See on Dan 9:2 for the period of seventy years with respect to exile.

82. Walter Brueggemann, *Ichabod Toward Home: The Journey of God's Glory* (Grand Rapids: Eerdmans, 2002), 8. See also *The Strength of the Weak God*, pp. 70–72.

cration of a rebuilt second temple—and although the text is ambiguous about *why* it happened, there is room to think the sin of the people was again to blame.[83]

The loss of the ark to the Philistines, Solomon's temple to the Babylonians, and perhaps even the Second Temple to the Seleucid tyrant Antiochus IV Epiphanes were the devasting results of sin. Sin makes it impossible for a holy God to "stay present." While his plan from the beginning was to dwell with the people he created, the sin of those same people wrestled hard against his presence. Then he covenanted with Israel to be their God and dwell among them, and he implemented a way for that to happen through the ark and the temple and the priesthood. It did not take long for their sin to bring the Philistines, the Babylonians, and the Seleucids. The pattern seemed impossible to break.

Then came one more temple—the culmination of all the previous temples. They had been but a shadow of the reality: the fullness of God dwelling on earth, tabernacled in a human being. The glory of God, confined to ligaments, tendons, and skin of a man who squalled, sweat, and spit. The glory of God in a thoroughly human being.

Then came one more devasting loss because of sin—the accumulation of all sins from all times. That human temple was destroyed, forsaken by God. Surely this was the most devastating loss of all.

But it was this destroyed, forsaken temple that was rebuilt three days later, breaking forever the oppressive cycle of sin. God could now live among people forever—he could live *in* people in a *new* temple built of living stones. The problem of sin had been taken care of for all time. And what is more, because of Jesus, God's people have a high priest who understands suffering and stands before the throne of God with full understanding of their pain. And they have a God who himself suffered great loss *for them*, a Father whose heart has been broken. And in the Spirit, they have an empathetic intercessor (Heb 4:15; Rom 8:26).

---

83. See on 8:12–13 above.

Daniel 9:1a–27d

B. Narrative 2: *Repentance and God's Promise of Restoration*

Main Idea of Narrative 2 (9:1a–27d)

As Daniel reflects on the writings of the prophet Jeremiah, he understands that the end of Israel's seventy-year exile is near. In response, he intercedes for his people, confessing their sin and imploring God to be merciful and to forgive them for his own name's sake. Daniel pleads for the restoration of God's people and God's city, Jerusalem. In response to Daniel's prayer, Gabriel brings a word of revelation, showing Daniel that the seventy years of exile were part of a bigger plan for God's people. In the revelation of the seventy weeks, history moves forward under God's control, and God's people have a promise of hope rooted in his character and faithfulness.

Literary Context of Narrative 2 (Dan 9:1a–27d)

Daniel 9 is the third of four visionary experiences Daniel has in the apocalyptic half of the book (chs. 7–12). Like ch. 8, this experience is recounted entirely in the first person (cf. 7:1; 10:1). While Daniel's first two visions occurred during the reign of Belshazzar (7:1; 8:1), this third vision is set in the first year of Darius (9:1), who was introduced into the narrative at the end of Dan 5 when Belshazzar was killed and his kingdom passed to Darius the Mede (6:1[5:31]). The narrative that followed in Dan 6 took place during the time of Darius (6:2[1]). As in the other apocalyptic chapters, the date formula in 9:1 positions the vision in the chronology of the book, linking it to the narrative chapters where each of the kings is introduced.[1] The historical

---

1. Belshazzar in ch. 5; Darius the Mede in ch. 5–6; Cyrus the Persian in Dan 1:21.

context of the first two visions in the reign of Belshazzar (chs. 7 and 8) evoked an emotional expectation for the visions.[2] In the two later visions (chs. 9 and 10–12), the historical context provided by each date formula will be a meaningful part of understanding the purpose of each vision (see further below).

Each of Daniel's four visionary experiences is unique. The visions of Dan 7 and 8 are symbolic visions, requiring an angelic interpreter. Their reports include introductions to the visions (7:1; 8:1), reports of the visions with their interpretations (7:2–27; 8:2–25), the end of each vision (7:28a; 8:26), and Daniel's reaction to what he had seen (7:28b; 8:27).[3] The visions of Dan 9 and 10–12 do not follow this pattern, nor is their content of the same nature. Daniel 9 and 10–12 are not symbolic visions requiring interpretation; rather, they are verbal revelations transmitted by divine beings. Lucas calls them "*epiphany visions*, in which a supernatural being appears and conveys a message."[4] The elements included in these visions are (1) the surrounding circumstances (9:1–2; 10:1), (2) supplication (9:3–19; 10:2–3), (3) the appearance of a messenger (9:20–21; 10:4–9), (4) a word of assurance (9:22–23; 10:10–11:1), (5) the revelation (9:24–27; 11:2–12:3), and (6) a charge to the seer (12:4).[5] While these elements are present in each of the last two visions, they do not form the structures or outlines of the chapters, which are determined by the syntax and discourse features of the sections (e.g., 9:1–3; 9:4–19; 9:20–27).

In addition to these differences of content and form, the revelation of Dan 9 differs from the other three in its role in the narrative. In the other visions, the revelation comprises most of the narrative and is its primary focus. In Dan 9, however, the narrative is dominated by a penitential prayer offered by Daniel on behalf of his people in response to his study of Jeremiah (Dan 9:1–19), events that culminate in the relatively short revelation of the seventy weeks (9:24–27).[6] This structure and emphasis dictate the approach of the commentary to follow.

In the literary context of the book's four apocalyptic visions, Dan 9 further narrows the imagery begun in the vision of ch. 7. Chapter 7 gave a glimpse of the entire cosmos and world history. The vision of ch. 8 narrowed that focus, bringing into view the all-important Jerusalem and temple. The revelation of ch. 9 and the events leading up to it focus entirely on Jerusalem and the temple. The final vision (chs. 10–12) will incorporate the second-century-BCE backdrop of events in Syria-Palestine into the larger picture of the visions' specific focus: the reign of Antiochus IV Epiphanes. Together Daniel's visions portray this particularly horrific

---

2. See on 7:1 and 8:1 above.

3. Lucas, *Daniel*, 31. This fits the general pattern of ANE dream reports as described by Oppenheim, *The Interpretation of Dreams in the Ancient Near East*, 187.

4. Lucas, *Daniel*, 32 (emphasis his).

5. Lucas, *Daniel*, 35.

6. This structure and emphasis of the chapter are not reflected in Daniel scholarship, where the voluminous material on the Seventy Weeks has been famously called "the dismal swamp of O.T. criticism" and "the trackless wilderness of assumptions and theories" (Montgomery, *Commentary on the Book of Daniel*, 400–401).

period in Jewish history, while also portraying a biblical pattern of evil rulers that will culminate in the book of Revelation.

> III. Macro Unit 3: Encouragement until God's Eternal Kingdom Comes (8:1a–12:13c)
>   A. Narrative 1: God's Leash on Evil (8:1a–27f)
> → **B. Narrative 2: Repentance and God's Promise of Restoration (9:1a–27d)**
>   C. Narrative 3: The Ultimate Conflict and God's Final Victory (10:1a–12:13c)

1. The Context of Repentance (9:1a–3b)

Main Idea of the Passage

Daniel 9:1–3 introduces the context for Daniel's prayer of repentance. As he reads the scrolls of Jeremiah during the first year of Darius, he realizes that the prophesied seventy years of Jerusalem's desolation were completed. He turns to God in penitential prayer.

Literary Context

Daniel 9:1–3 is the opening section of the Dan 9 narrative. As such, it functions in at least five ways in its broader literary context. First, it establishes the context for the chapter's events during the first year of Darius. In so doing, it positions the chapter in the chronology of the book of Daniel—namely, in the year following the death of Belshazzar and the fall of Babylon in ch. 5. Third, it explicitly connects what follows in the chapter to the prophecies of Jeremiah. Fourth, its mention of the seventy years of Jerusalem's desolation sets up Gabriel's revelation of "seventy weeks of years" at the conclusion of the chapter. Finally, its description of Daniel's prayer "with fasting and sackcloth and ashes" indicates the sorrowful and confessional nature of what follows.

> B. Narrative 2: Repentance and God's Promise of Restoration (9:1a–27d)
> **1. The Context of Repentance (9:1a–3b)**
> 2. Daniel's Prayer of Repentance (9:4a–19f)
> 3. The Revelation of Restoration (9:20a–27d)

Translation and Exegetical Outline

(See page 455.)

Structure and Literary Form

The opening section of the Dan 9 narrative (9:1–3) sets the context for the repentance that follows. It is comprised of two subsections: 9:1–2 and 3.

The first subsection (9:1–2) establishes the timing of the chapter's events: "in the first year of Darius, son of Ahasuerus, from Median descent" (9:1a). It also provides Daniel's "place"—that is, "in the scrolls . . . the word of YHWH to Jeremiah the prophet" (9:2b–c).

The second subsection (9:3) begins with a *wayyiqtol* clause that details Daniel's response to his time (in the first year of Darius) and "place" (in the scrolls of Jeremiah the prophet): "and I set my face to the Lord God" (9:3a). Daniel set his face to pray and petition, with fasting and sackcloth and ashes (9:3b).

Since the entire narrative of Dan 9 is Daniel's first-person report of the events, it is all set as reported speech (shaded on the charts).

Explanation of the Text

a. Daniel's Time and "Place" (9:1a–2d)

Daniel 9 opens with a date formula that sets the historical context for what follows and comprises the bulk of the chapter: Daniel's penitential prayer in section 2. However, the formula also serves as part of the space/time referent for the vision Daniel will receive at the end of the chapter (see on 9:20–21 below).[7]

The timing of the chapter's events is "in the first

---

7. Korner, "'And I Saw . . . ,'" 162. See Literary Context of Narrative 6 (Dan 7:1–28), pp. 348–50, for discussion of "space/time referent."

Daniel 9:1a–3b

1a	בִּשְׁנַת אַחַת לְדָרְיָוֶשׁ בֶּן־אֲחַשְׁוֵרוֹשׁ מִזֶּרַע מָדָי	"In the first year of Darius, son of Ahasuerus, from Median descent,	B. Narrative 2: Repentance and God's Promise of Restoration (Dan 9:1a–27d)
1b	אֲשֶׁר הָמְלַךְ עַל מַלְכוּת כַּשְׂדִּים׃	↑ who was made king over the kingdom of the Chaldeans,	1. The Context of Repentance (9:1a–3b)
2a	בִּשְׁנַת אַחַת לְמָלְכוֹ	in the first year of his reign,	a. Daniel's Time and "Place" (9:1a–2d)
2b	אֲנִי דָּנִיֵּאל בִּינֹתִי בַּסְּפָרִים מִסְפַּר הַשָּׁנִים	I, Daniel, understood in the scrolls the number of years,	
2c	אֲשֶׁר הָיָה דְבַר־יְהוָה אֶל־יִרְמִיָה הַנָּבִיא	↑ which was the word of YHWH to Jeremiah the prophet,	
2d	לְמַלֹּאות לְחָרְבוֹת יְרוּשָׁלִַם שִׁבְעִים שָׁנָה׃	for the fullness of the desolation of Jerusalem—seventy years.	
3a	וָאֶתְּנָה אֶת־פָּנַי אֶל־אֲדֹנָי הָאֱלֹהִים	And I set my face to the Lord God	b. Daniel's Response to His Time and "Place" (9:3a–b)
3b	לְבַקֵּשׁ תְּפִלָּה וְתַחֲנוּנִים בְּצוֹם וְשַׂק וָאֵפֶר׃	↑ to seek by prayer and supplication, with fasting and sackcloth and ashes."	

year of Darius" (9:1a), a temporal clause echoed in 9:2a: "in the first year of his reign." Between these repetitious clauses are several details about Darius. The narrator, not revealed as Daniel until 9:2b, reports that Darius was the son of Ahasuerus and of Median descent (9:1a). Then the narrator notes that this Darius was made king (הָמְלַךְ, 9:1b) over the kingdom of the Chaldeans.

These additional phrases describing Darius go beyond what the reader might expect at this point. While it is appropriate to include some description to reintroduce Darius into the narrative since he last appeared in Dan 6, an introduction that simply identifies him as "the king" would suffice (cf. 7:1; 10:1). That he is the son of Ahasuerus seems irrelevant, since there is no reference to this king elsewhere in Daniel, nor is genealogical information provided for any other king in Daniel. That he is of Median descent seems unnecessarily repetitive since we have already been told he is a Mede (6:1[5:31]). That he was "made king over the kingdom of the Chaldeans" also seems like unnecessary repetition (cf. Dan 6:1[5:31]). As Whitcomb notes, "the Book of Daniel gives far more information concerning the personal background of Darius the Mede than of Belshazzar or even of Nebuchadnezzar. For he is the only monarch in the book whose age, parentage, and nationality are recorded."[8] While the identity of Darius the Mede as a historical person remains uncertain, we can nonetheless consider what function all this extra information serves in the narrative.[9]

Darius is said to be the son of Ahasuerus, or Xerxes (9:1a). There is some evidence to suggest that "Xerxes" was a dynastic name—and certainly later Persian history knows several kings named "Xerxes" (e.g., Esth 1:1). If this is the case, then being called the son of Xerxes establishes Darius as Persian royalty.[10] In the same clause, he is also said to be of Median descent (9:1a).[11] Thus, the narrative reintroduces Darius as both Persian and Median.

This Medo-Persian king is said to have been "made king over the kingdom of the Chaldeans" (9:1b). The passive voice here aligns well with the unseen divine hand at work behind the rise and fall of kingdoms in the book of Daniel.[12] Beginning with God's "gift" of his temple vessels and his king into the hand of Nebuchadnezzar (1:2) and continuing through Daniel's visions of the four beasts (ch. 7) and of the ram and goat (ch. 8),[13] kings have been raised up and taken down (cf. Dan 2:20–23). A central theme of the book of Daniel is the relationship between divine and human kingship—namely, that God appoints and is sovereign over all kings. This is the theology behind Dan 9:1b—God is the one who raised up this Medo-Persian king and appointed him over the kingdom of the Chaldeans.

The use of the more cumbersome phrase that Darius was made "king over the kingdom of the Chaldeans" rather than, for example, saying he was made "king of the Chaldeans" or "king of Babylon" (cf. 1:2; 5:30; 7:1) highlights a theme of Daniel: the

---

8. J. C. Whitcomb, *Darius the Mede* (Eerdmans, 1959), p. 8, cited in Baldwin, *Daniel*, 27–28.

9. See ch. 5, n95 on the problem of Darius the Mede's identity.

10. If Darius was the same person as Cyrus, which is the position favored in this commentary, then his father was Cambyses I. While there is not any evidence that Cambyses was ever referred to as Xerxes, it is possible that the name derives from his maternal lineage instead: Cyrus's maternal great-grandfather was named Cyaxares, who led the Median forces that helped destroy the Assyrian Empire (Lucas, "Daniel," 556).

11. Cyrus was the son of a Median mother, who was herself royalty—the daughter of Median king Astyages.

12. Proponents of the theory that Darius was an official/general appointed over Babylon by Cyrus find support for the idea in the passive language of Dan 9:1 (and 6:1[5:31]).

13. See on the passive verbs in 7:4–6, 12; 8:11–12 above.

raising up and taking down of kingdoms. In the raising up of king Darius, another kingdom was brought down. In a book that portrays the temporal and destructible nature of human kingdoms, Babylon is no more. What is more, Babylon has fallen to a Median king. This too is purposeful in the narrative, which is concerned to show that Babylon was judged by the Medes in fulfillment of Jeremiah's prophecies (Jer 51:11, 28; cf. Isa 13:17). Median Darius was made king over the kingdom of the Chaldeans. But Daniel is also keen to demonstrate the fulfillment of Isaiah's prophecy that Babylon would fall to Elam (Persia) and Media (Isa 21:2), thus he makes a point of saying that Darius is the son of Xerxes and of Median descent. Darius represents the joint kingdom of Medo-Persia through which God punished the wicked Babylon.

The opening verse of Dan 9 affirms that Babylon has fallen to a Medo-Persian king, and its date formula (9:1a) identifies the timing of the events to follow.[14] A variation of the date formula is repeated in 9:2a, repetition that functions as a narrative hint that the date is important. The first year of Darius, regardless of Darius's exact identity, corresponds with the fall of Babylon in 539 BCE. This timing sets the context for understanding the rest of 9:2, which details Daniel's "place"—namely, reading the scrolls of Jeremiah the prophet.

Verse 2b begins with Daniel's identification of himself as the speaker (אֲנִי דָנִיֵּאל). He then reports, "I ... understood in the scrolls the number of years" (9:2b), a clause followed by two explanatory clauses (9:2c and 2d). The first is a relative clause (אֲשֶׁר הָיָה דְבַר־יהוה אֶל־יִרְמְיָה הַנָּבִיא) that grammatically modifies מִסְפַּר, "number," though broadly speaking, it modifies "in the scrolls the number of years" (9:2b). Daniel's understanding came from preserved writings of what YHWH had said through the prophet Jeremiah.[15] The second explanatory clause (9:2d) modifies הַשָּׁנִים, "the years" (9:2b): "for the fullness of the desolation of Jerusalem—seventy years." These two explanatory clauses give us a pretty good idea of what Daniel was considering in the writings of Jeremiah.[16] The seventy-year exile is mentioned in two sections of the book of Jeremiah: 25:1–15 and 29:1–14. The first is a preexilic prophecy to Judah warning them that God was going to punish them by sending Nebuchadnezzar to destroy their land and take them captive for seventy years. When seventy years had passed, he would punish Babylon for its sin. The second section, Jer 29:1–14, includes a letter Jeremiah wrote to the Jews in exile. He told them they would be in Babylon for seventy years, but he also promised that after seventy years, God would restore the people to their land.

Given Daniel's time and "place," it would have been clear to him that the time for promised restoration had come. God had punished his people through Nebuchadnezzar, seventy years had passed,[17] and by the first year of Darius, Babylon had been punished.

b. Daniel's Response to His Time and "Place" (9:3a–b)

The writings of Jeremiah promised restoration for Daniel's people, but they also included the people's need to confess their sins and seek (בקש)

---

14. Date formulae, when included, are part of the more general characteristic of apocalyptic literature in which visions are set in a narrative framework. See further above on Dan 7:1.

15. This is the first occurrence of the divine name (YHWH) in the book, which only occurs in Dan 9. See further below on 9:4a.

16. We do not know what stage the "book" of Jeremiah was in at the time Daniel read these scrolls, nor how Daniel had access to them. But in whatever form, the scrolls—as the word of YHWH—would have been considered sacred.

17. There are at least three ways to account for the prophesied seventy years of exile. (1) A literal approach begins

YHWH (Jer 29:12–13). Jeremiah promised the exiles that if they sought (בקשׁ) God wholeheartedly, he would restore them (Jer 29:13). As Daniel understood YHWH's words to Jeremiah, he responded in obedience. He sought (בקשׁ) the Lord in prayer and supplication, with fasting, sackcloth, and ashes. His prayer was intended to remind God of the prophecy and promise made through Jeremiah and to petition for mercy.[18]

Just as Solomon had implored YHWH to forgive the people when they reaped the consequences of their disobedience and then turned to him in confession (1 Kgs 8:46–51), so Daniel will confess the sin of the people and plead for the restoration of Jerusalem and God's people. In this confession and petition, Daniel will fill the role of a traditional prophet representing his people before YHWH and interceding for them.

2. Daniel's Prayer of Repentance (9:4a–19f)

Main Idea of the Passage

In Daniel 9:4–19, Daniel intercedes on behalf of his people. He confesses their generations of sin, acknowledges the deserved consequences, and proclaims the open shame of all the people. Then Daniel implores YHWH to forgive and restore his city and his people because of his righteousness and for the sake of his own name. While YHWH's people failed to listen to him at every step, Daniel pleads with YHWH to listen to his prayer and act.

Literary Context

Daniel 9:4–19 is the second section of the ch. 9 narrative and comprises the heart of the chapter—both in length and content. It follows the introductory section in which Daniel established the time and "place" of the chapter's events, and it functions

---

counting years with the 587 BCE destruction of Jerusalem and ends with the 517 BCE dedication of the Second Temple. However, the Jeremianic context of Daniel's prayer in Dan 9 suggests that the end of exile was in 539 BCE when Babylon fell. (2) Taking 70 as a round number instead, if exile began in 605 BCE (Dan 1:1) and ended in 539 BCE, it lasted a literal 66 years. This may be the approach of 2 Chr 36:17–23. (3) A third way to account for the prophesied seventy years is simply to take the number symbolically. Seventy can symbolize completeness or totality (see, e.g., Gen 46:27 [cf. Exod 1:5; Acts 7:14]; Deut 10:22; and Ps 90:10)—or, in the words of Dan 9:2, "the fullness of the desolation of Jerusalem." The Black Stone of Esarhaddon, written within a century of Jeremiah's seventy-year prophecy, has an inscription describing a god-decreed seventy-year desolation for Babylon. It seems that in the ancient Near East, "seventy years" was "a perfectly proper period for [a city] to lie desolate" (D. D. Luckenbill, "The Black Stone of Esarhaddon," *AJSL* 41.3 [April, 1925]: 167). Willis suggests that this length of time may have represented the lifespan of the king (*Dissonance and the Drama of Divine Sovereignty*, 140).

18. Lucas, *Daniel*, 236.

in at least three ways in its broader literary context. First, it gives voice to Daniel's confession, detailing both the nature of the people's sin and the basis for his request that God restore his people and city. Second, it establishes Daniel's prophetic role as he represents his people before God and intercedes for them. Finally, it provides the context for understanding Gabriel's revelation to follow.

> B. Narrative 2: Repentance and God's Promise of Restoration (9:1a–27d)
> 1. The Context of Repentance (9:1a–3b)
> **2. Daniel's Prayer of Repentance (9:4a–19f)**
> 3. The Revelation of Restoration (9:20a–27d)

Translation and Exegetical Outline

(See pages 460–62.)

Structure and Literary Form

The second section of the narrative in Dan 9 (9:4–19) is the longest section of the chapter and is comprised entirely of a penitential prayer by Daniel on behalf of his people. It consists of three subsections: 9:4–14, 15–16, and 17–19.

The first subsection (9:4–14) is Daniel's confession. It begins with a quotative frame in which Daniel introduces his prayer: "I prayed to YHWH my God, and I confessed, and I said" (9:4a–c). His actual prayer begins with an invocation and initial confession (9:4d–5). In this opening confession, he summarizes the sin of the people, saying they have sinned (חָטָאנוּ), done wrong (עָוִינוּ), done wickedly (הִרְשַׁעְנוּ), and rebelled (מָרַדְנוּ). He continues with a refrain that will characterize the remainder of his prayer: "We did not listen" (לֹא שָׁמָעְנוּ, 9:6). This refrain occurs again in 9:10, and together the repeated refrains form an *inclusio* around Daniel's contrast between the Lord's nature and his people's shame (9:7–9). Daniel then recounts how the people's failure to listen resulted in the threatened curse coming upon them (9:11–13). He concludes the subsection of confession by summarizing YHWH's righteous administration of the curse because of the people's failure to listen (וְלֹא שָׁמָעְנוּ, 9:14).

The second subsection (9:15–16) is a bridge between the two main subsections of confession (9:4–14) and supplication (9:17–19). As such, it repeats where Daniel has been and previews where he is going in his prayer. It begins with a second invocation (9:15a–c) and a brief confession (9:15d–e) before it gives Daniel's basic request (9:16).

Daniel 9:4a–19f

2. Daniel's Prayer of Repentance (9:4a–19f)
   a. Confession: "We Did Not Listen" (9:4a–14e)
      (1) Invocation and Confession (9:4a–5e)

      (2) The Open Shame of All Israel (9:6a–10c)

4a	"I prayed to YHWH my God,
4b	and I confessed,
4c	and I said,
4d	'Ah, Lord, the great and awesome God,
4e	↑ keeping covenant and lovingkindness to those who love him and keep his commandments,
5a	we have sinned,
5b	and we have done wrong.
5c	We have done wickedly,
5d	and we have rebelled,
5e	↑ turning from your commandments and your judgments.
6a	We did not listen to your servants, the prophets,
6b	↑ who spoke in your name to our kings, our princes, and our fathers, and to all the people of the land.
7a	To you, O Lord, belongs righteousness,
7b	but to us belongs open shame, as this day—to the men of Judah and to those dwelling in Jerusalem and to all Israel, those who are near and those who are far away in all the lands, where you scattered them there because of the treachery
7c	↑ which they committed against you.
7d	YHWH, to us belongs open shame—to our kings, to our princes,
8a	and to our fathers,
8b	because we sinned against you.
9a	To the Lord our God belongs compassion and forgiveness,
9b	although we have rebelled against him.
10a	We did not listen to the voice of YHWH our God
10b	↑ to walk in his torah,
10c	↑ which he gave to us by the hand of his servants the prophets.

Daniel 9:1a–27d

(3) The Curse Fulfilled (9:11a–13e)

11a	All Israel transgressed your torah
11b	turning aside,
11c	not listening to your voice,
11d	and the curse and the oath has gushed over us,
11e	which is written in the Torah of Moses, the servant of God,
11f	because we have sinned against him.
12a	And he fulfilled his words
12b	which he spoke against us and against our rulers,
12c	which ruled us,
12d	to bring on us great calamity,
12e	which has not been done under all the heavens
12f	like what has been done in Jerusalem.
13a	As it is written in the Torah of Moses,
13b	all this calamity came upon us.
13c	Yet we have not tried to appease YHWH our God
13d	by turning from our iniquity
13e	and giving attention to your truth.

(4) The Summary (9:14a–e)

14a	YHWH kept watch over the calamity,
14b	and he brought it upon us,
14c	for righteous is YHWH our God over all his deeds
14d	which he has done,
14e	and we did not listen to his voice.

b. The Bridge (9:15a–16b)

(1) Invocation (9:15a–c)

15a	And now, O Lord our God,
15b	who brought your people out from the land of Egypt with a strong hand
15c	and made a name for yourself, as at this day,

(2) Confession (9:15d–e)

15d	we have sinned.
15e	We have been wicked.

Continued on next page.

462 — Macro Unit 3: Encouragement until God's Eternal Kingdom Comes

	Continued from previous page.		
16a	אֲדֹנָי כְּכָל־צִדְקֹתֶךָ יָשָׁב־נָא אַפְּךָ וַחֲמָתְךָ מֵעִירְךָ יְרוּשָׁלִַם הַר־קָדְשֶׁךָ	O Lord, according to all your righteous acts, let your anger and your wrath turn from your city, Jerusalem, the mountain of your holiness,	(3) Supplication (9:16a–b)
16b	כִּי בַחֲטָאֵינוּ וּבַעֲוֹנוֹת אֲבֹתֵינוּ יְרוּשָׁלִַם וְעַמְּךָ לְחֶרְפָּה לְכָל־סְבִיבֹתֵינוּ׃	for, on account of our sins and the iniquities of our fathers, Jerusalem and your people have become a reproach to all those around us.	
			c. Supplication: "Please Listen" (9:17a–19f)
17a	וְעַתָּה שְׁמַע אֱלֹהֵינוּ אֶל־תְּפִלַּת עַבְדְּךָ וְאֶל־תַּחֲנוּנָיו	But now, listen, our God, to the prayer of your servant and to his supplications,	(1) "Listen to My Prayer" (9:17a–b)
17b	וְהָאֵר פָּנֶיךָ עַל־מִקְדָּשְׁךָ הַשָּׁמֵם לְמַעַן אֲדֹנָי׃	and shine your face upon your desolate sanctuary, for the sake of the Lord.	
18a	הַטֵּה אֱלֹהַי אָזְנְךָ	Incline, my God, your ear	(2) "Listen and See!" (9:18a–g)
18b	וּשְׁמָע	and listen!	
18c	פְּקַח [פְּקַח] עֵינֶיךָ	Open your eyes	
18d	וּרְאֵה שֹׁמְמֹתֵינוּ וְהָעִיר	and see our desolations and the city	
18e	אֲשֶׁר־נִקְרָא שִׁמְךָ עָלֶיהָ	which your name is called over it!	
18f	כִּי לֹא עַל־צִדְקֹתֵינוּ אֲנַחְנוּ מַפִּילִים תַּחֲנוּנֵינוּ לְפָנֶיךָ	For not on account of our righteousness are we pleading our supplications before you,	
18g	כִּי עַל־רַחֲמֶיךָ הָרַבִּים׃	but on account of your great mercy [we are pleading].	
19a	אֲדֹנָי שְׁמָעָה	O Lord, please listen!	(3) "Please Listen!" (9:19a–f)
19b	אֲדֹנָי סְלָחָה	O Lord, please forgive!	
19c	אֲדֹנָי הַקְשִׁיבָה	O Lord, give attention	
19d	וַעֲשֵׂה	and act—	
19e	אַל־תְּאַחַר לְמַעַנְךָ אֱלֹהַי	Do not delay for your sake, my God,	
19f	כִּי־שִׁמְךָ נִקְרָא עַל־עִירְךָ וְעַל־עַמֶּךָ׃	because your name is called over your city and over your people."	

This subsection also contains the grounds for Daniel's request—namely, YHWH's righteousness (9:16a).

The third subsection (9:17–19) is Daniel's supplication. It consists of three requests in which Daniel implores the Lord to "listen" (שְׁמָעָה . . . שְׁמַע . . . שְׁמַע, 9:17a, 18b, 19a). He first pleads that God listen to his prayer and respond for his own sake (9:17). Then he asks God to listen with his ears and see with his eyes (9:18). He concludes his supplication with a series of staccato requests, beginning with the cry to "listen" (9:19a).

Explanation of the Text

a. Confession: "We Did Not Listen" (9:4a–14e)

Daniel frames his prayer by saying he "prayed" (*hithpael* of פלל) "to YHWH my God" (9:4a). The use of the divine name, YHWH, in Daniel only occurs in ch. 9, beginning with the reference in 9:2c to "the word of YHWH to Jeremiah the prophet." YHWH had given his name to his covenant people at the time of the exodus, and while the name appears late in the book of Daniel, the covenant it represents is in the background of Daniel's earlier prayers. In Dan 2:23, he blessed the "God of my fathers" for revealing the king's dream to him, and in Dan 6, his habit of prayer reflected the temple dedication prayer of Solomon in 1 Kgs 8.[19] Here, for the first time in the book, the explicit use of the divine name puts the covenant at the center of the chapter's events. It will be at the heart of everything Daniel confesses and requests in his prayer, and it will also be foundational to Gabriel's revelation in 9:20–27. By saying he prayed to "YHWH his God," Daniel invokes the covenant before he utters a word of confession.

Daniel also frames his prayer by saying he "confessed" (*hithpael* of ידה; 9:4b; cf. 9:20c). The use of this word is rare in the Old Testament, occurring only ten times with the meaning "to confess."[20] Six of these occurrences are associated with a kind of prayer classified by scholars as penitential[21]—a prayer that is "a direct address to God in which an individual, group, or an individual on behalf of a group confesses sins and petitions for forgiveness as an act of repentance."[22] Among the penitential prayers, Dan 9:4–19 is most similar to the great prayers of Ezra (9:6–15) and Nehemiah (9:5b–37), and all three of these prayers echo Solomon's prayer of dedication of the temple (1 Kgs 8:22–53). In that great prayer, Solomon had envisioned a day when YHWH's people would not be faithful to him; they would violate the covenant and be wantonly rebellious. Solomon had pleaded that

---

19. See above on 2:23 and 6:11[10].

20. Leviticus 5:5; 16:21; 26:40; Num 5:7; Ezra 10:1; Neh 1:6; 9:2–3; Dan 9:4, 20. The occurrences in Ezra, Nehemiah, and Daniel are associated with penitential prayers.

21. Samuel E. Balentine, "'I Was Ready to Be Sought Out by Those Who Did Not Ask,'" in *Seeking the Favor of God, Volume 1: The Origins of Penitential Prayer in Second Temple Judaism*, SBLEJL 21, ed. Mark J. Boda, Daniel K. Falk, and Rodney A. Werline (Atlanta: Society of Biblical Literature, 2006), 8.

22. Rodney A. Werline, "Defining Penitential Prayer," in *Seeking the Favor of God, Volume 1: The Origins of Penitential Prayer in Second Temple Judaism*, SBLEJL 21, ed. Mark J. Boda, Daniel K. Falk, and Rodney A. Werline (Atlanta: Society of Biblical Literature, 2006), xv.

YHWH be merciful when that day came, that he hear his people when they prayed toward Jerusalem and the temple. He asked YHWH to forgive his people when they confessed. While Ezra and Nehemiah had offered their penitential prayers in the postexilic years—that is, after the decree of Cyrus that effectively ended the exilic period—the book of Daniel positions his prayer on the verge of the postexilic period (i.e., the first year of Darius, ca. 539 BCE).

A basic understanding of the format and function of penitential prayers can be helpful for analyzing Daniel's prayer. Scholars agree that six elements characterize penitential prayers:[23] (1) praise; (2) supplication—with the depiction of a need, a "muted lament,"[24] and an implicit request; (3) confession of sin that includes admission of culpability, "declaration of solidarity with former generations," and consistent use of the *hithpael* of the root ידה; (4) history that involves an "anthological use of historical sources" and the use of the contrast motif of God's grace versus Israel's disobedience; (5) themes of covenant, land, and law; and (6) the purpose of bringing an end to the devastating effects of captivity, oppression, or "the sorry state of Palestine."[25] All of these characteristics are evident to some degree in the prayer of Dan 9.

Related to the format and function of Dan 9 as a penitential prayer is its extensive intertextuality—that is, the way in which it incorporates language from other biblical texts, and specifically language from Deuteronomy. In his commentary, Towner calls Daniel's prayer "a meditation of Scripture upon earlier Scripture."[26] Montgomery details every word or phrase that can be found elsewhere in the Old Testament, with the result that more than 85 percent of Daniel's prayer could be considered a quotation.[27]

Understanding both the general characteristics of penitential prayers and their use of other texts can be valuable, and I will refer to both in the commentary that follows. However, the focus of the analysis here will be the *discourse* of the text—that is, how the words, sentences, and paragraphs shape the flow of thought and the overall message of the text.

Daniel's prayer begins with words of invocation and praise, as he calls upon the "Lord, the great and awesome God" (9:4d).[28] This pair of adjectives[29] describing God or his works is used elsewhere in

---

23. This list is found in various forms. Mine is a nearly verbatim representation of Mark J. Boda's list in *Praying the Tradition: The Origin and Use of Tradition in Nehemiah 9*, BZAW 277 (Berlin: de Gruyter, 1999), 28.

24. Boda says in penitential prayers, the pray-er's "complaint against Yahweh was muted and the emphasis shifted to admitting the guilt of the suppliants and justifying Yahweh's actions of judgment" (*Praying the Tradition*, 41).

25. Boda elaborates on this final point: "Each composition was concerned with the reversal of the deplorable results of the fall of the state: either the return of the people or the restoration of their land and city" (*Praying the Tradition*, 41).

26. Towner, *Daniel*, 129.

27. Montgomery, *Commentary on the Book of Daniel*, 361–68. Towner provides the rough percentage (*Daniel*, 129). While all this intertextuality makes for rich commentary, it is hard to know to what extent the intertexts would have resonated with Daniel's original audience. Newsom explains: "It is difficult to say whether contemporary readers and hearers would have simply noticed the biblicizing style or whether they would have made the connections to specific intertexts. In antiquity, education included memorizing extensive repertoires of culturally important texts; thus it is possible that the better-educated members of the ancient audience would have heard the text in all of its allusive richness, a feat of understanding that modern readers can accomplish only with the laborious use of concordances" (*Daniel*, 292). Daniel himself, as an elite member of Jerusalem society (Dan 1:4), would have known the texts, and so would later editors who shaped the book of Daniel as it developed—so the intertexts *are* meaningful. The uncertainty is the extent to which a less educated audience would have recognized them.

28. Lucas observes that generally throughout Daniel's prayer, he addresses "Adonai (Lord)" when he is pleading with God, but "when he is simply addressing God or, more usually, speaking of God in the third person," he addresses him as "YHWH" (*Daniel*, 236).

29. נוֹרָא is a *niphal* participle functioning adjectivally.

the Old Testament (e.g., Deut 7:21; 10:21; Neh 1:15), but the significance of the word נוֹרָא, "awesome," in particular, often gets lost in English translations.[30] A word that once described something that inspired terror or awe (another diluted word) more commonly describes, at best, something that provokes wonder ("Those mountains are awesome"). At worst, it simply describes something that impresses ("Your cooking is awesome") or makes a person happy ("You're free for lunch? Awesome!"). But when used of God in the Old Testament, נוֹרָא describes his "numinous nature"[31]—that is, a sense of his divine presence, his otherness, his God-ness. It is a word that reminds us that YHWH is "terrible and dreadful"[32]—that is, he is a God with a power and presence deserving of fearful respect. He is the kind of God before whom Isaiah was undone (Isa 6:5), and Ezekiel was stunned silent for an entire week (Ezek 3:15). He is the God whose voice shakes the skies (Jer 10:13), whose hand stretched out the heavens like a tent (Ps 104:2), whose outstretched arm terrified the Egyptians when Israel was in bondage (Jer 32:21), and whose feet rest on the earth as a footstool (Isa 66:1). He is the God whose enemies should cringe before him (Ps 66:3). This is the God Daniel invokes in 9:4. The great, terrible, and dreadful God. Of Daniel's invocation, Goldingay observes, "There is some courage about beginning with recognition of the majestic aspect to God, which is a threat to people who fail to yield to him, whether foreigners or Israelites.... It is precisely such failure that Daniel will have to go on to acknowledge."[33]

The clause that follows modifies this great and awesome God (9:4e). He is the one "keeping covenant and lovingkindness to those who love him and keep his commandments." Certainly this can be considered praise, a characteristic of penitential prayers, but it is more than that. It establishes the character of this God before Daniel utters a word of confession or petition. This is the God who keeps covenant. This is the God who shows lovingkindness. Daniel qualifies this divine action by identifying the recipients of such loving faithfulness: those who love God and keep his commandments. Lest we consider these two distinct actions, the Old and New Testaments alike are clear that those who love God *do* keep his commandments (e.g., Deut 11:13; John 14:23). We might say we love God *by* keeping his commandments, or that it is impossible to love God *without* keeping his commandments.[34]

From these words of praise and acknowledgment, Daniel moves into his initial words of confession (9:5–6). In four single word independent clauses, Daniel confesses: "we have sinned" (חָטָאנוּ, 9:5a); "and we have done wrong" (וְעָוִינוּ, 9:5b); "we have done wickedly" (הִרְשַׁעְנוּ, 9:5c); "and we have rebelled" (וּמָרָדְנוּ, 9:5d). While there are different nuances to each Hebrew word,[35] the effect here is that the people's sin is comprehensive. In these four abrupt confessions, Daniel hammers home the point: We have sinned in every possible way.[36]

---

30. For a similar translation problem, see on the word "dreadful" (דְּחִילָה) in Dan 7:7 above.

31. H. F. Fuhs, "ירא," *TDOT* 6:300.

32. M. V. Van Pelt and W. C. Kaiser, Jr., "ירא," *NIDOTTE* 2:532.

33. Goldingay, *Daniel*, 462.

34. Balentine notes, "The penitence motif is accented with a complementary emphasis on God's sovereignty, mercy, and justice. A repeating affirmation—'the great and awesome God who keeps covenant and steadfast love to those who love you and keep your commandments' (Dan 9:4; Neh 1:5; 9:32)—undergirds the summons to contrition as the only appropriate response to God, whose 'righteousness' (צְדָקָה; 3x in Dan 9; vv. 7, 14, 16; cf. v. 18) is tempered with 'mercy' (רַחוּם; 6x in Neh 9: vv. 17, 19, 27, 28, 31 [twice])" ("'I Was Ready to Be Sought Out by Those Who Did Not Ask,'" 8).

35. See Goldingay, *Daniel*, 473–74; Miller, *Daniel*, 245.

36. Note that these four abrupt confessional clauses are matched by the four staccato petitions at the end of the prayer. See below on 9:19.

The first three confessional clauses (9:5a–c) are "virtually a verbatim repetition" of Solomon's prayer in 1 Kgs 8:47.[37] In echoing Solomon's prayer, Daniel implicitly acknowledges that his people's present situation—namely, captivity—is because of their sin.[38] The Old Testament is not bashful about blaming Israel for the exile, which makes it noteworthy that the book of Daniel—a book set entirely during the exilic years—says nothing of this culpability until ch. 9. Instead, the book opens with God's "gift" of his temple, king, and city into the hand of Nebuchadnezzar (Dan 1:2–4), and nary a bad word about the rebellion of God's people occurs for eight chapters (Dan 1–8).[39] The focus instead has been on the superiority of Israel's God over all other kings—especially the gentile kings of captivity—and the book has highlighted the faithfulness of God's choice servants in their exilic context. But now, as the years of exile near an end, Daniel's prayer brings his people's sin into full view. He acknowledges the sin that made exile a reality and restoration a necessity.

The fourth independent clause (וּמָרָדְנוּ, "and we have rebelled," 9:5d) is followed by a subordinate clause that explains how the people rebelled: "turning from your commandments and your judgments" (וְסוֹר מִמִּצְוֺתֶךָ וּמִמִּשְׁפָּטֶיךָ, 9:5e). This description of Daniel's people contrasts with his opening description of God as the one who keeps covenant and lovingkindness for those who love him and "keep his commandments" (שֹׁמְרֵי מִצְוֺתָיו, 9:4e). Daniel is praying on behalf of people who did not keep his commandments but turned from them.[40]

In these opening words of invocation and confession, Daniel makes it clear *to whom* he is praying and *for whom* he is praying. He is praying to "the great and awesome" God who keeps covenant with those who obey him, and he is praying for people who have violated that covenant in every possible way. This prayer starts where every prayer should start—with a recognition of who God is and an honest acknowledgment of who we are. Such a prayer can only lead to contrition and a plea for mercy.

From these opening words of praise and confession, in which Daniel contrasts the greatness of God with the depravity of his people, the prayer moves to a more extended contrast in 9:6–10, specifically a contrast between the righteous and compassionate nature of God and the shame that belongs to Daniel's people—a contrast common in penitential prayers. The section is structured

  A "We did not listen" (9:6)
    B "To you . . . righteousness" (9:7a)
      C "To us . . . open shame" (9:7b–d)

---

37. Balentine, "'I Was Ready to Be Sought Out by Those Who Did Not Ask,'" 8. Cf. also Neh 1:6–7; 9:16–18; and Ezra 9:6, 7, 13, 15.

38. While he will say this explicitly in what follows, Daniel's use of Solomon's words in this initial confession helps set the agenda for what follows.

39. The possible exception to this is the ambiguous "transgression" (פֶּשַׁע) in Dan 8. See on Dan 8:16–26 above, and esp. nn33 and 34. However, even if Israel's transgression is in view in Dan 8, the reference is oblique, while in Dan 9 Israel's guilt could not be clearer.

40. Much of the language of Daniel's prayer is Deuteronomic, including this clause about turning aside from YHWH's commands (Deut 5:32; 9:12, 16; 11:28; 17:20; 28:14; 31:29; cf. Josh 1:7; 1 Kgs 9:6; 2 Kgs 17:13; 2 Chr 7:19), though as Goldingay observes, "it goes back to the very beginning of Israel's covenant relationship with Yahweh," first appearing as a description of Israel's behavior in the aftermath of the golden calf (Exod 32:8; *Daniel*, 474).

C′ "To us . . . open shame" (9:8)[41]
   B′ "To the Lord our God . . . compassion and forgiveness" (9:9)
      A′ "We did not listen" (9:10)

chiastically, and the shame of God's people is its central theme:

The two outer sections (A, A′) begin with "We did not listen" (וְלֹא שָׁמַעְנוּ, 9:6a, 10a), while the B and C sections all begin with a *lamed* preposition and object: לַאדֹנָי אֱלֹהֵינוּ, לָנוּ, לְךָ—each form showing possession (but see on 9:8a below). Having these parallel prepositional phrases in the first position of each clause sharpens the contrast being made between what the Lord is like and what Daniel's people are like.

The A segments of the chiasm include the first two occurrences of the verbal root שמע, "to listen," a verb that is used seven times in the prayer (9:6, 10, 11, 14, 17–19). Its use extends to both major sections of the prayer—the confession (9:4–14) and the supplication (9:17–19)—and in them, Daniel plays on the different meanings of the word שמע. In his confession, he repeatedly says that his people did not listen—that is, they did not obey (9:6, 10, 11, 14). In his supplication, he repeatedly pleads that the Lord listen—that is, hear and respond (9:17, 18, 19). The word שמע captures both the offense and the need, and its thematic repetition helps the audience follow the flow of thought.

In his first confession that the people did not listen (וְלֹא שָׁמַעְנוּ), Daniel specifies that they did not listen to "your servants, the prophets" (9:6a). The prophets were the ones who spoke in YHWH's name (9:6b) to Israel's kings and princes, to "our fathers"—that is, the ancestors—and to "all the people of the land" (9:6b).[42] While the prophets' role in the life of Israel entailed many things, their primary function was calling the people—from the king to the commoner—to live according to YHWH's torah, to live according to their covenant with YHWH. Daniel's confession here is that they did not heed the prophets' calls. They did not listen to the prophets.[43]

Prophets not only spoke YHWH's word to the people; they spoke for the people to YHWH. They were intercessors, and in Daniel's confession he fulfills this prophetic role. However, he does not just speak *for* the people before YHWH—as Moses did when the Israelites worshiped the golden calf: "Oh, what a great sin these people have committed!" (Exod 32:31). Nor does Daniel just speak of what the people did wrong—as Samuel did when the Israelites begged for a king: "You have done all this evil; . . . As for me, far be it from me that I should sin against YHWH by failing to pray for you'" (1 Sam 12:20, 23). In his intercession, Daniel speaks as one of the people: "We have sinned . . . we have . . . we have . . . we did not listen." Daniel's confession has no hint of "them" and "me." While he had no doubt committed his own acts of covenant unfaithfulness—don't we all?—he took responsibility for sins he had not committed. He stands in solidarity with his people, taking every last offense as his own.

From this confession, Daniel makes the first of two statements about the Lord's character (the B segments, 9:7a and 9:9): "To you, O Lord, belongs

---

41. This clause actually begins with the vocative יהוה, "YHWH." See further below on 9:8a.

42. Note that standing in solidarity with past generations is a feature of penitential prayers.

43. Israel's need and failure to listen is a common theme in Deuteronomy and literature related to it (e.g., Deut 4:30; 8:20; 9:23; 28:62; 2 Kgs 17:14; 18:12; 21:9; Jer 26:4; 32:33; 44:23).

righteousness" (9:7a). This is followed by the first of two statements about Israel's shame: "but to us belongs open shame" (9:7b). Daniel's statement about the Lord's character is concise; his statement about the people's shame is not. He calls it "shame of face," that is, public shame (cf. 2 Chr 32:21; Ezra 9:7), and it is shame the people still bear (כַּיּוֹם הַזֶּה, "as this day," 9:7b). Newsom notes that the contrast between the Lord's righteousness and the people's shame "is not expressed in semantically opposite terms"—that is, the expected opposite of "right" is "wrong" or "guilt," but instead Daniel attributes "shame" to the people.[44] Newsom discusses the powerful concept of shame in biblical thought, especially highlighting its "objective, social dimension: people who are dishonored through defeat and apparent abandonment by their God become objects of mockery and disgrace." The use of the word "face" (פָּנִים) in the idiom points to the social dimension of shame, but the concept also includes psychological dimensions, as evident in texts like Lev 26:29–40, where the people experience "shame and self-loathing when they belatedly recognize and confess their sins against God." In Daniel's expression "shame at the recognition of sin is the emotion that both impels the confession and makes it difficult to approach God" (cf. also Ezra 9:6; Jer 3:25).[45]

Then Daniel details who bears this shame: the men of Judah, the inhabitants of Jerusalem, and every last Israelite, whether living near or far away—those living in the land and those living in exile ("those who are far away in all the lands," 9:7b; cf. 1 Kgs 8:46). Just as Daniel had made the offense clear (i.e., the people had sinned in every possible way; 9:5), so he makes the offenders clear—every Israelite everywhere bore this shame.

This language of "all Israel" in Daniel's prayer (9:7b, 11a; cf. 9:20c) is important. "Israel" was originally the name of the whole people descended from Jacob/Israel. When that "whole people" split into two separate kingdoms after the death of Solomon in the tenth century BCE, the larger northern nation adopted the name "Israel" for itself, while the smaller southern nation adopted the name of its largest tribe—Judah. The Northern Kingdom, "Israel," fell to the Assyrians in 722 BCE, leaving only the Southern Kingdom of Judah with its capital city, Jerusalem. When Jerusalem and the nation of Judah fell to the Babylonians under Nebuchadnezzar in 587 BCE, many Judeans were taken into exile, while others remained in the land, and still others scattered among the nations. That Daniel, part of "the little community of surviving Judahites,"[46] uses the expression "all Israel" in his confession is a "theological claim that, despite all that has happened, the covenant community that originated from Jacob/Israel and took shape at Sinai still exists, though now scattered."[47] Goldingay adds that "Daniel has not abandoned an awareness that 'Israel' was designed to be a much bigger entity than 'Judah and Jerusalem' (9:7). The latter is the nucleus of Israel, but as such it does not exclude others; it is rather a 'representative centre, to which all the children of Israel should be welcomed if they return.'"[48]

But Daniel is still not finished. In two relative clauses, he further describes the faraway lands where some of the people were living. Specifically, he details which lands and why some of the people lived there. They were the lands where God scat-

---

44. Newsom, *Daniel*, 294.
45. Newsom, *Daniel*, 294.
46. Goldingay, *Daniel*, 470.
47. Lucas, *Daniel*, 238.
48. Goldingay, *Daniel*, 470, citing H. G. M. Williamson, *1 and 2 Chronicles* [London: Marshall, Morgan & Scott, 1982] 26, referring to Williamson, *Israel in the Books of Chronicles* [Cambridge: CUP, 1977] 87–140).

tered them (9:7c; cf. Jer 16:15; 23:3; 32:37) because of the treachery they had committed against him (9:7d).[49] Lest there be any question about the guilt causing the people's shame, Daniel summarizes: Some of the people are living in exile because they broke the covenant. There are no loopholes. There is no wiggle room. Everyone is guilty, and everyone bears the disgrace.

The second of Daniel's two statements about the people's shame follows in 9:8a. This statement begins with the vocative "YHWH" before the prepositional phrase "to us" (לָנוּ), breaking the pattern of clause-initial prepositional phrases depicting possession (9:7a, 7b, 9a). This is also the only use of the divine name as a vocative in Daniel's prayer and in the entire chapter. These two features of the discourse draw special attention to the name "YHWH" at this point. As the personal name of Israel's God, "YHWH" represents the covenant made between Israel and their God at Sinai (Exod 24) and renewed at Shechem (Josh 24). By addressing the Lord, the great and awesome God, as "YHWH," Daniel makes the people's shame very personal and their offense that much more egregious. YHWH was the one who rescued Daniel's people from slavery, who set his affection on them, who loved them even though they spurned him repeatedly. YHWH was the one who was a father to them, fought for them, and forgave them repeatedly. During centuries of such gracious provision, attention, and love, Daniel's people had done nothing but thumb their noses, roll their eyes, and leap brazenly over every boundary drawn to protect them. "Oh, YHWH." Bound up in that name was the people's sordid, sorry past, and Daniel could well have whispered it with a grimace, head hung low.

Then Daniel repeats "to us belongs open shame" and, for a second time, specifies who bears the disgrace: "our kings . . . our princes . . . our fathers" (9:8a; cf. 9:7b). Whereas the first time Daniel highlighted that everyone everywhere was guilty, this time the categories are political.[50] The leaders and commoners alike bear the shame because they all sinned against YHWH (9:8b).

This second statement about the people's shame is followed by the second of Daniel's two statements about YHWH's nature (9:9). On the heels of saying kings and commoners bear the shame of the people's sin, Daniel says the "Lord our God" is compassionate and forgiving (9:9b). The clause that follows this statement contrasts these traits with the rebellion of the people, affirming that Daniel's people know the truth of God's character from experience: "although we have rebelled against him" (9:9b). Daniel's hope has a history: the "Lord our God" had shown himself to be compassionate and forgiving when the people had rebelled. In these two clauses, Daniel "begins to establish the ground upon which" his supplication will be made in 9:15–19.[51] Newsom observes that although "the people have no claim of being in the right, they can still make an appeal based on the nature of God as a deity more disposed to gracious forgiveness and mercy than to prolonged punishment." She notes that this affirmation of God's character comes out of God's own words to Moses in Exod 34:6–7 after the people sinned with the golden calf. While God characterized himself then as one who "does not leave the guilty unpunished," he also revealed that his "inclination to forgive is exponentially greater."[52]

This section of Daniel's confession (9:6–10)

---

49. The language of being scattered (פוץ), banished (נדח), or dispersed (זרה) among the nations is a common Old Testament theme (e.g., Lev 26:33; Deut 4:27; 30:3; Jer 30:11; Ezek 11:16).

50. Newsom, *Daniel*, 294.
51. Ibid.
52. Ibid., 294–95.

concludes with another "we did not listen" refrain (לֹא שָׁמַעְנוּ, 9:10a), echoing what was said in 9:6a. There Daniel had said the people did not listen to the prophets, speaking in God's name. Here he says they did not listen "to the voice of YHWH our God" (9:10a), removing the intermediary prophets and speaking the bottom line: they did not listen to (i.e., obey) YHWH himself. The infinitive clause that follows (9:10b) explains what it means to listen to the voice of YHWH: to walk in (i.e., obey) his instructions (תּוֹרֹתָיו). The section concludes with a relative clause modifying "his torah"—it was the instructions "which he gave to us by the hand of his servants the prophets" (9:10c).[53] This clause echoes 9:6 in its mention of YHWH's servants, the prophets, while the entire "we did not listen" refrain of 9:10 rounds out the chiasm of confession in 9:6–10. It both echoes and elaborates on the refrain in 9:6: Not listening to the prophets meant not listening to YHWH himself—that is, they did not walk in his instructions, which they knew through the prophets.[54]

From this full confession, Daniel moves into a description of the consequences of Israel's sin—namely, YHWH's enactment of the covenant curses (9:11–13).[55] This announcement that the curse was fulfilled also falls loosely into a chiastic structure, with the central theme being the fulfillment of the covenant curses:

A Israel's sin, turning aside (סוּר), and not listening (שמע) (9:11a–c)
  B The curse, written in the Torah of Moses, came (9:11d–f)
    C YHWH fulfilled his word against us (9:12)
  B′ The calamity, written in the Torah of Moses, came (9:13a–b)
A′ Israel's failure, not turning (שׁוּב), and not giving attention (שׂכל) (9:13c–e)

The three opening clauses comprise another confession: "All Israel transgressed your torah," or your "instruction" (9:11a)—again indicating the all-encompassing nature of the people's sin.[56] This statement is followed by two dependent clauses describing how Israel transgressed: they turned aside (סוּר, 9:11b), and they did not listen to YHWH's voice (לְבִלְתִּי שְׁמוֹעַ בְּקֹלֶךָ, 9:11c). Both of these clauses recall Deuteronomy's many warnings against turning (סוּר) from YHWH's commands and not obeying (שמע) him, lest the covenant curses come upon them (e.g., Deut 5:32; 9:12, 16; 11:16, 28; 28:14–15).

Daniel is acknowledging that Israel has done exactly what Moses warned them against, and thus in 9:11d, he recounts that "the curse and the oath"[57] did come (נתך, "pour, gush") on the people, exactly as described in "the Torah of Moses, the servant of God" (9:11e).[58] The final clause of 9:11 verifies that the curse was deserved: "because we have sinned against him" (9:11f).

At the heart of the section detailing the fulfill-

---

53. The theme of law evident throughout this section (9:6–10) and the next (9:11–13) is a feature of penitential prayers.

54. This section (9:6–10) and the next (9:11–13) involve an "anthological use of historical sources" as Daniel rehearses the people's sins and YHWH's faithfulness (Boda, *Praying the Tradition*, 28).

55. The theme of covenant emphasized in this section (9:11–13) is characteristic of penitential prayers.

56. On the use of "all Israel," see on 9:7 above.

57. "Curse and oath" is likely a hendiadys, so "solemn curse" (Goldingay, *Daniel*, 442) or "the curse (pronounced) under oath" (Lacocque, *The Book of Daniel*, 176) (cf. Num 5:21; Neh 10:30[29]). The people had ratified the covenant, along with its curses, by solemn oath, and it was legally binding.

58. The most detailed description of the covenant curses is found in Deut 28:15–68, a description Newsom calls "harrowingly graphic" (*Daniel*, 295). See also Lev 26:14–45.

ment of the curse is the declaration that YHWH did exactly as he said he would. He fulfilled his word (9:12a). This clause is modified by the relative clause of 9:12b and the infinitive construct clause of 9:12d. This was the word "which he spoke against us and against our rulers" (9:12b), reiterating that the covenant and the curse were for commoner and king alike, and it was his word "to bring on us great calamity" (9:12d).

Daniel does not detail the covenant curses as "the Torah of Moses" does, but he communicates their horror in the verb נתך, "pour out, gush," a verb that elsewhere describes God's anger and wrath (Jer 7:20; 42:18; 44:6; 2 Chr 12:7; 34:25). The verb in Daniel's prayer is a recognition that the administration of the covenant curses is an expression of divine rage (cf. Deut 29:20–27[21–27]). Daniel also indicates the horror of the covenant curses when he describes the "great calamity," which was brought upon the people as that "which has not been done under all the heaven like what has been done in Jerusalem" (9:12e–f). While the Old Testament often refers to Sodom and Gomorrah as the example of utter destruction (Gen 19:24–28; Deut 29:22[23]; Isa 1:9; 13:19; Jer 49:18; 50:40; Amos 4:11; Zeph 2:9; Lam 4:6), Daniel describes Jerusalem's fate as unique "under all the heavens" (cf. Deut 2:25; 4:19), perhaps suggesting "that it would replace Sodom and Gomorrah as the benchmark for the destruction of a sinful city."[59]

Daniel reiterates that "all this calamity" (9:13b) came upon the people just as the written Torah of Moses had said it would (9:13a; cf. 9:11d–e). The main clause is in 9:13b, and it is an unusual construction in Hebrew: אֵת כָּל־הָרָעָה הַזֹּאת בָּאָה עָלֵינוּ, "all this calamity came upon us." The particle אֵת usually marks the direct object, but in this case "all this calamity" is clearly the subject. The best explanation seems to be that the אֵת "seems solely designed to bring the noun into prominence."[60] The covenant curse (9:11d), the great calamity (9:12d), the horror of what befell the people is the central idea of this section (9:11–13).

In this section (9:11–13) Daniel acknowledges that the devastation the people had experienced was the direct result of their violation of the covenant, a direct fulfillment of YHWH's words. Daniel concludes this acknowledgment much as he began it in 9:11a–c, reviewing the nature of the people's sin—with one notable difference. In 9:11a–c, he described their sin in the positive—that is, what the people did: they transgressed, turned aside, and did not listen. This time, he describes it in the negative—that is, what the people failed to do: they had not tried to appease YHWH, not turned from their iniquity, and not given attention to YHWH's truth. In everything they did and failed to do, the people had offended YHWH. In theological parlance, these are sins of commission and omission, respectively. In the preceding section (9:6–10), Daniel made it clear that the people's sin was all-encompassing in participation—every Israelite everywhere, from the palace to the lands of exile, bore the shame. Here, he makes it clear that the people's sin is all-encompassing in scope—in everything they did and did not do, they violated the covenant. The curse was well deserved and even required by the terms of the covenant.[61]

The confession portion of Daniel's prayer (9:4–14) concludes with a summary in 9:14. YHWH kept

---

59. Newsom, *Daniel*, 295.
60. Joüon §125j. See also GKC §117m, where אֵת "introduces a noun with more or less emphasis."
61. While none of the violated laws are specifically cited, this "anthology of related laws" is "an essential element" of penitential prayers, "used in every case to explain the reason for judgment upon the people" (Boda, *Praying the Tradition*, 31).

watch (שקד) over the calamity and brought it upon the people (9:14a–b). The reason for this is found in 9:14c and 9:14e. While 9:14e is an independent clause, it could also make good contextual sense to read it as governed by the כִּי, "for," of 9:14c. Both clauses provide the reason for YHWH's action of bringing the curse: YHWH is righteous and we did not listen (i.e., obey) his voice. This is a summary of the confession. YHWH is righteous; we are utterly sinful and disgraced; the curse has rightly come upon us.

b. The Bridge (9:15a–16b)

The second subsection of Daniel's prayer begins in 9:15 with וְעַתָּה, "and now," a form that is often used in penitential prayers to mark "the transition from past to present."[62] In this case, Daniel has rehearsed the history of Israel's sin and now he prepares to move into supplication. Verses 15–16 comprise a transition from one to the other and, as such, contain elements of each. Daniel begins by invoking the name of God for the second time (9:15a–c), confessing his people's sin in summary (9:15d–e), and stating his principal request (9:16a), along with the bases for it (9:16a–b).

Daniel invokes the name of the "Lord our God." He began his prayer and confession with the invocation "Ah, Lord, the great and awesome God," followed by a clause further describing the nature of God (9:4d–e). This second invocation includes two dependent clauses describing past acts of God. In particular, Daniel notes that the "Lord our God" had "brought your people out from the land of Egypt with a strong hand" (9:15b). He is also the God who "made a name for yourself, as at this day" (9:15c)—the second time Daniel has said something is the case "as at this day." The first time it was the people's open shame (9:7b); here, in sharp contrast, it is the name that God has made for himself by acting on behalf of his people.

In these words of invocation, Daniel refers to the people of Israel as "your people," pleading that YHWH act on behalf of the people he brought out of Egypt. The deliverance from Egypt was the redemptive act in which YHWH established the grounds for the covenant he made with Israel at Sinai: he became their God and they his people (cf. Exod 20:2). It is noteworthy that this reference to Israel as "your people" is the first such reference in Daniel's prayer (9:15b; cf. 9:16b, 19f). Up to this point, Daniel has maintained a distance between YHWH and Israel, referring to Israel in terms of "we," "us," and "our." Used with respect to YHWH thus far, "your" has identified all the things that the people rebelled against: "your commandments and your judgments" (9:5e); "your servants" (9:6a); "your name" (9:6b); "your torah" (9:11a); "your voice" (9:11c); "your truth" (9:13e). Here Daniel reminds YHWH that he has acted in the past on behalf of his people, and he will ask that he do it again.[63]

Daniel again identifies with the people and their sin in his words of confession (9:15d–e), an abbreviation of his opening confession (9:5): "We have sinned" (חטא) and "been wicked" (רשע). Then in

---

62. Boda, *Praying the Tradition*, 30.
63. Of the expression "your people," Newsom notes that other texts use "this irrevocable relationship ... as a means of appeal to God to act for his own name's sake to rescue an undeserving people (cf. Deut 9:26–29; Ezek 20:22). Even though the people's sin is responsible for their devastation and thus the mockery to which they are subjected (Dan 9:16b), their own actions have also put at risk the honor of God, who might appear to be powerless to redeem them and to defeat the human enemies who have been the instruments of their punishment (cf. Ps 79:9–13). The appeal to God's honor is intensified in Dan 9:18–19, where twice it is emphasized that God's own name is attached to Jerusalem" (*Daniel*, 296).

9:16a, he provides the grounds for the requests he is going to make: "according to all your righteous acts . . ." Daniel had earlier professed that righteousness belonged to the Lord, a reference to his character (cf. 9:14c). Here he recalls God's deeds, his actions "on behalf of Israel when it is attacked or afflicted by oppressors in Egypt, in the wilderness, in the judges period, and in the exile" (Judg 5:11; 1 Sam 12:7; Isa 45:24; Mic 6:5; Ps 103:6).[64] Goldingay observes that Daniel's reference in 9:15b to the exodus, the act of righteousness in which YHWH "established his reputation for doing what is right . . . leads into the generalization about Yahweh's צדקת" in 9:16.[65] Further, as Towner notes, this appeal to the righteous acts "by which God founded and brought forth the nation is language proper for asking God now for a new public and universal manifestation of his saving nature. . . . Now the use of exodus language can establish the hope that God will save Israel after all and will restore her."[66]

According to YHWH's reputation for doing what is right, Daniel asks that he let his anger and wrath turn from his city, Jerusalem, the mountain of his holiness (9:16a). The combination of "anger" and "wrath" is hendiadys, intended to show the degree of YHWH's rage: "furious wrath" or "raging anger" (NET) captures the idea.

Then in 9:16b, Daniel provides both the reason for and result of YHWH's anger and wrath: generations of Israelite sin had caused it, and being a reproach to everyone around resulted from it. Implied in the statement that YHWH's city ("your city") and people ("your people") had become a reproach is another reason YHWH should act: his own honor and reputation. Daniel will make this appeal to YHWH's honor explicit in his full supplication to follow, but here he lays the foundation. When YHWH's city and YHWH's people look bad, YHWH looks bad.[67]

c. Supplication: "Please Listen" (9:17a–19f)

In 9:17 Daniel moves into his full supplication, the transitional וְעַתָּה, "and now" (9:17a), signaling the shift. The supplication includes three short sections that each revolve around the word שמע, "listen" (9:17, 18, 19). Just as שמע had characterized Daniel's confession, so it also typifies his supplication. However, the supplication incorporates wordplay with the word שמע, "to listen." In the confession, it referred to the people's failure to obey. In the supplication, it refers to YHWH's hearing the people's confession and responding in mercy. In the שמע of the confession and the שמע of the supplication, the prayer captures both the problem and the solution: the people's failure to "listen" necessitated YHWH's listening. Daniel's disobedient people desperately needed YHWH to hear their cry.

The first "listen" section is in 9:17, where Daniel makes two requests. First, he implores "our God" to "listen . . . to the prayer of your servant and to his supplications" (9:17a; cf. 1 Kgs 8:28). Daniel addresses God as "our God" and refers to himself as "your servant." He is speaking on behalf of the people, as a mediator between the people and their God. The second request is that God "shine

---

64. Goldingay, *Daniel*, 465.
65. Ibid.
66. Towner, *Daniel*, 138.
67. Moses made a similar plea in the aftermath of the golden calf incident when YHWH threatened to destroy the people: "Why should the Egyptians say, 'It was with evil intent that he brought them out, to kill them in the mountains and to wipe them off the face of the earth'?" (Exod 32:12; cf. Num 14:13–19).

your face upon your desolate sanctuary" (9:17b). The idiom of "shining one's face" means to show favor, and it is first used of God's favor in the Aaronic blessing (Num 6:25): "YHWH make his face shine on you and be gracious to you" (cf. also Pss 31:17[16]; 67:2[1]; 80:4, 8, 29[3, 7, 28]; 119:135). Here Daniel asks that God show favor on his desolate sanctuary—the temple in Jerusalem. He provides the reason for this request in the latter half of 9:17b: "for the sake of the Lord." Daniel makes explicit what was implicit in 9:16—namely, YHWH should restore his sanctuary for his own sake.

The second "listen" section is in 9:18, where Daniel asks God to both hear (שְׁמַע) and see (רְאֵה) by, first, making the hearing and seeing possible: "Incline your ear. . . . Open your eyes" (9:18a, 18c; cf. 1 Kgs 8:29). These are idiomatic expressions and common in the Old Testament, but they nonetheless suggest that from the perspective of the speaker, God has his ears turned away and his eyes closed (cf., e.g., 2 Kgs 19:16; Pss 17:6; 88:2; 119:18; Prov 22:17; Jer 11:8).[68] Daniel begs God to pay attention to "our desolations and the city" (9:18d), and he again implies the reason that God should pay attention by describing the city as the one "which your name is called over it" (9:18e): YHWH's reputation was at stake. The temple in Jerusalem was spoken of from the time of the wilderness wanderings, when Moses rehearsed the law for the second generation of Israelites out of Egypt in preparation for their renewal of the covenant at Moab (Deut 29–30; cf. Deut 12:5, 11, 14; 14:23, 25; 16:2). Its significance was that YHWH had brought the people out of bondage and kept his covenant with Abraham, Isaac, and Jacob so that he could live among them—he their God, and they his people. The Jerusalem temple represented the heart and soul of the covenant YHWH had initiated and implemented with the people of Israel. He had chosen them, and he had chosen the mount in Jerusalem. And by doing so, he had tied his reputation to those people and to that place. Daniel pleads with YHWH to act for the sake of his own name, and in the final clause of this second "listen" section, he repeats the grounds of his request: YHWH's great mercy (רַחֲמֶיךָ הָרַבִּים, 9:18g), not any merits of Daniel's people (9:18f).

The third "listen" section is in 9:19, and it consists of a series of four staccato requests, the first of which is "O Lord, please listen!" (אֲדֹנָי שְׁמָעָה). At the beginning of his prayer, Daniel had confessed the people's sin in four abrupt clauses (9:5a–d), and here he matches this with four abrupt requests.[69] He concludes these requests with a final plea that God not delay, and in that plea he repeats yet again the grounds of his request: "for your sake, my God, because your name is called over your city and over your people" (9:19e–f). As Goldingay observes, Daniel's supplication "is dominated by motive clauses and phrases that indicate the reasons why God should forgive and restore"[70]—that is, his for his own name's sake. Daniel had no grounds to appeal on Israel's account. After generations of Israel's brazen sin, only God's great mercy could overcome the damage that sin had done to his sanctuary, his city, and his people, and in overcoming it, God would restore the glory of his name.

---

68. Use of these expressions is another echo of Solomon's prayer of dedication. See, e.g., 1 Kgs 8:28, 29, 30, 32, 34, 36). Cf. also Neh 1:6.

69. These requests also reflect Solomon's dedicatory prayer (e.g., 1 Kgs 8:30, 32, 34, 36, 39, 50).

70. Goldingay, *Daniel*, 453.

3. The Revelation of Restoration (9:20a–27d)

Main Idea of the Passage

In Daniel 9:20–27 Gabriel comes to Daniel with a word of revelation in response to his supplication. He reveals to Daniel that the prophesied seventy years of exile were only part of a longer and greater "exile" for his people: seventy "weeks of years."

Literary Context

Daniel 9:20–27 is the third and final section of the narrative that comprises ch. 9. It follows the lengthy section in which Daniel confessed his people's sin and implored God to restore his people and his city for the sake of his own name (9:4–19). In this broader literary context, the third section functions in at least six ways. First, it provides a response to Daniel's prayer, albeit in a strange and difficult way. Second, it pulls together themes of the chapter, such as confession, intercession, and the desolation of Jerusalem and the temple. Third, it links the revelation of Dan 9 with the vision of Dan 8, with the desolation of the temple dominating both. Fourth, it offers an expanded interpretation of Jeremiah's seventy-year prophecy that lays out a pattern for the future. Fifth, its emphasis on the determined nature of events to come reinforces the comfort of Dan 8 that, no matter how desperate the times may be, God has evil on a leash. Finally, its subtle incorporation of Jubilee concepts suggests hope for the future.

> B. Narrative 2: Repentance and God's Promise of Restoration (9:1a–27d)
>   1. The Context of Repentance (9:1a–3b)
>   2. Daniel's Prayer of Repentance (9:4a–19f)
> → **3. The Revelation of Restoration (9:20a–27d)**

Translation and Exegetical Outline

(See pages 476–77.)

Daniel 9:20a–27d

20a		"And while I was speaking
20b		and praying
20c		and confessing my sin and the sin of my people, Israel,
20d		and presenting my supplication before YHWH my God on behalf of the holy mountain of my God—
21a		while I was speaking in prayer,
21bα		the man Gabriel…
21c		whom I had seen in the vision at the beginning,
21d		wearied with weariness,
21bβ		…approached me at the time of the evening offering.
22a		He instructed
22b		and he spoke with me,
22c		and he said,
22d		'Daniel, now I have come forth
22e		to instruct you in understanding.
23a		At the beginning of your supplication,
23b		a word went out,
23c		and I, even I, came
23d		to declare [it],
23e		for you are treasured.
23f		Consider the word,
23g		and understand the vision.

3. The Revelation of Restoration (9:20a–27d)

  a. The Setting and the Agent (9:20a–21d)

  b. Gabriel's Revelation (9:22a–27d)

   (1) The Reason for the Revelation (9:22a–23g)

(2) The Seventy Weeks (9:24a–27d)

24a	Seventy weeks are determined for your people and for your holy city
24b	to finish the transgression,
24c	and to make an end of sin,
24d	and to atone for iniquity,
24e	and to bring in everlasting righteousness,
24f	and to seal up vision and prophet
24g	and to anoint a holy of holies.
25a	Know
25b	and understand:
25cα	From the going out of a word . . .
25d	to restore
25e	and to build Jerusalem
25cβ	. . . until an anointed one, a ruler, will be seven weeks.
25f	And for sixty-two weeks it will be rebuilt with a plaza and a moat, but in distressed times.
26a	And after the sixty-two weeks, an anointed one will be cut off
26b	and have nothing.
26c	And the city and the holy place, the people of the ruler who is coming will destroy,
26d	and its end will come with a flood.
26e	And until (the) end will be war,
26f	desolations are determined.
27a	He will confirm a covenant for the many for one week.
27b	But in the middle of the week he will stop sacrifice and offering,
27c	and upon the wing of abominations will be a desolator,
27d	until complete destruction—one that is decreed—pours out on the desolater."

Structure and Literary Form

The third section of the narrative in Dan 9 (9:20–27) continues and concludes Daniel's first-person report of the penitential prayer he offered on behalf of his people in response to what he understood from Jeremiah's prophecies concerning the length of exile. This third section details the revelation Daniel received in response to his prayer, and it consists of two subsections: 9:20–21 and 9:22–27.

The first subsection (9:20–21) begins with a pair of repetitious temporal clauses that establish the timing of the revelation: "and while I was speaking . . ." (וְעוֹד אֲנִי . . . מְדַבֵּר, 9:20a, 21a). Following this temporal setting, Daniel introduces the agent of the revelation, "the man Gabriel" (9:21bα).

The second subsection (9:22–27) is the content of Gabriel's revelation, beginning with the quotative frame for his speech (9:22a–c). Gabriel first provides the reason for his presence and for the word (דָבָר) he was sent to declare (9:22d–23). Then he declares the vision (מַרְאֶה, 9:23g) that Daniel was to consider and understand: the word regarding the "seventy weeks" (שָׁבֻעִים שִׁבְעִים, 9:24a) decreed for Daniel's people (9:24–27).

The entire section of 9:20–27 is shaded on the charts because it still represents Daniel's reported speech. However, Gabriel's revelation as recounted by Daniel is demarcated as embedded reported speech and so indents every independent clause once and indents dependent clauses beyond that, according to how they relate to their respective independent clauses.

Explanation of the Text

a. The Setting and the Agent (9:20a–21d)

The main clause of the subsection in 9:20–21 is 9:21b: "the man Gabriel . . . approached me." However, before Daniel provides this information, he sets the context with a lengthy series of temporal clauses (9:20a–21a). The first four clauses (9:20a–d) are each governed by the temporal adverb עוֹד, "still" (9:20a), while 9:21a repeats in summary form the clauses of 9:20. In these clauses, Daniel establishes that what follows happened while he was "still" (עוֹד) engaged in all the activities of the previous section (9:4–19): "speaking . . . praying . . . confessing . . . and presenting my supplication" (. . . מְדַבֵּר מִתְפַּלֵּל . . . מִתְוַדֶּה . . . מַפִּיל תְּחִנָּתִי, 9:20a–d). Collins says 9:20 echoes the language of Daniel's prayer and serves as a summary,[71] but it does more than that. If the purpose was merely to summarize, 9:21a would have sufficed ("while I was still speaking in prayer," וְעוֹד אֲנִי מְדַבֵּר בַּתְּפִלָּה), or Daniel could have simply said he prayed, confessed, and presented supplications (cf. 9:3, 4a–c, 17a). Instead, 9:20 includes

---

71. Collins, *Daniel*, 351.

overspecifying details that recall the main themes of Daniel's prayer.

In 9:20c Daniel says he was confessing his own sin and that of his people, Israel. In this statement, Daniel reiterates his identification with his people, owning their sin as his. Israel's offense is corporate, and Daniel stands in solidarity with his people as he intercedes for them. His position as intercessor is highlighted first by his reference to "Israel" as "my people" (עַמִּי) in 9:20c and then in his subsequent reference to YHWH as "YHWH my God" in 9:20d. Goldingay explains:

> When Israel is "my people," the pronoun usually refers to Yahweh. In prayer, they would normally be "your people": so vv. 15, 16, 19 (as Daniel speaks of "your city" and "your sanctuary" in vv. 16, 17, 19). The expression indicates Yahweh's special relationship with Israel, which is fundamental to the basis on which one prays for them. On the other hand, Yahweh can use the expression "your people" in speaking to their representative (Exod 32:7; 34:10; contrast 32:11, 12; 33:13, 16); he is then dissociating himself from them. Here Daniel takes the initiative in identifying himself with the people whom Yahweh has every ground for repudiating. His speaking of them as "my people" links to his addressing Yahweh on their behalf as "my God." It is by their association with him that he commends them to Yahweh. Daniel belongs to that company of persons such as Israel's ancestors, the prophets, kings, priests, and heavenly beings whose prayer can be expected to find a hearing with God. . . . He prays as one who is *persona grata* with Yahweh, though the passage does not quite make the explicit assumption that an intercessor's personal merits may "count" on behalf of people for whom he prays.[72]

Daniel also reiterates the reason for his request: "the holy mountain of my God" (9:20d; cf. 9:16a, 17b, 19f). At the center of Daniel's prayer was the issue of YHWH's reputation—for the city, temple, and people that he had chosen for his own name's sake (cf. 9:15c, 16, 17b, 18d–e, 19e–f). The reason YHWH should act is that his name was at stake. Israel's longstanding sin had made Jerusalem, his holy mountain (where his name dwelled), the target of his anger and his wrath (9:16). Daniel says, "It is our fault! We, Israel, deserve your wrath, but act in mercy for the sake of Jerusalem."

After the lengthy temporal reference of 9:20, Daniel repeats the adverb עוֹד, "while," in 9:21a in a repetitious summary of 9:20: "I was speaking in prayer" (אֲנִי מְדַבֵּר בַּתְּפִלָּה; cf. 9:20a–b). The purpose of this restatement is likely to refocus the reader on "the synchronicity of the prayer and the arrival of the angel" after the lengthy detail of 9:20c–d.[73] The synchronicity itself suggests that the coming of "the man Gabriel" may be a response to Daniel's prayer, and the repetition of the temporal reference supports the idea (cf. 9:22–23 where Gabriel himself says as much).

The main clause in 9:21b is separated into two sections—the subject ("the man Gabriel") in 9:21bα, and the predicate ("approached me at the time of the evening offering") in 9:21bβ. Between these parts is a relative clause overspecifying the identity of the subject, Gabriel: "whom I had seen in the vision at the beginning" (9:21c), followed by an adverbial clause describing Daniel when he saw Gabriel at that time (מֻעָף בִּיעָף, "wearied with weariness," 9:21d).[74] Gabriel had appeared to Daniel in his vision of ch. 8, which is probably what "at the beginning" refers to here (see NASB, NIV). When he first saw Gabriel in Dan 8, Daniel was terrified

---

72. Goldingay, *Daniel*, 470–71.
73. Newsom, *Daniel*, 297.

74. The Hebrew expression מֻעָף בִּיעָף translated here as "in my extreme weariness" is difficult. There are at least three ways

and required an angelic touch for strengthening (Dan 8:17–18), but here, he simply reports the angel's arrival. Thus, the point of overspecifying his identity may be to explain Daniel's lack of surprise and terror at the presence of an angel. A secondary reason for the overspecification may be to connect the visions of Dan 8 and Dan 9. In his earlier vision, Daniel had witnessed the desolation of the Jerusalem temple under Antiochus IV Epiphanes. Here Gabriel will reveal more to him about that future time.

Daniel includes another temporal reference in 9:21bβ when he notes that Gabriel approached him "at the time of the evening offering." This reference to the second daily sacrifice that would have been offered in the Jerusalem temple connects the revelation to come in 9:24–27, which is concerned with the disruption of sacrifice, and the vision of Dan 8, which involved taking away the daily sacrifice (8:11–12) for 2,300 "evenings and mornings," a reference to the sacrifices missed during the time of the temple's desolation. Newsom observes that "in the Second Temple period the 'time of the evening sacrifice' (Exod 29:41; Lev 6:20[13]; Num 28:4; 2 Kgs 16:15) came to be seen as a particularly appropriate and efficacious time to offer prayer (Ezra 9:4–5; Jdt 9:1; cf. Luke 1:10)."[75] Additionally, in the context of Dan 9, this reference to the temple recalls the focus in Daniel's prayer on YHWH's city, holy mountain, and sanctuary.

The revelation that follows also falls within the time and "place" of the entire narrative of Dan 9 established in the opening verses of the chapter: the first year of Darius as Daniel was considering YHWH's word to Jeremiah the prophet regarding the "fullness of the desolation of Jerusalem" (9:1–2). The allusions in 9:20–21 to the Jerusalem temple (9:20d and 9:21bβ) reflect what Collins calls "the preoccupation with the disrupted cult,"[76] but such preoccupation is easily explained by the time and "place" of Dan 9—namely, the verge of promised restoration.

b. Gabriel's Revelation (9:22a–27d)

The second subsection of the passage in Dan 9:20–27 includes the content of Gabriel's revelation, and it begins with Daniel's quotative frame introducing Gabriel's embedded speech: "he instructed and he spoke with me, and he said" (וַיָּבֶן וַיְדַבֵּר עִמִּי וַיֹּאמַר, 9:22a–c). The first two verbs should be read as verbal hendiadys and so could be translated "he explained." The verb בין, "to discern, understand," first appeared in Dan 9 in Daniel's statement about what he "understood [בִּינֹתִי] in the scrolls" (9:2), and Gabriel will use the nominal form בִּינָה in his explanation of why he has come (9:22e). Then he will use the verb twice more in his exhortation to Daniel to "consider" (בִּין) and "understand" (הָבֵן) what he is going to reveal (9:23f–g). The same verb

---

scholars have made sense of it: (1) "in my extreme weariness" (e.g., NASB; cf. NET), where the two Hebrew forms derive from the same root, i.e., יעף, meaning "to be weary." In this case מֻעָף is a *hophal* participle ("to be weary or faint") and בִּיעָף is a בְּ preposition on the noun יְעָף ("weariness, faintness"). Grammatically, the phrase could refer to Gabriel or Daniel, but the word order suggests Daniel is the referent (Goldingay, *Daniel*, 446; cf. Miller 1994, 250–51). (2) "in swift flight" (ESV, NIV, NRSV), where the two Hebrew forms derive from the root עוף, "to fly." מֻעָף is still a *hophal* participle, and בִּיעָף is the בְּ preposition on "an otherwise unattested nominal by-form" of the root עוף (Newsom, *Daniel*, 285; cf. Lucas, *Daniel*, 229; Collins 1993, 352). (3) "being made to fly in weariness" (Young, *The Prophecy of Daniel*, 189–90), where מֻעָף derives from עוף, "to fly," while בִּיעָף is a בְּ preposition on a noun derived from יעף, "to be weary." The latter two options, both involving Gabriel's flight, seem unlikely given the word "man" to describe Gabriel's appearance in v. 21bα. For the initial description of Gabriel as a "man," see Dan 8:15–16.

75. Newsom, *Daniel*, 298.
76. Collins, *Daniel*, 352.

is used with respect to Gabriel's interpretation of Daniel's vision in ch. 8. Gabriel was commanded to "explain" (הָבֵן) the vision to Daniel (8:16d), and then Gabriel instructed Daniel to "understand" (הָבֵן) that the vision was for an end time (8:17f). Daniel 8 concluded with the statement that Daniel was appalled by what he had seen, but "there was no one to explain" (וְאֵין מֵבִין, 8:27f).

The thematic importance of the root בין (as well as שׂכל) in the book of Daniel, and especially in the apocalyptic portion, becomes clear near the end of the book's final revelation. Newsom observes that in the visions of Dan 8 and Dan 9, angelic interpreters are the ones explaining (בין), but in Dan 11:33–34 the ones explaining (בין) are the "wise" (*maśkîlîm*; מַשְׂכִּילִים); thus the angel who is able to interpret for Daniel the hidden meaning of visions and texts is the model for the "wise," who will similarly bring understanding to the people during the Antiochene persecution.[77]

Gabriel's embedded speech begins in 9:22d and continues through the end of the chapter (9:27). He starts by addressing Daniel by name, the first character to do so since Darius called to him after his night in the lion's den (see on 6:21[20]).[78] The use of the vocative is not semantically necessary since it is clear in the text who is being addressed, so its use here may serve as a call to pay attention to the important information that follows.[79]

Gabriel first explains why he has come—namely, to instruct Daniel in understanding (לְהַשְׂכִּילְךָ בִינָה). As noted, Gabriel similarly instructed Daniel in Dan 8, but there he was explaining a vision (8:16–17). Daniel has not had a vision in ch. 9; rather, he had been considering the prophecies of Jeremiah regarding the end of exile, and in response, he had prayed for forgiveness and restoration—for the end of the prophesied seventy-year exile. Thus, it is not immediately clear what Gabriel will be explaining.

Before getting to the content of the revelation, Gabriel further explains his presence. The initial clause of 9:23 is temporal: "At the beginning of your supplication" (בִּתְחִלַּת תַּחֲנוּנֶיךָ, 9:23a). This clause situates the main clauses that follow in 9:23b–c and indicates that Gabriel's presence and the revelation he will give are related to Daniel's prayer: "a word went out, and I, even I, came" (יָצָא דָבָר וַאֲנִי בָּאתִי, 9:23b–c). Specifically, Gabriel sets the time of the word going out at the beginning of Daniel's supplication (תַּחֲנוּנֶיךָ), not simply the beginning of his prayer. While supplication is part of prayer, Daniel himself seems to distinguish between his supplication and the rest of his prayer, which is primarily comprised of confession (9:3b, 4, 17a, 18f, 20b–d). If this distinction is in play in Gabriel's words, then the word went out after Daniel confessed the sins of his people, in accordance with what Moses had said needed to happen for restoration (Lev 26:40–43).

Gabriel also provides a reason for the message and his appearance in 9:23e, when he says, "for you are treasured." Newsom says Daniel's actions showed him "to be worthy of understanding."[80] The presence of the semantically unnecessary אֲנִי, "I," before the verb בָּאתִי, "I came," in 9:23c also suggests this before Gabriel says it: Daniel prayed and a *divine being* appeared to give him insight. With full knowledge of the rest of the chapter, we know that Daniel's prayer for restoration will not be answered in quite the way he was hoping. That God sent Gabriel simply to explain this to him demonstrates how treasured and unique Daniel was.[81]

Gabriel's introductory words conclude with his

---

77. Newsom, *Daniel*, 298.
78. The only other character who will address Daniel by name is the figure in Dan 10, a divine being that many consider to be Gabriel. See below on Dan 10:10–20.
79. Runge and Westbury, *LDHB: Introduction*, 2.3 Thematic Address.
80. Newsom, *Daniel*, 298.
81. Cf. also Dan 10:11, 19.

exhortation to Daniel in 9:23f–g that he should "consider the word and understand the vision." Just as Daniel had originally considered and understood (בִּינֹתִי, 9:2b) the word of YHWH (דְבַר־יְהוָה, 9:2c) to Jeremiah about the years of exile, he should now consider and understand (הָבֵן/בִין, 9:23f–g) the word (דָּבָר, 9:23b, 23f) that went out and that Gabriel has come to declare.

Gabriel's revelation begins by recalling Daniel's reflection on the prophecies of Jeremiah. Daniel had concluded his reflection with the phrase שִׁבְעִים שָׁנָה, "seventy years" (9:2d), and Gabriel's revelation begins with שָׁבֻעִים שִׁבְעִים, "seventy weeks" (9:24a). Most scholars understand these "weeks" to mean "weeks of years," making "seventy weeks" equivalent to seventy times seven years—i.e., 490 years.[82] Background for the idea of "weeks" meaning "weeks of years" is found in Lev 25, where YHWH instructs Moses about the Sabbath Year and the Year of Jubilee—ideas many scholars see in the revelation of the Seventy Weeks. After six years of working the land, the Israelites were to let it rest for during the seventh year as "a sabbath to YHWH" (Lev 25:2, 4). Then they were to "count off seven sabbath years—seven times seven years—so that the seven sabbath years amount to a period of forty-nine years" (Lev 25:8). The fiftieth year was the Year of Jubilee—a year in which debts were canceled, slaves were freed, and land was restored to its original owners. After these instructions about Sabbath Year and the Year of Jubilee in Lev 25, the next chapter entails reminders of the rewards for covenant obedience and, more relevant to the context of Dan 9, the sevenfold punishment that would result from disobedience (Lev 26:18, 21, 24, 28; see on Dan 9:11–13 above). The revelation of Dan 9:24–27 intertwines ideas of covenant, punishment, exile, restoration, and Jubilee.

Gabriel brings a revelation that reinterprets Jeremiah's prophecy. Daniel had been concerned about seventy years, but Gabriel's revelation is concerned with *weeks* of years. Gabriel's words do not contradict Jeremiah's prophecy, but instead "disclos[e] a hidden meaning."[83] Anderson calls this hidden meaning a hallmark of apocalypticism:

> The seventy years predicted by Jeremiah are not to be taken at face value. The real meaning lies below

---

82. Scholars widely agree in their understanding of the "weeks" of Dan 9:24 as a reference to "weeks of years" totaling 490 years (but see Sidney Greidanus, *Preaching Christ from Daniel: Foundations for Expository Sermons* [Grand Rapids: Eerdmans, 2012], 297–98n31). However, they differ in their views of whether the numbers in the Seventy Weeks should be understood literally, symbolically, or in some combination of both. If the numbers are understood literally, then the prophecy fits within a schema of roughly 490 years, depending how literal the numbers are. (See Collins, *Daniel*, 352–53, and Miller, *Daniel*, 253–58 for perspectives that are primarily literal.) If the numbers are understood symbolically, then there is some flexibility in identifying the historical referents. However, there are also different views on how "literal" the symbolism is (i.e., should the sixty-two weeks comprise a proportionately longer period of time than the seven weeks or is the actual time irrelevant? (See Baldwin, *Daniel*, 195–97, and Newsom, *Daniel*, 299–301, for symbolic perspectives on the numbers.) Scholars who take the numbers to be symbolic point out that even non-apocalyptic Old Testament texts use "seventy" and "seven" to represent fullness or totality, a symbolism also common in the literature of the ancient Near East. Additionally, since apocalyptic literature is characteristically symbolic, one might expect the numbers to be symbolic. Other apocalyptic literature of the Second Temple period even uses the symbolism of "weeks" to structure history (e.g., in 1 Enoch there are seventy generations from the flood to the end, and a Qumran text uses seventy "weeks" to structure the same period of time; in the Testament of Levi a portion of history is segmented into seventy weeks; in Jubilees, all of human history is structured according to ten Jubilees, or 490 years. See Goldingay, *Daniel*, 451). That Daniel's Seventy Weeks are best understood symbolically seems clear enough from its integration of ideas from Jeremiah and Leviticus (cf. later 2 Chr 36). However, in God's providential control of history, 490 years also roughly corresponds to the length of time between Daniel and Antiochus IV.

83. Newsom, *Daniel*, 299. Newsom describes some accepted exegetical practices that may explain Gabriel's interpretation: "One possible hermeneutical key to Gabriel's interpretation is that of double reading. Since the Hebrew of the time was

the surface. This is the hallmark of apocalypticism. For the divinely enlightened, in this instance, it is not merely seventy years but seventy weeks of years.... [This interpretation] comes only as the result of fresh inspiration, divinely ordained. This is the secret and the stance of the apocalyptist.[84]

This fresh, divinely ordained inspiration delivered by Gabriel is that the end of the seventy-year exile predicted by Jeremiah and prayed for by Daniel was just a small part of an even greater seventy—"seventy 'sevens'" (9:24). While Daniel prayed for restoration, Gabriel foretells a fresh devastation for his people, for the holy city, and especially for the temple. However, while the combination of seventy and seven in the Seventy Weeks suggests that this new devastation represented the sevenfold punishment of Lev 26, the backdrop of Lev 25:8 also hints that the restoration would be multiplied. YHWH had instructed his people to celebrate a Year of Jubilee after "seven sabbaths of years" (49 years), a time of canceled debts, freedom, and restoration. In the 490 years of the Seventy Weeks is a tenfold Jubilee after a sevenfold season of chastisement.

In 9:24a, Gabriel refers to the Jews and Jerusalem as "your people ... your holy city." Daniel had been praying on behalf of *God's* people and *God's* city (9:19f), but as their intercessor, he held God's people and God's city "near [his] heart, dear and precious unto [him]."[85] Since the Jews were God's people, they were his people, and Jerusalem was his city.

This initial revelation is followed by six infinitival clauses in which Gabriel identifies six purposes for the Seventy Weeks (9:24b–g). The significance of this list is evident by its length, its placement before the main part of the prophecy (9:25–27), and its expansive nature. While some of the purposes roughly correspond to the historical circumstances under Antiochus IV Epiphanes, they also transcend them in eschatological expectations—much as Daniel's earlier visions had. These purposes give Jeremiah's prophecy a theological and cosmic dimension that centered "around the temple and its sanctity, rather than the land and the people (though the question of sin is central in both prophecies), and [referred] to an apocalyptic end time, not just the return of the exiles."[86]

The first three clauses address the problem of "the transgression" (הַפֶּשַׁע, 9:24b), "sin" (חַטָּאת, 9:24c), and "iniquity" (עָוֹן, 9:24d). The use of הַפֶּשַׁע, "the transgression" (9:24b), recalls "the transgression" of Dan 8. There it referred to Antiochus IV's desecration of the Jerusalem temple (see on Dan 8:12–13 above), which was permitted for just a time. Similarly, the revelation of Dan 9:24b indicates הַפֶּשַׁע, "the transgression," will end. The two purposes that follow this—making an end of sin

---

written only consonantally, the letters for the word 'seventy' and the letters for 'weeks' look the same, and the consonants of Jeremiah's prophecy, šb'ym, could be pronounced either šib'îm ("seventy") or šābū'îm ("sevens," "weeks"). The potential for double reading was undoubtedly activated by another hermeneutical practice, that of interpreting one text in light of another. Leviticus 26:18 (cf. v. 28) is one possible intertext. There, in the context of promised blessings and threats for covenant obedience or disobedience, God declares that he will punish the people 'sevenfold' because they did not listen. Thus Jeremiah's seventy years can be multiplied by seven, and one might translate the rest of the line as '[they] are decreed *against* ['*al*] your people and your holy city' (so Montgomery 373)" (*Daniel*, 299). She also discusses the influence of 2 Chr 36 on the Seventy Weeks prophecy (*Daniel*, 300).

84. R. A. Anderson, *Signs and Wonders: A Commentary on the Book of Daniel* (Grand Rapids: Eerdmans, 1984), 111.

85. Otto Zöckler, *A Commentary on the Holy Scriptures: Daniel*, eds., J. P. Lange et al., trans. James Strong (Bellingham, WA: Logos Bible Software, 2008), 194.

86. Lester L. Grabbe, "'The End of the Desolations of Jerusalem': From Jeremiah's 70 Years to Daniel's 70 Weeks of Years," in *Early Jewish and Christian Exegesis: Studies in Memory of William Hugh Brownlee*, ed. C. A. Evans and W. F. Stinespring (Atlanta: Scholars Press, 1987), 68.

(לְהָתֵם חַטָּאת, 9:24c) and atoning for iniquity (לְכַפֵּר עָוֹן, 9:24d)—may include Antiochus's offenses, but since Daniel just confessed both in his prayer (9:5a–b, 13d, 16b), it seems more likely that the sin and iniquity of the Jews is the referent.[87] While Antiochus would be destroyed, the Jews would be punished and then redeemed.

With the problems associated with sin addressed by the first three infinitival clauses, the remaining three are positive in nature. The first is "to bring in everlasting righteousness" (9:24e), a purpose that may have been partly fulfilled when the desecrated temple was restored (i.e., made right or legitimate) in 164 BCE by the Maccabees (cf. 8:14). The second is "to seal up vision and prophet" (9:24f) and reflects the ancient Near Eastern practice of placing a seal on a rolled up document to preserve it (cf. 8:26) and to verify the authenticity of the sender. The sixth and final purpose of the Seventy Weeks is "to anoint a holy of holies" (לִמְשֹׁחַ קֹדֶשׁ קָדָשִׁים, 9:24g), which may have its first historical referent in the restored temple of 164 BCE.

While these purposes are focused on Israel and Jerusalem, they also likely speak "of the accomplishment of God's purposes for history"[88] and provide what Collins calls "an eschatological ideal."[89] Making an end of sin and bringing in everlasting righteousness, especially, transcend the events of the second century BCE, and the language in 9:26d that "its end will come with a flood" recalls both the global destruction of the Genesis flood and the final battle of Gog and Magog.[90] The Seventy Weeks had its first fulfillment in Antiochus IV, but he was only a "pale foreshadowing"[91] of greater evil to come. This pattern in the book of Daniel begins with Belshazzar, whose evil was superseded by Antiochus, whose evil would also be superseded. Such patterning is common in the Bible and is usually referred to as typology—that is, portraying one figure in the light of a predecessor. Neither Belshazzar nor Antiochus were the first of their kind. That (dis)honor goes to Adam, the first "king" who defied God (Ezek 28). The Seventy Weeks is both a prophecy and a pattern. God will accomplish his purposes for humanity when history repeats itself for the last, and worst, time.

Having established the purposes of the Seventy Weeks, Gabriel again calls Daniel to know and understand (תֵּדַע וְתַשְׂכֵּל) what is to follow (9:25a–b; cf. 9:23f–g).[92] This admonition to "know and understand" is a metacomment—a speaker's pause in the flow of information to comment on what he or she is about to say. In English, a speaker might say, "Listen," or "I want you to know that . . ."[93]

---

87. Lucas cautions against making a "simplistic distinction . . . between the sins of Israel and those of her oppressors in Dan. 9:24" (*Daniel*, 242). He cites approvingly Porteous's (*Daniel*, 140–41) comment: "It is important to notice that the writer intends to imply that an end will be brought, not only to the wickedness of Antiochus, but also to the rebellion of Israel," and he observes that Dan 11:30–35 and 12:12 will refer to Jews who supported Antiochus (*Daniel*, 242).

88. Baldwin, *Daniel*, 169.

89. Collins, *Daniel*, 353.

90. Wells and Sumner, *Esther and Daniel*, 191.

91. Lucas specifically uses this expression to refer to Belshazzar (*Daniel*, 222), but it applies here as well.

92. Would that Gabriel had provided a few more details for later interpreters trying to "know and understand" the Seventy Weeks. Daniel 9:24–27 is easily the most difficult section in the book of Daniel and one of the most controversial texts in the entire Bible. It is impossible and unnecessary to detail the many views in this commentary, so I will offer what I consider to be the best reading and note particular difficulties in footnotes. See John H. Walton, "Views Concerning Daniel's 70 Weeks" in *Chronological and Background Charts of the Old Testament* (Grand Rapids: Zondervan, 1994), 106, for a helpful overview of the main interpretive options. See also Miller, *Daniel*, 252–57, for a description of four representative views.

93. Runge and Westbury, *LDHB: Introduction*, 1.3 Metacomments. For other Old Testament examples, see Moses's "See" in Exod 33:12 and "Hear" in Deut 6:4; and Joseph's oath, "by the life of Pharaoh," in Gen 42:15–16. See also on Dan 3:18 above.

These clauses are semantically unnecessary but are the speaker's way of emphasizing the importance of what is about to be said.

What is about to be said is the prophecy itself, broken into three time frames, each punctuated with a significant event that involves the root מׁשח, "to anoint": seven weeks and the coming of an anointed one (9:25c);[94] sixty-two weeks and the cutting off a second anointed one (9:26a–b);[95] and a final week in which a covenant is confirmed but broken at midweek before the end comes (9:27). The conclusion of this final week and the entire Seventy Weeks is described in 9:24—namely, when the purposes (and specifically the last one, "to anoint a holy of holies") of the Seventy Weeks have been accomplished.[96] This repetition of the root מׁשח, "to anoint," and its use to signal the end of "each slice of history"[97] reinforce an important theme of the vision: the temple and the priesthood, both central to the life of postexilic Jews, who no longer lived under a Davidic king.[98]

Gabriel addresses the first seven weeks in 9:25a–e. The main clause is verbless and is comprised of the two parts of 9:25c: the lengthy subject is "From the going out of a word . . . until an anointed one, a ruler" (מִן־מֹצָא דָבָר . . . עַד־מָשִׁיחַ נָגִיד), and the predicate is "seven weeks" (שָׁבֻעִים שִׁבְעָה). The two infinitive clauses of 9:25d–e contain the content of the דָבָר, "word," that went out: "to restore and to build Jerusalem.". These infinitive verbs comprise a verbal hendiadys—that is, the "word" was to rebuild Jerusalem.

There is little agreement among scholars about the referent for this "word" to rebuild Jerusalem, but the context of the chapter may be helpful. The word דָבָר occurs several times in Dan 9. In 9:2c, Daniel refers to the דְבַר־יְהוָה, "word of YHWH," to Jeremiah, and in 9:12a, he speaks of the "word" (דְבָרוֹ) God spoke against Israel. Most relevantly, in 9:23b, Gabriel refers to the "word" (דָבָר) that "went out" (יצא; cf. 9:23f). Thus, all occurrences of דָבָר, "word," in Dan 9 prior to 9:25 refer to words of YHWH. It makes good contextual sense to understand the "word" in 9:25 as also being the word of YHWH, and specifically the word to Jeremiah that prompted the events of the entire chapter (9:2c).[99]

From this word until the appearance of "an anointed one, a ruler" (מָשִׁיחַ נָגִיד) would be seven

---

94. Interpreters disagree about whether to read the seven weeks and the sixty-two weeks in Dan 9:25cβ–f as one unit of time (e.g., NIV, NASB, KJV) or two (e.g., ESV, NRSV). One's understanding of how to read these time periods determines how the Seventy Weeks relate to the life and ministry of Jesus. If the seven and sixty-two comprise one period of time, then the "anointed ones" of v. 25 and v. 26 are the same person: Jesus (e.g., NIV, NASB, KJV). If the two timeframes are read as distinct periods of time, then the "anointed ones" have different referents, and neither is Jesus. (This latter reading does not preclude the belief that Jesus was the Messiah; it only means that the Seventy Weeks prophecy does not refer directly to his life and ministry.)

The debate arises from whether one accepts the Masoretic accents as faithful to the intention of the original Hebrew text or whether one considers them to represent a later scribal addition by Jews who wanted to counter the Christian messianic interpretation of the Seventy Weeks. For a defense of the first view, see Thomas McComiskey, "The Seventy 'Weeks' of Daniel against the Background of Ancient Near Eastern Literature," *WTJ* (1985) 47:18–45; for a defense of the second view, see Roger T. Beckwith, "Daniel 9 and the Date of Messiah's Coming in Essene, Hellenistic, Pharisaic, Zealot and Early Christian Computation," *Revue de Qumrân* 40 (1981): 521–42. Either reading is possible, but my view is that reading the time periods as distinct is the better reading. However, I also consider it possible that the ambiguity is intentional and significant; see further below, "Jesus *in* the Seventy Weeks" (489–93).

95. Translations of מָשִׁיחַ in vv. 25–26 as "the Anointed One," "Messiah," and "the Messiah" (e.g., KJV, NIV, NASB) suggest the presence of the definite article on מָשִׁיחַ that is not in the Hebrew (i.e., הַמָשִׁיחַ), where both anointed ones are indefinite: "an anointed one."

96. Lacocque, *The Book of Daniel*, 194.
97. Ibid.
98. See p. 487n106 below on the history of postexilic Judah.
99. There are three basic interpretations of what the "word" in v. 25c refers to: one of Jeremiah's prophecies, a decree of Persian kings, or Gabriel's word of revelation (cf. v. 23). With respect to the "word" being one of Jeremiah's prophecies, scholars

weeks, an echo of the instructions about the Year of Jubilee in Lev 25. "Seven times seven years," or forty-nine years, was "the maximum period that land could be alienated from its ancestral heirs or that a person could be kept in indentured slavery,"[100] a key idea as the captive Daniel reflected on the years his people had been alienated from the land of promise. Given the symbolism of Jubilee behind the first seven weeks, we expect the מָשִׁיחַ, "anointed one," who appears at the end of the "seven 'sevens'" to have a role in the restoration of Israel's land. While a מָשִׁיחַ, "anointed one," in the Old Testament can refer to a prophet (e.g., 1 Kgs 19:16), a king (e.g., 1 Sam 24:7), a priest (e.g., Lev 4:3), and even a gentile king (i.e., Cyrus in Isa 45:1), the centrality of the temple in Dan 9 (and the rest of Daniel's visions) suggests the מָשִׁיחַ of 9:25cβ is a priest. Among the known figures associated with the return from captivity, Joshua the high priest is the best candidate for the first מָשִׁיחַ of the Seventy Weeks.[101] The overspecification that this מָשִׁיחַ is also a ruler (נָגִיד, 9:25cβ) may reflect the importance that the temple and the priesthood would assume during the Second Temple period, when the Jews were still subjects of foreign kings, the Hasmonean dynasty excepting.[102]

The second period of time is sixty-two weeks (9:25f–26b), a period of time with no significance other than filling the time between the first seven weeks and the final week.[103] Of the three periods of time in the Seventy Weeks (seven weeks, sixty-two weeks, one week), Newsom notes, "Only the first and last are of interpretive significance. The middle section is simply what remains after the times of significance have been subtracted."[104] During this time, Jerusalem would be completely restored, including "its socioeconomic infrastructures and its defensive system"—that is, from its plazas (the commercial hubs of ancient Near Eastern cities) to its defensive moats.[105]

Despite this restoration, Gabriel characterizes the sixty-two weeks as "distressed times" (9:25f).

---

note that דָּבָר "frequently denotes prophetic word, but almost never means 'decree,'" for which the word *dāt* would be expected (McComiskey, "The Seventy 'Weeks' of Daniel," 26). The exact prophecy was either about the seventy years of exile (Jer 25:12 [605 BCE]; Jer 29:10 [597 BCE]) or the future restoration (Jer 30:18–22; 31:38–40 [587 BCE]). If the "word" refers to a royal Persian decree, there are four options: (1) the decree of Cyrus in 539 BCE (Ezra 1:1–4); (2) the decree of Darius I in 521 BCE (Ezra 6:1–12); (3) the decree of Artaxerxes I in 458 BCE (Ezra 7:12–26); (4) the decree of Artaxerxes II in 445 BCE (Neh 2:7–9). For discussion of these options, see Lucas, *Daniel*, 242–43. The third position—that the "word" in v. 25 is the same as the "word" in v. 23—is argued by Collins (*Daniel*, 354–55), who says this makes the best sense in the context. I like Collins's thinking here, but agree with Newsom that if Daniel's prayer/confession triggers the start of the Seventy Weeks, this would seem to "trivialize the prophetic word that Daniel had been pondering, which seems unlikely" (*Daniel*, 304). Young (*The Prophecy of Daniel*, 201–203) takes a "both/and" position, agreeing in part with Collins that the referent for the "word" is the same in v. 23 and v. 25, but also calling the issuance of a divine word "an invisible event" that is enacted in history—and in the case of Dan 9:25, the divine word "became evident in history during the first year of Cyrus"—i.e., 539 BCE (*The Prophecy of Daniel*, 202).

100. Collins, *Daniel*, 352. This idea also underlies the Chronicler's interpretation of Jeremiah's prophecy of the seventy-year desolation (2 Chr 36:18–21).

101. Scholars with non-Messianic approaches to the Seventy Weeks (see p. 485n94 above) generally understand the first anointed one to be Cyrus (called "his anointed" in Isa 45:1) or one of the "sons of oil" (Zech 4:14) during the early postexilic years: the Jewish governor Zerubbabel or the high priest Joshua. I previously favored Cyrus (Widder, *Daniel*, 203), but after several more years of reflecting on the chapter/book and especially its focus on the temple, I now consider Joshua the more likely choice.

102. Of the prominence of temple and priest in the postexilic period, Newsom observes that "the way of calculating time in relation to sabbatical and Jubilee periods, and the focus on high priests—both suggest that for the authors of Daniel, the temple and the priestly staff who serve it are the objects by which the well-being of the nation as a whole are to be measured" (*Daniel*, 305).

103. See p. 485n94 above.
104. Newsom, *Daniel*, 204.
105. Seow, *Daniel*, 149.

Even the long-anticipated end of exile and the restoration of Jerusalem were not going to usher in the glorious vision foretold by the prophets. The coming of the first מָשִׁיחַ would not lead to the "everlasting righteousness" of 9:24e.[106] Instead, centuries after the restoration, the last legitimate (i.e., Zadokite) high priest in Jerusalem, another מָשִׁיחַ, was assassinated (2 Macc 4:23–29; Dan 11:22), and his sacred office passed on to the highest bidders. The sixty-two weeks of "distressed times" came to an end with the "cutting off" (9:26a) of this anointed one, high priest Onias III in 171 BCE, and the final week began.

The events of the final week are summarized in 9:26c–f: the city and holy place would be destroyed, and "its end" (קִצּוֹ)—i.e., Jerusalem and the temple with it—would come "with a flood" (בַּשֶּׁטֶף). While the subject of the clause in 9:26c is "the people of the ruler who is coming," the object occupies initial position in the clause: "the city and the holy place." Thus, 9:26c could be translated as I have: "and the city and the holy place, the people of the ruler who is coming will destroy." This word order again brings the central theme of Jerusalem and the temple to the fore.[107] Verse 27 offers some details of the tumultuous seventieth week: the confirmation of a covenant (9:27a), the violation of the covenant and the cessation of temple practices (9:27b), an abomination in the temple (9:27c), and destruction of the desolator (9:27d).[108]

History fills in this sketch of the seventieth week,[109] but in terms of the text itself and its discourse, several comments are relevant. First, "the ruler who is coming" (נָגִיד הַבָּא) marks the second occurrence of "ruler" (נָגִיד) in the Seventy Weeks (9:26c). The first "ruler" was the first

---

106. Much of Judah's postexilic history has been lost to history, but we do know that the restored nation still lived under the rule of foreign kings—just from afar as vassals rather than as captives in exile. In the first two centuries after the return from exile, "Yehud" (Judah) was a Persian province. After the rise and fall of Greek Alexander the Great and the subsequent shuffle of territory among his generals, the Jews were caught in the "land between" the ever-scuffling Syrian Seleucids and Egyptian Ptolemies. During this time the Jewish (specifically Zadokite) high priest became the most important local official in Jerusalem, the one responsible for answering to foreign overlords and maintaining religious and civic life in Jerusalem. One of his more difficult tasks was deciding which foreign power was more powerful under any given monarch—and then currying favor with it in order to keep the peace at home and abroad. Beginning in the third century BCE, power struggles between the Zadokite high priest and a non-Zadokite clan, the Tobiads, ultimately led to the assassination of Onias III, the last Zadokite (and thus legitimate) high priest in Jerusalem (2 Macc 4:23–29; Dan 11:22). The esteemed office of high priest devolved into a position "anywhere between an annually tendered office and a royal title or benefice" (Athas, "In Search of the Seventy 'Weeks' of Daniel," 12n24).

107. Verse 26 has several syntactic difficulties. Some interpreters organize the clause structure differently, resulting in a translation like that of Goldingay, beginning with the final phrase of v. 25 (וּבְצוֹק הָעִתִּים): "But in the pressure of the times and after the sixty-two sevens, an anointed will be cut off and will have neither the city nor the sanctuary. A leader to come will devastate a people, and its end: with the flood" (*Daniel*, 443; see also Lucas, *Daniel*, 227, 244).

108. Verse 27 also has several difficulties, beginning with the referent for "he," the subject of הִגְבִּיר (v. 27a). I understand it to be Antiochus, but others consider it a reference to Jesus, and still others think "he" is the antichrist. Obviously, the referent for "he" determines what the בְּרִית, "covenant," is. The verb הִגְבִּיר (hiphil of גבר, "make strong") is not used elsewhere with בְּרִית, making it difficult to be certain what it means to "make strong" a covenant. In view of this difficulty, some scholars read בְּרִית as the subject rather than the object (i.e., "a covenant will prevail," as in Goldingay, *Daniel*, 442, 449).

109. The seventieth week entails the tumultuous final years of Antiochus IV's reign. Antiochus's troops ("the people of the ruler who is coming") desecrated the temple and nearly annihilated Judaism, acts that effectively devastated the holy city. Prior to this, Antiochus made an alliance with Hellenizing Jews (1 Macc 1:11), and in the middle of the last week (167 BCE) he replaced acceptable sacrifice in the Jerusalem temple with an "abomination" (v. 27c; cf. 8:13). The particular offense is described in 1 Macc 1:54 as a structure placed on the altar of burnt offering. While it is hard to be certain what exactly the structure was, most scholars think it may have been sacrificed swine (2 Macc 6:5) or even the statue of a Greek god. Antiochus's death in 164 BCE brought an end to the atrocities of the seventieth week. See further below on Dan 10–12.

מָשִׁיחַ, "anointed one," whose coming was associated with the restoration of Jerusalem (9:25cβ). By contrast, this second נָגִיד is associated with a fresh destruction. Second, the repetition of the root שׁמם, "to desolate" (9:26f, 27c, 27d), links this revelation to Daniel's prayer (9:17–18), to the vision of ch. 8 (8:13), and to the revelation yet to come in Dan 11–12 (11:31; 12:11). It also recalls the covenant curses of Lev 26, where it refers to the streets and land (Lev 26:22, 32, 34–35, 43) and to the sanctuary (Lev 26:31). Third, the repetition of חרץ, "to decree," offers assurance that although the desolation of Jerusalem and the temple was determined by decree (נֶחֱרָצָת, 9:26f), so was the complete destruction (כָּלָה) of the desolator (נֶחֱרָצָה, 9:27d)—that is, the one who desolates the sacred places will not get away with it. Finally, the actions of the desolator in confirming a בְּרִית, "covenant," for one week evoke another covenant—namely, the covenant that YHWH made with Israel and that drives Daniel's prayer of confession and supplication; the covenant that set apart Jerusalem and its temple as holy places; the covenant of a loving and merciful, faithful and forgiving God; a covenant whose maker will never be destroyed. All these stand in contrast to the בְּרִית made by the desolator. Daniel had pleaded with the great and awesome God whose covenant and character gave him hope of forgiveness and restoration.

The revelation and the chapter end abruptly—with the prediction of the temple's desolation (9:27b–c) and of complete destruction decreed and poured out on the desolator (9:27d). Unlike the other three visions of the apocalyptic chapters, this revelation contains no concluding instructions by the interpreter (cf. 8:26; 12:9–13) or remarks by Daniel (cf. 7:28; 8:27; 12:8). The final thoughts of Dan 9 are the desolation of the temple and the destruction of the desolator. The reader/listener is left with the question "And then what?" The text answers this question—only not here at the end where we might expect it. It answered it at the beginning of Gabriel's revelation when he detailed the sixfold purpose of the Seventy Weeks (9:24b–g): the transgression will be finished, sin will be ended, iniquity will be atoned for, everlasting righteousness will have been brought in, vision and prophet will have been sealed up, and a holy of holies will have been anointed. As discussed above (see on 9:24), some of these purposes have historical referents in the Antiochene crisis of the second-century BCE. But that initial fulfillment hardly accounts for the eschatological language and symbolism of the Seventy Weeks. As with Daniel's earlier visions, the initial fulfillment was not the end of the revelation's significance. The events of the Seventy Weeks as described in Dan 9 are allusive enough to be applied again and again when God's people encounter similar patterns of sin, suffering, and despotism.[110] Perhaps that is part of the reason for the abrupt ending—the pattern continues while we await the ultimate fulfillment of the Seventy Weeks with its complete destruction of God's enemies and the arrival of everlasting righteousness.

---

110. See further below, Prophecy, Patterns, and Prayer, pp. 493–95.

Canonical and Theological Significance

Jesus in the Seventy Weeks

Daniel's prayer in Dan 9 and its subsequent answer are prefaced by the statement that Daniel had been considering the scrolls of Jeremiah, and specifically YHWH's words to Jeremiah that Jerusalem's desolation would last seventy years. As noted (see on Dan 9:2 above), this context suggests that Daniel was pondering Jer 25 or Jer 29—or both. In these writings, YHWH had told the people that he was going to punish them by means of Nebuchadnezzar, but then after seventy years, he would also punish Nebuchadnezzar and Babylon.

By the first year of Darius, seventy years had passed. Babylon had been destroyed. As Daniel reflected on the writings of Jeremiah in light of the history he was living, he was compelled to acknowledge Israel's full culpability for the exile, confessing generations of systemic and individual sin and pleading for merciful restoration. His heartfelt prayer reveals that, in addition to considering Jeremiah's words, he was also recalling Moses's writings from centuries earlier about the covenant between YHWH and the motley little nation he had redeemed from Egyptian bondage. Moses had detailed the stipulations of the covenant, telling of the blessings that would result from obedience and warning of the curses that would result if Israel disobeyed YHWH's instructions—his torah to them. Daniel had lived through the sevenfold punishment for sin described in Lev 26, and he offered a confession rooted in the promise of restoration at the end of Lev 26:

> But if they will confess their sins and the sins of their ancestors—their unfaithfulness and their hostility toward me, which made me hostile toward them so that I sent them into the land of their enemies—then when their uncircumcised hearts are humbled and they pay for their sin, I will remember my covenant with Jacob and my covenant with Isaac and my covenant with Abraham, and I will remember the land. For the land will be deserted by them and will enjoy its sabbaths while it lies desolate without them. They will pay for their sins because they rejected my laws and abhorred my decrees. Yet in spite of this, when they are in the land of their enemies, I will not reject them or abhor them so as to destroy them completely, breaking my covenant with them. I am YHWH their God. But for their sake I will remember the covenant with their ancestors whom I brought out of Egypt in the sight of the nations to be their God. I am YHWH. (Lev 26:40–45)

From Daniel's place in history, Israel's worst days were surely behind them. The hope of restoration lay ahead, and what a restoration the prophets had said it would be! Isaiah had said YHWH would return the people from every corner of the globe. Jerusalem would be rebuilt, and the temple restored. Israel's deserts would become like Eden, and those returning home would "enter Zion with singing; everlasting joy [would] crown their heads. Gladness and joy [would] overtake them, and sorrow and sighing [would] flee away." The brokenhearted would be bound up, the captives freed, and the mourners comforted (Isa 43:5–7; 44:26–28; 51:3, 11; 61:1–3). Jeremiah had promised peace and security in Israel as the restored people served YHWH and their Davidic king. YHWH would bring the scattered people of Israel home, where they would "shout for joy on the heights of Zion . . . rejoice in the bounty of YHWH . . . be like a well-watered garden, and . . . sorrow no more." In place of sorrow, YHWH would give them comfort and joy, and he would fill his people with his bounty. He would make a new covenant with them, inscribing it on their hearts, and the restored city of Jerusalem would "never again be uprooted or demolished" (Jer 30:9; 31:10–14, 33, 40). The prophet-in-exile, Ezekiel, had promised that when YHWH regathered the people, he would save them from their idolatry and "all their sinful backsliding," and they would live forever in the promised land. David would rule them forever under an everlasting covenant. YHWH would put his sanctuary among them forever—and he even gave Ezekiel the plans for a new temple and priesthood, as well as directions for new gates to the city that would henceforth be called "YHWH Is There" (Ezek 37:23–28; 40–48:35). Joel had told of threshing floors filled with grain and vats overflowing with wine. YHWH would live in Zion, Jerusalem would be holy, never again to be invaded. Mountains would drip new wine, hills would flow with milk, and Judah's ravines would run with water (Joel 2:24; 4[3]:17–18; cf. Amos 9:13). Amos had promised that Israel would never again be uprooted (Amos 9:15). Micah envisioned the mountain of YHWH's temple "established as the highest of the mountains," people streaming to it to learn the ways of YHWH. Implements of war would be remade into farm tools. War would be a thing of the past, and there would be prosperity for all (Mic 5:1–5).

Yes, from Daniel's place with his people, scattered among the nations of the world, it must have appeared that the worst was over and the best was just around the corner, and so he pleaded with Israel's covenant God to forgive his people and bring about restoration.

Then Gabriel appeared, announcing that he had come in response to Daniel's prayer to give him understanding, a strange answer to Daniel's prayer. What Gabriel gave Daniel was a new interpretation of Jeremiah's seventy years—an interpretation only possible through new revelation. Gabriel affirmed to Daniel that the end of exile was indeed just around the corner—at the end of the first seven "weeks." Jerusalem *would* be rebuilt and restored, and the temple with it. However, that is where the glorious prophecies would stop—or rather, be delayed. Everlasting peace and prosperity would have to wait. Sixty-two troubled "weeks" lay ahead, followed by a final "week" of suffering, betrayal, and destruction. Gabriel's words end with the destruction of the city and the temple—with no promise of restoration beyond that. He said the sacrifice and offering would be stopped, and he gave no word of it restarting.

As already noted, while that is the end of the *text*, it is not the end of the Seventy Weeks. Gabriel had revealed the end before he told the beginning. When he announced that Seventy Weeks had been determined for Daniel's people and for his holy city, he also said what would be accomplished by them (Dan 9:24). The sixfold purpose that introduced the events of the Seventy Weeks is their end. The transgression would be finished, sin would be ended—*and* atoned for. Everlasting righteousness would come. Vision and prophet would be sealed up. And "a holy of holies" would be anointed.

How could atonement be made without sacrifice? How could a holy of holies be anointed without a temple? Perhaps Gabriel's words imply that both would be restored. Or perhaps the allusive language suggests more. Baldwin, who sees initial fulfillment of the Seventy Weeks in the tumultuous history of both the Antiochene persecution and the Roman destruction of 70 AD,[111] suggests that these six purposes comprise progressive stages in which God is working to achieve his ends.[112] She suggests that the finishing of the transgression and the end of sin (9:24b–c) represents "sin in general and in its many forms," and if it is to be finished, "we are being told about the final triumph of God's kingdom and the end of human history." The last of the three clauses concerned with sin in 9:24d, "to atone for iniquity," marks the climax of God's dealings with sin: "It is announcing that God has found a way of forgiving sin without being untrue to His own righteousness. This assurance was what the prayer had been feeling after; it was the great longing expressing in the Old Testament as a whole."[113] With the problem of sin addressed, God promised to bring in everlasting righteousness—an "attribute of God alone" (cf. Jer 23:6) that makes it a "short step to justification by faith" (Rom 3:25, 26; cf. also Zech 3:4). The sealing of prophet and vision indicates that God will have accomplished everything he promised through Jeremiah. Of the sixth and final purpose, "to anoint a holy of holies," Baldwin notes the absence of an object—that is, the Hebrew simply says "to anoint a holy of holies"—and says the ambiguity is best explained by the context:

---

111. Baldwin reads the seven weeks and the sixty-two weeks as a single unit, which typically signals a messianic view of the Seventy Weeks (see p. 485n94 above). However, she makes no specific comment on the identity of the anointed ones in Dan 9:25–26. I read the time frames separately because I consider it a more natural reading of the text, and I also think it is the reading that makes better sense in the larger context of Daniel's visions. However, I recognize both readings are possible and even plausible—and I think the ambiguity of the Hebrew syntax may even be intentional such that, in the mystery and wonder of divine inspiration, both readings are plausible because both readings are part of the prophecy.

112. Baldwin, *Daniel*, 168. Baldwin's discussion summarized here is found on pp. 168–69.

113. Baldwin, *Daniel*, 169.

In 539 BC concern was centred on the holy place in Jerusalem, and the rededication of the Temple was not excluded, but the Lord's anointed was ultimately to be a man [cf. Matt 12:6, "something greater than the temple is here"] who was the subject of "vision and prophet."[114]

If we may tentatively interpret the verse, it is speaking of the accomplishment of God's purpose for all history. If we look at this from our vantage point it was accomplished partly in the coming of Christ, but it still has to be consummated (Eph 1:10; 1 Cor 15:28). If the historical work of Christ and his second coming are telescoped, this is not unusual, even in the New Testament.

Gabriel's revelation showed Daniel's vision of restoration to be too small. A restored nation of Israel, worshiping God in the confines of a new temple, was never God's end game. From the creation of the garden and its keepers, to his covenant with Abraham and his descendants, to his miraculous incarnation in the womb of a young Jewish girl named Mary, God's intention was to fill the earth with his presence, to restore every corner of creation, to live with his people from every tribe and every nation forever. *This* was the purpose of the Seventy Weeks. And this purpose is wrapped up in the person of Jesus, *the* anointed one.

Just as there are hints in Daniel's earlier visions that the prophecies both foretold and transcended the second-century-BCE events of the Antiochene persecution, so there are hints in the Seventy Weeks that it both foretells and transcends the events surrounding either Antiochus IV or Roman Titus. The prophecy involves Jesus because everything in the Bible in some way involves Jesus.[115] Most significantly, the use of symbolic numbers steeped in the concepts of Sabbath and Jubilee in the structure of the Seventy Weeks points to Jesus. Jesus had inaugurated the kingdom of God by declaring himself to be the fulfillment of Jubilee as prophesied by Isaiah:

> The Spirit of Sovereign YHWH is on me,
>   because YHWH has anointed me
>   to proclaim good news to the poor.
> He has sent me to bind up the brokenhearted,
>   to proclaim freedom for the captives
>   and release from darkness for the prisoners,
> to proclaim the year of YHWH's favor
>   and the day of vengeance of our God,
> to comfort all who mourn . . . (Isa 61:1–2)[116]

---

114. Baldwin, *Daniel*, 169.

115. One such hint may be the use of מָשִׁיחַ, "anointed one" or "messiah," which occurs nowhere else in Daniel. This word is not an Old Testament code word for "Jesus," but the fact that its root appears three times in Dan 9 and one of these occurrences describes the cutting off of a מָשִׁיחַ should at least give us pause.

116. See Jesus's adaptation of Isaiah's prophecy (Luke 4:16–21). The interpretive significance of Jesus's proclamation can

Jubilee in the Mosaic law was but the shadow of a future hope for the restoration of all things. Jesus was the reality, coming to restore all things forever. While other "anointed ones" were connected with the return from Babylonian captivity, Jesus was the one who would bring the end to the ultimate exile—separation from God and bondage to sin. His restoration and freedom, unlike those initiated in 539 BCE, would be complete and permanent. He was the one whose death would make obsolete the rituals of the temple, and he himself would become the ultimate high priest, making intercession for us before the throne of God. God's purposes would be fulfilled without a physical temple and without the ongoing ritual of sacrifice. Because of the restoration wrought by Jesus's death, burial, resurrection, and ascension, God's dwelling place will fill the whole earth, and he will live with his perfected people without the limitations of temple curtains forever.

Prophecy, Patterns, and Prayer

The book of Daniel—and specifically his visions—have often been read for their contribution to end-times theology. These contributions have been detailed on charts showing how the tentacles of the beastly Roman empire reach into modern times, when the antichrist will destroy a new temple in Jerusalem, and when God's faithful people can expect to be rescued from the horrors of the end times.[117]

This is not my approach to nor my conclusions about Daniel's visions. Rather, I see in Daniel's visions a portrayal of human kings typified by their "beastly" character—that is, their ways of ruling and reigning that fall outside God's intent for his image-bearers, created to rule and reign on planet earth. I see a pattern of rulers who defy God and oppress his people. I see a portrayal of human kingdoms characterized by their pride and rebellion against God. I see a suffering that persists for the righteous and a reward that lingers in the distance. I see sacrilege, despotism, and injustice. I see God's people crying, "How long?"

What I see is the news feed from any given day, in any given place in the world.

---

be found in many Luke commentaries. See, e.g., Joel B. Green, *The Gospel of Luke*, NICNT (Grand Rapids: Eerdmans, 1997).

117. I suspect one of the reasons the American church, especially, has focused on an end-times theology in Daniel's apocalyptic chapters is because it fails to understand how the message of the visions is immediately relevant to us. Our culture has been relatively comfortable and safe. Evil happens, but for most of us, it happens a fair distance from where we live. We are allowed to worship freely and live by our convictions with minimal fear of physical or even emotional harm. The worst "oppression" we know is social censure or loss of political power. The apocalyptic horror of Daniel's visions is not very real in our immediate surroundings, as it is for many of our brothers and sisters around the globe. Suffering is not an abstract concept for followers of Jesus in many countries and cultures of the world, where a high price is exacted from those who align themselves with Jesus. These brothers and sisters know the reality of oppression and suffering, and they do not have to wonder how bad the world will get and when. Things are bad now. For these dearly loved people of God, the apocalyptic message of Daniel is profoundly relevant. They little care how the book of Daniel might chart the future or foretell the demise of a madman. Their comfort is that God is on his eternal throne and victory is assured. Their comfort is that one day God will reward them and judge their oppressors.

Are some days worse than others? Oh, yes. Are some periods of history worse than others? Certainly. Are some places on the globe worse than others? Without a doubt.

Daniel's exilic and postexilic audiences were uncertain about their future and their place in the plan of God, and they suffered greatly at the hands of rulers who had no regard for the ways of God. It is this uncertainty and this suffering that the book of Daniel addresses, affirming that God still had a good plan for his people. He would restore them—but, as the Seventy Weeks especially indicates, this restoration would be much bigger, much farther away, and more glorious than they had hoped for. The Seventy Weeks revealed that although the years of Babylonian exile were nearly over, Jeremiah's "seventy years" would take much longer to complete. "Exile"—that is, living under the rule of idolatrous foreign kings, living away from the promised land of Sabbath rest—was going to characterize life on earth for some time yet to come. The fullness of God's kingdom on earth was going to take longer to come than the people had anticipated.

Jesus himself tried to help his disciples understand this, and he did so by reapplying the Seventy Weeks to their situation.[118] Prompted by their questions about the destruction of the temple and the end of the age (Matt 24:3), Jesus told them of the difficulties that lay ahead (i.e., natural and man-made disasters, persecution, apostasy, and false messiahs and prophets; Matt 24:4–14), and he said they should flee to the mountains when they saw the "the abomination that causes desolation" standing in the holy place (24:15; cf. Dan 9:27). Some interpreters consider this a reference to the Roman destruction of the temple in AD 70, and others consider it a reference to the time leading up to Jesus's second coming. The problem is that neither view completely answers the disciples' questions about the temple's destruction, the end of the age, and Jesus's return. Was Jesus referring to the Roman conquest? Was he speaking of the eschatological end? Yes. But by invoking the imagery of the abomination of desolation in Daniel, Jesus drew on "a complex typology of prophecy and fulfillment stretching all the way from Nebuchadnezzar to the eschatological antichrist."[119] Nebuchadnezzar had desecrated the temple in 587 BCE. Antiochus had desecrated the restored temple in 167 BCE. The Romans under Titus desecrated the temple in 70 AD. Each of these desecrations was part of a "continuum of fulfillment" leading to the ultimate sacrilege of the antichrist (e.g., 2 Thess 2:3–4; Rev 13:8).[120]

---

118. He also alluded to Daniel's other visions when he spoke of incomparable distress (Matt 24:21; cf. Dan 12:1) and the coming of the Son of Man on the clouds (Matt 24:30; cf. Dan 7:13–14).

119. Turner, *Matthew*, 579.

120. Turner's continuum has eight desecrations of the Jerusalem temple: "1. Nebuchadnezzar's conquest in 605 BCE (Dan. 1:1; 5:1–4, 22–23); 2. Antiochus IV Ephiphanes's sacrilege, which led to the Hasmonean revolt in 167 BCE; 3. The Roman conquest of the Hasmonean kingdom in 63 BCE; 4. The unfulfilled plot to set up a bust of Caligula in the temple (40–41 CE); 5. The Zealots' misuse of the temple grounds before the Roman destruction of Jerusalem; 6. The Roman destruction in 70 CE; 7. The further desolation of Jerusalem by the Romans in 135 CE in response to the second Jewish revolt led by Bar Kokhba (Dio Cassius, *Roman History* 69.12.1–2); 8. The ultimate sacrilege of

All the fulfillments leading up to that final fulfillment warn God's people against false messiahs and prophets, encouraging them to persevere through suffering with the confidence that God's kingdom will one day fill the earth.

Daniel responded to Jeremiah's prophecy of seventy years with repentance and hope. The text offers no details of his response to the Seventy Weeks prophecy, though it seems likely he continued to repent of his people's sins and hope that God would act out of his gracious character. Would that our response to God's words would also be repentance and hope. We repent of our own sins and the sins of our own "family," our brothers and sisters in Christ.[121] While we do not stand in a national covenant with God as Daniel's people did, the New Testament indicates that we are a spiritual family bound together even more tightly by the blood of Christ. Like it or not, we stand together with "one another"—a phrase that pervades the apostolic writings to the fledging early church. We confess and we hope for that ultimate restoration. Lord Jesus, come!

---

the antichrist (Matt. 24:15; 2 Thess. 2:3–4; 1 John 2:18, 22; 4:3; 2 John 7; Rev. 13:8 . . .)" (*Matthew*, 579).

121. Corporate confession has a long history in the formal worship of the church, and we would do well to revive the practice in our local churches. Bryan Chapell also addresses the responsibility of believers to confess national and familial sin: "If I am so swept into a culture of materialism that I do not see or fight against the impoverishment of the disadvantaged, then I need to confess my personal sin. In addition, if I see and object to the sin but still live in, and benefit from, the society driven by such aims, then my confession of our corporate sin is appropriate. If I find racism abhorrent but still have advantages from the slave-owning heritage of my family or the oppression-ignoring history of my church, then I should confess the sin of my family and ecclesiastical affiliations. If I personally find the sins of abortion, sex trafficking, and chemical addictions abhorrent but find my life entwined in a culture that promotes such evil, then I have a responsibility to confess *our* sin with the prayer that God would bring his mercy and power to bear upon all of these evils. Grace is great enough to cover all our sin—individual and corporate—but that does not free us from responsibilities to confess both" (*The Gospel according to Daniel: A Christ-Centered Approach* [Grand Rapids, Baker Books: 2014], 160).

Daniel 10:1a–12:13c

C. Narrative 3: *The Ultimate Conflict and God's Final Victory*

Main Idea of Narrative 3 (10:1a–12:13c)

In the book's final vision, Daniel encounters a divine being, "a man clothed in linen," who reveals what would happen to Daniel's people in a future time. The appearance of the man overwhelms Daniel, who requires significant ministration to be able simply to receive the revelation. The revelation is a recounting of history from the period of the Persians through the reign of the Seleucid king Antiochus IV Epiphanes in the second century BCE. It also reaches into the future, providing a glimpse of the continuing pattern of evil rulers and promising that the faithful among Daniel's people will receive their reward in the resurrection, while the oppressors of his people will be judged. Daniel himself is promised reward at the end of days. Through this revelation Daniel is again assured that everything that befalls his people is under God's control, and God will reward the righteous and punish the wicked in his time.

Literary Context of Narrative 3 (Dan 10:1a–12:13c)

Daniel 10–12 is the last of Daniel's four visionary experiences in the apocalyptic half of the book (chs. 7–12). Like the vision in ch. 7, this experience is recounted in a first-person vision report that is embedded in a third-person narrative framework (cf. 7:1; cf. 8:1; 9:1–2). While Daniel's first two visions occurred during the reign of Belshazzar (7:1; 8:1), and the third was set in the first year of Darius (9:1), this final vision is dated to the third year of Cyrus, king of Persia (10:1). As in the other apocalyptic chapters, the date formula in 10:1 positions the vision in the chronology of the book by linking it to the narrative chapters where each of the kings is introduced.[1]

---

1. Belshazzar in ch. 5; Darius the Mede in chs. 5–6; Cyrus the Persian in Dan 1:21.

Cyrus's introduction into the book's narrative is in Dan 1:21, where the narrator established the time frame of Daniel's service in the royal court. He is also mentioned at the end of the Dan 6 narrative when Daniel is said to have prospered during his reign (6:29[28]). In this fourth vision, as in the third vision, the historical context provided by this date formula is a meaningful part of understanding the vision's purpose (see further below).

In the literary context of the book's four apocalyptic visions, Dan 10–12 is the last and longest of Daniel's visions. In it the imagery begun in the vision of ch. 7 is further narrowed as Daniel envisions the future beyond his people's suffering and catches a glimpse of resurrection and reward for God's faithful. In the vision of the four beasts and the divine throne room (Dan 7), Daniel caught a glimpse of the entire cosmos and world history. In the vision of the evenings and mornings (Dan 8), the focus narrowed to bring the all-important Jerusalem and its temple into view.[2] The revelation of Dan 9 (9:24–27), as well as the events leading up to it, focused entirely on Jerusalem and the desecration of the temple. This final vision will continue the focus on the temple, but it will do so by incorporating the second-century-BCE events in Syria-Palestine that led to the temple's desecration. Together, Daniel's visions portray this particularly horrific period in Jewish history, while also portraying a biblical pattern of evil rulers that will culminate in the book of Revelation.

Since Dan 10–12 is apocalyptic literature, the discussion that follows will incorporate Korner's language as used in the commentary above on Dan 7.[3] However, as previously discussed, each of Daniel's four apocalyptic visions is unique. The visions of Dan 7 and 8 are symbolic visions, requiring an angelic interpreter, but the visions of Dan 9 and 10–12 are verbal revelations transmitted by divine beings and do not require interpretation. Lucas calls them "*epiphany visions*, in which a supernatural being appears and conveys a message."[4] The elements included in these visions are (1) the surrounding circumstances (9:1–2; 10:1), (2) supplication (9:3–19; 10:2–3), (3) the appearance of a messenger (9:20–21; 10:4–9), (4) a word of assurance (9:22–23; 10:10–11:1), (5) the revelation (9:24–27; 11:2–12:3), and (6) a charge to the seer (12:4).[5] While these elements are present in Daniel's visions of Dan 9 and Dan 10–12, they do not form the structures or outlines of these chapters, which are determined by the syntax and discourse features of the sections (e.g., 10:1–11:2a; 11:2b–12:4; 12:5–13). Such diversity of form has required an individualized approach to the structure of each vision.

---

2. While themes from each of Daniel's visions appear in the revelation of Dan 10–12, this final vision is most tied to the vision of the evenings and mornings in ch. 8. Willis (*Dissonance and the Drama of Divine Sovereignty*, 159) discusses how it echoes or reworks nearly every verse of that chapter in order to provide what Newsom calls "both a more finely grained historical account and the fully resolved ending that was absent from ch. 8" (*Daniel*, 328).

3. Korner, "'And I Saw . . . ,'" 160–83. See Literary Context of Narrative 6 (Dan 7:1–28) above, pp. 348–50.

4. Lucas, *Daniel*, 32 (emphasis his).

5. Lucas, *Daniel*, 35.

For the sake of consistency and simplicity in the analysis of Dan 10–12, we will retain the language of "vision block" for the three large segments that comprise the entirety of Daniel's vision report (10:1a–11:2a; 11:2b–12:4d; 12:5a–13c) and "individual vision" for visionary elements within each block as relevant (10:4a–9d; 10:10a–15c; 10:16a–11:2a). However, the use of formulaic statements to organize the vision report into sections is less pronounced in this final vision report than it was in Dan 7 and Dan 8 (e.g., "I looked, and I saw" and "I looked, and oh!").[6] The first and third vision blocks include such statements to indicate the major and minor sections (וְהִנֵּה, "וָאֶשָּׂא אֶת־עֵינַי וָאֵרֶא וְהִנֵּה "I lifted my eyes, and I looked, and oh!" [10:5a-b[7]]; וְהִנֵּה, "And/Then oh!" [10:10a, 16a]; וָרָאִיתִי אֲנִי דָנִיֵּאל וְהִנֵּה, "I looked—I, Daniel—and oh!" [12:5a-b]), and both blocks also recount visionary experiences. The second vision block, however, is less a vision than a verbal revelation, and it simply begins with the messenger's הִנֵּה, "Listen" (11:2b).[8]

> III. Macro Unit 3: Encouragement until God's Eternal Kingdom Comes (8:1a–12:13c)
>   A. Narrative 1: God's Leash on Evil (8:1a–27f)
>   B. Narrative 2: Repentance and God's Promise of Restoration (9:1a–27d)
> ➤ **C. Narrative 3: The Ultimate Conflict and God's Final Victory (10:1a–12:13c)**

1. Vision Block 1: *The Vision of a Heavenly Messenger* (10:1a–11:2a)

Main Idea of the Passage

Daniel 10:1–11:2a recounts Daniel's vision of a divine figure, described as "a man clothed in linen" (10:5b). Overwhelmed by the being's appearance such that he is without strength, Daniel falls into a trance-like sleep on the ground. After several enabling touches and encouraging words, Daniel is ready to receive the revelation sent to him by way of the divine being. The heavenly messenger announces that he is going to tell Daniel what is inscribed in a "book of truth" (10:21a).

---

6. Such statements were absent altogether from the vision report of Dan 9.

7. This first vision block begins properly in 10:5a, but for the sake of simplicity I have included in it the lengthy space/time referent for the vision (10:1–4).

8. The attention-getting הִנֵּה is common in BH, and its use in vision reports typically expresses the speaker's surprise at the unexpected nature of what he is seeing. See on 8:3 above and 10:5, 10, 16 below for discussions of הִנֵּה.

Literary Context

Daniel 10:1–11:2a is the opening section of the lengthy narrative of Dan 10–12. As such, it functions in at least three ways in its broader literary context. First, it establishes the context for the chapter's events during the third year of Cyrus, positioning the narrative in the chronology of the book of Daniel. The context further includes Daniel's circumstances—namely, that he had been mourning for three weeks along the banks of the Tigris River. Second, it provides a summary of the revelation Daniel would receive as being true and concerning a great conflict (10:1). Finally, it draws attention to the significance of the revelation by its emphasis on the appearance of the messenger (10:5–6), the effect of the messenger's appearance on Daniel (10:7–11; 15–19), and the challenges the messenger faced trying to deliver the message (10:12–14, 20–11:1).

C. Narrative 3: The Ultimate Conflict and God's Final Victory (10:1a–12:13c)
→ **1. Vision Block 1: The Vision of a Heavenly Messenger (10:1a–11:2a)**
   2. Vision Block 2: The Revelation from the Book of Truth (11:2b–12:4d)
   3. Vision Block 3: The Vision of Two Others (12:5a–13c)

Translation and Exegetical Outline

(See pages 500–503.)

Structure and Literary Form

The opening section of the Dan 10:1–12:13 narrative (10:1a–11:2a) is Daniel's vision of the divine messenger who will give him the revelation contained in 11:2b–12:4, and it offers a behind-the-scenes glimpse of events surrounding his appearance. The passage is comprised of five subsections: 10:1, 2–3, 4–9, 10–15, and 10:16–11:2a.

The first subsection (10:1) is the third-person narrative introduction to the first-person vision report that begins in 10:2 and continues through the rest of the narrative. It establishes the timing of the chapter's events: "in the third year of Cyrus, king of Persia" (10:1a). It also describes the nature of the revelation that will follow—it was a word that was true but entailed great conflict (10:1d)—and it notes that Daniel would understand (בִּין) the revelation (10:1e–f).

Daniel 10:1a–11:2a

C. Narrative 3: The Ultimate Conflict and God's Final Victory (Dan 10:1a–12:13c)
  1. Vision Block 1: The Vision of a Heavenly Messenger (10:1a–11:2a)
    a. The Narrative Introduction (10:1a–f)

1a	↓ In the third year of Cyrus, king of Persia,
1b	a word was revealed to Daniel,
1c	↑ whose name was called Belteshazzar.
1d	True was the word—and a great conflict.
1e	But he understood the word,
1f	and he had an understanding about the vision.

    b. Daniel's Introduction to the Vision (10:2a–3c)

2a	↓ "In those days,
2b	I, Daniel, was mourning for three weeks of days.
3a	Pleasant bread I did not eat,
3b	and meat and wine did not enter my mouth.
3c	I did not anoint myself at all until the fullness of three weeks of days.

    c. Individual Vision: The Appearance of the Man (10:4a–9d)
      (1) The Time and Place of His Appearance (10:4a–c)
      (2) The Man Clothed in Linen (10:5a–6e)

4a	↓ On the twenty-fourth day of the first month,
4b	I was along the bank of the great river—
4c	↑ that is the Tigris—
5a	and I lifted my eyes,
5b	and I looked, and oh! A man clothed in linen!
5c	His waist was girded with gold of Uphaz.
6a	His body was like topaz.
6b	His face was like the appearance of lightning,
6c	and his eyes were like torches of fire.
6d	His arms and legs were like the gleam of burnished bronze,
6e	and the sound of his words was like the sound of a tumult.

(3) The Effects of the Vision (10:7a–9d)

7a	And I, Daniel, alone saw the vision.
7bα	The men ....
7c	↑ who were with me
7bβ	... did not see the vision.
7d	However, a great fear fell upon them,
7e	and they fled
7f	↑ to hide themselves,
8a	and I alone remained.
8b	I saw this great vision,
8c	and no strength remained in me.
8d	My vigor was changed for ruin,
8e	and I did not retain strength.
9a	I heard the sound of his words,
9b	and as I heard the sound of his words,
9c	↓ I fell on my face into a deep sleep,
9d	and my face was on the ground.

d. Individual Vision: An Enabling Touch and an Encouraging Word (10:10a–15c)

(1) Who Daniel Was (10:10a–11g)

10a	And oh! A hand touched me,
10b	and it set me trembling on my knees and palms of my hands.
11a	He said to me,
11b	'Daniel, highly favored man, understand the words
11c	↑ which I am about to speak to you.
11d	Stand in your place,
11e	↑ for now I have been sent to you.'
11f	And when he spoke this word with me,
11g	I stood trembling.

Continued on next page.

Continued from previous page.

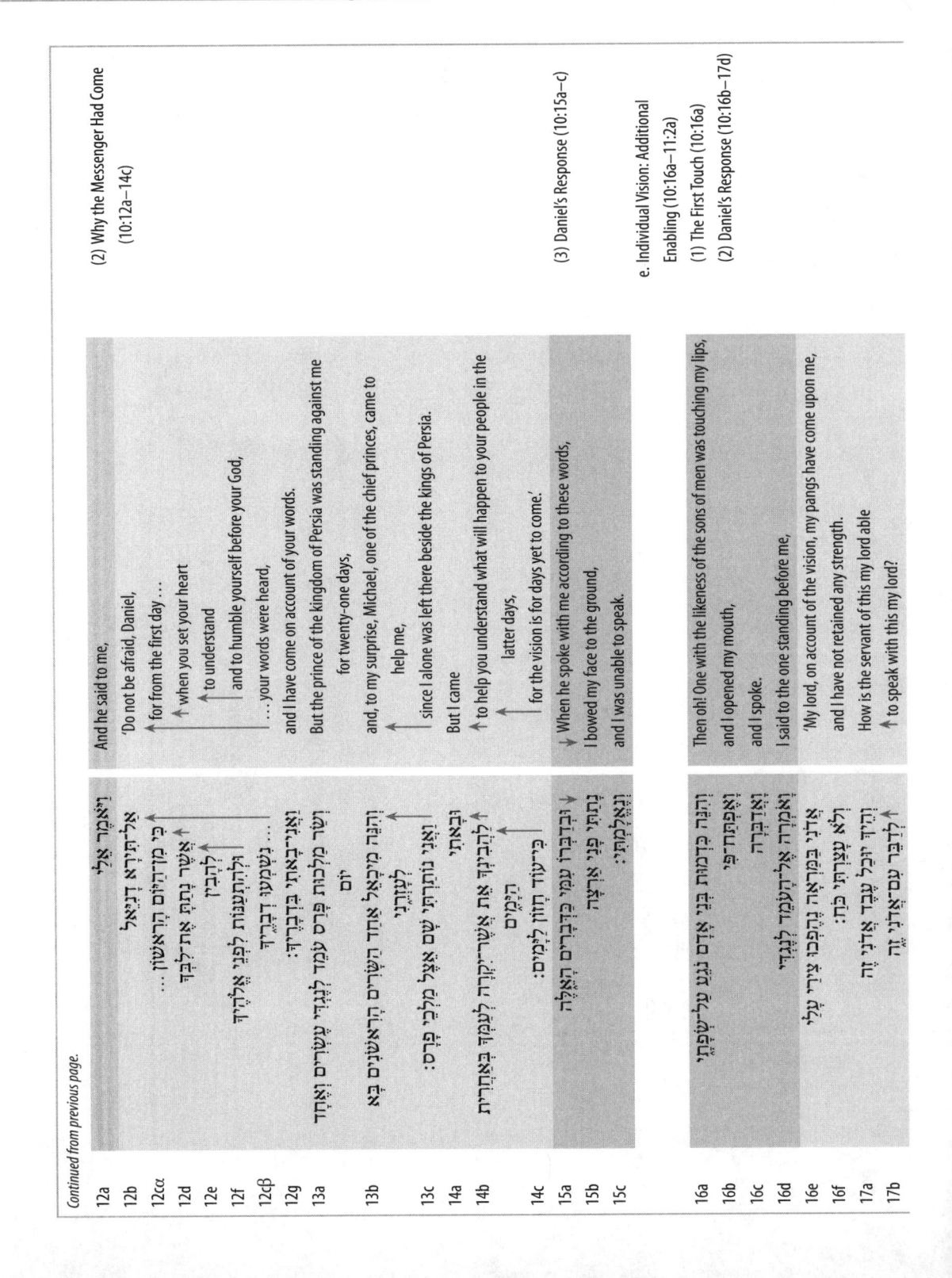

12a	And he said to me,	וַיֹּאמֶר אֵלַי	(2) Why the Messenger Had Come (10:12a–14c)
12b	'Do not be afraid, Daniel,	אַל־תִּירָא דָנִיֵּאל	
12cα	for from the first day ...	כִּי מִן־הַיּוֹם הָרִאשׁוֹן ...	
12d	← when you set your heart	אֲשֶׁר נָתַתָּ אֶת־לִבְּךָ	
12e	to understand	לְהָבִין	
12f	and to humble yourself before your God,	וּלְהִתְעַנּוֹת לִפְנֵי אֱלֹהֶיךָ	
12cβ	... your words were heard,	נִשְׁמְעוּ דְבָרֶיךָ	
12g	and I have come on account of your words.	וַאֲנִי־בָאתִי בִּדְבָרֶיךָ׃	
13a	But the prince of the kingdom of Persia was standing against me for twenty-one days,	וְשַׂר מַלְכוּת פָּרַס עֹמֵד לְנֶגְדִּי עֶשְׂרִים וְאֶחָד יוֹם	
13b	and, to my surprise, Michael, one of the chief princes, came to help me,	וְהִנֵּה מִיכָאֵל אַחַד הַשָּׂרִים הָרִאשֹׁנִים בָּא לְעָזְרֵנִי	
13c	since I alone was left there beside the kings of Persia.	וַאֲנִי נוֹתַרְתִּי שָׁם אֵצֶל מַלְכֵי פָרָס׃	
14a	But I came	וּבָאתִי	
14b	to help you understand what will happen to your people in the latter days,	לַהֲבִינְךָ אֵת אֲשֶׁר־יִקְרָה לְעַמְּךָ בְּאַחֲרִית הַיָּמִים	
14c	for the vision is for days yet to come.'	כִּי־עוֹד חָזוֹן לַיָּמִים׃	
15a	When he spoke with me according to these words,	וּבְדַבְּרוֹ עִמִּי כַּדְּבָרִים הָאֵלֶּה	(3) Daniel's Response (10:15a–c)
15b	I bowed my face to the ground,	נָתַתִּי פָנַי אַרְצָה	
15c	and I was unable to speak.	וְנֶאֱלָמְתִּי׃	
16a	Then oh! One with the likeness of the sons of men was touching my lips,	וְהִנֵּה כִּדְמוּת בְּנֵי אָדָם נֹגֵעַ עַל־שְׂפָתָי	**e. Individual Vision: Additional Enabling (10:16a–11:2a)** (1) The First Touch (10:16a) (2) Daniel's Response (10:16b–17d)
16b	and I opened my mouth,	וָאֶפְתַּח־פִּי	
16c	and spoke.	וָאֲדַבְּרָה	
16d	I said to the one standing before me,	וָאֹמְרָה אֶל־הָעֹמֵד לְנֶגְדִּי	
16e	'My lord, on account of the vision, my pangs have come upon me,	אֲדֹנִי בַּמַּרְאָה נֶהֶפְכוּ צִירַי עָלַי	
16f	and I have not retained any strength.	וְלֹא עָצַרְתִּי כֹּחַ׃	
17a	How is the servant of this my lord able	וְהֵיךְ יוּכַל עֶבֶד אֲדֹנִי זֶה	
17b	← to speak with this my lord?	לְדַבֵּר עִם־אֲדֹנִי זֶה	

17c	As for me, from now no strength remains in me,	
17d	and breath is not left in me.'	
18a	The one with the appearance of a man touched me again,	(3) The Second Touch and Another Encouraging Word (10:18a–19d)
18b	and he strengthened me.	
19a	He said,	
19b	'Do not be afraid, dearly loved man.	
19c	Peace be yours.	
19d	Be strong, yes, be strong.'	
19e	↓ And when he had spoken with me,	(4) Daniel's Response (10:19e–i)
19f	I was strengthened.	
19g	And I said,	
19h	'May my lord speak	
19i	↑ for you have strengthened me.'	
20a	And he said,	(5) The Messenger's Explanation (10:20a–11:2a)
20b	'Do you know why I came to you?	
20c	But now I will return	
20d	↑ to fight with the prince of Persia,	
20e	I must go forth—	
20f	Oh! The prince of Greece is coming.	
21a	However, I will tell you what is inscribed in a book of truth.	
21b	There is no one supporting me against these—except Michael, your prince.	
11:1aα	I . . .	
11:1b	↓ in the first year of Darius the Mede,	
11:1aβ	. . . arose	
11:1c	↑ to strengthen and be protection for him.	
11:2a	But now truth I will tell you.'"	

The second subsection (10:2–3) is the beginning of Daniel's first-person report of the vision he saw, and Daniel begins by describing his context: fasting, mourning, and abstaining from lotions for three weeks.

The third subsection (10:4–9) includes the first of three individual visions in the passage: the appearance of a man clothed in linen (10:5b). Daniel provides the specific time and place of this vision: "on the twenty-fourth day of the first month" and "along the bank of the great river—that is the Tigris" (10:4a–c). The vision proper begins in 10:5 with Daniel's statement "and I lifted my eyes, and I looked, and oh!" (וָאֶשָּׂא אֶת־עֵינַי וָאֵרֶא וְהִנֵּה). He then describes the appearance of the man (10:5–6), as well as the effect the vision had on him (10:7–9).

The fourth subsection (10:10–15) is the second individual vision in the first vision block. It begins with Daniel's announcement that הִנֵּה, "oh!"—a hand had touched him as he lay asleep on the ground (10:10a). The hand raised him up, and the man clothed in linen spoke to Daniel, encouraging him (10:11) and explaining why he had come (10:12–14). Daniel responded by returning to the ground, unable to speak (10:15).

The fifth and final subsection (10:16–11:2a) is the last individual vision in the first vision block. It begins with וְהִנֵּה, "Then oh!" (10:16a), as Daniel recounts additional touches and encouragement he received, enabling him to receive the revelation. First, a humanlike figure (כִּדְמוּת בְּנֵי אָדָם, 10:16a) touched his lips and Daniel responded by speaking (10:16b–17). Then the figure touched him again, giving him strength (10:18). Then the messenger encouraged him, and Daniel finally responded that he was strengthened (10:19). The messenger then explained why he had come, as well as what he had left behind to bring his message to Daniel (10:20–11:2a).

Since all but the first verse of the Dan 10–12 narrative is Daniel's first-person report of the vision and revelation, everything after Dan 10:1 is set as reported speech (shaded on the charts).

Explanation of the Text

a. The Narrative Introduction (10:1a–f)

Daniel 10–12 opens with a date formula that serves as part of the space/time referent for the vision Daniel is about to receive in the narrative.[9] The narrator reports that the events happened "in the third year of Cyrus, king of Persia" (10:1a). Cyrus is first named in the book of Daniel in the conclusion of Dan 1, where the narrator positions Daniel in the royal court "until the first year of Cyrus the king"

---

9. Korner, "'And I Saw...'," 162. See Literary Context of Narrative 6 (Dan 7:1–28) for discussion of "space/time referent" (pp. 348–50). The rest of the space/time referent will be in Daniel's introduction of the vision (see below on 10:2–3) and his specification of place/time in 10:4.

(1:21). He is mentioned again at the conclusion of Dan 6, where Daniel is said to have prospered in the reign of Darius, "that is, in the reign of Cyrus the Persian" (6:29[28]).[10] In this third and final mention, he is called "king of Persia," a title that sets up the revelation to follow, where Persian kings head the survey of history (11:2).

That Daniel's vision occurs during the reign of a "king of Persia" firmly moves the chronology of the book to the third empire in its "inexorable march of the four kingdoms"[11] (chs. 2 and 7).[12] This move sets up the lengthy climax of Daniel's visions in which the fourth kingdom (Greece) will spawn the persecutor Antiochus IV Epiphanes.

Cyrus came to power in the ancient Near East in 559 BCE, but his third year in the context of the book of Daniel should be understood as the third year after his conquest of Babylon in 539 BCE. Taken literally, this would date the revelation of Dan 10–12 to 536 BCE. However, if the dates in Daniel are not intended to be precise, this may be the narrator's way of saying "not long after the beginning" of Cyrus's reign.[13] Either way, the "third year" fits well in a discourse pattern of the book, where key events are linked to the first and third years of kings' reigns (cf. 1:1; 7:1; 8:1; 9:1; 10:1; 11:1; the only exception is Dan 2:1). This similarity of dates at key transitions throughout the book may be the narrator's way of affirming God's sovereignty in history[14]—God was in charge when a king began his reign, and he remained active and in control even after the king had established himself.

The truth of God's control over the course of history is particularly relevant to the circumstances behind Daniel's final vision. Three years earlier (the time of the revelation of Dan 9), Cyrus had issued an edict allowing captive people—including the Jews—to return to their homelands and rebuild their temples.[15] Several thousand Jewish exiles did return to Israel under the leadership of their Persian-appointed governor, Sheshbazzar (Ezra 1:1–4; 5:14). They began to rebuild, but their efforts were quickly frustrated by local opposition (Ezra 1; 3; 4:1–5). It did not take long for repatriated Jews to realize that they were not living in the glorious restoration promised by the prophets. They were still subjects of a gentile king, not a Davidic one (cf. Ezek 37:24; Jer 23:5–6). The foundation of the new temple made the old men wail, as they remembered the splendor of the first temple (Ezra 3:12–13; cf. Ezek 37:26–28). The people faced fierce opposition and even danger in their own land (Ezra 4:4–5; cf.

---

10. See ch. 5, p. 286n95 on the equation of Cyrus with Darius.

11. Pace, *Daniel*, 184. Understanding Persia as the third kingdom assumes the Greek view of the kingdoms in Dan 2 and 7. Scholars with the Roman view of the kingdoms consider the third kingdom to be Greece. See IN DEPTH: The Identities of the Kingdoms, pp. 15–17, and IN DEPTH: The Identities of the Kingdoms, Take 2, pp. 386–90.

12. Collins (*Daniel*, 372) notes (following H. G. M. Williamson, *Ezra, Nehemiah*, WBC 16 [Nashville: Nelson, 1985], 9, 11) that, although the Nabonidus Chronicle and some postexilic narratives (2 Chron 36:22; Ezra 1:1) refer to Cyrus as "king of Persia," he does not appear to have used the title for himself. More commonly, he was known as "king of Babylon" after his conquest there.

13. See on Dan 1:1 (i.e., "the third year of the reign of Jehoiakim").

14. Goldingay, *Daniel*, 152–53.

15. Cyrus's famous edict is described on the sixth-century-BCE Cyrus Cylinder, an inscription that summarizes the Persian king's rise to kingship in Babylon and his release of captive peoples to rebuild their worship sites destroyed by the Babylonians: "I returned the (images of) the gods to the sacred centers [on the other side of] the Tigris whose sanctuaries had been abandoned for a long time, and I let them dwell in eternal abodes. I gathered all their inhabitants and returned (to them) their dwellings" ("Cyrus Cylinder," trans. by Mordechai Cogan [*COS* 2.124: 315–16]). Cyrus's foreign policy differed from that of his predecessors inasmuch as he assumed conquered people groups would be better subjects if they were allowed to live in their homelands and worship their own gods in their temples.

Jer 32:37). They were hungry, and their tattered clothes could not keep the cold out (Hag 1:6; cf. Isa 60). Their circumstances represented only a partial fulfillment of the prophets' grand visions of restoration. Although Daniel, as far we know, was not among those who returned to the land, he likely knew about the postexilic difficulties his countrymen were encountering.[16] That the narrator of Dan 10 overspecifies Daniel's identity as the one "whose name was called Belteshazzar" (10:1c) may well be a reminder that, although the enforced exile was officially over, Daniel and his people were still not free.

The narrator describes the revelation (הַדָּבָר) to Daniel as "true and a great conflict" (אֱמֶת וְצָבָא גָדוֹל, 10:1d). The phrase וְצָבָא גָדוֹל, "and a great conflict," is ambiguous. It may refer to the revelation itself (i.e., that it detailed a period of great conflict;[17] see, e.g., NIV, NET), the difficulty Daniel had understanding the revelation (see, e.g., NJPS),[18] or the difficulty he had simply receiving the revelation.[19] The ambiguity allows us to consider all these possibilities—and perhaps all of them are meant to some degree.

This introduction by the third-person narrator summarizes all that follows: Daniel receives a revelation that was true, and it was associated with great difficulty. Daniel understood what he was told, though, as Collins notes, this statement "anticipates the end of the revelatory process, not Daniel's initial reaction," which was a lack of understanding (12:8).[20]

b. Daniel's Introduction to the Vision (10:2a–3c)

In 10:2 the narrative shifts to Daniel's first-person account, beginning with the temporal clause "in those days" (10:2a)—that is, the days of Cyrus's third year when Daniel received the revelation (10:1). Daniel summarizes what he is about to say by saying he had been mourning for "three weeks of days" (שְׁלֹשָׁה שָׁבֻעִים יָמִים). This overspecification that the weeks were "weeks of days" may be to distinguish between the three literal weeks represented here and the seventy symbolic "weeks" in Dan 9:24–27.

In 10:3 Daniel details what his mourning entailed: not eating "pleasant bread" (לֶחֶם חֲמֻדוֹת), meat, and wine,[21] and abstaining from anointing himself with oil—a sign of rejoicing (e.g., Ps 45:7) as well as a common practice in the arid climate of the Middle East.[22] Daniel mourns by "fasting in the sense of abstention from festal food and even from the everyday grooming of a respectable person (2 Sam 12:20; 14:2; Qoh 9:7–10; Jdt 10:3)."[23]

His introduction concludes with repetition of

---

16. Newsom assumes he is still serving in the royal court but says the date formula "suggests that Daniel was among the returnees" (since the reader knows Cyrus's decree occurred in his first year). She considers this "discrepancy" the result of later "incomplete editing" (*Daniel*, 328). While I assume Daniel was not among the returnees, I consider the question of his royal service into the third year of Cyrus to be open—that is, he remained in Babylon, but may not have been active in the royal court by this time.

17. Lacocque considers the phrase צָבָא גָדוֹל to be "a succinct and allusive résumé of Isa. 40:2," such that the revelation of Dan 10–12 "is going to show us on what 'true' basis the prophet [Isaiah] could have announced the end of Jerusalem's 'great slavery.'" In this way, Dan 10 stands parallel to Dan 9, which took up the prophecy of Jeremiah and provided Daniel with additional understanding about that prophet's word (*The Book of Daniel*, 204).

18. This is Newsom's view (*Daniel*, 329).

19. This is the view of Collins, who translates, "and the service was great," understanding "the service" to be "that of Daniel in receiving the vision" (*Daniel*, 372.)

20. Collins, *Daniel*, 372.

21. Miller observes that the *waw* conjunction between the clauses "Pleasant bread I did not eat" and "meat and wine did not enter my mouth" could be translated as "even," and so explaining what the "pleasant bread" (NIV's "choice food;" NASB's "tasty food") was—i.e., meat and wine (*Daniel*, 278).

22. Collins calls the abstention from anointing "a traditional sign of mourning" (e.g., 2 Sam 14:2; cf. Isa 61:3) (*Daniel*, 373).

23. Goldingay, *Daniel*, 525.

the time period involved: "three weeks of days" (שְׁלֹשֶׁת שָׁבֻעִים יָמִים, 10:3c). While there are longer fasts in the Bible (e.g., forty days for Moses atop Sinai [Exod 34:28; Deut 9:9–10], Elijah en route to Horeb [1 Kgs 19:8], and Jesus in the wilderness [Matt 4:2]), Daniel's twenty-one-day fast is "extraordinary."[24] Its length is also important enough that Daniel states it twice in two verses.

Daniel's behavior recalls Dan 9, where his prayer of repentance was accompanied by fasting in sackcloth and ashes (9:3). However, in Dan 10, he does not specify that he was praying—though the messenger will later acknowledge that he was there in response to Daniel's "words" (דְּבָרֶיךָ, 10:12g) as he humbled himself before God and sought to understand (10:12c–f).[25] But Daniel himself never makes this explicit. Instead, he focuses on the extent and length of his mourning such that his act of mourning and its potential cause dominate the reader's impressions. Daniel 9 was driven by Daniel's repentance. Daniel 10 is driven by Daniel's grief—a grief that overwhelms him in the third year of Cyrus (cf. Neh 1:4).

c. Individual Vision: The Appearance of the Man (10:4a–9d)

Daniel's vision of the heavenly messenger begins in 10:5a–b (וָאֶשָּׂא אֶת־עֵינַי וָאֵרֶא וְהִנֵּה, "and I lifted my eyes, and I looked, and oh!"), but he prefaces the vision itself with the final component of the extensive space/time referent (10:4; cf. 10:1a, 2a).

The time reference is a second date formula: "On the twenty-fourth day of the first month" (10:4a). The "space" reference is in 10:4b–c: "I was along the bank of the great river—that is the Tigris."

While date formulae are common in the book of Daniel, this final one is unique because it is not linked to a regnal year (cf. Dan 1:1, 21; 2:1; 7:1; 8:1; 9:1; 10:1). Instead, the date formula in 10:4a recalls the Jewish calendar and invites the audience to consider the significance of the twenty-fourth day of the first month. The first month of the Jewish calendar, the month of Abib/Nisan,[26] is the month of Passover and the Feast of Unleavened Bread, a joint celebration beginning on the fourteenth of the month and continuing for seven days. As the commemoration of the deliverance from Egyptian bondage, Passover was one of the most significant celebrations of the year, yet Daniel fasted through it.

The unique dual date formulae for this vision suggest the significance of both dates and quite possibly a connection between them and Daniel's extensive mourning. As discussed above, the third year of Cyrus was a short time after the edict allowing captive Jews to leave their land of exile, return to their own land, and reestablish the worship of their God. A number of Jews did return, but full restoration proved allusive. The fact that Daniel's three weeks of mourning in the early years of this "new exodus" extended through Passover and the Feast of Unleavened Bread implies that his grief may have been over the diminished deliverance and "exodus" from Babylonian exile.[27] It is this

---

24. Newsom, *Daniel*, 330. Goldingay (*Daniel*, 525) observes that the three-week period is explained by the messenger's words in 10:13, while Lacocque (*The Book of Daniel*, 205) notes "that the traditional three days for sanctification ... are here expanded to three weeks" (Exod 19:10–15; Ezra 4:16).

25. Fasting in later apocalyptic literature was frequently a way a person prepared to receive a revelation (e.g., seven-day fasts in 2 Esd 5:13; 2 Bar. 9:1; 12:5; 20:5–6).

26. The name "Abib" (Exod 13:4; 23:15; 34:18; Deut 16:1) was the preexilic name for the first month of the Israelite calendar (March/April), but after the exile, Jews adopted the Babylonian name "Nisan" for the first month.

27. Goldingay notes that Antiochus's hostility against the Jews will make it impossible for them to observe Passover properly (1 Macc 1:39, 45)—turning their celebration into mourning. Thus "Daniel shares in anticipation in this 'mourning'" (*Daniel*, 526).

less-than-expected restoration that the final revelation given to Daniel will ultimately address.

The space reference for Daniel's vision in 10:4b–c puts him on the banks of the Tigris River, the more easterly of the two great Mesopotamian rivers—the Tigris and the Euphrates, the river on which the city of Babylon was built. Elsewhere in the Old Testament, הַנָּהָר הַגָּדוֹל, "the great river," refers to the Euphrates (e.g., Gen 15:18; Deut 1:7; Josh 1:4), but its use here for the Tigris fits well with Daniel's post-Babylonian setting. Unlike earlier visions in which he appears to have been in a trance or dreaming, Daniel is on location for this revelatory experience (cf. 7:1; 8:1; see also Ezek 1:1; 11:1).[28]

Daniel's vision begins in 10:5a–b with his statement "and I lifted my eyes, and I looked, and oh!" (וָאֶשָּׂא אֶת־עֵינַי וָאֵרֶא וְהִנֵּה). The use of הִנֵּה here indicates Daniel's surprise at what he sees—"a man clothed in linen" (10:5b). Linen in the Old Testament is traditional priestly garb (e.g., Exod 28:42; Lev 16:23, 32; Ezek 44:17), but it is also worn by the heavenly scribe in Ezek 9–10. Most basically, it signifies holiness (Lev 16:4). What follows this initial description is a lengthy description of the appearance of the man: he was wearing a golden sash, his body was like topaz with arms gleaming like burnished bronze, his eyes and face flashed (10:5c–6d). Daniel concludes his description with the statement that the sound of the man's words was like the sound of a tumult (קוֹל דְּבָרָיו כְּקוֹל הָמוֹן, 10:6e)—though, at this point, Daniel reports nothing that the man actually said, and it may be that all he heard was an "inarticulate but terrifying roaring."[29]

Then Daniel notes that he alone saw the vision (10:7a). Prior to this comment, the reader had no reason to think otherwise, since neither the narrator (10:1) nor Daniel (10:2–6) had indicated that anyone else was present with Daniel during his three weeks of mourning. Yet here Daniel first comments that he alone saw it, and then he expands his statement by saying the men who were with him did not see it (10:7b–c). Despite not seeing anything, these men were impressed by a great fear, so they fled to hide (10:7d–f). Then Daniel again emphasizes his solitude: "and I alone remained" (10:8a).

The presence (and then absence) of these other men is important in the text for at least two reasons. First, their reaction to a vision they could not see but only sensed underscores the awesome nature of what Daniel saw. Perhaps they heard the "sound of a tumult"—though Daniel does not say so—but even without seeing anything, they were still terrified enough to run for their lives. Second, their inability to see the vision highlights Daniel's value to the one sending the message—a fact made explicit by the messenger in 10:11–12 (cf. 10:19). The vision and the message were for him and him alone.[30]

In the remainder of 10:8, Daniel describes what happened when he saw the vision: no strength remained in him, his vigor was changed "for ruin" (לְמַשְׁחִית), and he was without strength. This threefold statement that Daniel's strength was sapped seems like overkill—but the point is that the vision was utterly overwhelming. Men who could not even see it were terrified by it, and the one who *did* see it was undone. The vision drained him of whatever energy he had. Then the man began to speak and Daniel fell into a deep sleep, facedown on the ground (10:9; cf. 8:18).

The identity of the man clothed in linen is never

---

28. The text, however, does not say why Daniel was in the region of the Tigris—whether he was there on government business or whether he had left Babylon for the purpose of this extended fast, as Miller suggests (*Daniel*, 280).

29. Newsom, *Daniel*, 331.

30. Cf. Exod 20:18; 2 Kgs 2:11–18; Acts 9:7.

made explicit—unlike the identity of the interpreter of Daniel's vision in Dan 8 and the messenger of the revelation in Dan 9 (i.e., Gabriel, 8:16–17; 9:20–21). While many commentors assume the man in linen is also Gabriel,[31] at least three things suggest otherwise. First, Daniel does not name the man, when he has already named Gabriel in his visions twice. Second, Daniel's reaction here is dramatically different from his reaction to Gabriel in previous appearances. Admittedly, when Gabriel first approached him in Dan 8:17, Daniel fell to the ground, but when Gabriel appeared in Dan 9, Daniel shows no such fear. Third, the description of the "man clothed in linen" goes beyond any of Daniel's descriptions of "holy ones" (i.e., angelic beings) and instead echoes much of Ezekiel's language to describe his visions of God by the Kebar River (Ezek 1). Daniel is seeing someone greater than Gabriel—and arguably someone greater than any angel. Daniel is seeing a theophany—that is, an appearance of God in human form.[32]

d. Individual Vision: An Enabling Touch and an Encouraging Word (10:10a–15c)

The second individual vision of the first vision block begins in 10:10a, when Daniel reports, "And oh! A hand touched me." This hand set him trembling on all fours and then "He said to me" (10:11a). The speaker ("he") is not explicitly identified, leaving the reader to assume it belongs to the only other being introduced so far—the man clothed in linen. But whose hand touches Daniel? Beginning at this point and continuing through the rest of ch. 10, determining how many beings are involved in Daniel's vision and what role each plays is difficult. My view, which I detail below, is that there are two distinct figures: the man clothed in linen (who, we learn in 12:6, is above the waters of the river) and another humanlike figure on the riverbank near Daniel. The man clothed in linen is the one who does all the speaking, and the humanlike figure is the one who administers all the strengthening touches to Daniel.[33]

It is important to remember that the events of 10:10–19 are recounted from Daniel's perspective, and in 10:10, that perspective has him face down on the ground in a trance-like sleep. What he suddenly realizes (הִנֵּה) is that a hand is touching (נֹגַעַת) him. Given what this hand does, "touch" may be an understated translation: he is pulled from a prostrate position to a "four on the floor" position. In neither of these positions would Daniel have necessarily seen the being to whom the hand belonged. What he does know is that a hand has pulled him out of his sleep and set him on all fours.

---

31. See, e.g., Montgomery, *Daniel*, 420; Newsom, *Daniel*, 330; Hill (*Daniel*, 180) considers the man to be either Gabriel or another angel.

32. Commentators who consider the "man clothed in linen" to be a theophany (or a christophany—a preincarnate appearance of Christ)—include, e.g., Young, *The Prophecy of Daniel*, 225; Miller, *Daniel*, 281–82 (but see p. n33 below); cf. Longman, *Daniel*, 248–50. See also Chapell, *The Gospel According to Daniel*, 171–72. The primary problem with this view is what the "man clothed in linen" says in 10:13–14. See p. 510n36 below.

33. While my view has long been that there are two figures (a theophany and an angel) in the Dan 10 scene, I have changed my view about each one's role since writing my earlier commentary (see *Daniel*, 220–22). Most scholars consider the hand and the voice to belong to the man clothed in linen (as I did), though most also see a second figure in the scene by 10:16. Miller sees the second figure entering the scene in 10:10 (as I do), but he assigns all the speaking to this second figure (as I do not). Following G. C. Luck (*Daniel* [Chicago: Moody, 1958], 109) and Walvoord (*Daniel*, 243–45), Miller considers this second figure (10:10–14) to be an interpreting angel, while the "man clothed in linen" is God (for some of the reasons I discuss above). Miller thinks a second figure must be in view here because the "language of vv. 11–14 is inappropriate as applied to deity" (*Daniel*, 282n26). I think a second figure is in view here because the text itself leads me in this direction—that is, my view is textual, while Miller's is theological. See further on Dan 10:13–14.

Then "he" speaks to Daniel (וַיֹּאמֶר, 10:11a). From Daniel's perspective, this "he" is the only other figure he knows to be in the vision: the man clothed in linen. While "a hand" roused him and raised him, Daniel has not yet seen whose hand it is.[34] The man uses Daniel's name and calls him אִישׁ־חֲמֻדוֹת, "highly favored man" (10:11b). Gabriel had used similar language in 9:23 in his explanation for coming to Daniel (כִּי חֲמוּדוֹת אָתָּה). In the context of Dan 10, this title is further affirmation of Daniel's unique value as the recipient of this revelation (see on 10:7 above). The man then issues two commands to Daniel: first, he was to understand the words that were about to be told to him, and second, he was to stand up to hear the message. When Daniel heard "this word" (אֶת־הַדָּבָר הַזֶּה) from the messenger, he was able to stand as commanded (10:11f–g). There was encouragement in "this word"—Daniel was highly treasured, and this man had been sent to give him a message.

Then the man spoke again, offering further explanation for his presence. He tells Daniel not to be afraid because his words had been heard from the first day (10:12b–c), and it was because of those words that the man had come (10:12g). The man makes explicit what the reader could only infer earlier—that is, that Daniel had been praying during his extended period of mourning (see on 10:2 above). Between the two parts of clause 10:12c, the man details the nature of Daniel's prayer: he had set his heart to understand (לְהָבִין) and to humble himself (לְהִתְעַנּוֹת) before his God (10:12d–f). The man's encouragement to Daniel is that from the time he started praying, he had been heard, and the man with his message was a response to those prayers.

This is similar to what happened in ch. 9: Daniel had understood (בִּין) Jeremiah's prophecy (9:2); he had confessed his people's sin, humbling himself before God (9:3–4, 20); Gabriel, dispatched "at the beginning of [Daniel's] supplication," was sent to help Daniel understand (בִּין, 9:22–23). However, in Dan 9, the response was nearly instantaneous, whereas here in Dan 10, the messenger is "three weeks of days" late. Newsom comments that this "contrast between the two situations . . . suggests the heightened importance" of the situation in Dan 10.[35] What the man says next also amplifies the importance of this situation. He explains his twenty-one-day delay: he had been prevented from coming by the antagonistic prince of the kingdom of Persia (10:13a), and he was unable to get away until Michael, one of the chief princes, came to his aid (10:13b).[36] God does not owe an explanation for his delays—and there is no textual evidence that Daniel even asked for one—yet the man provides

---

34. While many commentators assume the hand belongs to the man clothed in linen, the text does not require this. In Dan 12:5, the man clothed in linen is said to be above the waters, and given Daniel's position on the banks of the river in ch. 10, it is entirely plausible—even probable?—that the man is also there in the initial vision, while the one touching him is next to him on the riverbank.

35. Newsom, *Daniel*, 332.

36. Herein lies the primary opposition for viewing "the man clothed in linen" as an appearance of God. As Longman says, "What power could resist God for twenty-one days, as the 'prince of the Persian kingdom' apparently had done? Can we really imagine God being thwarted in his purposes so effectively, even if temporarily?" Similarly, Miller says, "No being could resist the power of God himself (certainly not the omnipotent, sovereign God described time and time again in the Book of Daniel) for a moment much less for twenty-one days" (*Daniel*, 282). But, as I have said elsewhere, "perhaps this is theology dictating interpretation. First, who can say what God's purposes might have been in such a struggle, much less whether they were thwarted? Second, given the paucity of information we have about how the supernatural world operates, how can we say what God does and does not allow in heavenly struggles? Third, this divine struggle to overcome would not be the first of its kind in the biblical story: consider Jacob's wrestling match with the angel of Yahweh (Gen 32:22–33). Sometimes God limits himself to the 'rules' he embedded in creation" (*Daniel*, 220).

the explanation, perhaps another indication of how special Daniel was (cf. 10:11, 19).

The explanation in 10:13 answers fewer questions for us than it raises—questions about the nature of divine beings and spiritual warfare.[37] What we can say, based on Deut 32:8–9, is that the "prince of Persia" was presumably the divine being YHWH had assigned to rule the territory of Persia, while Michael, here called "one of the chief princes" and later identified as the "prince" (שַׂר) of Daniel's people (10:21b; 12:1), was the divine being YHWH assigned to rule Israel.[38] For reasons the text does not say, the prince of Persia stood in the way of the messenger bringing the message to Daniel. Although the text does not provide an explicit reason for the opposition, it does explain why the messenger was bringing the message: to help Daniel understand what was going to happen to his people at a future time (10:14). Given this, Newsom's assessment of the prince of Persia's opposition seems correct:

> Why does he try to detain Gabriel, and what does he hope to accomplish by doing so? As Gabriel's message will make clear, the duration of Persian sovereignty has already been determined (11:2). The prince of Persia cannot change that by his actions. All he can do is try to prevent Gabriel from

communicating the future course of history to Daniel and thereby prevent that knowledge from reaching its ultimate recipients during the persecutions under Antiochus IV. For the authors of Dan 7–12, insight into "the truth" was vital; it was the only basis not only for courage and confidence but also for knowing the proper actions to take in response to the persecutions (see 11:33–35). Thus the actions of the prince of Persia appear to be part of a general Gentile hostility toward God and Israel.[39]

The messenger says the vision pertains to the "latter days" and "days yet to come" (10:14b-c). The expression "the latter days" (בְּאַחֲרִית הַיָּמִים) occurs elsewhere in the Old Testament, and while it can refer to the future day when God establishes his kingdom (e.g., Isa 2:2; Hos 3:5), it can also have a noneschatological day in view (e.g., Gen 49:1; Num 24:14; Deut 4:30; 31:29). Here in Daniel the time frames seem to refer to *the* end as well as to a specific turning point in Israel's future.[40]

When Daniel heard these words (כַּדְּבָרִים הָאֵלֶּה) from the messenger, he dropped his head, and he was unable to speak (10:15). Which part of "these words" affected him the most is impossible to say, but it seems reasonable to assume it was everything: hearing that he was about to learn more about

---

37. While the Old Testament reflects ancient Near Eastern ideas about divine beings ruling over nations (e.g., Deut 32:8–9; 2 Kgs 18:33–35; cf. Sir 17:17) and assumes the involvement of heavenly beings in earthly affairs—particularly with respect to warfare (e.g., Num 10:35–36; Deut 33:2–3; Judg 5:19–20; Hab 3:12–13; Lucas, *Daniel*, 275–76)—we get few clear pictures of what that looks like. The clearest picture of such affairs is in the book of Daniel. We do know that YHWH assigned the territories of the world to heavenly beings ("sons of God") after the events at Babel, but he kept Israel as his own territory/property (though Michael also becomes "prince of Israel"—see further n38 below).

38. Michael only appears a handful of times in the Bible (Dan 10:13, 21; 12:1; Jude 9; Rev 12:7), but in Second Temple literature he is identified as one of the archangels and specifically as the one given authority among the divine beings (e.g., 1 En. 20:5; 1QM 9:15–16; 1QM 17:6–7). See Newsom, *Daniel*, 332–33.

39. Newsom, *Daniel*, 333. Miller suggests that that the "struggle involved all of the decisions and relationships pertaining to the Jews during the Persian period (e.g., the reconstruction of the temple, deliverance for the Jews during the time of Esther, permission for Ezra and Nehemiah to return, and their subsequent construction of the city)" (*Daniel*, 288).

40. Lucas, *Daniel*, 277.

"the latter days" for his people (cf. his response to such knowledge in 7:28 and 8:27) and hearing the enigmatic allusions to the heavenly realm.

e. Individual Vision: Additional Enabling (10:16a–11:2a)

The third and final individual vision of the first vision block begins in 10:16a when Daniel reports, "Then oh! One with the likeness of the sons of men was touching my lips" (וְהִנֵּה כִּדְמוּת בְּנֵי אָדָם נֹגֵעַ עַל־שְׂפָתָי). This occurrence of הִנֵּה, as with the hand in 10:10, indicates Daniel's perception of something new in his vision. Here, he sees (and feels) one with the "likeness of the sons of men" touching his lips. I consider this "new" figure to be the same one whose hand touched Daniel in 10:10, except at this point he sees the whole being instead of just sensing the touch of its hand. He describes this figure comparatively—that is, it looks *like* a human being—whereas he had described the first figure of his vision as a man (אִישׁ־אֶחָד, 10:5b). Perhaps Daniel "does not make bold to identify [this] figure clearly"[41] because his head is down and the being is in such close proximity (it is, after all, touching his lips) that Daniel cannot adequately take in the whole of its shape.

This second touch enabled Daniel to open his mouth and speak. Unlike Isaiah and Jeremiah before him, who received angelic touches on their lips in preparation for their prophetic tasks (cf. Isa 6:5–7; Jer 1:9), Daniel receives this touch so that he can respond to "the one standing before me" (הָעֹמֵד לְנֶגְדִּי, 10:16d)—that is, the man clothed in linen. Daniel is responding to the one who has been speaking to him since 10:11.

What follows in the rest of this section is a dialogue between Daniel (10:16d–17, 19g–i) and the man clothed in linen (10:19a–d, 10:20a–11:2a). Daniel addresses the man clothed in linen as "my lord" (אֲדֹנִי) and tells him in four clauses the effects of the vision on him. First, "pangs," like those of a woman in labor, have come upon him (10:16e; 1 Sam 4:19; Isa 13:8; 21:3). Then, he had not retained any strength (10:16f); no strength remained in him (10:17c); and he had no breath left (10:17d). In the middle of these four clauses is the heart of the matter for Daniel (10:17a–b): "How is the servant of this my lord able to speak with this my lord?" (הֵיךְ יוּכַל עֶבֶד אֲדֹנִי זֶה לְדַבֵּר עִם־אֲדֹנִי זֶה). The meaning of this awkward syntax is best captured by the translation, "How can I, your mere servant, speak with one such as you?" Daniel has been completely undone by the vision of the man in linen, and he has yet to hear the message the man is bringing.

In 10:18 the second figure touches him again, strengthening him, and in 10:19 the man clothed in linen encourages him: "Do not be afraid, dearly loved man . . ." (10:19b).[42] He tells him, "Be strong! Be really strong!" (NET), and at these words, Daniel is finally strengthened (10:19e–f) and so tells the man in linen to speak because he has strengthened him (10:19g–i).

The man in linen responds to Daniel in 10:20–11:1, offering further explanation of the extenuating circumstances. He asks a rhetorical question in 10:20b that he will answer in 10:21a—namely, "Do you know why I came to you? . . . I will tell you

---

41. Collins, *Daniel*, 375.

42. The "he" of וַיֹּאמֶר in 10:19a may well refer to the second figure, the one who touched him in 10:18, but in the entire context of 10:10–20, it also makes good sense for this to be the man clothed in linen. In my view, the man does all the speaking, while the second figure administers all the enabling touches.

what is inscribed in a book of truth."[43] Between this question and answer, the messenger returns to the topic of his struggle with the prince of Persia, noting that he must go because the prince of Greece is coming—perhaps suggesting that the heated battle is about to get more heated, and his presence is very much needed. Then after his answer in 10:21a, he speaks again about the celestial struggle, noting this time that his only strong ally in the fight is "Michael, your [pl.] prince" (מִיכָאֵל שַׂרְכֶם, 10:21b). As confirmation of this strong alliance, the man comments that he arose to strengthen and protect him during the first year of Darius the Mede.[44]

Although we are not told what challenge Michael faced in the first year of Darius that required reinforcement, this is the book's second explicit reference to the first year of Darius the Mede (cf. Dan 9:1–2), inviting us to consider the relationship between the two. In ch. 9, Daniel had been praying for the restoration of his people and the Jerusalem temple as he reflected on Jeremiah's prophecy of a seventy-year exile. The first year of Darius the Mede coincided with the decree of Persian Cyrus to allow captive people groups to return to their homelands and rebuild their worship sites.[45]

As Michael's people—the Jews—anticipated their return to Palestine, one wonders if other heavenly princes really wanted the Jews restored to their land. The text only teases us, but perhaps Israel's prince, Michael, faced significant heavenly conflict in the days leading up to Cyrus's important decree, and the man clothed in linen came alongside Michael to fight on behalf of God's exiled people and their release from captivity.[46]

The back-and-forth thoughts expressed by the messenger in 10:21–11:1 have vexed scholars, some of whom conclude the text is "jumbled" or "disturbed."[47] As it stands, the discourse effect of the messenger's explanation is that he appears torn between two urgent and important matters. The celestial conflict is raging and Michael awaits his return, but the message of truth for the dearly loved Daniel is pressing enough to have required the man in linen leave the heat of battle to deliver it.[48]

By 11:2a the man clothed in linen is finally ready to deliver his message: "But now truth I will tell you." The long introduction to the man's message (10:10–11:1) is remarkable and points to the significance of the message, the messenger, and the recipient.

---

43. The "book of truth" is likely a reference to a record of the course of history as determined by God (cf. 1 En. 93:2).

44. The referent for "him" in 11:1c ("I . . . arose to strengthen and be protection for him") is ambiguous and could syntactically refer to Michael or Darius. My understanding is that "he" is Michael, but if it is Darius, my interpretation is little affected.

45. For the identity of Darius the Mede, see discussion in ch. 5 at p. 286n95.

46. If this reading is correct, then we may also see evidence in 11:1 that God was actively answering Daniel's prayer for restoration in Dan 9—as Daniel prayed in the first year of Darius, God was moving to restore his people through the decree of Cyrus.

47. Hartman and Di Lella, The Book of Daniel, 285; and Newsom, Daniel, 335.

48. My comments about what spiritual warfare may actually look like are intentionally vague. I do not think the Bible gives us enough information to say much more. Heavenly beings are real and their warfare is real, but how their struggles transpire I am not willing to say.

2. Vision Block 2: *The Revelation from the Book of Truth* (11:2b–12:4d)

Main Idea of the Passage

In Daniel 11:2b–12:4, the man clothed in linen discloses to Daniel a detailed prophecy that traces events from the time of the Persian Empire to the resurrection and reward of the righteous. The focus of the prophecy is the tumultuous period that encompasses the activities of the "king of the north," a collective expression for Seleucid kings—most notably, Antiochus the Great (III) and Antiochus IV Epiphanes.

Literary Context

Daniel 11:2b–12:4 is the second and longest section of the narrative in Dan 10–12. It follows the appearance of the "man clothed in linen" in ch. 10 and contains the entirety of the message he came to deliver. In this broader literary context, the section functions in at least four ways. First, it details the revelation given to Daniel after his three weeks of mourning on the banks of the Tigris River. Second, as Daniel's fourth apocalyptic vision and the book's final revelation, the section serves as the climax of the book in its king who embodies the sum total of all wicked kings. Third, it provides resolution to the book's question of the suffering faithful by offering the promise that the wicked will be judged and the faithful will receive their reward in the resurrection. Finally, in its patterned portrayal of wicked gentile kings, the revelation provides a template that can be applied repeatedly until the end time.

> C. Narrative 3: The Ultimate Conflict and God's Final Victory (10:1a–12:13c)
>   1. Vision Block 1: The Vision of a Heavenly Messenger (10:1a–11:2a)
> ➡ **2. Vision Block 2: The Revelation from the Book of Truth (11:2b–12:4d)**
>   3. Vision Block 3: The Vision of Two Others (12:5a–13c)

Translation and Exegetical Outline

(See pages 516–22.)

Structure and Literary Form

The second section of the narrative in Dan 10–12 (11:2b–12:4) continues Daniel's vision report begun in 10:2, and it contains the message the man clothed in linen brought to Daniel. This message consists of six subsections: 11:2b–e; 11:3–4; 11:5–35; 11:36–45; 12:1–3; and 12:4.

The first four subsections (11:2b–45) survey the rise and fall of successive empires and/or kings, beginning with the Persian Empire (11:2b–e) and continuing on to "a king of strength" (מֶלֶךְ גִּבּוֹר, 11:3–4, i.e., Alexander the Great of Greece) and then to a series of "kings of the north" and "kings of the south" (11:5–35) before culminating in the rise and demise of "the king," a king who embodies the worst of all kings (11:36–45). This survey of kings and kingdoms has what Newsom calls "structural repeatability," that is, "discernible repetitions, recurrences of analogous phenomena."[49] This pattern is established by repetition of words/roots and phrases such as עמד ("arise, stand," 11:2–4, 6–8, 11, 13–17, 20–21, 25, 31), חזק ("be strong," 11:5–7, 21; cf. גִּבּוֹר, 11:3), כִּרְצוֹנוֹ ("as he pleases," 11:3, 16, 36), and משל ("to rule;" 11:3–5, 39, 43), and it depicts the rise, growth, and demise of successive powers.

The fifth subsection (12:1–3) concerns a time of great distress that occurs "at that time" (בָּעֵת הַהִיא, 12:1a)—that is, a time concurrent with the rampage of the last king in the preceding verses. At that time (בָּעֵת הַהִיא, 12:1e), Daniel's people will experience deliverance and reward. The six and final subsection (12:4) consists of the messenger's charge to Daniel to keep the revelation secret and seal the scroll.

The entire section (11:2b–12:4) is shaded on the charts because it still represents Daniel's reported speech. However, the section is also the embedded speech report of the messenger, and so is bordered with lines indicating this. Every independent clause is indented a minimum of twice: once for being Daniel's reported speech and again for being embedded speech within Daniel's speech. Dependent clauses are indented further, according to their relationship to their respective independent clauses.

---

49. Newsom, *Daniel*, 327. In her discussion of the structure of ch. 11, Newsom references the work of Reinhart Koselleck (*The Practice of Conceptual History: Timing History, Spacing Concepts*, trans. T. S. Presner et al. [Stanford: Stanford University Press, 2002]), and it is unclear whether the phrase "structural repeatability" is hers or his.

Daniel 11:2b–12:4d

			2. Vision Block 2: The Revelation from the Book of Truth (11:2b–12:4d)
			a. The Kings of Persia (11:2b–e)
2b		"Listen, another three kings are arising for Persia,	
2c		and the fourth will gain much more wealth than all of them.	
2d		And when he has become strong in his wealth,	
2e		he will stir up everything—that is, the kingdom of Greece.	
			b. A King of Strength (11:3a–4h)
3a		A king of strength will arise.	
3b		He will rule with great authority,	
3c		and he will do as he pleases.	
4a		↳ But when he has arisen,	
4b		his kingdom will be broken,	
4c		and it will be divided to the four winds of the heavens—	
4d		but not to his descendants	
4e		and not according to his authority	
4f		↑ which he ruled,	
4g		↳ for his kingdom will be uprooted	
4h		and (given) to others besides these.	
			c. The Kings of the North and the South (11:5a–35e)
			(1) Attempted Alliance and Repeated Invasions (11:5a–9b)
5a		And the king of the south and one of his princes will grow strong,	
5b		and he will grow strong over him.	
5c		And he will rule.	
5d		His dominion will be a great dominion.	
6a		At the end of years they will ally,	
6b		and the daughter of the king of the south will come to the king of the north	
6c		↑ to make an agreement.	
6d		But she will not retain the strength of arm,	
6e		and he will not stand, or his arm.	
6f		And she will be given over, and the ones who brought her, and he who fathered her, and he who supported her in that time.	

7a	וּבָא אֶל־הַחַיִל	One of the shoots from her root will arise in his place,	
7b	וּמִצְעַד מִנֶּזֶר שָׁרָשֶׁיהָ כַּנּוֹ יַעֲמֹד	and he will come to the army,	
7c	וְיָבֹא אֶל־הַחַיִל	and he will enter the fortress of the king of the north,	
7d	וְיָבֹא בְמָעוֹז מֶלֶךְ הַצָּפוֹן	and he will deal with them,	
7e	וְעָשָׂה בָהֶם וְהֶחֱזִיק׃	and he will prevail.	
8a	וְגַם אֱלֹהֵיהֶם עִם־נְסִכֵיהֶם עִם־כְּלֵי חֶמְדָּתָם כֶּסֶף וְזָהָב בַּשְּׁבִי יָבִא מִצְרָיִם	And also their gods with their molten images, with their precious vessels of silver and gold into captivity he will take to Egypt.	
8b	וְהוּא שָׁנִים יַעֲמֹד מִמֶּלֶךְ הַצָּפוֹן׃	And he for years will withdraw from the king of the north.	
9a	וּבָא בְּמַלְכוּת מֶלֶךְ הַנֶּגֶב	Then he [the king of the north] will come into the realm of the king of the south,	
9b	וְשָׁב אֶל־אַדְמָתוֹ׃	but he will return to his own land.	
10a	(וּבְנוֹ) [וּבָנָיו] יִתְגָּרוּ	But his sons will mobilize	
10b	וְאָסְפוּ הֲמוֹן חֲיָלִים רַבִּים	and gather a multitude of great power.	
10c	וּבָא בוֹא	It will keep coming	
10d	וְשָׁטַף	and overflow	
10e	וְעָבָר	and pass through	
10f	וְיָשֹׁב	and return	
10g	(וְיִתְגָּרוּ) [וְיִתְגָּרֶה] עַד־(מָעֻזֹּה) [מָעֻזּוֹ]׃	and wage war as far as [his] fortress.	(2) Exploits of the King of the North (11:10a–19d)
11a	וְיִתְמַרְמַר מֶלֶךְ הַנֶּגֶב	But the king of the south will be enraged,	
11b	וְיָצָא	and he will go out,	
11c	וְנִלְחַם עִמּוֹ עִם־מֶלֶךְ הַצָּפוֹן	and he will fight with him, with the king of the north.	
11d	וְהֶעֱמִיד הָמוֹן רָב	He will raise up a great multitude,	
11e	וְנִתַּן הֶהָמוֹן בְּיָדוֹ׃	but the multitude will be given into his hand.	
12a	→וְנִשָּׂא הֶהָמוֹן	→ When the multitude is carried away,	
12b	(וְרָב) [יָרוּם] לְבָבוֹ	his heart will be lifted up,	
12c	וְהִפִּיל רִבֹּאוֹת	and he will throw down tens of thousands,	
12d	וְלֹא יָעוֹז׃	but he will not remain strong.	
13a	וְשָׁב מֶלֶךְ הַצָּפוֹן וְהֶעֱמִיד הָמוֹן רַב מִן־הָרִאשׁוֹן	Again, the king of the north will raise up a multitude greater than the first,	
13b	וּלְקֵץ הָעִתִּים שָׁנִים יָבוֹא בוֹא בְּחַיִל גָּדוֹל וּבִרְכוּשׁ רָב׃	and at the time of the end, some years, he will again come with a great army and abundant supplies.	

Continued on next page.

Continued from previous page.

14a	וּבָעִתִּים הָהֵם רַבִּים יַעַמְדוּ עַל־מֶלֶךְ הַנֶּגֶב	And in those times, many will stand against the king of the south,
14b	וּבְנֵי פָּרִיצֵי עַמְּךָ יִנַּשְּׂאוּ	and the sons of the violent ones of your people will be lifted up
14c	לְהַעֲמִיד חָזוֹן	↑ to establish a vision,
14d	וְנִכְשָׁלוּ׃	but they will stumble.
15a	וְיָבֹא מֶלֶךְ הַצָּפוֹן	Then the king of the north will come,
15b	וְיִשְׁפֹּךְ סוֹלֲלָה	and heap up an assault ramp,
15c	וְלָכַד עִיר מִבְצָרוֹת	and he will capture a fortified city.
15d	וּזְרֹעוֹת הַנֶּגֶב לֹא יַעֲמֹדוּ וְעַם מִבְחָרָיו	And the strength of the south will not stand, not even his choice troops.
15e	וְאֵין כֹּחַ לַעֲמֹד׃	There will be no strength to stand.
16a	וְיַעַשׂ הַבָּא אֵלָיו כִּרְצוֹנוֹ	The one coming against him will do as he pleases.
16b	וְאֵין עוֹמֵד לְפָנָיו	No one will stand before him.
16c	וְיַעֲמֹד בְּאֶרֶץ־הַצְּבִי	He will stand in the Beautiful Land,
16d	וְכָלָה בְיָדוֹ׃	and destruction will be in his hand.
17a	וְיָשֵׂם פָּנָיו	He will set his face
17b	לָבוֹא בְּתֹקֶף כָּל־מַלְכוּתוֹ וִישָׁרִים עִמּוֹ	↑ to come with the power of his entire kingdom, and a proposal with him,
17c	וְעָשָׂה׃	and he will make it.
17d	וּבַת הַנָּשִׁים יִתֶּן־לוֹ	And the daughter of women he will give him
17e	לְהַשְׁחִיתָהּ	↑ to ruin it [the kingdom],
17f	וְלֹא תַעֲמֹד	but it will not stand,
17g	וְלֹא־לוֹ תִהְיֶה׃	and it will not be for him.
18a	וְיָשֵׁב (וְיָשֵׂם) פָּנָיו לְאִיִּים	Then he will set his face to coastlands,
18b	וְלָכַד רַבִּים	and he will capture many.
18c	וְהִשְׁבִּית קָצִין חֶרְפָּתוֹ לוֹ	But a commander will stop his scorn against him—
18d	בִּלְתִּי חֶרְפָּתוֹ יָשִׁיב לוֹ׃	moreover, he will return his scorn to him.
19a	וְיָשֵׁב פָּנָיו לְמָעוּזֵּי אַרְצוֹ	So he will set his face to the fortresses of his land,
19b	וְנִכְשַׁל	but he will stumble,
19c	וְנָפַל	and he will fall,
19d	וְלֹא יִמָּצֵא׃	and he will not be found.
20a	וְעָמַד עַל־כַּנּוֹ	Then one will stand in his place,
20b	מַעֲבִיר נוֹגֵשׂ הֶדֶר מַלְכוּת	↑ who sends out a tax collector for the splendor of the kingdom.
20c	וּבְיָמִים אֲחָדִים יִשָּׁבֵר	But within few days he will be shattered,
20d	וְלֹא בְאַפַּיִם וְלֹא בְמִלְחָמָה׃	↑ but not in anger and not in battle.

(3) Exploits of the King of the North, the Despicable One (11:20a–35e)

Daniel 10:1a–12:13c

21a	Then in his place will stand a despicable person,
21b	but the honor of kingdom will not be given to him.
21c	He will come with ease,
21d	and he will seize the kingdom by intrigues.
22a	The overflowing forces will be overwhelmed before him,
22b	and they will be broken—and also a ruler of a covenant.
23a	↳ And after he makes an alliance with him,
23b	he will act deceitfully.
23c	He will go up,
23d	and he will become powerful with a few people.
24a	With ease and into the richest province he will come,
24b	and he will do
24c	↑ what his fathers and his fathers' fathers had not done.
24d	Booty and plunder and property to them he will distribute,
24e	and against fortified cities he will devise his plans—but only for a time.
25a	He will stir up his power and his heart against the king of the south with his great army,
25b	and the king of the south will prepare for battle with his very great and large army,
25c	but he will not stand,
25d	↑ because plans will be devised against him.
26a	The ones eating his choice food will break him,
26b	and his army will overflow,
26c	and many will fall slain.
27a	As for these two kings—their hearts will be for evil,
27b	and at the same table lies they will speak,
27c	but it will not succeed,
27d	↑ for still there will be an end at an appointed time.
28a	Then he will return to his land with great wealth,
28b	but his heart will be against the holy covenant.
28c	He will take action,
28d	and he will return to his land.

Continued from previous page.

29a	At an appointed time he will return,	
29b	and enter the south,	
29c	but the latter will not be like the former—	
30a	The ships of Kittim will come against him,	
30b	and he will be humbled.	
30c	He will return,	
30d	and he will be angry against the holy covenant.	
30e	He will take action,	
30f	and then he will return.	
30g	He will show regard for those who abandon the holy covenant.	
31a	Forces from him will arise,	
31b	and they will desecrate the sanctuary fortress.	
31c	They will remove the daily sacrifice,	
31d	and they will set up the abomination that desolates.	
32a	The wicked ones of the covenant he will pollute with smooth words,	
32b	but the people who know their God will be strong,	
32c	and they will act.	
33a	And the wise of the people will instruct the many,	
33b	but they will stumble by the sword, by fire, by captivity, or by plunder for days.	
34a	↳ And when they stumble,	
34b	they will be given a little help,	
34c	and many will join them insincerely.	
35a	But some of the wise will stumble,	
35b	↳ to refine them,	
35c	and to purify,	
35d	and to make them pure until an end time,	
35e	↳ for it is still for the appointed time.	
36a	The king will do as he pleases,	
36b	and he will exalt himself.	
36c	He will make himself greater than any god,	
36d	and against the God of gods he will speak great things.	

d. A King of Kings (11:36a–45c)

Daniel 10:1a–12:13c

36e	וְהִצְלִיחַ ↑	He will prosper
36f	עַד־כָּלָה זַעַם	until wrath is finished,
36g	כִּי נֶחֱרָצָה נֶעֱשָׂתָה׃	↑ for that which is decreed has been done.
37a	וְעַל־אֱלֹהֵי אֲבֹתָיו לֹא יָבִין	The gods of his fathers he will not regard——nor the one beloved of women.
37b	וְעַל־חֶמְדַּת נָשִׁים	
37c	וְעַל־כָּל־אֱלוֹהַּ לֹא יָבִין	He will not regard any god,
38a	כִּי עַל־כֹּל יִתְגַּדָּל׃	for he will magnify himself against them all.
38bα	וְלֶאֱלֹהַּ מָעֻזִּים ...	But a god of fortresses instead he will honor,
38c	עַל־כַּנּוֹ יְכַבֵּד	and a god ...
38bβ	וְלֶאֱלוֹהַּ אֲשֶׁר לֹא־יְדָעֻהוּ אֲבֹתָיו ↑	↑ which his fathers did not know
	יְכַבֵּד בְּזָהָב וּבְכֶסֶף וּבְאֶבֶן יְקָרָה וּבַחֲמֻדוֹת׃	... he will honor with gold and with silver and with costly stones, and with treasures.
39a	וְעָשָׂה לְמִבְצְרֵי מָעֻזִּים עִם־אֱלוֹהַּ נֵכָר	He will act against a fortress of fortresses with a foreign god.
39b	אֲשֶׁר (הִכִּיר) [יַכִּיר] ↑	↓ The one he regards
39c	יַרְבֶּה כָבוֹד	he will show great honor,
39d	וְהִמְשִׁילָם בָּרַבִּים	and he will make them ruler over the many,
39e	וַאֲדָמָה יְחַלֵּק בִּמְחִיר׃	and the land he will divide up for a price.
40a	וּבְעֵת קֵץ יִתְנַגַּח עִמּוֹ מֶלֶךְ הַנֶּגֶב	But at an end time, the king of the south will make war with him.
40b	וְיִשְׂתָּעֵר עָלָיו מֶלֶךְ הַצָּפוֹן בְּרֶכֶב וּבְפָרָשִׁים וּבָאֳנִיּוֹת רַבּוֹת	The king of the north will storm against him with chariot and horsemen and with many ships.
40c	וּבָא בַאֲרָצוֹת	He will enter the lands,
40d	וְשָׁטַף	and he will overflow,
40e	וְעָבָר׃	and he will cross over,
41a	וּבָא בְּאֶרֶץ הַצְּבִי	and he will enter the Beautiful Land.
41b	וְרַבּוֹת יִכָּשֵׁלוּ	And many will stumble,
41c	וְאֵלֶּה יִמָּלְטוּ מִיָּדוֹ אֱדוֹם וּמוֹאָב וְרֵאשִׁית בְּנֵי עַמּוֹן׃	but these will be rescued from his hand——Edom, Moab, and the chief sons of Ammon.
42a	וְיִשְׁלַח יָדוֹ בַּאֲרָצוֹת	He will stretch out his hand against the lands,
42b	וְאֶרֶץ מִצְרַיִם לֹא תִהְיֶה לִפְלֵיטָה׃	and the land of Egypt will not escape.
43a	וּמָשַׁל בְּמִכְמַנֵּי הַזָּהָב וְהַכֶּסֶף וּבְכֹל חֲמֻדוֹת מִצְרָיִם	He will rule over the hidden treasures of gold and silver and all the treasures of Egypt.
43b	וְלֻבִים וְכֻשִׁים בְּמִצְעָדָיו׃	The Libyans and Cushites will be in his steps.

Continued on next page.

Continued from previous page.

44a		Then reports will alarm him from the east and the north,
44b		and he will go out in great fury
44c		↳ to destroy
44d		and to devote many to destruction.
45a		He will pitch his royal tents between the seas and the beautiful holy mountain,
45b		but he will come to his end,
45c		and there will be no one to help him.
12:1a		At that time Michael will arise,
12:1b		↳ the great prince standing over the sons of your people.
12:1c		It will be a time of distress
12:1d		↳ which has not been from the beginning of a nation until that time.
12:1e	e. The Time of Distress (12:1a–3b)	And at that time your people will be delivered—
12:1f		↳ all the ones found written in the book.
12:2a		And many of those sleeping in the dusty earth will arise—
12:2b		↳ these to life everlasting,
12:2c		and these to shame and to everlasting abhorrence.
12:3a		The wise will shine like the shining of the expanse of the heavens,
12:3b		and the ones who make many righteous like the stars forever and ever.
12:4a	f. The Charge to Daniel (12:4a–d)	'But now, Daniel, keep these words secret,
12:4b		and seal the scroll until a time of the end.
12:4c		Many will roam about,
12:4d		and knowledge will increase.'

Explanation of the Text

The revelation of Dan 11 is an extraordinary prophecy of events that concerned the Jews from the fourth to the second-century BCE. The level of detail in the revelation is astounding (and anomalous) in terms of biblical prophecy, such that a reader can fill in the specific names and identify the specific events of nearly everything described.[50] While Dan 11 covers a multi-century swath of history, it does so in a formulaic and patterned way. Since the approach of this commentary is considering how the structure of a text contributes to its meaning, this patterning of the text is of primary interest in the comments that follow. I have included the basic history depicted by the prophecy but have footnoted as appropriate a more detailed history as well as other issues.

a. The Kings of Persia (11:2b–e)

The second vision block of the Dan 10–12 narrative begins with הִנֵּה (11:2b), which signals that what follows is the message the man clothed in linen was sent to deliver.[51] Since the "vision" to follow is not properly a vision but rather an auditory revelation, I have translated הִנֵּה as "listen!"

Dated to the third year of Cyrus (10:1), the revelation begins by announcing that "another three kings are arising [עֹמְדִים] for Persia, and the fourth will gain much more wealth than all of them." History knows of many more than four Persian kings after Cyrus, so "four" is symbolic for the totality of Persian kings from the time of Cyrus to the end of the Persian Empire.[52] When the fourth king, said to

---

50. Such detail is unknown elsewhere in the Bible, but it is similar in form to a Babylonian prophecy that appears to have been written during the reign of Nebuchadnezzar's son and successor, Amēl-Marduk (Evil-Merodach in Jer 52:31; 2 Kgs 25:27–30), predicting what his reign would be like. While the destination of the Uruk Prophecy (one of five main texts in a collection of texts called the Akkadian Prophecies) is the reign of Amēl-Marduk, en route to this destination, it "prophesies" and evaluates the reigns of several Babylonian kings leading up to Amēl-Marduk—depicting their reigns as future events, though in fact they had already occurred—that is, the Uruk Prophecy employs the literary device of *ex eventu* ("after the fact") prophecy to establish a pattern of kingship leading to Amēl-Marduk. It uses the formulaic statement "After him a king will arise," followed by an evaluative summary of that king's reign. After this series of *ex eventu* prophecies, the Uruk Prophecy gives way to predictive prophecy when it arrives at the reign of Amēl-Marduk, predicting a glorious reign for Nebuchadnezzar's successor. In reality, he reigned only two years before being assassinated. While none of the Babylonian kings is named, it is not hard to fill in names based on the historical events described. See Hermann Hunger and Stephen A. Kaufman, "A New Akkadian Prophecy Text," *JAOS* 95.3 (July–September, 1975): 371–75.

The revelation in Dan 11 is equally specific, allowing a reader to fill in the names and details of nearly every person and event described in general terms by the prophecy. While critical scholarship is nearly unanimous in its acceptance of Dan 11 as *ex eventu* prophecy, evangelical scholars debate whether Dan 11, like the Akkadian Prophecies, uses the literary device of *ex eventu* prophecy and ends in a similar way as the Uruk Prophecy—namely, with an erroneous prediction about the destination of the vision (Amēl-Marduk in the Uruk Prophecy and Antiochus IV Epiphanes in Dan 11). Daniel 11 with its question of *ex eventu* prophecy is the driving force of the debate about Danielic authorship. See further below on 11:36–45 and the Introduction, pp. 26–29.

51. Miller-Naudé and van der Merwe, "הִנֵּה and Mirativity in Biblical Hebrew," 54. Cf. the use of הִנֵּה in 8:19.

52. Cf. the use of "four" elsewhere in Daniel's visions, and see commentary on Dan 7:2–3, 6, 17; 8:8; 11:4. In additional to the symbolism of totality, a Hebrew idiom may be at play in the pattern of "three . . . and a fourth" in 11:2. Goldingay discusses this "numerical saying" as used in Wisdom literature (e.g., Prov 30:15, 18; cf. Amos 1–2) (*Daniel*, 531). Lucas similarly sees symbolism at work, and in the 3+1 idiom, he sees a "summarizing [of] the nature of the Persian Empire as rulers who amass wealth, grow strong and provoke conflict with the Greeks" (*Daniel*, 279). Commentators who think "four" represents specific kings suggest several combinations of monarchs dating from Cyrus (see, e.g., Collins, *Daniel*, 377; Miller, *Daniel*, 291; Longman, *Daniel*, 273).

"gain much more wealth than all of them" (11:2c), reaches the peak of his wealth (כְּחֶזְקָתוֹ בְעָשְׁרוֹ, 11:2d), he attracts the attention of the kingdom of Greece—that is, his wealthy strength "serves only to excite the envy of the Greeks and their hostile entry into the east."[53] In the next verse, the Dan 11 prophecy moves on to the next empire: Greece under Alexander the Great. Two hundred years of Persian world dominance merit a single verse.[54]

b. A King of Strength (11:3a–4h)

On the heels of the Persian kings, "a king of strength" would arise (וְעָמַד מֶלֶךְ גִּבּוֹר, 11:3a). This king, agreed by all to be Alexander the Great, rules (מָשַׁל, 11:3b) with great authority and does as he pleases (כִּרְצוֹנוֹ, 11:3c; cf. 8:4; 11:16, 36). Nonetheless, he ends up with a broken kingdom that is parceled out to the "four winds of the heavens" rather than to one of his descendants (11:4c–d). Alexander the Great, great conqueror of the ancient world, died suddenly in Babylon in 323 BCE, and since he had no viable heir, his vast empire was divided among his generals.[55] Clifford summarizes the "ignoble end of the great Alexander" as depicted in Dan 11:4: "At the point of his greatest success, his kingdom is broken and scattered, and inherited by none of his children."[56]

c. The Kings of the North and the South (11:5a–35e)

Beginning in 11:5, the prophecy moves into its depiction of the kings of the north and the south. The "king of the north" and the "king of the south" are titles that represent the dynasties of two generals who received portions of Alexander's empire—Seleucus (Syria) and Ptolemy (Egypt), respectively. These are the kings of interest in Dan 11 because they represent the dynasties that warred over "the land between," Palestine. While 11:5–35 encompasses more than a dozen Seleucid and Ptolemaic kings who reigned over the course of more than a century, their individual identities "are assimilated into the symbolic figures of the king of the south (Ptolemies) and the king of the north (Seleucids)."[57] The prophecy describes their collective exploits in terms of their strength (חזק, 11:5–7, 21) and their surges of power and/or their inability to maintain it (עמד, 11:6–8, 11, 13–17, 20, 21, 25, 31).

The account in Dan 11 of the tug of war between the Seleucids and Ptolemies builds up to the reign of Seleucid king Antiochus IV Epiphanes (11:20–35). Embedded in this account is what Newsom calls a "pattern of containment":

> Despite alternating patterns of aggression, neither the king of the north nor the king of the south can "effect a permanent rule by reason of their containment of each other" (Clifford 24). So long as the king of the north cannot successfully sweep away the king of the south, that is, so long as the Syrian Seleucids cannot capture and hold Ptolemaic Egypt, history remains in balance. Only when Antiochus IV does conquer much of Egypt, and then seeks to challenge a heavenly rather than an earthly kingdom, will history break loose from

---

53. Richard J. Clifford, "History and Myth in Daniel 10–12," *BASOR* 220 (Dec., 1975): 24.
54. Clifford observes that in this single verse (11:2), "the glory of Persia is slighted by lumping all the kings anonymously together" ("History and Myth in Daniel 10–12," 24).
55. For a more detailed history of the events described in Dan 11, see Newsom (*Daniel*, 336–53) or Lucas (*Daniel*, 278–90). For a very readable full-length treatment, see Tomasino, *Judaism Before Jesus*.
56. Clifford, "History and Myth in Daniel 10–12," 24.
57. Newsom, *Daniel*, 340.

its moorings and the determined vision of eschatological events unfold.[58]

This pattern emerges early in the prophecy as it traverses the early history of the Ptolemies' and Seleucids' attempts at alliance and their invasions of each other's territory (11:5–9). Alexander's general Ptolemy I Soter (323–285 BCE) was the first "king of the south" (11:5a), and Seleucus I Nicator (312–281 BCE) was also Alexander's general. However, after Seleucus received his part of the vast empire, he was driven from power and fled to Egypt. Ptolemy took him in and took him along on a military campaign in Palestine (11:5a). After this successful campaign, Ptolemy gave Seleucus a small fighting force that he used to regain his original territory.

During the middle of the third century BCE, the successors of Ptolemy and Seleucus attempted a marriage alliance that ultimately caused more problems than it fixed. Ptolemy's granddaughter Berenice was married to Seleucid king Antiochus II Theos (grandson of Seleucus I), who divorced his then-wife, Laodice, and sent her into exile with their son and would-be heir, Seleucus II. The alliance stipulated that only a son of Ptolemaic Berenice and Seleucid Antiochus could succeed Antiochus for the Seleucid throne. However, after Antiochus II died, the exiled Laodice murdered her rival Berenice, along with the heir-apparent infant son of Berenice and Antiochus II.[59] This bloodbath removed all Ptolemaic connections in the Seleucid royal house, assuring that Laodice's son, Seleucus II, would ascend the Seleucid throne.

The Ptolemaic response to Laodice's revenge is depicted in 11:7–9. In 246 BCE Berenice's brother Ptolemy III avenged his sister by attacking the Seleucids and killing Laodice. Ptolemy then made his way home with plunder, most notably, statues of Egyptian gods lost in the long-ago conquest of Egypt by Persian Cambyses (525 BCE).[60] Following this round of Ptolemaic-Seleucid fighting, there was a lull in hostilities that Seleucus II broke in 242 BCE with his unsuccessful invasion of Egypt (11:8b–9).

From this early history, the prophecy moves on to the exploits of the greatest "king of the north," Antiochus III, or Antiochus the Great (222–187 BCE; 11:10–19). This lengthy section foreshadows the career of Antiochus IV. Clifford describes this foreshadowing:

> As in Dan 11:21–35, the perspective is Seleucid and there are two campaigns against Egypt. The first ends in stalemate (Dan 11:10–12). The second is successful. No one can withstand Antiochus. He stands in the "beautiful land" and does as he pleases (Dan 11:16). Provoked by Seleucid success, "lawbreakers of thy people" arise to assist the victor and to "establish the vision," just as the success of the later Antiochus will encourage a group (Dan 11:30, 32). Intoxicated by these triumphs, Antiochus III sets out on further conquest. He is stopped by Rome

---

58. Newsom, *Daniel*, 327, 337. In this discussion, Newsom interacts with Clifford's "History and Myth in Daniel 10–12." Clifford is the one who identifies the "containment" motif in Dan 11. Both Clifford and Newsom consider Dan 11:36–45 to be (erroneous) predictions about Antiochus IV, whereas I see a shift in 11:36 to the eschatological figure of the antichrist—the one under whom history will "break loose from its moorings and the determined vision of eschatological events unfold." See further discussion below.

59. Antiochus II may have been poisoned by Laodice. Furthermore, she may have killed some of Berenice's Egyptian attendants. It is not entirely clear to whom "the ones who brought her" and "he who supported her in that time" refer (11:6f).

60. Newsom notes that "'godnapping' . . . was a regular practice of war in the ancient Near East, a way of symbolizing that the defeated nation's deities were powerless against the victor and his gods." Cf. the events of Dan 1:1–2. It was the restoration of these items that earned Ptolemy the epithet of "Benefactor" (Greek *Euergetes*; see Newsom, *Daniel*, 341).

in the person of L. Cornelius Scipio. Up to the second campaign of Antiochus III, the check on the unbridled rule of Seleucid or Ptolemaic power was provided by each of Alexander's successors on the other. Now a third power, Rome, enters to frustrate the Seleucid plans, as it will in the days of Antiochus IV (Dan 11:30). The last pointer to Antiochus IV in this account is the dynastic marriage of Antiochus' daughter Cleopatra to Ptolemy V in Dan 11:17. It recalls the earlier unsuccessful marriage in 11:6, and prepares us for yet another piece of royal intrigue which cannot succeed (Dan 11:26–27).[61]

Antiochus III was the son of Seleucus II (and the grandson of Laodice), and while many details of his career are sketchy, he did launch at least two campaigns against the Ptolemies. He lost the first to Ptolemy IV, losing control of Palestine in the process (11:10–12). However, Ptolemy's victory led to "an unwise overconfidence and even grandiosity" that resulted in his foolish and costly behavior and "a near collapse of the Ptolemaic state" as peasants revolted and seditious groups vied for power (11:12–14).[62] Antiochus III was victorious in his second campaign against Egypt, and so regained lost territories. He eventually gained control over all the territory of Palestine: he did "as he please[d]" (כִּרְצוֹנוֹ), and "no one [was able to] stand before him" (וְאֵין עֹמֵד לְפָנָיו, 11:16a-b). As he stood victorious in the Beautiful Land (11:16c), he was at the peak of his power.

However, the marriage alliance of his daughter Cleopatra to Ptolemy V was the beginning of his demise. Cleopatra "appears to have embraced Ptolemaic ambitions," to the detriment of her Seleucid father (11:17).[63] Antiochus turned his attention to coastal territories in Asia Minor (11:18a), but this brought him into conflict with Rome and ultimately led to a humiliating defeat (189 BCE) that resulted in loss of territory, a hefty tribute, and political hostages (including his son Antiochus IV) in Rome. Antiochus III was then killed in 187 BCE during the pillaging of a Persian temple in Elemaïs, where he was confronting a rebellion (11:19).

The transition from Antiochus III to Antiochus IV went by way of Seleucus IV Philopater (187–165 BCE), the son and immediate successor of Antiochus III. The prophecy in Dan 11 reports that the one who would "stand in ... place" of Antiochus III (עָמַד עַל־כַּנּוֹ, 11:20a) sent out "a tax collector for the splendor of the kingdom" (נוֹגֵשׂ הֶדֶר מַלְכוּת, 11:20b). In order to chip away at the debt he inherited, Seleucus IV dispatched his finance minister, Heliodorus, to Jerusalem to seize temple funds. However, Heliodorus was unsuccessful, and in 175 BCE he assassinated Seleucus.[64]

This launched "a complex and messy struggle for succession"[65] that ultimately resulted in the accession of Antiochus IV Epiphanes to the Seleucid throne. Daniel 11 reports that this "despicable person" stood (עָמַד ... נִבְזֶה, 11:21a) in the place of the

---

61. Clifford, "History and Myth in Daniel 10–12," 24.
62. Newsom, *Daniel*, 343.
63. Newsom, *Daniel*, 345.
64. See 2 Macc 3 for an account of these events.
65. Newsom, *Daniel*, 346. Antiochus IV was one of the Seleucid hostages in Rome, as was the son and rightful heir of the Seleucid throne, Demetrius I. Seleucus IV died shortly after Antiochus IV had been freed, and Heliodorus had seized the throne. Antiochus returned to Syria with a small army (acquired with the help of Eumenes II, king of Pergamon), Heliodorus disappeared (or fled), and the wily Antiochus IV assumed the throne—"nominally as regent for his nephew Demetrius, with his other nephew, Antiochus, as co-regent" (Lucas, *Daniel*, 283). He married Seleucus's wife (another Laodice), and they had their own son—and, not surprisingly, his coregent was then murdered, securing Antiochus's grip on his brother's throne. All this lay behind the statement in Dan 11:21d that the "despicable person" would "seize the kingdom by intrigues."

"shattered" king (11:20c), prefacing the full report of this new king "by insisting he did what none of his predecessors had done" (11:24b-c).[66] The account of Antiochus IV's reign builds on the report of Antiochus III, as the prophecy recounts two campaigns against Egypt—the first characterized by "intrigue and lying table fellowship"[67] (11:25-28), and the second ending with his humiliation at the hands of the Romans (צִיִּים כִּתִּים, 11:30a-b). This defeat prompts him to lash out against "the holy covenant" (בְּרִית־קֹדֶשׁ, 11:30d-31), action that led to "division among Jews into supporters and resistors" (11:32-35).[68] The section ends by saying that the appointed time of the end is still to come (11:35d-e).

The historical events portrayed in 11:21-35 concern Antiochus IV Epiphanes, the little horn of Daniel's vision of the evenings and the mornings in ch. 8.[69] The portrayal begins with a description of Antiochus's character and the nature of his reign (11:21-24)—namely, he was known to be treacherous, "lacking honor and legitimacy."[70] The effects of his reign were catastrophic (11:22a) and ultimately resulted in the death of the last legitimate high priest in Jerusalem (Onias III), as well as the slaughter of many faithful Jews.[71]

Antiochus IV's first incursion into Egypt (169 BCE) is recounted in 11:25-28 (cf. 11:10-12). His opponent, the young Ptolemy VI, had attempted to regain Palestinian territory from the Seleucids, but Antiochus's forces overwhelmed him (1 Macc 1:17-19).[72] The two monarchs negotiated a treaty in which each played their own political game (11:27).[73] Meanwhile, a rebellion had broken out in Jerusalem, and Antiochus saw that it was soundly quashed (11:28).[74]

---

66. Clifford, "History and Myth in Daniel 10-12," 24.
67. Ibid.
68. Clifford, "History and Myth in Daniel 10-12," 23.
69. In the Greek view of Daniel's four empires, Antiochus is also the little horn in the vision of Dan 7.
70. Newsom, *Daniel*, 346.
71. The reference to a "ruler of a covenant" in 11:22b is usually understood to be a reference to events that involved the Jewish high priest Onias III later in Antiochus's reign. During the Second Temple period, the Jewish high priest was the most important local official in Palestine, serving both the Jews and the empire. During the era of the Ptolemies and Seleucids, as control of Palestine shifted from one empire to the other, the Jewish high priest was in the complicated position of needing to pick the right ruler to favor. If he picked the Seleucid king and then power shifted to the Ptolemaic king, the high priest could lose his political power. Onias II, the grandfather of Onias III, had done exactly this, with the result that he lost civil authority to the affluent pro-Ptolemy Tobiad family. However, when power shifted again, the victorious Seleucid king (Antiochus III) rewarded the son of Onias II (Simon the Just) for his father's loyalty, and the high priest was reinstated as chief civil authority. When Antiochus III's successor, Seleucus IV, needed to pay down his inherited debt, it was not hard for the opportunist Tobiad family to bribe him into appointing a "temple captain" of their choosing to take over administration of temple finances from Onias III. Then when the same debt passed on to Antiochus IV, he was more than willing to accept a bribe to depose Onias III altogether and install the highest bidder in his place (Onias III's brother Jason). The corruption of the holy office only got worse, and when the deposed Onias III tried to expose some of it, he ended up dead. Since Antiochus IV had deposed Onias III and appointed his successor (Menelaus), Dan 11:22b credits him with the death of "a ruler of a covenant."
72. The extent to which Antiochus gained control over Egypt is unclear.
73. Newsom notes the complexity of the title "king of the south" at this point in the prophecy: "From 180 to 176, the widowed queen Cleopatra had been regent for her son, Ptolemy VI Philometor. After her death, the regency of the still-underaged child passed to two members of the court.... They also made Ptolemy VI's sister, Cleopatra II, his queen and consort, and in 170 added their younger brother Ptolemy VIII Physcon as the third coregent. Rivalry between the two brothers encouraged factions at court. Following the initial victories of Antiochus IV, two members of the Alexandrian aristocracy... staged a coup and replaced [the two court members] as regents" (*Daniel*, 348).
74. The number of assaults Antiochus IV unleashed on Jerusalem is unclear in the historical record. There are two attacks described in 1 Macc 1:20-40, but 2 Macc 5 appears to conflate the events into one attack. The historical record is clear, however, on the fact that Antiochus IV's aggression against the Jews increased over time.

A prophecy describes a second Egyptian campaign in 11:29–30b. In 168 BCE Antiochus IV attempted to regain control he had lost in Egypt, but "the latter will not be like the former" (11:29c). Like Antiochus III before him (11:18), the Romans put a humiliating stop to his expansionism ("The ships of Kittim will come against him," 11:30a).⁷⁵ On his way home, the humiliated Antiochus vented his anger on the Jews. His forces made the Jerusalem temple a pagan shrine, slaughtered Jews, and torched Jerusalem. Pigs and other unclean animals were killed in the temple precincts and sacrificed to Zeus by gentile priests. Jewish religious practices such as circumcision and observance of Sabbath were forbidden, and sacred scrolls were destroyed, along with their owners (11:30c–31; see 1 Macc 1:20–57).

Daniel 11:32–34 introduces a separation that occurred among the Jews during the reign of Antiochus IV. His policies of hellenization created two groups: those who had been "pollute[d] with smooth words" (11:32a)—that is, Jews who forsook the covenant in favor of hellenization (1 Macc 2:18; 2 Macc 7:24)—and "the people who know their God" and stood firm (11:32b–c). Some of this latter group were "the wise of the people" (מַשְׂכִּילֵי עָם) who instructed "the many" (רַבִּים) and paid a high price for it (11:33a–b). In their suffering, they would receive "a little help" (עֵזֶר מְעָט, 11:34a–b), and their suffering would refine and purify them.⁷⁶ The section ends with the reminder that the end time and an appointed time (עֵת קֵץ . . . מוֹעֵד, 11:35d–e) still lay in the future.

d. A King of Kings (11:36a–45c)

In 11:36 the prophecy references "the king" (הַמֶּלֶךְ), an anomalous title in this final vision, where the kings are called "the king of the south" (מֶלֶךְ הַנֶּגֶב, 11:5–6, 9, 11, 14, 25, 40), "the king of the north" (מֶלֶךְ הַצָּפוֹן, 11:6–7, 11, 13, 15, 40), or, most commonly, "he." The identity of this king has been much debated, with many scholars seeing a continuation of the prophecy concerning Antiochus IV Epiphanes and others seeing a shift to the eschatological leader, the antichrist.⁷⁷ The best answer

---

75. Rome had determined that Antiochus IV had to be stopped in order to maintain the balance of regional power. They sent an envoy with an elderly consul of Rome, Gaius Popillius Laenas, who told Antiochus to go home. The consul "drew a circle round the king with the stick he was carrying and said, 'Before you step out of that circle give me a reply to lay before the senate'" (Livy, *History of Rome* 45.12, ed. Canon Roberts [Medford, MA: Dutton]). Antiochus had no choice but to comply.

76. There are several issues in these verses. The first is the identity of the "wise" (מַשְׂכִּילִים), a group that appears four times in this final revelation (11:33, 35; 12:3, 10). While some scholars think they represent the Hasidim, a Jewish resistance group that assisted the Maccabees in their revolt against the Seleucids (1 Macc 2:42; 7:13; 2 Macc 14:6), most think the only connection between the two groups is that they both seem "to have constituted a distinct group and to have been active in some way in the resistance to Antiochus Epiphanes" (Collins, *Daniel*, 69). Another question with respect to the מַשְׂכִּילִים has to do with the purpose of their suffering (11:35). The syntax of 11:35 is ambiguous, so it is unclear who or what is refined, purified, and made pure by the suffering. A third question is what "a little help" (עֵזֶר מְעָט, 11:34b) refers to. There are at least three suggestions: (1) it is a criticism of the Maccabees' violent resistance in contrast to the presumed nonviolence of the מַשְׂכִּילִים, "wise"; (2) it means the help offered by the Maccabees was small compared to the deliverance that would come at the appointed time; (3) it has no particular group in mind but only refers to "the general vulnerability" of "the wise" (Seow, *Daniel*, 181). For further discussion, see Lucas, *Daniel*, 288–89, 312–15; Collins, *Daniel*, 66–69; Newsom, *Daniel*, 352–53; Miller, *Daniel*, 302–4.

77. Scholars with the view that this prophecy was written in the second century BCE understand 11:36–45 to be about Antiochus IV. Everything up to 11:36 is considered *ex eventu* prophecy—that is, a narration of known historical events styled as prophecy. Then 11:36–39 summarize, more or less, his reign (details do not match the historical record precisely), and in 11:40–45 the author foretells the demise of Antiochus IV from his vantage point in 167–165 BCE. However, the events predicted do not align with what is known of Antiochus's downfall, so the prophecy proves to be erroneous. The author's

may be found between these two views—that is, the prophecy has eschatological significance, but its first application is to Antiochus IV Epiphanes to the extent he fulfills it. It will have continuing application to the successors of Antiochus, until the end of time when it is completely fulfilled.[78] Biblical scholars sometimes refer to this multilayered fulfillment as "telescoping"—that is, the prophecy merges near and far predictions into a single prophecy, such that the timing of various events is indistinguishable.[79]

Another phenomenon at work in Dan 11:36–45 is the patterning that has been seen in the book since at least ch. 5, where Belshazzar exhibited a belligerent blasphemy that would only be intensified by his successors. Meadowcraft describes how Dan 11:40–45 further illustrates patterns or trends that will intensify until their final resolution: the king of the north will continue to expand, Israel's enemies will continue to oppose them, and "the general unpleasantness that has characterized Antiochus IV will be writ ever larger," while the effect all these things have on God's faithful and their land comes "ever more sharply into focus."[80] He concludes, "As a result, [11:40–45] stand between the historical present and the culmination of history. They reflect the trends that are seen in the ongoing tussle between the Hellenist kingdoms while pointing towards a larger significance and culmination in the future that may be glimpsed in only the broadest outlines."[81]

In terms of this patterning, this final king in the book of Daniel is described in language that echoes and exceeds the descriptions of all the other proud, wicked kings in Daniel's visions. He is a king who will "do as he pleases" (עָשָׂה כִרְצוֹנוֹ, 11:36a), an expression used of the ram (8:4, Cyrus), the "king of strength" (11:3, Alexander the Great), and "the king of the north" (11:16, Antiochus III). This last king will "exalt himself" (יִתְרוֹמֵם, 11:36b), as did the little horn (8:11) and the king of the south (11:12; Ptolemy IV). While his predecessors made themselves great (the ram in 8:4; the goat in 8:8) or made themselves as great as God (the little horn in 8:11; cf. the king in 8:25 [Antiochus IV Epiphanes]), this king outdoes them all and sets out to "make himself greater than any god" (11:36c). And "against the God of gods" this ruler "will speak great things" (11:36d), much as the little horn did in the ch. 7 vision (7:20, 25). The king of Dan 11:36–45 "will

---

purpose for using the literary device of *ex eventu* prophecy was to encourage his suffering second-century-BCE audience by reminding them of God's control of history. Many scholars with the view that the prophecy of Dan 11 is predictive from start to finish believe 11:36–45 refers to the antichrist. While the text does not clearly introduce a new character in 11:36, there are hints (discussed in the commentary) that "the king" may refer to more than Antiochus—although the second-century-BCE despot may have been in view as well. Additionally, the discrepancies between the details of 11:36–45 and the historical record has prompted Christian interpreters since at least the time of Jerome to see the antichrist in Daniel's final prophecy (and Jerome saw the antichrist in the prophecy as early as 11:21 [Stevenson and Glerup, *Ezekiel, Daniel*, 291]). At the end of the day, every interpretation of this difficult text has enough problems that its interpreters should exercise "humility and charity" (Hill, *Daniel*, 199).

78. Baldwin comments on this section (and others in the book), "The writer is never speaking only about one era of history, even though the prediction was to be applied to Antiochus as the first of many oppressors" (*Daniel*, 222).

79. This prophetic phenomenon is evident in Jesus's prediction in Matt 24 and Mark 13 of the fall of Jerusalem and the end of the age. In light of this, Baldwin discusses the challenge of interpreting Dan 11:36–45: "If one takes the view that what we have here is history, then this account is mistaken; but if the book is allowed to provide the genre, and what we have here is prophecy, there is no problem. Biblical prophecy regularly exhibits this characteristic of telescoping the future, so that the more distant event appears to merge with the nearer so as to become indistinguishable from it" (*Daniel*, 201–2).

80. Tim Meadowcraft, "Who Are the Princes of Persia and Greece (Daniel 10)? Pointers Towards the Danielic Vision of Earth and Heaven," *JSOT* 29.1 (2004): 108.

81. Meadowcraft, "Who Are the Princes of Persia and Greece (Daniel 10)?" 108.

prosper" (11:36e), as did the little horn and the king it represented, Antiochus IV Epiphanes (8:12, 24–25). This king is further described as one who would not regard the gods of his father or any god, for that matter, because he would "magnify himself against them all" (עַל־כֹּל יִתְגַּדָּל, 11:37c). This last king embodies the worst of all kings.[82] He is the culmination of the pattern begun in the book of Daniel by Belshazzar. The history of royal opposition to God reaches its apex in this last king, and when he finally comes to his end, there will indeed be no one to help him (11:45b–c; cf. 8:4, 7).

e. The Time of Distress (12:1a–3b)

The revelation continues into ch. 12, but its focus shifts from "the king" to his impact on Daniel's people. Much of this shift revolves around the word "time" (עֵת), an important concept in the book of Daniel, where God is the one in control of time (e.g., 2:21; 7:25; 8:17, 19; cf. מוֹעֵד, 8:19; 11:27, 35; זְמָן, 2:16; עִדָּן, 4:13[16]; 7:12, 25). The word עֵת, "time," occurs four times in the first verse of this final chapter (12:1a, c, d, e), creating the sense that "the time" toward which the entire book has been driving finally arrives with the fulfillment of this prophecy.[83]

The first event associated with this "time" is the appearance of Michael, who will "arise" (יַעֲמֹד, 12:1a) "at that time" (בָּעֵת הַהִיא, 12:1a)—that is, the time of the last king's rampage and ultimate demise (11:40–45). After the lengthy prophecy of ch. 11 in which the verb עמד ("to stand") repeatedly described the rise and reign of kings and their waging of battles (11:2–4, 7, 11, 13–17, 20, 21, 25, 31), one more being "arises": Michael, who is described as "the great prince standing over the sons of your people" (12:1b). The text does not immediately say what Michael will do, but given what has already been said about celestial conflicts in this last narrative, one might infer that Michael will fight on behalf of the people he "stands over"—which may mean he intervenes militarily or he executes judgment on the enemies of his people (cf. 10:13; 10:20–11:1).

The second marker of this "time" is a twofold qualitative statement: it would be a time of distress (עֵת צָרָה, 12:1c), unlike any distress experienced by a nation of people "until that time" (עַד הָעֵת הַהִיא; 12:1d; Jer 30:7). Thankfully, this is not the last word on "time." The fourth and final occurrence of "time" in the first verse is in 12:1e, a repetition of the verse's beginning: "and at that time" (וּבָעֵת הַהִיא). In the first occurrence, Michael arose. This time Daniel's people will be delivered.[84] The repetition suggests that the people's deliverance is a result of Michael's action on their behalf.

This is the second time Michael factors into the Dan 10–12 narrative. It was his presence alongside the messenger in his conflict with the prince of Persia that enabled the messenger to bring the revelation to Daniel (10:13; cf. 10:21). His presence over and on behalf of Daniel's people at the end of the revelation will result in their deliverance (12:1). His appearances bookend this last extraordinary reve-

---

82. Additional reasons many scholars see the antichrist in 11:36–45 are (1) the eschatological overtones of the section and those that follow in ch. 12—namely, resurrection, reward for the righteous, and judgment for the wicked; and (2) the ambiguous syntax in 11:40, such that it is unclear whether two or three kings are engaged in battle. Longman identifies several hints in the text that more than Antiochus IV is in view, including its "bigger-than-life" cosmic and mythical language (*Daniel*, 281).

83. This preoccupation with time continues into the rest of the chapter (12:4b, 6c, 7e, 9c, 11a, 11c, 12b).

84. Daniel 12:1f describes Daniel's people as "all the ones found written in the book." This book is one of several mentioned in the book of Daniel (cf. 7:10; 9:2; 10:21). This final book is considered to be "a list of those who belong to God's people, the citizen list of the true Jerusalem" (Goldingay, *Daniel*, 546). Elsewhere this book is called a "book of life" (cf. Exod 32:32–33; Ps 69:29[28]; Isa 4:3; Mal 3:16–18).

lation, a fitting reminder that the events it depicts are more than earthly. They are cosmic, and they are part of a conflict that finally reaches its climax when God's people are delivered and vindicated.

The messenger reveals in 12:2 that "many of those sleeping in the dusty earth will arise"—that is, the dead will be raised. Some of them will be raised to everlasting life, while others will be raised to everlasting judgment. Resurrection is not a common idea in the Old Testament. For people of the ancient Near East, including the Israelites, death was a shadowy existence in the underworld. The Israelites called this place "Sheol," and it was a place people "slept," unable to praise the Lord (2 Kgs 4:31; Job 14:12; Isa 26:19; Pss 6:5; 30:9; 115:16–17). A suffering person who thought himself in or near Sheol could implore God to raise him up from it (1 Sam 2:6; Pss 88; 40:3[2]), but ultimately, death itself was irreversible. Resurrection was rare, miraculous, and temporary—that is, a person raised from the dead (e.g., 1 Kgs 17:17–24; 2 Kgs 13:21) eventually died again.[85]

Resurrection is used as a metaphor in the Old Testament (e.g., in Ezek 37 of Israel's restoration), but the resurrection promised here appears to be an actual and individual resurrection for both the righteous and the unrighteous—that is, it results in reward and punishment.[86] Daniel is further promised that "the wise" (הַמַּשְׂכִּלִים)—also called "the ones who make many righteous" (מַצְדִּיקֵי הָרַבִּים, 12:3b)—will shine forever and ever like the shining of the expanse of the heavens and like the stars (12:3). This is best understood as metaphoric language and may well be a jab at Antiochus IV Epiphanes who, though "wise in intrigues, grasping for the stars, is upstaged by those truly *wise*, who do not grasp for stars but receive the gift of shining like the stars—and not just for a human lifetime, but *forever and ever*."[87]

f. The Charge to Daniel (12:4a–d)

With the promise of 12:3, the revelation concludes, and the messenger addresses Daniel in 12:4 with instructions to keep the words secret and to seal the scroll. In Dan 8:26, Daniel was instructed to "seal up the vision," but here the instructions may include the entire book of Daniel. The seal authenticated a document and preserved it from unauthorized opening, and since this scroll was to be sealed "until a time of the end" (עַד־עֵת קֵץ, 12:4b), Newsom notes that "whoever reads the book of Daniel has the sense of standing in the time of the end, since the book is now unsealed."[88] The message of the book of Daniel has been relevant to every generation that reads it. Though written in a faraway time and place to an audience that has long been asleep "in the dusty earth" (12:2a), its prophecies and promises continue to encourage the faithful people of God. As we await its final fulfillment, we cling to its promise of resurrection to life everlasting and judgment.[89]

---

85. Newsom, *Daniel*, 362. Collins includes a lengthy discussion of the concept of resurrection in ancient Judaism (*Daniel*, 394–98).

86. Most scholars agree that this is the case in Dan 12 (but see Seow, *Daniel*, 187, who thinks the imagery of resurrection here "convey[s] hope in the revival of the Jewish people after a history of suffering and death"). However, Dan 12 is vague on the details of what this resurrection entails. The full Christian doctrine of resurrection depends on later teachings of the New Testament.

87. Paul M. Lederach, *Daniel*, BCBC (Scottdale, PA: Herald Press), 255 (emphasis his).

88. Newsom, *Daniel*, 365.

89. The messenger's closing words in 12:4c–d are difficult. They may be an allusion to Amos 8:11–12, where there was a famine for the word of YHWH. The promise in Dan 12:4 is an increase of knowledge, "such that the dire situation Amos described will be reversed" (Newsom, *Daniel*, 364–65). See also Seow, *Daniel*, 189–90.

3. Vision Block 3: *The Vision of Two Others* (12:5a–13c)

Main Idea of the Passage

In Daniel 12:5–13 Daniel's vision report concludes with his vision of two additional beings who converse with the man clothed in linen about the timing of the revelation's events. Daniel also questions the man, who instructs Daniel to go his way and await his inheritance at the end of days.

Literary Context

Daniel 12:5–13 is the third and final section of the narrative that comprises chs. 10–12. It is also the third vision block of the narrative, and it is the passage that concludes the book of Daniel. In this broader literary context, this section functions in at least two ways. First, it brings the events of the narrative to a conclusion. Second, it provides the book's final word on the mysteries of God's ways in past and future events, encouraging the reader (by way of Daniel) to persevere in confident faith until the end.

> C. Narrative 3: The Ultimate Conflict and God's Final Victory (10:1a–12:13c)
> 1. Vision Block 1: The Vision of a Heavenly Messenger (10:1a–11:2a)
> 2. Vision Block 2: The Revelation from the Book of Truth (11:2b–12:4d)
> ➡ **3. Vision Block 3: The Vision of Two Others (12:5a–13c)**

Translation and Exegetical Outline

(See pages 534–35.)

Structure and Literary Form

The third section of the narrative in Dan 10–12 (12:5–13) continues and concludes Daniel's first-person report of his experience on the banks of the Tigris River (10:4). It is a new vision block, indicated by the use of visionary language: . . . וָרְאִיתִי וְהִנֵּה, "I looked . . . and oh!" and Daniel's self-reference (אֲנִי דָנִיֵּאל) (12:5a–b). This third section reports a vision Daniel saw after he received the revelation detailed in the second vision block (11:2b–12:4), and it consists of two subsections: 12:5–7 and 8–13. Each subsection includes a question asked of the man clothed in linen and his response.

The first subsection (12:5–7) begins with a formulaic statement: וָרְאִיתִי . . . וְהִנֵּה, "I looked . . . and oh!" (12:5a–b; cf. 10:5, 10, 16), indicating the beginning of the vision block and its single visionary element: the appearance of two additional heavenly beings and the subsequent dialogue among them and Daniel. Daniel describes the location of the three heavenly beings, and then reports with embedded speech the question one asked of the man clothed in linen (12:6). The subsection concludes with the man's response (12:7).

The second subsection (12:8–13) begins with Daniel's statement that he did not understand what he had heard. It then reports in two embedded speeches a question Daniel asked of the man clothed in linen (12:8) and the response he received (12:9–13).

The entire section of 12:5–13 is shaded on the charts because it still represents Daniel's reported speech, and it also reflects embedded speech reports of each participant (12:6c; 12:8d; 12:9b–13c). As Daniel's vision report, every independent clause is indented once, while independent clauses of the embedded speech reports are indented twice. Dependent clauses are indented accordingly.

Daniel 12:5a–13c

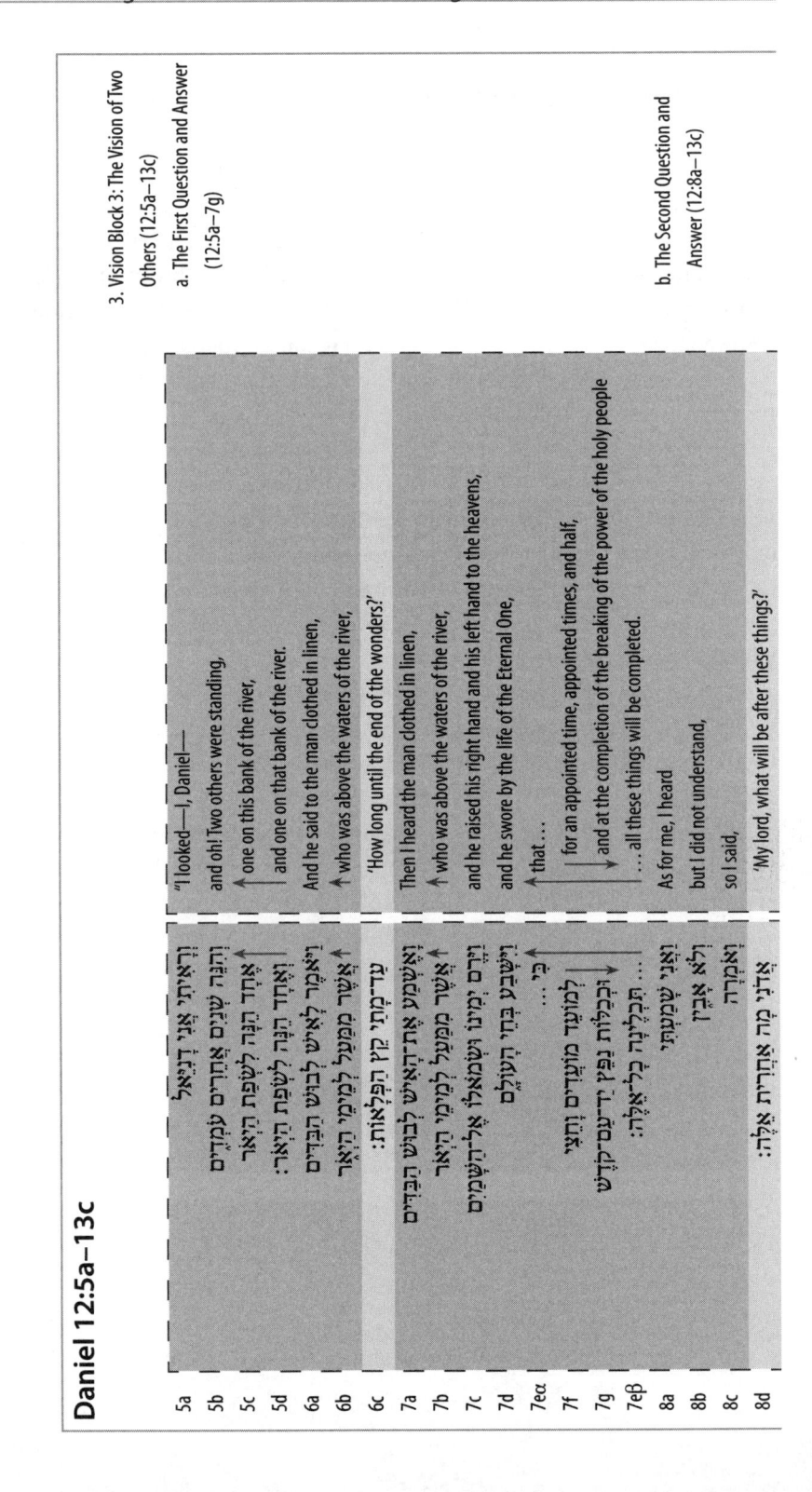

3. Vision Block 3: The Vision of Two Others (12:5a–13c)

   a. The First Question and Answer (12:5a–7g)

5a	"I looked—I, Daniel—	וָאֶרְאֶה אֲנִי דָנִיֵּאל
5b	and oh! Two others were standing,	וְהִנֵּה שְׁנַיִם אֲחֵרִים עֹמְדִים
5c	one on this bank of the river,	אֶחָד הֵנָּה לִשְׂפַת הַיְאֹר
5d	and one on that bank of the river.	וְאֶחָד הֵנָּה לִשְׂפַת הַיְאֹר׃
6a	And he said to the man clothed in linen,	וַיֹּאמֶר לָאִישׁ לְבוּשׁ הַבַּדִּים
6b	who was above the waters of the river,	אֲשֶׁר מִמַּעַל לְמֵימֵי הַיְאֹר
6c	'How long until the end of the wonders?'	עַד־מָתַי קֵץ הַפְּלָאוֹת׃
7a	Then I heard the man clothed in linen,	וָאֶשְׁמַע אֶת־הָאִישׁ לְבוּשׁ הַבַּדִּים
7b	who was above the waters of the river,	אֲשֶׁר מִמַּעַל לְמֵימֵי הַיְאֹר
7c	and he raised his right hand and his left hand to the heavens,	וַיָּרֶם יְמִינוֹ וּשְׂמֹאלוֹ אֶל־הַשָּׁמַיִם
7d	and he swore by the life of the Eternal One,	וַיִּשָּׁבַע בְּחֵי הָעוֹלָם
7eα	that…	כִּי…
7f	for an appointed time, appointed times, and half,	לְמוֹעֵד מוֹעֲדִים וָחֵצִי
7g	and at the completion of the breaking of the power of the holy people	וּכְכַלּוֹת נַפֵּץ יַד־עַם־קֹדֶשׁ
7eβ	…all these things will be completed.	תִּכְלֶינָה כָל־אֵלֶּה׃

   b. The Second Question and Answer (12:8a–13c)

8a	As for me, I heard	וַאֲנִי שָׁמַעְתִּי
8b	but I did not understand,	וְלֹא אָבִין
8c	so I said,	וָאֹמְרָה
8d	'My lord, what will be after these things?'	אֲדֹנִי מָה אַחֲרִית אֵלֶּה׃

9a	וַיֹּאמֶר	And he said,
9b	לֵךְ דָּנִיֵּאל	'Go, Daniel,
9c	← כִּי־סְתֻמִים וַחֲתֻמִים הַדְּבָרִים עַד־עֵת קֵץ׃	for hidden and sealed are the words until an end time.
10a	יִתְבָּרֲרוּ	Many will be purged,
10b	וְיִתְלַבְּנוּ	purified,
10c	וְיִצָּרְפוּ רַבִּים	and refined.
10d	וְהִרְשִׁיעוּ רְשָׁעִים	But the wicked will do wickedness,
10e	וְלֹא יָבִינוּ כָּל־רְשָׁעִים	and none of the wicked will understand,
10f	וְהַמַּשְׂכִּלִים יָבִינוּ׃	but the wise will understand.
11a	→ וּמֵעֵת הוּסַר הַתָּמִיד	From the time the daily sacrifice is taken away
11b	וְלָתֵת שִׁקּוּץ שֹׁמֵם	and the desolating abomination is set up
11c	יָמִים אֶלֶף מָאתַיִם וְתִשְׁעִים׃	there will be 1,290 days.
12a	אַשְׁרֵי הַמְחַכֶּה	Happy is the one who waits
12b	וְיַגִּיעַ לְיָמִים אֶלֶף שְׁלֹשׁ מֵאוֹת שְׁלֹשִׁים וַחֲמִשָּׁה׃	and reaches 1,335 days.
13a	וְאַתָּה לֵךְ לַקֵּץ	And now, go to the end
13b	וְתָנוּחַ	and rest,
13c	וְתַעֲמֹד לְגֹרָלְךָ לְקֵץ הַיָּמִין׃	and you will stand for your inheritance at the end of days."

Explanation of the Text

a. The First Question and Answer (12:5a–7g)

The beginning of the third and final vision block includes the formulaic statement "I looked" (וָאֶרְאֶה), followed by Daniel's reference to himself. This self-reference echoes the beginning of Daniel's vision report (10:2b) and also reorients the audience to the speaker after the lengthy embedded speech of the messenger (10:20–12:4).

Daniel reports seeing "two others" (12:5b), that is, two other heavenly beings in addition to the messenger (the man clothed in linen) and perhaps the ministering angel of 10:10, 16–19, assuming he is still present.[90] These two others were standing on opposite sides of the river (12:5b–d), and one of them addressed the man clothed in linen, whose specific location is provided for the first time in the narrative: he was "above the waters of the river" (מִמַּעַל לְמֵימֵי הַיְאֹר, 12:6b; cf. 10:16d).

The question asked is similar to the one asked in Daniel's vision of the evenings and the mornings, where Daniel overheard a holy one ask, "How long is the vision?" (8:13c). Specifically, how long would the removal of the daily sacrifice last, along with the desolating transgression and the giving over of the holy place and the host to be trampled (8:13d–e)? Here the question is "how long until the end of the wonders [הַפְּלָאוֹת]?" The root of the word translated "wonders" also appears in 8:24 and 11:36 to describe the arrogant words and actions of Antiochus IV and the last king, respectively.[91] In this context, it likely refers to all the events depicted in the revelation—and more specifically, those of the end time.

Daniel reports that he heard the answer from the man clothed in linen (12:7a–b), but he summarizes the man's response rather than reporting his direct speech. More important than the actual words in this context are the actions accompanying them. First, the man raised his right hand and then his left, and then "he swore by the life of the Eternal One" (12:7c–d; cf. Deut 32:40). Usually the swearing of an oath was accompanied by the lifting of one hand, and most commentators consider the dual action here "especially emphatic."[92] The contents of the response include two temporal references that are dependent on the clause in 12:7e—namely, "that . . . all these things will be completed." The first temporal reference—"for an appointed time, appointed times, and half" (לְמוֹעֵד מוֹעֲדִים וָחֵצִי, 12:7f)—recalls the Aramaic "time, times, and half of time" of Dan 7:25 (עִדָּן עִדָּנִין וּפְלַג עִדָּן). The second temporal reference—"at the completion of the breaking of the power of the holy people" (כְּכַלּוֹת נַפֵּץ יַד־עַם־קֹדֶשׁ, 12:7g)—is difficult, though most think it refers generally to the actions of Antiochus against the Jews (cf. 11:29–39).

---

90. Many scholars assume one of these "two others" was also present during the vision of Dan 10, making the total number of participants four (the man, Daniel, two others). I think five participants are possible (the man, Daniel, the ministering angel of Dan 10, and two others).

91. The form in the earlier occurrences is a *niphal* participle, whereas here it is a noun.

92. Collins, *Daniel*, 399. Cf. also Rev 10:5–6. However, Newsom says this claim has no support (*Daniel*, 366). She considers more likely the explanation of Eugene P. McGarry that the imagery arose from a variant of Deut 32:40, upon which the text is based ("The Ambidextrous Angel (Daniel 12:7 and Deuteronomy 32:40): Inner-Biblical Exegesis and Textual Criticism in Counterpoint," *JBL* 124 [2005]: 211–28).

b. The Second Question and Answer (12:8a–13c)

The second subsection of the book's final section begins with another self-reference by Daniel: "As for me, I heard" (וַאֲנִי שָׁמַעְתִּי, 12:8a). Daniel then reports that despite hearing the messenger's response, he did not understand it (12:8b), so he follows up with a question of his own in 12:8d. His question is an embedded speech report, in which he addresses the messenger as he did earlier: "My lord" (אֲדֹנִי; cf. 10:16–17, 19). Daniel's question appears to be a request for more information, not just a restatement of the angel's question. He asks, "What will be after these things?" (מָה אַחֲרִית אֵלֶּה, 12:8d)[93]—that is, Daniel assumes something will happen after the resurrection of reward and judgment.

The man's response is recorded as direct speech, and his words conclude the book (12:9–13). He addresses Daniel directly ("Go, Daniel," 12:9b), although he does not answer his question. The apparent reason for not answering is in 12:9c, "for hidden and sealed are the words until an end time." By recalling his earlier directions to Daniel (12:4a–b), the messenger says the revelation is finished. He then summarizes what was prophesied in 11:32–35: The "many" (רַבִּים) will be purged, purified, and refined, but the wicked will go on being wicked and without the understanding that the wise (הַמַּשְׂכִּלִים) have (12:10).

What the wise will presumably understand is the revelation and, in context, the messenger's last word about the timing of events provided in 12:11–12. Returning to the thematic events surrounding the desecration of the temple (8:11–14; 9:26–27; 11:30–31), the messenger says there will be 1,290 days between the removal of the daily sacrifice and the setting up of the desolating abomination (12:11). He follows this with a blessing for the one who "waits and reaches 1,335 days" (12:12). These two numbers have vexed interpreters, but Newsom offers an interpretation that makes good sense of them in context.[94] She considers them in light of the other time frames in Daniel's visions (7:25; 8:14; 9:27; 12:7) and concludes that, although we cannot say definitively what the numbers mean, "that matters less . . . than the fact that the numbers lend themselves to symbolic patterns that feature prominently in other parts of the book of Daniel. The 'outcome of these things' (10:8) is, as the angel said, 'concealed and sealed' (10:9), but 'the wise will understand' (10:10). The book entrusts the reader with this one last puzzle."[95]

---

93. The uncertainty of Daniel's meaning is reflected in the variety of translations: "What will be the outcome of these events" (NASB; cf. ESV, NIV, NRSV, NJPS); "What shall be the latter end of these things" (JPS; cf. KJV); "What will happen after these things" (NET). Jerome is credited with the translation used here (Collins, *Daniel*, 400).

94. There are three main approaches to interpreting the two numbers: (1) literally, and so explain their correspondence to the "appointed time, appointed times, and half" (12:7; cf. 7:25) with respect to Antiochus's actions in the second century BCE or to the actions of the antichrist in the end times (see, e.g., Collins, *Daniel*, 401, and Miller, *Daniel*, 325–26, respectively); (2) symbolically, such that the significance is the delay and the need for the faithful to endure until the end (see, e.g., Baldwin, *Daniel*, 231–32, and Newsom, *Daniel*, 368); (3) consider them inexplicable—that is, their obscurity is intentional, with the point being that God alone knows their meaning and controls the future, and the believer's task is to trust and persevere (e.g., Longman, *Daniel*, 287; cf. Lucas, *Daniel*, 298).

95. Newsom, *Daniel*, 368. Newsom's proposal goes like this: (1) each of Daniel's visions dealt with the length of the Antiochene persecution in different ways (3.5 years/42 months in 7:25; 2,300 mornings and evenings or about 3.5 years in 8:14; the last "half week" in 9:27; 3.5 years/42 months in 12:7); (2) 1,290 days equals 43 months of 30 days, and 1,335 days equals 44.5 such months (based on the observation of Hartman and DiLella, *The Book of Daniel*, 314); (3) the pattern of what is left over from the prediction in 12:7 (3.5 years/42 months) is "1 extra month in the first part, and 2 1/2 months in the second part. The length of the delay would have the same numerical pattern as the original prediction—a time, two times, and half a time. This pattern would also account for why the 2 parts of the final period are not presented as of equal duration" (*Daniel*, 368).

The man's final words to Daniel reinforce that even though much about the revelation, including its timing, is unknown, God's faithful people must wait with confidence that God will keep his promises. One day the righteous will receive their reward, and the wicked will receive their due punishment.

This closing section of the book and the revelation that precedes it are challenging. There are numerous interpretive difficulties, and the prophecy pertains to a complicated time and place in history that is foreign to most of us. But throughout this last narrative are echoes of an earlier era and its prophet. In the late seventh-century BCE, Habakkuk struggled to understand God's approach to punishing the wicked. He was told that God would judge at the appointed time. Until then, the righteous needed to wait and to continue believing (Hab 2:2–20; cf. Dan 10:14; 11:14, 27, 35). So too for Daniel, and so too for the readers of his book.

Canonical and Theological Significance

The book of Daniel roars to its conclusion in a three-chapter narrative set in the third year of Cyrus. By this time in history, the enforced exile of the Jews was over, and the people were allowed to return to their homeland to rebuild their lives there. Some of Daniel's countrymen had already returned, but they found life back in the land difficult. Others remained in Babylon, not willing or able to uproot and start over again. While the prophesied end of Babylon and exile had occurred, the hope—nay, expectation—for full restoration awaited fulfillment.

Daniel's visions thus far of his people's future indicated that the difficulties they faced would only grow, reaching unfathomable and even unprecedented proportions. For the grief-stricken Daniel, it was a time of confusion and angst. Into this mire of expectation and disappointment, God spoke to his highly favored servant, overwhelming him with a vision of himself, letting him glimpse the sovereign steering of history to its consummation, and comforting him with the promise of resurrection, reward, and judgment.

The encouragement of Dan 10–12 is its perspective. In its vision of God, its sweep of history, and its look at the future, it offers the bird's-eye view of things. It shows the big picture, and in doing so, it encouraged Daniel to persevere in confident faith because his ultimate hope was in the God who was and ever would be on the throne. We, as Daniel's successors on the other side of Easter, also hope in this God—but we do so in the triumph of the cross and the empty tomb. Our comfort is that God has already triumphed over evil through the finished work of Christ, and it is the glorious eternal kingdom that came to earth with the ministry of Jesus that will one day fill the earth.

The lengthy narrative at the conclusion of the book of Daniel unfolds in three stages: Daniel's vision and preparation to receive it (ch. 10), the revelation itself (11:2–12:4), and an epilogue of encouragement (ch. 12). The canonical and theological significance of each stage is discussed below.

What Daniel's Vision Reveals

Daniel's vision in ch. 10 has at least a twofold significance in the canon. First, the text's emphasis on the effort required for Daniel to receive the revelation of Dan 11–12 reminds us that our God is an awesome God—that is, he is terrible and dreadful, entirely "other" than we are.[96] When the "man clothed in linen" appeared, Daniel was utterly undone.[97] Multiple acts of angelic strengthening were required before he could even remain on his feet to hear the man's words.

We can easily lose sight of the terrifying nature of God. Some of us prefer to think about God in terms of Jesus, who appears to be approachable, relatable, and even downright good company. These impressions of Jesus have led people since at least the time of Marcion (ca. 80–150) to distinguish between the "God of the Old Testament" and the "God of the New Testament"[98]—seeing the Old Testament God as "angry, sexist and racist"[99] and the New Testament God as loving to all.[100]

Such charges against the "God of the Old Testament" do not hold up under a careful reading of the ancient book in its original context,[101] but without this careful reading, many people—including many Christians—skip over what the Old Testament reveals of YHWH, preferring instead to focus on Jesus in the Gospels and New Testament. We are not wrong to focus on Jesus—he is the destination of the Old Testament, the center of the New Testament, and the exhilarating consummation of the complete story of the Bible. But sometimes in this focus, we actually forget who Jesus is. We forget that this person *like* us is also entirely *other* than us. We forget that the holy transcendence of God is also present in the very immanent Jesus. We become so comfortable with the humanity of Jesus that we forget his "God-ness." The vision of God that overwhelmed Daniel in ch. 10 reminds us that our God, revealed fully in Jesus, is an awesome God—worthy of deep reverence and even fear.

---

96. See discussion of "awesome" in Dan 9:4 above.

97. See on Dan 10:4–9 above for my view on the "man clothed in linen" as a theophany, not an angelophany.

98. Marcion was a second-century heretic who rejected Judaism, the Old Testament, and thus the God of the Old Testament: "Preaching a gospel of love, Marcion focused on what he implied was a second, higher and better God of the NT" (A. G. Padgett, "Marcion," *DLNT*, 705).

99. David T. Lamb, *God Behaving Badly: Is the God of the Old Testament Angry, Sexist and Racist?* (Downers Grove, IL: InterVarsity Press, 2011), 11.

100. Orthodox Christianity affirms that these "Gods" are one and the same. Jesus was fully man and fully God—the God of the Old Testament. He declared himself to be one with the Father (John 10:30), and he told his disciples that if they had seen him, they had seen the Father (John 14:9). John introduces Jesus as "the Word," saying "the Word was God" who became flesh and dwelled among us (John 1:1–14), and Paul calls Jesus the "image of the invisible God" (Col 1:15). The Bible knows of no distinction between an Old and New Testament God.

101. Lamb likes to turn the idea of the Old Testament God "behaving badly" on its head: "How does one reconcile the loving God of the Old Testament with the harsh God of the New Testament? When I ask this question of students, at first they are shocked, and then most assume that I have simply misspoken, as I am prone to do. They typically have heard the question inverted, along these lines: 'How did the mean Old Testament God morph into a nice guy like Jesus?' I assure them that this time, at least, I have not accidentally inverted by words. I then observe that God in the Old Testament is consistently described as slow to anger and abounding in steadfast love, but Jesus speaks about hell more than anyone else in Scripture. The word *hell* does not even show up in English translations of the Old Testament" (*God Behaving Badly*, 9).

A second area of significance that Daniel's vision in ch. 10 provides is what it reveals about the cosmic nature of reality. While most of the Bible concerns itself with life on earth, in a few places the text takes us into heavenly territory and allows us to glimpse an otherwise unseen realm.[102] The book of Daniel is one of those places, and its glimpses into the heavenly realm help us see beyond the familiarity of life on planet earth. Its perspective pulls us out of our own narrow perspectives and reveals a reality far greater than anything we see. A handful of texts in Daniel give us this cosmic perspective, including the throne room vision of ch. 7, the little horn's reach to the host of heaven in ch. 8 (8:10), and the man in linen's explanation for his delay in 10:13–11:1.

In the vision of the divine throne room in Dan 7, Daniel receives a glimpse of the transcendent nature of God's rule. The vision was part of the cosmic perspective on God's kingdom that Dan 2 and Dan 7 offer. Together, the chapters portray the nature of human and divine kingdoms, with ch. 7 especially highlighting the highest throne and its sovereignty over all human kings. In the vision of the evenings and mornings in ch. 8, Daniel witnesses the astonishing rise of the little horn and its level of success against the "host of heaven" and its commander—a heavenly success that played out in the earthly conflict between Antiochus IV Epiphanes and the faithful Jews in second-century-BCE Jerusalem. Daniel's vision of the man clothed in linen in ch. 10 makes the book's most explicit foray into celestial territory as the man explains his delay in responding to Daniel's prayers: the prince of Persia had opposed him for twenty-one days, and the man was unable to get away until Michael came to his aid. He concludes this explanation by saying he must return to fight the prince of Persia, noting that the prince of Greece is coming, and commenting that Michael alone has been supporting him—as he supported him in the first year of Darius.

While we cannot be sure what earthly conflicts lie behind these heavenly conflicts, it is clear that at least some conflicts happening on earth reflect conflicts in the heavenly realm—or vice versa. Paul says as much when he admonishes that standing against the devil's schemes requires that we "put on the full armor of God. . . . For our struggle is not against flesh and blood, but against the rulers, against the authorities, against the powers of this dark world and against the spiritual forces of evil in the heavenly realms" (Eph 6:11–12). We can take comfort in this greater reality—that our struggles often involve greater forces and higher stakes than what we see. We are part of a greater story that God is writing as he brings history to its consummation under the earthly rule of his Anointed One.

---

102. The most extensive scholarly treatment of this topic is Michael S. Heiser's *The Unseen Realm: Recovering the Supernature Worldview of the Bible* (Bellingham, WA: Lexham Press, 2015); see also his more accessible version of the same material, *Supernatural: What the Bible Teaches about the Unseen World and Why It Matters* (Bellingham, WA: Lexham Press, 2015), and his website: https://faithlife.com/michael-heiser.

The Relevance of the Revelation

The revelation Daniel received in 11:2–12:4 is not among the Bible's easiest texts to preach. We struggle to see how Paul's words to Timothy that "all Scripture is God-breathed and is useful for teaching, rebuking, correcting and training in righteousness, so that the servant of God may be thoroughly equipped for every good work" (2 Tim 3:16–17) hold true with texts like Dan 11. However, while much of the revelation Daniel received may not particularly equip us "for every good work," it can instruct us in the ways of God, and in doing so it encourages us to trust what he is doing—whether we can see it clearly or not. The closing words of the revelation also provide the encouragement we need to endure whatever the ways of God bring across our paths.

With respect to the ways of God, the revelation in Dan 11 shows us that God cares about and is in control of every detail of history. In its march of kings and kingdoms and its sordid details of the Seleucid-Ptolemaic history, Dan 11 affirms that God is working every detail into his greater plan and moving history to its God-appointed times. Through the struggles of the second century BCE, God was shaping the world that Jesus would enter in the "fullness of the time" (Gal 4:4). But all of history—not just the events detailed in Dan 11—has been part of God's glorious plan "to bring unity to all things in heaven and on earth under Christ" (Eph 1:10). What we encounter every day is part of that same glorious plan. Anything that concerns us concerns him. Nothing goes unnoticed, and it is all important—though we may never fully understand how.

There is great comfort in this truth—comfort for the big things of life as well as the small things. The God who is actively raising up human "kings" and taking them down again is also actively at work in our individual lives. While we may hear the headlines and want to worry, we need not. While we may fret about our families, friends, or careers, we should not. The path God's people travel has always been difficult and riddled with great injustice. Nonetheless, the sovereign king of an eternal kingdom is on the throne, and the events happening around us reflect God's design and control—no matter what it may look like. The book of Daniel began with a subtle affirmation that God was at work, despite appearances, and it ends with the assurance that the times are in God's hands (11:27, 29, 35)—and so are we.

The final words of the revelation in Dan 12:1–4 speak of resurrection, reward, and vindication. As discussed in the commentary, resurrection is not a common idea in the Old Testament, and this portion of Daniel is the only place where it appears to be actual and individual (rather than metaphorical and collective). Later New Testament teaching will give a fuller picture of this promised resurrection, grounding it in the death, burial, and resurrection of Christ himself. We have a great high priest interceding for us because Jesus came to earth and suffered (Heb 4:14–15). We have confidence that all spiritual forces in opposition to him have been vanquished because Jesus died and rose again (Col 2:14–15). We believe that we will one day rise from the dead because Jesus rose (1 Cor 15:21–23). We know that a new order is at work in our present world because Jesus ascended. If none of this were true, we would indeed be most miserable (1 Cor 15:19), but because all of it is true, God's people can have unfettered joy and hope.

In the closing words of the revelation to Daniel, who suffered through four visions of his people's tumultuous future, God gave him a glimpse into the future that would enable him and all God's faithful people after him to endure until the end. No matter the intensity of the suffering, God's victory is secure and his eternal kingdom will prevail. He will bring judgment for the wicked and reward for the faithful, who will reign with him forever.

Awaiting the Next and Last Chapter[103]

When the revelation was finished, questions remained. How long would these things last? What would happen then? These questions linger still today, and with Daniel we wait for yet more appointed times. We endure the struggle as God moves history to its appointed end.

As I finish this book, I see suffering all around. Some of it is the suffering that comes to us all simply because we live in a broken world, a world wracked by sin, disease, and death. Some of my dear friends are traversing the dark valley of a brain tumor. Another friend awaits the outcome of a stem-cell transplant, praying that the acute myeloid leukemia that besieged his body and his family in the spring will be eradicated. My own beloved father is shuffling his last few steps into the arms of Jesus.

But some of the suffering I see around me is targeted at my brothers and sisters around the globe because they believe in Jesus, because they believe in the one who will make that broken world new at his appointed time. Like many in the original audience of the book of Daniel, they will suffer unto death for keeping their covenant with the God who saved them.

My prayer is that those of us the world over who follow Jesus may live well—and that we may die well, whenever and however that may happen. That we may live and die with the full confidence that God is on the throne, that he has defeated every evil, that his glorious kingdom will one day fill the earth—and on that day, all these bitter tears will be wiped away, never to be shed again. All these sorrows will be done away with, never to be revisited. All the old will be new, and the new will be ever newer. We will live and reign with our friend, brother, and savior—Jesus—over an everlasting kingdom that radiates the light of the Lamb . . . forever.

---

103. C. S. Lewis calls this present life the cover and the title page of the Great Story, and he says we await "Chapter One of the Great Story, which no one on earth has read: which goes on for ever: in which every chapter is better than the one before" (*The Last Battle* [New York: Collier Books, 1956], 184).

Ancient Sources Index

Old Testament

Genesis
1 . . . . . 53, 73, 146, 390, 394, 395, 422
1:1–10. 394
1:2. 395
1:3. 174
1:26–28. 395
1–11 53
2:10. 358
2:16–17. 240
2:21. 428
3:16–19. 341
9:13–14. 378
10:10. 52
11 . . . . 53, 137, 182, 244
11:1–9. 53, 289
11:2. 52
11:4. 53
12:2–3. 128
14:1, 9. 52
15:16. 430
15:18. 508
15:21. 428
16:7. 174
18:3. 51
19:24–28 471
21:33. 368
22:4. 91
24:3, 7. 102
24:50. 91
25:24. 138
27:34–40, 37, 39 91
31 174
31:32. 174
31:47. 31
32:22–33 510
37 . . . . 93, 136
37:5–10. 128
37:18–20 345
37:22. 345
37:23–24 345
37:24. 345
37:25. 345
37–50 128
39:2–6. . . . . 64, 133, 342
39:6. . . . . 64, 133
39:9. . . . . 339, 342
40 126
40:6. 97
40–41 90
40–42 77
41 . . . . 64, 83, 87, 123–37
41:1. 87
41:2, 2–7, 4–5, 5 125
41:6, 7. 126
41:8. . . . . 83, 126, 127
41:13–26 129
41:14, 15. 126
41:15–16 127
41:16. . . . . 112, 123, 126
41:17. 126
41:25. . . . . 123, 126, 134
41:27. 129
41:38. . . . . 93, 123, 136
41:39. . . . . 64, 133
41:39–46 123
41:45. 126
41:46. 69
41–42 25
42:15–16 . . . . 164, 484
45:8. 51
47:25. 129
47:27. . . . . 129, 458
49:1. 511
49:9. . . . . 14, 17, 21, 27, 395

Exodus
1:5. 458
2:24. 174
3:1–3. 174
3:2. 368
3:13–16. 104
4:5. 104
4:21. 295
5:2. 295
7:3. 202
7:4–5. 281
7:5. . . . . 73, 193
7:13. 295
7:15. 71
7:17. . . . . 73, 193
8:15[19] 258, 295
8:18[22] 73, 193
9:12. 295
10:3. 448
13:4. 507
13:21. 368
14:4, 18. 73, 193
15:5. 412
15:6. 281

15:15.................................71
15:18...............................391
16:28...............................448
19:1–7..............................185
19:4................................186
19:6................................237
19:8................................186
19:10–15............................507
19:18...............................368
19:19–20............................186
20:2......................166, 186, 472
20:3–4..............................186
20:3–6..............................166
20:7................................292
20:18..........................186, 508
21:28–2............... 31–32, 36, 413
23:15...............................507
24..................................469
24:16...............................379
25–27...............................147
25–31...............................287
25:31–40............................259
26:35...............................259
27:20...............................259
28:42...............................508
29:41...............................480
29:38–42............................420
29:45–46.............................93
30..................................147
31:18...............................258
32:12...............................473
32:16...............................258
32:31...............................467
32:32...............................162
32:32–33.......................369, 530
33:12..........................164, 484
34:1................................258
34:6–7..............................469
34:18, 28...........................507
35–40...............................287
40:24...............................259
40:34–35............................379

Leviticus

4:3.................................486
5:5.................................463
6:13[20]............................480
10..................................369
11..................................359
16:4................................508
16:21...............................463
16:23, 32...........................508
19:26................................61
24:5–9..............................259
25......................187, 482, 486
25:2, 4.............................482
25:8...........................482, 483
26:3................................469
26:14–33............................237
26:14–45............................470
26:18..........................482, 483
26:21...............................482
26:22...............................488
26:24...............................482
26:28..........................482, 483
26:29–40............................468
26:31, 32, 34–35....................488
26:40...............................463
26:40–43............................481
26:40–45............................489
26:43...............................488

Numbers

5:7.................................463
5:21................................470
6:25................................474
           7:10–11, 84, 88, 150
7:89................................428
10:35–36............................511
11:28................................51
12:7................................138
14:11...............................448
14:13–19............................473
14:14...............................379
14:24...............................138

14:27...............................448
22–24...............................277
23–24...............................272
23:19...............................396
23:21...............................391
24:14...............................511
28:2–8..............................420
28:4................................480

Deuteronomy

1:7.................................508
2:25................................471
4:11–12, 15–16......................186
4:19...........................186, 471
4:19–20.............................368
4:20, 24, 25–28.....................187
4:27................................469
4:28...........................254, 280
4:29–31.............................187
4:30...........................467, 511
4:31................................428
5:6.................................166
5:26................................329
5:32...........................466, 470
6:4...........................164, 484
6:22................................202
7:19................................202
7:21................................465
8:2–3................................75
8:20................................467
9:9–10..............................507
9:10................................258
9:12, 16......................466, 470
9:23................................467
9:26–29.............................472
10:21...............................465
10:22...............................458
11:13...............................465
11:16...............................470
11:28.........................466, 470
12:5..........................104, 474
12:11, 14...........................474
13:2................................202

14 359	24 469	19:9[8] 368
14:23. 474	24:14–15 185	
14:24. 104	**Judges**	**1 Kings**
14:25. 474	2:15. 281	1:17. 51
15 187	5:11. 473	2:1–4. 185
16:1. 507	5:19–20. 511	3:2. 53
16:2. 474	6:11–7:25 71	3:5–15. 93
16:11. 93	**1 Samuel**	5 77
17:14–20 237	2 443	5:3–5. 53
17:20. 466	2:1 443	6:13. 93
24 187	2:6. 531	6:20–35. 147
26:8. 202	2:6–7. 278	7–8 287
28:14. 174, 466	2:8. 443	7:49. 259
28:14–15 470	2:19 54	8:11 379
28:15–68 470	3 136	8:16–20. 104
28:62. 467	4:1–5:2 . . . . 71, 448	8:16–29. 53
29:5[6] 75	4:3, 8. 448	8:22–53. 463
29:16[17] 254	4:19 512	8:28 . . . . 473, 474
29:20–27[21–28]. 471	4:21 449	8:29–30. . . . . 316, 474
29:22[23] 471	5:3–4. 71	8:32, 34. 474
29–30 474	5:7, 11 449	8:35. 316
30:3. 469	7:10. 428	8:36. 474
30:11–20 185	12:6–15. 185	8:38. 316
31:15. 379	12:7. 473	8:39. 474
31:29. . . . . 466, 511	12:20, 23. 467	8:42, 44. 316
32:8–9. . . . . 368, 511	15:23. 61	8:46. 468
32:39. 278	16:21. 69	8:46–51. 458
32:40. 536	17 71	8:47. . . . . 316, 466
33 395	17:26. 329	8:48, 49. 316
33:2–3. 511	17:45–47 188	8:50. . . . . 316, 474
33:17. 413	24:7. 486	8:54. 316
34:11. 202	26:12. 428	8:51. 187
		8:63. 150
Joshua	**2 Samuel**	9:6. 466
1:4. . . . . 357, 508	7 237	12:10. 254
1:7. 466	7:13. 104	14:18. 138
2:9, 24. 71	7:26. 413	15:13. 266
3:10. 329	12:1–14. 293	17:8–16. 71
3:11. 51	12:20. 506	17:17–24 531
5:14. 419	14:2. 506	18:16–40 193
6:1–27. 71		18:20–21 185
7 331		18:20–40 71
7:21. 52		18:32. 448

19 121	24–25 253	6:1–12 486
19:5–8 174	25:13–17 52	6:11 92
19:8 507	25:27–30 523	7:12–26 .... 31, 486
19:13 428		7:13 137
19:16 486	**1 Chronicles**	7:24 380
20:28 73	3:1 27	8:2 27
21:20–24 293	5:26 286	9:4–5 480
22:11 413	9:32 259	9:5 316
22:19 419	23:30 316	9:6 .... 466, 468
	28:15 259	9:6–15 463
2 Kings		9:7 .... 466, 468
2:11–18 508	**2 Chronicles**	9:13, 15 466
4:1–7 193	4:7, 19 259	10:1 463
4:8–37 443	6:13, 20–21, 26, 29, 34, 38 316	
4:31 531	7:9 150	**Nehemiah**
4:38–5:27 193	7:19 466	1–2 25
5 277	12:7 471	1:4 507
8:19 259	18:10 413	1:5 465
9:36 138	32:21 468	1:6 .... 463, 474
9–10 252	34:25 471	1:6–7 466
13:21 531	36 .... 482, 483	1:15 465
14:25 138	36:5–21 288	2–3 463
16:15 480	36:6 49	2:7–9 486
17:3 466	36:7, 10 52	9 316
17:4 467	36:17–23 458	9:5 104
18:12 467	36:18 52	9:5b–37 463
18:29–35 183	36:18–21 486	9:10 202
18:33–35 511	36:22 501	9:16–18 466
18–19 443	36:22–23 70	9:17, 19, 27, 28, 31, 32 465
19:14–19 74		10:7[6] 27
19:16 329	**Ezra**	10:30[29] 470
19:19 193	1 505	12:27 150
19:28 281	1:1–4 .... 70, 486, 505	
19:35 174	1:5–11 288	**Esther**
21:9 467	1:7–10 253	1 251
23:29–35 49	3 505	1:1 456
23:29–24:17 288	3:12–13 505	1:19 310
23:36–24:6 50	4:1–5 505	4:8–11 98
24:1–17, 6, 8–12, ... 49	4:8–6:18 31	8:8 310
24:10 50	4:16 507	
24:12–16 49	5:12 138	**Job**
24:13 52	5:14 505	1:8 138
24:17 49		

1:21 104	30:9. 531	88 531
4:13. 428	31 76	88:2. 474
7:12. 394	31:3–4[2–3]. 113	89 237
9:12. 233	31:17[16]. 474	89:6–8[5–7]. 368
14:12. 531	32 104	89:11–12[10–11]. 394
14:14, 20. .27	34 . . . . .76, 104	89:27[26] 113
19:5. 413	35 446	89:47[46] 444
26:8. 378	35:17. . . . . .51, 444	90:2. 368
26:12–13 .394	35:26. 413	90:10. 458
34:8. 48	39 443	92 104
41 394	40:3[2] 345, 531	92:15. 113
42:2. 233	41 104	93 394
	42:9. 113	94:3. 444

Psalms

2 393	44:6[5] 413	94:22. 113
2:1. 308	44:12[11] .76	95:1. 113
3 . . . . .339, 446	45:7. 506	95:6. 316
6:5. 531	50 368	96:10–13 .368
8 395	50:3. 369	97:3. 369
8:4[3]. 258	55:17. 316	103 104
8:5[4]. 396	56:8–9. 369	103:6. 473
9 104	61 76	104:2. 465
10 445	62:3[2], 7–8[6–7] 113	104:3. 379
11 76	66 104	104:7. 394
13 445	66:3. 465	110 393
13:3[2] 444	67:2[1] 474	110:1. 74
17:6. 474	68:5[4] 104, 379	113:1–3. 104
18 . . . . .104, 443	69:15[14] .345	114:7. 51
18:2. 113	69:29[28] 369, 530	115:3. 233
18:28. 384	71:3. 113	115:4–7. . . . . .254, 280
18:31, 46. 113	72:2. .225, 237	115:16–17 531
19:14. 113	73 104	116 104
21 443	74:13–14 .394	118 104
22 445	75:8[9]. 278	118:25. 185
23 193	77 445	119:18. 474
25 446	77:5. 83	119:84. 444
25:15. 232	77:17–21 .394	119:164. 316
28 . . . . .76, 446	78:35. 113	120–34 76
28:1. 113	79:5. 444	120 76
29 394	79:9–13. 472	121 183
29:3. 428	80:4[3], 8[7], 29[28] 474	121:1–2. . . . . .185, 232
30 104	82:1. 368	122 76
30:1. 150	82:6. .174, 369	122:4. 104
	83 446	122:5. 368

123 . . . . 76, 443
123:1–2 232
126 443
129 76
132:11–12 237
135:3 104
135:6 233
135:9 202
135:15 254
135:15–18 280
136:12 70
137 443
138 104
138:2 413
139:16 369
141:8 232
141–44 76
144:1 113
145:13 202

Proverbs

1:6 430
1:31 341
2:16 431
5:3 431
6:16–19 367
6:24 431
7:5, 13, 21, 22, 27 431
21:4 384
22:17 474
30:15, 18 523
30:30 358

Ecclesiastes

1:12 209
9:7–10 506

Isaiah

1:9 471
2:1–5 237
2:2 511
2:2–3 113
2:11 367
2:20 254
4:3 530
5:15 384
6:1 392
6:3 113
6:5 465
6:5–7 512
7:7 24
7:14 237
9:6 368
10:5 367
11:4 . . . . 225, 237
11:9 113
11:11 52
13:8 512
13:17 . . . . 286, 457
13:19 471
14:4, 9–11 440
14:12–20 . . . . 281, 440–41
14:27 281
17:12–13 358
19:1 379
20:3 138
21:2 . . . . 286, 457
21:3 512
21:9 174
22:20 138
27:1 394
29:10 428
30:22 254
31:4 24
31:7 254
33:24 341
36:18 183
37:10–11 183
38:16 51
40–66 191
40:2 506
40:17 233
40:18–20 280
40:19–20 . . . . 122, 191
40:24 . . . . 122, 191
40:28 368
41:2 434
41:3 387
41:7 . . . . 122, 191
41:8 138
41:14–15 113
42:16 . . . . 122, 191
42:18–43:13 . . . . 146, 191
43:1–2 193
43:5–7 490
44:7 . . . . 122, 191
44:9–10 191
44:9–20 . . . . 146, 189, 254
44:12–13 122
44:12–20 189–90
44:17 191
44:26–28 490
44:28 367
44:28–45:1 74
45:1 . . . . 239, 486
45:1–8 70
45:3 . . . . 122, 191
45:7 369
45:24 473
47 65
47:1–7 122
48:6 . . . . 122, 191
49:7 . . . . 122, 191
49:23 122
51:3 490
51:9–10 394
60 506
60:10–14 . . . . 122, 191
61:1–2 . . . . 244, 492
61:1–3 490
61:3 506
65:6 369
66:1 . . . . 72, 74, 237, 390, 465

Jeremiah

1:9 512
2:5 24
3:12–14 185

Ancient Sources Index

3:19 419
3:25 468
4:1–4 185
4:13 379
7:2–11 449
7:20 471
7:25 138
9:12–15[13–16] 237
10:3–5 254
10:10 368
10:11 31
10:13 465
11:4 187
11:8 474
13:18 266
14:14 61
15:3 357
16:15 469
21:7 138
22:1–17, 13–17 49
22:15–16 . . . . 225, 237
23:3 469
23:5–6 505
23:6 491
25–26 49
25:1 49
25:1–15 . . . . 35, 457
25:9 . . . . 114, 138, 189, 239
25:12 . . . . 288, 486
25:12–14 70
25:29 367
26:4 467
27:5–6 114
27:6 . . . . 51, 74, 138, 189, 239, 367
27:16–22 . . . . 52, 253
27:22 288
28:1–9 52
28:3 253
28:14 114
29:1–14 . . . . 35, 457
29:10 . . . . 70, 288, 486
29:11 365
29:12–13 458

29:22 152
30:2 357
30:7 530
30:9 490
30:10 138
30:11 . . . . 76, 469
30:18–22 486
31:10–14 490
31:33 490
31:38–40 486
31:40 490
32:20–21 202
32:21 . . . . 70, 465
32:27 469
32:33 467
32:36 506
33:21 138
36 49
37:20–21 345
37:23–28 490
38:2–3 345
38:4, 5, 6 345
39:2 345
39:3 368
40–48:35 490
42:18 471
43:10 . . . . 114, 138, 189, 239, 367
44:6 471
44:23 467
46:25–26 138
48:25 412
49:18 471
49:19, 22 358
49:36 357
49:38 368
50:40 471
51:11 . . . . 286, 288, 387, 457
51:27–29 387
51:28 286
52:12 69
52:29 147
52:31 523

Lamentations

1:9 413
2:3 412
3:44 379
4:6 471

Ezekiel

1 . . . . 359, 368, 509
1:1 . . . . 49, 392, 508
1:3, 4, 7, 14, 16, 22 365
1:24 . . . . 365, 428
1:26, 27 365
1:28 . . . . 365, 378
2:1, 3 428
2:3–8 237
2:4 24
3:4–9 237
3:15 . . . . 49, 465
8:1–3 412
8:5 407
9–10 508
10:4 379
11:1 . . . . 412, 508
11:16 469
17 395
17:13 412
17:22–23, 24 243
19:10–14, 11 243
20:6 419
20:22 472
26:7 . . . . 114, 137, 236
28 484
28:3 27
28:13–14 438–39
28:15–19 439
31:6 243
31:13 244
34:17 412
34:21 413
36:19 76
36:24–28 237
37 531

37:1 412
37:1–14 400
37:24, 26–28 505
38:9 378
43:11 357
44:17 508
45:12 282

Daniel

1 . . . 31, 32, 33, 40, 43–77, 45, 66, 79, 81, 87, 88, 114, 133, 140, 163, 202, 235, 238, 245, 251, 403–4
1–4 . . . . 235, 248
1–6 . . . . . 23, 24, 25, 28, 34, 35, 38, 51, 61, 131, 411
1:1–2:4a 85
1:1 . . 38, 39, 45, 49, 50, 51, 62, 68, 87, 147, 301, 458, 494, 501, 507
1:1a 46, 48, 51, 83
1:1b 46, 48, 54
1:1b–c 46
1:1c 48, 54
1:1–2 . . . . . . 48, 57, 61, 166, 237, 248, 253, 356
1:1–3 105
1:1–5 . . . . 45, 46, 47, 56, 60, 66, 71, 72
1:2 . . . . . 50, 51, 52, 53, 56, 60, 72, 103, 114, 132, 137, 138, 187, 236, 244, 288, 289, 290, 391, 456
1:2a 46, 48, 51, 52, 60, 63
1:2b 48, 52, 54
1:2b–c 46, 51, 54
1:2c 48, 52, 54
1:3 54
1:3a 46, 48, 54, 56, 61
1:3b 46, 48, 54, 56, 61, 68
1:3–5 . . . . 57, 68
1:3a–5b 46
1:3a–5c 54
1:4 . . . . 64, 65, 133, 149, 464
1:4b 55, 56, 69
1:4c 48, 54, 55, 56, 60, 61
1:4c–5c 46
1:5 89

1:5a 46, 48, 55, 56, 61
1:5b 48, 56, 61
1:5b–c 66, 68
1:5c 46, 54, 55, 56, 69
1:6 . . . . 57, 60
1:6a 60
1:6–7 . . . . 60, 112, 179
1:6–17 . . . . 56, 58, 59, 69, 58–59
1:7 62
1:7a–b 61
1:7b 57
1:7–8 61
1:8a 57, 61
1:8b–d 57, 62
1:8c 57
1:8c–d 60, 64
1:8d 62
1:8–14 98
1:8–17 . . . . 55, 61, 68
1:9 . . . . 48, 51, 54, 60, 63, 65, 103
1:10 38
1:10b 63
1:10b–f 57, 60, 63
1:11–13 94
1:11a 64
1:12–13 . . . . 57, 60, 64
1:12a 64
1:12b 46
1:13a 46
1:15 . . . . 62, 64, 133
1:16 . . . . 64, 65
1:17–20 . . . . 64, 133, 203
1:17 . . . . 51, 54, 65, 103, 149
1:17a 60, 65
1:17a–b 57
1:17b 48, 60, 63, 65
1:17b–c, 17c 60
1:18 54
1:18–20 88
1:18–21 . . . . 65, 66, 67
1:18a–b, 18c 66, 68
1:18a–19a 66, 68
1:19–20 130

1:19 . . . . 69, 88, 89, 102
1:19a 68
1:19a–c 66
1:19b 68, 69
1:19b–c 66
1:19c 56, 68
1:20 . . . . 64, 66, 69, 88, 133
1:20a 68
1:20b 66, 69
1:20b–c 68
1:21 . . . . . 38, 39, 49, 51, 62, 66, 68, 70, 117, 286, 336, 356, 451, 496, 497, 501, 507
2 . . 31, 32, 33, 40, 64, 69, 73, 79–139, 81, 123–37, 140, 142, 147, 148, 149, 155, 181, 195, 196, 197, 203, 210, 214, 219, 234, 235, 238, 239, 247, 251, 260, 261, 285, 286, 293, 297, 335, 338, 349, 365, 385, 389, 432–33, 434, 501, 540
2–4 . . . . 202, 235
2–6 . . . 33, 80, 81, 103, 140, 195, 246, 296, 348, 349
2–7 . . . . 31, 32, 40, 79, 81, 83, 105, 121, 131, 140, 142, 195, 200, 235, 246, 297, 299, 348, 352, 403–4
2:1–2 129
2:1–3 . . . . 83, 121
2:1–11 . . . . . . 82, 83, 84–86, 90, 94, 95, 100, 105
2:1–12 . . . . 92, 130
2:1–16 195
2:1 . . 38, 39, 49, 50, 97, 121, 147, 209, 356, 380, 381, 386, 387, 501, 507
2:1a, 1b, 1c, 1d 83
2:2 . . . . 89, 97, 153, 261
2:2a 89, 271
2:2b, 2c, 2d, 2e 89
2:3–5 129
2:3 . . . . 83, 90, 93, 99, 112
2:3b 89
2:4 . . . . . 32, 83, 89, 102, 112, 153, 317
2:4a, 4b 83, 90
2:4c 92
2:4c–d 90, 92
2:4d 90

2:5–6 . . . . 83, 89, 90, 93, 99, 112	2:15–16 131	2:24 . . . . 98, 106, 111, 112
2:5 . . . . . . .85, 91, 92, 93, 96, 107, 119, 156, 159, 162, 163, 168, 171, 177, 178, 212, 215, 228, 264, 270, 353	2:15 . . . . .91, 103, 112	2:24a, 24a–h, 24b–c, 24d, 24e, 24f, 24g 111
	2:15a–b 98	2:24h 90, 111
	2:15a–c 95	2:25–26 87
2:5a–b 85, 90	2:15c 98	2:25–45 106
2:5b 89	2:15d 98, 99	2:25 . . . . .98, 106
2:5c 92	2:15d–16d 95, 98	2:25a, 25b, 25c 111
2:5d 90, 92	2:16–19 129	2:25d 90
2:5e–f 92	2:16 . . . . 95, 98, 99, 100, 111, 121, 530	2:26–27 91
2:6 . . . . 90, 129	2:16a 102	2:26–28 131
2:6a 90, 92	2:16d 90	2:26 . . . . 106, 112, 121
2:6b 92	2:17–18 . . . . .100, 140	2:26c, 26d–f 112
2:6c 90	2:17–23 . . . . 94, 99, 101, 131	2:26e 90
2:7–9 131	2:17 . . . . 103, 121	2:27–29 73
2:7 . . . . 83, 91, 92, 112, 156, 318	2:17a, 17b 102	2:27–30 . . . . .106, 277
2:7b 90, 92	2:17a–b 100, 102	2:27–45 . . . . .106, 112
2:7c 90	2:18–19 73	2:27 . . . . 93, 103, 106, 129, 130
2:8–9 . . . . 83, 93, 98, 99, 213	2:18 102	2:27c 90
2:8 . . . . 91, 98	2:18a, 18b 102, 103	2:27c–e 106, 112
2:9 . . . . .88, 92, 112	2:18a–b 100	2:28–29 . . . . .123, 130
2:9a–f, 9h 90	2:19–23 . . . . .100, 103	2:28 . . . . .103, 130
2:10–11 . . . . 83, 93, 97, 112, 112	2:19 102	2:28a–b 112
2:10 . . . . 91, 103, 156, 318	2:19a 102, 103, 111	2:28a–d 106
2:10a 89	2:19b 102, 103, 104	2:28c–d 112
2:10d 90	2:20–22 236	2:28e–29d 106
2:11 . . . . 102, 103, 123, 136, 210	2:20–23 . . . . . . .73, 102, 103, 112, 114, 122, 129, 132, 456	2:29–30 261
2:11d 90		2:29 . . . . 112, 134, 278
2:11e 93	2:20 .91, 97, 228	2:29c 112
2:12–13 . . . . 87, 95, 97	2:20a–b 102, 103	2:30 . . . . . 103, 106, 112, 123, 130, 131
2:12–16 . . . . . . 94, 95, 96, 99, 100, 105	2:20c 104	2:31–33 147
2:12 . . . . 88, 91, 95, 96, 97, 99	2:20c–d 102, 104	2:31–36 . . . . .106, 112
2:12a, 12a–b 97	2:20c–23e 100	2:31 . . . . .148, 278
2:13–23 130	2:21 . . . . . .99, 102, 104, 239, 278, 383, 392, 436, 530	2:31a 106, 112, 114
2:13a 99		2:31b–d 113
2:13b 97	2:22 . . . . .102, 104	2:33, 34–35 366
2:13b–d 99	2:23 463	2:34 366
2:13c 97, 102	2:23a, 23b 104	2:34a 112
2:14–15 . . . . 100, 111	2:23a–b 102, 104	2:35 147
2:14 . . . . .131, 147	2:23c–e 102, 103, 104	2:35a 113
2:14a 97, 98	2:24–25 . . . . .98, 100	2:35d 114
2:14a–c 98	2:24–30 130	2:37–38 . . . . 73, 147, 219, 239
2:14a–15b .97	2:24–45 . . . . 94, 104, 105, 106, 107–10, 111	2:37–39 149
2:14a–15c 95, 99		

2:37–40 435
2:37–45 . . . . 106, 112, 117
2:37 . . . . 73, 102, 234, 236, 278
2:37a 106, 112, 114, 137
2:37b 114, 229
2:37a–38c 114
2:38 . . . . 114, 147, 382
2:38d 114
2:39a 116
2:40–43 114
2:40–45 109
2:40 . . . . 365, 366
2:41–42 366
2:42 365
2:43 116
2:44 . . . . 73, 290, 380, 384
2:44–45 366
2:45 . . . . 123, 147, 281
2:45b 117
2:45e, 45f, 45g–h 114
2:46–47 . . . . 118, 120
2:46–49 . . . . 117, 118, 119, 121
2:46 . . . . 118, 120, 147, 149, 285
2:46a 118, 120, 121
2:46a–b 149
2:47–49 . . . . 149, 294
2:47 . . . . 73, 91, 103, 118, 203, 210,
238, 285, 290, 329
2:47c 138
2:48–49 . . . . 118, 121
2:48 . . . . 87, 104, 118, 123, 285
2:48a 118, 121
2:49 . . . . 118, 141, 162, 181
3 . . . 25, 30, 32, 34, 40, 53, 69, 79, 92,
97, 116, 118, 121, 138, 140–94,
189, 197, 203, 235, 238, 248, 254,
255, 265, 293, 297, 301, 335,
338, 380
3–6 . . . . 34, 288
3–7 102
3:1–4 265
3:1–7 . . . . 141, 142, 143–44, 145,
152, 158
3:1 . . . . . . 145, 147, 149, 152, 169, 189,
235, 251, 301

3:1a 145, 147, 148, 149, 155
3:1b 145
3:1b–c 148
3:1c 145, 148
3:1d 145, 155
3:2–3 . . . . 156, 254
3:2 . . . . 145, 149, 169, 179, 189,
255, 335
3:2a 149, 173
3:2a–d 149
3:2b 145, 150, 152, 176
3:2c–d 145, 150, 155
3:2d 145, 149, 173
3:3 . . . . 145, 149, 150, 152, 169,
179, 255
3:3a 145, 149, 151, 176, 179
3:3a–d 150, 155
3:3b 145, 149, 152, 173
3:3c 145, 151, 152
3:3d 145, 151
3:4–6 . . . . 145, 151, 162, 343
3:4 . . . . . . 150, 151, 179, 209, 261, 380
3:4–7 254
3:4a 151
3:4b 145, 151, 152
3:4b–6a 156
3:5–6 155
3:5 . . 145, 149, 151, 169, 189, 209, 255
3:5a 145, 151, 155
3:5b–c 149, 151
3:5c 145, 152, 155
3:5d 145, 149, 152, 155, 173
3:5g 151
3:6 . . . . 145, 151
3:6a 145, 151, 155
3:6a–c, 6b–c 151
3:7 . . . . . 145, 149, 150, 151, 152, 155,
162, 169, 179, 189, 209, 255, 380
3:7a 145, 152, 155
3:7b 145, 152, 153
3:7c 145, 152, 155
3:7d 145, 149, 155, 173
3:8–12 . . . 142, 145, 153, 154, 155, 158

3:8 . . . . 155, 331
3:8a–b 155
3:9–11 156
3:9–12 155
3:9 . . . . 90, 91, 156, 163, 317, 318
3:9a 149, 156, 162, 173
3:10–11 . . . . 155, 156
3:10–12 162
3:10 . . . . 149, 169, 189, 255
3:10c, 10d 145, 155
3:11a 145, 151, 155
3:12 . . . . 148, 149, 156, 161, 165, 169,
189, 255, 304, 318, 380
3:12a 153
3:12a–b, 12c, 12d 156
3:12e 145, 156
3:12e–f 145, 155
3:13–18 . . . 142, 145, 157, 158, 159–60
3:13 . . . . 149, 158, 161, 179
3:13a 161, 169
3:13b 161
3:14–15 . . . . 158, 161, 162
3:14 . . . . . . 91, 148, 149, 165, 169, 189,
255, 380
3:14a–b 162
3:14c–e 161, 162
3:14d 162
3:14e 145
3:14e–f 145, 162
3:15 . . . . . . 53, 149, 156, 165, 169, 181,
182, 185, 189, 201, 255, 329
3:15a–d 165
3:15a–e 161, 162
3:15b, 15d 145
3:15e–g 165
3:15f 162
3:15f–g 161, 162
3:15g 145, 162
3:15h–i 149, 158, 161, 162, 164,
173, 175, 180
3:15i 164
3:16–18 . . . . . . 158, 161, 163, 185, 188,
309, 317, 339
3:16 . . . . 91, 156

Ancient Sources Index

3:16a 163
3:16b 163, 164
3:16b–c 163
3:16–17c 161
3:17–18 . . . . 165, 317, 380
3:17, 17a–c 165
3:17b 164
3:17c 151
3:17d 145, 161
3:18 . . . . 149, 161, 165, 169, 189, 255, 484
3:18b 164
3:18c 164, 165
3:18c–e 161, 164
3:18d–e 145
3:19–20 . . . . 145, 167, 168
3:19 . . . . 91, 169
3:19a 161, 169
3:19b 145, 161, 169
3:19c–f 169
3:19c–20d 169, 172
3:19e–f 161, 169
3:20, 20a–b 169
3:20d 145, 151
3:21 149
3:21a 172, 179
3:21a–b 172
3:21b 145
3:21d 151
3:21–23 172
3:21–25 . . . . . . 145, 170, 171, 172, 175
3:22 . . . . 169, 172
3:22a, 22b 172
3:22c 172, 179
3:23 . . . . 149, 172, 180
3:23a 145, 151, 173, 179
3:24–25 . . . . . . 162, 172, 173, 182, 260
3:24–26 91
3:24 149
3:24a 149, 173
3:24a–b 161, 172
3:24c–d 173
3:24d 179
3:24e 172, 173, 180
3:24f–g 173
3:24h 172, 173
3:25 . . . . 149, 172, 173
3:25a–b 173
3:25e 180
3:25g 174
3:26 . . . . 73, 176, 201, 294
3:26a 145, 151
3:26a–e, 26b–c 176
3:26d 176, 179, 180, 201
3:26d–e 176
3:26f 176, 179, 180
3:26–27 . . . . 151, 209, 330
3:26–30 . . . . . . 145, 175, 176, 177–78
3:26f–27f 176, 179
3:27 176
3:27a 176, 179
3:27b 145, 176, 179
3:27c, 27d, 27e, 27f 179
3:28–29 . . . . 73, 174, 176, 179, 182, 185, 203, 238, 294, 329
3:28 . . . . 91, 170, 174, 290, 380
3:28c 180
3:28c–e 149, 173, 175
3:28d, 28e, 28f, 28g, 28h, 28i, 28j . . 180
3:28c–29g 176, 181
3:29 . . . . 170, 180, 335
3:29b 145
3:29e–g 149, 173, 180, 201
3:30 . . . . 141, 176, 181
3:31–32[4:1–2] 234
3:31–33[4:1–3] . . . 103, 197, 198, 199, 200, 203, 230, 279
3:31–4:15[4:1–18] 196, 198, 204, 211, 230, 232
3:31[4:1] 197, 198, 200, 201, 205, 226, 232, 333, 335, 380
3:31a[4:1a] 200, 214, 232
3:31a–b[4:1a–b] 200, 201
3:31c[4:1c] 200
3:32–33[4:2–3] . . . 198, 200, 201, 202, 218, 329, 332, 335
3:32[4:2] 73, 201, 298, 301
3:32a[4:2a], 32b[4:2b] . . . 200, 201, 205
3:32c[4:2c] 200, 201
3:33[4:3] 73, 202, 380, 384
3:33a[4:3a], 33b[4:3b] 202
3:33c–d[4:3c–d] 233
3:34[4:2] 102
4 . . . 32, 33, 34, 40, 53, 64, 69, 79, 87, 90, 114, 116, 118, 121, 135, 138, 147, 194, 195–245, 246, 247, 251, 261, 274, 278, 279, 290, 291, 293, 298, 301, 333, 335, 356, 380, 381, 382, 433
4:1–5[4–8] 205, 209, 307
4:1–15[4–18] 200, 202, 204, 205, 206–8, 212
4:1[4] . . 197, 205, 209, 212, 228, 229, 232, 233, 234, 380
4:1a–b[4a–b] 209
4:2[5] 218, 261, 385
4:2a[5a] 209, 210
4:2b–d[5b–d] 209
4:2c[5c], 2d[5d] 210
4:3[6] 271
4:3c[6c] 210, 261
4:4a[7a] 209
4:4b[7b] 209, 210
4:4c[7c] 209, 210, 213
4:5–6[8–9] . . . 121, 266, 279, 294, 329
4:5[8] 93, 123, 136, 213, 268
4:5a[8a] 210
4:5a–b[8a–b] 211
4:5b[8b] 218
4:5c[8c] 211
4:5d[8d] 205, 210
4:6–15[9–18] 205, 211, 214, 224
4:6[9] 93, 210, 213, 268
4:6a[9a] 210, 211
4:6a–f[9a–f] 211
4:6b–d[9b–d] 211, 213
4:6d[9d] 211
4:7–9[10–12] 205, 211
4:7–14[10–17] 197, 220–22
4:7[10], 7a[10a] 211
4:7b–c[10b–c] 405
4:7c[10c] 211

4:7c–d[10c–d] 219	4:16d–f[19d–f] 214	4:24a–d[27a–d] 225
4:7d[10d] 211	4:16e–h[19e–h], 16g–j[19g–j] . . .218	4:25–27[28–30] 228
4:8[11] 234	4:16i[19i] .219	4:25–30[28–33] 197, 214, 220–22, 226, 227
4:8a–b[11a–b] 202	4:16i–24[19i–27] 220–22, 242	
4:9[12] 234	4:16g–24d[19g–27d] 197, 218	4:25–34[28–37] 73
4:9c[12c] 219	4:17–18[20–21] 218	4:25[28] 228
4:9f[12f] 211, 219	4:17–19[20–22] 382	4:26–27[29–30] 226, 229
4:10–14[13–17] . . . 205, 211, 212, 229	4:17–20[20–23] 149	4:26[29] 228
4:10[13] 212, 234, 279, 286, 381	4:17 . . . . .219, 234	4:27[30] 91, 219, 229, 279
4:10a–b[13a–b] 205, 211	4:17a[20a], 17b[20b], 17c[20c] . . .219	4:27c–d[30c–d] 228
4:10b[13b] .229	4:17c–d[20c–d] 202	4:27d[30d] 228, 229
4:11[14] 261	4:18[21] 219, 225, 228, 234	4:28[31] 234, 279
4:11a–b[14a–b] 205, 212, 224	4:18c[21c] 219	4:28a[31a] 228
4:11c–13[14c–16] 212	4:19[22] 218, 234, 278	4:28b[31b] 229
4:11c–14g[14c–17g] 205	4:19a[22a] 219	4:28c[31c] 228
4:12[15] 234	4:20–21[23–24] 219	4:28d[31d] 229
4:12a[15a] .225	4:20[23] 212, 224, 229, 234, 279, 381	4:28c–29h[31c–32h] 229
4:12b[15b] .229		4:28–29[31–32] 228, 229
4:13[16] 530	4:20a[23a] 219	4:29[32] 149, 239, 383
4:13a–b[16a–b] 225	4:20a–b[23a–b] 229	4:29b[32b] 229
4:13c[16c] 212, 229, 232	4:20b–i[23b–i] 219	4:29d[32d] 229, 232
4:14[17] 73, 211, 212, 232, 233, 239, 278, 279, 381	4:20a–c[23a–c] 218	4:29e–h[32e–h] 233, 274, 279
	4:20c[23c] 212, 224	4:30[33] 228, 229, 234, 258
4:14a–b[17a–b] 212	4:20d–e[23d–e] 224	4:30a[33a] 228
4:14c[17c] 212, 225	4:20d–i[23d–i] 218	4:30e–f[33e–f] 232
4:14c–g[17c–g] 225, 274, 279	4:20f[23f] .225	4:30–31[33–36] 209
4:14d[17d], 14e–f[17e–f] 212	4:20g[23g] 229	4:31–32[34–35] 73, 103, 116, 202, 232, 234
4:14g[17g] 212, 225	4:20i[23i] 229, 232	
4:15–16[18–19] 121, 329	4:21–23[24–26] 218	4:31–33[34–36] 232
4:15[18] 73, 93, 123, 136, 200, 205, 213, 232, 233, 234, 266, 268, 279, 294	4:21[24] 224, 278, 279	4:31–34[34–37] 196, 198, 200, 204, 222–23, 230, 231, 232, 232, 279, 285, 294, 329
	4:21a[24a] 219	
	4:21b[24b] 224, 229	
4:15a[18a] .212	4:21c[24c] 224	4:31[34] 232, 234, 234, 290, 380, 383, 384
4:15b[18b] .213	4:22[25] 229, 234, 239	
4:15b–f[18b–f] 211	4:22a–d[25a–d] 224	4:31a[34a], 31b[34b] 232
4:15c–f[18c–f] 213	4:22d[25d] 229	4:31c–34e[34c–37e] 198
4:16–24[19–27] 197, 213, 214, 215–17	4:22e[25e] 225, 229, 232	4:31d–f[34d–f] 233
	4:22f[25f] .225	4:32[35] 233, 234, 281
4:16–30[19–33] . . . 197, 204, 214, 226	4:22f–i[25f–i] 233, 274, 279	4:33[36] 209, 232, 233, 291, 382
4:16[19] 91, 261, 433	4:23[26] 225, 234	4:33a[36a] 232, 233
4:16a[19a] 214, 218	4:23d[26d] 225	4:33d–e[36d–e] 233
4:16b[19b], 16c[19c] 218	4:24[27] 218, 228	4:34[37] 196, 202, 232, 234, 236
4:16a–c[19a–c] 214		4:34a[37a] 233, 280
4:16a–f[19a–f] 197, 218		

5 . . . . . . .32, 33, 34, 40, 52, 53, 79, 116, 117, 118, 120, 163, 195, 196, 234, 235, 246–95, 298, 301, 336, 348, 356, 411, 438, 442, 451, 453, 496, 529
5:1–4 . . . . .248, 249, 250, 255, 265, 267, 494
5:1–5 54
5:1 . . . . 250, 251, 301
5:1a 250, 263, 266
5:1a–b 250
5:2–3 . . . . 248, 254, 280, 288
5:2–5 . . . . .52, 280, 288
5:2 . . . . 250, 251, 252
5:2a 250, 251, 263
5:2b 250, 251, 259
5:2c 251, 252, 253, 258, 259, 265
5:2c–d 250, 251, 259
5:2d 252
5:2e 250, 251, 263
5:3–4 . . . . 250, 252, 287
5:3 . . . . .250, 252
5:3a 252, 259
5:3b 252, 253, 258, 259
5:3b–d 259
5:3c 252, 253
5:3d 252
5:3e 251, 252, 263
5:4 . . . . 250, 254, 263
5:4b 254
5:5–8 . . . . 255, 256, 257, 262, 265
5:5 . . . . 256, 258, 259
5:5a 256, 258, 281
5:5a–b 258
5:5b 256, 258, 259
5:5b–c 263
5:5c 256, 258, 260, 281
5:6–7 .256, 260
5:6 . . . . 256, 261, 385
5:6a 256, 260, 263, 265
5:6b 256, 260, 265
5:6c 256, 260, 267
5:6d 256, 260
5:7–8 73
5:7 . . . . .91, 261
5:7a 261, 263, 271
5:7a–b 256
5:7c–i .258, 277
5:7d 263, 285
5:7e–g, 7e–i 258
5:8 . . . . 256, 258, 261, 263
5:8a, 8d 263
5:9–12 . . . . 262, 263, 264, 268, 269
5:9 . . . . 263, 265, 268, 385
5:9a 263, 265
5:9a–b 266
5:9b 260, 265
5:9c 263, 265, 266
5:10 . . . . . . .90, 91, 261, 263, 265, 266, 268, 317
5:10a 263
5:10d .263, 266
5:10d–f 263
5:10e–f 260, 266
5:10f 263
5:10b–12 277
5:11–12 . . . . .263, 281
5:11 . . . . .93, 252, 272
5:11b .266, 272
5:11b–c 267
5:11c .266, 272
5:11c–d 265
5:11d 263, 265, 266, 272
5:12 . . . . 121, 266, 268, 298
5:12a .267, 272
5:12b .265, 267
5:12c 263
5:12c–d 268
5:12d .266, 268
5:13–14 . . . . .269, 271
5:13–16 . . . . 268, 269, 270, 274
5:13 . . . . . 91, 252, 273, 304, 318, 329
5:13a 263, 269, 271
5:13c 263
5:13d 269
5:13d–f 267
5:13e 272
5:13e–f 269
5:13f 263, 271
5:13d–14c .269
5:13b–16 277
5:14–17 73
5:14 . . . . .93, 281
5:14a .269, 272
5:14b 272
5:14b–c 269
5:14c 272
5:15 . . . . .269, 272
5:15a, 15b, 15c, 15d, 15e 269
5:16 . . . . 269, 272, 285
5:16a–c 271, 281
5:16b–c 272
5:16d–i 271, 272, 285
5:17–28 . . . . 255, 268, 273, 274, 275–76, 277
5:17 . . . . 91, 274, 277, 280
5:17b 263
5:17c–d 274, 277
5:17c–f 277
5:17e 263
5:17e–f 274, 277
5:18–19 . . . . .149, 274
5:18–21 . . . . .274, 277
5:18 . . . . . .73, 102, 234, 252, 263, 265, 274, 278, 279, 280
5:19 . . . . 279, 280, 380
5:19a .278, 279
5:19b 278
5:19c .274, 280
5:19c–d, 19e–f 278
5:19e .274, 280
5:19g .274, 280
5:19g–h 278
5:19i 274, 280
5:19i–j 278
5:20–21 . . . . 149, 274, 279
5:20 279
5:20a, 20a–b, 20c–e 280
5:21 . . . . .73, 102, 234
5:21f 274

5:21f–i 279, 280
5:21h–i 280
5:22–23 . . . . 53, 54, 274, 278, 280, 494
5:22 . . . . .252, 294
5:22a .263, 280
5:22b–c 277
5:23 . . . . 254, 280, 288, 293
5:23a .277, 281
5:23b–c 280
5:23d .277, 280
5:23e–g, 23h 280
5:23i .277, 280
5:24–25 277
5:24–28 . . . . 274, 277, 281
5:24 . . . . .278, 281
5:24a .258, 281
5:24b 281
5:25–28 262
5:25 282
5:25a–b 281
5:25c, 26a .282
5:26b–c 277
5:26–28 282
5:27–29 387
5:27 291
5:27a–b 277
5:28a–b, 28a–b 277
5:29a .263, 285
5:29b–d 285
5:29b–e 285
5:29–6:1[5:31] 273, 283, 284, 285
5:30 . . . . 285, 286, 288
5:30a 263
5:30–6:1[5:31] . 70, 285, 289, 296, 456
6 . . . . 25, 32, 34, 69, 70, 79,
   116, 118, 140, 150, 197, 235,
   258, 296–347, 356, 380, 496
6:1[5:31] 70, 116, 285, 286, 288,
   298, 336, 355, 451, 456
6:2–3[1–2] 299, 301
6:2–5[1–4] 298, 299, 300
6:2–29[6:1–28] 40
6:2[1] 38, 285, 301, 451

6:2a[1a], 2b[1b], 2c[1c] 301
6:3[2] 302, 336
6:3a[2a], 3b[2b] 301
6:3c[2c] 301, 302, 307, 308
6:3d[2d] 299, 301
6:4–5[3–4] 121, 324, 328
6:4–6[3–5] .342
6:4[3] 298, 299, 302, 337, 340
6:4a[3a] 302, 336
6:4a[3b], 4c[3c] 302
6:5–6[4–5] 303, 304, 317
6:5–24[4–23] 73
6:5[4] 299, 302, 303, 307, 331,
   337, 340
6:5a[4a] 302, 308
6:5a–b[4a–b], 5c–d[4c–d] 303
6:5c–f[4c–f] 299, 305, 307
6:5d[4d], 5e[4e], 5f[4f] 303
6:6–10[5–9] 304, 305, 306
6:6[5] 90, 302, 305, 331, 336, 340
6:6a[5a] 307, 308, 322, 330
6:6b[5b] 307, 323, 336
6:6b–c[5b–c] 303
6:6c[5c] 307, 312
6:7–9[6–8] . . . 305, 307, 308, 317, 340
6:7–10[6–9] 323
6:7[6] 308
6:7a[6a] 302, 307, 308, 317, 322
6:7c[6c] 308, 309, 317, 322
6:7c–8d[6c–7d] 305
6:8–10[7–9] 343
6:8[7] 303
6:8a[7a] 308, 309
6:8a–c[7a–c] 310
6:8b[7b] 310, 317
6:8b–c[7b–c], 8d–e[7d–e] 308
6:8e[7e] 303, 309
6:9–10[8–9] 335
6:9[8] 305, 308, 335
6:9a[8a] 309, 310, 317
6:9a–b[8a–b] 309
6:9b[8b] 310, 317
6:9c[8c] 310, 322

6:9c–d[8c–d] 317
6:9d[8d] 310
6:10[9] 305, 308, 310, 311, 315,
   317, 323, 333, 335
6:11–12[10–11] 166, 312, 315
6:11–15[10–14] 305, 311, 312,
   313–14
6:11[10] 309, 312, 315, 316, 328,
   335, 337, 340, 463
6:11a[10a] 315, 319
6:11a–c[10a–c] 319
6:11b[10b] 315
6:11b–c[10b–c] 315, 319
6:11c[10c] .317
6:11e–i[10e–i] 315
6:11f–h[10f–h] 316
6:11h[10h] 323
6:12–14[11–13] 316
6:12[11] 308, 312, 315, 316, 331
6:12a[11a] 308, 317, 322, 330
6:12b–c[11b–c] 303
6:12b–d[11b–d] 316, 317
6:12h[11h] 323
6:13–14[12–13] 312, 317, 317,
   335, 340
6:13[12] 91, 307, 308, 322
6:13a[12a] 317
6:13a–d[12a–d] 312
6:13b[12b], 13c[12c] 317
6:13e[12e] 303
6:13f–i[12f–i] 312, 317, 322
6:13h[12h] 322
6:13h–i[12h–i] 317
6:14[13] 91, 156, 307, 312, 318
6:14b[13b] 317, 318
6:14c[13c] 296, 304
6:14e[13e] 303
6:15[14] . 312, 318, 320, 322, 328, 340
6:15a[14a] 318, 330
6:15a–b[14a–b] 312, 318
6:15b[14b] 318
6:15c–f[14c–f] 312
6:15d[14d] 324
6:15e–f[14e–f] 318

Ancient Sources Index

6:16–19[15–18]. 319, 320, 321
6:16[15] 307, 308, 317, 320, 322, 340
6:16a[15a] 308, 317, 322, 330
6:16b[15b], 16c[15c] 322
6:16d[15d]. 317
6:16d–e[15d–e]. 322
6:16c–17c[15c–16c] 308
6:17–18[16–17]. 323
6:17[16] 91, 309, 320, 330, 337, 340, 380
6:17a–c[16a–c] 322, 323
6:17d–h[16d–h] 322
6:17f–g[16f–g] 323
6:17f–h[16f–h] 328, 329
6:17g[16g] 323
6:17h[16h]. 323, 324
6:18[17] 322
6:18b–d[17b–d] 330
6:18d[17d]. 324
6:19[18] 320, 322, 324, 328, 340
6:19b–d[18b–d] 324
6:20–21[19–20]. 328
6:20–25[19–24]325, 326–27, 328, 332
6:20a–b[19a–b] 328
6:21[20] 90, 91, 309, 337, 340, 380, 481
6:21a[20a] 328
6:21c[20c] 329
6:21e[20e] 323, 329
6:21e–g[20e–g] 328
6:21f[20f]. 330
6:22–23[21–22] 308, 328, 329, 330, 339
6:22[21] 317, 330
6:23[22] 309, 316
6:23a[22a] 323, 330
6:23b[22b], 23c[22c] 330
6:23d[22d] 303, 330, 331
6:23e[22e] 330
6:24–25[23–24]. 328, 330
6:24[23] 337, 340
6:24a[23a] 328, 330, 340
6:24b–c[23b–c] 330

6:24b–f[23b–f] 328
6:24d[23d] 330
6:24e[23e] 330, 331
6:24f[23f] 303, 331
6:25[24] 303, 328
6:25a–d[24a–d] 330, 331
6:25b[24b] 308, 322
6:26–28[25–27] . . . 103, 308, 333, 340
6:26–29[25–28] 332, 333, 334
6:26[25] 116, 335, 380
6:26a[25a], 26a–b[25a–b], 26c–28d[25c–27d] 333
6:27–28[26–27]. 102
6:27[26] 73, 290, 384
6:27b[26b] 323
6:27c[26c] 323, 335
6:27d[26d], 27e[26e] 335
6:28[27] 335, 336
6:27a[26a], 28c[27c] 335
6:29[28] . . . 38, 39, 117, 286, 296, 302, 333, 336, 337, 340, 348, 497, 501
7 . . . 31, 32, 33, 34, 35, 37, 40, 73, 79, 81, 105, 115, 116, 131, 235, 247, 286, 297, 348–401, 349, 356, 404, 405, 406, 411, 432–33, 433, 434, 437, 438, 442, 443, 452, 456, 496, 497, 498, 501, 540
7–10 203
7–12 . . . 23, 24, 25, 27, 28, 34, 38, 131, 291, 297, 356, 400, 451, 496
7:1–6. . . . . 350, 351, 352, 353–54, 355, 361
7:1 . . 27, 38, 39, 49, 50, 147, 350, 352, 355, 356, 357, 405, 410, 411, 438, 451, 452, 456, 457, 496, 501, 507, 508
7:1a, 1b. 355
7:1c 357
7:1d 385
7:2–27. 452
7:2 . . . . 31, 91, 278, 350, 381, 395, 435, 523
7:2a–b. 357
7:2c 350, 357
7:2c–d. 350, 357, 358, 365, 378
7:2–4b 352, 357

7:2c–4b. 357
7:3–7. 435
7:3 . . . . 278, 381, 523
7:3a 358, 378
7:3b 358, 366
7:4–6. . . . . 378, 395, 456
7:4 . . . . 350, 352, 381
7:4a 358, 365
7:4a–b. 358, 359
7:4b 358
7:4c 350
7:4c–g. 350, 352, 359
7:4d 358
7:4d–g 370, 378
7:4e, 4f, 4g 358
7:5 . . . . 350, 352, 359
7:5a 350, 358, 359, 365
7:5b 378
7:5d–f 370, 378
7:5e–f 359
7:6 . . . . 350, 352, 359, 523
7:6a 365
7:6a–b. 350, 359
7:6b 359
7:6e 359, 370, 378
7:7–8. 367, 382
7:7–10. 383
7:7–12. . . . . 350, 360, 361, 362–63, 364
7:7–14. 73
7:7 . . . . . . 350, 361, 365, 378, 383, 465
7:7a 361
7:7a–b. 350, 365, 378
7:7b 361, 365
7:7c 366, 382
7:7d–e. 366
7:7d–f. 366, 378, 382
7:7f, 7g 366
7:7g–h 382, 383
7:7i 367
7:8 . . . . 369, 383, 384, 413, 420
7:8a 367
7:8a–b, 8a–c. 361, 367
7:8b 350, 367, 382, 384

7:8c 367, 384
7:8d 350, 367
7:8d–e 361, 367, 384
7:8e 383, 384
7:9–10 . . . . 361, 367, 379
7:9 383
7:9a 350, 367
7:9b 367
7:9b–c 368
7:9c 367, 368
7:9d–e, 9f–g, 9d–10d 368
7:10 530
7:10a–b 368
7:10c–d 368, 380
7:10e–f 369
7:11–12 . . . . 361, 369, 378
7:11 . . . . 366, 368, 369, 420
7:11a 350, 369
7:11a–b 369
7:11c 350, 369
7:11d, 11e, 11f 370
7:11c–12 369
7:11d–f 370, 378
7:11d–12b .350
7:12 . . . . 36, 73, 395, 456, 530
7:12a 370, 380
7:12a–b 378
7:12b 370
7:13–14 . . . . . . 371, 378, 385, 398, 494
7:13–28 . . . . .350, 361, 370, 371, 372–74, 375–78
7:13 . . . . .37, 368
7:13a–b 350, 357, 365, 378
7:13b 371, 378, 379
7:13c 378
7:13d 378, 380
7:14 .37, 73, 380
7:14a 378, 380
7:15–20 . . . . .359, 371, 375–76, 377–78, 380
7:15 . . . . .371, 385
7:15a 380
7:16 429

7:16a 427
7:16a–b 371
7:16b 382
7:17–18 . . . . 368, 380, 387, 427
7:17 . . . . . 358, 359, 371, 381, 383, 523
7:17a 380
7:17b 381, 383
7:17c 381
7:18 . . . . . 336, 371, 380, 381, 384, 435
7:18b 381
7:19–20 382
7:19 . . . . .383, 429
7:19b 371
7:19c 382, 383
7:19f, 19g–i 382
7:20 . . . . 413, 420, 529
7:20a, 20c–d 371
7:20c–h 383
7:20e, 20f–h, 20g 384
7:20h 21 382
7:21–22 . . . . 350, 371, 382, 383
7:21–25 73
7:21 382
7:21a 350, 382
7:21b 371, 382
7:21c 384
7:22 . . . . 336, 368, 381
7:22a 383, 384
7:22b, 22c .383
7:22d 383, 385
7:23–27 . . . 359, 371, 376–77, 378, 383
7:23 . . . . 371, 383, 429
7:23c, 23d .383
7:24 383
7:24a 375
7:24c 383, 384
7:24b–26 375
7:25 . . . . . .73, 388, 413, 421, 436, 437, 529, 530, 536, 537
7:25a–b, 25e 384
7:26 . . . . .73, 389
7:27 . . . . . .73, 375, 380, 381, 384, 385, 389, 435

7:27a 384
7:28 . . . . . .85, 357, 371, 375, 377, 378, 385, 429, 433, 452, 512
7:28a, 28b .385
8 . . . . .31, 32, 35, 40, 73, 115, 116, 192, 286, 348, 349, 350, 356, 385, 388, 389, 405–50, 451, 452, 456, 475, 479, 480, 497, 498, 509, 540
8–10 31
8–12 . . . . . .31, 32, 33, 40, 79, 80, 349, 384, 388, 403–4
8:1–2 . . . . .406, 411
8:1–4 . . . . 406, 409, 410, 414, 423
8:1 . . . 38, 39, 49, 50, 85, 90, 147, 267, 350, 356, 357, 405, 407, 408, 410, 411, 451, 452, 496, 501, 507, 508
8:1a 410
8:1b, 1c 411
8:2–25 452
8:2 . . . . .408, 411
8:2a 406, 408, 411
8:2a–d 407
8:2b, 2c 411
8:2c–d 408
8:2d 411
8:2e 406, 408, 411
8:2e–f 407
8:2f 408, 411
8:3 . . 406, 408, 412, 418, 427, 429, 498
8:3a 407, 408, 411, 412
8:3a–b 406
8:3b 406, 418
8:3b–c 406, 408, 411, 412, 414, 423, 427
8:3c 418, 429
8:3c–g 408
8:3g 412
8:4 . . . . .408, 412, 420, 429, 524, 529, 530
8:4a 406, 408, 412
8:4b, 4c 413, 419, 421
8:4d, 4e 413, 421
8:5–6 . . . . .414, 418
8:5–7 429

8:5–14. . . . . . .406, 413, 414, 415–16, 417–18, 422, 423	8:13b. 421	8:24a–b. 430, 431
8:5. . . . . .412, 427	8:13c. 421, 536	8:24b. 430
8:5a. .414, 418	8:13c–e. 417, 421, 427, 429	8:24c–e, 24f. 431
8:5a–b. 406, 412, 423, 427	8:13d. 421, 430, 536	8:25. . . . . 281, 413, 432, 437, 529
8:5b. .418, 429	8:13e. 536	8:25a, 25b, 25c, 25d, 25e 431
8:5c, 5d. .418	8:14. . . . . 428, 437, 484, 537	8:26. . . . . 369, 452, 484, 488, 531
8:6. 419	8:14a. 421	8:26a, 26c, 26d–e 432
8:6a, 6c. .418	8:14b. 421, 427, 429, 432, 436	8:27 . 267, 423, 429, 433, 452, 488, 512
8:7–12. . . . . 414, 417, 418	8:15–27. . . . . .406, 414, 422, 423, 424–25, 426–27	8:27f. 481
8:7. . . . . 417, 419, 530	8:15. . . . . 412, 423, 427, 480	9 . . . . .35, 51, 54, 316, 348, 356, 388, 404, 406, 438, 442, 451–95, 497, 498, 501, 507, 509
8:7a. 406, 417, 418	8:15a. 423, 427	
8:7b, 7c, 7d, 7e. 419	8:15a–b. 408, 423	
8:7e–f. 413, 419, 421	8:15a–c. 408, 412, 414	9–12 . . . . 35, 349, 349, 356
8:7g, 7h. .419	8:15b. 406, 418, 427	9:1–3. . . . . 452, 453, 454, 455
8:7i 413, 419, 421	8:15b–c. 406, 423, 427	9:1–19. 452
8:8. . . . . .413, 417, 419, 420, 429, 523, 529	8:15c. 418, 427, 428, 429	9:1 . . . . . .40, 49, 50, 70, 147, 286, 290, 350, 356, 400, 411, 451, 501, 507
8:8a. .413, 419	8:16–26. . . . . .423, 428	9:1a. 454, 456, 457
8:8c, 8d. .419	8:16. . . . .357, 423, 428, 480, 481, 509	9:1b. 456
8:9–12. . . . . 417, 429, 431	8:16a. 406, 423, 428	9:2. . . . . .339, 449, 457, 458, 489, 510, 530
8:9–14. 73	8:16d. 428, 429, 481	
8:9. . . . . .413, 419	8:16f. 481	9:2a. .456, 457
8:9a, 9b. .419	8:17. . . . . 428, 481, 509, 530	9:2b. 456, 457, 482
8:10–12. .444	8:17a, 17d, 17f. 428	9:2b–c. 454
8:10–14. 73	8:17f–g. 428, 429	9:2c. 457, 463, 482, 485
8:10. . . . . 384, 413, 419, 435, 540	8:17–18. . . . . .423, 480	9:2d. .457, 482
8:10a, 10b. 419	8:18. .428, 508	9:3–4. .51, 510
8:10c. 419, 421	8:18a–b, 18c, 18d 428	9:3–19. . . . . .452, 497
8:11. . . . 281, 413, 419, 448, 456, 480, 529, 537	8:19–26. . . . . .423, 428	9:3. . . . . 454, 457, 507
	8:19. . . . . . . 36, 73, 412, 428, 523, 530	9:3a. 454
8:11a. 419	8:19a. 428	9:3b. .454, 481
8:11b. 420, 421, 430	8:19b, 19b–d, 19c, 19d 429	9:4–14. . . . . . . 138, 459, 463, 467, 471
9:1–2. . . . . . .38, 39, 48, 452, 454, 480, 496, 497, 513	8:20–21. .381	9:4–19. . . . 52, 452, 458, 459, 460–62, 475, 478
	8:20. 429	
8:11c. 420, 421, 436	8:21. . . . . 116, 286, 429	9:4. . . . . 316, 463, 465, 481, 539
8:12 419, 420, 436, 448, 450, 456, 480, 483, 530, 537	8:21a. 430	9:4a. 457
	8:22. . . . . 429, 435, 448	9:4b. 463
8:12a. 420, 421, 430	8:22c. 430	9:4a–c. 459, 478
8:12b. 420	8:23–25. .429	9:4d. 464
8:12c, 12d. 421, 432	8:23a. 430	9:4d–e. 472
8:13–14. . . . . 414, 417, 421	8:23b. 430, 431	9:4e. .465, 465
8:13. . . . . 444, 450, 483, 487, 488, 537	8:24–25. . . . . .73, 530	9:5–6. 465
8:13a. 406, 417, 421	8:24. . . . . .448, 536	9:5. . . . . .468, 472
		9:5a, 5b. 465, 484

9:5c, 5d 465	9:15d–e 472	9:24–27 . . . . 73, 290, 452, 478, 480, 482, 484, 497, 506
9:5e 472	9:16 . . . . 459, 465, 473, 479	9:24 . . . . 369, 430, 482, 483, 484, 485, 488, 491
9:6–10 . . . . 470, 471	9:16a 463, 472, 473, 479	9:24a 478, 482, 483
9:6 . . . . 459, 470	9:16a–b 472	9:24b 483, 488
9:6a 467, 472	9:16b 472, 473, 484	9:24c 483, 484, 488
9:6b 467, 470, 472	9:17–18 488	9:24d 483, 484, 488
9:7–9 459	9:17–19 . . . . 459, 463, 467, 473	9:24e 483, 484, 487, 488
9:7 . . . . 51, 465, 468, 470	9:17 . . . . 467, 473	9:24f 483, 484, 488
9:7a 467, 468, 469	9:17a 463, 473, 478, 481	9:24g 483, 484, 488
9:7b 468, 469, 472	9:17b 479	9:25–27 483
9:7c, 7d 469	9:18–19 472	9:25 . . . . 485, 486, 487, 491
9:8 467	9:18 . . . . 463, 465, 467, 473	9:25a, 25b 484, 485
9:8a 467, 469	9:18b 463	9:25c 485, 486, 488
9:8b 469	9:18d–e 479	9:25d, 25e 485
9:9 . . . . 467, 469	9:18f 481	9:25f 486
9:9a, 9b 469	9:19 . . . . 51, 465, 467, 473	9:26 . . . . . . 73, 485, 486, 487, 491, 537
9:10 . . . . 459, 467, 470	9:19a 463	9:26a 487
9:10a 467, 470	9:19a–c 459	9:26a–b 485
9:10b, 10c 470	9:19d–e 459	9:26c, 26c–f 487
9:11–13 . . . . 459, 470, 471, 482	9:19e-f 479	9:26d 484
9:11 . . . . 467, 470	9:19f 472, 479, 483	9:26f 488
9:11a 468, 470, 472	9:20–21 . . . . 452, 454, 478, 480, 497, 509	9:27 . . . . . . 73, 481, 485, 487, 494, 537
9:11a–c 470, 471	9:20–27 . . . . 452, 463, 475, 478	9:27a 487
9:11b 470	9:20 . . . . 463, 478, 479, 510	9:27b, 27c, 27d 487, 488
9:11c 470, 472	9:20a 478, 479	10 . . . . . 31, 70, 388, 438, 538, 539–40
9:11d, 11d–f, 11e, 11f 470	9:20b 478, 479, 481	10–12 . . . . . 29, 40, 192, 348, 385, 404, 406, 429, 438, 452, 496–542
9:12 470	9:20c 463, 468, 479	10:1–4 498
9:12a 471, 485	9:20d 478, 479, 481	10:1–5 350
9:12b, 12d, 12e–f 471	9:21 428	10:1–11:2a . . . 497, 498, 499, 500–503
9:13a–b, 13c–e 470	9:21a, 21b 478, 479	10:1 . . . . . 27, 31, 38, 39, 49, 50, 62, 70, 117, 147, 286, 356, 411, 451, 452, 456, 496, 497, 499, 504, 501, 506, 507, 508, 523
9:13d 484	9:21c, 21d 479	
9:13e 472	9:22–23 . . . . . . 452, 478, 479, 497, 510	
9:14 . . . . 459, 465, 467, 471	9:22–27 . . . . 356, 478, 480	
9:14a–b 472	9:22a–c 478, 480	
9:14c 472, 473	9:22d 481	10:1a 499, 504, 507
9:14e 472	9:22e 480	10:1b 507
9:15–16 . . . . 459, 472	9:23 . . . . 481, 485, 486, 510	10:1c 506, 507
9:15–17 51	9:23a 481	10:1d 499, 506
9:15–19 469	9:23b 482, 485	10:1e, 1f 499
9:15 . . . . 281, 472	9:23b–c, 23c, 23e 481	10:2–3 . . . . 452, 497, 499, 504
9:15a–c 472	9:23f 480, 482, 484, 485	10:2–6 508
9:15b 472, 473	9:23g 478, 480, 482, 484	10:2 . . . . 499, 506, 510, 515
9:15c 472, 479		

10:2a 506, 507	10:16 . . . . 498, 509, 533, 536, 537	11:8 . . . . .515, 524
10:3 . . . . .62, 506	10:16a 498, 504, 512	11:8b–9 525
10:3c 507	10:16b–17 504	11:9 528
10:4–9 . . . . . . .452, 497, 498, 499, 504, 507, 539	10:16d 512, 536	11:10–12 . . . . .526, 527
10:4 . . . . 38, 504, 507, 533	10:16e, 16f 512	11:10–19 525
10:4a 507	10:17 . . . . 512, 536, 537	11:11 . . . . 515, 524, 528, 530
10:4a–c 504	10:17a, 17b, 17c, 17d 512	11:12–14 526
10:4b–c 508	10:18 . . . . 504, 512, 536	11:12 529
10:5–6 . . . . 499, 504, 508	10:19 . . . . .481, 504, 508, 511, 512, 536, 537	11:13 . . . . 515, 524, 528, 530
10:5 . . . . 498, 504, 533	10:19a, 19b, 19c, 19d, 19e, 19f, 19g, 19h, 19i 512	11:14 . . . . 515, 524, 528, 530, 538
10:5a 498, 507, 508		11:15 . . . . 515, 524, 528, 530
10:5b 498, 504, 507, 508, 512	10:20–11:1 . . . . .499, 530	11:16 . . . . . . .413, 419, 515, 524, 525, 526, 529, 530
10:6e 508	10:20–11:2a 504, 512	
10:7–9 504	10:20–12:4 536	11:17 . . . . 515, 524, 526, 530
10:7–11 499	10:20b 512	11:18 . . . . .526, 528
10:7 510	10:21–11:1 513	11:19 526
10:7a, 7b, 7c, 7d, 7e, 7f 508	10:21 . . . . 369, 428, 511, 530	11:20–35 524
10:8 . . . . .508, 537	10:21a 498, 512, 513	11:20 . . . . 515, 524, 530
10:8a 508	10:21b 511, 513	11:20a, 20b .526
10:9 . . . . .508, 537	11 . . . . 28, 30, 31, 388	11:20c 527
10:10–15 . . . . 498, 499, 504, 509	11:1 . . 38, 39, 49, 50, 70, 286, 501, 513	11:21–24 527
10:10–19 509	11:1c 513	11:21–35 . . . . .525, 527
10:10–20 . . . . .481, 512	11:2–12:3 . . . . .452, 497	11:21 . . . . 515, 524, 529, 530
10:10–11:1 . . . . 452, 497, 513	11:2b–12:4 . . .497, 498, 499, 514, 515, 516–22, 533, 538, 541–42	11:21a, 21d 526
10:10 . . . . 498, 509, 512, 533, 536, 537		11:22 . . . . .487, 527
10:10a 498, 504, 509	11:2 . . 28, 381, 387, 501, 511, 515, 530	11:24 527
10:11–12 508	11:2a 513	11:25 . . . . 515, 524, 527, 528, 530
10:11 . . . . 481, 504, 511, 512	11:2b 498, 523	11:26 . . . . .526, 527
10:11a .509, 510	11:2b–e .515, 523	11:27 . . 36, 73, 526, 527, 530, 538, 541
10:11b, 11f, 11g 510	11:2d 524	11:28 527
10:12–11:1 435	11:3–4 515	11:29–39 536
10:12–14 . . . . .499, 504	11:3 . . . . 413, 515, 529, 530	11:29 . . . . 36, 73, 528, 541
10:12b 510	11:3a, 3b, 3c 524	11:30–35 . . . . .36, 484
10:12c, 12d, 12e, 12f, 12g 507, 510	11:4 . . . . 357, 515, 523, 530	11:30–43 73
10:13–11:1 . . . . .384, 540	11:4c, 4d 524	11:30 . . . . 525, 526, 527, 528, 537
10:13 . . . . 428, 507, 509, 511, 530	11:5–9 525	11:31–35 73
10:13a, 13b .510	11:5–35 .515, 524	11:31 . . . . .420, 488, 515, 524, 527, 528, 530, 537
10:14 . . . . 509, 511, 538	11:5 . . . . 515, 524, 528	
10:14b, 14c .511	11:5a 525	11:32–35 . . . . .431, 537
10:15–19 499	11:6 . . . . 515, 524, 525, 526, 528	11:32 . . . . 525, 527, 528
10:15 . . . . .504, 511	11:7–9 525	11:33–34 481
10:16–11:2a 498, 499, 504, 512	11:7 . . . . 515, 524, 528, 530	11:33–35 . . . . .28, 511
		11:33 . . . . .527, 528

11:34 . . . . 527, 528
11:35 . . . . . . 36, 73, 528, 530, 538, 541
11:36–45 . . . . 515, 525, 528, 529, 530
11:36 . . . 281, 413, 515, 524, 525, 528, 529, 530, 536
11:37–39 528
11:37 . . . . 413, 530
11:39 515
11:40–45 . . . . 28, 528, 529, 530
11:40 . . . . 28, 528, 530
11:41 419
11:43 515
11:45 530
12 . . . . 31, 538, 542
12:1–3 . . . . 73, 317, 431, 515, 530
12:1–4 541
12:1 . . . . 73, 428, 494, 511, 530
12:1a 515
12:1b, 1c, 1d 530
12:1e 515, 530
12:1f 530
12:2, 2a 531
12:2b 536
12:3 . . . . 28, 384, 528, 531
12:4 . . . . . . 31, 369, 452, 497, 515, 531
12:4a 537
12:4b 530, 537
12:4c, 4d 531
12:5–7 . . . . 533, 536
12:5–13 . . . 497, 498, 523, 533, 534–35
12:5 . . . . 510, 533
12:5a 533
12:5a–b 498
12:5b 533, 536
12:5c, 5d 536
12:6 . . . . 509, 533
12:6b 536
12:6c 530, 533
12:7 . . . . 533, 537
12:7a, 7b, 7c, 7d 536
12:7e 530, 536
12:7f, 7g 536
12:8–13 . . . . 533, 537
12:8 . . . . 488, 506, 533
12:8a, 8b 537
12:8d 533
12:9–13 . . . . 488, 533, 537
12:9 369
12:9b 537
12:9c 530, 537
12:10 . . . . 528, 537
12:11 . . . . 420, 488, 537
12:11a, 11c 530
12:12 . . . . 484, 537
12:12b 530

Hosea

1 188
3:5 511
6:4 378
8:4 254
13:7–8 366
14 185

Joel

2:24 490
4[3]:1–2, 12 368
4[3]:17–18 490

Amos

1–2 523
1:3 24
4:11 471
8:11–12 531
9:11–15 237
9:13, 15 490

Jonah

1:9 102

Micah

2:3 24
3:5, 11 277
5:1–5 490
6:5 473

Nahum

1:3 379

Habakkuk

1:5–11 367
1:12–2:1 138
2:2–20 538
3:12–13 511

Zephaniah

2:9 471

Haggai

1:6 506
2:23 138

Zechariah

1 380
1:2–4 185
2:5[1] 407
2:10[6] 357
3:4 491
3:8 138
4:14 486
5:1, 9 407
5:11 52
6:1 407
10:9 76
14:1–5 368

Malachi

3:16–18 530

New Testament

Matthew

3:2 244
4:2 507
4:17 244
5:21–22 242
5:35 74
5:43–48 243

6:5............316
6:5–6...........315
6:10............244
6:25.............75
9:6............397
10:7............244
12:6............492
12:8............397
13:31...........290
13:31–33........139
13:32...........244
14:13–21, 22–33..71
15:29–31.........71
15:29–39........193
16:21............72
16:27...........381
17:12...........397
17:17...........448
17:22–23.........72
19:19, 28.......397
20:17–19.........72
21:9............185
22:21...........315
23:37...........448
24:1–51.....442, 529
24:3, 4–14......494
24:15......24, 27, 494, 495
24:21, 30.......494
25:31...........381
25:31–35........239
26:2........72, 346
26:3–5, 14–16, 23.....346
26:24.......346, 397
26:36–55........346
27:11...........346
27:40–43.........72
27:42–43........192
27:46............72
27:60...........346
27:62–66........447
27:64–66........346
28:1............346
28:3............369
28:18...........398
28:20...........193

Mark

1:15............244
2:10, 27........397
4:31............290
4:39–41.........394
5:35–43..........71
6:45–52..........71
6:51............394
7:24–30.........193
8:1–10...........71
8:31......72, 346, 397
8:38............381
9:2–3...........369
9:19............448
10:45...........397
11:25...........316
13:1–37.....442, 529
13:22...........202
14:1, 10, 32....346
15:2, 14, 15, 46.....346
16:2............346

Luke

1:10............480
1:19, 26........428
4:16–21.........492
4:18–19.........244
5:24............397
6:5.............397
7:11–17..........71
8:24............394
9:10–17..........71
9:22.............72
9:26............381
9:41............448
9:44–45..........72
10:25–37........243
11:2............244
11:30...........397
12:40...........397
13:9............162
13:19...........290
17:11–19........193
18:11, 13.......316
18:31...........397
18:31–33.........72
19:10...........397
20:43............74
21:5–36.........442
22:2, 4–6, 39–45, 41.....346
23:1–3, 4, 18–25.....346
23:56...........448
24:1............346

John

1:1–14..........539
1:46............139
4:39–42..........71
6:1–15...........71
6:68............188
8:6.............258
9:1–3...........341
10:22...........150
10:30...........539
11:1–44..........71
11:47–53........346
12:8............187
12:34...........396
14:9............539
14:23...........465
18:1–2, 38, 39–40.....346
19:19...........346
20:1............346

Acts

2:14–41..........71
2:35.............74
3:1–10...........71
5:12–16..........71
4:13–22..........71
4:18–20.........315

4:27 239	1:21 74	**2 Peter**
4:27–28 72	1:22 239	1:3–4 188
5:29 . . . . 315, 339	6:11–12 540	3:9 448
7:14 458	**Philippians**	
7:49 74	2:9–11 240	**1 John**
7:56 396	2:12–13 294	2:18 . . . . 390, 442, 495
7:60 . . . . 188, 316	4:12 75	2:22 . . . . 442, 495
9:7 508		4:3 . . . . 442, 495
9:36–43 71	**Colossians**	
9:40 316	1:15 539	**2 John**
17:24–28 75	2:14–15 541	1:7 . . . . 442, 495
20:36 316		
21:5 316	**1 Thessalonians**	**Jude**
	2:3 . . . . 494, 495	1:9 . . . . 428, 511
Romans	2:4 . . . . 442, 494, 495	
1:18–25 188		**Revelation**
3:25, 26 491	**2 Thessalonians**	1:13 396
8:18 192	2:3 390	4:1–2 412
8:26 450	2:9 202	5:6 393
9:17 239		5:6–9, 13 37
13 34	**1 Timothy**	10:5–6 536
	2:1–2 . . . . 239, 240	11:13 102
1 Corinthians		11:15 245
11:30 341	**2 Timothy**	12:7 . . . . 428, 511
15:19 . . . . 392, 442, 542	3:16–17 541	13 . . . . 34, 394, 442
15:20–28 185		13:8 . . . . 494, 495
15:21–23 541	**Hebrews**	14:8 . . . . 137, 236, 289
15:23–25 290	2:6 396	14:14 396
15:24–28 239	4:14–15 541	16:11 102
15:28 492	4:15 450	16:19 . . . . 137, 236, 289
	10:13 74	17 442
2 Corinthians	11:17–19 188	17:3 412
2:14 77	12:5–12 448	17:5 . . . . 137, 236, 289
12:7–10 341	12:5–13 341	17:14 137
		18 . . . . 182, 442
Galatians	**James**	18:2 . . . . 137, 139, 236, 289
3:7–9 77	1:17 369	18:10 . . . . 137, 236, 289
4:4 541	5:15–16 341	18:21 . . . . 137, 139, 236, 289
		19:1–10 73
Ephesians	**1 Peter**	19:16 137
1:10 . . . . 492, 541	4:12–14 188	20:7–15 73
1:16–23 185	5:13 . . . . 137, 236, 289	

21:1–4 73
22:1 393

Deuterocanonical Books

Sirach

8:18 103
17:17 511

1 Maccabees

1–2 436
                         1:2–4
1:11 487
1:11–15 431
1:16–20 435
1:17–19, 20–40 527
1:20–57 . . . . 436, 528
1:20–64 388
1:39 507
1:43 431

1:45 507
1:54 487
1:54–55, 59 436
2:18, 42 528
3:27–37 435
4:41–44 436
6:1–4 435
7:13 528

2 Maccabees

3 526
4:23–29 487
5 527
6:5 487
6:14 43
7 . . . . 192, 436
7:18 431
7:24 528
14:6 528

1 Esdras

3–4 . . . . 123, 124

2 Esdras

12:11–12 116

4 Maccabees

8 192

Pseudepigrapha

1 Enoch

1–36 212
1:3–9 368
20:5 511
25:3 368
90:20–27 368
93:2 513

Subject Index

Abednego, 1, 4–6, 32, 34, 118–21, 140–41, 149, 201–297. *See also* Azariah
  accused by Chaldeans, 153–57
  belief in God's ability to rescue, 163–66, 188
  defiance of Nebuchadnezzar, 145–46, 163–66, 309, 318, 337
  in the fiery furnace, 170–74, 192. *See also* fourth figure in the fire
  Nebuchadnezzar's response to defiance of, 157–63, 167–69, 174–81
  Nebuchadnezzar's response to deliverance of, 175–81
  refusal to eat or drink, 54–65
  service in Babylonian court, 65–70, 117–21, 141, 162, 181, 297
abomination of desolation, 18, 21–22, 397, 477, 487, 494, 520, 535, 537
Abraham, 53–54, 73, 77, 91, 128–29, 138, 187–88, 396, 474, 489, 492
Abrahamic covenant, 77, 128–29, 187–88, 474, 489, 492
Ahasuerus, 16, 25, 454, 456
Ahiqar, 25
Ahura Mazda, 92, 309
Alexander the Great, 115–16, 286, 387–88, 434–35, 487, 515, 524, 529
Amel-Marduk, 117, 224, 523
Ancient of Days, 13–14, 348, 362, 364, 367–68, 372–73, 375–80, 383–84, 392–95
antichrist, 202, 386, 388–90, 433, 437, 442, 487, 493–95, 525, 528–30, 537
Antiochus II Theos, 525
Antiochus III (the Great), 388, 525–29
Antiochus IV Epiphanes
  downfall of, 28, 389, 437, 487, 528–29
  persecution of Jews and, 80, 192, 336, 388, 403–4, 430–32, 435–37, 450–52, 496, 480–84, 487, 511, 527–28, 536–37, 540
  political history of, 435–47, 487, 496, 524–28
  prophecies concerning, 28, 523, 528–30
  significance of, 389–90, 437–42, 484, 492, 494, 528–30
  symbols for, 386, 388, 432–35, 437, 505, 514, 527, 531
apocalyptic literature, 26, 296, 348–50, 356–57, 365, 369, 380, 383, 385–86, 390, 392, 406, 411, 443–44, 457, 482, 497, 507
Aramaic chiasm, 31–35, 38, 43–44, 79–80, 83, 105–6, 115, 121, 131–32, 140, 142, 195–96, 200, 202, 235, 246–47, 250, 291, 297, 299, 348–49, 352, 403–4, 434
Aramaic language, 31–35, 90, 150, 259, 282, 302
Arioch, 3, 95–100, 106–7, 111–12, 131
Artaxerxes, 25, 137, 486
Ashpenaz, 1, 47, 54–56
Assyria, Assyrian Empire, 25, 49, 74, 136, 147, 172, 183, 193, 243, 252, 286–87, 366, 412, 443, 456, 468
attention-getting device, 173, 211, 350, 367, 412, 498
authorship of Daniel, 27–31
Azariah, 1–3, 30, 44, 57, 58–60, 66–67, 74, 101, 121. *See also* Abednego

Baal, 187, 357, 368, 379, 394, 448–49
Baal Cycle, 357, 379, 394
Babel, tower of, 53, 244, 289–90, 511
Babylon
  birth of, 53, 289–90
  culture of, 61–62, 74–75, 77, 146, 266
  exilic community in, 40–50
  fall of, 247, 251, 285–90, 329, 336, 453, 456–57
  gods of, 61, 123–24, 357, 394. *See also* Marduk
  in vision of Daniel, 73, 350–55, 357–59, 365–66, 381, 386–87, 399, 432–33
  language and literature of, 55–56
  mythology, 88–89, 114, 243, 357–58, 394, 395
  rebuilding of, 458
  ritual celebrations, 251
  seventy-year desolation for, 458
  symbol of, 289–90
  temple treasure, 1, 47–48, 51, 53–54
Belshazzar
  banquet of, 248–55
  fall of Babylon and, 251, 285–91
  interpretation of writing and, 246–55, 260, 262–63, 266–29, 271–87, 290–91, 293–95
  mother of, 121, 262–68, 271–72
  Nebuchadnezzar and, 246–55, 260, 262–63, 266–29, 271–87, 290–91, 293–95
  prototype of defiant kings, 281, 290–91, 356, 389–90, 411, 438, 441, 484, 493, 496, 529–30
  speaking to Daniel, 268–73
  writing on the wall before, 268–73
Belteshazzar, 1, 3, 7–8, 10, 18, 58, 61, 107, 112, 121, 205–6, 208, 210–11, 213, 215, 218, 264, 267, 329, 500, 506. *See also* Daniel

black obelisk of Shalmaneser, 252
blasphemy, 52, 181, 235, 246–58, 290–95, 399, 411, 437–38, 442, 529

canon and genre of Daniel, 23–27
Cleopatra, 526, 527
changed reference, 54, 68, 286, 333
chiasms, 466–67, 470–71. *See also* Aramaic chiasm
clause-initial position. *See* fronting
composition and structure of Daniel, 31–35
confession, corporate, 479, 495
cosmic tree imagery, 212, 243–45
court stories, 25, 31–32, 39, 80–81, 123–37, 145, 150–51, 169, 172, 181, 210, 267
Cyrus
    anointed one, 74, 239, 486
    context for prophecy of war given to Daniel, 39, 49, 496–97, 499–500, 504, 507, 523, 538
    Darius the Mede as, 286, 336, 456
    expansion of Medo-Persian under, 251, 387, 410, 434, 505
    freeing of captives and Israel's restoration, 51, 66, 70, 288–89, 309, 464, 486, 505–7, 513, 538
    in Daniel's visions, 115–17, 434, 486, 505, 529
    instrument of YHWH, 74, 366
    role in chronology of book, 39, 49, 51, 62, 70
    successor of Belshazzar, 137, 286–87, 296, 334, 336, 348, 356, 451

Daniel, 136, 209–10, 213, 262–68, 271–72, 298–302, 336
    abilities and knowledge of, 54, 65–60, 87–88, 97–99, 111–12, 117, 120, 123
    as a prophet, 24–27, 225, 457–59, 463–74
    Belshazzar and, 39, 268–85, 294
    commitment to God, 61–65, 99–105, 208, 213, 266–68, 296–318, 325–31, 336–47, 463–74, 480–81, 504–13, 537–38
    conspiracy against, 296–311, 317–24

context of prayer for end of seventy-year exile, 356, 451–58, 478–80
Darius's interactions with, 302, 325–31, 336
dreams/visions of, 32, 39, 348–90, 403–37, 451–53, 475–88, 496–98, 514–31
fasting by, 16, 62, 453–55, 457–58, 504, 506–7
Gabriel's interactions with, 404–5, 422–32, 434–37, 451, 453, 459, 463, 475–76, 478–88, 490–92, 510
in the lions' den, 39, 319–30
interpretation of Nebuchadnezzar's dreams by, 111–17, 213–25, 240–43
interpretation of writing on the wall by, 246–55, 260, 262–63, 266–29, 271–87, 290–91, 293–95
Nebuchadnezzar's response to, 69–70, 87, 111–12, 209–13, 218
prayer and, 315, 317, 458–74, 463–64, 513
refusal to eat and drink, 54–65
respect for Babylonian monarchs, 98, 163–64, 213–19, 225, 240–43, 277
response to Darius's decree, 311–19
response to his visions, 385, 433
service in royal court, 56–70, 87–88, 121, 156, 266–68, 285, 298–302, 336, 385, 433
throne room vision, 39, 367–80, 390–93
vision of a great conflict, 39, 514–31
vision of four beasts, 39, 348–90
vision of the evenings and mornings (ram and goat), 39, 403–37
vision of the man in linen, 39, 498–13
vision of two others, 39, 532–38
Daniel, book of
    as apocalyptic literature, 24–31, 523, 528–29
    authorship and dating of, 27–31
    canon and genre of, 23–27
    composition and structure of, 31–35
    historical information in, 31, 63, 203
    historical setting of, 24–27, 35–37, 43, 48–54, 202, 317, 338

languages of, 31–35
purpose and theology of, 35–37, 53, 166, 239, 286–87, 336, 379–80, 456, 493, 510
Darius I Hystaspis, 92, 124, 412, 486
Darius the Mede. *See also* Cyrus
    conspiracy against Daniel and, 296–311, 317–24
    historical difficulty of, 286
    praise of Daniel's God, 297, 332–36
    punishment of daniel, 319–30
    seventy-year exile and, 451, 453–58, 513
date formulae, 38–39, 45–46, 48, 83, 147, 203, 351, 355–56, 407, 410–11, 451–52, 454, 457, 496–97, 504, 506–7
dating of Daniel, 27–31
David, King, 51, 71, 138, 185, 188, 293, 329
Davidic king, 35, 51–52, 71, 74, 237, 243, 400, 485, 490, 505
Dead Sea Scrolls, 103, 224–25, 436, 482
demonstratives, near and far, 172–73, 302–3, 307–8, 336–37
diaspora, 27, 74, 75–77, 124, 157, 182, 202, 236, 287, 316–17, 337, 434
discourse features, 37–38, 91, 164, 191, 265, 452, 497
    attention-getting device, 173, 211, 350, 367, 412, 498
    changed reference, 54, 68, 286, 333
    demonstratives, near and far, 172–73, 302–3, 307–8, 336–37
    forward-pointing reference, 156, 281–82
    fronting, 48, 52, 102–3, 157, 266, 277, 280, 378, 380, 469
    left dislocation structure, 60, 65, 68, 120, 256
    metacomment, 164, 484
    overspecification, 51–52, 63, 98, 102, 111, 120, 148–52, 164, 173, 176–77, 209, 212, 228, 232–34, 252–54, 259, 263–65, 278, 280, 323–24, 330, 480, 486, 506
    redundant quotative frame, 90–92, 212
    thematic address, 112, 151, 164, 211, 309, 322, 329, 481

Subject Index

topical frames, 52, 151–52, 157, 250, 258, 266, 277, 280

vocatives, 89–90, 106, 112, 114, 151, 162–64, 211, 266, 278–80, 308–10, 317–18, 322, 329, 330, 467, 469, 481

divination, 61, 88–90, 93, 103, 136, 213, 360

divine council, 367–68, 379–80, 398–99

dreams. *See* visions/dreams

Egyptian gods, 243, 525

El, 368, 379

Enmeduranki, King, 88–89

Enuma Elish, 357, 394

Esarhaddon, 458

evil, 33–34, 90, 99, 192–94, 289–91, 384–85, 399–401, 432–33, 437–50, 475, 484, 493, 495–98

Evil-Merodach. *See* Amel-Marduk

ex eventu prophecy, 26–29, 523, 528–29

exile of Israel
Cyrus's decree regarding end of, 51, 66, 309, 464, 486, 506, 513
length of, 35–36, 51, 70, 287–90, 356, 400, 449, 451, 453, 455, 457–58, 475, 478, 481, 483, 485–86, 489–90, 494, 512

faith/faithfulness, 185–89, 339–42
presence of God and, 35, 170–74, 180, 191–94, 330
reward and resurrection and, 26, 34, 80, 403–4, 482, 496–97, 514, 531, 537–38, 541–42. *See also* resurrection
suffering and dying in, 185–89, 342–45, 442–48, 493–95, 530–31, 541–42

fasting, 16, 62, 453–55, 457–58, 504, 506–7

Festival of Lights, 150, 436

"finger of God," 9, 256–60

forward-pointing reference, 156, 281–82

four kingdoms in Daniel 2 and 7
four kings view, 115–17
Greek view of, 115–17, 286, 297, 386–90, 432, 437, 505, 527
Roman view of, 115–17, 386–90, 433–35, 437, 505

fourth figure in the fire, 173–74, 180, 191–94, 330

fronting, 48, 52, 102–3, 157, 266, 277, 280, 378, 380, 469

Gabriel
interpreter of Daniel's vision (ch. 8), 404–5, 422–32, 434–37
"man in linen" and, 508–9
response to Daniel's prayer (ch. 9), 451, 453, 459, 463, 475–76, 478–88, 490–92, 510

genres of Daniel, 24–35

gentiles, 37, 77

goat in Daniel's vision, 15–16, 39, 42, 116, 389, 405, 412–26, 429–30, 432–35, 456, 529

God
ability to save, 157–66, 173–74, 179–85
blasphemy against, 52, 181, 235, 246–58, 290–95, 399, 411, 437–38, 442, 529
covenant with Israel, 35–37, 54, 185–89, 252–53, 258–60, 317, 339–42, 368–69, 400–401, 458–74, 482–83, 487–93
"finger of," 9, 256–60
forgiveness of, 315–16, 397, 451, 458–69, 473–74, 481, 488, 490
human–divine interaction. *See* spiritual warfare
judgment and, 53, 239, 242–43, 293–95, 368–70, 442, 43. *See also* judgment by God
Nebuchadnezzar's proclamations regarding, 120–21, 179–81, 201–4, 230–38
silence and, 442–48
sovereignty of, 23, 33–34, 36, 50–54, 70–75, 103–5, 111–14, 126–27, 129–32, 134–39, 166, 191, 201–3, 213, 225, 232–40, 243–45, 253, 279, 285–87, 297, 310, 333–34, 370, 390–93, 403, 445, 456, 505, 509–11, 539–42
wisdom of, 103–5, 122–23

Greek Empire, 16, 19, 115–17, 172, 387–90, 412, 425–26, 429–30, 432–35, 5–3, 505, 513, 515–16, 524, 529, 540. *See also* four kingdoms in Daniel 2 and 7

Hananiah, 1–3, 44, 57, 58–60, 66–67, 74, 101, 121. *See also* Shadrach

Hanukkah, 150, 436

Hasmoneans. *See* Maccabean revolt and era

Hathor, Egyptian goddess, 243

Hezekiah, 74, 121, 183, 193, 329

hinneh. *See* attention-getting device

historical contexts of Daniel's visions, 39
vision of a great conflict (chs. 10–12), 496–99, 504–7
vision of Seventy Weeks (ch. 9), 356, 451–57, 478–80
visions of beasts/ram/goat (chs. 7–8), 351–52, 355–57, 405, 407–8, 410–11, 438

historical setting of book of Daniel, 24–27, 35–37, 43, 48–54, 202, 317, 338

"holy ones (of the Most High)," 7, 14, 208, 212, 348, 350, 371–78, 380–85, 388, 399, 401, 413, 416–17, 421–22, 427–28, 437, 444, 509

hope, 34–35, 76, 122–23, 240

human government, 33–34, 163–64, 182, 235, 238–40, 383–85, 392, 493

humanity. *See also* faith/faithfulness
divine–human interaction, 385, 419–20, 435, 513, 530, 540. *See also* prayer; spiritual warfare
eternal life through resurrection, 26, 37, 400, 448, 496–97, 514, 530–31, 537–38, 541
heirs of the eternal kingdom and, 35–37, 443, 348, 380–81, 384–85
image of God and, 240–43, 393–400, 539

idolatry, 35, 43, 49, 61–62, 77, 93, 138–49, 151–66, 181–91, 254, 258, 292–93, 297, 338

Isaiah, 23, 113, 121–22, 137, 146, 189–91, 233, 244, 281, 286, 387, 392, 394, 440–41, 457, 465, 490, 492, 506, 512

Jehoahaz, 49

Jehoiakim, King, 1, 39, 44, 47, 52, 54, 60, 62, 66, 68, 70–72, 132, 288, 391, 505

Jeremiah, 23, 49, 344–47, 449, 512. *See also* Jeremiah's prophecies

Jeremiah's prophecies. *See also* Seventy Weeks, Jeremiah's prophecies and
- Babylon and Nebuchadnezzar in, 70, 138, 182, 286, 288–89, 358
- exile and restoration in, 35, 70, 253, 288–89, 339, 400, 404, 451–58, 463, 475, 478, 480–86, 489–91, 494–95, 506, 510, 513

Jerusalem Temple, destruction of. *See* temple

Jesus Christ
- Daniel as a prophet and prefigure of, 24, 344–47
- Olivet Discourse, 27, 379, 442, 494–95, 529
- as our Jubilee, 485, 489–93
- as son of man, 37, 135, 379–81, 389, 393–400
- suffering of, 344–47
- trial of, 399

Jews/Israel
- Cyrus's edict and Israel's restoration, 51, 66, 70, 288–89, 309, 464, 486, 505–7, 513, 538
- Daniel's prayer for, 315, 317, 458–74, 463–64, 513
- destruction of temple and, 127, 248, 403, 413, 435–36, 457–58, 480, 483, 487–88, 491, 528
- exile of, 35–36, 45–56, 51, 70, 287–90, 356, 400, 449, 451, 453, 455, 457–58, 475, 478, 481, 483, 485–86, 489–90, 494, 512
- Festival of Lights, 150, 436
- suffering under Antiochus, 80, 192, 336, 388, 403–4, 430–32, 435–37, 450–52, 496, 480–84, 487, 511, 527–28, 536–37, 540
- victory of Nebuchadnezzar over, 45–57, 60–61, 70–74

Job, 23, 27, 29, 233, 340–41, 446

Joseph, 25, 49, 51, 77, 83, 93, 164, 339, 342, 484. *See also* Joseph and Daniel, similarities between

Joseph and Daniel, similarities between, 64–65, 87, 112, 123–37, 342, 344–47

Josephus, 24, 116, 120

judgment by God, 53, 239, 242–43, 293–95, 442, 43
- Babylon and, 70, 287–89, 285–89
- Belshazzar and, 283–87, 246, 258–60, 293–95
- Nebuchadnezzar and, 226–35
- oppressors of God's people and, 37, 360–70, 383–85, 401, 541–42, 442–43, 496, 530–31, 537–42

lament, 345, 421, 442–48, 464, 593, 542
- against Tyre, 27, 438–39
- in Daniel's visions, 416–18, 421, 429, 534, 536

law, the. *See also* t/Torah
- of God, 11, 25, 37, 296, 303–13, 315, 317, 323–24, 331, 337, 339–42, 346
- of the Medes and Persians, 11–12, 304, 306, 308, 310–11, 314, 317–18, 322, 339, 391

kingdom, people of the, 14, 374, 377, 380–81, 384–85, 401. *See also* "holy ones (of the Most High)"

kings. *See* human government

left dislocation structure, 60, 65, 68, 120, 256

lions' den, Daniel in the, 319–31, 344–47

little horn in visions of Daniel, 73, 116, 235, 281, 348, 350, 360–62, 367, 371–75, 382–90, 413, 421, 432–33, 436–38, 441–42, 448, 527, 529–30, 540

Maccabean revolt and era, 28, 116, 134, 431, 435–36, 484, 494, 528

man clothed in linen in Daniel's vision, 18, 22, 496, 498, 500, 504, 507–10, 512–15, 523, 532–36, 539–40

Marduk, 123–24, 357, 394

Median Empire, 115–17, 283, 286, 297, 336, 386–89, 410–12, 429, 432–34, 456–57

Medo-Persian Empire, 77, 115, 308–10, 323, 386–87, 410, 412, 433–34, 456–57

Meshach, 1, 4–6, 32, 34, 118–21, 140–41, 149, 201–297. *See also* Mishael
- accused by Chaldeans, 153–57

belief in God's ability to rescue, 163–66, 188
- defiance of Nebuchadnezzar, 145–46, 163–66, 309, 318, 337
- in the fiery furnace, 170–74, 192. *See also* fourth figure in the fire
- Nebuchadnezzar's response to defiance of, 157–63, 167–69, 174–81
- Nebuchadnezzar's response to deliverance of, 175–81
- refusal to eat or drink, 54–65
- service in Babylonian court, 65–70, 117–21, 141, 162, 181, 297

Mesopotamian religions, 93, 136, 186–87, 308–9, 368

metacomment, 164, 484

Michael, 18–19, 21, 428, 502–3, 510–13, 522, 530, 540

Mishael, 1–3, 44, 57, 58–60, 66–67, 74, 101, 121. *See also* Meshach

Nabonidus, 117, 224–25, 251–52, 356

Nabonidus Chronicle, 505

Nabopolassar, 48, 50

near and far distinction. *See* demonstratives, near and far

Nebuchadnezzar, King
- "king of kings," 4, 109, 114, 137–39, 147, 189, 219, 236, 239
- acknowledgment of God's sovereignty, 201–4, 230–38
- arrogance of, 147–49, 158–64, 195–96, 226–29
- Belshazzar and, 246–55, 260, 262–63, 266–29, 271–87, 290–91, 293–95
- Daniel and friends brought into service of, 45–65
- dream fulfillment and restoration of, 226–38
- dreams of, 83–89, 105–14, 195–97, 204–25
- in vision of Daniel, 357–59. 381–82
- interpretation of dreams by Daniel, 111–17, 213–25, 240–43
- prototype of gentile kings, 181–83, 441
- response to saving of Shadrach, Meshach, and Abednego, 179–81, 191–94

responses to Daniel and his interpretations, 69–70, 87, 111–12, 209–13, 218
statue of gold and, 147–49. *See also* statue built by Nebuchadnezzar
taking of captives by, 45–65
Neco, Pharaoh, 49–50

Olivet Discourse, 27, 379, 442, 494–95, 529
Onias II, 527
Onias III, 426, 487, 527
overspecification, 51–52, 63, 98, 102, 111, 120, 148–52, 164, 173, 176–77, 209, 212, 228, 232–34, 252–54, 259, 263–65, 278, 280, 323–24, 330, 480, 486, 506

Paul, apostle, 34, 74–75
Persian Empire, 387, 412, 434–35, 514–15, 523. *See also* four kingdoms in Daniel 2 and 7; Cyrus
Philistines, 71, 448–50
Potiphar, 128, 339, 342, 344
prayer
as human–divine dialogue, 337–39
as modeled by Daniel, 315, 317, 458–74, 463–64, 513
toward Jerusalem, 315, 317, 337–39, 463–64, 513
Prayer of Nabonidus, 224–25
prophets, Old Testament, 16, 23–24, 27, 35, 137–38, 185, 187, 202, 237, 253, 290, 345, 366, 379, 389, 400, 442, 446, 467–69, 479, 487, 490, 494–95, 505–6. *See also* Isaiah; Jeremiah
pseudonymity, 26–29. *See also* ex eventu prophecy
Ptolemies, 116, 487, 524–27, 541
Ptolemy I, 435, 524, 525
Ptolemy III, 525
Ptolemy IV, 526, 529
Ptolemy V, 526
Ptolemy VI, 527
Ptolemy VIII Physcon, 527
purpose and theology of Daniel, 35–37, 53, 166, 239, 286–87, 336, 379–80, 456, 493, 510

Qumran. *See* Dead Sea Scrolls

ram, 360
in Daniel's vision, 15, 39, 42, 384, 405, 407–10, 412–26, 429–34, 456, 529
symbolism in Old Testament, 412
redundant quotative frame, 90–92, 212
repentance, 25, 35, 40, 42, 187, 224–25, 240, 293–95, 301, 432–35, 443, 451–54, 457–74, 507
resurrection, 26, 37, 400, 448, 496–97, 514, 530–31, 537–38, 541
of Jesus, 72, 139, 185, 346, 392–93, 399, 493, 541
Old Testament portrayal of, 531
Roman Empire, 115–16, 192, 386, 433, 493. *See also* four kingdoms in Daniel 2 and 7

Seleucids, 80, 148, 386, 388, 403–4, 432, 435–36, 450, 496, 514, 524–28, 541
Seleucus, 388, 435, 524–25
Seleucus II, 525–26
Seleucus IV, 388, 526–27
Sennacherib, King, 74, 183, 193
Seventy Weeks, 39
context of Daniel's prayer and, 356, 451–58, 478–80
Daniel's prayer for, 458–74
Gabriel's revelation of, 475–88
interpretations of, 452, 482–87, 489–95
Jeremiah's prophecies and, 35, 70, 253, 288–89, 339, 400, 404, 451–58, 463, 475, 478, 480–86, 489–91, 494–95, 506, 510, 513
Shadrach, 1, 4–6, 32, 34, 118–21, 140–41, 149, 201–297. *See also* Hananiah
accused by Chaldeans, 153–57
belief in God's ability to rescue, 163–66, 188
defiance of Nebuchadnezzar, 145–46, 163–66, 309, 318, 337
in the fiery furnace, 170–74, 192. *See also* fourth figure in the fire
Nebuchadnezzar's response to defiance of, 157–63, 167–69, 174–81
Nebuchadnezzar's response to deliverance of, 175–81

refusal to eat or drink, 54–65
service in Babylonian court, 65–70, 117–21, 141, 162, 181, 297
Year of Jubilee and, 475, 482–83, 486, 492–93
Shalmaneser, 252
Sheol, 531
Shinar, 1, 47–48, 52–54, 244, 288–90
Solomon, King, 93, 185, 254, 315–16, 431, 458, 463, 466, 468, 474
son of man
Daniel as, 15, 424, 426, 428
in Daniel's context, 14, 35, 37, 42, 348–49, 370–82, 384–86, 389, 393–401, 432–33, 443
Jesus as, 37, 135, 379–81, 389, 393–400
spiritual warfare, 384–85, 420, 433, 435, 510–11, 513, 530, 540
statue of Nebuchadnezzar's dream, 4, 32, 108–9, 112–17, 130–31, 142, 147, 195, 210, 219, 235, 247, 282–83, 335, 349, 365, 385, 387, 392, 434
statue built by Nebuchadnezzar, 142, 145, 147–49, 152–53, 157, 165, 169–70, 179, 235, 248, 251, 254–55, 265, 380
suffering
faith and, 35–37, 163–66, 302–4, 315–17, 323–24, 330, 342–44, 390–92, 530–31, 537–38, 542
God's presence in, 174, 180, 192–93, 433, 448–50
lament and, 345, 421, 442–48, 464, 593, 542
of Jesus, 344–47
of Jews under Antiochus, 80, 192, 336, 388, 403–4, 430–32, 435–37, 450–52, 496, 480–84, 487, 511, 527–28, 536–37, 540
sin as cause of. *See* "transgression/transgressors, the"
temple, 260, 463–64, 474, 480, 494
dedication of by Solomon, 315–16, 463–64, 474
desecration by Antiochus, 403, 413, 435–36, 480, 483, 487–88, 491, 528
destruction by Nebuchadnezzar, 127, 248, 457–58

temple vessels, 56, 71, 250
    Belshazzar and, 9–10, 246, 248–61, 271–72, 277, 280, 282, 290–92, 356, 438
    God's ownership of, 43, 45, 54, 60, 61, 74, 51–52, 287–89, 391, 456
    importance in Israel, 287–89
    Nebuchadnezzar and, 1, 47–48, 51–54, 60–61, 71, 250–52, 271–72, 290–91, 391, 456

Ten Commandments, 158, 166, 186–87, 258, 292

thematic address, 112, 151, 164, 211, 309, 322, 329, 481

theology of Daniel, 53, 166, 239, 286–87, 336, 379–80, 456, 493, 510

throne room vision of Daniel, 34, 348, 360–61, 367–69, 371, 379, 383, 497

Tiamat, 357, 394

Tobiads, 487, 527

topical frames, 52, 151–52, 157, 250, 258, 266, 277, 280

t/Torah, 16–17, 124, 340, 436, 460–61, 465–67, 470–72, 489

"transgression/transgressors, the," 15–17, 416, 418, 420–21, 425–26, 430, 461, 466, 477, 483, 488, 491, 536

trees, kings portrayed as, 7–8, 138, 196, 202, 204–7, 211–12, 215–19, 224–26, 229, 234, 243–44, 282

Ugarit, 287, 357, 368, 379, 384

Ulai Canal, 15, 408–9, 412, 424, 426, 428–29

Uruk Prophecy, 523

visionary literature, 348–40. *See also* apocalyptic literature

visions/dreams, 88–93, 135–37, 210, 213
    angel's interpretation of Daniel's, 116, 370–78, 380–85, 406, 422–32, 497, 507–9
    Daniel's interpretations of Nebuchadnezzar's, 111–17, 213–25, 240–43
    Joseph and Pharaoh's, 64–65, 87, 123–37
    little horn in Daniel's, 73, 116, 235, 281, 348, 350, 360–62, 367, 371–75, 382–90, 413, 421, 432–33, 436–38, 441–42, 448, 527, 529–30, 540
    man in linen in Daniel's, 18, 22, 496, 498, 500, 504, 507–10, 512–15, 523, 532–36, 539–40
    of Daniel. *See* Daniel
    of Nebuchadnezzar. *See* Nebuchadnezzar
    ram and goat in Daniel's, 15–16, 39, 42, 116, 384, 389, 405, 407–10, 412–26, 429–35, 456, 529
    setting of Daniel's, 39. *See also* historical contexts of Daniel's visions

vocatives, 89–90, 106, 112, 114, 151, 162–64, 211, 266, 278–80, 308–10, 317–18, 322, 329, 330, 467, 469, 481

watcher(s), 7–8, 205–8, 286, 211–12, 216, 218, 224, 229

wisdom, 1–2, 77, 93–97, 438–39
    as characteristic of kings, 73, 81, 93, 105, 431, 438–39
    of Babylonian wise men, 82, 94, 97, 112, 121–22, 129, 149
    of Daniel, 1–2, 3, 10, 64–65, 87–88, 94, 112, 131, 210, 261, 266, 272
    of God, 3, 73, 81–82, 97, 99–105, 112, 121–23, 131–32, 149, 191, 219, 329, 335, 338
    of Shadrach, Meshach, and Abednego, 1–2, 65, 80

wisdom literature, 64, 80, 124, 523

Xerxes, 251, 456–57

YHWH. *See* God

Year of Jubilee, 475, 482–83, 486, 492–93

Zedekiah, King, 49, 288, 345, 392

ziggurats, 53

Zoroastrianism, 308–9

Author Index

Ackroyd, P. R., 287, 288
Adeyemo, Tokunboh, 88
Allen, Leslie C., 183
Alstola, Tero, 50
Althaus, Paul, 241
Anderson, R. A., 483
Arnold, Bill T., 258, 308
Athas, George, 51, 487
Avalos, Hector I., 146, 152

Baldwin, Joyce G., 336, 359, 367, 421–22, 437, 456, 482, 484, 491, 492, 529, 537
Balentine, Samuel E., 463, 465, 466
Bar-Efrat, Shimon, 60, 63
Bauer, Dieter, 436
Beale, G. K., 383, 395, 398
Beckwith, Carl L., 174
Beckwith, Roger T., 485
Bedenbender, Andreas, 25
Belcher, Richard P., 104
Berlin, Adele, 163, 173–74, 337
Bloch, Ariel A., 166
Block, Daniel I., 26, 27, 49–50, 392, 396, 438
Blomberg, Craig L., 194, 389
Boda, Mark J., 464, 470, 471, 472
Bottéro, Jean, 89, 90
Brueggemann, Walter, 449
Butler, Alban, 192

Callaway, Mary C., 345
Calvin, John, 69, 75, 87, 386
Card, Michael, 447
Carr, David M., 55

Carson, D. A., 444
Casey, P. M., 27
Chapell, Bryan, 495, 509
Chaplin, Jonathan, 239
Clermont-Ganneau, C., 282
Clifford, Richard J., 524, 525, 526, 527
Cogan, Mordechai, 183, 505
Collins, John J., 24, 26, 27, 28, 31, 61, 62, 87, 90, 92, 93, 103, 117, 123, 147, 148, 150, 155, 197, 224–25, 251, 265, 287, 316, 356, 380, 383, 384, 388, 412, 430, 431, 478, 480, 482, 484, 485–86, 486, 505, 506, 512, 523, 528, 536, 537
Cook, John A., 91, 96, 97, 101, 103, 109, 111, 114, 150, 156, 162, 163, 165, 169, 209, 209–10, 219, 224, 225, 265, 301, 318, 357, 358, 359, 366, 380, 381
Cory, I. P., 89
Coxon, Peter W., 145, 150, 151, 169, 172
Cross, Frank M., 120

De Zorzi, Nida 360
deSilva, David A., 116, 435
DiLella, Alexander A., 434, 513, 537
Doran, Robert, 124, 181
Driver, S. R., 87, 292

Eissfeldt, Otto, 282
Eklund, Rebekah Ann, 447
Evans, Craig A., 397

Fee, Gordon D., 191, 192, 390
Fewell, Danna Nolan, 87–88, 103, 112, 113, 146, 150, 157, 201, 204, 229, 253, 254, 255, 261, 265, 266, 268, 272, 273, 278, 281, 282, 301

France, R. T., 244, 245
Fuhs, H. F., 465
Futato, Mark D., 379

Getty, Keith and Kristyn, 392
Gleddiesmith, Stacey, 446
Glerup, Michael, 174, 528–29
Gnuse, Robert, 64, 124, 125, 133
Goldingay, John E., 34, 36, 50, 51, 61, 65, 70, 92, 93, 98–99, 102, 117, 124, 133, 141, 146, 148, 149, 155, 165, 173, 174, 202, 225, 232, 234, 250, 251, 260, 267, 278, 279, 286, 287, 293, 315, 316, 329, 330, 349, 356, 358, 360, 366, 368, 369, 374, 380, 382, 385, 386, 391, 421–22, 430, 432, 433, 434, 465, 466, 468, 470, 473, 474, 479, 479–80, 482, 487, 505, 506, 507, 523, 530
Gooding, David W., 32, 385
Goswell, Greg, 260, 316
Grabbe, Lester L., 483
Grayson, A. K., 50
Green, Joel B., 492–93
Greidanus, Sidney, 482
Gunn, David M., 146
Gurney, Robert J. M., 386–87

Hamilton, James H., 29, 32
Hartman, Louis F., 434, 513, 537
Heiser, Michael S., 368, 379, 540
Hellholm, David, 26
Hill, Andrew E., 157, 174, 202, 224, 308, 318, 367, 384, 509, 528–29
Horton, Michael, 400
Hubbard, Robert L., Jr., 389
Humphreys, W. Lee, 124

Hunger, Hermann, 523

Johns, Alger F., 180, 370
Jones, David W., 188
Josephus, 24, 116
Joubert, W. H., 70

Kaiser, W. C., Jr., 465
Kalimi, Isaac, 253
Kaufman, Stephen A., 523
Kelly, J., 259
Klein, William W., 389
Korner, Ralph J., 349, 350, 355, 406, 410, 454, 497, 504
Koselleck, Reinhart, 515

Labonté, G. G., 125
Lacocque, André, 272, 388, 434, 470, 485, 506, 507
Ladd, George Eldon, 397, 398
Lamb, David T., 539
Lambdin, Thomas O., 64
Lederach, Paul M., 531
Lenglet, Adrien, 32, 150
Lewis, C. S., 542
Li, Tarsee, 101, 150, 232, 265, 328, 359
Long, V. Philips, 50, 203
Longman, Tremper, III, 48, 50, 53, 55, 62, 64, 92, 117, 136, 201, 210, 252, 259, 265, 267, 289, 294, 297, 310, 319, 330, 386, 430, 509, 523, 530, 537
Lucas, Ernest C., 26, 34, 50, 60, 61, 62, 55, 70, 76, 97, 98, 116, 139, 148, 155, 157, 173–74, 188, 201, 204, 211, 224, 259, 281, 356, 358, 367, 370, 381, 385, 387, 393, 396, 438, 452, 456, 458, 464, 468, 484, 485–86, 487, 497, 511, 523, 524, 526, 528, 537
Luck, G. C., 509
Luckenbill, D. D., 457–58
Lundbom, Jack R., 345
Luther, Martin, 72, 241

McComiskey, Thomas, 485, 485–86
McGarry, Eugene P., 536
Meadowcroft, Tim, 529

Merrill, Eugene H., 390
Metzger, Bruce M., 29
Michalowski, Piotr, 55
Millard Alan R., 61, 120, 252
Miller, Cynthia L., 91, 97
Miller, Stephen R., 29, 259, 318, 388, 421–22, 430–31, 435, 479–80, 482, 484, 506, 508, 509, 510, 511, 523, 528, 537
Miller-Naudé, Cynthia L., 412, 429, 523
Mohammed, Ravelle, 292
Moltmann, Jürgen, 239
Montgomery, James A., 87, 197, 210, 308–9, 316, 359, 369, 387, 421–22, 434, 452, 464, 482–83, 509
Mott, Stephen C., 239
Mowinckel, S., 383
Muraoka, Takamitsu, 149

Newsom, Carol A., 52, 54, 61, 64, 68, 69, 70, 87, 89, 98–99, 103, 112, 113, 114, 120, 150, 155, 156, 157, 162, 164, 165, 174, 181, 196, 202, 203, 203–204, 210, 224, 225, 228, 232, 234, 235, 254, 258, 260, 261, 282, 287, 293, 324, 338, 356–57, 366, 367, 368, 369, 370, 381, 382, 395, 420, 421, 430, 431, 432, 433, 435, 436, 441, 464, 468, 469, 470, 471, 472, 479, 479–80, 480, 481, 482, 482–83, 485–86, 486, 497, 506, 507, 508, 509, 510, 511, 515, 524, 525, 526, 527, 528, 531, 536, 537
Niditch, Susan, 124, 181, 431
Niebuhr, H. Richard, 76
Niehaus, Jeffrey J., 51
Noll, Mark A., 72
North, Christopher R., 387

O'Connor, M., 48, 63, 64, 420
Oppenheim, A. Leo, 90, 93, 218, 452

Pace, Sharon, 87, 103, 113, 124, 147, 247, 253, 259, 267, 281, 308, 323, 430, 505
Padgett, A. G., 539
Patterson, Richard D., 124
Peterson, Eugene, 365

Porteous, Norman W., 265, 419, 430–31, 434, 484
Powell, Mark A., 239
Prinsloo, G. T. M., 102, 104
Provan, Iaian, 50
Purvis, James D., 253

Rae, Scott B., 239
Reed, Esther D., 239, 240
Rindge, Matthew S., 125, 133, 133–34
Runge, Stephen E., 51, 52, 54, 60, 65, 68, 90, 112, 149, 151, 157, 164, 173, 176, 211, 212, 258, 265, 277, 281, 302, 307, 309, 322, 323, 329, 333, 481, 484
Ryken, Leland, 25, 259, 289

Sandy, D. Brent, 30, 31
Schreiner, Thomas R., 391
Schuele, Andreas, 307
Segal, Alan F., 399
Segal, J. B., 50
Segal, Michael, 260, 261, 261–62, 265
Seow, C. L., 87, 90, 105, 113, 117, 120, 166, 210, 250, 251, 252, 277, 268, 279, 285, 297, 331, 384, 406, 486, 528, 531
Sittser, Jerry, 342
Smelik, Klaas A. D., 138
Smith-Christopher, Daniel L., 401
Steinmann, Andrew E., 32
Sternberg, Meir, 126, 127
Stevenson, Kenneth, 174, 528–29
Stuart, Douglas, 191, 192, 390
Stutzman, Barronelle, 343, 344
Sumner, George, 37, 419, 484

Tomasino, Anthony J., 116, 435, 524
Towner, W. Sibley, 104, 234, 282, 342, 346, 464, 473
Turner, David L., 243, 396, 494–95

Van Dam, C., 89
van der Merwe, C H. J., 412, 429, 523
van der Toorn, Karel, 136
Van Pelt, M. V., 465
Vroegop, Mark, 445, 446, 447

Author Index

Waltke, Bruce K., 48, 63, 64, 420
Walton, John H., 29–30, 31, 53, 286–87, 308–9, 386–87, 387, 388, 484
Walvoord, John, 149, 509
Wells, Samuel, 37, 419, 484
Wenham, Gordon J., 128
Werline, Rodney A., 463
Westbury, Joshua R., 51, 52, 54, 60, 65, 68, 90, 91, 112, 149, 151, 157, 164, 173, 176, 211, 212, 258, 265, 277, 281, 302, 309, 322, 323, 329, 333, 481, 484

Westermann, Claus, 104
Whitcomb, J. C., 456
Widder, Wendy L., 123, 166, 345, 486, 509, 510
Wilhoit, James C., 259, 289
Williamson, H. G. M., 468, 505
Willis, Amy C. Merrill, 34, 457–58, 497
Wills, Lawrence M., 303
Wilson, John A., 55
Wiseman, D. J., 49, 50, 286
Wittmer, Michael E., 295

Wolters, Al, 260, 282
Wright, Christopher J. H., 53–54

Yancey, Philip, 444
Young, Edward J., 87, 308–9, 430–31, 434, 437, 479–80, 485–86, 509
Younger, K. Lawson, Jr., 252

Zimmerli, Walther, 392
Zöckler, Otto, 483